Books by William L. Shirer

20th CENTURY JOURNEY

THE NIGHTMARE YEARS

1930-1940

William L. Shirer

VOLUME II

THE NIGHTMARE YEARS

1930-1940

20TH CENTURY JOURNEY

JOURNEY

A Memoir of a Life
and the Times

LITTLE, BROWN AND COMPANY · BOSTON · TORONTO

LIBRARY OF CONGRESS CATALOGING IN PUBLICATION DATA
(Revised for volume II)

Shirer, William L. (William Lawrence), 1904–
    20th century journey.

    Includes indexes.
    Vol. 2-   published: Ist ed. Boston: Little, Brown.
    Contents: [1] The start, 1904–1930 — v. 2. The
nightmare years, 1930–1940.
    1. Shirer, William L. (William Lawrence), 1904–
2. Authors, American — 20th century — Biography.
3. Journalists — United States — Biography.   I. Title.
PS3537.H913Z52   070′.92′4 [B]   75-41417
ISBN 0-316-78703-5 (v. 2)

VB

DESIGNED BY DEDE CUMMINGS

Published simultaneously in Canada
by Little, Brown & Company (Canada) Limited

PRINTED IN THE UNITED STATES OF AMERICA

To
Deirdre, Caitlin,
Christina, and Alexander —

May the world of these grandchildren have peace.

The end and the beginning of beings are unknown. We see only the intervening formations. Then what cause is there for grief?

— BHAGAVADGITA

We know little of the past and nothing of the future, and the present is so immense that it exceeds our range of experience.

— RADHAKRISHNA PARAPHRASING SANKARA

Contents

BOOK TWO
Life and Work in the Third Reich, 1934–1937

BOOK THREE
The Road to Armageddon, 1935–1938

BOOK FOUR
The Coming of World War II, 1939–1940

Introduction

For me, as for millions of others on this small globe, the decade 1930–1940, with which these memoirs deal, was a time of growing upheaval. My work as an American foreign correspondent in Europe and Asia became more and more concerned with revolutions, uprisings and a spreading intolerance, violence, repression, aggression and barbarism in supposedly civilized countries. One watched it all leading inexorably toward war.

These were the nightmare years. I was twenty-six when the decade began. For the previous five years, ever since arriving in Paris fresh out of a small Iowa college, I had worked as a newspaperman in most of Europe's great capitals, sensing the crumbling of the old order, of the gradual breakdown of the structure of peace set up by the victorious Western democracies at Versailles in 1919 on the conclusion of the Great War.

The status quo in Europe was being challenged by the totalitarian dictatorships, of the left and right — Stalin's Bolshevik Russia, Mussolini's Fascist Italy — and by the sudden rise of Hitler in Germany as the 1930's began. It was also being undermined by the onset of the Depression, with its massive unemployment, failing banks and businesses, falling currencies and spreading hunger.

Still, there had been a decade of peace after the terrible bloodletting of the war, and a certain well-being of the people, weary from so murderous a conflict. In Paris, full of so much light and beauty, which I had come to passionately love, but also in London, Rome, Vienna and Geneva (the site of the League of Nations), I had covered the news for the *Chicago Tribune*. It had been an interesting life — and a great education — for a naïve, ignorant young American.

Then one August day in 1930 in Vienna, where I was then stationed, I received a curt cable from Colonel Robert Rutherford McCormick, the eccentric publisher of the *Tribune*, ordering me to fly out to India. Mahatma Gandhi's Civil Disobedience movement was threatening British rule there and rocking the foundations of the Empire. Gandhi was emerging as a unique figure, preaching a new kind of revolution through nonviolent noncooperation with British authority, tramping about the country in a loincloth to arouse his fellow Indians from the torpor they had sunk into during centuries under the foreign yoke. To most Indians Gandhi had become a saint and a savior. To some in the West he was a Christ-like figure, caring for the poor, practicing what he preached. Deeply religious, Gandhi was also a shrewd politician and a charismatic leader.

Of all the world leaders, he had already struck me as the greatest and the most original. I was anxious to talk to him and to try to understand him and the revolution he had launched. That experience and his impact on me, on India, on the British, and indeed on the world, I have described in *Gandhi — A Memoir*.

I lingered on in Asia, going up the Khyber Pass to Kabul, the capital of primitive, tribal Afghanistan, to see a new king establish himself after another bloody civil war, then traveling overland back to Europe through Mesopotamia, Syria and Turkey, stopping at such places as Ur, Babylon and Bagdad, meeting with some adventure in these faraway, seething areas and in Ur stumbling across two of the greatest archaeological discoveries of our time.

Back in Vienna, I married, got fired, took a year off in a Spanish fishing village, where I watched the fledgling Spanish Republic falter, read in the newspapers of Adolf Hitler taking over in Germany, wrote my first book, which was unpublishable, returned to Paris in time to cover a Fascist assault (backed by the Communists) on the Third Republic and the bloodiest rioting on the Place de la Concorde since the Commune — and at the end of the summer of 1934 I went on from there to Berlin.

This was, as it turned out, a fateful move for me. It determined my life and work for years to come. Like the experience with Gandhi, it left an indelible impression on me. Recounting it fills the bulk of the pages of this memoir.

With increasing fascination and horror I watched Hitler crush freedom and the human spirit in Germany, the country of Luther, Kant, Beethoven, Goethe and Schiller, persecute the Jews and prepare to massacre them, destroy all who opposed him, and drag this great nation toward war, conquest and destruction. To my consternation most Germans joined joyously in this Nazi barbarism.

I left Germany in December, 1940, fifteen months after Hitler plunged Europe into war. As a war correspondent I had followed the German army through some of its early campaigns, in Poland and in the West, reporting on how it had revolutionized modern warfare with the *Blitzkrieg,* in which an overwhelming concentration of tanks and planes on a narrow front would break through the enemy lines, cut off and surround whole armies, and quickly annihilate them. When I departed Berlin, German troops, after their quick and easy conquests of Poland, Denmark, Norway, Holland, Belgium and France, stood watch from the North Cape to the Pyrenees, from the Atlantic to beyond the Vistula. Britain stood alone. Few doubted that Hitler would emerge from the conflict as the greatest conqueror since Napoleon. Not many believed that Britain would survive.

But history, as it does so often, took an unexpected turn. The Nazi dictator, spoiled by early success, overreached himself. He turned on Russia, which under Stalin had been his virtual ally, and then he took on the United States, which had largely held aloof. These were potentially the two most powerful nations on earth. Dragging them into the war against him sealed Hitler's fate.

At the war's end in 1945, I was back in Germany to survey the ruins and to try to find out at first hand how the Third Reich had reached its sorry end.

Berlin, the once proud capital, was a mass of rubble, indescribable in its desolation. So were most of the other cities of Germany. The German people, so arrogant over their conquests when I had last seen them, were shivering, hungry and homeless, struggling only to survive the first miserable winter of peace. Hitler was dead, a suicide, as were two of his closest henchmen, Goebbels and Himmler. Seven million Jews and a like number of Slavs — Poles and Russians — were also dead, massacred in cold blood by the leaders of this Christian country. Göring, Ribbentrop, Rosenberg, Hess and most of the other men around Hitler were alive, imprisoned at Nuremberg, awaiting trial as Nazi war criminals. I went down to Nuremberg to see them in the dock, to follow the first weeks in the courtroom, and to reflect on the ups and downs of history, of which these memoirs have been so full. I felt that in this case, justice after all, for once, had caught up with the perpetrators of some of the most coldblooded and massive crimes men had ever committed. One seldom lived to see that happen. I had not believed, in the despairing years I labored in Berlin, that I would ever see it.

The two years in India with Gandhi, the six years in Nazi Germany under Hitler, the long war, which had begun for me on September 1, 1939, taught me something about life. In the introduction to the first volume of these memoirs I tried to sum up what I had learned from them and also from the years that followed, when for the first time since my youth, I lived and worked at home in my own country.

Truth and the meaning of life were what concerned me. What was truth? Men sought it — Gandhi said his whole life was spent mostly in the pursuit of truth — but did he or any other man, or saint, attain it? Fully? Even the truth about oneself? That was the most difficult of all. "What manner of man am I?" Stendhal kept asking all through his life and books, finally admitting: "In truth, I haven't the faintest idea."

Can you tell the truth in memoirs like these? I have tried to. But I am conscious that memory, blurred and disjointed by the passage of time, and brightened by the imagination, can lead one often to recount more fiction than fact. I remember Isadora Duncan pondering this in Paris while she was writing her memoirs. "How can we write the truth about ourselves?" she would ask. "Do we even know it?"

Luckily I have not had to depend only on memory in putting down what appears in these pages. I was able to save and bring home from Asia, Europe and the war a great deal of material that documented my life and work: my diaries, my newspaper dispatches, the texts of my broadcasts, letters, photographs, clippings and mementos. These have enabled me to write of events and myself, not as I remember them after a lapse of thirty or forty or fifty years, but as they appeared to me at the time. I have often been struck by what a difference there is between the two. Whenever — and it has often happened — my memories conflicted with the evidence of my papers, I have stuck to the latter.

I have been fortunate, too, in other respects so far as these memoirs reflect most of the main currents and events of the twentieth century. Sheer survival has enabled me to live through most of the century, which began with the horse-and-buggy days and extended into the computerized nuclear age, when Americans journeyed by rocket to the moon, photographed planets tens of millions of miles away, and mankind suddenly came into the possession of the means to blow up the world. This one life span saw more changes on this planet than had taken place in the previous thousand years. Today, toward the end of the century, we take them for granted. But when I was born in Chicago early in 1904, the motor car was just coming in. There were only fifteen thousand automobiles in the entire country, and no paved roads to run them on. There were no airplanes, radios, television sets, electric refrigerators, washing machines and dishwashers, oil burners, air conditioners, gasoline-driven tractors, filling stations, shopping centers, parking lots, traffic lights, computers, income taxes, social welfare, napalm, nuclear bombs, world wars and much else that is commonplace today.

Finally, the nature of my job as an American foreign correspondent enabled me personally to witness many of the great happenings and developments of the century. Thus the account of them in these pages is firsthand. I saw and felt them happen.

Without these direct, immediate experiences I never could have gained at least some understanding of, much less have got the feel of, what happened and why in that nightmare time. They helped later in the writing of some history and of these pages. They enlivened my journey through the twentieth century.

BOOK ONE

The Road to Berlin
1930–1934

CHAPTER 1

Home to Vienna from India (I)
1930 An Interlude in Kabul

One stifling October day in 1930, at a party in Bombay, I ran into the crown prince of Afghanistan. He had arrived by boat a couple of days before from Paris and was on his way to Kabul to mark the first anniversary of his father's becoming king. The Indian press had been referring to the occasion as a "coronation," but the young prince informed me that this was a misnomer. Afghan kings did not wear crowns — it would have looked ridiculous to the wild, mountain tribesmen.

On October 16, ten days hence, his father would formally assume the throne as Nadir Shah. As General Nadir Khan, he had entered Kabul just a year ago, overthrown the usurper Bacha-i-Saqao (who ten months previously had ousted King Amanullah), and had been acclaimed king by the tribal chiefs. But there had been a great deal of mopping up to do and it was only now that Nadir felt sufficiently in the saddle to take over as king.

For some days I had been pestering the Afghan consulate for a visa so that I could cover the festivities. With Gandhi and some fifty thousand of his followers in jail, the Civil Disobedience movement for the moment had slackened. I was restless to find a good story for my newspaper, the *Chicago Tribune*, which had sent me out to India that summer from my post in Vienna. Perhaps, unconsciously, I felt ready for a new adventure, for a taste of danger. A journey to Afghanistan, if the British would let me through the embattled Khyber Pass, promised all three. No correspondent had been able to get into the country for more than a year, and no one outside it knew what had been going on.

During the previous year, 1929, four men in succession had occupied the throne in Kabul, and the tribes had gone to war for or against each of them. Amanullah, who had made himself king when his father was murdered in 1919, was overthrown in January by angry tribesmen, stirred up by mullahs (priests) who resented his unveiling the women and otherwise trying to modernize and secularize the backward, intensely Moslem country. His elder brother Inayatullah, whom he had cheated out of the rightful succession in 1919 but whom he now named to succeed him, lasted but three days. Bacha-i-Saqao, the doughty water carrier's son (his name identified himself as such) and a famous bandit and Robin Hood, who had driven them both out, now proclaimed himself Amir and reigned nine months, only to be overthrown by Nadir Khan, who after promising to spare his life, had had him executed in a rather Afghan manner — by degrees: first stoning, then shooting, and finally hanging.

The primitive, warring country provided a further interest for an American reporter. Strategically situated between the Asian empires of Soviet Russia and Great Britain, Afghanistan had become a center of their rivalry. The Soviet and British legations in Kabul, I had heard, were swollen with secret agents stirring up trouble on each other's borders and striving to keep Afghanistan on their side with subsidies, bribes and covert military support. To the British, Soviet dominance would be a threat to India, already embroiled in Gandhi's revolution. Through the Indian government the British, I had good reason to believe, had financed and armed the successful effort of their old enemy, Nadir Khan. They hoped he would be their man. Bacha had turned out to be pretty much Moscow's man.

During the party I struck up a conversation with the sixteen-year-old crown prince that was to solve all my problems. For not only did I need the permission of the Afghan government to journey to Kabul, I had to have the permission of the British to go up through the Khyber Pass in order to get on the road to the Afghan capital. Since spring, when the Afridis had come down the Khyber to attack Peshawar, the Pass had been closed to civilians, and British and Indian troops had been fighting ever since to clear it. A few weeks before, I had gone up to the northwest frontier to see how the fighting was going. I had pleaded with the authorities to let me at least *see* the fabled Khyber Pass. I had been flatly turned down. Too much risk, the hard-pressed British general in charge of operations had decided.

In Delhi I had received the same runaround. The government could not take the responsibility of allowing a Westerner to cross into Afghanistan, especially an American, whose government had no diplomatic or consular representation in the country and therefore could offer no protection to its citizens.

"Your life wouldn't be worth a rupee in that wild place," a friendly British official had said in turning me down.

Still, I wanted to take the chance. The British were exaggerating the danger, I felt certain, because having scarcely appreciated my coverage of Gandhi's Civil Disobedience movement, they did not intend now to allow me to poke my nose into a country where they, like the Russians, were conniving for control.

But even if they weren't exaggerating? An old cliché was much in my mind in those days of my brash youth: "Nothing risked, nothing gained." That was what newspapering was all about, at least for a roving correspondent.

Mohammed Zahir Khan, as the young prince was named, spoke French but little English, and this proved to be a break for me. Few Indians or English at the party spoke French. So the prince seemed relieved to find someone he could talk to, and soon we were deep in a conversation comparing our experiences in Paris. He already missed it, he said, and so, I said, did I — I would always miss it. As we chatted on I soon felt enough at ease to enlist his help.

"Let me see," he said, reflecting for a moment. "No problem with the visa. I can arrange that. But with the British — that's more difficult." He paused for a moment and then smiled.

"If you like," he said, "I can make you an official member of our party. We're already cleared to go through the Khyber."

The idea of putting something over on the British seemed to appeal to him. His father, he reminded me, had beaten them when he commanded the Afghan army in the third Anglo-Afghan war in 1919.

On October 8, I boarded the Frontier Express at Bombay for Peshawar, listed as a member of His Highness's official party. There was only one bad moment — at the entrance to the Khyber Pass two days later. Our caravan of four cars and a truck with the baggage had been stopped for a final look at our papers. A bristling, young, mustached British border official told the prince, with profuse apologies, that he could not let me through.

I felt my journey coming to an end at its beginning. The prince broke in:

"I have to insist. This American gentleman is a member of our official party."

❦ ❦ ❦

The famed Khyber Pass was awesome in its desolation and the way it wound through narrow defiles in the barren mountains that rose steeply above it, but it was scarcely romantic, as Kipling and other English writers (and later, American movies) depicted, unless you saw romance in the long camel caravans that were slowly moving with their loads of goods from Turkestan by way of Kabul toward India and its rich markets.* And in the fighting that was now under way.

On the heights above the Pass, rifles were crackling and guns pounding as Indian and British troops engaged the elusive Afridis, but unlike Kipling I did not find war then, nor later, the least romantic. In this gray, bare, forlorn, rock-strewn place it seemed grim and senseless.

As we edged through the Pass, keeping an eye out for hostile tribesmen who, though armed only with rifles, were stubbornly contesting each hilltop with the British, my mind kept turning over the history of this ancient road.

Darius of the Persians had come in 510 B.C. and Alexander the Great in 326 B.C., and long before them the Aryans from Central Asia to settle permanently in India and become the great Hindu people, and after them the Tatars, Moguls, Scythians, Afghans, Turks and Arabs. Probably no other mountain pass in the world had seen so many warring, conquering peoples sweep through it nor so many bloody battles fought in its narrow confines.

All along the thirty miles of the zigzagging road we passed columns of troops. There were sentinels, in their native garb, every few yards and manned machine-gun blockhouses every few hundred yards. Atop almost every mountain peak was a fortress, from which British artillery was firing. The trim sweep of their battlements made them look like grounded battleships. Running down from them were barbed-wire entanglements. We had been warned that stray Afridis

---

* Kipling had celebrated the camel caravans, called *kafilas,* in a verse from the *Ballade of the King's Jest,* which young British army officers on the northwest frontier never tired reciting.

> *When springtime flushes the desert grass*
> *The Kafilas wind through the Khyber Pass,*
> *Lean are the camels, but fat the frails,*
> *Light are the purses, but heavy the bales,*
> *As the snowbound trade of the north comes down*
> *To the market square of Peshawar town.*

The camel caravans lined the Pass not only in the spring, but after the fierce heat of summer, all through the autumn. I saw one column that October that must have been five miles long.

might infiltrate the defenses and descend on our little caravan — the prince had turned down an offer of a military escort — but nothing like that happened. After a couple of hours we reached the Afghan frontier at Dakka. On the British side there was a huge sign in English: IT IS ABSOLUTELY FORBIDDEN TO CROSS THIS BORDER INTO AFGHAN TERRITORY. But a British outpost waved us through and we were greeted on the other side by a battalion of ragged Afghan troops and a makeshift band that struggled through some tune — perhaps the Afghan national anthem. Soon we were on our way again over a bumpy road full of potholes and shellholes toward the winter capital at Jalalabad, where we put up for the night.

The royal palace was in ruins, but a small wing had been roofed and patched up. It offered at least shelter from the chilly night. Jalalabad, a town of some sixty thousand inhabitants, was the center of the fierce Shinwari tribes, and where the revolution that had toppled King Amanullah had broken out twenty months before. The battles of the ensuing civil war had left hardly a house standing.

Prince Zahir apologized for the primitive accommodations in the palace. Soldiers lugged in a large wobbly table and some half-broken chairs for our simple dinner by the light of a couple of lamps, for there was no electricity. Two orderlies spread bedrolls on the floor to sleep on. The prince also apologized for the lack of plumbing, but the makeshift toilet did not bother me. It consisted of a hole in the floor in one corner of the big room in which we ate and slept.

One of the members of the party that the prince had brought from Paris was a pleasant but fussy French archaeologist, who did not like squatting over the hole in the full view of the rest of us.

"It is unique," he said, pronouncing it "unike" (as in "bike") when he switched to English so that the prince could not catch his words.

"Not so 'unike' at that," I chided him. "There was a stand-up toilet like that in the hotel in Paris I lived in for years."

"*Impossible!*" he exclaimed in French. "Perhaps in the slums . . ."

"The hotel, monsieur," I said, "was a stone's throw from some of the centers of French civilization: the Sorbonne, the Odeon Theatre, the Medici Palace of the Luxembourg. It was once the home of some of your greatest poets: Baudelaire, Verlaine. And you had to stand over a hole in the floor to shit."

"Very 'unike' for Paris," he muttered. I would soon learn that almost everything in this primitive land struck him as "unike."

Our little motorized caravan struggled the next day up the steep grade of the rocky road to Kabul over the 8,000-foot-high pass at

Jagdalak, where a British brigade had been ambushed and destroyed in 1842 during the first Afghan war. We spent the night under tent at Fort Barikab, where Bacha-i-Saqao had annihilated the troops of Amanullah. The town below was in ruins. This, I learned, was not entirely friendly territory, and that evening the commander of the company of troops we had picked up at Jalalabad as an escort threw out strong posts on the heights above.

We made it into Kabul the afternoon of the third day. Cheering tribesmen, perhaps assembled for the purpose, greeted the crown prince. The king's brother, the prime minister, welcomed us and led our little convoy through the dusty, unpaved streets to the royal palace for tea.

I did not have much stomach for the buns and cakes. I felt a bit exhausted from three days of bumping over the roughest roads I had ever traversed. And my stomach had turned a little at a sight in the great central bazaar, past which we had driven. A dozen bodies dangled stiffly from ropes that stretched down from the roof of the dome, the heads turned slightly, as they are apt to do after a hanging, a gruesome grin on the waxen faces, the hands still tied.

"Very 'unike,' " my French friend muttered, his face turning pale, as I'm sure mine did.

That night I was put up in the Café Wali, one of the shabbiest hotels I have ever encountered. But it was the capital's only hotel left standing and I was glad to find shelter in one of its four bare rooms.

The king had requested that the festivities be kept simple, but they turned out, for me at least, to be a strange and colorful pageant, continuing for four days. Thousands of tribesmen had flocked through the passes and down the valleys from all parts of the kingdom, on foot, on their camels, horses and donkeys, brandishing their trusty rifles and often joyously discharging them into the air, as they poured into Kabul to help the new ruler celebrate. However hard and primitive their lives in the desolate hills, they had a capacity for laughter and high spirits, shouting wildly the opening day at the parade grounds as they dashed past the reviewing stand on their mounts; cheering their favorites at the races, of which there were three different kinds (one for elephants — the first and last time I saw this particular sport — a second for camels and a third for horses); working themselves up to fine fettle in their dances, which resembled those I had seen among American Indians, with the same beat of the drums; and gazing wild-eyed at the fireworks that blazed each night from the lofty mountains of the Hindu-Kush that encircled the capital. There was no drinking, since Moslems are forbidden alcohol by Islamic law and in Afghanistan particularly this was strictly enforced. But there was no need. The special occasion was enough to give them all the pleasures they wanted.

Formal dress, grotesque as that seemed in this wild place, had been requested for the opening ceremonies at the parade grounds, where the king, in a scarlet uniform, received the diplomatic corps, tribal chiefs and a scattering of European visitors, delivered a speech to the nation, and reviewed the forces, some twenty thousand men. The royal request for formal dress brought out the oddest assortment of clothing I had ever seen. The tribal Sardars stuck to their native garb, long coats or robes, with baggy Turkish trousers, daggers hanging from their embroidered cartridge belts and various types of turbans on their heads. Most of them wore shoes of some sort, but their followers were largely barefoot despite the crisp autumn air. The British minister and his aides were resplendent in gold-embroidered uniforms, white topis and long swords. The French wore brown topis and long afternoon coats, the Turks ordinary jackets and ordinary felt hats, as did the Russian minister, who sported a beautifully beat-up fedora. A Chicago businessman, who had flown in from Russia to try to get some mineral concessions from the new king, showed up in white tie and tails and a silk hat. I borrowed a dinner jacket from the French legation.

Several hundred tribesmen stared at the unveiled wife of the Turkish minister striding with her husband from their car toward the royal enclosure. She was the only woman present, and the minister had purposely brought her, I was told, to remind the Afghans that Turkey under the great Kemal Ataturk had, as Amanullah had proposed to do, cast off the old orthodox Moslem ways, chased the caliph from Constantinople, curbed the mullahs and their religious hold on the people, decreed Western dress and taken the veils off the women (as well as the fezes off the men). The Turkish lady was attired in a chic Parisian hat and dress.

Watching her reminded me that since reaching Kabul I had scarcely seen a woman except for some of the veiled ladies in the Amir of Bukhara's famed harem. The numerous men of the royal family kept their women out of sight. The wives and secretaries in the various legations had long since been evacuated.

The parade of the troops past the king was scarcely orderly. Nadir's best forces had been the more warlike tribes, campaigning and fighting in their native garb under their own leaders, who would have disdained attending the army war college — they had their own ideas of how best to fight in the mountains. The king's regular troops in their old-fashioned, ill-fitting uniforms of the prewar Austrian army were a ragged lot. But a large band of Waziri and Mangal tribesmen, in their tall turbans and flowing robes, were a splendid sight as they led the parade. Tall and fierce looking, they were reputed to be the best warriors in Afghanistan. Those on mounts dashed by, raising their long spears and shouting wildly; the foot soldiers surged by on bare feet in one great mass, out of step and line, but looking formidable.

Behind them marched the Royal Guard in scarlet coats, gold-braided dark-blue trousers and bearskin hats, apparently hand-me-downs from Buckingham Palace or the viceregal palace in Delhi. What did it matter if they were a bit threadbare, somewhat soiled, unpressed and ill-fitting? The Guard marched proudly behind a tiny puffing band similarly uniformed. Then came the regular troops in Austrian field-gray. Not nearly as formidable as the tribesmen, they more or less kept in step. What interested me most were the camel corps and the elephant corps, particularly the latter, which brought up the rear. I had never seen an elephant corps before. I thought they had gone out with Hannibal.

"They're useful in hauling guns up the mountain passes," someone explained to me.

The king, who despite his scarlet uniform looked more like a kindly professor than a man who had spent most of his life fighting in the rugged mountains, talked gently, like a father, to his people, his words carried for the first time to the vast throng by loudspeakers — a gift, I believe, of the Russians, as were the four planes of the Royal Air Force, antiquated rickety biplanes that zoomed overhead after he had spoken. The king kept addressing the people as "My dear children, my dear brothers," and promised them, as kings have done everywhere, "peace and prosperity," but few of the hardy tribesmen, like large audiences elsewhere, seemed to pay much attention to the words. They seemed restless to see the parade and then to get to the fun and games.

The British minister, R. R. Maconachie, had been in a jovial mood that morning when we struck up a conversation.

"Coming from Chicago, you must feel at home here in Afghanistan," he quipped.

"Why so?" I said. I knew what he meant, but I did not let on. (The killings in the Chicago gang wars and the murderous doings of Al

Capone had been front-page stuff in the English newspapers of India, which reached the British legation in Kabul.)

"I mean ... uh ... there's a lot of wild shooting there ... like here," he laughed.

There was much more to report from Kabul than the royal celebrations, picturesque as they were. From the day I arrived I had been digging out accounts of more substantial events, all of them unreported up to now, since the country had been closed to foreign journalists two years before. It was a young newspaperman's dream. I had a unique and colorful story to myself. The only problem would be to get it out. Communication with the outside world was still difficult. Telegraph lines were down, the mails uncertain. Only a feebly powered radio station connected us with Peshawar in India, manned here by an operator who did not know a word of English. It was my only hope. In Peshawar I had arranged with the radio station to receive my dispatches from Kabul and relay them, collect, to London. I had left a sizable deposit to facilitate the operation and make it worthwhile.

Feeling rather puffed up that I had a "world scoop," I wrote a lengthy dispatch for Chicago, telling not only of the royal celebration but, more importantly, what had happened in this forbidden mountain kingdom during the two years it had been shut off from the rest of the world.

I had the first account of the fall of Amanullah, who had become somewhat of a celebrity in Europe and America for thumbing his nose at the British and for trying to Westernize and modernize his backward kingdom; of how Bacha-i-Saqao had chased him from Kabul and ruled as a bandit-king for nine months; of Nadir Khan's return and the part the British played in it; of the struggle for influence here between Moscow and London, which maintained immense legations, bigger than their embassies in Paris or Berlin, from which they directed their intrigues against the other.

Both legations were full of fascinating characters, secret agents and spies, who had spent their lives in the vast area of mountains and deserts, knew the tribes and their languages. Both missions suspected that I was a spy myself, disguised as an American newspaperman. They were too cynical to believe that a legitimate American journalist would risk his neck to come to this out-of-the-way place. In time, I think, my naïveté impressed them. They began to feed me fantastic tales, some of them true.

I kept stumbling across the most weird characters. The ex-Amir of

Bukhara, for one, who until recently had been the absolute sovereign of the large state of that name in Russian Turkestan, possessor of a treasury said to have amounted to a hundred and fifty million dollars, and also of one of the most famous harems in Asia. I met him in a shabby room next to mine in the Café Wali, and later lunched with him in his modest palace outside Kabul, where he lived with a few faithful followers, thirty or so of his young children and a much reduced harem, and plotted to regain his lost kingdom from the Bolsheviks. There was an interesting fellow from Chicago, a priest, the Reverend George Blatter, who had come to Kabul with the noble determination to convert this most fanatical Moslem nation in all of Islam to Jesus and who escaped in the nick of time having his throat cut by angry mullahs.

There was a vast ghost city to see, the dream city called Dar-ul-Aman, which Amanullah, with the help of French, German and Italian architects and engineers and at the cost of millions of dollars, had built outside of Kabul — and never occupied, nor had anyone else. It was to be the glittering new capital of Afghanistan, an Afghan Versailles. It had a Renaissance palace for himself on a hill overlooking the city, a huge building for government offices below, a Bauhaus hotel, schools and hospitals, spacious Munich-style villas for the rich and apartment buildings for the rest. The buildings still stood, but Amanullah had decamped before anyone could move into them, and now their windows were boarded up and plaster was scaling off their walls. Weeds had overgrown the broad avenues, lawns, parks and the railroad tracks that connected the new town with the old — the first and last railroad built in the country. Two rusty locomotives, still attached to some passenger cars, were marooned on a siding. There was not a soul about.

There was another town Amanullah built and in it I had the first of two brushes with danger that I had been anticipating on this assignment. This was at Paghman, the summer capital, eight thousand feet up in the mountains sixteen miles north of Kabul, where the king and his government sojourned in summer to escape the capital's suffocating heat. By the time I got to it most of what Amanullah had built had been abandoned: the sprawling three-story European-style hotel (with running water in every room and a bath on every floor), the theater, the movie house, scores of spacious villas. Weeds grew over the playing fountains, the tennis courts, the cricket grounds, the vast square in the middle of which stood an arc de triomphe, and most of the streets. But Nadir Shah had kept open the palace, a ramshackle Bavarian-style country house.

In July, three months before I arrived, the king and his ministers and families had had a narrow escape when ten thousand armed Kohistanis, followers of Bacha, swept over the mountain peaks and swarmed down on Paghman. The monarch escaped, but just barely, and for several days Kabul itself was threatened.

Now on a bright October day I had driven up to Paghman to attend a lunch Nadir Shah was giving in the gardens of the palace. He offered a sumptuous meal of roast beef and mutton and fowl with all the trimmings and I was enjoying it, putting down huge amounts of food with my fingers, as I had by now learned to do. But the meal was never finished.

Suddenly I looked up as I was wiping my hands and mouth with a hot towel, between courses, and there upon the mountain ridge above us appeared a band of tribesmen about a thousand strong — probably the same Kohistanis who had shown up there in July. They proceeded to swoop down the mountainside, firing away with their rifles at us but fortunately not very accurately. Led by the royal family we made a hasty departure from the great table to our cars near by, covered by the King's Guard, which blazed away at the approaching army until we were in our automobiles and soon out of range.

It was my first time under fire, the first time I had ever heard the whistle of a hostile bullet whizzing by. I cannot say that I was not frightened. In fact, for a few moments that day in the mountains, as we rushed pell-mell from the table to our cars, I was terror-stricken. I did not want to die in this distant place, and so soon.

So the first few days in Kabul had given me a good, colorful story, as yet unreported to the outside world, and knowing I had it exclusively I pounded out a dispatch of some three thousand words. The Afghan operator at the radio station thought it a little much, especially as it was in a language he did not understand. However, he agreed to go to work on it.

The next day when I returned to thank him and to offer him a small token of my gratitude, he informed me that he had been unable to raise the radio operator in Peshawar. He said he would try again. But the next day the story was the same. The man in Peshawar simply would not answer his call. This could only be British sabotage, I thought. The British in India had never liked me anyway.

I felt absolutely defeated. Here was one of the most unusual stories I had ever had, and an exclusive one at that, and I couldn't get it out. I suddenly remembered a secretary of the Soviet legation having mentioned casually to me that he also served occasionally as a correspondent for TASS, the Soviet news agency, and that he might get out a little story on the celebrations and on the first year of Nadir's rule. He could file it to Moscow, he said, over the legation's radio. He seemed in no hurry, and this had given me some assurance. But by now he probably had gotten around to it. So Moscow would receive the news first, and TASS would give it to the foreign news agency correspondents there, and there would go my "world scoop." The *Chicago Tribune* would publish it as an A.P. dispatch from Kabul and wonder what the hell had happened to its correspondent, supposedly the only newspaperman on the scene, and at some expense to the home office.

The cost of transmitting my dispatch from Kabul to Chicago, at a dollar per word, would come to $3,000. If my lengthy cable arrived late, after the *Tribune* had already published the story from the A.P., Colonel McCormick, my eccentric publisher, would have a fit. He had fired some of his correspondents for less. Each day as I waited vainly for the Peshawar operator to receive my copy I had growing visions of suddenly becoming jobless in this out-of-the-way place, five thousand miles from my post in Vienna, nine thousand miles from home in America. I realized I didn't have enough saved up to pay the fare back to Vienna, much less to Chicago. I would be stranded in the remotest land in all of Asia. There was no U.S. legation to appeal to for help; I could certainly not wheedle anything out of the British. The Russians had already turned down my request for a place on the plane that left Kabul for Moscow once a week.

So I began to pare down what I thought was the most important scoop and certainly the most colorful dispatch I had ever written. Each day I would sit at the desk of the wireless operator and anxiously watch him tap out his appeal to his opposite number in Peshawar to answer. After an hour's wait, with no sign of life from the other end, I would sink further into despair, and ask him to try again the next day. Then I would cut five hundred words or so from the cable. By the afternoon of the third day, when there was still no response from Peshawar, I had halved my dispatch to fifteen hundred words. This chopping of such a good story depressed me, but it pleased the radio operator. "It gets easier to send each day," he said, in his few words of German.

On the fourth day, for some reason, the operator in Peshawar came miraculously to life, consented to receive fifteen hundred words and forward it to London for transmission to Chicago.

The *Chicago Tribune* published it on October 20 in the first column on the first page. Luckily for me, though the story was four days old, it was still a scoop, and the *Tribune* affixed a copyright notice under my byline to make sure that competitive journals did not filch my report. Obviously my friend at the Soviet legation had not yet got around to filing *his* report.

In London, where the *Daily Telegraph* published the dispatch, my story turned out to be almost too much of a scoop. The Afghan legation there, which apparently was one or two kings behind, protested that it was a fake. Not until the diplomatic cables came through from Kabul to the Foreign Office, I was told later, were the editors satisfied that it was not.

In November, 1930, I took leave of Kabul and set out with Walter Bosshard, a Swiss photographer and explorer, who knew well Central Asia and its languages (the suspicious Soviet minister had sworn to me that Bosshard was a British agent) for the Khyber Pass and India.

The evening before, the king had invited me in for a farewell talk. I noted again his almost perfect English, from which he occasionally lapsed into fluent French, which he had picked up during his years of exile in Europe. He did not seem tough enough, ruthless enough, to rule over these feuding, warring tribes, though I realized that deep down he was — he had dispatched Bacha most barbarously, and I knew that the week before I arrived in Kabul he had had thirty of the ringleaders in the attack on Paghman in July blown to bits at the canon's mouth. I soon became conscious that Nadir Shah deemed me more important than I was. Shyly he suggested that when I returned home I might call the attention of Washington to his nation's existence, the opportunities for American development of Afghanistan's vast, untouched natural resources and the desirability of diplomatic recognition. "You are the one great country in the world which has no political interests in Afghanistan. If we can establish commercial relations with you, why not diplomatic relations? Perhaps you can mention this in Washington. I have no one there to do it."

I promised to do it, not having the heart to tell him how futile that would be.

"After all," I said, "we don't recognize the existence of the Soviet Union thirteen years after the Bolshevik revolution."

"That astonishes me," the king said. "How is that?"

"I don't know," I said. "We have a peculiar blindness, I guess."

"I can't afford to be blind," he said, smiling. "The Russians are my neighbors. They're big. They're strong. And they keep after me."

I thanked the king for his many courtesies, wondering as I left how long this gentle-appearing man with the iron insides would last on his throne. The experience of having four kings during the previous year did not indicate that being the sovereign was a very permanent thing in this country. Amanullah's father had been assassinated, Amanullah himself overthrown, Bacha-i-Saqao executed. Seldom did an Afghan king die peacefully in his bed, at least if he remained in his kingdom.

The next morning Bosshard and I set out from Kabul by car, arriving an hour after dark at a small place called Nimla, where we spent the night at a newly built government rest-house, guarded by a platoon of regular troops. I was glad to have an old Asian hand such as Bosshard along. He not only spoke Pushtu, the native language in these parts, but knew his way about.

We had had a bad moment soon after dark that terrified me. Winding through a high mountain pass we had suddenly seen in our headlights a band of armed men standing before a small bridge over a gully and waving at us wildly to stop, which we did.

"Could be bandits," Bosshard said calmly. "Keep cool."

Pointing their rifles at us, the men motioned us to get out of the car. I noticed for the first time that Bosshard was carrying a revolver and that as we alighted he unbuttoned the holster and unclicked the safety catch. I was of course unarmed and would not have known how to handle a pistol if I had one. I had not handled a gun since my childish soldiering at Camp Funston when I was fifteen. Besides, two pistols would scarcely have been a match for the six or seven rifles pointing at us.

To my surprise Bosshard started yelling at the men most belligerently in what I took to be Pushtu. This had an unexpected result; the bandits lowered their rifles.

"They're not bandits," Bosshard turned to me to say in English, "they're government soldiers. And they want some money for allowing us to cross this miserable little bridge. It can't be more than thirty feet."

Bosshard dropped his voice and began haggling. Finally he took some silver from his pocket and handed it over to one of them. We climbed back into the car and started to proceed. But the men formed a new line in the middle of the bridge and would not let us over.

"Goddamned bastards!" Bosshard muttered and sprang out of his car. I thought for a moment he was going to pull his gun, and that would be the end of us in this godforsaken place in the blackness of the night. Then suddenly he did something I thought was worse. He walked up to the ringleader and resoundingly slapped his face. Watching him through the windshield, in the car's lights, I froze. To my astonishment, and relief, the men parted and waved us through. I started breathing again.

"I thought they were going to blow your brains out when you slapped the fellow," I said as we coasted down the grade to Nimla.

"No. That's the language they understand."

He used it again the next day at Jalalabad. We had stopped there for a few minutes shortly before noon so he could take some photographs of the bazaar. The crowd, mostly boys and old men, was friendly enough as Bosshard started snapping pictures with his Leica. He would stop to give the youngsters some silver foil from his film packs and joke with them in Pushtu. The old men grinned toothlessly.

Suddenly a couple of young mullahs appeared and started angrily to harangue the crowd. In an instant the amiable crowd was transformed into an angry, threatening mob. Led by the mullahs they started shouting the one word I could understand. *Kafirs! Kafirs!* Infidels we were, nonbelievers, the slashing of whose throats hastened one to the Moslem heaven. A verse from the Koran that someone had recited to me in Kabul came running through my mind.

> And whenever the sacred months are past, kill those who join other gods with God wherever ye shall find them; and seize them and slay them and lay in wait for them with every kind of ambush.

The youngsters, who a moment before had been laughing with us, started to pick up loose stones and hurl them at us. I had never been stoned before — it was something one read about in the Bible.

I looked back at our car, some hundred yards down the street, and turned to run for it.

"Don't!" Bosshard said sternly. "Don't run!"

Again he took his revolver out and held it up.

"Keep facing them. And step backward slowly," he said calmly.

Once or twice we had to jerk our arms up to our faces to ward off a missile. We kept treading backward toward the car. The crowd kept edging closer. Their aim was getting better. The damned street seemed to be loaded with stones. Finally Bosshard brandished his gun and fired a couple of shots in the air. The crowd stopped. By this time we had nearly reached our car. We back-treaded the last thirty feet as fast as we could, Bosshard covering our retreat.

"Jump in fast! On the other side. Don't turn your back!" He was calm, but decisive. He put his gun down, threw himself into the car behind the wheel, and turned the starter. In a second we were off, a few parting stones falling harmlessly on the roof of the car.

There was considerable firing going on in the Khyber Pass as we approached it after crossing the border at Dakka. I noticed a new sign, in English: THIS IS HOSTILE TERRITORY. PROCEED AT YOUR OWN RISK.

Three or four times we heard a bullet whistling overhead. It was a warm day and we had the windows down.

"Might as well," Bosshard had said. "They're not bulletproof."

A short distance into the Khyber a British patrol stopped us.

"You drew a little fire from that ridge to the north," a young British officer said cheerfully. It seemed to amuse him. We showed him our papers. "Well, how are things in Kabul?" he laughed. "Still shooting up there?"

It was very hot now and the young officer gave us a drink from his canteen.

"I got orders to see you through the Pass," he said. "Break for us. Means a night off in Peshawar. A warm shower. And some cool drinks."

The colorful old capital of the Northwest Frontier looked good to us too. The interlude in Afghanistan was over.

I had seen one of the last of the remote lands in Central Asia on the verge of being pushed into the twentieth century. I had had a glimpse of it the way it must have been for more than two millennia, since Darius and then Alexander had come to Kabul. A tribal society, primitive, savage, living off its flocks and barren fields, roving up and down the mountain valleys on camels, asses, or on foot, its people spending most of their time in mere survival, foraging for grazing lands, pausing here and there to plant and harvest a crop on the rocky soil, fighting off or attacking hostile tribes and government tax collectors, fearless of death in a way I envied, illiterate, uncivilized to a Westerner, but conscious of a long and continuous history, handed down by word of mouth from generation to generation.

Quickly in the years after I left, the tribal country became a nation. Capital poured in from the West to develop and transform it. New roads were built and the old ones improved. Many tribal chiefs abandoned their camels and asses for shiny American motor cars. The dirt streets of the Kabul I knew were paved — by the Russians; those of Kandahar, the second largest town — by the Americans. In 1934 the country was admitted to the League of Nations. The world had at last accepted Afghanistan as a full-fledged nation. But Nadir Shah was not around to see the country's recognition at Geneva. Just three years after I last saw him — on November 8, 1933 — he was assassinated in Kabul by a young student whose father had been executed the previous year for taking part in a rebellion in the south.

His son, Mohammed Zahir Shah, who had taken me with him to Kabul that autumn of 1930, became one of the world's longest-reigning monarchs and set a record for his own unruly country. Becoming king at age nineteen in 1933, he lasted forty years. But for the first thirty years he was largely a figurehead; the country was run by his numerous uncles and cousins. For fifteen years his cousin and brother-in-law, Mohammed Daud Khan, virtually ruled the kingdom as prime minister. I had met this young man in Bombay with the crown prince; he had journeyed with our party to Kabul for the celebrations in honor of Nadir Shah becoming king. Daud had struck me then as an exceptionally able and ambitious young man. And cunning.

Not until 1963, thirty years after becoming king, and already forty-nine, did King Zahir apparently feel himself strong enough to dismiss his cousin and take over himself. At any rate, he fired Daud. But ten years later, on July 17, 1973, while King Zahir was in Italy for a health cure, Daud seized power and abolished not only the king but the monarchy.

The usurper, in turn, did not last very long. Five years later, on April 27, 1978, a military junta of young army and air force officers besieged the presidential palace, killed Daud, his wife and children, and most of the rest of his immediate family and more distant relatives, and seized power in the name of "revolutionary justice."

The new prime minister, Nur Mohammed Taraki, was unlike any other ruler this tribal, feudal country had ever seen. He was a soft-spoken intellectual, novelist and journalist, who founded and led Afghanistan's first political party with any mass following, which he named Khalq (The Masses). It was considered "leftist" in Kabul and often suppressed, along with Taraki, who spent a good deal of his time in prison. He was there when the coup erupted and Western correspondents, hastening to Kabul, reported that one reason for the timing of the uprising was to free Taraki before Daud had him murdered. The real power behind Taraki, the correspondents believed, was a group of young officers. Behind them, probably, was Moscow.

This would soon become more apparent. In September, 1979, Taraki was overthrown and murdered by one Hafizullah Amin. Apparently Amin had, or would win, the backing of the Soviet Union, which was becoming concerned with a widespread Moslem tribal revolt against the pro-Communist regime and felt that Taraki was not doing enough to put it down. But Amin, though more brutal, was no more effective than Taraki in suppressing the rebellion.

Suddenly, two days after Christmas, 1979, the Russians took matters into their own hands. Amin was overthrown in a "coup" and killed. The Russians replaced him with Babrak Karmal, who was hastily flown to Kabul from his exile in Czechoslovakia, and installed in power. On the same day, Soviet troops invaded Afghanistan. Within a few weeks a Red Army force of nearly a hundred thousand men was reported to have been deployed in the mountainous country in the dead of winter. They also were reported to be meeting the usual reception which Afghans gave foreign invaders. Soon they became bogged down as the Moslem rebels continued to resist. To the surprise of no one who knew the land, the Russian troops apparently were having a more difficult time than Moscow had envisaged.

Advertisement in December 29, 1930, issue of the Chicago Tribune *featuring the author's world scoop in Afghanistan*

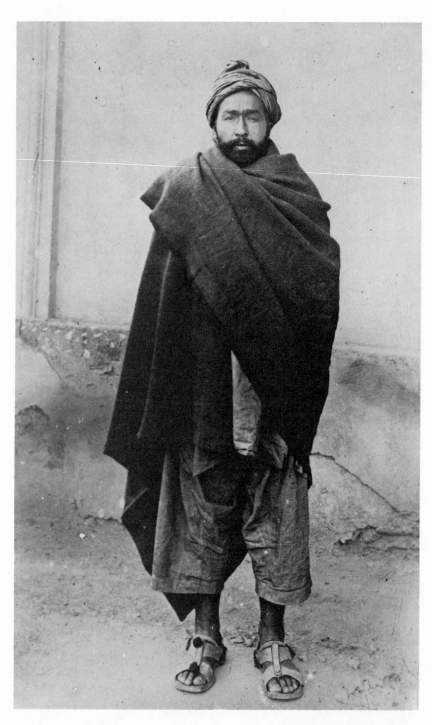

Bacha-i-Saqao, the water carrier's son, who ruled as amir of Afghanistan after overthrowing Amanullah. Photo taken just prior to his execution by Nadir Khan.

Bodies of the followers of Bacha-i-Saqao.

The author (extreme right) walking to the ceremonies proclaiming Nadir king of Afghanistan, 1930

Three tribesmen in the Khyber Pass, 1930

Elephant races, Kabul, 1930

*Royal ceremonies in Kabul, 1930. The author is to the right
of the man with the cane.*

*The author speaking with Mohammed Zahir Khan, then crown prince of
Afghanistan, in Kabul, 1930*

*The author (third from left) lunching with the ex-Amir of Bukhara,
in Kabul, 1930*

The Khyber Pass

United Press International Photo

CHAPTER 2

Home to Vienna from India (II)
1930 A Stopover in Ur

Back in Delhi in November I took a couple weeks off to digest my experiences in Afghanistan and write a mail series on them for the *Chicago Tribune*. Gandhi, Nehru and the rest of the Congress leaders and their fifty thousand followers were still in jail, and there was little to write from India. I could not shake my malaria, which had been chronic since my arrival. In Kabul the poisonous food had given me another case of dysentery.

I began to long to get back to my post in Vienna — not only to recuperate but to have a new story to write. The Austrian capital, I knew, had been hard hit by the Depression. Friends wrote about long breadlines in the streets and the terrible poverty and unemployment. Tension between the Socialists, who controlled the city, and the conservative Catholic Christian Socials, who ran the country, was threatening to erupt into civil war. Central Europe and the Balkans, which were part of my Vienna beat, were reported to be even more restive than usual. There was a growing revolt among the masses against the inept dictatorship and semidictatorships of the region.

In Germany, next door to Austria, the Nazis under Adolf Hitler were reported to be staging a sensational comeback. I had started to look into Hitler's background in Vienna the year before. As an Austrian he had spent his formative years there before moving on to his beloved Germany and fighting as a common soldier throughout the Great War. In the bitter first years of defeat, chaos and the catastrophic fall of the mark he had launched his Nazi party, staged the abortive coup in Munich in 1923, which the world had laughed at as the "Beer Hall Putsch," and served a couple of years in prison. Then little was heard of him, and in Berlin toward the end of the 1920's my friends among the correspondents and diplomats told me Hitler was a forgotten man. He had, as the British ambassador put it, "passed into oblivion."

He had, however, recently emerged from oblivion, and was again agitating for the overthrow of the Weimar Republic and attracting an astonishingly large and growing following. Indeed, this very autumn of 1930, he had astounded even Germany by a staggering victory in the national election. From 810,000 votes and twelve members elected to the Reichstag just two years before, the Nazis had jumped to six and a half million votes that brought them one hundred and seven seats and propelled them from the smallest party in Parliament to the second largest. The Nazis under Hitler obviously were on the move, threatening to tear up Germany and take it over. From nearby Vienna I could cover part of that story.

There was a further reason for my wanting to get back to Vienna. I was in love with a young woman there. Our correspondence since I came out to India had deepened our love. She was a beautiful, lovely, lively, dark-blond Viennese of twenty.

The Afghan series over, I cabled Colonel McCormick, who personally ran the foreign service of the *Chicago Tribune*, which he also owned, published, and edited. I had to give some thought to the wording. He apparently had liked my work in India and obviously wanted me to stay on. If I merely cabled I was ill from malaria and dysentery and wanted to return to Vienna for a cure, he might suggest I go to the Himalayas for rest and recuperation. It would be more effective if I proposed a return to Europe overland by way of some of the most historic and picturesque towns in the world. It promised some colorful stories, and would respond to the colonel's reputed interest in history and geography.

I thereupon cabled McCormick I would like to return to Vienna overland by way of Basra, Babylon and Bagdad. Those historic, alliterative names, I thought, would strike his imagination. They did. Back came a message from Chicago: SHIRER COME BACK VIA BABYLON. MCCORMICK.

Toward the end of November I journeyed down to Bombay, took leave of the few Indian friends who were not in jail, and sailed for Basra. From there I planned to catch the first train for Babylon and tarry there to see what time had done to the fabled capital of Nebuchadnezzar, where much later, in 323 B.C., Alexander had died of fever at thirty-three on his way back from India, and been buried. It would be a good dateline from which to write my first dispatch. Bagdad, another fabled name, would follow.

As it turned out, it was not at Babylon or Bagdad, but at Ur, which I thought had disappeared from the face of the earth some time after the biblical era, when it was known as Ur of the Chaldees, the birthplace of Abraham, that I found the most exciting and the most important story of the trip home.

At about 6 one morning at the end of November, 1930, on the train carrying me up from Basra to Babylon and thence to Bagdad, I was awakened by the jolting of my sleeping car coming to a sudden stop. I looked out the window to see what was happening. There was a large sign in English on the little railroad station. UR-JUNCTION. Could it possibly be the Ur I had read about in the Bible?

Surely even the prosaic British, who ruled Mesopotamia, would not desecrate the memory of such an historic town by calling it Ur-Junction. Still . . . I noticed a little rest-house beyond the station. I could put up there until the next day's train for Babylon. I dressed hurriedly, tossed my bedroll and luggage out the window, and got out.

At the rest-house a Turk in charge greeted me as though he had half expected me. He spoke quite a bit of German.

"Great excitement over there the last few days," he said, pointing out the window at a great mound that rose in the desert a mile or two away. "I'll take you over after breakfast," he said. "My donkeys need some exercise."

"Fine. Thank you very much," I said. I wondered what the hell was the cause of the excitement, but I tried to hide my ignorance.

After breakfast my host saddled a couple of mangy donkeys and we set out across the sand toward the place. From a distance it looked like a forlorn hillock rising a couple of hundred feet out of the monotonous desert.

"The professor is expecting you, *ja?*" the Turk said, as we jogged along.

"*Ja,*" I lied. I wondered what a "professor" could possibly be doing in this sandy waste.

"By the way," I added, "is this Ur-Junction possibly the Ur of the Chaldees — you know, the one in the Bible, the one Abraham was said to have lived in?"

"Oh, *ja,*" he beamed. "That's it. Ur of the Chaldees, certainly. But . . ."

So the "professor," I thought, could be some archaeologist and scholar, excavating perhaps the ruins of Abraham's town. If so, that would be a good story for me. The churchy Christians of Chicago would love it. As we approached the place I could make out great stone walls that must have been dug out of the sand along the side of the mound. And suddenly I saw a great pit, at the bottom of which Arab workmen were digging.

"The professor," the Turk said, "he has two hundred men working down there. Great excitement, I tell you."

He turned back, tying my donkey to a jutting piece of rock. I took out my Kodak and started snapping some pictures of the dig. I also took some shots with my Pathé movie camera.

But not many.

Suddenly a man in a topi who was not an Arab came running up the slope toward me. Obviously he did not approach as a friend.

"You can't do that here!" he shouted, and I knew at once he was an Englishman. "It's strictly forbidden!" Then, after looking me up and down as though I might be a grave robber, he said:

"Who are you, anyway? What are you doing here?"

When I started to respond that I was the correspondent of an American newspaper, the *Chicago Tribune*, he cut me short.

"We do not want journalists here," he said. "The *Times* of London has exclusive rights to our story. I am writing it myself. Your newspaper can buy it from the *Times*."

"I'm terribly sorry," I tried to explain. "In truth, sir, I haven't the faintest idea what this is all about. Or who you are. I was just —"

"I'm C. Leonard Woolley," he said, "director of — I'm sure you know or you wouldn't be here — of the joint expedition of the British Museum and the University of Pennsylvania." As though he was aware that he might be sounding pompous, he began to melt, though warily.

"I was on my way to Babylon and Bagdad," I told him, "en route home to my post in Vienna. When I saw the sign, Ur-Junction, I just decided on a hunch to get off, thinking it might be Ur of the Chaldees."

By the look on his face, he obviously thought it a most unlikely story.

"Where did you come from?" he asked.

Instinctively, I thought this was the chance to break through his suspicion. If you have something new and unusual to tell a man like this, he may reciprocate.

"I've just come from Kabul," I said.

"I say, that's interesting," he said. "I didn't know one could get into that wild country at present. Come along and tell me about it."

Over tea I quickly disposed of the subject of Afghanistan. Then through lunch and for the rest of the day Professor Woolley, at last convinced of my innocence, talked to me of one of the most remarkable and historically important archaeological discoveries of our time. He had just found physical evidence of what up to now had been believed to be a sacred legend: the biblical Flood.

The story in the Bible of Noah's Ark and the Flood, like many legends, had been based, he said, on an actual occurrence. He had established that some time before 3200 B.C., the whole area of the lower Euphrates and Tigris had been engulfed in a great inundation that had wiped out its towns and villages and most of its inhabitants. For the people who had lived there this was the whole world. The Sumerians, who had then occupied the area and who heard what happened from the few survivors, retained it in their memories and later, more than two thousand years before Christ, and therefore some centuries before Abraham, preserved the story of the flood in their tablets, which Woolley had unearthed at Ur. That account was taken over subsequently by the Hebrews and incorporated, with certain embellishments and moral lessons, in the biblical story of Noah's Ark.

The first inkling that Woolley's expedition had hit upon the physical remains of the flood had come the year before. The treasures discovered during years of excavating the Royal Cemetery at Ur had revealed a Sumerian civilization of a remarkably high order. What Woolley and his party then wanted to ascertain was how the inhabitants of Ur had reached such an astonishing level of culture and art. They decided to dig deeper. Because the coming of hot weather would soon end their season's labors, they had time to sink beneath the cemetery only a small shaft not more than five feet square — just large enough for one man to dig in. Suddenly, after going down some fifty feet past layer after layer of broken pottery and other shards, they came upon a layer some eight feet thick in which there were no remains of human activity at all — just clean water-laid mud. They believed that they had hit virgin soil, and that the digging of the shaft had been a waste of time. But Woolley decided to dig a little deeper and soon he came upon fragments of pottery and flint instruments more primitive than they had discovered in the cemetery above. These obviously had been left by a people who had lived there before the thick layer of silt had covered up their settlement.

Woolley said he himself was quite sure what he had hit upon but wanted to check with the staff first. Two members studied the bottom of the shaft but could not think of any explanation for the deep layer of sediment below which was a scattering of artifacts.

"My wife happened to come along," Woolley said, "and I asked her if she had any idea."

"Well, of course," he said she answered. "It's the Flood."*

It was, he was fairly confident, the right answer. But on the strength of a pit only a yard and a half square he could not be absolutely sure. It was not large enough to give positive evidence of a deluge. The next season, he decided, he would excavate a large pit to see if his first findings would be confirmed.

It was on this he had been working, with his aides and some two hundred Arab workmen, before my arrival. After tea he took me down to the immense pit, which measured some seventy-five feet by sixty, dug below the graves of the Royal Cemetery. It went down sixty-four feet. As we descended, Woolley noted the various layers from whose artifacts he had deduced the course of history of the splendid civilization of Sumeria, from which all the others in the West, he believed, had sprung.

Toward the bottom Woolley paused to show me what he called the physical remains of the flood. It was a layer of clean silt ten to eleven feet thick. Microscopic analysis showed that it was water-laid, built up by gentle currents which had piled up the silt.

"So here you see the evidence," he said, "of a flood such as Mesopotamia never experienced afterward."

He had calculated that ten or eleven feet of silt must have meant floodwaters at least twenty-five feet deep. (The Genesis story says the waters rose to twenty-six feet.) In the lowland of the lower Euphrates and Tigris valley, he pointed out, that would mean that the inunda-

---

* One of Woolley's young assistants remained skeptical. This was Max Mallowan, who barely two months before had married Agatha Christie and obviously was not happy about this first separation. Since he had met her the previous spring at Ur, he would have liked, I gathered, to have brought his bride back to the site that autumn. But the formidable Mrs. Woolley was there, and while she was present, I also gathered, there was no place in the Woolley camp for another woman. Agatha Christie stayed put back in England, and I missed meeting a woman who later would become the most prestigious writer of mystery novels of our time. (There are 85 of them.)

Her husband would also become one of the most eminent of the British archaeologists working in the Near East, going on from Ur up to Nineveh and later to Syria and finally to his greatest triumph at Nimrud, one of the four capitals of Assyria.

Agatha Christie's novel *Murder in Mesopotamia*, incidentally, is about the dig in Ur and the leading characters, I can now see, are based on the Woolleys and Mallowan and their life and work together at Ur about the time I broke momentarily onto that scene.

tion covered an area some three hundred miles long and a hundred miles wide. Thus the inhabitants believed that the whole world had been engulfed and in time this conception became the basis of the story in the Old Testament.

In Genesis, the Hebrews took over another aspect of the Flood, as recounted by the Sumerians. Woolley told me that in the Sumerian legend, which is in the form of a religious poem, the surviving inhabitants are depicted as having seen in the disaster the vengeance of their gods on a sinful people. This is the lesson the Hebrews drew, and the one I was taught, and believed, in the Sunday School of the First Presbyterian Church when I was growing up in Cedar Rapids, Iowa.

I can still see in my mind our teacher declaiming lugubriously the stern words of the Lord from Genesis VI.

> The Lord saw that the wickedness of man was great. . . . And the Lord was sorry that he had made man on the earth, and it grieved him to his heart. So the Lord said: "I will blot out man whom I have created from the face of the earth, man and beast . . . for I am sorry that I have made them. . . . I will bring a flood of waters upon the earth . . . everything that is on the earth shall die."

That would have blotted out mankind, along with the beasts and the birds and "every creeping thing," but since they did survive, the Hebrews invented the story of Noah and his Ark — "But Noah found favor in the eyes of the Lord."

The Sumerians, in their poem, were more historical.

Professor Woolley, having finished with the story of the Flood, now showed me something of additional interest. The layers beneath the silt of the flood disclosed to him an antediluvian civilization of surprising sophistication. There were three superimposed layers beneath the flood level and in them, he said, he was finding richly decorated pre-Sumerian pottery in abundance, a good many terra-cotta figurines modeled with considerable skill and artistry, various flint instruments, and seals with elaborate geometric designs and others with rows of animals depicted with a lively naturalness. He thought it probable that where such seals were employed the art of writing might well have been known, though no examples of a written language had yet been found.

"The inhabitants may have been in the Neolithic stage," he said. "But their culture was considerable. They knew a good deal about the arts and crafts. And from the evidence we have found they carried on a trade that extended to the Orontes river, hundreds of miles to the north, and to India, a thousand miles to the east."

This culture was not entirely snuffed out by the flood. It contributed to that of the Sumerians which followed and which, to Woolley, became one of the glories of human civilization.

"I would say," he exclaimed, "on the basis of what we and others have found in Mesopotamia, that the Sumerians were the pioneers of the progress of Western man!"

At a time, he said, when the Egyptians, who until now historians had believed to have had the oldest human civilization, were still barbarians, the Sumerians at Ur and other towns along the Euphrates were living in a civilization of the most urban type, with architects who employed all the basic principles of construction known to us today and artists who combined a vivid realism with an imaginative style.

Craftsmen, he went on, worked in metals — gold, silver and copper — with great skill; potters, abandoning hand work for the potter's wheel, produced objects of extreme beauty, enhancing them by painting, and hardening them in kilns, which at Ur became virtual factories. Merchants carried on a brisk trade not only within the Euphrates valley but as far north as the mountains of Anatolia, the Mediterranean five hundred miles to the west, and India.

The season before, Woolley had unearthed a mosaic in lapis lazuli and shell which he called the "Standard" and which revealed for the first time a great deal of information about the Sumerian army, its weapons, organization and formations, which had enabled Sumeria to dominate for so long most of the world it knew. No other military force matched it.

The "Standard" also showed that the use of swarms of chariots, which, according to the Book of Judges, struck such terror in the Hebrews, had first been employed two thousand years before by the Sumerians. In fact the mosaics depicting the chariots in action, when I recalled them years later during the Second World War, seemed to me to have foretold the use of cavalry, even "mechanized" cavalry, in our time. Chariots drawn by asses dash through the enemy while other chariots carrying javelin throwers weave about the battlefield like modern tanks — indeed like the German panzers I followed through Poland, Belgium and France in 1939 and 1940 — bombarding the enemy with a hail of javelins and causing its ranks to break. The figures in the "Standard" disclosed something more that was equally fascinating. The phalanx, which until then we thought had been invented by Greek military genius, was the crux of the Sumerian army's attack more than two thousand years before Alexander.

The whole mosaic is not only fine art but a fascinating documentation of how wars were waged at the beginning of our bloody, warring history. It keeps reminding me of a sober fact: apparently from the outset mankind has wasted its fortunes, its energies, its blood and its youth in making war. And just as today in the twentieth century, the world powers have always been those which build up the most military might. Sumeria was an early, perhaps the earliest, example.

I asked Professor Woolley about his belief that his discoveries proved that not the Egyptians, as had been believed up to that time, but the Sumerians were the first, at least in the Western World (he apparently did not know much about early China and India), to build up a great civilization.

"Look," he said, warming to my question. "We have found that by 3500 B.C. this Sumerian civilization is already many centuries old. Now, in 3500 B.C. Egypt was still barbarous, a place of many petty kingdoms. The First Dynasty, which united it, came much later — at least five hundred years later. It borrowed from the much older civilization of Mesopotamia. But we can go further. Not only the Egyptians, but the Babylonians, Assyrians, Phoenicians, Greeks and, in the end, ourselves, owe much of their culture to the Sumerians. That is why, to repeat, I call them the pioneers of the progress of Western man."

So my chance visit to this ancient site, which had begun so inauspiciously, ended amicably and with enormous benefit to me. I had stumbled across a good story for my newspaper. I thanked Woolley for his courtesy and generous help. As I was taking my leave he reminded me of his commitment to the *Times* of London and asked me to promise that I would not publish anything in the *Chicago Tribune* before it appeared in the *Times*, which I readily did.

By this time he had become warm and friendly. To assist me in getting down as accurately as possible what he had told me, he lent me some books and articles of his, suggesting I check my notes against them. Our agreement about publication had an amusing sequel, though at the time I cannot say I was especially amused.

In Bagdad a few days later I pored over the material Woolley had given me, compared it to my notes, and when I had finally got the story straight, I wrote a lengthy article. I was rather pleased with my piece. It divulged something interesting and important about the course of history. It was a little above the cut of our usual reporting on the events of the day. It ought to hit the front page. I mailed it to Colonel McCormick himself, mindful of his interest in history, particularly military history. And I advised him of my agreement with Woolley to hold up publication until the archaeologist's own report appeared in the London *Times.* Woolley had been a little concerned that my newspaper, if only out of carelessness, might break the release date.

Neither he nor the esteemed *Times* need have worried. For the London newspaper and for the journals throughout the world to whom it sold Woolley's account of his discovery, the story was somewhat of a sensation, a bit like the one years before of the opening of the tomb of Tutankhamen in Egypt. It was played up in large headlines.

Not in the "World's Greatest Newspaper," as the *Chicago Tribune* proclaimed itself on its masthead. Its editor buried my learned piece in the back pages of the travel section of the bulky Sunday edition, using it as mere filler between the ads.

The wonders of Sumerian civilization, which I thought might interest even our gang-ridden Chicagoans, were lost among the ads promoting the wonders of the modest resorts along the sandy shores of Lake Michigan. The wonder of the discovery of the remains of Noah's Flood and the light it shed on the biblical story, lost too.

After Ur, Babylon was a disappointment, and Bagdad even more. The glories of the Babylon of the great lawgiver Hammurabi at the beginning of the Second Millennium B.C. and of Nebuchadnezzar, fifteen hundred years later, had turned to dust. There was practically nothing to see. No great ruins to bear witness to vanished magnificence. One could only re-create the past here by an act of memory and imagination. What Isaiah, after hurling his biblical curses at the fallen city of iniquity, admitted was "the glory of kingdoms, the beauty of the Chaldee's excellence," was a site of utter desolation.

I pondered, as I suppose many who have paused at this ancient site have done, what happens on this fickle earth to even the greatest of cities, centers so long of the finest achievements of man. Babylon had endured longer than most — four thousand years. I wondered if my native Chicago, and New York, and those much older cities that had become the place of my life and work, London and Paris and Vienna, would last as long, and then end this way — buried under the rubble.

Nothing much was left either of old Bagdad, the city on the Tigris

I had marveled at during my schooldays, the glittering capital of Harun-al-Raschid, of the Arabian Nights, the center of learning of Arabia at a time when Islam constituted the highest civilization of the West. It had fallen victim to the twentieth century and to the lure of Western European values. It turned out to be a squalid, noisy place.

There was one person in particular I wanted to see in Bagdad, and that was King Feisal. He had been the darling, I knew, of T. E. Lawrence, who had helped make him commander of the Arab forces, which had joined the British under Allenby in the push north across the deserts to drive the Turks out of the holy cities of Mecca and Medina and finally out of Jerusalem and Damascus during the Great War. One December morning he invited me to the palace for a talk.

Lawrence had described Feisal as he was at thirty-one, in 1916, when the two met for the first time in the Hejaz. He found the young Arab chief "tall, graceful and vigorous . . . and with a royal dignity of head and shoulders . . . [but] impetuous, hot tempered, even unreasonable. . . . His personal charm, his imprudence, the pathetic hint of frailty as the sole reserve of his proud character made him the idol of his followers."

Now in 1930, at forty-five, when I met him, he had mellowed. He had a finely chiseled, aristocratic, still handsome bearded face, but there was sadness in it and weariness. Perhaps, I thought as we chatted in French before the fireplace at one end of his neat office, this was because of the failed dream. Lawrence and Churchill had held out to him the prospect of becoming the ruler of the whole Arabian peninsula after the war. Now the formidable Ibn Saud had achieved that, by his own genius and without British help. Feisal was left to be king of a small country, which though Arab was almost a foreign land to a man brought up in the shadow of the holy cities, Mecca and Medina. By now, I felt, as we talked, he had become a fatalist. What had happened to him was what Allah had wanted.

Like Nadir Shah, Feisal did not have much longer to live. He also died three years later, in 1933, in Berne, Switzerland. But unlike the Afghan king, he died in bed. His kingdom lasted longer, but like Nadir's it too came to an end. In 1958 a revolution replaced it with a Republic.

I wanted very much to get back to Vienna for Christmas. And so late in December I set out overland for there. The overnight train from Bagdad took me as far as Kirkuk, where the railway ended, and from there our party of a dozen or so, mostly English officers and officials going home on leave, proceeded by car to Mosul. We passed forests of oil rigs but the pumps were idle. At Mosul I had hoped to skip over to see the ruins of nearby Nineveh, once capital of the Assyrian Empire which reached its golden period under Sennacherib, but there was no time.

From Mosul our motor caravan crossed the northeast tip of Syria, a desolate, rocky mountain strip. It was full of French troops, who looked like raw recruits and who had brought a little bit of France with them. In the villages they sat at tables outside makeshift cafés, sipped wine, and fondled their women companions, whom they must have brought with them from home, for they were French.

At the little station in Nisibin, the railhead of the old Berlin–Bagdad railway across the frontier in Turkey from Syria, all was confusion, reminding me of scenes of provincial railway stations in Russia which Tolstoy so graphically depicted. The departure of the twice-weekly train to Istanbul was almost too much to handle for the dozen Turkish rail officials and another dozen customs men. It took four or five hours for the wrangle — over tickets, sleeping berths, passports, health certificates — to subside. It was nearly midnight on a Saturday night before the little train finally chugged out of Nisibin and made its way west slowly across Anatolia, dipping down to Aleppo in Syria and then up past the Taurus mountains toward the Sea of Marmara, arriving finally on the following Tuesday at the Bosporus, from which we took a ferry across to Istanbul.

From Bagdad to Istanbul, a distance of a thousand miles as the crow (and plane) flies, it had taken five days by car and by train. Today a jet makes it in a couple of hours.

Istanbul had always seemed to me to be the beginning of Asia when I had arrived there from Paris or Vienna, but now approaching it from Asia it struck one as the beginning of Europe. The streets were like those of London, Berlin, Paris, Rome. There were smart shops and chic women, grand hotels and bars and gaudy movie fronts. Under the constant prodding of Mustapha Kemal, Turkey in ten years had shed its oriental ways, broken the hold of Islam and become European.

Kemal had taken the veils off the faces of the women, the fezes off the heads of the men (it was *verboten* to wear them), and changed the characters of the alphabet from Arabic to Latin. He had abolished the sultanate and the caliphate, which for centuries had been one —

the sultan had been the caliph and thus temporal ruler of the Turkish Empire and spiritual ruler of Islam. He had suppressed the ulema and the Mohammedan religious orders, separated State and Church, replaced Moslem law by civil law, and secularized the schools. And to break the millennium-old hold of religion on the country he had put through a law providing that the use of religion as a means of exciting popular discontent, whether in speech or print, would be deemed high treason.

As it happened, the Ghazi (the Victorious), as Kemal was known, was in Istanbul when I arrived, though he had long since moved the capital from there to Ankara, in the heart of Anatolia. I duly applied to see him, for he seemed to me to be one of the great men of our time. But he was extremely busy. There was uneasiness in the country over the swift pace of his drastic reforms and this had led to two uprisings recently, one by the Khurds and the other by Moslem fanatics at Menemen, near Smyrna, both of which Kemal had ruthlessly put down. When his secretary informed me that I would have to wait a week or two for an appointment, I decided to forget it. Christmas was but a few days away and I very much wanted to get back to Vienna.

It was snowing heavily in Budapest as the Orient Express pulled into the station an hour before dawn. Tess was waiting on the platform in the icy semidarkness. She had come down from Vienna to meet me. She was bundled up in a heavy winter coat but her head was bare, her face eager and beautiful in the dim light. We fell into each other's arms. By the time we proceeded on to Vienna a couple of days later, we had decided to marry.

CHAPTER 3

Married, Fired, Vienna

1931-1932

Shortly before noon on the sunny, wintry day of January 31, 1931, Tess and I took a taxi to the *Rathaus* and there were married by the Socialist vice-burgomaster of Vienna, a genial, bearded man. My German had become somewhat rusty, and during the brief marriage ceremony Tess had to nudge me at the proper moments to say *"Ja."* I did not fully grasp the remarks in German which the vice-burgomaster proffered at the end, though Tess said they were felicitous and quite humorous about how to be happy though married. I had not the slightest doubt that we were going to be happy together, married, forever! Emil Vadnai, a Hungarian friend who worked for the *New York Times*, and his lovely, dark-haired Viennese wife were our only witnesses, and after the ceremony we four took a taxi to Schoener's, the best restaurant in Vienna, for a festive lunch and champagne.

I went about in the clouds those first days of February, 1931. In a few days, on the twenty-third, we would celebrate my twenty-seventh birthday. Tess's twenty-first birthday would come in August.

Back in Vienna, a city I loved, and married to a beautiful young Viennese I loved, I looked forward to a life that, for a change, would be relatively stable. I was keen to get the Vienna bureau of the *Tribune* functioning again, reorganizing the news coverage of a rather vast territory that stretched down the Danube through six countries to the Black Sea. There would be plenty to write about. And Tess, with her background in this part of the world and her knowledge of its languages (for she was among other things a gifted linguist), would be of immense help.

In my euphoria I forgot that life rarely turns out as planned. A few days after the wedding, as we were about to move into our apartment, a cable came from Colonel McCormick in Chicago:

"SHIRER. RETURN INDIA."

Gandhi had just been released from prison and had agreed to confer with the viceroy about a peace settlement in India. It was the development I had waited for in vain all through the last half of the previous year out there. The prospect of meeting Gandhi and of reporting on whatever next step he took to further his revolution excited me. But the prospect of leaving Tess, after only a few days of marriage, tore me apart.

She came down with me to Trieste, where I was to catch the Lloyd-Triestino S.S. *Ganges* to Bombay, sharing a stateroom overnight to Venice, where we spent a last day together, walking and gondolaing around the wondrous city, and in the room we took at the Danieli. We had a rather sad parting at the dock — all our fond hopes to start living together suddenly crushed. From the very beginning of our marriage, then, the pattern of our life together for the next fourteen years was fixed.

By early summer, the story in India had simmered down. It was no longer necessary to follow Gandhi about. He was lying low for the moment, resting and preparing for the Round Table Conference in the fall in London, where I would join him. I had cabled the colonel suggesting I return to my post in Vienna — I was determined to link up with Tess, one way or another. When he replied asking me to remain in India for the time being, I cabled Tess to come out. We would have a second honeymoon on the cool Himalayan heights at Simla for the rest of the summer.

I met her boat in Bombay, where we lingered a week so that she could get a feel of the country. Sarojini Naidu was in town and immediately took Tess in tow. The poet was in a relaxed mood after the strain of a year leading salt marches, of stretches in prison and of helping Gandhi negotiate in Delhi with the viceroy and then with the Indian Moslems. She loved elaborate weddings and parties, and took us to several. She introduced Tess to some of the women leaders of the Congress; she took her shopping. It was an exciting week for my bride.

But the food and the heat — Bombay was stifling hot in June before the monsoons came — were too much for her. We decided to hasten north to Simla. With her uncanny knack of picking up foreign languages, Tess quickly learned enough Hindustani to talk with Indians. Soon she began writing pieces for some of the leading German and Austrian newspapers. In Vienna, despite her youth, she already had made a good beginning in journalism. She had become the Vienna correspondent of *Drama*, a London magazine, for which she wrote about the Austrian theater. And she had been assistant to the Vienna correspondent of the London *Daily Telegraph*.

In Simla there was not much spot news to cover, and we had time for ourselves and our love. It was an idyllic interlude. But even the mountain climate did not agree with my bride. She came down with dysentery, from which I was still suffering along with malaria, and a mysterious fever, and pains and cramps in her stomach. We laughed at being such young invalids, but it was not really funny. At the beginning of August I cabled Chicago that I was ill and returning to Vienna. I would pick up Gandhi in London in September.

In Delhi a few days later, on our way to Bombay to catch a boat for Marseilles, I almost lost Tess — just six months after we were married. On the train coming down the mountains from Simla she collapsed, and by the time we got to Delhi she was so deathly ill that she had to be driven in an ambulance directly from the railroad station to the hospital.

For a week the English doctors — civil surgeons with military titles — despaired for her life. They could not diagnose what was wrong. She had a high fever and she could not hold down nourishment. They thought at first she was pregnant, then that she had acute appendicitis. One day the colonel-doctor in charge said he would have to operate the very next morning. By evening he had changed his mind. There was no air-conditioning then, even in the hospital, and Tess seemed to suffer most from the unbearable heat. During the day the thermometer would rise well above one hundred in her room, even after the monsoons came, and it was a damp, sticky, stifling heat. Brave and stoic as Tess was, she would cry out: "Bill, I can't stand the heat! It's killing me! I can't breathe!"

I spent the whole day, from early morning until late in the evening, when the nurses asked me to leave, at her side, frustrated that there was nothing I could do except comfort her in her waking hours. The doctors seemed of little help, but they were all we had. At one juncture I proposed to take her back to Vienna. The physicians there were the best in Europe, and might save her. But the colonel-doctor said Tess was much too weak even to make the train journey to Bombay. Back in my room in the Cecil Hotel late at night I could not sleep. I threshed over one plan after another — anything to save her life.

Early in the second week she began to show signs of recovery. She was able to take some nourishment. Ice packs seemed to relieve her from some of the fever and the heat. The doctors still couldn't find out what was causing her illness, but at least they discerned that there was a turn for the better.

"She's over the worst," announced the colonel-doctor. "She's going to get well. Fast."

Back in Vienna I asked the *Tribune* for a brief sick leave, and Tess and I took off for Edlach in the foothills of the Alps below the Semmering to recuperate. By early September we both felt fairly fit again, and I was able to go down to Marseilles in time to meet Gandhi and proceed with him from there to London for the Indian Round Table Conference. Returning to Vienna late in the autumn after its breakup, I plunged heartily into my work and, for the first time, a married life in an apartment of our own. It was a new beginning, and we loved it. Our life and work together settled down, bringing much fulfillment.

But not for as long as we had hoped and planned.

At first, all went well. Ever since my return from India, Colonel McCormick, for all his imperiousness and frigidity, had expressed surprising concern about my tropical illnesses and had urged me to take all the time I needed to get well. He wrote at length offering rare praise for my work in India and especially my covering of Gandhi at the Round Table Conference in London. At his direction the *Chicago Tribune* had published several full-page ads boasting of some of my "exclusive" dispatches: from Kabul, about Afghanistan; from Marseilles and London about Gandhi; and, after I had returned to Vienna, there would be one more, about Gandhi's cabling me from Poona Prison explaining why he was "fasting unto death."

Even some of my reporting from Central Europe began to attract the favorable attention of the eccentric owner of the *Tribune*. Thus when I sent a story about the long imprisonment of Dr. Adalbert Tuka, a Slovak and a former professor of jurisprudence at Bratislava

University, who was regarded by many Slovaks as the Dreyfus of Czechoslovakia, the colonel dashed off a note to me:

Dear Shirer:
I like this story. It is stories like these that set the Tribune Foreign News Service in a class by itself. Other papers do not cover them.

He was pleased also that I had saved cable tolls by sending it by mail.

On another occasion he lauded the "objectivity" of my reporting, and this led him to further thoughts about the superiority of his newspaper.

The fact is that we print the news and the truth and we are the only newspaper that prints the news and the truth on international affairs. All the other American newspapers either through their proprietors or through their correspondents are reached in one way or another. Mostly they are over-impressed; sometimes they are socially seduced and, I think, never bribed.

The colonel could be quick too to criticize, and when he did he would usually follow the expression of his displeasure with another disquisition, more fantastic than those which went with his praise. Thus when once I compared the living conditions of the Vienna workers in the beautiful apartment complexes, built for them by the Socialist government of the capital, with what it had been like for them in the dreary slums under the Hapsburgs before the war, he shot back a clipping of my dispatch with the curt comment: "Mr. Shirer: How do you know this?" followed by a more lengthy letter a few days later.

Dear Shirer:
I cannot imagine how you could know what conditions in Vienna were like before the war.
Reading your article I gathered the impression that you were either reading the New York newspapers pretty assiduously or associating with New York newspaper men. They are not good teachers.
New York newspaper men are pretty well confirmed in the habit of parlor socialism. It is nothing but a form of mental laziness somehow translated into dreamy egotism. Writers of the parlor socialist type do not bother to seek the facts, and their small entourage does not want facts; it wants lazy ecstasy.
The principal achievement of the Chicago Tribune in the last fif-

teen years has been to insist on facts on economic and semi-historic matters.

A blanket approval of Bolshevism in the abstract furnishes many a man an excuse for not supporting his family. You should be careful not to get in the frame of mind where a similar approval of all the effects of Vienna socialism justifies you in your own mind in not doing a real day's work.

Yours sincerely,
Robt. R. McCormick

I should have been mature enough not to answer the colonel's aberrations. It was ridiculous to hold that if you were not present to witness something, like the prewar condition of the workers, you couldn't find out what they were. Life in Vienna's slums before the war was fully documented — you had only to read the official reports. Dozens of writers, domestic and foreign, had described them firsthand. As to my dangerous association with New York newspapermen, there weren't any in Vienna to contaminate me. "The *New York Herald-Tribune*," I wrote back, "is represented here by an Austrian official, the *New York Times* by two Britishers, one of whom has never seen America."

It was a mistake to shoot back a reply, though I did not realize it at the time. I was still not wise enough to know that you did not cross the autocratic lord of the *Chicago Tribune*, who hurled his dictates and dictums to his hirelings from the lofty Tour de Beurre* above Michigan Avenue.

All through that year of 1932, which toward its end was to bring another turning point in my life, the *Tribune*, like all other American newspapers, was preoccupied by domestic news. We were told to cut down on our cables by twenty-five percent, not only to save money but because there would be little space available for foreign news.

For weeks the kidnapping of the Lindbergh baby and its bitter, sad aftermath took over the front page. Sharing it, month after month, was the latest news about the Depression, which got worse and worse. Business and banking were at a standstill. Some fifteen million citizens were out of work. No one in America knew what to do about it, not President Hoover, the Congress, the financial, business and labor leaders, the newspapers. When summer came other domestic stories crowded onto the front page: the chasing of the veterans' bonus army from Washington by federal troops under General

---

* The Tribune Tower was a replica of the famous Tour de Beurre of the Rouen Cathedral. McCormick's office, as described in Volume I, was at the top of it.

Douglas MacArthur, with an unknown Major George S. Patton commanding the charging horse-cavalry and tanks, and another unknown major, Dwight D. Eisenhower, photographed at the side of the general, whose aide he was. It was a famous victory, and a shameful one.

But most extensive of all that summer was the reporting of the Republican and Democratic conventions, both of which were held in Chicago. Reading copies of the home paper in my pleasant retreat in Vienna, I was struck by the foreboding of Colonel McCormick and his newspaper on the eve of the conventions. Herbert Hoover would be automatically renominated for President by the Republicans, and the *Tribune* would support him against whatever Democrat was nominated. Yet Colonel McCormick was in despair about the future of the Republic.

In an editorial that took two whole columns on the front page on the eve of the Republican convention in June, the colonel proclaimed that the "Reds" were taking over Washington (despite Hoover being in the White House!)* and fast ruining the country. By raising federal taxes from less than a billion to four billions "in less than a generation," "they" were destroying business and bankrupting the taxpayer.

"The tide [of life in America]," the colonel exclaimed, "has been running strongly in the direction of serfdom since the war." And he concluded ominously: "The National conventions this year may be the last held in the United States by a free people. . . . Unless we have a new birth of freedom, the death of our civilization is near and inevitable."

With such dire thoughts about the state of the nation — there was no mention in the editorial about the creeping Depression, which was what most worried Americans that year — the colonel had little interest in what we were covering in Europe except, I think, the news from Germany.

The Republic of Germany, in contrast to our own, was really going down the drain that summer.

In the spring Hindenburg had been reelected President in a runoff election, but the upstart Adolf Hitler, as most people, even in Germany, I thought, regarded him, had run the venerable old field mar-

---

* Adjacent to the page-one editorial was a cartoon by Orr, "the colonel's hatchetman," as he was called in the *Trib* newsroom, depicting the familiar statue of Lincoln in the Memorial at Washington. But Lenin has replaced the great Emancipator on the pedestal. Ragged-looking members of the "Radical Congress" are seen slouching away, carrying a pail of "red paint" and their brushes after having painted out Lincoln's name and substituted Lenin's. "Will It Come to This?" the cartoon's caption asks.

shal a close race. The results of the election had reassured some and alarmed others, both in and out of Germany. For the rest of Europe, if not faraway America, had become increasingly concerned about the floundering Weimar Republic and the threat of a Nazi dictatorship replacing it. Hindenburg's reelection had seemed to give the Republic a new lease on life. But Hitler's challenge, which had won him thirteen and a half million votes (against Hindenburg's nineteen and a third million), showed that his drive for power was not to be taken lightly.

This became more evident in midsummer that year. The national elections on July 31 brought a resounding victory for the Nazis. With 13,745,000 votes, they won 230 seats in the Reichstag, making them by far the largest party in Parliament, though still short of a majority in a house of 608 members. Hitler was knocking at Hindenburg's door, demanding that as head of the largest party he be entrusted to take over the government as chancellor.

Though eighty-five and senile, and weary of his job of trying to save the Republic, in which he did not much believe, for he had remained an ardent monarchist and wished the Hohenzollerns back on the throne, Hindenburg resisted Hitler's demands all through the summer. But he entrusted power to two weird, intriguing misfits, who were as cool to the Republic as he and just as royalist.

The first was Franz von Papen, a ludicrous figure who, as the French ambassador in Berlin, André François-Poncet, a veteran diplomat, said, was taken seriously by neither his friends nor his enemies. He had not been able even to get himself elected to the Reichstag. His own party, the Catholic Center, completely disowned him. Yet Hindenburg named him chancellor in June. Having no support in the Reichstag he was forced to rule by presidential decree. But not for long.

The man who foisted him upon the German Republic was another devious figure, General Kurt von Schleicher, the power behind the throne due to his influence with Hindenburg, his position in the army, and his undoubted gift for intrigue. His name was the word in German for "intriguer" or "sneak." It was Schleicher who had induced the befuddled Hindenburg at the end of May to dismiss Heinrich Brüning, the last chancellor with the backing of a major parliamentary party in the Reichstag the Republic would see. From midsummer that year the Reichstag was shorn of its constitutional powers, as the elected body representing the people, to govern the country. It never got them back.

Papen misgoverned the country until December 2, when Schleicher withdrew his backing of him and in turn took over as chancellor, the last one of the Weimar Republic which he and Papen had done their best to undermine and destroy.

In Austria, across the border from Germany, we watched uneasily that year the signs that Hitler would soon take over the torn and chaotic country. The Austrians knew that if he did, one of his first acts would be to join his native Austria to the German Reich. In the very first paragraph of *Mein Kampf* he had sworn to accomplish this "by every means."

Ironically enough, with all the ominous news from Germany and home, life in Vienna that last year was pleasant and tranquil. Tess and I shed the worst effects of our tropical maladies, rebuilt our health, and for the first time had a quiet and lovely personal life together. I could not compete for headlines with Germany nor with the compelling events at home. But since a journalist, like an author, has a compulsion to write and find material to enable him to write, I traveled about a good deal in the vast territory of my beat, seeking to find out what was going on in the increasingly repressive Danube dictatorships and semidictatorships. It might be helpful in measuring what Hitler would do if he grabbed power, though we already had some evidence from Mussolini's strutting dictatorship in Italy. And there were always "human interest" stories.

Colonel McCormick, busy as he was in Chicago trying to avert the collapse of American civilization, somehow found time occasionally to give me a specific assignment. But in a peculiarly perverse way.

One day toward the end of May he sent me a clipping from the Paris weekly *L'Illustration* showing a collapsed bridge over a small river. "Shirer — go there," read his letter, in its entirety. But he had carefully cut out the text accompanying the illustration. The bridge was unidentified. There were thousands of bridges in my part of the world, and some, being badly built or not properly maintained, were liable to collapse and sometimes did. Fortunately, I remembered seeing a photograph similar to the colonel's. It was of a bridge across the Dniester river between Rumanian Bessarabia and Moldavia in the Soviet Ukraine. It had been blown up by the retreating Bolsheviks toward the end of the war, and there had been reports recently of a thousand Moldavian peasants fleeing the Soviet paradise to the Rumanian side — over the ice until the April thaws came, and in the month since then by boat, raft and swimming. So I took it I was to go there, if my bridge was the same as the colonel's, and see for myself.

Picking up a friend in Bucharest who knew Russian and Moldavian — I wouldn't have trusted Rumanian police or military interpreters — I journeyed up through Bessarabia to the Dniester and found the broken bridge near a dreamy little town called Tighina on the banks of the river. There I got my first glimpse of Russia. Red guards patrolled the opposite bank, not more than fifty yards away. In the distance you could see peasants plowing their fields, behind a team of horses.

For a week I talked through my interpreter to scores of peasants who had fled across the river, sometimes, when their tales of woe seemed almost incredulous, gathering them together in groups and asking each one whether the others were telling the truth or at least exaggerating. Though I quickly perceived that there was no love lost between the richer kulaks and the poorer serednjaks and bedniaks — a distinction they themselves had pointed out to me — their accounts of hunger and persecution on their side of the frontier held together.

Though the Ukraine was the "breadbasket" of Russia, the chief complaint of these refugees was that they never had enough to eat. They grew enough grain on their small plots, they said, but most of it was taken away from them by Soviet officials. And not only their grain. Police confiscated their livestock and farm implements and carted them away to the collective farms. Some of them had been carted away themselves to work in the mines of the Urals. They had managed to escape, make their way back to the Dniester and finally cross over. Not much more than half of the nearly two thousand who tried that spring made it. The rest were cut down by the machine guns of the Red guards.

God knows these primitive Slav peasants expected little enough from life, not much more than to be able to work, eat, breed, and in the end, perhaps, go to heaven — some I talked to were obviously deeply religious. Used to misery and hardship though they were, in Soviet Russia that year they had found limits to their endurance.

I remember that last year an idyllic week in August with Tess in Salzburg. The entertainment editor in Chicago had asked me to do some mail articles on the Salzburg Festival, which for a month at the end of the summer became the music center of Europe. It afforded us a brief escape into a baroque, Mozartean dreamland.

The serenity and unfathomable mystery of Wolfgang Amadeus

Mozart, born on January 27, 1756, a century and three-quarters before, in a simple little house on Market Street, still hung over the baroque town, making it, at least during the music festival that honored his life and works, a place unlike any other I had ever seen.

It was a place, we found, where one's anxieties over the death-throes of the Weimar Republic across the nearby frontier, and over the coming elections and growing Depression at home, and over all the other ills that beset this chaotic, meaningless world, seemed to evaporate — to be replaced by the spell of glorious music and the dreaminess which floats over the baroque façades and the flat baroque roofs to the edge of the Alps, which tower over this serene and tranquil town. The world might be in a bad fix — it undoubtedly was. But Salzburg, during the festival, forgot it — if it ever knew, or cared.

My diary reflects this.

August 24. Strolled through the town; down the Getreidesgasse, past Mozart's birthplace, an unimposing old building (but Herman Bahr says that none of the buildings in Salzburg impose by themselves, but only together do they give the town its atmosphere and beauty) now made into a museum. Past the Kollegiankirche, an ugly structure, though built by Fischer von Erlach, Austria's great architect of the baroque. . . . At noon went up on the Mönchs Berg and walked along the ridge overlooking the town. The view superb. The baroque towers, the flat roofs, the hills which stab so suddenly out of the earth, the Salzach river hurrying busily along.

Wandered over the ridge to the Restaurant Katz, about half-way up the Hohen Salzburg. It commands another splendid view. The town gibbet used to stand here, exhibiting to the populace the dangling bodies of the condemned. The thought almost spoiled our lunch, which otherwise was excellent.

Home by way of Noonberg, where an abbey and a Gothic church look over the town below. . . . In the evening we walk upstream to Mulln, where we found an old Renaissance church and the greatest beer hall I've ever seen. It is part of a monastery. When you enter, a statue of the crucifixion stares you in the eye. Further on are little shops selling sausages, ham, garlic salad and rolls. Further on still you come into a great beer hall. You take a stein from the shelves and hold it under the barrel tap until it is filled. At long wooden tables the local guzzlers sit, puffing at their long pipes whose bowls rest on their laps and tossing down the excellent beer. As you put down your beer and sausages, Christ on the Cross looks down on you. Monks drift in, make the sign of the cross at the statue, and join you. Much beer has bloated their faces. . . .

The innumerable wine gardens at the end of many a stroll were just as good.

After nearly half a century the memory of Salzburg during the festival lingers pleasantly in the mind. Refreshed by our week there, we returned to Vienna eager for the life and work we believed lay ahead for us.

In the spring the first of two disasters that year had struck me.

The snows in the Alps lasted late that season, and toward the end of March John MacCormac of the *New York Times* and his wife, Molly, joined Tess and me for a final weekend of skiing on the Semmering. There were no lifts then and we spent the time cross-country skiing from one village to the next. On the Sunday morning we decided to climb a mountain, have lunch in an inn at its top and in the afternoon make a good downhill run, the last we would have until next year.

By the time we reached the peak the noon sun was so warm that we ate lunch outside in our shirtsleeves. The snow, we noticed, was beginning to melt and become soggy, and by the time we started down skiers before us had made deep ruts on the trails. Once you were in the ruts it was hard to get out.

About four o'clock we reached a small flat where the slope leveled off. A thousand feet below us was a valley through which the main railroad line from Vienna to Italy ran. We could see the village and its railroad station, from which we had planned to catch a train at five o'clock back to Vienna — in time for Jack and me to get to work that Sunday evening. The run down the rather steep slope was a half mile or so. There would be time to get a beer and a sandwich at the station before the train arrived.

We held a moment's consultation and decided to follow the track other skiers before us had made. It was now a foot and a half deep. Once in it you could not get out of it. But it went in a straight line down to the little square in front of the station. I followed the Mac-Cormacs and Tess down. The way seemed clear. All three had reached the bottom and stepped aside, waiting for me. The going was faster than I had expected because ice had formed at the bottom of the rut. Halfway down I suddenly noticed a figure none of us had seen. It looked like a woman. She apparently had fallen, taken her time to get up, and was just putting her skis down in the deep rut of the trail to continue to the bottom. She was some two hundred yards ahead when I first saw her. I yelled at her and at the same instant tried to steer my skis out of the rut. But I could not get out. I could not break my speed. And she was barely moving. In a few seconds, unless I did something, I would hit her. I did the only thing I could think of doing. I took a tumble, coming to a stop upside down a few yards from her. Unfortunately, I had somehow lost the rubber grip at the top of my right ski pole. As I tumbled and rolled over, its bare end hit me square in the right eye. I went blind.

I lay there until Jack and Tess climbed up to help me. They led me on foot down the slope. Molly had gone to try to find a doctor. They laid me out on a bench at the station. Soon the doctor arrived, washed away the blood, and bandaged my face. Vision in the left eye had come back partly. I could see blurred figures. The doctor left a crack open so I could see.

For ten days as I lay in the hospital in Vienna with both eyes and the rest of my face bandaged, there was some fear among the doctors that I might become totally blind. I refused to believe it. I could not bring myself to face that prospect. For the first time I heard talk among the ophthalmologists about the threat of something they said they still knew little about: the working of the sympathetic optic nerve. If one eye was badly damaged, they explained, the sympathetic nerve might at any time cause blindness in the other.

At the end of a fortnight the bandage over the left eye was removed and the vision in it, though blurred, seemed promising enough and soon the blur began to recede. In the right eye, however, a blood clot had formed. When the bandage was taken off, I could see light through it, but that was all. For weeks, indeed for months and years, I took various treatments to dissolve the clot but they did not work. By midsummer, though not abandoning hope that someday the clot might disappear, I became reconciled to seeing through one eye. It was easier than I had expected.

And I had some good luck, after the bad. Twice during the first year of the war that came in 1939 (to skip ahead) my face got slightly banged up, once in Berlin when I barged through a glass door in the blackout, and again in June, 1940, when I was following the German army on its dash to Paris. One night in an abandoned house near Maubeuge in northern France a few British bombers came over. A bomb fell near, broke the windows and a couple of small splinters of glass hit my face. In both cases, only the bad eye suffered. At Maubeuge German army medics removed the splinters and bandaged the eye, but it became infected, and when we reached Paris I had to go out to the American hospital to have it treated. There the physicians advised having it out, again explaining the threat of the mysterious sympathetic optic nerve. But there was no time.

One evening in Baltimore in the late spring of 1944, when I was dining at H. L. Mencken's, I noticed that one of the guests kept staring at my blinded eye. This was Professor Alan C. Woods, an eminent ophthalmologist at Johns Hopkins. As we parted he asked me if I could come to see him at the hospital the next morning. His tone was so urgent that I agreed. "You must excuse me," he said when I arrived at his office, "for giving your eye a clinical glance last evening. But I did not like the looks of it." After examining the eye, he said, rather gruffly: "This eye must come out. At once!" And he too expounded on the mysterious threat of the sympathetic nerve. It might bring total blindness at any moment, he warned. I was a fool to take any further chances.

And so toward the end of May that year I had the eye removed at the Institute of Ophthalmology of the Columbia Presbyterian Medical Center in New York. This cost my participation in one of the most important and exciting assignments of the war: the Allied landing in Normandy on June 6. I felt a terrible frustration at having to miss it. By the time I was able to catch up with General Eisenhower's forces in Western Europe they had entered Paris.

One eye, I found, is enough for a human being, or at least it has been for me. For nearly half a century since my skiing accident (as these lines are written), that is, for more than half my life, I have been able to read voraciously for both my work and my pleasure without the slightest trouble or any sign of eye strain. About the only thing I have had to give up is tennis, where the lack of binocular vision and the sense of depth it gives is a handicap. But I was never any good at it anyway. No loss.

The end of my relatively brief career as a foreign correspondent for "The World's Greatest Newspaper" came suddenly out of the blue in the autumn that year of 1932 in Vienna.

That was the second disaster of that fateful year for me. One fine mid-October day I found myself out of a job. On the very evening the *Chicago Tribune* was about to publish a full-page ad* boasting about the scoop I gave its readers with the cable sent to me by Mahatma Gandhi from Poona Prison in which he explained his "fast unto death," and praising its young Vienna correspondent to the skies,

---

* The full-page ad about my "Gandhi Scoop" had to be "wrecked," as the cable editor later wrote me, just as the *Tribune* went to press. There was a "big blow-off" that evening, he said, in McCormick's office.

Colonel McCormick ordered his managing editor to cable me, as follows:

SHIRER THIS NOTIFICATION YOUR SERVICES WITH TRIBUNE
TERMINATES TODAY OCTOBER SIXTEENTH STOP YOU WILL BE
PAID ONE MONTH'S SALARY COVERING TO NOVEMBER SIX-
TEENTH.

> E. S. BECK TRIBUNE

I was, I admit, stunned. I had no idea why I was fired. There had been no warning of any kind. I got off a letter to Beck, who personally and as managing editor had shown me many kindnesses, asking why.

Five weeks later I received a reply from him. "The reason you were dropped from the staff," he wrote, "was that your recent dispatches and mail articles had not been satisfactory to the management." In addition, Beck added, there was a specific reason.

This had to do with a routine dispatch I had recently sent in which the Austrian police mistakenly identified an American actress, Mary Wong, involved in a minor traffic accident, as Anna May Wong, a Hollywood movie star. The latter took exception to the report in the *Tribune*, threatened to sue, and my newspaper paid her $1,000 and printed a retraction. The whole matter seemed to me to be scarcely of world-shaking importance, though I regretted any embarrassment to Anna May Wong. Dozens of other American newspapers published the story from news agency dispatches, as did the *New York Times* from its Vienna correspondent.

For several days I felt dazed, then bitter and finally, I regret to say, rather sorry for myself. I could not comprehend why this trivial mistake in one brief dispatch outweighed in the colonel's mind all the serious reporting I had done over the years. Only later did I realize that probably I was just another casualty of the Depression, one of millions. Some months before, the colonel had abruptly fired his favorite among us, Henry Wales, our veteran Paris correspondent, while he was on his way to the Far East on an assignment McCormick himself had given him. My successor in India, Egbert Swenson, had recently been sacked. Jay Allen, the most brilliant among us younger men, would soon be let out. McCormick was drastically cutting down his foreign staff to save money.

I quickly found out that it would not be easy to find another job in Europe. As the Depression deepened at home, the few newspapers

that had a foreign staff — the *New York Times*, the *New York Herald-Tribune*, the *Chicago Daily News* — and all three American
news agencies, also were cutting down. I telephoned their European
chiefs in London or Paris. They said they would keep me in mind.
But for the moment they were not hiring any correspondents.

Tess and I had a grim and dreary Christmas that year. Even some
of our friends, we thought, had begun to view us somewhat differently now that I was jobless. The Gunthers, our closest friends,
reneged on a skiing holiday we had planned together, and instead
went off to the big house party Dorothy Thompson and Sinclair
Lewis were throwing on the Semmering. We decided to remain in
Vienna over the holidays and conserve our dwindling resources. The
Tribune had not paid — and would never pay — the promised one
month's severance pay.

After New Year's our spirits began to revive. I had managed to
save a thousand dollars over the last five years. We would, we decided, take a year off in Spain, where living was incredibly cheap.
There we would regain our health, read all the books there had never
been time to read, and I would try to write one. Perhaps I could
make a modest living as a writer — and never again be at the mercy
of the whims of a mad publisher. At any rate, we would have a year
to think things over and plan a new life — so far as one could. We
wrote friends in Spain, went over brochures and maps, and decided
we would look for a place on the Costa Brava above Barcelona. We
felt relieved to have come to a decision. We booked passage on a Yu-
goslav tramp steamer leaving Trieste for Barcelona on February 15.
We would celebrate my birthday on February 23 aboard, for the little boat, stopping at a dozen ports in Italy en route, took three weeks
to reach its destination.

On January 20, 1933, we abruptly halted our planning. A letter
dated December 20, 1932, arrived from Colonel McCormick in Chicago.

Dear Shirer:
    You did some excellent work in India, but since then you have al-
most vanished from the picture as a European correspondent. Is it
that your health is so bad, or do you think that your field is non-pro-
ductive? We might transfer you elsewhere, if that is so.
    It seems to me, however, that your part of the world should pro-
duce as much interesting reading as the Baltic, although heaven
knows, you haven't made it do so.

Sincerely,
McC.

I was as dumbfounded by this message as I had been at the one of my dismissal. But it offered hope of my resuming my work with the *Trib*. The colonel, forgetful though he was, seemed to be in a surprisingly mellow mood regarding me.

I thought this letter over for an hour. Did I really want to go back to work for him, badly as I needed the job? Tess came in, and we decided that, however reluctantly, we did. I would swallow my pride. And so, rather buoyed up, I cabled that I was answering his letter by mail.

Though "rather surprised" at his letter, I wrote, I "appreciated his sympathetic inquiries and criticism." The reason I had "almost vanished from the picture as a European correspondent," I said, was that on October 16 last he had fired me. I thought my old beat in Central Europe could still be very productive.

I tacked on a P.S. "I had planned to leave here February 15, and would appreciate a cable about all this, since a letter wouldn't reach me in time."

Thinking that I was about to be reemployed, I took Tess out that evening to Sacher's and we splurged on much good wine and food. We hated to give up the prospect of a year off in Spain; it had seemed like a beautiful dream. But the prospect of reemployment, especially during the Depression, seemed too good to pass up.

When we returned to our apartment from Sacher's, a cablegram from Chicago was awaiting us. I was sure it was from the colonel and that he would be saying I could start work again immediately. I tore it open.

SHIRER DISREGARD LETTER THIRTIETH. MCCORMICK

A week or so later, as we were preparing to get off to Spain, a letter came from the colonel's secretary. It was dated January 11.

Dear Mr. Shirer:
On December 30th Colonel McCormick addressed a letter to you in care of the Tribune Office in Vienna commenting on the lack of stories and news from you.
He asks that you disregard it, if it has been delivered to you, as at the time of writing he did not know that you were off the payroll.
Very truly yours,
G. W. Burke
Secretary to Colonel McCormick

So the old boy hadn't known I was "off the payroll"! He who alone, so far as the foreign staff was concerned, decided who was put off it. What a contemptible son-of-a-bitch!

"The old bastard," I said to Tess as she finished reading the letter, "didn't have the guts to write it, and sign it, himself."

During the three months we remained in Vienna after my discharge I tried, as soon as the shock wore off, to do a little stocktaking. Without deadlines to meet and without, for the first time since I became a foreign correspondent, having to scurry here and there in Europe and Asia to cover a story, I at last had time for a little sizing-up of myself and of the world I was trying to make my way in.

I have a letter I wrote to my brother from Vienna on November 18, 1932, just a month after McCormick rid his newspaper of me. It recalls how I saw myself and the world then — in contrast to what, after nearly half a century, I imagine myself thinking at that juncture. It rather surprises me to see what kind of a person I was at twenty-eight, and what hopes and aspirations and views I had then, when adversity first struck after the good times and the exciting unfolding of the first seven years of working at journalism in Europe and Asia.

I think it [getting fired] came in time for me yet to make something out of my life. . . . I think last summer when you were here I told you that [John] Gunther and I had agreed that we would get out of our racket when we were 30. Gunther has gone over the time-limit and is still with the *Chidailynews*, but he soothes his soul by writing for the *Nation* and turning out an occasional novel. He wants to quit his job, but he has no money. He has a wife and a youngster.°

Fortunately that part of the problem has been solved for me. But I realize that an important problem — which road to take at this turning — remains to be faced.

I have a lot of spiritual and intellectual cravings which my job has not allowed me to satisfy. There are the books one has wanted all his life to read. I want to write a lot . . . I have just finished a play and am busy revising it. It is about what the Indian revolution did to some In-

---

° He solved the problem three years later, in 1935, by taking a year off in London to write *Inside Europe*, the first of his "inside" books. Published in 1936 it quickly brought him fame and fortune and enabled him to give up daily newspaper work forever.

My other friend and colleague from Chicago, Vincent Sheean, fared likewise. He had been fired by the *Chicago Tribune*, he always maintained, for taking too much time out for dinner one evening in Paris, at about the time I had gone to work there for the *Trib* in 1925 — and this after he had given our newspaper a world scoop by risking his life to penetrate the French lines in the Riff, during the war there, to interview the rebel leader Abd-el-Krim. His first book, an account of his adventure, had not gone very well, but his next book, *Personal History*, published in 1935, a year before Gunther's *Inside Europe*, was an immediate best-seller, and allowed him to devote most of the rest of his life to writing more books. Sheean was the best writer, the most philosophical and learned, of the three of us.

dians and some British. Probably it will never see the light of day.* . . .
Probably also I will dash off a book based on my flight to Delhi, my
contacts with Gandhi, Nehru, Patel, Raman, the Viceroy and the fantastic interlude in Afghanistan.

There was much more — the letter was ungodly long — that reveals the intellectual confusion (and pretensions) of a twenty-eight-
year-old American abroad, and adrift. Now that I had the time, I
wrote, I was going to study the philosophers, "from the Greeks to
Kant and Hegel and Marx down to Santayana, if anybody believes in
him any more." Recently I had begun to read *Das Kapital* but found
Marx "hard-going" in German. I was halfway through Spengler's
Decline of the West but had got stuck on his chapter on mathematics.
I intended to delve into Rutherford, whom I understood to have
"disproved the stability of matter"; and into the Michelson-Morley
experiments, "which proved that science had been wrong in taking
the mere earth as a standard of measurement," and this would lead
me to Einstein and "his theory of relativity and the discarding of
mankind's millennium-old ideas of space and time." Finally,

> Tess has succeeded in interesting me a bit in the Viennese industry,
> psycho-analysis. I'm reading a book of Freud's lectures, and once a
> week we go to a lecture at the university by one of Freud's bright
> young men.

Rereading the letter almost takes my breath away — even after
forty-six years. Such intellectual ambition! Or was it pretension?
I remember that writing it brought a sense of release. Forgotten
now was the shock and the bitterness at having been fired and the
despair at being unable to find a new job. The immediate future
looked brighter than seemed possible a few weeks before.
Not even Hindenburg's naming of Adolf Hitler on January 30,
1933, shortly before we departed Austria, to take over the government in Berlin gave us pause about taking the year off in Spain as we
had planned. Maybe the Germans deserved a dose of this Nazi char-
latan to bring them to their senses. They would, I thought, soon see
the light, and that would be the end of this once-Austrian vagabond.
At any rate, there was no way for an unemployed foreign correspondent to get involved in reporting the German mess. I didn't even
want to. I was determined to have a year off from all of that.
It never occurred to me, as Tess and I prepared to depart for

* Mercifully, it never did.

Spain, that another turn of fate, within a year and a half, would en-
mesh me in the tangled, barbarian world of Adolf Hitler and the
Germans and set me to reporting over the years the most momentous
story I would ever experience and, in the end, to get it down in a
book of history.

All that lay ahead, in the unknown.

John Gunther and the author in Vienna, 1932

The author ice-skating in Vienna, 1931

The author skiing in Semmering, Austria, with his wife, Tess, 1931

The author and Tess in Vienna, 1932

CHAPTER 4

The Year Off in Spain

1933

It had begun to snow when we left Vienna on February 19 and it had become a blizzard that evening on the Semmering, where we paused for a final day of skiing and to say goodbye to Frances Gunther (John had gone to Berlin to help cover Hitler's takeover) and to Dorothy Thompson and Sinclair Lewis. (Dorothy and Red, their marriage on the rocks, were feuding again, and he had declined to come to the little farewell party she got up for us.)

But by the time our wandering freighter made it down the Italian coast from Venice to Sicily and up the other side to Genoa and to Barcelona three weeks later, spring had come in Spain. Spring had come to our spirits too.

Excerpts from my diary tell of the idyllic voyage.

On Thursday, February 23, I was 29, and at noon we slipped into Ancona. After prowling through the narrow streets of the Old Town, which sloped down to the port, we had a birthday feast in an old Albergo — fettucini washed down with Chianti. . . .

Catania, Sicily, Sunday February 26. After Bari we swung around the heel of Italy to Catania, which we were surprised to find is an enterprising trading town of 300,000. To the north beyond the groves of almond trees in full blossom and orange trees laden with their yellow fruit, we could see Mount Etna, snow covered and belching smoke. . . .

At noon we drove down to Syracuse, once the largest colony of the Athenian empire. The great theater, hewn out of rock on the side of a hill that sloped down to the bay, was in good condition. It was, I believe, the largest Greek theater outside of Greece.

On Saturday, March 4, we steamed into the Bay of Naples, as enchanting as I had remembered it. To the south, Mount Vesuvius was puffing smoke.

Lunch along the bay overlooking Vesuvius. Oysters, spaghetti, fritta mista, gorgonzola and wine, from which we returned to ship in fine fettle.

The Neapolitan newspapers were headlining the inauguration of President Roosevelt that day and stressing that all the banks at home had been closed down. "Panic in America!" read one headline. We couldn't believe it.

Sunday, March 5, into Livorno, passing on the way Elba, a beautiful island rising sheer out of the sea. Napoleon was a fool to leave its beauty for another war.

Early Monday, March 6, into Genoa, the greatest port in the Mediterranean. . . . We wandered through the narrow little streets, stopping to get a look at one old palace after another. Around noon we stopped at the American Express to exchange some traveler's checks for Spanish pesetas. We were told that since all the banks in America had shut down there were no quotations for the dollar. . . . We were pretty depressed at the news because our whole holiday depends on the dollar being good and staying strong.

Lloret de Mar (Spain). March 22, 1933. At last the very spot we dreamt of!

A little fishing village of some 3,000 souls, perched along a half-moon, wide, sandy beach between two rocky promontories. Back of us the mountains, rising gently toward the snow-capped peaks of the Pyrenees, the slopes terraced with vineyards and olive groves and tracts of cork-oak trees.

We had stumbled across Lloret de Mar on a hike up the Costa Brava from Barcelona. The village was picturesque, but we feared accommodations might be primitive. The house we found, however, was anything but that. It was a large three-story double-villa along the beach, and our half had ten rooms — a large living room with fireplace, a spacious dining room, seven bedrooms and two baths —

and there was central heating. The living room had been beautifully furnished by a Catalan painter, and the other rooms tastefully done. When the proprietor, a genial Barcelona physician and a professor on the faculty of the university medical school, told us the price would be fifteen dollars a month, furnished, we hid our pleasant surprise and promptly forked over the rent for a year, somewhat to *his* surprise. At least we would have a roof over our heads for the next twelve months.

It had been difficult to raise even that modest sum for so great a bargain. During our first few days in Barcelona we had no money at all. The banks in America were still closed and the bank in Barcelona refused to exchange our dollars until a new exchange rate was established. We wondered how we would pay our inexpensive little pensione for room and board when a check arrived from a Paris bank, where I had kept a small account. It was for $250 in pesetas, which the bank had changed a day or two before the U.S. bank holiday. It was more than enough to pay our pensione bill and the year's rent at Lloret. We felt relieved.

In the meantime the rest of our life's savings, some $800, had arrived from London and been deposited in the Barcelona bank. But a few weeks later, when we journeyed in to Barcelona to get some cash, the teller mournfully informed us that the mighty U.S.A. had gone off the gold standard and that our dollars were now worth only sixty percent of what they had been. Our $800 would fetch only some $480 in pesetas.

We were dumbfounded. Another illusion gone! It seemed incomprehensible that the almighty dollar, the most stable currency in the world, had suddenly lost forty percent of its value. Our hope of living in Spain for a year on our thousand bucks was suddenly dashed. We need not have worried. Food, wine, clothing and all the other items of daily living turned out to be as cheap as our rent. We soon calculated that, if we were careful, we had enough to tide us over to the end of the year. We lived well enough, had plenty to eat, and even entertained visiting friends on expenditures which, including rent, averaged sixty dollars a month.

So our year in this coastal paradise was secure. We never again gave our finances another thought. As the warm spring months passed we settled down to living the life we had intended to have — utterly free from the pressures of deadlines and events, beautifully independent of the rest of the world, of publishers and editors, of relatives and friends. As I look back nearly half a century later on that year off in Spain, it seems like a dream, a dream that became true.

We swam in the blue waters of the Mediterranean four or five times a day, lolled on the beach in front of our house, hiked up and around the lower reaches of the Pyrenees above the village past groves of olives and acres of vineyards, returning on a warm early evening for another dip in the sea, a hearty dinner, and, often, an hour at the plaza in front of the town hall, where we sat on the terrace of the café and watched the villagers dance the *sardana*, loving the strange Catalan music that accompanied it.

We plunged into the books there had been no time to read, and I soon began to write a book of my own. It was sheer luxury to have several hours a day for reading books. I finished Spengler's *Decline of the West*, brilliant in the sweep of its probe into past civilizations but flawed by its outlandish interpretations of their history and even more by its foolish prophecies based on them. I raced through Trotsky's three-volume *History of the Russian Revolution*, carried away by the narrative he unfolded, fascinated by his sharp and ironic portraits of the chief Bolsheviks who had been his comrades until Stalin expelled him from the Soviet Union. I went back to Tolstoy's *War and Peace*, marveling not only at his genius as a novelist but at his novel grasp of history.

I read or reread a lot of novels that year, especially by Hemingway, Huxley, D. H. Lawrence, Dos Passos and Dreiser, but the novel that most impressed me came out of France: Céline's *Voyage au bout de la nuit*. Trotsky had hailed it in a long review in a French literary weekly as the first great proletarian novel and apparently believed that Céline was a Communist, depicting the drab lives of the poor and unwashed of Paris and dissecting the hypocrisy and greed of the bourgeoisie. Trotsky would have been surprised, had he lived, to see Céline emerge as a champion of the Far Right and a collaborator of the Nazis during the German occupation of France. What fascinated me most about Céline was that he shook up the French language with a new syntax and an original style, his prose crackling with short, jabbing sentences and with the argot you heard in the slum streets of Paris but never, previously, saw in books.

These works were just a beginning, as I began to devour more books in a week than I had previously in a year. I read a lot more of European history but paused to go through Beard's *Rise of American Civilization* and some of Veblen to orient me on the history of my own country. With philosophy I did not do well. I tried to read Plato and Aristotle, Kant and Bergson, but not much of their wisdom seeped through to me. Probably I was still too immature to grasp it.

That I was too immature to write a book well only dawned on me some time after I wrote my first one that year in Spain. Nearly every morning from 8 A.M. to 1 P.M. I labored away at an autobiographical novel of my experience in India. I was exhilarated. At last I was writing a book. I felt it was pretty good. Only later did I see that it was dreadfully immature and sentimental. That I could be sentimental shocked me. I was not aware of that side of me.

But the time writing that first book was not entirely lost. I began to get out of my system an awful lot of bad writing that dashing off daily cables and meeting deadlines had bred in me. And I began to achieve the discipline every writer needs. Each morning I stuck at my typewriter from four to six hours, no matter how I felt, no matter how slowly, painfully, the words came.

A good many of those working hours in Lloret were spent in writing articles and short stories for magazines, from which I hoped to derive enough income to prolong our stay in Spain in case I could not find a job at the year's end. Not a single one was ever accepted for publication, in America or in England.

This not only disheartened me but puzzled me. Admittedly I did not have an "in" with editors in New York and London. Outside Chicago, and Paris, where my by-lines in the *Tribune* were fairly familiar, I was unknown. But still I thought my articles and two or three short stories were not badly done. They contained a good deal of original material and background from my firsthand experiences in Asia and also now in Spain, where the Republic, born only two years before, was in trouble. Yet all my pieces were rejected summarily and sometimes with editorial condescension.

Thus the editor of the esteemed *Nation* wrote that an article on Gandhi was "too elementary" for his readers. If my piece on Gandhi was too elementary for the *Nation's* readers, it struck Carl Brandt, my agent in New York, as just the opposite. He wrote saying it would interest "only some of our more serious, historically-minded magazines." But it did not. It drew instead a large number of rejection slips from them. Most of them were mimeographed form letters, such as the following:

> We regret that the enclosed manuscript is not adapted to the present needs of *The New York Times.*

Even Irita Van Doren, the editor of the *New York Herald-Tribune Books,* who later would become one of my dearest and closest friends and who would pressure me to write more for her than I had time for, turned me down when I wrote to ask her if I could review books for her publication.

I knew of course that a young writer trying to break into publication was bound to receive a flock of rejection slips. But I was being turned down totally. What kind of animals were these editors, anyway? I wondered. Wythe Williams, the veteran foreign correspondent of the old *New York World* and then of the *Times*, answered:

> Personally I think most of them should either be in the grocery or plumbing line or lower. . . . The average American editor today seems to be a mongrel offspring of a jellyfish and an eel. So why should you care whether they take your stuff, which is much too intelligent for them anyway.

I cared, of course, because I was jobless and needed the money.

Later (to skip ahead) when I had made a certain name for myself by my radio coverage of Nazi Germany and the war, and from the publication of my first book, *Berlin Diary*, I was besieged to write articles for them by many of the same editors who previously had shown no interest in my work. By then I didn't need the money or have the time.

I had a curious experience in this regard with the editors of several American magazines during the early part of the Second World War. I had sent Brandt a long section of my diary which recounted from day to day my experiences as a correspondent with the German army as it raced across Holland, Belgium and France to Paris in May and June of 1940. Believing that it was the first eyewitness account in depth of the German *Blitzkrieg*, which revolutionized warfare that spring and humbled in six weeks the formidable French army, I thought my agent could easily sell it to one of the "slick" magazines for a tidy sum. I had just sent my family home from Europe to America and needed the money to pay the expenses.

All the "slicks" — *Life, Look*, the *Saturday Evening Post, Colliers, Reader's Digest* — turned it down, their editors telling Brandt the German conquest of the West was over and that their readers were no longer interested in it.

Brandt finally sent it to the *Atlantic Monthly*, writing me that the piece would not fetch much money there but it was better than no publication at all. In Boston, as I learned later, Ted Weeks, one of the best editors in the country, read the piece, stuck it in one of his desk drawers, and forgot it.

A year later, when *Berlin Diary*, which contained the war diary I had submitted separately as an article, began to climb to the top of the best-seller list, Ted Weeks remembered the forgotten manuscript, retrieved it, and telephoned Brandt that he wished to publish it, after all, in the *Atlantic*.

"It will now cost you ten times what you could have had it for a year ago, when I first submitted it," said Brandt.

So the *Atlantic Monthly* paid what for it was a whopping fee and published it a whole year after receipt of it. And *Reader's Digest*, which the year before had rejected it, rushed to publish it along with other excerpts from the book. Its payment was so large it took my breath away.

In Spain that year I could not, of course, foresee such a stroke of luck. All that I wrote that year was rejected as unpublishable.

I fared no better in lining up a job for the time when our year off in Spain would be over. Toward the end of the year I had to face the fact that I was not going to make even a modest living by writing. I would have to go back to newspapering — or to anything else that paid wages. I sent off letters, telegrams and cables to editors back home and to bureau chiefs in Europe saying I was looking for employment at the end of the year. Most of them were old colleagues and friends (Edwin L. James, for instance, had gone home from Paris to be managing editor of the *Times*) and all replied warmly that they were keeping me in mind, but with the Depression on at home, they simply were not hiring new correspondents.

So far as I can recall, and it seems a little strange, I did not become dejected. We were young, and we were having the time of our life in Spain and I felt certain that by the time our money was gone, something would turn up. One had to trust to luck, and I had had my share of the good, as well as the bad. An unexpected turn of fortune, after all, had landed me a newspaper job in Paris eight years before, just as I was about to return home, enabling me to stay on in Europe and pursue a new course I had followed happily ever since.

The occupant of the other half of our house that summer in Spain turned out to be Andrés Segovia. I had first heard the great guitarist play in Paris seven years before, and had marveled that he could get such a rich and vibrant music, especially classical music, from a guitar. I had heard him again in Vienna and we had met casually at a reception after his concert.

Sharing the house in Lloret, we became good friends. He proved to be as fine a person as he was a musician, courtly and gracious, like most Spaniards, modest and simple in his manners and extremely considerate. When he learned that I was writing a book he went to the farthest corner of the house to practice, as he did daily from 7 A.M. till noon, so as not to disturb me with the sound of his music. All my protests that this generous gesture was unnecessary, that my writing was quite unimportant compared to his playing, he waved aside.

Three or four evenings a week he joined us in our living room to listen to the recordings of the Asian equivalents of the guitar which I had picked up in Bombay, Kabul, Bagdad and Istanbul. He seemed fascinated by this music from the East and would ask me to play the records over and over. Sometimes he would take up his guitar and strum through some of the Asian melodies. Many of them, he remarked, were not so very different from those of the Spanish flamencos, which derived from the Moors and the gypsies of his native Andalusia and were part of his repertoire.

The evening invariably wound up with Segovia playing some of the works he had been practicing. These could be compositions from Albéniz, Manuel de Falla and other Spanish composers, but more likely they were transcriptions from Bach and Mozart that he made for the guitar. Segovia was the first guitarist, I believe, to play Bach and Mozart. Until you heard him render them you could scarcely imagine them on a guitar, but on his instrument they were magnificent, full of tone colors and subtle nuances.

"I imagine Bach would have been surprised," I remarked one evening, "if he had been told that some of his finest works would one day be rendered on a guitar."

"On the contrary," Segovia said. "I believe that some of Bach's solo suites were originally written for the lute. Afterward he transcribed them for other instruments. So some of his greatest music is natural for the guitar."

Unlike many musicians I have known, Segovia had a deep interest in literature. From his conversation it was obvious that he had read a great deal of fiction, poetry, history and philosophy. He never tired of talking of the wonders of Cervantes. (His farewell present to us was a beautiful edition of *Don Quixote*, in Spanish.) He introduced me to the works of Miguel de Unamuno — he was a personal friend and admirer of the philosopher — urging me to read Unamuno's great work *The Tragic Sense of Life*, which I did that summer and fall, as soon as I had learned Spanish.

Occasionally friends came down to stay with us, bringing a whiff of the outside world. Russell and Pat Strauss arrived from London as soon as the House of Commons, of which he was a young Labour member, adjourned for the summer. The Jay Allens (Jay was covering Madrid for the *Chicago Tribune*) came over from Madrid, bringing with them the ebullient Luis Quintanilla, one of the best of the young Spanish painters. A fierce Republican, Quintanilla had distinguished himself during the last hours of the monarchy two years before by climbing to the balcony of the royal palace and unfurling the flag of the Republic. He was a friend of Hemingway, whose letters to him, in Spanish, he used to read to us. They were mostly, if my memory is correct, about bullfights and fishing trips. Heinrich Kranz, a Viennese literary critic, journeyed down from Vienna, read the manuscript of a play about India I had dashed off during the months of unemployment there after my firing, and perused the pages of the novel I was writing. He must have been blind because he thought both of the scripts were very good and made me promise that I would give him the rights in German to both, with him as translator. Tess's brother, a student at the University of Vienna, biked all the way down to Lloret and lingered with us most of the summer. He brought disturbing news that the Austrian Nazis, encouraged by Hitler's takeover in Germany, were becoming so strong that they soon might take over Austria.

These visitors and a few others brought us up to date on what was going on in the world we had temporarily withdrawn from. We were grateful, but we had no wish to return to it for the time being.

That fall, after the last of our friends had left, we did journey about Spain a little — so far as our slender pocketbook allowed. In Toledo and at the Prado in Madrid we discovered El Greco. It was an unforgettable experience, one of the peaks in our lives. A diary entry of November 28 recalls it.

> Tess and I were strolling through the Prado. . . . Halfway down the long gallery we wandered into a small side-room to the left. It was like stepping off the world into a fantastic new one — Greco's world, which is unlike any you have ever seen or imagined. I felt a chill of excitement race down my spine, as had happened perhaps half a dozen times when I had beheld for the first time some wonder of art or nature.

The paintings in the Greco room in the Prado were only a foretaste to those we found a week later in various churches in Toledo. The one I remember best is the *Burial of Count Orgaz* (*El Enterrio*) in the little church of St. Tomé. It was badly lit when we saw it but one could see it well enough in the dim light to realize that it was a masterpiece, one of the greatest works of this transplanted Greek genius from Crete who became the most Spanish of painters.

I have never been able to get down in words an adequate or accurate description of a work of art that moved me profoundly, whether a painting or a sculpture, a symphony or a chamber-music piece. In the presence of Greco I felt tongue-tied. I could find no words to express his tremendous impact on me. Here was a new and volcanic kind of dramatic expression in painting, unlike any you had seen in the works of the Italians or the Dutch or the French except perhaps in Rembrandt, Leonardo and Michelangelo, though it was utterly different from those masters. Here are strange figures such as no other painter depicted, the human body and especially the face distorted, elongated, contorted, the limbs twisted, the eyes burning, the dark skies suddenly broken with blazing streaks of light, the clouds a bleak, cold whitish gray. Greco does not depict nature as it is but as his weird, restless imagination demands to complete a picture of men and women caught up in dynamic movement, in tumult, strife, agony, suffering, terror and religious zeal in a nightmarish world. No wonder that some of Greco's rivals thought him crazy and others that his distortions were due to an astigmatism that made it impossible for him to see straight.

After Greco, it was difficult for us to appreciate the genius of Velázquez. To return from Toledo to view again the latter's beautiful paintings in the Prado at Madrid was like coming from a tormented night into the tranquil light of day. Velázquez seemed to do everything easily and lightly.

Goya, the third of the great Spanish painters, was also for a time a court painter, like Velázquez, but how different! His portraits of a succession of Spanish sovereigns and their families are far from flattering. He viewed them cynically, as he did the world, as somewhat of a cruel farce. But what I remember him most for is his depicting of the horrors of war and the way men suffer in them. Though our wars have become far more frightful in their carnage than those observed by Goya, no other painter has caught the terror of them as he did.

We stood mesmerized in the Prado one day before his *Execution of May 3, 1808*. On May 2 that year the French troops of Murat had entered Madrid and the common people of the capital had resisted them with sticks and stones, for they were unarmed. Next day Murat began executing them before firing squads at the city's gate. Goya was a witness to the massacre, and he was outraged. Wild with loathing for the conquerors but full of compassion for the victims, he painted the grim scene. No one who has seen the work can ever forget it. Lit up against the blackness of the night, French troops are aiming their rifles at the ragged captured civilians a few feet in front of them. The faces of the doomed are frozen in fear. Some try to hide them with their hands. Others clench their fists in defiance. One man, about to be shot, throws his hands up and glares frightenedly into the muzzles of the guns. Before him are the dead bodies of those already slain, lying in pools of blood. You gaze at the scene as if it were a nightmare, but Goya keeps reminding you that it is real, that this is war, that organized killing such as this is barbarous.

An assistant curator, who saw us pausing in horror before the painting, whispered to us that we must go to the top floor of the Prado to see the extent of Goya's portrayal of war and its depravity. That is how we came to see Goya's great etchings — I believe there were some four hundred of them — which he called *Los Desastres de la Guerra,* a record, the curator said, of the French atrocities in Spain during the Napoleonic war. We spent an hour looking at them, until we could stand it no longer. Taken as a whole, they are the most devastating indictment of war I have ever seen.

The Spanish Republic, which had done so much in the bare two and a half years since its birth to liberate Spain from its medievalism, already was tottering that fall. There could be no doubt of that after the national elections, which had taken place while we were in Madrid. The balloting had turned out of office the men who had founded the Republic and who, through a new Constitution and a bevy of new laws rushed through the Cortes, had brought Spain abruptly — perhaps too abruptly for such a backward, conservative, Catholic country — into the modern world. The Right, which was lukewarm and, in part, hostile to the Republic, had triumphed — largely, some of my Spanish friends like Quintanilla insisted, because the government had given the women the vote for the first time, and the women had voted as the priests told them.

From all I could learn since coming to Spain, the Republic had gotten off to a surprisingly promising start. In the spring of 1931 the old monarchy had fallen — of its own weight. King Alfonso had quit and departed Spain, peacefully and quietly, the last of the Bourbons, who had ruled Spain for five centuries. There was no bloodshed, no revolution. The Republic took over by default. Its leaders were mostly middle-class intellectuals, lawyers, doctors, professors and writers, backed by the Socialist party and the socialist trade unions.*

What they had accomplished for the Republic in its first two years was truly remarkable, or so it seemed to me.

The stranglehold of the Church on Spain was broken. Church and State were separated, religion disestablished, Church property nationalized. The Jesuits were dissolved and other religious orders restricted. Religious schools, as most in Spain had been, were to be replaced by secular schools, and primary education was to be made compulsory and free. Women were given the vote for the first time and equal rights in all other matters. Divorce, which the Church had forbidden, was made relatively easy, and civil marriages legally recognized. All titles were abolished. The medieval penal laws were drastically revised and liberalized. Minimum wages were established and the state recognized the right of the workers to organize. Land reform broke up the large estates. The state was to take over those of more than fifty-six acres which had not been tilled, compensate the owners according to the taxes they had paid,† and redistribute the land to the peasants.

Catalonia, which had clamored for centuries for a measure of autonomy, was granted limited self-rule, as were the Basques in the north.

The army, which with the Church had been a pillar of the monarchy, was brought under the direct control of civilian government and its officers' ranks purged of those who would not take an oath of loyalty to the Republic. But ten thousand of them, including over a hundred generals (the Spanish army was top-heavy with generals), were retired with full pay for life.

All these changes and reforms and many lesser ones, hurriedly legislated within a couple of years, were the equivalent for an American of those brought about in our country by Woodrow Wilson and Franklin D. Roosevelt over a period of a quarter of a century. But since Spain before the Republic had been so backward, what the new Republican regime accomplished in so short a time was even more impressive. But it did not have time to put the drastic new laws into effect. The Rightist coalition, which triumphed in the autumn elections that year, began immediately to set them aside.

---

* The three million organized Spanish workers were almost equally divided between the Socialist UGT (*Unión Generale del Trabajadores*) and the anarchist CNT (*Confederación Nacional del Trabajo*). The anarchists were against *any* government, republican or monarchist. The Spanish Communist party in 1933 numbered only some 3,000, and was politically insignificant.

† Since tax evasion by the wealthy landowners had been notorious, compensation was often less than the real value of the land.

The Republic began to be undermined not only by the reactionary politicians and their backers, the Church, the wealthy landowners and capitalists, and the pensioned army generals, but, most outrageous of all, by the anarchists, whose mass following among the workers and peasants the Republic in two short years had done so much to liberate.°

So the fledgling Republic, in its first two years, knew who its enemies were — on the Left and on the Right. It sought to curb them, but the mild, tolerant liberals and socialists who ran it could not bring themselves to be drastic enough to render their foes incapable once and for all of overthrowing it. They deprived the Church of many of its privileges but left it with enough power and determination to strike back.† They dissolved the Jesuits but did not expel them. They forbade the Jesuits and other Catholic orders to teach, and did nothing when their teaching continued. They tried to eliminate the army as a political power by weeding out the anti-Republican officers, but then, by retiring them at full pay, left them the means and the leisure to conspire against the Republic.

All that fall and early winter, after the liberal government fell and was replaced by a Rightist bloc, I reflected gloomily on the swift decline of this still very young Republic, so splendid in its ideals, so inept in guarding its strength, so innocent of the threats of its determined enemies.

The Weimar Republic of Germany, whose liberal constitution and legislation had inspired the Spanish Republicans, had disintegrated in much the same way. And at the very beginning of this year, 1933, it was in its death throes. Adolf Hitler, who had become its chancellor in January, was fast picking it to pieces, wiping out one by one all the freedoms it had achieved for the German people. Was the Spanish Republic following it? I was afraid it was. Only a miracle, it seemed to me, or some immense stroke of luck, could save it now.

As I prepared to leave at the end of the year, I sensed that the whole lovely country was rapidly drifting into anarchy and violence. No figure in Spain, no group or party, seemed wise enough or strong

---

° Spain was the only country in the world where the anarchists had won over large sections of the workers and peasants.

† The Primate of the Church in Spain, Cardinal Segura, the archbishop of Toledo, had struck back within a month of the proclamation of the Republic. In a violent pastoral letter he called on all Spanish Catholics "to fight like intrepid warriors prepared to succumb gloriously" against the Republic. The Republican government demanded his removal and he was forced to leave Spain. He returned clandestinely a few months later but was arrested and escorted under guard to the French frontier. From exile he championed General Franco's rebellion and returned to Spain at the end of the Civil War to become archbishop of Seville.

enough to halt it. Or even willing enough to try. The amiable and fraternal spirit that had prevailed at the beginning of the Republic was degenerating into bitter fratricide. For the first time there was a serious threat of civil war.

Toward the end of that idyllic year off in our fishing village in Spain our money began to run out.

Once more, I began to scratch around for a job. Wires and letters to bureau heads of American newspapers and news agencies in Paris and London brought no results. Nor did cables and letters to newspaper editors in New York. America was beginning to dig itself out of the Depression, thanks mostly to President Roosevelt's buoyant efforts, but there were still ten million unemployed at home, my companions in forced idleness, and there was a long way to go to restore the stagnant economy. The newspapers in New York, I was informed, were not taking on new hands, especially foreign correspondents.

We spent the Christmas and New Year's holidays in London, where we stayed with Pat and Russell Strauss, who had spent a summer's fortnight with us in Lloret. In their spacious house on the edge of Hyde Park we forgot our poverty and bleak prospects and enjoyed for a moment the luxury of the rich. Russell, a left-wing Labour M.P., had inherited a prosperous family business.

I called on my old colleagues, who ran the London bureaus of the American wire services and those newspapers that maintained a foreign staff. All were under strict wraps to do no hiring.

It was discouraging, but Christmas and New Year's were no time for moping. Something, I was sure, was bound to turn up. So Tess and I abandoned ourselves to the holiday spirit, revisiting the National Gallery and Tate to see the paintings and the British Museum to see the sculpture Lord Elgin had carted away from Greece, tripping up in the afternoon to St. Paul's Cathedral past Fleet Street, where I had spent some of my youthful summers working on the *Tribune*, and to the theater and concerts in the evening, and on New Year's Eve packing off, with the Strausses, to a wild masquerade ball at Albert Hall.

We saw old friends, like Nye Bevin, the bad boy of the Labour party and a warm and captivating man, and Jennie Lee, who was a Labour M.P. from a Scottish mining district, and still not only the youngest but the prettiest woman in Parliament. Nye and Jennie, I gathered, had begun to fall in love — these children of coal miners, in Wales and Scotland — and they raged with life. Later they would be married and climb the political ladder to posts in the cabinet when Labour returned to power.

The Strausses entertained a good deal that holiday fortnight, and we met a number of politicians, artists, editors, writers and reporters, of whom I remember most vividly Henry Moore, who was carving forceful, exciting and original sculpture. He had not yet received the renown that would later come. Even more interesting to me was Harold Laski, the brilliant but erratic theoretician of the Labour party, a spellbinding conversationalist in a small group, with a mind that sparkled and exploded, and with a curious penchant for dropping names. He would tell you that he had just received a letter from his old friend President Roosevelt or from his dear friend Justice Frankfurter, and what they had had to say about the state of the world. Or say that he had had a violent argument the other day about communism with Bertrand Russell and of course come out on top. Still, I liked him immensely. He challenged your mind, shook you up.

For reasons I never understood, Laski never made it to the top of the Labour party, never was named to the cabinet or to any other important post, though he was an ambitious man. Perhaps he was too gifted. British politicians, not only Tory, but Labour, seemed to me to be distrustful of first-class, sparkling minds.

Stanley Baldwin, the leader of the Tory party and the real power in the "nationalist" government of the ailing old Labourite Ramsay MacDonald, was a good example. No one accused him of being sparkling or brilliant, though he was not unintelligent. He was as stolid as John Bull. The country seemed to like him for just muddling along — it was so rather British.

Britain, despite its Empire and Commonwealth and its prestige in the world, was becoming insular, it seemed to me. I found little concern in London about Adolf Hitler's increasingly brutal dictatorship in Germany and none at all about the shaky Spanish Republic. The Labour people did not like Hitler, of course, and dimly perceived that Nazism was a threat. The Tories were inclined to give the Nazi Führer the benefit of the doubt. Several of their politicians had visited Berlin that summer or fall and returned to report that Hitler had reestablished order in the Reich. No more political armies were roaming the streets, killing. Hitler had destroyed all of them but his own, but the good Tories did not seem to have heard of it. They also were pleased that Hitler had suppressed the Godless Communists.

My Labour friends were not much interested in what I had to tell of the faltering Spanish Republic and of the probability of civil war that would tear the country apart and perhaps pave the way for another fascist state. Probably they didn't believe me. Most of the Tories were hostile to the Madrid government, blaming it for the church burnings and the strikes. At least King Alfonso had kept order — there it was again: the old bugbear of the conservatives, for whom "law and order" came first.

On our way back to Spain we stopped in Paris, where Eric Hawkins, the amiable Englishman who was editor of the American Paris *Herald*, held out some hope that there might be a place for me on the copy-desk in the coming months. I did not tell him — I was too proud — that I could not hold out for more than a month or two. We were down to our last one hundred dollars. Hawkins would wire me, he said, if anything turned up.

Tess and I spent a gloomy week on our return to Lloret de Mar. The January weather had turned cold and raw, with heavy seas lashing our beachfront. We did not dare spend another peseta on coal for the furnace, so we tried to keep warm by donning extra sweaters and wrapping blankets around us on top of them, as the poor in Spain did when winter came, hoping the Mediterranean sun would come out again and provide a little free warmth. We gave up eating meat, which was relatively expensive, and bought fish directly from the fishermen when they came in with their daily catch. They did not charge much. And they threw in a few extra and much appreciated sardines for good measure. Because they knew we lived in a big house and were Americans they didn't suspect that we had become poorer than they.

Try as we might, Tess and I could not think of a way out, or figure what we would do when our last little hoard of pesetas gave out in a few weeks. I had, I thought, exhausted every possibility of a job. Perhaps, it began to dawn on us, we would have to go back to America, if we could borrow the money for the ship's fare, though my brother, then working in New York, had warned me how difficult it would be to find employment there — any kind of employment. Well, if we couldn't, we told ourselves, and were able to make it home, we could always join the breadlines in Manhattan. A lot of others who had once had it good, we had read in the newspapers, had joined them.

In the meantime, for another few weeks, we decided, the only thing left to do was to live as cheaply as possible (our rent was paid to April) and trust that something would turn up. If it didn't, we would cross that bridge when we came to it.

We never quite got to that bridge. A wire finally came from Hawkins in Paris. How soon could I report for work? He wanted me to take over the day copy-desk of the *Herald*.

This was a comedown of course. After six years as a foreign correspondent in Europe and Asia I would be returning to where I had started nearly nine years before: on the copy-desk of an American newspaper in Paris. That was progress? The thought depressed me. But like everyone else, we had to eat. Besides, I was getting back into newspaper work, which I loved, and in a city I loved above all others on earth.

The year off in Spain had convinced me that I still had a lot of maturing and honing to do to become a writer, and especially to try to live from writing. The truth was that though I still felt a drive eventually to end up writing books, journalism was what I was so far best at. I loved the work and the life. Europe was stirring again, increasingly fragmented between the fascist authoritarianism of the Right in Germany and Italy, and the threat of it in Spain, and of the Left in Russia, and of the decaying democracies, Britain and France, in the West. It was a new turn in the history of this ancient continent. I wanted to sink my teeth in it, follow it, try to understand it and write about it.

The telegram from Paris was a potent tonic to our lagging spirits. We bought a hundred pounds of coal to heat up the house and a gallon of local wine to warm up our spirits. We celebrated our luck with a feast.

After all, we agreed, we had had a wonderful year off in Spain — "the best," I noted in my diary that evening, "the happiest, the most uneventful year we have ever lived together." By the side of the sea we had regained the health we had lost in India. For nearly a year we had lived in this picturesque Catalan fishing village exactly as we had dreamed.

> This year [I wrote in my diary] we had time to know each other, to loaf and play, to wine and eat, to see the bull-fights in the afternoon and Barcelona's gaudy *Barrio Chino* at night; time to sense the colors, the olive green of the hills, the incomparable blues of the Mediterranean in the spring, and the wondrous, bleak, gray-white skies above Madrid; time to know the Spanish peasant and worker and fisherman, men of great dignity and guts and integrity despite their miserable lives; and at the Prado and Toledo just a little time for Greco....
>
> It has been a good year.

I left Tess to pack up our books and other belongings and to close up the house, and toward the end of January, 1934, I boarded the train at nearby Gerona for Paris. In a month or so I would be thirty years old. At thirty most men were well on their way in their life-work or had given up and dropped out of the race. As the train chugged northward toward France I thought of that. And I won-dered what lay beyond this latest turning point in our lives.

Tess Shirer in Lloret de Mar, Spain, during the Shirers' "year off" in 1933

Andrès Segovia, Tess Shirer, Luis Quintanilla (a painter and friend of Hemingway) and, at left, Michael Allen, later a prominent American clergyman, in Lloret de Mar, 1933

The author and Segovia chatting on the beach in Lloret de Mar, 1933

CHAPTER 5

Return to Paris

1934

All that unhappy season of my return to Paris, where my adult life and work had begun so luminously nearly nine years before, I felt depressed and defeated.

It was hard to face the dismal fact that with this job on the copy-desk of the Paris *Herald*, grateful as I was to get it, I was back to where I had begun that summer of 1925, when at twenty-one, fresh out of a small Iowa college, I had landed a job on the copy-desk of the Paris edition of the *Chicago Tribune*. I could not forget all those subsequent, exciting years as a foreign correspondent in Europe and Asia. And now back to this. It hurt my pride and laid me low with a deadening sense of failure. Still, one had to be thankful, I suppose, for whatever crumbs fell to one in those earliest and worst years of the Depression. They kept one alive.

Paris and France had changed and, like my own life, for the worse. I scarcely recognized them.

When I had departed just four years before for Vienna, France was still regarded as the greatest power on the continent of Europe. The country was prosperous, the people confident and relaxed, basking in the peace and well-being of the old continent finally recovered from the devastations and the hatreds of the Great War. No nation threatened France or its hegemony in Europe.

The Depression had not yet come to France. The day I left Paris in January, 1930, the State Treasury, which had been empty in 1926, reported a surplus of 19 billion francs for 1929. Industrial production had reached a new high. The country's trade balance was exceptionally favorable. There were only 812 persons out of work, as against the millions in America, Britain and Germany.

Paris itself, it seemed to me then, had never been lovelier. The French, as well as visiting or resident foreigners, especially Americans, still saw it as the City of Light, the cultural capital of the world, the most beautiful metropolis ever built. Life bustled in it. The theaters, concert halls, cabarets, restaurants, cafés were crowded. Prices were reasonable. The art museums and galleries attracted great throngs. Books poured from the presses and were bought and read. No city in the world had so many bookstores nor so many — and so lively — literary and art reviews. No other provided so much intellectual and artistic excitement.

French governments, it is true, came and went with startling rapidity. But that was nothing new. The citizens seemed to regard it as the price of democracy in a republic of fierce individualists. Stumbling and mediocre as most governments were, at least they had stabilized the franc, more than balanced the budget and created an era of prosperity and euphoria.

Those last golden years of the 1920's, which promised to stretch into the next decade, would be remembered by historians and memoirists as one of the happiest times of the Third Republic, a second *Belle Époque*, as good as the quarter of a century before the war came in 1914. Strife and controversy were muted. An unusual spirit of tolerance prevailed. Life was good.

Now, in the bleak January of 1934, that Paris, that France, seemed gone. What struck me first was the shrill pitch to which strife between Frenchmen had risen. Rancor and intolerance poisoned the air. Insults and threats were hurled at each other by the Right and the Left. The former professed to fear the coming of Godless communism; the latter of totalitarian fascism.

I was astounded by the strength of incipient fascism in this democratic republic. In my first years in Paris there had been no sign of the totalitarian bug that had bitten such a large number in Italy and later, even more, in Germany. Only Action Française, the royalist movement, had clamored for the downfall of the Third Republic. But no one had taken it seriously. Monarchy was a dead duck in France.

Now, I found to my surprise that rowdy, antiparliamentary Fascist leagues had sprung up in France like mushrooms. And while one or two seemed to be merely offshoots of the old anti-Republican and anti-Semite groups that had come and gone during the last quarter of the nineteenth century and which in their Bonapartism and Boulangism were traditionally French, most of them appeared to me to have the new and uglier quality that I had seen in the Blackshirts of Italy and in the Brownshirts in Germany. In France too — and I could scarcely believe it — they were now prowling the streets in their variously colored shirts, their jackboots echoing on the pavement, beating up decent citizens and harmless politicians and howling for the destruction of the Third Republic.

Nearly every day after I arrived in Paris they were rioting in the streets, overturning kiosks and cars and setting them on fire, and battling the gendarmes and the Garde Mobile to get to the Chamber of Deputies to "throw the rascals out" and burn down the House of the Representatives of the People.

Hawkins had quickly taken me off the copy-desk of the *Herald* and sent me out as a reporter to cover the mounting disorder. I was grateful to become a reporter again. In the excitement of the new assignment, I pretty much shed the depression I had felt on my demotion from foreign correspondent. This was a big story. To my utter astonishment it began to look to me as if France, which had seemed so stable and peaceful when I had left just four years ago, was drifting, like Spain, toward civil war. Within a few days of my arrival it would totter to the edge of it.

How, in the four years of my absence, had France come to this? Obviously, I had a lot of cramming to do to find an answer and put some depth and meaning into my reporting. Uprisings do not just occur. There had to be reasons for this once splendid democracy to have arrived at such a critical point — its very survival at stake.

One reason, of course, was the Depression.

It had finally hit France in the autumn of 1931, following the crash of the great Kreditanstalt bank in Vienna, the financial panic in Germany and the abandonment by Great Britain on September 21 of the gold standard and the forty percent devaluation of the pound sterling. Stocks plummeted on the Bourse (as they had on the New York Stock Exchange on the "Black Friday" of two years before), the Treasury surplus quickly turned into a deficit, the trade balance turned unfavorable, industrial production fell, and, for the first time, unemployment rose astronomically.

The Depression was never quite as bad in France as in more industrialized Germany, Britain and the United States. Unemployment seldom rose above half a million. But the slump was bad enough, the worst economic and financial crisis the country had experienced in more than a hundred years. And it was aggravated and prolonged by the failure of the fumbling Parliament and the rapidly changing governments of the Third Republic to take sensible measures to cope with it.

It was obvious that after the United States in 1933 followed Britain in devaluating its currency by forty percent, France would have to follow suit or be shut out of the world markets. But the French people had developed a neurosis about the franc as the result of its disastrous fall in the mid-twenties, which had wiped out most of their savings. No government dared to devaluate it now. The result was that France alone clung to the old gold standard and priced itself out of the foreign markets. The government followed a calamitous policy of severe deflation. Production was curbed, wages and salaries cut. Misery spread. And resentment.

But whereas in England and America the resentment took the form of grumbling against the government in power (President Hoover had been blasted out of office in the American elections in 1932), in France, as in Germany, it was directed more against the parliamentary republican regime itself. In Berlin this had brought Hitler to power; in Paris it spawned a number of right-wing leagues whose objective was to overthrow the Third Republic and set up some sort of authoritarian fascist form of government. By the beginning of 1934 it seemed to rightist leaders that their time had come.

Who were these leaders? What was the strength of the storm troops they were throwing into the streets? And what exactly were they up to? I worked long hours those first weeks in Paris to try to find out. It was not easy. Even the government and the police, as the rioting grew day after day, seemed to be ignorant and confused about the forces opposing them.

The origins of these forces went back much farther than I had suspected. As early as 1926, when the franc had fallen to new lows and the government was facing bankruptcy, Ernest Mercier, the electricity magnate, had founded an antiparliamentarian movement called Redressement Français (French Resurgence). Its message was that a parliament of *politicians* was incompetent to handle the affairs of state in the complicated postwar world, where the intricacies of national and international business and finance called for specialized knowledge. It wanted a parliament and government of "technicians" who knew how modern capitalist society functioned, and it assured the country that the great business and financial enterprises could furnish these trained men. In other words, it wanted its own men to control directly what up to now they controlled only indirectly. Mercier saw in Mussolini's corporate state a form in which his aims could be realized. Gradually he built up a following among his fellow magnates. Together they dispensed millions propagating their ideas.

By the time I arrived in Paris Mercier was becoming restless. On January 24 he told a mass meeting of his followers:

> There is only one solution — and circumstances will soon impose it — and that is a government of authority. . . . Not one among us will stop until it has been accomplished.

The business and financial community knew well what he meant by a "government of authority." Some of its leaders were more explicit. In the columns of one of their organs, the *Revue Hebdomadaire*, they demanded a corporate state on the Italian style. In the same newspaper François Le Grix, a spokesman of big business, predicted that a *coup de force* was inevitable and imminent.

> It will take place very simply and very quickly. The Chamber will be adjourned *sine die* and Paris put in a state of siege after demonstrations by tax-payers and unemployed.

The "leadership," he predicted, was ready to act.

Jacques Lemaigre Dubreuil, the peanut-oil king, was more specific. On January 29 he told a rally of his Taxpayers League:

> We are going to carry out a march on the Chamber of Deputies, and if necessary we will use whips and sticks to sweep out this chamber of incapables.

The shaky government paid no attention to these warnings. Perhaps this was because it was more concerned with the militant leagues, whose toughs were rioting daily in the streets.

Among the most active and effective of these was the royalist Action Française, whose storm troopers were organized as Camelots du Roi. Their spirits roused by the daily dose of inflammatory articles by Charles Maurras, the poet-philosopher of the royalists, and by Léon Daudet, who possessed the most vituperative pen in Paris, in the daily newspaper *L'Action Française*, they had staged a big demonstration on January 9, just before I arrived. They had tried to storm the Chamber of Deputies but had been hurled back by the police.

Neither the government nor the public knew that behind the sudden activity of the royalist street brawlers as the new year began lay more than a desire to take advantage of the revolt of rightist public opinion in Paris against Parliament. The leaders of Action Française had been secretly urged to become more active by the comte de Paris, heir of the Pretender to the throne, the duc de Guise. The young prince — he was twenty-six — believed that the time was ripe for a serious attempt to restore the Orléans monarchy. At the first of the year he and his father had summoned Maurras and the other royalist leaders to Brussels, where the "royal" family lived in exile, and had urged them to bring the Republic down. The other leagues and the rightist war veterans must be brought into a plot, he said, to stage a coup.

By the end of January I had been able to identify the other leagues and to size them up. Among the oldest was an organization of street brawlers called Jeunesse Patriotes, recruited mostly from university students, which a right-wing deputy, Pierre Taittinger, had founded in 1924 during the financial crisis of that time. According to police records I managed by hook and by crook to obtain, it had a membership of some ninety thousand in the country, of whom six thousand were in Paris. Its street fighters were organized in mobile squads of fifty men, outfitted in blue raincoats and berets, and commanded by a retired general named Desofy.

A somewhat similar group of street toughs was called Solidarité Française, founded the year before by the wealthy perfumer François Coty, who for a decade had dabbled in right-wing movements and newspapers. I had run into this pompous, empty-headed perfumer now and then during my first years in Paris and watched him gradually conceive himself as a savior of the nation, who, like another famous Corsican (Coty's born name was Spoturno), might end up a Napoleon. Ridiculous as the thought was, for Coty was a political nincompoop, he obviously had begun to take it — and himself — seriously by the time of my return to Paris in 1934.

A more serious threat than the old perfumer himself were his storm troops. They were commanded by a Major Jean Renaud, a tough retired colonial army officer with a gift for rabble-rousing oratory. His street fighters were outfitted in blue shirts, black berets and jackboots, and their slogan, which they shouted in the streets, was "France for the French." The major claimed his fighting force numbered one hundred eighty thousand, of whom eighty thousand were concentrated in Paris. The police assured me that its strength was probably less than a fifth of that. Still, a force of some fifteen thousand toughs in the capital, trained in street fighting, could cause trouble, and this it was doing in the riots the last days of January.

The most fascist of the movements was one calling itself Le Francisme, which drew its inspiration from Mussolini and Hitler. It had been founded the autumn before by a right-wing adventurer named Marcel Bucard who was under the delusion that eventually he would become the French Führer. Its rowdies, though numbering only about five thousand, were among the most adept street fighters in Paris and they had a fanatical belief in Nazism that the toughs in the other leagues did not share. Many of them would become collaborationists of the Germans after the fall of France and one of them, Paul Ferdonnet, would later achieve notoriety as the "radio traitor of Stuttgart," when he broadcast Nazi propaganda in French from the German radio station there.

More important in numbers and in the backing it received from a surprisingly large segment of conservative circles was the Croix de Feu, founded in 1927 as a nonpolitical association of decorated war veterans and taken over in 1931 by an energetic forty-five-year-old lieutenant-colonel by the name of François de La Rocque, who had recently retired from active army service. He quickly transformed it into a paramilitary, antiparliamentary league, able to mobilize street demonstrators on an hour's notice and determined to stamp out communism and pacifism and reform the Republic by curbing its erring Parliament.

Though Colonel de La Rocque struck me as a rather courtly gentleman — he was the idol of the elderly upper-class women in the Boulevard St. Germain, where he lived — he had demonstrated his tougher qualities by breaking up meetings of liberals and socialists and sending his troops into the street to battle the police. His initial and most famous assault had been on the final meeting of the International Disarmament Congress in 1931 when he led a battalion of Croix de Feu veterans into the great hall of the Trocadéro and chased from the platform one of the most distinguished gatherings of European statesmen and notables ever to assemble in Paris. All of France, and most of Europe, heard the tumult, for the proceedings were being broadcast, and La Rocque in a sense was made.

He was not a very intelligent man nor did he have much political sense. But he was a good organizer and he labored hard at working up a mystique about himself, for the movement's objectives were purposefully vague so as to draw as many adherents as possible. One of his strengths was that he had good contacts in the government itself. At the time of the Trocadéro riot he was in close touch with Pierre Laval and André Tardieu, who alternated as conservative premiers in those days, and who gave him not only moral support but — it seems certain — financial backing from secret funds of the state La Rocque was trying to undermine. Private funds were also not lacking — from such sources as Mercier and Coty. By the end of 1933, as the hostility against Parliament and government mounted in Paris, the Croix de Feu and its auxiliary bodies had sixty thousand members, of whom a third were in Paris. Its shock troops, organized and trained by former army officers, and directed by an able staff headed by La Rocque, were the most disciplined and certainly the most formidable in Paris.

Finally, one of the two great organizations of ex-servicemen, the conservative UFC (Union Fédérale des Combattants), with nearly a million members, fed up with the antics of the legislature and government, threatened to throw its men in Paris into the streets unless the political leaders shaped up and did something about the mounting problems of the Depression and the deflation. The UFC was potentially more of a threat than the rightist leagues. Neither the police nor the army, if the latter was called to assist in maintaining order, would dare to fire on or even beat up these veterans who had fought so valiantly for France in the Great War. They held a special place in the esteem of all Frenchmen.

Besides the dire effects of the Depression on everyone, there had been two developments during my absence from Paris that had aroused the ire of a great many people, and which the rightist leagues were now exploiting. Between June, 1932, and the time of my return eighteen months later, no less than six governments had been formed and overturned, each lasting an average of three months. To a growing number of citizens this seemed utterly irresponsible. No cabinet lasted long enough even to try to come to grips with the nation's gut problems. Eminent ministers, drawn from the Chamber and the Senate, twiddled their thumbs and let the country drift toward anarchy.

The second development that had caused deep and widespread resentment was the increasing number of financial scandals involving cabinet ministers, past or present, senators, deputies, the police, the prosecutor's office and even the courts themselves.

Beginning in 1928, there had begun a wave of politico-financial scandals, some of which I had covered for the *Chicago Tribune*. The most sensational had involved a dumpy, remarkably brazen lady of forty named Martha Hanau, who was arrested on charges of having swindled investors in her various financial enterprises of hundreds of millions of francs. For years she managed to postpone her various trials and then her convictions. Gradually the public learned that the redoubtable lady was able first to defraud the public and then to evade the consequences because she had "connections." She knew an astonishing number of cabinet members, senators and deputies, had close connections with the French Foreign Office, and used her ill-gotten gains to subsidize newspapers, including a leading daily journal of the Left, *Le Quotidien.*

A resourceful woman of great persuasive powers, she induced the most eminent statesmen and notables in France to contribute to her weekly financial journal, and thus give respectability to a publication whose chief purpose was to promote her swindles. No less eminences than Premier Poincaré himself, a man of complete probity, Foreign Minister Briand, Education Minister Herriot and even the cardinal archbishop of Paris, who were surely equally honest, wrote articles for her, none of them having the faintest notion of what Madame Hanau was up to. How could the innocent investors, confiding their life savings to the lady's get-rich-quick schemes, have any suspicion of one with such formidable connections? They couldn't, and didn't, and the lady swindler amassed millions before she was caught.

In those last years of the 1920's and stretching into the 1930's one financial scandal after another followed, all having the same pattern. Crooks, with the aid of bribed cabinet members, senators and deputies, were able to set up in business, including banking, and then, when they were caught, evade trial or have their cases continually postponed or the charges quashed, sometimes by the minister of justice himself, who was in on the deal.

The public, especially in volatile Paris, was getting fed up with such corruption in high places. If Parliament and government would not clean up their own houses, then the people of Paris, it was becoming evident by the time I returned, might take to the streets, as they had in 1789, 1830, 1848 and 1871, and overturn still another regime.

It was against this background that at the beginning of 1934 the affairs of a longtime swindler with remarkable connections in the highest and most respected circles of the Republic — in the government, the Parliament, the police, the Prosecutor's Office, even the courts — burst into light and provoked the gravest crisis in the history of the Third Republic.

On the morning of December 30, 1933, as the good citizens were getting ready to celebrate their survival of still another trying year, the newspapers announced that a warrant for arrest of one Serge Alexandre, alias Sacha Stavisky, had been issued in connection with certain frauds. The headlines were small, the name unknown to the public. Then suddenly the story burst like a fury through the press and the country.

Serge Alexandre (Sacha) Stavisky, born in 1886 at Kiev of Russian Jewish parents, had come with his family at the turn of the century to Paris, where the father began to practice dentistry in one of the poorer quarters. At twenty-two Sacha had his first brush with the law over a minor fraud, and in 1912, when he was twenty-six, received his first jail sentence for another. His father, out of chagrin, committed suicide but this seems to have had little effect on the young hustler. Shunning work, he had drifted into the petty underworld of Paris, living off women, drug-peddling, confidence games, forgery, the disposal of stolen bonds, and an occasional armed robbery, and developing a remarkable ability to escape the clutches of the law.

Gradually he rose in the world, accumulating money from his shady practices, frequenting the gambling salons of the French resorts, buying a theater, financing a newspaper, showing himself around with fancy mistresses, acquiring politicians and even ingratiating himself, whenever he felt the law breathing down his neck, with the Sûreté Générale, for whom he sometimes served as an informer in the shadowy world of crooks and adventurers.

Finally in 1926 he got into real trouble when he was arrested for mulcting the investors in one of his companies out of 7 million francs. Put behind the bars in the Santé prison in Paris, he languished there for eighteen months while the authorities tried to unravel the tangle of his swindles. He had been released in 1927 on provisional liberty ostensibly to face trial; thanks to his friends and supporters in the Justice Department, the courts, the police, the Parliament and in certain ministries, his trial kept being postponed until, at the beginning of 1934, it had been put off nineteen times over a period of seven years.

All this while Stavisky was back at his old practices, growing richer, buying two newspapers, one on the Left, the other on the Right, acquiring one of the capital's leading theaters, the Empire, and a stable of racing horses, and enlarging his circle of friendships among politicians, ministers and ex-ministers, police officials and newspaper publishers and editors. During this period his murky affairs, I was able to establish, came to the attention of the police on forty-five occasions. Not once was anything done about them. The obsessive swindler seemed to be above and beyond the law.

Responsible for the nineteen postponements of his trial was the head of the Paris Parquet, Chief Prosecutor Georges Pressard, who happened to be the brother-in-law of Camille Chautemps, a perennial cabinet minister, a longtime wheelhorse of the Radical party, and now, since the previous November, the premier. The official who actually did the postponing, under Pressard's direction, was one Dr. Albert Prince, an assistant prosecutor, whose body, shortly after the Stavisky storm broke, would be found mangled on the rails of the Paris–Dijon railroad line.

The longer his trial was put off, the more money Stavisky made in a whole string of new fraudulent enterprises. One of his favorite rackets was to have himself named, through his pull with the politicians, the agent for the floating of a city's municipal bonds. He would "cover" them with deposits of false or stolen jewels and by fictitious bookkeeping, discount them at a legitimate bank, and use the money to found a new company of dubious purpose. In this way he had made off with ten million francs of municipal bonds of the city of Orléans in 1928 but had managed to scrape up enough funds to repay them before he was caught.

He was not so lucky at Bayonne, where, practicing the same chicanery with the connivance of the mayor and other politicians, national and local, he could not make good on the municipal bonds becoming due. On Christmas Eve, 1933, one of his confederates in the city government there confessed that 239 million francs' worth of bonds now maturing, which had been floated by Stavisky, were worthless. The confederate was arrested. So was the distinguished mayor-deputy of Bayonne, along with various other politicians and the editors of two large Paris newspapers — all accused of aiding and abetting, for a price, Stavisky's swindle. A few days later a prominent cabinet member was exposed in the press as having helped to promote the sale of Stavisky's dubious Bayonne municipal bonds. The dam began to break.

In the meantime Stavisky had disappeared, and the police, whom he had sometimes served as a stool pigeon, appeared unable, or unwilling, to find and arrest him. The Sûreté, in fact, I discovered, had recently furnished him with a false passport apparently in the hope that he would flee abroad and once out of their reach would not have to reveal his "connections." But by now the aroused press of Paris was screaming that he be brought to justice, and with public indignation mounting, the police finally "found" him in the winter resort of Chamonix. On January 8 the newspapers announced that Stavisky had committed suicide just as the police were breaking into the villa where he had been hiding. Few Frenchmen believed it. Most were sure the police had murdered the crook to prevent him from exposing so many in high places, including the police, who were involved in his crimes and who had kept him out of jail so long.*

Next day the tempers of a good many people in Paris rose swiftly to the boiling point. This was the last straw, after the mounting revelations of the complicity of politicians and police with the longtime swindler. That morning, January 9, *L'Action Française* issued a ringing appeal on its front page for Parisians to gather after their day's work and march on the Chamber of Deputies to drive the "Robbers and Assassins" out.

The call enabled the royalists to mobilize their own forces. That evening, some two thousand of them tried to reach the Chamber, but were repulsed. Afterward, they had surged across the bridge into the Place de la Concorde and taken out their frustration by grabbing the minister of marine out of his car in front of the ministry and belaboring him.

Two nights later, on the eleventh, the Jeunesses Patriotes, led by a member of the Paris City Council, joined the royalist Camelots. The demonstrators tore down trees and railings and confiscated motorcars to form barricades in the streets. They overturned newspaper kiosks and set them on fire. They jammed the third-rail conduits furnishing electric power to the streetcars, which, along with the public buses, were halted. A police report I saw a few days later described the damage as the worst in Paris in twenty years.

The spirit of insurrection was spreading in the city. The next morning *L'Action Française* in blaring headlines called for "a revolt of Paris against the robbers," meaning the Parliament and government.

Premier Chautemps stubbornly refused to appoint a special parliamentary committee to investigate the whole Stavisky mess. No doubt

---

* A year later the special parliamentary investigating committee almost agreed. After mulling over all the evidence it concluded that while Stavisky undoubtedly had shot himself as the police broke into his villa, his suicide had been "partly forced" by the police. They found that the police had let the wounded man lie on the floor for more than an hour without succor while he slowly bled to death. "This extraordinary negligence," the committee held, "finished the task which Stavisky had begun. . . . Would it have been possible to take Stavisky alive? We believe the answer is yes. Beyond doubt there was no attempt by the police to make a normal arrest and conserve for justice an accused of this importance."

it was embarrassing to him that the public prosecutor responsible for postponing the swindler's trial nineteen times was his brother-in-law, and that his own brother, Pierre Chautemps, was a lawyer for one of the Stavisky companies. At any rate, backed by a parliamentary majority, thanks to the votes of the Socialist party, whose leaders feared that powerful reactionary forces were hoping to stage a Fascist coup, Chautemps chose to do nothing except to demand the muzzling of the press, which he held largely responsible for urging the rioters on.

The riots did go on, increasing in violence. There were violent outbreaks on January 22 and 23, and the biggest of all on January 27, which continued all through the afternoon and evening, during which much more property damage was done, and eighty policemen and several hundred rioters injured.

That evening Chautemps, his shaky government further compromised by the revelation that his minister of justice was involved in a new financial scandal, this one connected with a bankrupt bank, and he himself finally shaken by the seriousness of the rioting that day and perhaps by a new chant of the besieging mob that could be clearly heard in the Chamber — "Hang the Deputies!" — resigned. It was the first time in the history of the Third Republic that a government backed by a solid majority in both chambers had given way to the menace of the streets. The fascist leagues had won their first victory. They had overthrown a "leftist" government. The triumph merely whetted their appetite.

The President of the Republic, the ineffectual Albert Lebrun, tried to persuade the leaders of all the parties to form what he called "a national government of truce." But none of them wanted the responsibility. Finally Lebrun turned to Édouard Daladier, a Radical-Socialist untouched by the Stavisky scandal or by any other, widely believed to be a man of strong determination who could settle the crisis with a firm and fair hand.

It was at this time that my journalistic contact with this well-meaning but, in the end, rather tragic figure in French politics began.* He was a good man in many ways, but not big enough — no

---

* It would continue until near the end of his life, long after the war, when he discussed frankly with me what in his opinion had brought the fall of France, and his own major responsibilities for the catastrophe. In 1961 he became fascinated by the revelations in my book *The Rise and Fall of the Third Reich* about the weaknesses of Nazi Germany on the eve of the Anglo-French surrender at Munich, including a revolt of the German High Command and a plot of the German generals to overthrow Hitler. He had learned of them, he said, only after reading my book twenty-three years later. Had he known of them at the time, he said — and he was bitter that the British, who were aware of them, had not tipped him off (he was, after all, head of the French government) — he would not have given in so easily to Hitler at Munich. My exposures led him to write a series of articles on the subject

French politician was — to cope with the problems that now began to overwhelm France and that would continue to mount to the time of Munich and finally to the terrible disasters of the war.

But those first few days of February Daladier seemed to be the man of the hour. He had a reputation for being tough, intelligent, straightforward and utterly uncorruptible. Named minister for the first time in 1924, when he was forty, he had subsequently served in seven more cabinets. At the end of January, 1933, he had been named premier and his government had lasted nine months, three times longer than the average. As were so many politicians in France, he was self-made. Son of a provincial baker, he had worked his way through school and earned the degree of *agrégé d'histoire* at the University of Lyon. The study of history was, next to politics, his great passion, and he had taught it for several years.

During the Great War he had fought for four years as an infantryman in the trenches, survived the slaughter of Verdun, and risen from a private in the ranks to captain. I had once heard someone who had served in his company asked if Daladier had been a good officer. He had replied: "Better than that. He was a good soldier." The newspapers called him the "bull from Vaucluse" (his electoral district) not only because of his broad shoulders and thick neck but because of his stubbornness and his rather rude manner of attack. Now in February, 1934, as the battles in the streets of Paris grew in intensity, Daladier appeared to many to be the man France needed.

His first act as premier was to promise the country that he would set up a special parliamentary committee to investigate the Stavisky affair. In the meantime he himself would move "fast and firmly" against those already compromised in the scandal, no matter who they were. But in this he acted clumsily. Convinced by a hasty study of the evidence that the head of the secret police, the prefect of police in Paris and the chief prosecutor all bore a heavy responsibility in the Stavisky business, he got rid of them. But instead of firing them he kicked them upstairs. He appointed the popular but right-wing Paris police chief, Jean Chiappe, resident-general in Morocco; Pressard, the prosecutor, a judge; and the head of the Sûreté, director of France's great, classical theater, the Comédie-Française.

"A policeman running the House of Molière!" exclaimed the Parisians in derision. To the sober but liberal historian François Goguel this was "vaudeville," which was the last thing France needed in this critical hour.

---

in *Candide* in the fall of 1961. Daladier provided me with a great deal of inside information for my subsequent book on the fall of France.

Chiappe refused to accept his new post and announced that he had been "fired." To the burdens of *L'Affaire Stavisky* was added a new one, *L'Affaire Chiappe.* The hot-blooded prefect of police, a passionate Corsican, became overnight the new martyr of the Right, and began to intrigue with it against Daladier.

Despite the confusion and resentment caused by the premier's "firings," the streets of Paris were strangely quiet over the weekend of February 3. The leagues were waiting for Tuesday, February 6, when the Chamber of Deputies reconvened to vote on the new Daladier government.

On the morning and early afternoon of February 6, the big-circulation dailies, as well as the political newspapers of the Right, carried flaming appeals from the various leagues calling on their members and all good Parisians to take to the streets that evening in a massive demonstration against the government. As I read them, they were a call to insurrection, or at least to violence leading to insurrection. *L'Action Française* listed certain cabinet ministers as among those who would be "killed without mercy."

To further inflame the populace, most of the newspapers carried false reports that the government had secretly brought into the capital squadrons of tanks, machine-gun companies and black Senegalese troops to "mow down" the "peaceful" demonstrators. Finally, all the great newspapers published not only the hysterical appeals of the leagues but carefully noted on their front pages the exact time and place for each league and its sympathizers to meet — in case they had failed to receive more direct orders. The Paris press, I thought, was behaving even more irresponsibly than usual.

At the last moment the Communists got into the act. On the morning of February 6 *L'Humanité*, the party's daily paper, called on all members to join the demonstration that evening. Thus the Communists were joining their enemies on the extreme Right in demonstrations aimed at bringing down the Republican government. I was more surprised than I should have been. I had once seen this duplicity in Berlin toward the end of the Weimar Republic. There the German Communist unions had joined the Nazi unions in carrying out a strike that had paralyzed public transport. The French Communists must have forgotten, I mused, that their German brothers had been liquidated as soon as the Nazis triumphed.

Late on the afternoon of February 6 I was assigned by the Paris *Herald* to go down to the Place de la Concorde, across the Seine from the Chamber, to see if the threatened demonstrations were coming off. I found only a few hundred shock troops of Action Française, Jeunesses Patriotes and Solidarité Française, trying unsuccessfully to shove back the police toward the bridge that leads from the great square across the Seine to the Palais Bourbon, the seat of the Chamber of Deputies. I went into the Hotel Crillon on the north side of the Place for a bite to eat. It did not look as if it would turn out to be much of a story.

When I emerged onto the Place de la Concorde an hour later — about 6:30 P.M. — the scene had changed. The square was packed with several thousand demonstrators who were standing their ground against repeated charges of mounted, steel-helmeted Garde Mobile. Over by the obelisk a bus was on fire. I worked my way through the Guards, who were slashing away with their sabers, to the Tuilleries, which overlooks the Place on the east side from an elevation of ten or fifteen feet. A mob was crowded behind the railings, pelting the police and Guards with stones, bricks, garden chairs and iron grilles ripped up from around trees. It was here that I noticed for the first time Communists mingled with their supposedly Fascist enemies. Down on the broad square itself the fighting continued, with the crowd advancing and then retreating before the charges of the mounted Guards. It was by no means an unequal fight. The rioters were using sticks with razor blades attached to one end to slash away at the horses and the legs of the mounted men, and they were throwing marbles and firecrackers at the hooves. A number of horses went down and their riders were mauled. Both sides began to carry away their wounded.

To get a better view I fought my way out of the churning mass, got over to the Hotel Crillon, and went up to a third-floor balcony overlooking the Place. Twenty or so reporters, French and foreign, were standing there against the railing, and there was one woman I did not know, a few feet to my left.

The first shots we didn't hear. Suddenly the woman slumped silently to the floor. When we bent over her, blood was flowing from her face from a bullet hole in the center of her forehead. She was dead.

The firing now became general — from both sides. It was difficult to see what was going on; all the streetlights by now had been pelted or shot out. Later it would be established that a mob, mostly from the Solidarité Française, had started to break through the last police barricade guarding the Seine bridge leading to the Chamber, which the forces of order had been instructed to hold at all costs. A few policemen and Garde Mobile had panicked and opened fire with their automatic pistols, killing six rioters and the woman on the Crillon balcony across the square, and wounding forty more. Finally the officers in charge had got their men to stop firing. Several of the senior officers themselves had been wounded by flying missiles or bullets — by this time some of the rioters were firing back — and been carried off to a first-aid station hastily set up in one of the corridors of the Chamber.

Going over to the Chamber for a moment to see what was happening there, I found the corridor jammed with injured police and Guards lying on the floor. Two doctors and half-a-dozen wives of deputies were working over them. In the Chamber itself, I was told, there had been pandemonium for several hours. Daladier had been unable to read his ministerial declaration, so great was the clamor on the floor. Several times deputies left their benches to indulge in a free-for-all in the well of the House. Once the rightist deputy Jean Ybarnegaray strode over to the ministerial bench and tried to drag the premier off. Daladier, who had the build of a wrestler, had sent him sprawling. In the din and confusion Daladier finally concluded that debate on approving his new cabinet was impossible and demanded a vote of confidence.

Long before I arrived, one of my reporter friends told me, the sound of firing from the nearby Place de la Concorde was heard for the first time above the shouting within the Chamber. "They're firing!" the rightist deputy Scapini, who had been blinded in the war, shouted. "You are a government of assassins!" Between the sounds of firing could be heard the roar of the mob, and it seemed to be coming closer. A deputy yelled: "They are storming the doors of the Chamber!" My friend swore he saw several deputies hastily depart through a back door and steal out into the night.* As a member later told me, "The least courageous were not the last to depart." He added that the Speaker himself, Fernand Bouisson, a dignified gentleman with a white beard, had hidden a slouch hat and an old dark overcoat under his rostrum to replace his topper and cover his formal dress-suit, which the presiding officer customarily wore during the sessions.

* The valiant members of my own profession in the press gallery could not get away until they had written and telephoned in their stories. But they had sought to protect themselves in case the mob invaded the premises. On the door of the now deserted press room I found a hastily scrawled sign: *"NOTICE TO THE DEMONSTRATORS: NO DEPUTIES IN HERE!"*

The face of Édouard Herriot, three times premier and head of the Radical-Socialist party, was too well known to the public even if he had tried to disguise himself, which he had not. As he was making his way home on foot that night he was seized by fifty ruffians, roughed up, and, to their cries of "Throw him into the Seine," dragged toward the riverbank, where he was rescued by a platoon of gendarmes just as he was about to be tossed into the river's muddy waters.

Before adjourning, I learned, the Chamber had given Daladier a thumping vote of confidence, 343 to 237. The decisive majority was due to the support of the Socialists, whose leader, Léon Blum, had exclaimed during the debate: "Our vote for the government is not a vote of confidence. It is a vote of combat!" The Socialists, unlike the Communist unions, were not forgetful of what had happened to their party and to the democratic regimes in Italy and Germany when Mussolini and Hitler had taken over.

So Daladier had the confidence of a parliamentary majority, but on this night of wild rioting it was not enough. The rage of a lot of Parisians and the fierce determination of the ugly mob had to be taken into account too. The premier was to learn this in the next crucial hours. For though the deputies had gone home, the battle still raged in the Place de la Concorde and in the area around it. As I returned to the scene, it seemed to me to have grown uglier and more threatening.

During the long evening I worked my way several times through the melee to the Crillon to telephone to the *Herald* what I could — a confused account, to say the least. The lobby of the hotel had been turned into a dressing-station. Dozens of injured lay on the floor, attended to by volunteer doctors and well-dressed ladies serving as nurses. Once, soon after we had carried the body of the dead woman down from the balcony, the Ministry of Marine next door was set on fire. Fire trucks arrived, but before the firemen could get their hoses playing on the building the rioters had slashed them. They were now trying to force the entrance of the smoking ministry. Naval guards were holding them back at pistol point.

About 9 P.M. suddenly the roar of the mob subsided and the sporadic firing stopped. Into the Place de la Concorde from the Champs Élysees marched a long column of several thousand war veterans from the UNC, their decorations pinned on their breasts. They were singing the "Marseillaise" and holding high their flags and banners. Many carried signs: "UNC. WE WANT FRANCE TO LIVE IN

ORDER AND HONESTY."* Unlike the rioters, these ex-soldiers were not in a very militant mood, at least at first. The forces of order treated them with marked deference, saluting their flags. The main column turned north from the Place into the rue Royale. A smaller group of about a thousand — members, I judged from their banners, of the Association of Veterans Decorated for Action at the Peril of Their Life — headed south for the bridge. There its two leaders, General Lavigne-Delville and Colonel Josse, the latter a former deputy and senator, parleyed with the municipal police chief, who politely but firmly refused to let them pass over to the Chamber.

I fell in with them as they rejoined the main column of veterans, which in the meantime had turned toward the presidential palace. The ex-servicemen, stopped at a barrier by the police, now became belligerent, fighting their way through the barricade and then through a second one. At the gates of the presidential palace they were met by mounted Republican Guards with drawn sabers and pushed back. They returned to the Concorde in an ugly mood, having lost some fifty badly injured and most of the rest nursing bruises from the blows of police sticks and the sabers of the horse guards. As they retreated into the square, they were joined by thousands of brawlers from the leagues and a large number of Communists, who had been milling about the Place, pelting the guardians and setting fire to cars and autobuses.

This was now a considerable force — at least twenty to thirty thousand strong, I estimated — and it was in a crazed and brutal mood, determined to storm the bridge at any cost and seize the Chamber of Deputies. None of these angry men knew that the deputies already had cleared out of the Chamber. At about 10:30 P.M. this formidable mob, to whom the war veterans now gave some leadership and direction, surged across the square, assaulted the beleaguered forces defending the bridge, and almost carried it. During the next hour it made twenty successive charges, and though each was repulsed, the mob kept re-forming and making new attempts.

The strongest came shortly before 11:30. The guardians were driven back and some of them started to flee for their lives over the bridge. It was at this moment that the police and guards again opened fire, in self-defense, and the rioters were halted at the edge of the bridge.

* Perhaps none of these war veterans, indignant at the corruption that had come to light in the Stavisky affair, knew that their own leader, the president of the UNC, was on the board of a Stavisky company that had perpetrated one of the crook's last and most extravagant swindles. I didn't know it myself, until much later.

It was now approaching midnight and the enraged mob re-formed for what looked like one final desperate attack. It seemed doubtful to me that the defenders could hold this time. Exhausted by nearly six hours of fighting, weakened by the loss of more than a thousand injured, and frustrated by orders not to use their firearms — only a relative few had panicked and used them — the police and guards appeared to me to have neither the force nor the will to withstand another serious assault.

It was then that a surprising and abrupt change in the critical situation occurred. A Colonel Simon, commander of the First Legion of the Gendarmerie, had been asked by the Paris prefecture of police if he could scare up some gendarmes from the suburbs and surrounding towns, and he had arrived at sundown with some five hundred and had turned them over as reinforcements to the Paris police. He remained at the Concorde bridge, he testified later, merely to see how his men were doing. By 11:30, though, he realized that the forces of order were too weak and demoralized to stem another assault by merely trying to stand their ground. Part of the demoralization, he saw, came from the lack of leadership. Most of the seasoned officers had been wounded and carried off to the Chamber. Colonel Simon therefore simply stepped in on his own and took charge. His experience as an army officer in the war had taught him that in situations as critical as this the best, and perhaps the only, defense was to take the offensive; he therefore summoned the commanding officers and proposed that they mount a determined attack with all the forces left and clear the square. He asked the mounted guards to lead the charge and promised to follow at the head of the gendarmes and Garde Mobile on foot to mop up.

Suddenly a large squadron of Mobile and Republican Guard cavalry, with drawn sabers, surged into the square, followed by several hundred police and foot guards brandishing their white batons. The surprised rioters gave way; they started to run. I could scarcely believe it. With a few minutes the Place de la Concorde was cleared and the horse guards were chasing stragglers through the avenues that led from the square.

I glanced at my watch. It was ten minutes after midnight. I started to sprint up the Champs Élysees to the office to write the rest of my story. It was a good mile uphill along the broad avenue to the *Herald*, and I arrived badly out of breath and exhausted. But with the excitement of the evening still surging through my veins I managed to write a couple of columns before our final deadline.

When I returned to the shambles of the Concorde about 2 A.M., it was deserted except for a few army troops guarding the bridge and the Chamber beyond. They apparently had been hastily brought in to relieve the weary remnants of the police.

As I made my way home, dead with fatigue, on foot, for there was no public transport functioning nor any taxis, I wondered what had become of the Croix de Feu, by far the strongest of the leagues. I had not seen a sign of them all evening. They were supposed to have been the shock troops which, as their leader, Colonel de La Rocque, had boasted, would invade and occupy the Chamber. Twice that evening, I learned later, the colonel from a distant command post had ordered his troops, some four thousand strong, to halt just as they were overpowering the police and making ready to pour into the Palais Bourbon from the rear and chase out the deputies.

The colonel, it turned out, had been frightened by the extent of the insurrection and had lost his nerve. On the morning of February 7, however, he issued a grandiose statement: "The Croix de Feu invested the Chamber and forced the deputies to flee!" This was not true. The deputies had left on their own steam, if a bit hurriedly, after affirming their confidence in the government. What *was* true was that La Rocque's storm troops *could* have taken the Palais Bourbon, chased out the deputies, and assumed the lead in setting up a provisional government.* The colonel, through some fatal flaw, had held back and muffed his chance. History is full of lost opportunities.

The casualties in the Place de la Concorde that evening were considerable. Among the rioters, fourteen were killed by bullets and two died later from their wounds. Some 655 were injured. The police and guards lost one killed and 1,664 injured. According to the govern-

---

* This was also the view of one of La Rocque's fiercest enemies, Léon Blum, the Socialist leader. In testimony before the parliamentary investigating committee after the second war, Blum declared: "If, above all, the [Croix de Feu] column advancing on the Left Bank under the orders of Colonel de La Rocque had not stopped in front of the slender barricade of the rue de Bourgogne, there can be no doubt that the Assembly would have been invaded by the insurrection. . . ." Blum added that there could be "no doubt" either that the deputies would have been driven from the Chamber "and a provisional government proclaimed, as was done in the same place in 1845 and September 4, 1870.

"Who would have composed the provisional government?" Blum asked himself. "I do not know, of course, what the relations of Marshal Pétain with the organizers of the riots may have been [they were much closer than Blum knew]. But I believe his name would have been on the list of the members of the new government, along with those of Pierre Laval. . . ."

On the night of February 6, in fact, the seeds were sown that later would make Pétain and Laval the chief actors in burying the Third Republic and the main pillars of the defeatist, collaborationist, totalitarian regime of Vichy, which succeeded it.

ment the guardians fired 527 revolver shots; how many were fired by the rioters was never ascertained though I would have guessed around two or three hundred. It was the bloodiest encounter in the streets of Paris since the Commune of 1871.

The premier, who had seen four years of massive slaughter as an infantryman in the war, was appalled by the bloodshed. But as head of the government he was pledged to defend the Republic against any attempt, however bloody, to overthrow it. After an emergency cabinet meeting at the Ministry of Interior, which in the early morning hours resembled a fortified place — it was the safest place in town for the members to gather — a weary Daladier at 3 A.M. made his way through the now quiet streets to his residence at the Quai d'Orsay.

"What are you going to do?" the journalists asked him.

"Save the Republic," he said.

The next morning he had second thoughts. Most of the members of the cabinet, who at the meeting at the Ministry of Interior had backed him and urged him to call out the army to put down the Fascist leagues, also had had second thoughts and now urged that the government resign. The frightened president of the Republic was demanding it. Lebrun telephoned the premier and told him he must step down "in order to avert civil war."

Overnight Daladier had brought in to the outskirts of Paris heavy reinforcements from the army: the 512th Regiment of tanks, twenty battalions of infantry and twenty squadrons of cavalry. But Daladier did not fully trust the army. As minister of war in the last four governments he had been feuding for more than a year with General Maxime Weygand, commander in chief of the army, whose fierce and outspoken royalist sympathies might make him, Daladier thought, a lukewarm defender of the Republic.

The police and guards, Daladier felt, could scarcely be depended upon, at least for the next few days. Nearly two thousand of them had been wounded and the rest were weary and demoralized. Early on the morning of the seventh, police intelligence reported to the premier that the Fascist leagues were preparing another onslaught that evening and that this time several thousand of them would come armed with revolvers and hand grenades. There had been a run on every gun shop in Paris. Several groups, the police warned Daladier, had "condemned" various ministers to death and intended to carry out the "sentence" before dark.

Depressed at the prospect of further and perhaps greater bloodshed in the streets, Daladier gave up. Shortly after lunch he handed in his resignation to a relieved President Lebrun. For the second time in a fortnight — and in the history of the Third Republic — the "streets" had overthrown a government supported by the majority in a democratically elected Parliament.

In a final communiqué to the public, Daladier explained why he had stepped down:

> The government, which has the responsibility for maintaining order and security, refuses to assure it today by resort to exceptional means susceptible of causing a bloody repression and a new effusion of blood. It does not wish to employ soldiers against the demonstrators. I have therefore handed to the president of the Republic the resignation of the cabinet.

In this pathetic declaration, I thought, could be seen all the weaknesses of the Third Republic, of the Radical politicians who dominated it, and of Daladier himself. If the fascist-minded rioters would not shrink from bloodshed in order to overthrow the regime, was it not the duty of the Republican government and its premier to defend the Republic by force if necessary? From what I had seen of the mob the night before, especially its lack of determined leadership and cohesion, it seemed evident that a display of military force on the following day would have cowed the demonstrators and caused them to disperse. But Daladier, deserted by his hesitant colleagues in the cabinet and Parliament, harassed by an easily frightened president of the Republic, unsure of the loyalty of the army under its royalist chief, and reviled by a venal press, would not risk any show of force at all.

"Imagine Stalin or Mussolini or Hitler," I wrote in my diary that evening, "hesitating to employ troops against a mob threatening to overthrow their regimes!"

Were the Western democracies in an increasingly totalitarian world becoming too soft or too stupid or too tired to defend themselves and the freedoms and decencies they had won and maintained for their peoples? It was a question I began to ponder more and more from that night on through the next few years until the answer became increasingly and appallingly clear.

The melancholy at the turn of events, which I shared with many others in Paris that February 7, was relieved somewhat at the end of the day by a bit of comedy provided by the Pretender to the French throne. He issued a ringing declaration from Belgium.

Frenchmen! From foreign soil, where I am constrained to live by
the cruel law of exile, I bow with deep emotion before the dead and
the wounded, who at the cost or the risk of their lives, have risen up
against an evil government. To maintain itself in power . . . it has not
hesitated to fire on war veterans, on the war-mutilated, on a generous
youth, the hope of the country.

Frenchmen! That is where you have been led by sixty years of a Republic, by a government of parties.

Frenchmen of all parties and of every sort! Now is the hour to rally
to the principle of monarchy, on which was founded over the centuries the grandeur of France, and which alone can assure peace,
order and justice.

> In Exile, February 7, 1934
> Jean, duc de Guise

Most of Paris read the proclamation with amusement. The Parisians thought it was not bad theater. It helped to relieve some of
their aches and exasperation.

Instead of the good duke and a restored monarchy, the rebels got
instead merely another coalition republican government of all parties except the Socialists and Communists, led by the seventy-one-
year-old former president of the Republic, Gaston Doumergue, who
was a staunch republican, a Radical, and a Protestant and Freemason
to boot, possessing all of the qualifications which the royalists and
right-wingers said they had rebelled against.

Doumergue, a vain, mediocre, and now senile old man, who as
president had become as noted for his perennial smile as President
Lebrun was for his constant weeping, had retired to his native village
with his mistress, whom he shortly after married, and he was reluctant to return to Paris in the midst of such a grave crisis. But his van-
ity was touched by Lebrun's appeal to him to save his country, and
his wife was pleased at the prospect of becoming what she had not
been before, Madame la Presidente — even if it was "of the Council"
and not of the Republic.

So "Papa" Doumergue, as the press called him, became premier in
a government that included seven former premiers and, for the first
time, the illustrious Marshal Henri Philippe Pétain, hero of Verdun.
This last appointment would have important consequences. It
marked the beginning of the political career of a military man then
age seventy-eight, who in the end, more than any other, would bring
down the Third Republic forever.

But that is to look far ahead. After one more bloody night on February 7, which was mild compared to the evening before — only four rioters were killed and 178 injured, while the police and guards suffered only 289 wounded — Paris began to settle down under the benign leadership of Doumergue's all-party government. There was a sort of truce.

It was almost broken, though, by a murky affair, an aftermath of the Stavisky scandal. Less than a fortnight after Doumergue took over, the body of a Paris magistrate involved in the shady business of keeping Stavisky out of jail was found mangled on the tracks of the Paris–Dijon railway. Apparently he had been tied to the rails after having been drugged. The popular and rightist newspapers immediately charged that the judge, Dr. Albert Prince, had been murdered by the police of the Sûreté at the instigation of former Premier Chautemps and of his brother-in-law, Pressard, to keep him from revealing their complicity in the Stavisky business. It had been Prince who, as head of the financial section of the public prosecutor's office, had granted Stavisky the nineteen postponements of his trial, ostensibly at the command of Pressard.

Public opinion, stirred up by the sensational press, was outraged. It looked like another "police murder," like that of Stavisky himself, and for the same motive: to silence a witness to the corruption of the republican regime. The truth, as with so many of these affairs in France, was never completely established. I worked on the story for weeks and concluded that the judge had been murdered, for obvious reasons. But a parliamentary investigating committee, with more evidence than I was able to uncover, concluded that it was a suicide and not a murder. It found that Dr. Prince had "saved Stavisky by his dilatory tactics" and that because of this involvement and certain others connected with his private life he chose in a moment of depression to kill himself. I remained skeptical. How the magistrate managed to drug himself to the point of unconsciousness, as the committee contended he did, and then tie himself to the rails before being run over was never explained.

The Third Republic had had a narrow escape. But more than that, I felt, February 6, 1934, marked a crucial and probably fatal turning point in the affairs of the Third Republic. From now on it might be all downhill for a regime that, with all its faults and failings — and corruption — had given France a society as civilized and as free as any other in the world. Time would bear this out too, as the Western democracies, Britain as well as France, began their inexplicable drift toward impotence, confusion and appeasement, their self-confidence slipping away; their self-interests forgotten or sacrificed in foolish domestic bickering; their power, which victory in the Great War had made supreme only sixteen years before, allowed to rot; their short-comings and growing weaknesses glossed over with a stifling and fatuous complacency; their eyes blinded — and this was especially true of France — to the mounting threat of fascism from within and from abroad, especially from Nazi Germany. France — and Britain too — drowsed, while Germany awoke.

Busy as I was working as a *Herald* reporter on the big stories of France's travail that winter and spring, I began to be restless to become a foreign correspondent again. Four events outside of France that late winter and summer of 1934 provoked me to try once more.

On February 12, 1934, six days after the rioting on the Place de la Concorde, the Austrian chancellor, Engelbert Dollfuss, struck against the Social-Democrats, who controlled the capital of Vienna, massacring with the artillery and machine guns of the regular army hundreds of them, men, women and children, holed up in the great municipally built housing complexes that had been a model to the world for working-class homes. In destroying the Socialists, he also destroyed democracy in Austria, replacing it with a "Christian" dictatorship.

There had been a general strike in Paris that day, but I find in the notes for my diary I made that evening that my concern was mostly for what was happening in Vienna. I was surprised that Dollfuss could be so savage.

> It's only a little more than a year ago [I wrote in my diary] that John Gunther and I had a long talk with him. . . . I found him a timid little fellow, still a little dazed that he, the illegitimate son of a peasant, could have gone so far. But give the little men a lot of power and they can be dangerous. I weep for my Social-Democrat friends in Vienna, the most decent men and women I've known in Europe. How many of them are being slaughtered tonight? And there goes democracy in Austria, one more state gone.

It was not only that, but, as I also noted, that by destroying the Austrian Socialists, the chief source of democracy in the country, Dollfuss was paving the way for the Nazis to take over.

On July 25, six months later, they did try to take over, and though they failed because of their own bungling, they succeeded in murdering Dollfuss.

In the meantime, in Berlin, Hitler had struck against his own S.A. storm troopers, whose brawls in the street had helped him to power, and in one day, June 30, had slaughtered its leaders and a number of others against whom he nursed grudges, including his predecessor as chancellor, General Kurt von Schleicher (and his wife), and the man who once had been the number-two leader of the Nazi party, Gregor Strasser. It was a barbarous bloodbath such as even Germany had never before experienced, at least in modern, civilized times, and it shocked the country and all of Europe. Here was a bloody tyrant who would stop at nothing.

Following the Berlin story in Paris as best I could and repelled, like everyone else, by the reports of the Nazi slaughter, I nevertheless felt an urge, which I noted in my diary that very night of June 30:

Wish I could get a post in Berlin. It's a story I'd like to cover.

The urge became stronger at the beginning of August. My diary describes the events that made it so.

Paris, August 2. Hindenburg died this morning. Who *can* be President [of Germany] now? What will Hitler do?

Paris, August 3. Hitler did what no one expected. He made himself *both* President *and* Chancellor. Any doubts about the loyalty of the army were done away with before the old field marshal's body was hardly cold. Hitler had the army swear an oath of unconditional obedience to him personally.

The one-time Austrian had made himself absolute dictator of Germany. As long as the venerable old President Hindenburg lived, Hitler had had to share power in the Reich. Now he had it all to himself. Almost unconsciously I was filling my Paris diary with news from Germany. And I kept trying to figure out how I could get a job there, several times during the summer phoning my friends among the American correspondents in Berlin asking them to keep me in mind.

Nazi Germany, as abhorrent as it was, was the place to be. Hitler and the barbarous regime he was clamping on the Germans was making most of the world news, crowding France, Britain, Mussolini's Italy and Stalin's Russia off the front pages at home. At the risk of making a nuisance of myself, I kept in touch almost daily, by letter and telephone, with my American colleagues in Berlin, some of whom were among my oldest friends. They continued to assure me that they hoped to find me a job there. But I must be patient.

On the afternoon of August 9 I was sitting in the newsroom of the Paris *Herald* glancing through the late editions of the Paris newspapers from which we often got leads or simply plucked a story. I was bored by the job and feeling even more frustrated than usual. There was no local news of any importance. My phone buzzed.

> Paris, August 9. Dosch-Fleurot rang me at the office this afternoon from Berlin and offered me a job with Universal Service there. I said yes at once, we agreed on a salary, and he said he would let me know after talking with New York. . . . Must brush up my German.

Arno Dosch-Fleurot was an old friend. He had been a legendary war correspondent in the Great War and then a foreign correspondent in Europe for the old and wonderful *New York World* until its regrettable demise, and he had often helped me on a big political story when I became a fledgling foreign correspondent myself. Dosch, unlike some of his colleagues who talked out of the side of their mouths and played at being cynical and hard-boiled, was a gentleman of the old school, courtly, wise, warm, with a fine mind and a passion not only for journalism but for history, literature and the arts. He was one of the most civilized men I had ever known. I looked forward to working with him.

I remember putting down the phone in a daze and then, as I gazed about the news room, feeling a wondrous sense of release. I stalked out of the office and across the rue de Berri to the Hotel California and into the bar and ordered a double cognac.

At last I could be a foreign correspondent again. And in Berlin, where the big story was. I had turned thirty now, and it was time, I thought, to try to make something of myself. The years were racing by.

Riots on the Place de la Concorde, Paris, on the night of February 6, 1934

BOOK TWO

Life and Work in the Third Reich

1934–1937

CHAPTER 6

Hitler and the Third Reich:
First Impressions
1934-1935

Berlin, August 25, 1934 — *Tomorrow begins a new chapter for me.* . . .

I had no idea when I scribbled that line in my diary the evening we arrived in Berlin from Paris how big and horrible and long a chapter it would turn out to be, not only in my own life and work, but, as events unfolded in this raging Nazi German land, in the lives of hundreds of millions of others, here and abroad. Few in the Western World would escape its consequences. Millions would not survive them.

Nuremberg was a good place to begin.

We had scarcely arrived in the German capital when I was sent off to cover the annual Nazi party rally at Nuremberg. This was the best possible introduction to the nightmarish world Adolf Hitler was beginning to create in his adopted land. For a whole week in September, as hundreds of thousands of uniformed party leaders and troopers of the S.A. and S.S.* gathered to acclaim the Leader and to listen to his harangues, I could get at first hand a view of this strange man whom so many Germans hailed as a genius and a savior. I could

---

* S.A. for *Sturmabteilung*, the brown-shirted street brawlers; S.S. for *Schutzstaffel*, the black-coated elite guard. The S.A. numbered a million at this time; the S.S. some one hundred thousand. Rapidly in the ensuing years the S.S., under Heinrich Himmler, a former chicken farmer, would swell in numbers and become the chief paramilitary arm of the party and dominate the police and the secret police.

watch him day after day work his magic on the German masses and perhaps I could begin to grasp the reasons for something that was beyond my comprehension: the reputed hold of this vulgar, uneducated, fanatically bigoted Austrian, who had risen from the gutters of Vienna, on a great people who over the centuries had contributed their considerable share to the civilization of the West.

The party rally this September promised to be especially important — perhaps explosive. The summer of 1934 had been a bloody and crucial one for the Nazi dictator. On June 30, Hitler had massacred the leaders of the S.A., starting with Ernst Röhm, its chief and his only close personal friend, and then ordered the murder of several old political enemies, including his predecessor as chancellor, General Kurt von Schleicher and his wife.

The venerable Field Marshal Paul von Hindenburg, the president of the Republic, had died on August 2 in his eighty-seventh year, and Hitler, who until then was only chancellor, had immediately taken over his post too as head of state, suppressing a part of the old man's will that had asked for a restoration of the Hohenzollern monarchy. Hitler wanted no rival with whom he would have to share power, and especially no one with the prestige of a Hohenzollern.

Now as head of government and head of state, Hitler had made himself absolute dictator. The Reichstag, which under the constitution had the legislative power, had been reduced by the machinations of the Leader to a rubber stamp, convoked infrequently merely to voice approval of his acts.

In Berlin, during the few days I was there before departing for Nuremberg, one could feel the tension mounting about the party rally. Hitler, it was said, feared that disillusioned members of the S.A. might try to revenge the slaying of their leaders. The brown-shirted storm troopers had been the backbone of the Nazi movement, the tough street brawlers, a million strong, who had helped him to take over the country. Now they felt betrayed.

The army, though pleased that the Führer had destroyed the S.A. as its archrival for military power, had resented his scotching Hindenburg's wish to reestablish the Hohenzollern emperor. The generals, all through the fourteen years of the Republic, had been fervent monarchists. Many of them regarded Hitler as a vulgar upstart. Some were indignant at his murdering General von Schleicher, who had been one of their own. There were rumors in Berlin that the generals might take advantage of the presence of Hitler and all the Nazi bigwigs in Nuremberg to carry out a military coup in the capital and restore the monarchy.

❦ ❦ ❦

Those first ten days in Berlin had thrown me into a depression. Perhaps it was partly because I had seen a little of Berlin when it had been a carefree place during the heyday of the Weimar Republic. Memories came back of sitting up all night in smoke-filled studios, in bars, on the pleasant terraces of cafés with German men and women of my age, discussing everything under the sun with all the abandonment of youth: politics, art, literature, sports, love, sex, the past, the present, the future. Sometimes life in Berlin and Munich had seemed to me to be more free, more modern, more stimulating and exciting than even in Paris, and far more so than in London.

Now some of my old acquaintances — who had been ardent liberals or socialists, even Communists, usually pacifists and freewheeling in their passion for freedom, for poetry, for music, for the latest novels and biographies, and the latest turn of politics — were full of the Nazi bug, addressing me solemnly about Germany's destiny under the Führer, the rebirth of the Fatherland under National Socialism, the necessity for a strong and virile nation adequately armed and free of the shackles of Versailles, liberated too from the poison of liberalism, socialism and communism, a nation reborn and once more based on the solid traditions of the old Germany, which respected authority. I could scarcely believe that these were the same Germans I had once met and liked and admired. Freedom — to say and write and publish what you pleased, to vote as you wished, to belong to a party or a union or an association of your choice, all of which Hitler had quickly deprived them of — no longer seemed to matter. They depressed me.

Not all, of course. A few, happily, had not changed. But mostly they were afraid. They were careful of what they said. They did not trust you.

Platoons or companies of brown-shirted storm troopers of the S.A. and black-coated guards of the more elite S.S. were constantly marching through the streets, their jackboots echoing on the pavement. I was warned that anyone on the sidewalk who did not pause to salute their standards and flags was liable to be beaten up on the spot.* I soon learned to duck into a shop when they passed.

* Warned by the American ambassador as well as by my colleagues. William E. Dodd, the ambassador, had been particularly incensed by the treatment a few months before of a prominent American physician, Dr. Daniel A. Mulvihill, who had come to Berlin as a consultant on lung problems. He had been standing on the curb of Unter den Linden watching a band of S.A. men trooping by. When he failed to salute their swastika standard, several bully boys broke ranks and knocked him unconscious.

Sometimes it would be a Jewish shop. In 1934 quite a few of them were still open, but to a dwindling business. Storm troopers had painted crude signs in yellow paint on their windows designating them as "Not for Aryans," and the proprietors would not always be happy about my taking refuge in them. I might be followed, they feared, by the storm troopers, who would rough them up and perhaps smash their windows and close their shops. As far as the Jews were concerned, the Brownshirts were a law unto themselves. Few Jewish storekeepers dared to call on the police for protection. If, exceptionally, in desperation, they did, no policeman dared give it.

We had been introduced to the Gestapo the very moment we arrived in Berlin. The first persons to greet us at the Friedrichstrasse Bahnhof as we stepped out on the platform were two agents of the secret police. I had expected to meet the Gestapo eventually, but not quite so soon. The two plainclothesmen took me aside and asked me if I was Herr So-and-So. I denied it, but they insisted I was. They studied my passport. They kept looking at the photograph in it and then at my face, as if there was no resemblance between the two, which there wasn't, passport pictures being what they are.

"It could be a fake passport," I heard one of the men whisper to the other.

"Where did you get this passport?" he asked.

"In Paris," I said.

The two conferred in whispers. I wondered whether we would be turned back then and there, my job in Berlin gone before I had even begun. Finally they clicked their heels, affected a smile, handed my passport back, turned and left.

Next day an old friend, H. R. Knickerbocker, a veteran correspondent, whose ten-year love affair with the Germans had begun to turn sour, told us that the Gestapo probably suspected I was an accomplice of Dorothy Thompson, who under police escort had departed the railroad station an hour or two before we arrived. She had been given twenty-four hours to get out after an enraged Hitler had learned what she wrote of him in her book, *I Saw Hitler.** Knick himself was in trouble, he told us, for some pieces he had written about Joseph Goebbels, the propaganda minister. He expected to be booted out any day now.

* Dorothy had opened her book with an account of an interview she had had with Hitler just before he assumed power. The first paragraph read: "When I walked into Hitler's salon I was convinced that I was meeting the future dictator of Germany. In less than 50 seconds I was sure I was not. It took me just that time to measure the startling insignificance of this man who had set the world agog." This was a rather surprising judgment for so veteran and astute a Berlin correspondent.

❁ ❁ ❁

In Nuremberg, on September 4, ten days after my arrival in Nazi Germany, I saw Adolf Hitler for the first time.

Like a Roman emperor he rode into the medieval town at sundown, past solid phalanxes of wildly cheering Germans who packed the narrow streets that once had been the gathering place of Hans Sachs and the *Meistersinger*. Thousands of swastika flags blotted out the Gothic beauties of the city's architecture, the façades of the old houses, the gabled roofs. The streets, hardly wider than alleys, were a sea of brown and black uniforms.

I got my first glimpse of Hitler as he drove by our hotel to his headquarters at the Deutscher Hof, a favorite old hotel of his, which had been newly remodeled for him. He fumbled his cap, which he held in his left hand, as he stood in his car acknowledging the delirious welcome with somewhat feeble Nazi salutes with his right arm. Probably he was pacing himself, knowing that he would be raising that right arm in salute thousands of times before the week was over. He was clad in a rather worn gabardine trench coat, very much like the weatherbeaten ones we foreign correspondents wore in those days. His face, which was rather flabby, had no particular expression — I expected it to be much stronger — and I wondered what there was in his almost modest bearing, in his rather common look, that unleashed such hysterical acclaim in the mob, whose men, women and children were so wild in their joy at seeing him, their faces contorted in a way I had never seen before, ever.

The frenzy of the crowds fascinated me that evening even more than my first glimpse of the dictator. I had seen vast throngs in India moved by the sight of Gandhi and in Rome by Mussolini. But this German horde was different in a way I could not yet comprehend. Later that evening, I got caught up in a mob of these frenzied people, who jammed the moat in front of Hitler's hotel. They were swaying back and forth, like the Holy Rollers I had once seen in the back country of Arkansas and Louisiana, with the same crazed expression on their faces. They were shouting in unison: "We want our Führer!" When he appeared on the balcony for a moment and waved, they went mad. Several women swooned. Some, men and women, were trampled as the crowd surged toward the hotel to get a closer look at their Messiah. For such he appeared to be to them.

By the close of the next evening, after the events of the first day of the party rally had come to an end, I had "begun to comprehend," I boasted in my diary, "some of the reasons for Hitler's astonishing success." Borrowing from the Roman Church, I noted, he was restoring pageantry to the drab lives of Germans. The morning's opening meeting in the huge Luitpold Hall on the outskirts of Nuremberg was more than a colorful show. It had something of the mysticism and religious fervor of an Easter or a Christmas Mass in a great Gothic cathedral.

The hall was a sea of brightly colored flags. Suddenly the band stopped playing. There was a hush over the thirty thousand people packed in the immense arena. Then the band struck up the "Baden-weiler March," a rather catchy tune and played only, I learned, when the Leader made his big entrances. Hitler appeared in the back of the auditorium, dressed in a brown party uniform, and followed by his aides, Hermann Göring, Joseph Goebbels, Rudolf Hess and Heinrich Himmler, all in brown uniforms except Himmler, who wore the black garb of the S.S. He strode slowly down the wide center aisle while thirty thousand pairs of eyes were turned toward him and as many hands were raised in salute. It was a ritual, I was told, that had been followed at the opening of big party meetings for years.

As soon as the Nazi chiefs were seated on the huge platform a large symphony orchestra played Beethoven's stirring *Egmont* Overture. Great klieg lights played on the stage. Behind Hitler and his entourage of a hundred party officials and a scattering of army and navy officers was draped the swastika "blood flag," which had been carried through the streets of Munich by a Nazi column when the shooting began during Hitler's ill-fated Beer Hall Putsch of 1923. Behind this emblem, holy to the Nazis, stood some five hundred S.A. standards. When the music was over, Rudolf Hess, deputy to the Führer and at that time his closest confidant, rose and slowly read the names of the Nazi "martyrs" — Brownshirts who had been killed in the streets in the struggle for power. He read out the roll call of the dead slowly and solemnly and there was a hush over the hall, the members of the vast audience bowing their heads in reverence.

It was in such a hushed atmosphere that Hitler sprang his Proclamation to the People, which the Nazi press office had tipped us off the evening before would be the most important pronouncement ever made by the Führer. Everyone had expected him to read it himself. Instead, to save his voice for seven speeches he was scheduled to make during the week, he had it read by Gauleiter Adolf Wagner of Bavaria, who, curiously, had a voice and manner so like Hitler's that some of the correspondents who were listening on the radio back at the hotel thought it was the Führer himself.

The words of that proclamation I never forgot. They kept coming back to me in the ensuing years, a reminder of the way history turns out differently than some, even the mightiest, have planned.

> The German form of life is definitely determined for the next thousand years! For us, the nervous nineteenth century has finally ended. There will be no revolution in Germany for the next one thousand years!

So the Third Reich was to last a thousand years! The words stunned me. But they provoked the brown mass in the great hall into a frenzy. The thirty thousand leaped to their feet and wildly cheered and clapped.

It cannot be, I protested to myself, as the crowd continued to roar, that this evil thing, demeaning to a great people, could last for a thousand years — or even for a hundred. But I had a sinking feeling that it would last a long time. Hitler's grip on the German people was much greater than I had expected.

The throng was up on its feet, cheering again, when the Führer came, as was inevitable, to his customary outburst against communism.

"Germany has done everything possible to assure world peace. If war comes to Europe it will come only because of Communist chaos."

He was back at it again when he spoke at a so-called "Kultur" meeting in the afternoon. "Only brainless dwarfs," he stormed, "cannot realize that Germany has been the breakwater against the Communist floods, which would have drowned Europe and its culture."

It was not difficult for him to convince the German people of this and, in time, many in England and France, even in America. Much later, when Hitler had embarked on his aggressive war against the rest of Europe, Charles Lindbergh would use similar words to express his belief that Germany, Hitler's Germany, "held today the intangible eastern border of European civilization."

Beyond that eastern border lay Bolshevism, in the minds of Hitler, as well as Lindbergh, and his followers the destroyer of the civilization of Europe. But it was beginning to dawn on me, caught up in the Nazi delirium of Nuremberg, that European civilization, at least in Germany, might not survive Hitler's dictatorship.

I had not yet quite realized that in order to keep the German people stirred up Hitler needed enemies to blame for all that had gone wrong before and for all that threatened the new, awakened, authoritarian Reich. Besides the Bolsheviks there were the Jews! Twice that opening day he thundered against them. The chaos from which he had rescued the country, he said, had been the work of "Jewish intellectualism."

"The alien life and form of ideas," he said, "injected into and forced on nations by Jewish intellectualism, which is racially without a basis, led to an alien, rootless state and internationally to complete chaos in cultural life."

He had saved Europe, he boasted, not only from the Bolsheviks but from the Jews, and he wanted his listeners to remember it and be grateful.

Each day in Nuremberg that week, and often far into the night, there was a new pageant that thrilled and inspired the masses and that seemed to instill in them a renewed fervor for the Leader and what he was bringing into the life of the German nation.

On the third day Hitler introduced his new Labor Service Corps, the *Arbeitsdienst*. It was a highly trained group of fanatical Nazi youths who, though they carried only spades, obviously had received a good deal of military drill. The German army was still limited to one hundred thousand men by the Versailles Treaty and conscription was forbidden. But the Labor Service, which had been hailed as a German version of Roosevelt's CCC, was obviously military — indeed someone had told me its hundred thousand members were receiving basic training to be soldiers. This soon became evident.

Standing at attention on the Zeppelin Field in the early morning sunlight, which sparkled on their shiny spades, fifty thousand of them — the first thousand in the front ranks bared above the waist — listened to Hitler's short speech praising them for their service to the Fatherland. Then as they began to parade past the reviewing stand they broke into a perfect goose step — no Prussian sergeant in the old days probably did it better — and the huge crowd went mad. The goose step seemed to me ridiculous, but the spectators loved it. Spontaneously they jumped up and shouted their applause. As the young men, in dark green uniforms, paraded by they formed an immense *Sprechchor* — a chanting chorus:

> *We want one Leader! Nothing for us!*
> *Everything for Germany! Heil Hitler!*

Some historian — or perhaps it was a politician — had once remarked that if you wanted to capture a nation you first had to capture its youth. This, obviously, Hitler had done, or was doing. Besides the Labor Service, I was told, he was building up an even more massive organization of Hitler Youth, into which would be corralled every youngster from seven years old on.*

On the following night there was another impressive gathering. Two hundred thousand Nazi party officials were assembled, with their twenty-one thousand flags fluttering in the searchlights, on the grounds of the Zeppelin Wiese. They were all in uniform, a brown outfit with brown cap, which Hitler himself had designed.

"We are strong and we will get stronger," Hitler shouted at them through the microphone, his words echoing across the hushed field from the loudspeakers. There was a thundering roar that reverberated back to the speaker, who seemed to feed on it, just as this mass of petty leaders fed on his words. He was telling them what they — what all Germans — wanted to hear: that Germany was great and it was strong, and would, under his leadership and with their determination, grow greater and stronger.

"What we have won by fighting," he went on, "we will keep. We will extend the hand of peace to anyone who wants to take it. But we will be firm with all who believe they can deny Germany justice and equality."

With the inspired call for strength and greatness went reasonableness. The new Germany would be strong but peaceful, wanting only justice and equality. It was a theme I would hear the dictator dwell on dozens of times in the following years but it already began to have a hollow sound for me, if not for the Germans. What Hitler really meant, it would become clear, to me at least, was that Germany would keep the peace while preparing for war. It had to keep the peace while it was weak, shackled still by the restrictions of the peace treaty. But when it was once more powerful . . . ?

No one, obviously, in that brown mass was in the mood to be analytical. The impact of the man and of the staged pageantry fascinated me. In the crisp night air you could feel the collective joy. I tried to describe it in my diary that night.

* "We have begun, above all, with the youth," I would hear Hitler say later in a May Day speech in Berlin in 1937. "There are old idiots out of whom nothing can be made any more. [This was greeted with laughter.] We take their children away from them. We bring them up to be a new kind of German.

"When a child is seven it does not yet have any feeling about its birth and origin. One child is like another. At that age we take them and form them into a community until they are eighteen. But we don't let them go then. They enter the party, the S.A. and S.S. and other formations, or they march directly into the factories, the Labor Front, the Labor Service, and they go into the army for two years."

There in the floodlit night, jammed together like sardines, in one massive formation, the little men of Germany, who have made Nazism possible, achieved the highest state of being the Germanic man knows: the shedding of their individual souls and minds — with the personal responsibilities and doubts and problems — until under the mystic lights and at the sound of the magic words of the Austrian they were merged completely in the German herd.

Hitler, with his genius for arousing the deep instincts of his people, had revived the ancient custom of torchlight parades, which the Germans so loved. Later that night some fifteen thousand men picked from the two hundred thousand on the field staged a torch-light parade through Nuremberg's ancient winding streets, Hitler taking the salute in front of the station across from our hotel. It was the first such parade I had ever seen. It stirred the feelings of the marchers and spectators alike, who lined the streets. I was a little stirred myself as I watched the endless ribbon of bobbing torches pass by and dissolve into the night, the successive bands blaring out the old German martial tunes and the tramping men singing the old Nazi marching songs. It was like a scene in a Wagner opera — *Lohengrin,* or was it *Tannhäuser* or *Die Meistersinger von Nürnberg?*

The next day Hitler faced his S.A. storm troops for the first time since the bloody June purge of its leaders. In a harangue the Führer "absolved" them from blame in what he called the "Röhm revolt." There was considerable tension in the stadium, and Hitler himself, I thought, appeared nervous as he stepped to the podium. He had taken no chances though. The hundred thousand unarmed Brownshirts in the field were ringed by twenty thousand armed black-coated S.S., and Hitler's own elite bodyguard of twenty-five hundred S.S. men, their rifles at the ready, was drawn up before the platform, separating and protecting him from the mass of S.A. men on the field below.

There was no attempt on his life that day — nor, as far as I know, during the six and a half years he kept the peace. The foreign diplomats and the foreign correspondents often wondered why. It would have been easy enough to get him. A couple of days before, a group of us, British and American correspondents, had seen how easy. We were having a drink in the hotel room of one of the correspondents. Just then Hitler drove by, directly below us, returning from some meeting. How simple it would be, we mused, for someone in a room like this to toss a bomb on his car below, rush down into the street and escape in the crowd. That no one had done it, or, as far as we knew, attempted it — not even the friends or relatives of the scores of slain S.A. officers, nor those of the murdered General von Schleicher and his wife and of others who were summarily shot on June 30 — told us, we thought, something about this country and the hold Hitler had on it.

What the outside world had not realized and what I was just beginning to comprehend was that the Austrian-born dictator was giving the Germans — or most of them — what they wanted. In scarcely a year and a half he had unified the country, stamping out the old divisions of lands, states and provinces, humbling even Prussia, the foundation of modern, militaristic Germany. Not even Bismarck and the Hohenzollern monarchs had been able fully to accomplish this. Germany had until then remained a sort of confederation, with each member such as Prussia and Bavaria having its own government and parliament. Hitler had made short work of that. No more provincial governments or legislatures to put the brake on Berlin.

The swift and ruthless unification of the Reich had answered, I began to feel, a deep yearning in the Germans to be one. It had also made Germany stronger and, for Hitler, easier to govern. It was this urge to be strong again, to be equal to the other great unified powers in Europe after the humiliating defeat of 1918, that Hitler had played on so skillfully and that had so aroused the passions and the support of so many Germans.

Some three hundred thousand of them gave further vent to this feeling on the last day of the party rally at Nuremberg. They went wild with joy as ten thousand seasoned troops of the army staged a very realistic sham-battle in the Zeppelin Meadow. I was a little taken back at the enthusiasm of the huge crowd as it watched the soldiers go into action, heard the rat-tat-tat of the machine guns and the thunder of the light artillery and smelled the powder from the smoke of battle that floated into the stands. I had seen crowds at home and in France and England follow such military exercises with avid curiosity, but no more than that. The German audience seemed to become a part of the mock-battle.

Obviously they liked to play at war. Had they forgotten, I wondered, the great German novel *All Quiet on the Western Front,* which had depicted war as it really was — a senseless, brutal horror? It occurred to me that German militarism, of which we in the outside world had heard so much, was not just a product of spartan Prussia and the Hohenzollerns, from Frederick the Great to Kaiser Wilhelm

II. It was something deeply ingrained in these people, and, obviously, it had not died with the lost war of 1914–1918.

After seven days of ceaseless marching, goose-stepping, speech-making, and pageantry, the party rally came to an end. I was dead tired from trying to cover it. I had developed a bad case of crowd phobia. Each day and night one got caught up in the immense throngs: thirty thousand in the great Luitpold Hall, tens of thousands packing the narrow streets of Nuremberg to get a glimpse of Hitler and to watch the parades, a half million at the Zeppelin Meadow. Their hysteria and their joy had fascinated me. They seemed to love being caught up in such vast herds. I hated it. It wore down a man clinging to his sanity. Yet I was glad I had come. It was the sort of baptism in Nazi Germany I needed if I were going to write about it with any depth and understanding.

Late that night, after filing my last dispatch from Nuremberg, I jotted in my diary:

> You have to go through one of these to understand Hitler's hold on the people, to feel the dynamism in the movement he's unleashed and the sheer, disciplined strength the Germans possess. And now — as Hitler told the correspondents yesterday — the half-million men and women who've been here during the week will go back to their towns and villages and preach the new faith with new fanaticism.

Back in Berlin I tried to sort over my first impressions of Adolf Hitler. In looks and appearance he was rather different from what I had expected. In Nuremberg, except during the traditional hysterical outbreak against the Bolsheviks and the Jews, he did not look or behave like the mad, raging, brutish dictator I had been reading about and which he had proved himself to be by his merciless massacre of the S.A. leaders and political opponents less than three months before.

His face was rather common. It was coarse. It was not particularly strong. Sometimes, when he obviously was fatigued from the long speeches, the hours spent in reviewing his troops, it appeared flabby.

All through the week in Nuremberg, where I often sat or stood but a few feet from him in the stands, I tried to size up the features of the man. He was about five feet, nine inches tall and weighed around 150 pounds. His legs were short and his knees turned in slightly so that he seemed to be a bit knock-kneed. He had well-formed hands, with long, graceful fingers that reminded one of those of a concert pianist, and he used them effectively, I thought, in his gestures during a speech or when talking informally with a small group.

His nose betrayed the brutal side of him. It was straight but rather large and broadened at the base, where thick nostrils widened it. It was the coarsest feature of the face. Perhaps it was to soften it that he grew his famous Charlie Chaplin mustache. His mouth was quite expressive, and it could reflect a variety of moods.

The veteran correspondents maintained that Hitler had no sense of humor and never laughed. As to the first, I had yet no means of knowing, but at the party rally I saw him laugh heartily at least a dozen times. He would rear back his head as he did so, the forelock of his dark brown hair, which he parted on the right side, would fall over his left temple to the eye until, still laughing, he would shake it back by a jerk of the head or the swish of his hand.

It was the eyes that dominated the otherwise common face. They were hypnotic. Piercing. Penetrating. As far as I could tell, they were light blue, but the color was not the thing you noticed. What hit you at once was their power. They stared at you. They stared through you. They seemed to immobilize the person on whom they were directed, frightening some and fascinating others, especially women, but dominating them in any case. They reminded me of paintings I had seen of the Medusa, whose stare was said to turn men into stone or reduce them to impotence. All through the days at Nuremberg I would observe hardened old party leaders, who had spent years in the company of Hitler, freeze as he paused to talk to one or the other of them, hypnotized by his penetrating glare. I thought at first that only Germans reacted in this manner. But one day at a reception for foreign diplomats I noticed one envoy after another apparently succumbing to the famous eyes. Martha Dodd, the vivacious young daughter of the American ambassador, had told me a day or two before I left for Nuremberg, to watch out for Hitler's eyes. "They are unforgettable," she said. "They overwhelm you."

His oratory also was overwhelming, at least to Germans. It held them spellbound. At Nuremberg I grasped for the first time that it was Hitler's eloquence, his astonishing ability to move a German audience by speech, that more than anything else had swept him from oblivion to power as dictator and seemed likely to keep him there.

The words he uttered, the thoughts he expressed, often seemed to me ridiculous, but that week in Nuremberg I began to comprehend that it did not matter so much what he said but how he said it. Hitler's communication with his audiences was uncanny. He established a rapport almost immediately and deepened and intensified it as he went on speaking, holding them completely in his spell. In such a state, it seemed to me, they easily believed anything he said, even the most foolish nonsense. Over the years as I listened to scores of Hitler's major speeches I would pause in my own mind to exclaim: "What utter rubbish! What brazen lies!" Then I would look around at the audience. His German listeners were lapping up every word as the utter truth.

The pattern of his speeches I first heard at Nuremberg would be repeated in almost all the ones I listened to during the next six years. Indeed, I was told, he had fashioned it years before as a young agitator in Munich until it had become second nature with him. Repetitive though it was, his listeners never seemed to tire of it.

He would begin invariably in a low, resonant voice, beautifully modulated, speaking slowly and seeming to measure his words. In this mood he would recall the past, his own lowly beginnings as a penniless unknown, discharged soldier at the end of the war, the early years of struggle as leader of the Nazi party, the discouraging setbacks, the chaos of postwar Germany and his iron resolve to reawaken the Fatherland from the shame and misery of defeat to its true Germanic greatness, a course he had adhered to unflinchingly and, yes, fanatically, he was proud to say, though many scoffed and perhaps more laughed.

The deep, resonant voice in this opening part of his discourse, which so moved his listeners, was not, I was told by a veteran German journalist, God-given. Hitler had been endowed, he said, with a rather thin voice that had a fairly high register. Over the years he had learned to force it to a lower scale and make it more resonant and he had developed his lungs, gassed during the war, much as an opera singer does, to give his voice more volume and enable him to better modulate it.

As he worked toward the inevitable climax of his discourse, the natural voice would reassert itself, the tone rising in scale, and, as the words came tumbling out in a torrent, it would become shrill and he would begin to shriek hysterically and reach, as one Irish correspondent irreverently put it, an orgasm of sound and fury, followed by an ecstasy such as I had never seen in a speaker, and which the awed listeners seemed to fully share.

He appeared able to swing his German hearers into any mood he wished. He could stir up a burning hate, as when he spoke of the Bolsheviks and the Jews, and later on, of those who stood in his way:

the Czechs at the time of the Sudeten crisis, the Poles just before he attacked them. I shall never forget how he shrieked at them, in a paroxysm of hysteria, calling them animals, barbarians, pygmies, and threatening them with utter destruction — a threat he would make good.

Hitler could be ironic and sarcastic, provoking raucous laughter as he ridiculed his opponents and held them up to scorn. At such times the born actor in him would emerge and he would screw up his face and curl his lips like a comedian, rolling his eyes and rolling his "r's" broadly as the Austrians and Bavarians do, manipulating his voice to get the last drop of sarcasm out of it.

From early on Hitler had instinctively grasped the importance of the spoken word in public life. Realization of its unique power had come to him, he says in *Mein Kampf*, in the last years of his down-and-out youth before the war in Vienna.

> The power which has always started the greatest religious and po-litical avalanches in history rolling has from time immemorial been the magic power of the spoken word, and that alone.
>
> The broad masses of the people can be moved only by the power of speech. All great movements are popular movements, volcanic erup-tions of human passions and emotional sentiments, stirred either by the cruel Goddess of Distress or by the firebrand of the word hurled among the masses; they are not the lemonade-like outpourings of the literary aesthetes and drawing-room heroes.

He began to practice his oratory on the audiences he found in Vienna's flophouses, soup kitchens and street corners. But he had a long way to go.

In Munich after the war, in which he had served four years in the trenches as a common soldier in a Bavarian regiment, he got a job as an army educational officer, a Bildungsoffizier, assigned to harangue the soldiers on the evils of pacifism, socialism and democracy.

> All at once [he writes in *Mein Kampf*] I was offered an opportunity of speaking before a larger audience. And the thing that I had always presumed from pure feeling without knowing it was now corrobo-rated: I could speak!

The discovery pleased him greatly. He had been afraid that his voice might have been permanently weakened by the gassing he had received at the front. Now he found he had recovered sufficiently to make himself heard, he says, "at least in every corner of the small squad rooms."

Such was the beginning of a talent that was to make him the most effective orator in postwar Germany and lead him to the dictatorship of the great country. As part of my job as a correspondent, but also out of sheer fascination, I would listen over the next six years to nearly all of his great public utterances and marvel at their effect on the German people.

I, too, in my small way, had since my own youth been deeply interested in the art of public speaking. There was not much of it in our country; it had become pretty much a lost art and it would be lost almost entirely when radio came and the politicians and statesmen *read* their speeches so badly as to put you to sleep. By the time I entered college in 1921, William Jennings Bryan was about the only great orator left in our country. He was an eloquent speaker, with a deep, resonant voice that carried to the far corners of the biggest halls without benefit of loudspeaker. One summer, working on a Chautauqua tent crew, I heard him speak a dozen times, but I began to see, as later with Adolf Hitler, that while Bryan could sway an audience with the magic of his oratory, what he said was lacking in substance and was often banal.

In Paris, in my first years abroad as a foreign correspondent, I had been moved by the oratory of Aristide Briand, the perennial French foreign minister. He, like Bryan, had a golden voice, with the resonance of an old cello, and his words glowed and his gestures flowed — the gestures of hands and fingers so delicate and artistically expressive that they reminded me of Paderewski's at the piano. And in London I had often gone down to the House of Commons to hear Winston Churchill speak, awed by his eloquence and also by his command of language and the force of his ideas. I had gone abroad to work long before Franklin Roosevelt became president so that during my time in Nazi Germany I had not yet heard him speak in person, though I was able to catch a few of his broadcasts over the shortwave. These were impressive. He too had the art of communication.

So except for Churchill and possibly Roosevelt and Briand, Hitler, I concluded, was the most effective public speaker I had heard. Mussolini, his fellow Fascist dictator, was no match for him. In a dozen or so speeches of Il Duce which I personally listened to, he sounded monotonous, with his shrill voice and falsetto shrieking.

There was Gandhi, of course, in India, to whom I listened dozens of times. He could be eloquent and terribly moving speaking to a small group. But he was not an orator and never made any attempt to be one. He could cast a spell over an audience of a hundred thousand of his fellow countrymen, but this was because of his charisma, not his oratory — he never raised his rather thin voice nor made the slightest gesture with his hands.

It was often said by the few Germans not taken in by Hitler at the time, and by more Germans after the war, that the Nazi dictator spoke bad German. My own command of the language being far from perfect, I could not really tell, but I was inclined to go along with this opinion. On reflection, I am not so sure. Perhaps Hitler's blend of his native Austrian and his acquired Bavarian, both in the accent and the syntax, led some North Germans to conclude that his command of the spoken language was faulty. But I've been impressed by the opinion of Max Domarus, a German historian and archivist, who personally listened to even more speeches of the Führer than I did, from 1932 to the end, and who came to the conclusion that Hitler spoke very good German.

"Hitler built his sentences," Domarus wrote, "out of his Austrian idiom that North Germans sometimes found disturbing. Had Hitler spoken bad German, the German industrialists, diplomats and generals who listened to him would not have been so impressed as they were. His art of oratory and his command of the German language in all its nuances were the principal ingredients of his success."*

One would have to add his demonic personality and his personal magnetism which he imposed on his German listeners and which, as much as his rhetoric, and perhaps more, held them in his grip. It held them even when, abandoning his usual themes of politics, he addressed them on other matters — on art, for example.

One evening in Nuremberg I listened to Hitler declaim on the subject of "German Art — and Non-Art." He spoke for two hours without a note, and though what he said struck me as vulgar and nonsensical, I was again fascinated by his oratory, and how by his use of it he was able to impose his outlandish ideas on his audience. Two hours was a long time to sit in a damp church, where the meeting was held. To me the evening seemed interminable. But the longer the man talked, the more inspiring he became, obviously, to his awed listeners.

Art, I gathered, was a favorite topic of his. To the very end of his

* Hitler's writing was something else. One German pedant claims to have discovered 154,000 errors in German grammar and syntax in *Mein Kampf.*

frantic life, he regarded himself as an artist whose talents as a budding painter and architect had not been recognized by the stupid professors at the Academy of Art in Vienna, who had rejected his application to enroll in the school. In the middle of the Second World War, as the burdens of defeat began to weigh him down, he would assert that as soon as the conflict was over and won, he intended to step down as Führer and devote the rest of his life to architecture. During the years of his rule, he acquired a large collection of paintings, most of them bad, which he intended to leave to a great museum he would build in his hometown of Linz, Austria.

I was rather amused and intrigued at hearing the Führer's idiotic pronouncements on art. (What other world leader took time off to lecture the public on art?) But later, as my experience of life in the Third Reich lengthened and deepened, I became aware that there was something frightening about them, because they had become the basis on which he meant to become the arbiter of artistic taste in Germany. It was he, it became apparent, who would decide what art was good for Germans and what was bad. And this despite his atrocious taste! It was a depressing thought.

But in this Hitler was as good as his word. Already that first year of mine in Nazi Germany he had begun to remove from the state museums what would eventually turn out to be some sixty-five hundred modern paintings; not only the works of such fine contemporary Germans as Kokoschka and Grosz, but of Cézanne, Van Gogh, Gauguin, Matisse, Picasso and others.

The acquisitive Göring acquired some of the best of these and once offered to sell me a few of them for what he called bargain prices — and they were! — if I would pay for them in dollars instead of marks.

"I need the foreign exchange," he chuckled, "and you get some priceless paintings for next to nothing." He showed me some canvases, mostly by Kokoschka, whose acquaintance I had made in Vienna and whom, I told Göring, I much admired. The fat marshal was a little miffed when I turned him down. He seemed scornful that one would have any qualms about buying stolen art. He himself was to acquire a great deal of it. Indeed an entire freight train was commandeered to transport to Berlin his loot from the museums and private collections in Paris.

Hitler claimed, I believe, to have paid for *his* collections. But most of this expenditure must have come out of government funds, for it was discovered later that during 1943 and 1944, when the war had begun to go badly for him, he purchased for the proposed Linz mu-

seum some three thousand paintings at a cost of 150 million Reic..
marks, or 37.5 million dollars. Another two million dollars was ex-
pended during the last twelve months of the war, as the Allies closed
in on Berlin. American troops found cached away in the salt mines of
Alt-Ausee 6,755 paintings that were to go to the Linz museum. Certainly the Führer never did things in a small way.

But his appreciation of art was narrow and vulgar, and indeed, as
with most of his ideas of politics and history, half-baked and irratio-
nal. And he insisted on inflicting it on the German people. He made
no bones about it. Addressing an audience at the dedication of the
House of German Art in Munich on July 18, 1937, he said: "I was always determined, if fate ever gave us power, not to discuss these
matters [of artistic judgment] but to make decisions." And he had
made them in this first exhibition of Nazi German art.

I had gone down to Munich to cover Hitler's formal opening of the
place. The new museum, a vast pseudoclassic edifice in shining white
marble which the Führer had helped his favorite architect, Ludwig
Troost, to design and which he described as "unparalleled and inimitable" in its architecture, was in truth a monstrosity — the good citizens of Munich were already calling it the *Weisswurstpalast* (the
Sausage Palace). Inside were hung some nine hundred works, selected from fifteen thousand submitted, of the worst junk I had ever
seen.

Hitler had made the final selection himself. And in his accustomed
stormy fashion. He had become so incensed, some of his party comrades confided to me, at many of the selections made by the Nazi jury
presided over by Adolf Ziegler, a mediocre painter who was president of the Reich Chamber of Art,* that he not only had ordered
them thrown out but had kicked holes in several of the canvases.

In a long speech opening the House of German Art, he laid down
to the German people the Nazi line on "German Art." Let there be
no doubt about it! he warned.

> Works of art that cannot be understood, but need a swollen set of in-
> structions to prove their right to exist and find their way to neurotics
> who are receptive to such stupid or insolent nonsense will no longer
> reach the German nation. Let no one have illusions! National Social-
> ism has set out to purge the German Reich and our people of all those
> influences threatening its existence and character. . . . With the open-

---

* Ziegler owed his position as head of the Art Chamber to the happy circumstance that he
had painted the portrait of Geli Raubal, Adolf Hitler's great love.

ing of this exhibition has come the end of artistic lunacy and with it the artistic pollution of our people. . . .

And yet some Germans, I was pleased to see, preferred to be artistically polluted. In another part of Munich, in a ramshackle second-story gallery in the Hofgarten arcades that you reached by climbing a narrow, rickety stairway, was an exhibition of "Degenerate Art," which Dr. Goebbels had named and organized to show the people what the Führer was rescuing them from. It contained a splendid collection of modern paintings: Kokoschka, Chagall, George Grosz, Käthe Kollwitz, Max Beckmann and expressionist and impressionist works of a hundred other artists. The day I visited it, it was jammed, with a long line of people forming down the creaking stairs and out into the street. In fact, the crowds besieging the Exhibition of Degenerate Art became so great that Dr. Goebbels, incensed and embarrassed and fearing the Führer's wrath, soon closed it.*

Among the things I noted at that first party rally at Nuremberg which brought out the peculiar flavor of this dictatorship was the sight of Hitler, wherever he went, always surrounded by a pack of men in brown uniforms, a good many of whom looked like gangsters — the kind I imagined swarming around Al Capone back in my native Chicago. These were the S.A., S.S. and party leaders, cabinet ministers and cronies of Hitler. Most of them had coarse, hardened faces and rough manners. Their hair was closely cropped or shaven, their bellies pot, their cheeks scarred. Obviously the Führer liked to be surrounded by this brown swarm of male bodies. There was rarely anyone in civilian clothes. There were no women. It was a man's world, and the men were in uniform.

I kept reflecting on this as I prowled the jammed streets of Nuremberg that week. These Germans who surged around the Leader when he arrived at or departed from a meeting or ceremony, who drove in black Mercedes cars behind his in the processions and then leaped from their vehicles to surround him when there came a stop, and who hovered around the tribune where he spoke, had, most of them, come up from nowhere. But they were now ministers of government, chiefs of the party's paramilitary services and of a variety of party and public offices. They governed this great country for

---

* But not before it had drawn two million visitors, compared to the six hundred thousand who saw the Nazi collection at the House of German Art over a much longer time. A German art historian wrote after the war that the exhibition of "degenerate art" in Munich in 1937 "was probably the most popular art event [in Germany] of all time." (Berthold Hinz: *Art in the Third Reich*, p. 1.)

the Leader. Yet you looked in vain in them for some mark of intelligence, reflection, cultivation, sensitivity, compassion that one found occasionally in any civilian government elsewhere. They struck me as a band of roughnecks.

The civilizing, softening influence that women were beginning to bring in public life in other lands seemed totally lacking. Was this because of Hitler's attitude toward women? Was he a man without women in his private life? I knew practically nothing about that, yet. The gossip among the correspondents was that he had had one great love in his life — for a niece named Geli Raubal, who three years before had killed herself in Munich after a lover's quarrel. Since then, they said, Hitler was inconsolable. Women were fascinated by him, they added, and he would mildly flirt with some of them, especially pretty actresses who were invited to his receptions, but he would go no further than that.

He had shied away from bringing women into the Nazi party. What place, if any, I wondered, were women to have in this country, now that he had taken it over? One day at Nuremberg I heard that Hitler was going to address, for the first time, the National Socialist Frauenschaft — The N.S. League of Women. And though the foreign correspondents were not invited, I went to the hall to see what the Leader had to say to the women.

Not much! That became evident at once, though he spoke for nearly two hours. Emancipation of women? Hitler said the idea was absurd.

> Talk about the emancipation of women is an invention of Jewish minds. The German woman does not need to be emancipated. She has always possessed what nature has bestowed on her. . . . Her world is her husband, her family, her children and her home. Where would the great world [of men] be if the small world [of women] was not looked after? Providence has confided to women the care of their own world, on which the world of men can be built. These two worlds do not stand against each other. They complement each other, they belong together, as men and women belong to each other.
>
> We hold it wrong for the woman to invade the world of men. We feel it only natural that both worlds remain separated.

Was there, then, any place at all in public life for women in National Socialist Germany? Hitler quickly disabused the women of any such hope.

"For many years," he said, "we National Socialists have been against women entering public life, which for us seemed unworthy of them." And then, as if lecturing little children, he told his women listeners a story:

> Once a woman said to me: "You must see to it that women can enter Parliament — because they alone can improve it."
>
> "I do not believe," I answered her, "that mankind can improve what is so bad in itself. It would harm women." And I explained that I did not want to leave to women what I was taking away from men.*
>
> Our enemies said that with such a view we would never win over the women. But we've won over more than all the other parties combined. And I'm sure we would have won over the last German woman if only she had had the opportunity of studying our Parliament and the degrading influence it had on women.

So, Hitler told his feminine audience, there was to be no emancipation of women to the extent that they could take part in the public life of the nation. That was reserved for the German man. Let women follow their nature, be good wives and mothers, and builders of good homes.

There was an old saying in Germany that for women there were three things in life: *Kirche, Küche, Kinder* — the church, the kitchen, the children. Hitler, at war with the churches, did not mention the first. But he made it plain that in Nazi Germany the place of the woman was in the home, the kitchen, the nursery. That was all German women could look forward to.

It did not sound like much to me, but the ten thousand women in the audience, all in uniform, like their men, applauded him warmly.† They seemed to enjoy the prospect. It seemed to me to be a distressing throwback. More than in any other country in the West, German women, held down so long in the imperial times, had during the Weimar Republic played an increasingly important part in public and professional life. Many had won election to the Reichstag, the state legislatures, the town and city councils. Thousands had become doctors, lawyers, journalists. They had found personal fulfillment in careers.

Now, at the command of the Leader, it was back to the home and the duties of the household for them.

Adolf Hitler had become such a public figure and so reveled in it

---

* The Nazis had been the only party in the Reichstag that had no women among its members. Now that Hitler himself selected its deputies, there were none in the entire body.

† After listening to Hitler's speech, I was not surprised to learn, as I left this depressing assembly, that the head of the N.S. Frauenschaft, which was the umbrella organization for all the women's groups, was — a man.

and spent so much time exposing himself to the multitude that I wondered if he had any private life. A foreign journalist at Nuremberg could not pry any information about that from his aides. It was a well-kept secret, as it is in all dictatorships. No German newspaperman or broadcaster would dare to raise the subject, in print or on the air.

"You can say," one member of Hitler's entourage told me, "that he leads a Spartan personal life. He is a vegetarian, a teetotaller, a non-smoker and a celibate."

No one around the dictator dared, or at least ventured, to speak about the women, if any, in this celibate's life. One party member did confide that he was sure Hitler would never marry.

"Why not?" I asked.

"He considers he is married to Germany. Germany is his bride."

Of one thing I became sure after the week at Nuremberg. All of us in the West, our political leaders and our newspapers above all, had underestimated Adolf Hitler and his domination of this land and its people. His ideas might seem half-baked and often evil — to me they did. But the unpleasant fact was not only that he believed in them, fanatically, but that he was persuading the German people to believe in them. He might seem like a demagogue — he often was during those days in Nuremberg. But his oratory, his drive, his zeal, his iron will and the power of his personality were having an immense impact on the citizens of this country. He was convincing them that the new Germany, Nazi Germany, under his leadership, was great, was strong, and had a manifest destiny. He was demanding sacrifices and promising them glory. They were willing to make the first to achieve the second.

I heard no mention at Nuremberg of the loss of personal freedom and of other democratic rights. Apparently this was not much of a sacrifice. They couldn't have cared less. They had committed themselves to Adolf Hitler and his barbarian dictatorship.

The liberal, democratic West did not yet realize this, nor did the Soviet Union to the east.

I had been somewhat surprised on arriving in Berlin to find that though the German press was heavily censored and rigidly controlled there was no censorship of our dispatches (as there was, I believe, at that time of what the foreign correspondents filed from Moscow). A colleague had explained to me what I would learn very quickly on my own: that while you did not have to submit your copy for approval by the authorities before cabling it, you had to weigh carefully what you reported about Hitler and the Nazi regime. If he or his aides, especially Dr. Joseph Goebbels, the fanatical Nazi minister of propaganda and the watchdog of the foreign correspondents, found it unacceptable — out you went, as had happened to Dorothy Thompson the day of our arrival and to a few others in the months before.

Dr. Ernst (Putzi) Hanfstaengl, the Nazi party's foreign press chief, had given us a warning the day we arrived in Nuremberg to cover the party rally. In a speech of welcome he had asked us "to report on affairs in Germany without attempting to interpret them. History alone," he had laid it down, "can evaluate the events now taking place here under Hitler."

None of the foreign correspondents had taken him very seriously — that would have been impossible. Putzi, a tall, gangling, eccentric, incoherent, high-strung man, was rather a clown. The correspondents, especially the Americans, had taken quite a liking to him. A graduate of Harvard, where he was a classmate of Frankin D. Roosevelt, and half-American — his mother was a New England Sedgwick — Putzi and his wealthy, conservative Bavarian family had befriended Adolf Hitler in the early days in Munich. Putzi's chief value to the Führer was not his work as the party's foreign press chief, a job he often fumbled or neglected, but as court musician and court jester. He could soothe Hitler after a trying day with his endless jokes and tall tales, but above all with his piano playing. He pounded it like a maniac, thundering through Wagner, Beethoven, Liszt, Brahms, and others.

Once, during an evening at Knick's apartment a few days after we arrived in Berlin, a telephone call had come while Putzi was in the midst of hammering away at a Beethoven sonata. He was to come immediately to the Chancellery to play for the Leader, who apparently was having trouble falling asleep. Given the demonic way Putzi banged the piano, I wondered how it could induce slumber.

So we did not take seriously Putzi's warning that first evening in Nuremberg to leave to history the interpretation of events in Hitler's Germany that we were reporting. I was not willing to wait that long. But I soon learned to watch my step. All through my years in Berlin I was conscious of walking a real, if ill-defined, line. If you strayed too far off it you risked expulsion. One soon got the feeling of how far one could go. I made up my own mind from the very beginning that as long as I could tell the essential story of Hitler's Germany, fully, truthfully and accurately, I would stay, if I were allowed to. Once that became impossible I would go.

One by one over the next few years many of my colleagues — and they were usually the brightest, and the best — would get the axe. I myself would be threatened with it. When in time, after the war came, I realized that the Nazi censors would no longer allow me to report what I thought a foreign correspondent was obligated to report, even in wartime, I left — for good.* To be sure, my departure would be hastened by the knowledge that the authorities had begun to suspect that I was a spy, slipping military secrets by code words in my CBS broadcasts, which my government at home passed on to Britain, the only enemy Hitler had not conquered up to then. A well-placed German friend had warned me that I soon might be arrested and charged with espionage. Innocent though I was of such an absurd accusation, I had no faith that the dreaded Nazi People's Court would acquit me. If it did not — and this kangaroo tribunal rarely acquitted anyone, no matter what the lack of evidence — I might get the axe, literally. Convicted spies had their heads chopped off in Germany in those days.

So, after some difficulty, I would manage to get out in time and I would not return until the charred remains of Adolf Hitler lay buried in the shell-pocked ruins of the Chancellery in Berlin and the thousand-year Reich had come to an end.

But that time lay far ahead. For the moment I was getting my bearings in this strange, dynamic, paranoiac, totalitarian German land.

* Censorship of our broadcasts was instituted after the war began, as it was, I believe, in Paris and London.

Hitler relaxing in the country with his dog

Hitler's mother

Adolf Hitler inherited his eyes from his mother

The Führer inspecting paintings in the House of German Art

The House of German Art, in Munich

Hitler, the Orator

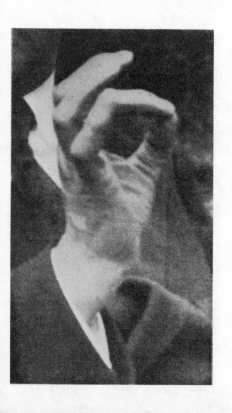

Memorial to the Nazis killed in the Munich Beer Hall Putsch

RIGHT: *May 1, 1933, Day of National Labor. Hitler leaving Lustgarten after a speech to the German youth. On this day, the Nazis arrested the labor leaders and broke the unions.*

CHAPTER 7

Life in the Third Reich

1934-1937

Fortunately for one so new to the frantic country, no big
stories broke the rest of that fall of 1934.

After a momentous year of triumph, massacre and consolidation of
his dictatorship, Hitler appeared to be taking it easy for the moment.
Not that any foreign correspondents or diplomats knew what he was
up to. A totalitarian regime, I was learning quickly, knew how to
guard its secrets. But the general feeling in the capital was that after
so many sensational developments during the summer just passed
there would be an interlude of quiet. This gave me an opportunity to
settle down in Berlin and to begin to get a feel of the churning country.

We rented a studio apartment in the Tauenzienstrasse, a stone's
throw from the top of the Kurfürstendamm. The owner, a Jewish
sculptor, and his wife, a well-known art historian, were anxious to get
out to England. Being Jewish, she was now unemployed and his
works could no longer be sold, at least to Aryans. We arranged to pay
them the rent in sterling in London, which was a violation of the new
currency laws. But it would help the couple at least to survive for a
while.

We felt lucky to get the place, which was furnished in a pleasant
modern style, and which contained a fine library of German works I
could make good use of. By now Tess and I had got accustomed to
living in apartments or houses that others had furnished: in Vienna,

in Spain, in Paris. But the migrant life we led made it impossible to furnish a home of our own — even if we could afford it. The apartments we saw in days of searching had been furnished in atrocious style, littered with junk and knickknacks. The stodgy German middle-class apparently liked their homes that way. The Jewish sculptor's place was just what we had hoped for.

Though there were no big stories to cover for the rest of that year, there was plenty of work to do. Brushing up on my German, for one thing. I had learned it fairly well in the years in Vienna but it had faded somewhat since. And the rather harsh German spoken in Berlin differed from the softer language acquired in Austria. Even Tess, a native Viennese, found it somewhat difficult at first.

There were contacts to make: with the Nazi officials who helped run the country; with German dissidents, if one could find them and win their trust; with German newspaper editors and reporters (all the good writers and artists had fled abroad); with the foreign diplomats and with my fellow foreign correspondents. And a reporter had to go out into the streets and ride the subways, buses and streetcars to try to catch the mood of the people.

It had turned out to be rather different than I had expected. What surprised me at first was that most Germans, so far as I could see, did not seem to mind that their personal freedom had been taken away, that so much of their splendid culture was being destroyed and replaced with a mindless barbarism, or that their life and work were becoming regimented to a degree never before experienced even by a people accustomed for generations to a great deal of regimentation.

One soon became aware, to be sure, that in the background there lurked the terror of the Gestapo and the fear of the concentration camp for those who got too far out of line or who had been Communists or Socialists or too liberal or pacifist or who were Jews. The Blood Purge of the past June was a warning of how ruthless Hitler could be.

Yet the Nazi terror in those early years, I was beginning to see, affected the lives of relatively few Germans. The vast majority did not seem unduly concerned with what happened to a few Communists, Socialists, pacifists, defiant priests and pastors, and to the Jews. A newly arrived observer was forced, however reluctantly, as in my own case, to conclude that on the whole the people did not seem to feel that they were being cowed and held down by an unscrupulous tyranny. On the contrary, and much to my surprise, they appeared to support it with genuine enthusiasm. Somehow Adolf Hitler was imbuing them with a new hope, a new confidence and an astonishing renewed faith in the future of their country.

What seemed to matter to them the most was that the Führer was setting out to liquidate the past, with all of its frustrations and bitter disappointments. He was promising to free Germany from the consequences of its defeat in 1918: the shackles of the peace treaty imposed on a beaten nation. He was assuring the people that he would make Germany strong again, the equal of the other great powers.

This was what most Germans, even those lukewarm toward Nazism or even opposed to it, wanted, and they accepted the sacrifices that the Leader demanded: the loss of personal freedom, a Spartan diet ("Guns before Butter") and hard work.

By the time I arrived in Germany, Hitler was beginning to make good on his promise to abolish unemployment. The previous year the registered unemployed had numbered six million. The figure already had fallen by more than a million; in another two years it would drop to less than a million and shortly thereafter disappear altogether. I soon found out what a job and a full dinner-pail meant to a German worker. When I went to some of the big industrial plants on the outskirts of Berlin, now humming at full blast thanks to the orders for secret rearmament, I expected workers to be sullen about the Nazi suppression of their trade unions, which had been the strongest in Europe and the backbone of the Weimar Republic. I found that they were not unhappy at all.

Didn't they resent the loss of their freedom to organize? I would ask.

"Freedom?" they would say. "Well, yes — that one." The unions had done a lot for the working man. But, on the other hand, there was one freedom, they said, they were glad to lose under Hitler.

"What is that?" I asked.

"The freedom to starve. Like we had before. Like you have in all your free-enterprise, capitalist countries. Like you have in your America, from all we hear. How many unemployed you got in your country? Ten million, we hear. Like it used to be here."

Most of the organized German workers had been socialists, quite a few Communists, until their parties were suppressed in the first year of Hitler's rule. The ones I talked to, with a few exceptions, had not become Nazis. They still mouthed the Marxist jargon, but they seemed content enough just to have a job and to leave politics, in which they had been so involved before 1933, to the Nazis. Hitler would make a great noise in herding them into one big "union," the so-called Labor Front. But the German worker was not unintelligent and he saw quickly that the Labor Front, which included also the employers, was a fraud. As time went on the regime would tighten the screws on the workers, reducing them to what looked to me like industrial serfdom. I would hear plenty of grumbling among them. But like everyone else in Nazi Germany they did what they were told, and with rather surprising docility.

As the country grew stronger, especially militarily, and Hitler struck out to retake what had been lost in the war and then to go on from there, the workers went along approvingly, as did almost all the other Germans. Their industriousness made possible the rapid German rearmament. There was never any revolt of the German proletariat, as there had been in 1918. That year, at the end of the Great War, they had overthrown the Hohenzollern monarchy. They were now in no mood even to attempt to strike, which Hitler had forbidden, much less to rebel. The German people, on the whole, had accepted the Nazi tyranny, and were helping to make it work. A newly arrived American correspondent had to recognize that startling reality. The outside world still did not believe it — or us — when we began to report it.

If not rebellion, there *was* a growing defiance in the churches that fall. Men of the cloth, both Protestant and Catholic, were not happy about what they began to perceive as persecution of their faiths. To allay the doubts and fears of the Catholics, Hitler, a nominal though nonpracticing Catholic himself, had the previous summer concluded a concordat with the Vatican, which guaranteed the freedom of the Catholic religion in Germany and the right of the Church "to regulate her own affairs." Coming as it did at the moment when the first excesses of the new regime, particularly against the Jews, had provoked worldwide revulsion, the concordat had given the Nazi regime much badly needed prestige abroad and at home and had tended to reassure German Catholics, who comprised one-third of the people.

But not for long. Five days after the signing of the concordat, the German government promulgated a sterilization law, which greatly offended the Catholic Church. Five days after that, Hitler took the first steps to dissolve the Catholic Youth League. Soon it was suppressed altogether, its members being forced into the Hitler Youth. During the next years thousands of Catholic priests, nuns and lay leaders would be arrested, many of them on trumped-up charges of "immorality" or of "smuggling foreign currency." Erich Klausener, leader of Catholic Action, had been murdered at his desk in the June 30 purge and his entire staff carted off to concentration camp. Scores of Catholic publications were suppressed, and even the sanctity of the confessional was violated by Gestapo agents, who posed as communicants and then arrested the priests who heard confessions, charging them with slander against the state.

All through the next few years I would listen to the tales of woe brought to me in secret by priests and nuns, for most of the assaults against the Church were not allowed to be reported in the controlled press. Sometimes the seat of the cardinal archbishop of Munich or the bishop of Berlin would be quarantined by the Gestapo. No one was allowed to enter or depart them. This usually occurred after the police had forbidden the reading in church of pastoral letters protesting against the latest persecution. Always, though, they would smuggle out copies to us foreign correspondents and we could keep the outside world, at least, informed.

By the early spring of 1937 the Catholic hierarchy in Germany, which, like the Protestant clergy, had at first tried to cooperate with the new regime, had become thoroughly disillusioned. The cardinal archbishop of Munich sent word to us that he was sick at heart. He and other German prelates, I knew, had turned in desperation to the Vatican for help. The Holy See could no longer overlook in silence what the Nazi regime was doing to the Church. And so it was that on March 14 that year, to the relief of the besieged German hierarchy but to the rage of Hitler and Goebbels, Pope Pius XI finally issued an encyclical, *"Mit Brennender Sorge"* (With Burning Sorrow), charging the Nazi government with "evasion" and "violation" of the concordat and accusing it of sowing the "tares of suspicion, discord, hatred, calumny, of secret and open fundamental hostility to Christ and His Church."

Goebbels forbade the publication of the encyclical in Germany. But many a Church father, at the risk of his life, got out mimeographed copies and they were soon being circulated surreptitiously to parishes all over the Reich.

"Have been covering the fight in the Protestant church," I noted in my diary on the evening of November 15 that first year in Berlin.

In some ways it was more interesting and important than the struggle of the Catholic Church to remain free. The Catholics, at least, presented a united front. But the Protestants were a divided faith. Almost all of the forty-five million of them, two-thirds of the people, belonged to twenty-eight Lutheran and Reformed churches, of which the largest was the Church of the Old Prussian Union, with eighteen million members. With the rise of National Socialism there came a further division among the Protestants. The year before the Nazi takeover of power, the more fanatical followers of Hitler had organized "The German Christian Faith Movement," which ardently supported the party's anti-Semitic doctrines and insisted on weeding out some of the "un-German impurities" of the Bible, especially those deriving from the Old Testament. It wanted Hitler's party leadership principles applied to a new Protestant Reich Church. It sought to bring all Protestants into one all-embracing congregation controlled by the state. Its members called themselves "German Christians." But after I had attended a few of their rallies I concluded they were more pagan than Christian.

The leader of the movement in Berlin, for instance, proposed the abandonment of the Old Testament "with its tales of cattle merchants and pimps" and the revision of the New Testament, with the teaching of Jesus made "to conform entirely with the demands of National Socialism." That fall and winter the German Christians demanded that all pastors take an oath of allegiance to Hitler and exclude converted Jews from their congregations. They also put up a hue and cry about "One People, One Reich, One Faith."

Opposed to the "German Christians" was another group, which called itself the "Confessional Church." It resisted the Nazification of the Protestant churches, rejected the Nazi racial doctrines, and denounced the anti-Christian declarations of the party leaders. At the time I arrived in Germany both groups, though about equal in strength, constituted together only about a third of the congregations. In between lay the majority of Protestants, who seemed too timid to join either of the warring groups. For the moment they were sitting on the fence, waiting to see which would come out on top and what Hitler, whom most of them supported politically, would do about it.

I soon became interested in the leader of the "Confessional Church," the Reverend Martin Niemöller, whose Church of Jesus Christ, at Dahlem, an affluent suburb of Berlin, I began to attend somewhat regularly — not, I must confess, because church services began to attract me, but because this congregation and its pastor had become a symbol of defiance to the totalitarian regime, at least so far as their Christian faith was concerned, and thus not only aroused my admiration but gave me something to report.

The defiant sermons of the Reverend Niemöller and the ringing declarations of his flock for religious freedom made news, if not in Germany, where it was not allowed to be published, at least for us foreign correspondents, who were free to make it known to the outside world.

No clergyman had seemed more unlikely to assume such a role than Niemöller. A much decorated submarine commander in the Great War and an ardent German nationalist in the chaotic years that followed, he had warmly welcomed Hitler's coming to power in 1933. In that year his autobiography, *From U-Boat to Pulpit*, had been published. In it he had noted that for him, as for so many Protestant pastors, the fourteen years of the Republic had been "years of darkness." In a final word inserted at the end of the book he added that Hitler's triumph had at last brought light to Germany. He was sure it would bring about the "National Revival" for which he himself had fought so long — for a time after the war in the rough and tumble Free Corps, from which so many tough Nazi party leaders had sprung. The Nazi press praised his book and made it a best-seller.

Less than two years later Niemöller had become completely disillusioned. That autumn of my arrival he called a meeting of likeminded ministers at his pastorate in Dahlem at which his "Confessional Church" declared itself to be the legitimate Protestant Church of Germany and promptly set up a provisional Church authority.

This was open defiance of the Führer. The year before, Hitler, after instigating a taste of terror carried out by his S.A. and Gestapo — several ministers were arrested and beaten, and others driven from their pulpits — had forced on the German Protestants a wooden-headed pastor, Ludwig Müller, as Reichsbishop of the new, supposedly unified "Reich Church." An early and devoted follower of Hitler, Müller had been snatched from his post as army chaplain of the East Prussian Military District, put at the head of the Church and told by the dictator to unify and Nazify it.

Hitler, it was said, had always had a certain contempt for German Protestants. Recently, according to one of my informants, he had confided to some of his party flunkies his disdain for them.

"You can do anything you want with them," he said. "They will submit. . . . They are insignificant little people, submissive as dogs, and they sweat with embarrassment when you talk to them."[*]

But that fall of 1934 he was finding that he could not do anything

---

[*] Confirmed by Hermann Rauschning, once a confidant of Hitler, in his book *The Voice of Destruction*, pp. 297–300.

he wanted with some of them. And this exasperated him. He could not understand, one heard in party circles, how a man like Niemöller, a former U-boat captain, a patriotic nationalist and a Nazi sympathizer, dared to oppose him. And he must have been more than exasperated when on the evening of November 8 some twenty thousand worshippers turned up at a rally in Dahlem to hear Niemöller and others denounce the attempt to Nazify German Protestantism. It was the first massive nonparty demonstration, I noted, since the Nazis came to power. The meeting had been prohibited by the authorities but it was held anyway, in defiance of them.

And never had the totalitarian regime heard such militant words of criticism. I noted Gestapo agents in the crowd, taking shorthand notes. "We are fighting," the Reverend Dr. Koch, one of the leaders, said, "against the defamation of Christ and true Christianity. There are false prophets abroad in this land preaching the doctrine of blood and soil and racial mysticism, which we reject." A manifesto, acclaimed by the crowd, asked for the abolition "of the whole system of heresy, untruthfulness and oppression. We reject the present Church regime."

Niemöller, who closed the meeting, refused any compromise. "For us," he said, "it is a question of which master the German Protestants are going to serve. Christ or another." He made it clear "the other" was Adolf Hitler, his fallen idol.

This rebellious element of the Protestant Church in the Third Reich, which was and remained a minority, gained some victories in the next year or two. But it was a losing battle. During the next twelve months the Gestapo would arrest seven hundred more "Confessional Church" pastors. But even with this help the bumbling Reichsbishop Müller was unable to carry out Hitler's orders to integrate the Protestant Church, and at the end of 1935 he resigned his office and faded out of the picture. That was a notable victory for Niemöller and his followers, but it was almost the last.

Hitler then appointed a Nazi lawyer friend, Dr. Hans Kerrl, to be minister for church affairs, with instructions to make another try at unifying the Protestants. But he proved to be almost as heavy-handed as Bishop Müller. When in May of 1936 Niemöller's group addressed a courteous but firm memorandum to Hitler himself, protesting against the anti-Christian tendencies of the regime, denouncing the government's anti-Semitism and demanding an end to the state's interference in the churches, the response was sudden and ruthless. Hundreds more of Niemöller's followers among the pastors were arrested; one of the signers of the memorandum, Dr. Weissler, was murdered in the Sachsenhausen concentration camp; the funds of the Confessional Church were confiscated and it was forbidden to make collections.

Finally the next year, on February 13, 1937, Dr. Kerrl publicly revealed his real attitude toward the churches and their Christianity. No doubt echoing his Master's voice, he told an audience of submissive churchmen:

> The party stands on the basis of Positive Christianity, and Positive Christianity *is* National Socialism. . . . National Socialism is the doing of God's will. . . . God's will reveals itself in German blood. . . . Dr. Zöllner and Count Galen° have tried to make clear to me that Christianity consists in faith in Christ as the Son of God. That makes me laugh. . . . No, Christianity is not dependent upon the Apostle's Creed. . . . True Christianity is represented by the party, and the German people are now called by the party and especially by the Führer to a real Christianity. . . . The Führer is the herald of a new revelation.

By 1937 Niemöller saw the end coming. He made no bones about it in his sermons and in the snatches of conversation I and other foreign correspondents had with him that spring. Gaunt and austere in countenance, with the feverish eyes of an early Christian martyr, he seemed in his pulpit as stoic toward fate as I imagined him to have been in the conning tower of his submarine during the war. On Sunday, June 27, that year I went out to hear him preach what we all felt might be his last sermon. The worshippers overflowed the church. As if he and his congregation knew quite well what was to come, he concluded his sermon: "We have no more thought of using our own powers to escape the arm of the authorities than had the Apostles of old. No more are we ready to keep silent at man's behest when God commands us to speak. For it is, and must remain, the case that we must obey God rather than man."

Three days later he was arrested and confined to Moabit prison in Berlin. After eight months there he was tried before a *Sondergericht*, one of the "special courts" set up by Hitler to try offenders against

---

° Dr. Zöllner, who enjoyed the respect of all the Protestant factions, had been named by Kerrl to head a committee to work out a general settlement. But early in 1937, after having been prevented by the Gestapo from visiting Lübeck, where nine Protestant pastors had been arrested, he resigned his post, complaining that his work had been sabotaged by the Church Minister.

Count Galen, the Catholic bishop of Münster, was one of the most fearless among the Roman prelates in criticizing the regime for the persecution of his Church.

the state. Though acquitted of the main charge of "underhand attacks against the State" — all his attacks had been in the open — he was fined two thousand marks and sentenced to seven months' imprisonment for "abuse of the pulpit" and for holding collections in his church. Since he had served more than his time, the court ordered his release. But as he was leaving the courtroom in the embrace of happy members of his family and his congregation, he was seized by the Gestapo, placed in "protective custody," and carted off to a concentration camp, first to Sachsenhausen and then to Dachau, where he remained for seven more years until he was liberated by American troops in the last days of the war.

By my count, 807 other pastors and leading laymen of the Confessional Church were arrested that year, most of them being sent off to concentration camps. The suppression pretty well broke the spirits of his followers. As for the majority of Protestant pastors, they, like almost everyone else in Germany, submitted in the face of Nazi pressure and terror.

By the end of 1937, somewhat to my surprise, though I understood it, the highly respected Protestant Bishop Marahrens of Hanover was induced by Dr. Kerrl to make a public declaration that must have seemed especially humiliating to tougher men of God such as Niemöller: "The National Socialist conception of life is the national and political teaching which determines and characterizes German manhood. As such, it is obligatory upon German Christians also." In the spring of 1938 the good bishop took the final step of ordering all pastors in his diocese to swear a personal oath of allegiance and obedience to Hitler.

This surprised me more than it should have. I had not known the history of how subservient the Protestant clergy in Germany had been to the authority of the state. Due mainly to the immense influence of Martin Luther, German Protestantism became an instrument of royal and princely absolutism from the sixteenth century until the kings and princes were dethroned in 1918. The hereditary monarchs and petty rulers had been the supreme bishops of the Protestant Church in their lands. Thus in Prussia the Hohenzollern king was the head of the Church.

In no other country, my friends said, with the exception of czarist Russia, did the clergy become by tradition so completely servile to the political authority of the state. The bishops and pastors, with few exceptions, stood solidly behind the sovereign, the Junkers and the army, and during the nineteenth century they opposed the rising liberal and democratic movements. Even the Weimar Republic, they explained to me, was anathema to most Protestant pastors, as it had been to Niemöller, not only because it had deposed the kings and princes, to which they owed allegiance, but because it drew its main support from the Catholics, the Socialists and the trade unions.

Looking back at that time in Nazi Germany, I can see that I and some of my colleagues among the foreign correspondents perhaps attached more importance to the persecution of the Catholic and Protestant churches than we should have. Resistance to a totalitarian regime makes news, and we played it up, such as it was.

What I myself failed to stress was that the church struggles never really affected, or even much interested, the vast majority of the German people in those early days of the Third Reich. I should have realized that a people who had so lightly given up their political, cultural and economic freedoms were not, except for a relatively few, going to die or even risk imprisonment to preserve freedom of worship.

What really aroused the Germans in the 1930's were the glittering successes of Hitler in providing jobs, creating prosperity, restoring Germany's military might, and moving from one triumph to another in his foreign policy, especially when it won back German lands lost in the war and acquired new ones that aggrandized the Third Reich. Not many Germans lost much sleep over the arrests of a few thousand pastors, priests and nuns, or over the quarreling of the various Protestant sects.

It seemed strange to me then, though, as it still does nearly half a century later, that this Christian people, whose Protestants had given us the Reformation, and whose Catholics had triumphed over Bismarck in the great *Kultur Kampf* in the latter part of the nineteenth century, did not realize that the Nazi regime intended eventually to destroy Christianity and substitute the old paganism of the early tribal Germanic gods and the new paganism of the Nazi extremists. Such Nazi leaders as Rosenberg, Bormann and Himmler made no bones about it in their public utterances, which could not have been made without the approval of Hitler. As Martin Bormann, one of the closest Nazi roughnecks to the Führer, once told a party meeting: "For us, National Socialism and Christianity are irreconcilable."

We know now what Hitler envisioned for the German Christians: the utter suppression of their religion. Early in the war a thirty-point program for the "National Reich Church" was drawn up by Alfred

Rosenberg, an outspoken pagan. Notwithstanding that he was the most stupid Nazi leader I ever met (with the possible exception of Joachim von Ribbentrop, the befuddled foreign minister), Rosenberg held, among other offices, that of "the Führer's Delegate for the Entire Intellectual and Philosophical Education and Instruction for the National Socialist Party."

Among the thirty "Articles" for the new "National Reich Church" were the following:

1. The National Reich Church of Germany categorically claims the exclusive right and the exclusive power to control all churches within the borders of the Reich: it declares these to be national churches of the German Reich.

5. The National Church is determined to exterminate irrevocably . . . the strange and foreign Christian faiths imported into Germany in the ill-omened year 800.

7. The National Church has no scribes, pastors, chaplains or priests, but National Reich orators are to speak in them.

13. The National Church demands immediate cessation of the publishing and the dissemination of the Bible in Germany. . . .

14. The National Church declares that to it, and therefore to the German nation, it has been decided that the Führer's *Mein Kampf* is the greatest of all documents. It . . . not only contains the greatest but it embodies the purest and truest ethics for the present and future life of our nation.

18. The National Church will clear away from its altars all crucifixes, Bibles and pictures of saints.

19. On the altars there must be nothing but *Mein Kampf* (to the German nation and therefore to God the most sacred book) and to the left of the altar a sword.

30. On the day of its foundation, the Christian Cross must be removed from all churches, cathedrals and chapels . . . and it must be superseded by the only unconquerable symbol, the swastika.

The lost war, disastrous as it was to their lives and to their nation, would spare the German people at least that pagan affliction.

There was also, that first fall of my arrival in Germany, a defiance of Nazi authority in, of all things, the world of music. We foreign correspondents seized eagerly on it, as we had on the resistance of the churches. Toward the end of November Wilhelm Furtwängler, one of the world's great conductors, got in trouble for making a spirited defense of Paul Hindemith in the columns of a leading Berlin morning newspaper. Hindemith had been under attack in party circles as a Jew and an opponent of National Socialist "culture," and the playing of his works had been forbidden. Furtwängler, though protesting to Goebbels himself, had reluctantly gone along with the Nazi *Verbot* of the playing of music by Jewish composers, especially the works of Mendelssohn. But Hindemith, he pointed out, was not a Jew. Moreover he was one of the few great living creative composers, and German cultural life would be enhanced by the hearing of his works. Further, said Furtwängler, he himself was concerned not only to defend Hindemith but to bring into the open the whole question of interference by political zealots in Germany's artistic life.

"What should we come to," he asked, "if political denunciation is to be turned without check against art?"

It was a good and defiant question and I got off a dispatch quoting the famous conductor's brave words. It was not the first time, I learned, that Furtwängler had opposed an attempt to Nazify the realm of music. He rejected the Nazi distinction between Jew and non-Jew, adding that the only distinction for him was between a good and a bad artist. He urged that other conductors who had been the pride of Germany, such as Bruno Walter and Otto Klemperer, both Jews, be allowed to continue to conduct.

Brave words. Few had dared to utter them since the Hitler takeover. The consequences were predictable. Early in December, Furtwängler was forced to resign as director and chief conductor of both the Berlin Philharmonic Orchestra and the Berlin State Opera, the two most prestigious musical organizations in Germany. He would eventually, a year or so later, make his peace with the authorities and resume conducting the Philharmonic, for which some, especially abroad, criticized him. But, to his credit, he insisted on keeping four or five Jews in his orchestra, despite the howls of Goebbels, Rosenberg and the rest of the Nazi pack. And when that finally became impossible, after the war came and plans began to be made for the "final solution" to the Jews, the old conductor, I heard, succeeded in getting his Jewish players out safely to Switzerland.

Despite my misgivings about Furtwängler's returning to his post, I sometimes, especially in the early war years in the blacked-out capital, found much solace in stealing away from my work on a dark night to hear the great conductor direct his still-fine orchestra in the works of some of the German masters, Bach and Mozart and Beethoven above all. One night during the first winter of the war, in 1940, I heard Furtwängler conduct a splendid performance of Tchaikovsky's *Eugen Onegin* at the Berlin State Opera, in which the leading tenor was a young, unknown American, Richard Tucker, later to become a star at the Met in New York. Goebbels did not like an American in the cast — by that time the propaganda minister was fuming against the United States for its support of beleaguered Britain. But how he would have shrieked, I thought, if he had known that the young American was also a Jew!

Richard Strauss, one of the world's leading living composers, curried favor with the Nazis from the beginning despite — or perhaps because of — the fact that the librettist of most of his great operas had been Hugo von Hofmannsthal, an Austrian Jew. Strauss was rewarded by being appointed president of the Reich Music Chamber, which decided what could be played and who would play it in Germany. He seemed to have no qualms at lending his great name to Goebbels's prostitution of German culture.

The persecution of the Jews, of course, was far worse than that of recalcitrant churchmen, socialists, communists, musicians and others, and in Berlin we would watch it grow, from month to month, from year to year, more mindless and inhuman. It weighed on an American correspondent in Berlin more than any other aspect of Hitler's primitive rule, provoking in me a constant depression of spirits and often sickness of heart.

From the moment of his takeover as chancellor, Hitler had lost no time in turning against the Jews. In his first year he had excluded them from public office, the civil service, journalism, radio, farming, teaching, the theater, the films. The next year, 1934, when I arrived in Berlin, he went further. He weeded the Jews out of the stock exchanges, the banks and the ownership of businesses, especially of the department stores, newspapers and magazines, and began to eliminate them from the practice of law and medicine. And all along there were the constant brutal beatings and the murders of Jews in the S.A. barracks, in the jails, prisons and concentration camps, where they were incarcerated merely because they were Jews.

Worse was to follow the next year, 1935, when the so-called Nuremberg laws were decreed. These deprived Jews of German citizenship, confining them to the inferior status of "subjects." They also forbade marriage between Jews and Aryans as well as extramarital relations between them. They even prohibited Jews from employing female Aryan servants under thirty-five years of age, Hitler being obsessed by the myth, as he made clear in *Mein Kampf*, that Jews continually raped, and therefore despoiled with their poisonous blood, young Gentile German maidens in their employ.

In the next few years it would be my sad duty to report on thirteen more decrees, supplementing the Nuremberg laws, that would outlaw the Jews completely, confining them to the ghetto and robbing them of the chance to earn a livelihood. The oppression of the Jews, which at first to a considerable extent had been carried on outside the law by the bully boys of the S.A. and S.S., now became legitimized by so-called German law. Hitler, as his party hacks never ceased to proclaim, had become the law. There was no other in the Third Reich.

We foreign correspondents tried to help the Jews the best we could. Tess and I sheltered some we knew, who had gone into hiding, until they could escape abroad. We used our contacts at the embassies and consulates of the U.S.A., Britain, France and Switzerland to facilitate their getting visas. We rounded up a little foreign currency, though this was against the law, to tide them over when they got out.

Sometimes Tess and I would put up a Jewish friend, or a friend of a friend, who had come out of jail badly beaten, caring for him until he had recovered enough to return to his family without shocking them too much. One of these had been a well-known Berlin lawyer, a much-decorated veteran of the war, in which he had lost an arm and a leg for the Fatherland. The head of the Jewish War Veterans Bund, he had been incarcerated without any formal charges and given the usual treatment. When he came to us one morning he was so battered in body and spirit he did not dare to face his family. We hid him in one of the rooms of our spacious studio-apartment until he was healed enough to go home. A few weeks later we were able to spirit him out to London. These efforts, we had to face it, were but a drop in the bucket. For most Jews there was no help.

There were some Jews in those early years of the Nazi dictatorship who did not seem to realize the predicament they were in and that it was bound to get worse. A rather surprising number, we thought, especially among the more affluent, believed that somehow things would get better for them. They had their roots and their stake in Germany, felt that they were good Germans, and were loath to leave. The virulent anti-Semitism, they thought, would pass. They did not take kindly to our counsel that they ought to leave while they could. They begged us to mind our own business. We ran into a number of them one weekend at Bad Saarow, a popular resort not far from Berlin. I noted in my diary:

> Bad Saarow, April 21, 1935. (Easter)
> Taking the Easter weekend off. The hotel mainly filled with Jews and we are a little surprised to see so many of them still prospering and apparently unafraid. I think they are unduly optimistic.

An American correspondent in Berlin had other concerns, right from the beginning. I soon learned how important it was to be careful to protect my sources, the men and women who at great risk furnished me with news the government tried to suppress. The slightest bit of carelessness on your part might result in your informant being arrested and charged with treason, which meant almost invariably a death sentence. This possibility kept weighing on my mind and sinking my spirits, and when sometimes one of my sources did get nabbed and, in two cases, sentenced to death, I would walk the streets of the capital, dazed and despairing, searching my conscience and my memory to try to discover if anything I had done, any slip I might have made, could possibly have implicated him.

They had also supplied information, I knew, to some of the other correspondents, and I would get together with my colleagues after work and we would wrack our brains to see if any of us, unwittingly, had been responsible for a leak.

We all had been visited by the Gestapo, in our offices and in our homes, and questioned regarding this suspected informant or that. My relations with the secret police, which had been established the first moment of my arrival in Berlin when they questioned me at the railroad station, turned out to be continuous. I never gave Himmler's agents any information whatsoever at these interrogations, and I'm sure my colleagues, with very few exceptions, did not either. After all, I had nothing to lose if I was found out; all they could do was expel me. My German informants risked their lives.

One of them, sentenced to death, had been a fearless young Protestant pastor who, disdaining many of the precautions we usually took, such as clandestine meetings after dark in a wooded area of the Tiergarten or in a busy street in a slum or in a crowded railroad station, came directly to my office or home and spilled out his heart and soul.

Another condemned to death was an editor of the *Börsen Zeitung,* a conservative morning newspaper in Berlin. Of him, I noted in my diary of January 4, 1936:

> X of the *Börsen Zeitung* is not to be executed. His death sentence has been commuted to life imprisonment. His offence: he occasionally saw that some of us received copies of Goebbels's secret daily orders to the press. They made rich reading, ordering daily suppression of this truth and the substitution of that lie. He was given away, I hear, by a Polish diplomat, a fellow I never trusted.

The death sentence of my pastor friend also was commuted to a life sentence, and I felt terribly relieved in both cases, though not wholly. I was glad they would live, but horrified that they faced spending the rest of their lives behind bars — for acts that in any civilized society were not crimes at all.

Sometimes, my Berlin diary reminds me, I became so depressed at the arrests of my pastor informants that I simply gave up, at least temporarily, trying to cover the church story so as not to get any more of them in trouble. Thus:

> Berlin, June 15 (1937). Five more Protestant pastors arrested yesterday, including Jacobi from the big Gedächtniskirche. Hardly keep up with the church war any more since they arrested my informant, a young pastor; have no wish to endanger the life of another one.

It was difficult for me to live with the savagery the Nazi regime inflicted on those it regarded as its enemies. I was not, at least in the early years in Berlin, tough enough to take the death sentences meted out, especially if I had known, however slightly, the recipients.

One morning that first winter in Germany I was stunned to read on the front page of the morning newspapers that two young German women I had met casually at embassy receptions and cocktail parties had been beheaded at dawn the day before. They were both from old aristocratic families, attractive, highly cultivated and intelligent, and they had not been backward in giving vent to their loathing of the Nazis. Probably this was what got them into trouble in the first place, though they were found guilty, the newspaper accounts said, of espionage for Poland. I had been having breakfast when the announcement caught my attention. It was a meal that was never finished. I was numbed at the thought of their heads — they both had silken dark hair and lovely, refined faces — being chopped off.

There was another beheading in Berlin a couple of years later that turned my spirits into ashes. On June 4, 1937, I noted in my diary:

> Helmut Hirsch, a Jewish youth of twenty who was technically an American citizen though he had never been to America, was axed at dawn this morning. Ambassador Dodd fought for a month to save his life, but to no avail.

Hirsch, a young poet who had been active in the German Youth movement before it was taken over by the Nazis, had fled Germany with his family to Prague to escape Hitler's persecution of the Jews and had renewed his studies in the university there. His parents had at one time lived in America and become naturalized citizens there, but on returning to Germany after the war they had failed to register their children as Americans, which they technically were.

Hirsch was convicted and sentenced to death by the dreaded People's Court, an inquisitional tribune set up by the Nazis a couple of years before to try offenders against the state, of planning to murder Julius Streicher, editor of the scurrilous anti-Semitic weekly *Der Stürmer*, and an old pal of Hitler from the earliest party days.

I had attended a couple of trials before this so-called court — usually it acted *in camera* — and concluded that the accused seldom had a chance. Four of the five "judges" were party members (the fifth was a regular judge), the proceedings were a travesty of justice, with the members of the bench yelling accusations against their hapless victim and the poor state-appointed defense lawyers too cowed to argue their client's case. The defendants, no matter what the evidence, or lack of it, were invariably found guilty and almost as invariably sentenced to death.

Actually, in this case, the Nazis had something on young Hirsch. So far as I could piece the story together, a Gestapo agent had infiltrated an anti-Nazi organization in Prague led by Otto Strasser, a former follower of Hitler who had been expelled from the party. The agent, along with some of Strasser's men, had persuaded Hirsch to travel to Germany with a suitcase full of bombs and a revolver, which were to be delivered to an undercover Strasser man in Nuremberg, who would use them to get the hated Streicher. When Hirsch's train crossed the border from Czechoslovakia to Germany, he was immediately arrested by the Gestapo and his incriminating luggage seized.

His trial was in secret. Ambassador Dodd himself, a courtly Virginian and a distinguished historian, whom President Roosevelt had persuaded to leave his chair at the University of Chicago to represent us in Berlin, had appealed to the Foreign Office, the Ministry of Justice and to Hitler himself to spare the life of the young man if he were convicted, as Dodd was sure he would be by such a court. The ambassador at first had sought to keep his efforts secret in the belief that publicity in the American press would only provoke Hitler. But when he saw that his appeals brought no response, he called me in one morning and outlined the whole affair. The next morning it was on the front pages of the newspapers at home which my news agency serviced.

Dodd had hoped, desperately, that this might stir up American opinion enough to make the Nazi government hesitate to behead the young man, whom the ambassador had contended was an American citizen. But in his heart, I think, he knew, as I knew, that Hitler was contemptuous of American public opinion. Neither the German Foreign Office nor the court, as far as Dodd knew, had contested Hirsch's right to American citizenship.

The morning of the execution I went over to the embassy to see the ambassador. He was utterly dejected. He read me, with tears in his eyes, the text of the last letter he had written Hitler asking that the death sentence be commuted. Dodd said he had tried the night before, when he learned that Hirsch was to be executed, to get Hitler to receive him personally for one last appeal, but he had been rebuffed. As he talked, Dodd grew bitter. There was no justice in Nazi Germany. His four years here as ambassador had been the cruelest and most depressing of his life. He had told President Roosevelt that he had had enough and was submitting his resignation. He would be relieved, he said, to escape this hell in Berlin and return to the campus in Chicago.

The last days before the execution I had been in touch with the lawyer and the sister of Hirsch in Prague. The day of the axing I received from them a copy of the last letter Hirsch was ever to write, addressed to his sister. He had just been informed, he said, that his last appeal had been rejected and that there was no more hope.

"I am to die, then," he wrote. "Please do not be afraid. I do not feel afraid. I feel released, after the agony of not quite knowing."

He went over his life and found meaning in it despite all the mistakes and its brief duration. It was a lyrical and brave farewell.

The Polish diplomat mentioned in the diary note of January 4, whom I suspected also of having implicated the two German women who had been beheaded, was not the only person I never trusted in Berlin. In truth, a foreign correspondent learned to trust very few. Sometimes the government would plant on you an agent who posed as a dissident. One of his ploys would be to give you some horrendous story, which the Propaganda Ministry would then prove was false. If you had sent it the Ministry could not only deny it, but kick you out for false reporting. Invariably these planted agents would try to win your confidence in them as genuine opponents of the regime and then attempt to worm out of you who you were seeing among the real enemies of the state. You learned quickly what they were up to.

Once in a while you were fooled. I took quite a liking to a young German in the Foreign Office, who fed me scraps of information and gossip, let me get by with murder sometimes when he was assigned as one of the censors of my broadcasts after the war came, and was outspoken in his criticism of everyone from Hitler on down, especially of his boss, Ribbentrop. I began to trust him until one night, in his cups, he admitted he was a member of the secret police and that one of his assignments was to check up on me.

And then there was Fatty. He was a tipster for a number of us American correspondents. Barred by Goebbels from employment by the German press because he refused to become a Nazi party member, or so he said, he eked out a miserable living furnishing tips and information to us. Fatty was a rather courtly, warm and amiable fellow. I liked him, as did my colleagues whom he also served. But I never fully trusted him. Occasionally he gave me valuable tips, but I always checked his information out, feeling that sometimes it might be a plant. We suspected him because Goebbels allowed him to operate as an informant of the foreign press. He did us many a favor, tipped us off occasionally to an important story, but we had to assume that his principal job was to keep the propaganda minister au courant of what we foreign correspondents were up to — whom we were seeing, what we were reporting. So we were guarded in what we told him. Though we liked him, we took him with more than a grain of salt.

There were a few Germans in the Nazi time who won my trust, and deserved it. One was a young woman who held a key post in the German Broadcasting Company. Secretly in love with a Jewish sculptor, who had been forced to flee abroad, she covered her anti-Nazi activities by sporting a Nazi party button on her bosom and in public by mouthing the Nazi gibberish. We became close friends, and I grew to trust her completely. She was able to feed me a good deal of inside information about what was going on in the government and party circles and on many occasions she tipped me off that I was in trouble with the authorities because of what I had written or broadcast or because of whom the Gestapo had caught me seeing. It was mainly she who warned me during the second winter of the war that the Gestapo was building up a case against me as a spy and that I should leave the country before it closed in on me.

During the war two officers of the High Command, at the risk of their hides, became trusted and valuable informants. One was a scion of an old, aristocratic family, which for generations had furnished officers to the army. The other was a former Austrian naval officer, recalled to duty when the war began. Both loathed the Nazis. More than that, they opposed the war because they believed it was unnecessary and in the end would be lost. Most of all they were sickened and revolted at Hitler's barbarous treatment of the conquered lands. They kept me informed of what was going on in the military command. Much of the information I couldn't use; to have done so would have cost me my head. But it helped me to be more knowledgeable in covering the war.

I could never repay these officers for what they did for me or for the risks they took. But one June day in 1940 in Paris, after the German army, to which I was attached as a correspondent, had entered the capital, I was able to do a small favor for my Austrian friend. He had just tipped me off that Hitler intended to humiliate the French by making them sign the armistice in the *Wagon-Lit* railroad coach at Compiegne, where Marshal Foch in 1918 had dictated the armistice terms to the Germans. But that was not what was primarily on his mind that day. He very much wanted to see a French woman he had known before the war. But she was a staunch French patriot and had forbidden him to appear in an enemy uniform. Would I lend him some civilian clothes, a pair of trousers, a jacket and a tie? (I had declined to wear a German army uniform offered us correspondents who followed the German army through Belgium and France that spring.) My clothes were rather dusty and rumpled by that time after several days in the field and they ill fitted him, and besides, I warned, as he struggled into them, that he would probably be court-martialed for doffing his uniform in wartime. He must have been in love with the woman because he took the risk.

His tip about Hitler and the Franco-German Armistice, incidentally, would lead me, with the help of the German army in defiance of the Führer himself, to one of the most notable world scoops I ever had.

The author watching a Nazi parade through the Brandenburg Gate, Berlin

The author's press pass, Nazi Party Congress, 1937

Hitler inspecting his army in Goslar, 1934

Hitler addressing a rally; Mussolini, lower left, listens

Wildly enthusiastic crowds greet Hitler. (Above) A typical scene in Berlin, March, 1933. (Right) It was no different in Vienna five years later, when Hitler entered the city after the Anschluss.

*The German people
greet their Führer*

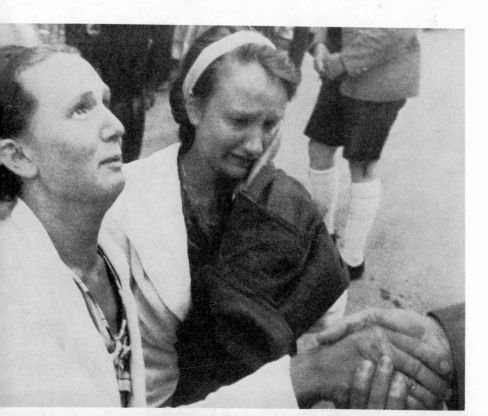

CHAPTER 8

The Men Around Hitler

Thanks mostly to one of the most doltish characters among the Nazi leaders, I began to get acquainted that first fall and winter with the men around Hitler.

They were the men, mostly misfits, who in the chaos that followed the defeat and the revolution in 1918 that overthrew the Hohenzollern monarchy had joined Hitler at the beginning of the 1920's in Munich when the just-formed Nazi party and its leader were regarded as pretty much of a joke, even by the Germans. They had, most of them, taken part in Hitler's ludicrous Beer Hall Putsch in Munich in 1923, shared in his subsequent imprisonment, and stuck with him through incredible ups and downs until the party rose, miraculously, phoenixlike, to power. Now they had been awarded the key posts in the Nazi regime. A foreign correspondent had to get to know them.

Every month or two the head of the Nazi party's Foreign Affairs Office, Alfred Rosenberg, a crackbrained, doughy-faced dolt, whom Hitler had also appointed, among other things, the party's official "philosopher," was host to the foreign correspondents and a few foreign diplomats at a *Bierabend.* Here one could listen to a specially invited Nazi chief expound on what he and his office were up to, and then meet and chat informally with him around a table over beer and sausage. Sometimes Rosenberg would invite in a general or an admiral. Smaller Nazi fry, deputies to the bigwigs, who often became news sources, would fill in at other tables — the big and little fry moving from one table to another every thirty minutes so that we, who remained at our places, got to talk with four or five of them in the course of an evening.

I had observed the whole lot of them at Nuremberg the very first days of my arrival in Nazi Germany. But it was at these "beer evenings" in Berlin that I first met them: among others, Hermann Göring, the fat, high-living, swashbuckling number-two man next to Hitler; Rudolf Hess, the somewhat dim-witted "deputy" to the Führer; Joachim von Ribbentrop, a vain, pompous, incredibly stupid man who eventually would become foreign minister; and Heinrich Himmler, who with his pince-nez looked like a harmless provincial schoolmaster but who in reality was the brutal, dreaded chief of the S.S. and Gestapo, and, in the end, exterminator of the Jews.

Also there would be the key men who secretly were building up the army, navy and air force, the first two greatly restricted, and the third forbidden, by the Versailles Treaty. The chief of these, in those early days of the Third Reich, were General Werner von Blomberg, minister of defense; General Freiherr Werner von Fritsch, commander-in-chief of the army; Admiral Erich Raeder, commander-in-chief of the navy, and of course Göring, head of the new and still secret air force. Göring, I had begun to feel, was the most forthcoming of the lot and one of the few Nazi leaders who had a sense of humor, albeit a crude one. Göring could be affable and even charming, but he was also an utterly ruthless man, as he had shown by the active part he took in the slaughter of June 30. And it was he who would be largely responsible for the shocking ends of the illustrious careers of General von Blomberg and General von Fritsch, against both of whom he brought charges relating to — of all things — sex!

Fritsch was present that first evening, and I had a few words with him. Blomberg would attend Rosenberg's next *Bierabend*, this time for Göring, a month hence.

Absent from Rosenberg's beer parties was the number-three man, Joseph Goebbels, the wily, glib, clubfooted minister of propaganda. He hated and despised Rosenberg. But we had opportunity enough to see Goebbels at the Propaganda Ministry, where he often conducted press conferences, or at his lavish parties, to which he might attract us by letting it be known that a number of beautiful actresses from the theater and screen (he was the czar of both) would be in attendance. To me Goebbels would become almost as insufferable as Ribbentrop — they shared a tremendous arrogance, though Goebbels was not unintelligent — but a foreign correspondent had to see him (and the others, equally if not more repugnant) to find out what was going on in the country. We learned to stomach more than I would have believed possible.

Alfred Rosenberg, our *Bierabend* host, for instance. Actually Rosenberg was not personally repulsive, as were Ribbentrop and Goebbels and Himmler. What Rosenberg lacked in repulsiveness, he made up in befuddlement. The official Nazi "philosopher" was the most muddled of men: tedious, dull, verbose and just plain stupid.

His theories of race, which insisted on the superiority of the "Aryan" Germans and the inferiority and sickness of the Jews — and also of the Slavs, Asians, Americans — were idiotic, and his ignorance of history was almost total. Yet in top Nazi circles, which included Hitler, Rosenberg was considered the chief intellectual of the party. In any other society he would not — he could not — have been taken seriously. Strangely enough, this archenemy of the Jews, Communists and the Soviet Union had taken a degree in architecture at the University of Moscow in 1917 in the midst of the Revolution, and his enemies in the Nazi hierarchy, who were numerous, claimed that Rosenberg had failed to become a Russian Bolshevik only because the party of Lenin had declined to give him a post. They also referred to him as "The Russian."

Actually, he had been born one in 1893 — in Reval (now Tallinn) in Estonia, which had been a part of the czarist empire since 1721. He came of German stock, or so he claimed — there were doubts even about that in Nazi party circles — but he was educated in Russian-language schools, at the Technical Institute in Reval, where he enrolled in the study of architecture, and when that school was moved to Moscow with the approach of the German army in 1915, he went along with it, graduating to the university there, where he won his degree.

He seems to have lingered on in Moscow for several months after the October Revolution, unable to make up his mind whether to support it.

After the war he emigrated to Paris and then to Munich, where he found a fertile climate for his growing anti-Communist, anti-Jewish, anti-Soviet sentiments. There he also found Adolf Hitler, then an unknown young right-wing agitator, who admired Rosenberg's staunch stand against the Jews and the Bolsheviks. Even more important, I think, Hitler, who had failed as a young man even to gain admission to the study of architecture at the School of Fine Arts in Vienna, was impressed by Rosenberg's diploma in that field, even though it came from the University of Moscow. From then on, despite Rosenberg's staggering incompetence and ineptitude, Hitler gave him one opportunity after another to gather power in the Nazi scheme of things.

That he didn't have the brains or the character to grasp them was becoming evident by 1935. Hitler had promised him eventually the key post of foreign minister, but now, two and a half years after coming to power, the Führer had not only not honored the promise but, it was obvious, never would. I always suspected that he began to have doubts about Rosenberg even as the official party philosopher, though he let him retain the title. In 1930 Rosenberg had published a book of some seven hundred pages entitled *The Myth of the Twentieth Century*, a ludicrous concoction of his half-baked ideas on Nordic supremacy. Hitler tried to read it only to confess to his cronies that it was impossible to get through. Nevertheless, it became a best-seller, next to the Nazi Bible, Hitler's *Mein Kampf*, in sales. I never met a party leader who had read it. This phenomenon prompted Baldur von Schirach, the Hitler Youth Leader, who fancied himself as a writer, to remark that "Rosenberg was a man who sold more copies of a book no one had ever read than any other author in German history."

Still, for all his bumblings and failures, Rosenberg kept trying. These monthly receptions at the Adlon for the foreign correspondents and diplomats were organized by him to remind Hitler and the party of his importance in foreign affairs. In a dictatorship, where access by a foreign correspondent to those wielding power is very limited, they were extremely valuable.

Most of the misfits around Hitler were so outlandish that it was almost impossible to believe that they were playing key roles in running this great and powerful country. Talking with them informally brought you abruptly down to the stark reality of the mad Hitlerian world.

My diary recalls that I attended the first of these Rosenberg *Bierabends* at the Adlon Hotel on November 15, 1934. The American ambassador, William E. Dodd, I noted, was present and "looked most unhappy." Dodd, as I have mentioned, was a distinguished historian. Unlike most American political appointees to embassies abroad, he not only spoke the language but he knew the history and the culture of the country in which he served. His education had made him a great admirer of the old Germany, but now, after only a year in Berlin, he had become disillusioned. He could not stomach the Nazis. He was frank and blunt about it, which did not endear him to Hitler and his henchmen or, he told me, to the striped-pants top bureaucrats in the State Department in Washington, who thought he ought to be more diplomatic. It was just that quality of frankness and bluntness that drew me to him, and we soon became good friends and he an important source of information for me.

The guest of honor that evening and the first Nazi cabinet member I was to meet was Dr. Bernhard Rust, the minister of education. His qualifications for the job of presiding over German education, once the envy of the Western World, were astonishing. In 1930 he had been dismissed by the Republican authorities as a provincial schoolmaster in Hanover for manifesting "an instability of the mind," which perhaps stemmed from his fanatical Nazism. On assuming power, Hitler had named Rust *Gauleiter* of Hanover and Prussian minister of education, in which latter post he was soon boasting that he was "liquidating the school as an institution of intellectual acrobatics."

So far as I could learn, Rust, whom Hitler had made Reich minister of education just seven months before, was now liquidating the educational system of the entire nation. He did not admit it, of course, in a lengthy speech during which, I noted in my diary, my mind wandered. He said he was merely Nazifying it — "according to the great ideas and ideals of the Führer."

Hitler, I remembered from reading *Mein Kampf,* had always showed a withering contempt for schoolteachers. They had failed to appreciate his genius in high school, which he quit before graduating, and they turned him down as being without talent when he attempted to get into the Vienna Academy of Fine Arts. To his dying day, Hitler never forgave nor forgot these teachers. No wonder then that Dr. Rust, on behalf of his Master, was firing teachers right and left. In the first five years of Hitler's rule he dismissed some twenty-eight hundred university professors and instructors — about a quarter of the total number. University enrollment declined rapidly. After six years of Nazism it would fall from 127,920 to 58,325. At the institutes of technology, once the envy of the world and on which Germany depended for its constant supply of scientists and engineers, the drop was even worse: from 20,474 to 9,554.

Academic standards fell dizzily. Publications devoted to various German industries, I noticed, began to complain about the poor quality of young executives, engineers and scientists recruited from the universities. They might be good Nazis, it was implied, but they were lousy at their jobs.

In the case of the scientists it was no wonder. The subject of "science and race" was already being taught in every high school and university throughout the Nazi land. Pupils had it drummed into them that there was "German Science," which was preeminent, and "Jewish Science," which was phony and evil. In the University of Berlin, where so many great scholars had taught in the past, the new rector, a Nazi storm trooper and a veterinarian, had already instituted twenty-five new courses in *Rassenkunde* (racial science), and before he had finished and wrecked the once great higher institution of learning, he had set up eighty-six courses connected with his own profession. The prestigious University of Berlin had, under the Nazis, become a vet's school!

The more I delved into the subject, the more unbelievable it became. The great German universities now began to teach what they called *German* physics, *German* chemistry, *German* mathematics. Even Professor Philipp Lenard of Heidelberg University, a Nobel Prize laureate in physics, became caught up in the racial aberrations fostered by Hitler. There was indeed a German physics, he proclaimed, because "science, like every other human product, is racial and conditioned by blood."

The megalomania of Nazi scientists became fantastic — and to me, fascinating because it was so ludicrous. To Professor Wilhelm Müller of the Technical College of Aachen, the publication of Einstein's Theory of Relativity, on which so much of modern physics is based, was in reality a bid for "Jewish world rule." To Professor Ludwig Bieberback of the University of Berlin, Einstein was "an alien mountebank." Even to Professor Lenard, "the Jew conspicuously lacks understanding for the truth . . . being in this respect in contrast to the Aryan research scientist with his careful and serious will to truth. . . . Jewish physics is thus a phantom and a phenomenon of degeneration of fundamental German Physics." Lenard too joined the Nazi pack in attacking Einstein and the Theory of Relativity.

Reading these eminent Nazi scientists made me feel as if I were living in a lunatic bin. Listening to Dr. Rust that first evening had given me that same feeling — so much so that when he sat down at our table for thirty minutes of informal talk, I found myself unable to ask him a single question. His idiotic remarks had left no room, at least in my mind, for querying him.

On leaving the Adlon *Bierabend* that night I asked Ambassador Dodd what he thought of Dr. Rust's views on education.

"Pure bunk," he said.

❦ ❦ ❦

Actually, as I would soon learn, Hitler was counting not so much on the public schools as on the Hitler Youth to educate the young men and women of the Third Reich. To build the Youth Movement he had selected a handsome young man of banal mind and, in part, illustrious American ancestry, who soon turned up at one of Rosenberg's beer evenings, where I first took his measure.

This was Baldur von Schirach, who looked rather like a sleek, shallow American college boy, the kind who made a good cheerleader at football games. Behind the Arrow-collar look was a dreadfully empty mind. Schirach's American cut and manner probably derived from his American forebears, who on his mother's side included two signers of the Declaration of Independence and a great-grandfather who as a Union officer had lost a leg at the Battle of Bull Run.

Even Schirach's insipid anti-Semitism had an American origin, or so he claimed. He always maintained that reading Henry Ford's book *The International Jew* at seventeen had made him a "lifelong" anti-Semite. That may have been true, but I doubted it. He became and remained a rabid anti-Semite because that was the way to advancement in the Nazi party. His rather silly paganism, which he preached to Germany's youth he got, I always thought, from Rosenberg. He was one of the very few Nazi leaders who took the party's official "philosopher" seriously.

Despite his banality and a certain appearance of softness, Schirach was possessed of a great driving force, a flare for organizing and a brutality shared by all who got ahead in the jungle world of the Brownshirts. He soon demonstrated this when he took over the Hitler Youth.

Until Hitler assumed power his youth organization had numbered but a hundred thousand in 1932, the last year of the Weimar Republic, compared to ten *million* enrolled in the various organizations united under the aegis of the German Youth Association. The statistic began rapidly to change soon after Schirach was named by Hitler to be "Youth Leader of the German Reich" in June, 1933. Schirach simply led a band of fifty armed Hitler Youth leaders into the national offices of the German Youth Association, occupied them and drove out the head, an old retired Prussian army officer. A new president, however, was named to head the association, the prestigious Admiral von Trotha, one of the most celebrated of Germany's naval heroes, who had been chief of staff of the High Seas Fleet in the

Great War and one of the "victors" of the Battle of Jutland. Young Schirach took on the admiral too, putting him to flight and confiscating millions of dollars of the Youth Association's property, including its hundreds of youth hostels scattered throughout the country.

The Catholic Youth Association, a million strong, was also dissolved despite the provisions of the concordat with the Vatican which specifically stipulated that it would not be molested. In 1936 Hitler formally decreed that *all* German youth, without exception, would be organized within the Hitler Youth organization.

"The German youth," the decree laid it down, ". . . shall be educated physically, intellectually and morally in the spirit of National Socialism . . . through the Hitler Youth."

From the age of six to eighteen the youth of Germany, boys and girls, was organized in the various cadres of the Hitler Youth. The first four years — from ages six to ten — a boy served a sort of apprenticeship as a *Pimpf*. He was given a performance book in which would be recorded his progress through the entire Nazi youth program, including his ideological growth. At ten, after passing suitable tests in athletics, camping and Nazified history, he graduated into the *Jungvolk*, where he took the following oath:

> In the presence of this blood banner, which represents our Führer, I swear to devote all my energies and my strength to the savior of our country, Adolf Hitler. I am willing and ready to give up my life for him, so help me God.

At fourteen the boy entered the Hitler Youth proper and remained there until he was eighteen, when he passed into the Labor Service or, after the spring of 1935, when Hitler, in defiance of the Versailles Treaty, decreed conscription, the armed services.

The Hitler Youth was a vast organization established on a paramilitary basis. The youngsters approaching manhood received systematic training not only in sports, camping and Nazi ideology, but in soldiering. On many a weekend while tramping through the great stretches of woodland that surround Berlin, I would run into companies of Hitler Youth scrambling through the forest, rifles at the ready and heavy army packs on their backs.

Sometimes you would run into the young ladies playing at soldiering too, for the Hitler Youth movement did not neglect the German maidens. From ten to fourteen girls were enrolled as *Jungemädel* — (Young Maidens) — and their training was much like that of the boys, including long marches with heavy packs on weekends and the usual indoctrination in Nazi ideology. A great deal of emphasis was put on their coming role as women in the Third Reich with strictures to be, above all, healthy mothers of healthy Nordic German children. This was stressed even more when the girls became, at fourteen, members of the B.D.M. — *Bund Deutscher Mädel* (League of German Maidens).

At eighteen, many of these young maidens did a year's service on the farms — their so-called *Land Jahr*, which was equivalent to the Labor Service of the young men. The young women were to help both in the house and in the fields. Inevitably, moral problems arose. The presence of a pretty young city girl sometimes disrupted a peasant's household, and angry complaints from parents, about their daughters having been made pregnant on the farms, began to be heard. Soon there was a lively little song about the maidens, a takeoff on the "Strength Through Joy" movement of the Labor Front.

> *In the fields and on the heath*
> *I lose Strength Through Joy.*

Similar moral problems arose during the Household Year, in which some half a million Hitler Youth maidens spent a year of domestic service in a city household. Actually such problems did not cause much concern among the party faithful. The more healthy Aryan children born, the better.

By the end of 1938, the Hitler Youth numbered 7,728,259. It was an impressive number, yet it was obvious that some four million youth managed to stay out of the organization. Hitler suspected that obstreperous parents were keeping their children out. In March, 1939, the last year of the precarious peace, he decreed a law conscripting all youth into the Hitler Youth. Recalcitrant parents were warned that their children would be taken away from them and put into state orphanages unless they were enrolled.

It was a disheartening experience to watch Hitler take over the youth of Germany, poison their minds, and prepare them for the sinister ends he had in store for them. I had not believed it possible until I saw it with my own eyes.

No wonder that in the very last months of the war in 1945, when all was lost and the great Führer of the Greater German Reich prepared to kill himself, it was a rag-tail force of German boys, fourteen to sixteen, from the Hitler Youth who tried to defend Berlin to the last.

None of us at the Adlon that autumn evening of 1934 could possibly have even faintly imagined such an end for this nation, however much a few of us might have wished it. Least of all, I think, the man who, next to Hitler, was responsible for the rapid buildup of the German army, General Freiherr von Fritsch, its commander-in-chief, who was among those present. It was the first time I had had a chance to have a word with him and I was a little surprised at how little he concealed his contempt for Rosenberg and the rest of the Nazis.

He would talk further along these lines when I saw him on an interesting occasion a few months later. Though he was a typical stiff-necked Prussian army officer of the old school, replete with monocle, he was an extremely intelligent man and I took a liking to him. I doubt if he ever even remembered my name for very long. He appeared merely to recognize my face as belonging to one of the American correspondents he could trust, vouched for by Karl von Wiegand, the veteran Hearst correspondent, who was a close friend of his, and through whom, mainly, I kept in touch with him, on and off, following his career to its sad, sudden and unexpected end.

Hermann Göring was the guest of honor at Rosenberg's next beer party at the Adlon in December that year, and the occasion gave me a chance to further a contact I had begun to make with the number-two man in Nazi Germany. It provided more than that: a meeting with perhaps the most sinister of the men around Hitler, Heinrich Himmler, chief of the S.S. and the Gestapo, and with two of Germany's most illustrious military men: Field Marshal August von Mackensen, the most brilliant of the German commanders on the Eastern front in the Great War and now, of course, at eighty-five, retired, and General Werner von Blomberg, the present minister of defense, who had swung the army over to Hitler and who was now feverishly busy — it was no longer a secret in Berlin — building up its strength in defiance of the restrictions of the Versailles Treaty. Knowledge of this seemed especially pleasing to Mackensen, who entered the hall arm in arm with Göring, whose latest fancy air force uniform which he himself designed — this one in crimson and blue — complemented the old field marshal's dress uniform of the Death's Head Hussars.

Next to Hitler, Göring was the most popular Nazi leader in the country and the most powerful. As prime minister and minister of the interior of Prussia, he had a great deal of power in the most important and largest part of Germany. He had control of the Prussian police and of most of the rest of the government apparatus. He set up the Gestapo, the secret police, to terrorize any lurking opposition and founded the concentration camps in which to incarcerate any who defied the Nazi authority or who were Communists, Socialists, liberals, pacifists, and/or Jews. He was president of the Reichstag. He was boss of German aviation, both civil and now military. He would soon be given more titles by Hitler that would make him pretty much the czar of the economy.

He got things done. He also loved luxury and opulence and already had begun to acquire several castles and to build a fantastic show-place outside Berlin which he called Karin Hall, after his deceased Swedish wife. He was also said to be a morphine addict, though he would kick the habit for fairly long periods only to fall back into it when the strain of life got him down. Göring was an authentic war hero, the last commander of the famed Richthofen Fighter Squadron, one of the rare holders of Germany's highest war decoration, *Pour le Mérite*, though he was only an army captain when he was mustered out.

Unable to cope with the immediate postwar chaos in Germany, Göring had gone first to Denmark and then to Sweden, where he eked out a living as a transport pilot and adviser to an aircraft company. In Sweden he had fallen in love with Karin von Kantzow, née Baroness Fock, a great Swedish beauty, who was married and the mother of an eight-year-old son. The husband, a young army officer, obligingly agreed to a divorce and the baroness and Göring were married in 1923 in Munich, to which Göring had returned and where, thanks to her means, they were able to live comfortably in a house of their own without his having to earn a living. Before going to Sweden he had enrolled in the university, and while there he had gone one day in 1922 to hear Adolf Hitler speak. Like others before him he was captivated by the Austrian's eloquence, joined the budding Nazi party and within a year was made commander of the S.A.

Severely wounded by police bullets as he marched at Hitler's side in the 1923 Beer Hall Putsch in Munich, he escaped across the frontier to Austria and eventually, with his wife, made his way to Sweden. Thanks to a general political amnesty which, ironically, the German Communists had helped the parties of the Right put through the Reichstag, Göring was able to return to Germany in 1927. He had fully recovered from his wounds and been cured of his drug addiction at the Langbro Asylum in Sweden. At thirty-four, the dashing, handsome war ace had become corpulent but had lost none of his energy, ambition and zest for life. He threw himself into renewed work for the Nazi party, hopeless as its situation appeared to be since the fiasco of the Beer Hall Putsch, earned his living as an adviser to the growing German airline, Lufthansa, and began to cultivate his business and social contacts. These were not inconsiderable, ranging from the former Hohenzollern crown prince and Prince Philip of Hesse, who had married Princess Mafalda, the daughter of the king of Italy, to Fritz Thyssen and other barons of the business world and, finally, to prominent officers of the army.

These were the very contacts which Hitler lacked but needed, and Göring soon became active in introducing the Nazi leader to his friends and in counteracting in upper-class circles the bad odor which some of the brown-shirted ruffians exuded.

In 1928 Hitler chose Göring as one of twelve Nazi deputies to represent the party in the Reichstag, of which Göring became president when the Nazis emerged as the largest party in 1932. The next year, with Hitler's ascent to power, Göring quickly grabbed the number-two spot for himself.

It is not necessary in a totalitarian dictatorship to be loved by the people. It is enough to be feared, as Stalin was in Soviet Russia. But that Hitler was beloved by the German masses — shocking as that seemed to me and to the outside world — there could be no doubt. Göring was next in their affection. They loved his down-to-earth saltiness, his jovialness, his crude sense of humor, his common touch. To them he was a hail-fellow-well-met. It never seemed to concern them that he was also a brutal, ruthless, unscrupulous killer. My gentle colleague Wally Deuel, the correspondent of the *Chicago Daily News* in Berlin, thought Göring was a "blood swiller."

Though he spoke well that evening — he had evolved a homespun manner on the platform — Göring's talk was a disappointment to me. I had hoped he would say something about the air force he was secretly building up, but he dodged the subject. During the question period we queried Göring mainly about three things — he did not seem to mind our probing, though serious questioning was rarely allowed German reporters.

Would he continue the secret police?

Ja.

Would he continue the concentration camps? (He had set up both.)

Ja.

Finally, some brave soul asked whether, in view of the reports

abroad that he himself had organized the Reichstag Fire, he had anything more to say on the subject. (A German reporter, I mused,
would be whisked off to a concentration camp for posing such a
question.)

He would, and did, deny once more, he answered, that he had anything to do with the fire or that anyone else in the Nazi party had. It
was the Communists alone, he reiterated, who had set fire to the
Reichstag.

Probably I imagined it (I wrote in my diary), but I thought he red-
dened slightly when he touched on the Reichstag Fire.

We did not further try to pin him down, though I wished we had.
Surely we would have failed to get any more out of him. But it was a
measure of how careful we were in this dictatorship that we did not
try.

Some of us were no bolder when the rotation brought Göring to
our particular table for twenty minutes or so. I asked him if he cared
to comment about the reports that he was building up a German air
force despite it being prohibited by the Peace Treaty. He answered
he did not care to at this moment. But his chuckle sort of gave him
away, as he intended, I think. He was genial enough. As you looked
at him and listened, it was hard to think he was Wally's "blood
swiller" — the killer who, in charge of the executions in Berlin while
Hitler was busy with them in Munich during the recent Blood Purge,
had carried out so many slayings.

As Göring got up to leave the table he asked me to come in to see
him about a matter I had brought up a few days before. I had not
asked him for a favor. I never asked for a favor, such as an exclusive
interview or an advance tip about some news break, from him, from
Hitler or from any other Nazi leader in all the time I was in Berlin. I
did not want to compromise my own freedom to write as much of the
truth as I could discover. On the other hand, I intended to establish,
if I could, some sort of contact with the men around Hitler in order
to try to follow what they were up to.

To develop such news sources in Germany was proving more difficult than in any other country I had ever worked. Most of Hitler's
henchmen had, like him, grown up without any contact with, or
knowledge of, foreign countries and snooping foreign reporters. They
were suspicious of us. They also were afraid that the dictator might
become suspicious of them if they saw much of the foreign correspondents. One of the reasons Hitler had publicly given for bumping
off his only close personal friend, Ernst Röhm, the S.A. chief, was
that Röhm had been in touch with the French ambassador.

This was a warning that any Nazi cabinet minister or party or government official ignored at his peril — at the peril, in fact, of his life. Still, there were times when they — and indeed the Führer himself — felt it important to influence foreign public opinion so as to further the policies and the goals of Nazi Germany. They would then call in a foreign correspondent they considered friendly and grant him an interview or tip him off to some coming event or change of policy that often made front-page news.

I myself was never called in on such occasions. More quickly than I had expected I was already becoming known in government and party circles as "anti-Nazi" or, as some put it, "unfriendly." My access to news sources became more and more limited.

What Göring had asked me to come to see him about was very simple. Universal Service wanted him to write a regular article every month or two. He had agreed to do so, if he could clear it with Hitler and if the price was right. (I knew of Göring's greed for money.)

Every Sunday the Hearst newspapers and other journals which subscribed to Universal Service published an article by a well-known foreign political figure. Lloyd George and Winston Churchill in England and Clemenceau and Poincaré in France had been regular contributors and Mussolini soon became one. Our New York office suggested getting, since we could not have Hitler, who had turned us down, the number-two Nazi. This had led me to call Göring.

He turned out to be, as I expected, a tough bargainer. We gave him a top price to begin with and he was always asking for more money for ensuing pieces. I must say he was genial enough about it, though persistent.

"Come on," he would say. "Your Mr. Hearst is a billionaire, *nicht wahr?* What's a thousand or two more dollars per article to him?"

This slight business relationship kept me in some touch for a while with the most important official, next to Hitler, in Nazi Germany. He sent me an invitation to a gala reception at the Opera the following spring on the occasion of his marriage to a provincial actress, Emmy Sonnemann, but lacking formal attire and much interest in such things, I did not go. Much later, as I have mentioned, he offered to sell me, at bargain prices in dollars, some German expressionist paintings he had confiscated from the museums and from Jews. I never wormed much news out of him, and let the contact fade. In retrospect, I think Göring, in writing these articles for us, wanted to impress the Western democracies that he had a moderating influence in Nazi Germany. This was scarcely true of domestic policy, such as the persecution of the Jews. In this he took an active part.° In foreign affairs it was to a certain extent true, and became more so as Hitler, crazed by easy success, raced down the road to war.

My diary reminds me that there was another important Nazi present at Rosenberg's December, 1934, *Bierabend* for Göring. When Göring reiterated to us that he intended to maintain the Gestapo and the concentration camps, I noted in my journal, "this makes Heinrich Himmler, Chief of the Secret Police and the S.S., who is here, smile."

> Himmler [I went on], who they say was the chief executioner on June 30, is an enigma to me. He does not look his part. Rather small, with thick spectacles covering small but animated eyes, he looks rather like a middling *beamte* (civil-service official). He does not look like the head of a Cheka should.

Himmler did not have much to say when the rotation brought him to our table. He seemed uncomfortable in the presence of non-Germans. He struck me as too insignificant, too mediocre, to succeed for long as such a key man in this repressive regime — already chief of the S.S. and Gestapo, already feeding victims into the brutal concentration camps. I couldn't have been more wrong, as it turned out.

But in this weird Nazi world there were a number of men of little competence and intelligence and no character — veritable thugs — who, to one's astonishment, would be given posts of key importance, with power over the life and death of millions.

Such a man was Fritz Sauckel, a piggish, brutal, stupid little man whom Hitler during the war put in charge of the millions of slave laborers. Another was Adolf Eichmann, a cipher of a man who became the Gestapo's manager of the "Final Solution" for the extermination of the Jews.

Himmler's background, like his looks and personality, was insignificant. After graduating in agronomy from the Munich Technische Hochschule, he became a chicken farmer in Bavaria and might have remained one had he not, like so many Bavarians, become involved in the right-wing activities of Hitler's Nazi party. He got his chance when Gregor Strasser, then the number-two man in the party, took

° "I would like to say that I would not like to be a Jew in Germany," Göring would remark laughingly one day some four years later after he had imposed a fine of a billion marks on the Jewish community.

him on as his secretary. (Himmler had repaid Strasser by murdering him in the recent Blood Purge.) Named head of the S.S. when that group was little more than a two-hundred-strong bodyguard for Hitler, Himmler showed his organizing abilities by rapidly building it up as a rival of the S.A. and now, since the purge of the S.A. chiefs, as its superior.

I confess that at this time, after seeing Himmler at this meeting and at others, I did not faintly imagine that before long he would become the party's and the regime's greatest killer, the man more responsible than any other German except Hitler for carrying out the attempted extermination of the Jews and of the Slavs in the occupied lands. Strasser in the beginning had called him "Our Gentle Heinrich."

Joseph Goebbels, a swarthy, dwarfish, most un-Nordic looking German from the Rhineland, with a crippled foot, a nimble mind and a complicated and neurotic personality, had succeeded Himmler as Strasser's secretary in 1925, when he was twenty-eight, and he, too, had turned against his boss to curry favor with Hitler. By early 1935, thanks to Hitler's confidence in him and his own abilities as a rabble-rousing orator, a brilliant organizer and a ruthless character in dealing with both his enemies and colleagues, he had become the number-three man in the Nazi party and government.

Contemptuous of Rosenberg, Goebbels refused to attend the party philosopher's *Bierabends* at the Adlon. But we saw him frequently at the Propaganda Ministry, where he presided over important press conferences. I personally could barely stand him. But then neither could most of the men around Hitler. He was too devious even for them. They used to refer to him in private as "that rat." He seemed to have no friends in the party — or anywhere else. But Hitler, to whom he was utterly loyal, appreciated his devotion, his talents and his ability to get things done. Named party *Gauleiter* of Berlin in 1926, when Hitler had few followers in northern Germany, he had helped to conquer the capital for the Nazis.

Goebbels now had great power in Germany. As minister of propaganda he controlled the press and the state-run radio. He also controlled the so-called Chamber of Culture, which enabled him to regulate all cultural activities in the country. He had the final say as to what music was played (Mendelssohn and other Jewish composers were *verboten*) and by whom, what books were published, what paintings and sculpture exhibited, what plays were staged and what movies produced.

That the culture of a great country was now being determined by the asinine ideology of Nazism was bad enough; but that it was subject to the dictates of this limited and neurotic man made it even worse. Unlike many of the men around Hitler, Goebbels, it is true, had had a solid university education, which had given him a background in German philosophy, history, literature and art, and also Greek and Latin. But you would never have guessed it when you listened to his speeches and read his writings. I found the content invariably banal, the product of a mind that though nimble was fundamentally mediocre.

For a man who was in charge of the nation's propaganda abroad as well as at home, and who had to deal with foreign correspondents from all over the globe but chiefly from the Western democracies, Goebbels was unbelievably ignorant of the world outside Germany. He appeared to know absolutely nothing of the history, the literature and the people of any foreign land. He understood no modern foreign language. His ideas of America, for instance, were childish.* This was a weakness shared by all the Nazi bigwigs, beginning with Hitler, and it began to occur to me that it might have ominous consequences for the Third Reich and, unfortunately, for much of the rest of the world. There is nothing more dangerous in the shaping of foreign policy than ignorance — of foreign lands and peoples. Hitler shortly would pick as his new foreign minister an ignorant nincompoop who would amply demonstrate this. This was the insufferable Joachim von Ribbentrop.

Ribbentrop was an ignoramus. Early in my observation of him I sized him up as incompetent and lazy, vain as a peacock, arrogant and without humor. He did speak French and English quite well, but his knowledge of these languages, picked up while knocking about Switzerland, France, England and Canada as a footloose youth, was not accompanied by the slightest comprehension of France and the French, and of the British and Americans and their countries. Ribbentrop was, in short, the worst possible man to be picked as foreign minister.

Why then, we would ask, did Hitler choose him? Only because, we concluded, Ribbentrop was doggedly loyal to the Leader and never crossed him or even questioned him. Göring and Goebbels, from all we could learn, apparently did, at least on rare occasions, though they doubtlessly kept in mind what had happened to Gregor Strasser

---

* Goebbels believed, for instance, that the United States was run by Jews and that it was being "racially" poisoned not only by a mixture of Jews and Gentiles, but of whites and blacks. He believed our level of culture was set by the gangsters.

and Röhm for daring to disagree. A few of the generals, certainly Fritsch, the commander-in-chief of the army, and Beck, the chief of the Army General Staff, did not believe for a moment that the dictator was infallible, and they were not backward in expressing their disagreements with him. Ribbentrop considered it treason to question the Führer or even to doubt that he was always right.

Unlike most of Hitler's henchmen, he came late to the Nazis. Like many of them he had little formal education, though he was born into a solid middle-class family — his father was a career officer in the imperial army. But he had quit high school at sixteen, worked a year at odd jobs in London and then for two years in Canada. He returned to Germany on the outbreak of the war in 1914, served as a lieutenant in the field, was wounded, and won the Iron Cross, First Class.

Whereas Hitler, Göring and most of the other party stalwarts returned from the lost war bitter at the defeat and at sea in the revolutionary postwar world, Ribbentrop seems to have adjusted easily. He got a job in a cotton-importing firm. In 1920 he met and married Annelies Henkell, daughter of the head of the well-known champagne company of that name, for whom he came to work as a wine salesman. Helping to expand the lucrative business by grabbing the German market for imported French brandies and Scotch whiskies, Ribbentrop soon became a partner in the firm and wealthy. In peddling his wares and in buying up stocks of liquor in France and England, Ribbentrop did a good deal of traveling, improved his English and French and made contacts in the business world of Western Europe. In Berlin, through his wealthy wife, he met the rich and the well-born.

To smooth his way, Ribbentrop in 1925, at the age of thirty-two, had managed to add a "von" to his name by inducing an aunt, whose late husband, an army general, had been awarded the title by the Kaiser, to "adopt" him. Everything about this simpleton seemed phony.

Yet Hitler took to him, as he did to so many mediocrities. Sensing that the Nazi leader might well be the man of the future, Ribbentrop arranged to meet him in August, 1932, a few days after the July 31 elections in which the Nazis had won a resounding victory that made them the largest party in the country and in Parliament. Always the opportunist, Ribbentrop saw it was time to jump on the Nazi bandwagon. He did, joining the party and offering his services to the Leader.

In the crucial secret negotiations in which Hitler engaged during the first days of the following January with, among others, the president of the Republic, Ribbentrop played a certain role. He and his wife were hosts to Hitler at their palatial residence in Berlin-Dahlem for a highly secret meeting on the evening of January 22, which they helped to arrange, between him and Oscar von Hindenburg, the weakling son of the old field marshal and president, who as a result endeavored to persuade his father to appoint the Nazi chief chancellor a week later.

Hitler remembered the favor. He was impressed by Ribbentrop's knowledge of French and English and by his connections with German big business and the aristocracy. On becoming chancellor he set Ribbentrop up as a sort of private adviser on foreign affairs. Later he sent him to London as German ambassador. This proved a disaster. At his very first attendance at a royal reception for the diplomatic corps Ribbentrop greeted the king of England with an outstretched hand in the Nazi salute, and shouted a "Heil Hitler!" There were cries in England for his recall.

But Hitler stuck by him — despite pleas from Goebbels and Göring that he be brought home because he was unnecessarily making an enemy of England. Göring later explained:

> When I criticized Ribbentrop's qualifications to handle British problems, the Führer pointed out to me that Ribbentrop knew "Lord So and So" and "Minister So and So."
> To which I replied: "Yes, but the difficulty is that they know Ribbentrop."

We foreign correspondents in Berlin got to know him too. Even while he was still serving as German ambassador in London he would rush back to Berlin to partake in some foreign policy shenanigans. I remember the ridiculous figure he cut, for example, on November 25, 1936, when we reporters were hastily summoned to the Propaganda Ministry for an "important" announcement, which turned out to be the signing of an anti-Comintern pact between Germany and Japan.

Ribbentrop strutted in, followed by the Japanese ambassador.

"Gentlemen," Ribbentrop said in his most unctuous manner, "this pact means that Germany and Japan have joined together to defend Western Civilization."

One of the British correspondents rose and asked Ribbentrop if he had heard him correctly.

"Ribbentrop," I noted in my diary, "who has no sense of humor, then repeated the statement without batting an eye."

Such were the men Hitler gathered around himself.

One got hardened to them. But it was not easy. I never got tough enough, for instance, to stomach Julius Streicher, the sadistic, pornographic Jew-baiter from Nuremberg, whom we could observe strutting through the streets of that ancient city cracking his whip. Almost to the last, Hitler had a warm heart for this psychopathic pervert, the Nazi boss of Franconia and editor of the unspeakably vulgar, anti-Semitic, mass-circulation weekly, *Der Stürmer.*

There were two other Nazi chiefs whom a correspondent ran into sometimes at Rosenberg's beer evenings or at other party gatherings and who were worth keeping track of. These were Rudolf Hess and Robert Ley.

Since the murder of Röhm, Hitler at this time, I believe, regarded Hess as the closest thing he had to a friend. He trusted him more than any other of his lieutenants. Of all these, Hess was the most loyal, the most selfless, the least ambitious. He was not the brightest, however. He had struck me from the moment I had observed him at Nuremberg as a very muddled man. By now he seemed to me to be a crackpot, devoted to astrologers, quacks and nature healers, as to a certain extent Hitler, Himmler and even Goebbels were, though Hess was much more so. He had a beetle-browed, brooding dark face that you first mistook for that of a thinker. He was an introvert, whereas most of the other Nazi biggies were extroverts, and it was obvious that he had psychopathic problems, as indeed they all did. All in all, he struck me as one of the more decent men around Hitler; at least he was less poisonous and repugnant than most of them.

Son of a German wholesale merchant in Egypt, Hess had spent the first fourteen years of his life growing up there and then had been sent back to Germany for an education. During the war he had served in the 16th Bavarian Regiment with Hitler, though they seem not to have become acquainted. He was wounded twice in the field and then became a flyer just as the war was ending. Drifting back to Munich, where he enrolled at the university, he became a protégé of Karl Haushofer, the famous German *Geopolitiker*, whose ideas, especially on the need of German territorial expansion, were absorbed by Hitler through Hess and became part of the tenets of National Socialism.

Hess joined the Nazi party shortly after Hitler did, in 1920, when it had only a handful of members, and shortly became the young Austrian's secretary, marching at his side during the Beer Hall Putsch in 1923 and sharing imprisonment with him at Landsberg, where he patiently took down the Leader's dictation of *Mein Kampf*, correcting the language as they went along.

Named deputy Führer of the party and a cabinet minister without portfolio when Hitler came to power in 1933, Hess by this time enjoyed a good deal of power in the Third Reich. He was boss under Hitler of the party machine. He carried out a number of fairly important government assignments. It was my guess at this time — the end of 1934 — that doubtful though he was of Hess's abilities, Hitler probably had secretly named him to succeed him in case of his own demise. Later, when the war came, Hitler publicly announced that the more resourceful Göring would be number two, but Hess would follow immediately as number three. In the end, the choice didn't matter. But for the moment, at the end of 1934 as Hitler prepared to celebrate his first two years in office, they both held considerable power as two of the Führer's principal aides.

I never got much out of Hess. Whereas Göring and Goebbels would take chances by occasionally speaking out, Hess remained silent. He did not speak badly in public, but he had nothing to say except to echo the Leader. I gathered he spoke tolerably good English from having grown up in British-controlled Egypt but when I addressed him in English he would reply in German without batting an eye.

Like his comrades, he seemed suspicious of foreigners — and surprisingly ignorant of foreign countries, despite his having grown up in one and having organized the Nazi party abroad. He believed, like Ribbentrop, that he understood Britain and the British and he certainly admired them. But his ignorance in this regard would be shown when he made his bizarre flight to Scotland during the war in the mistaken belief that he could talk the British into making peace with Nazi Germany and — even more ludicrous — joining the Third Reich in the coming onslaught on Bolshevik Russia.

Running into Hess now and then I gained the impression that he remained emotionally juvenile, that he had never escaped from mental adolescence. It amazed me that he had got so far in the jungle warfare of the Nazi party.

Later, for quite different reasons, I had similar thoughts about Robert Ley, who at this time was just emerging into the limelight. Fritz Thyssen, the steel magnate, referred to Ley as a "stammering drunkard" and indeed at one of Rosenberg's *Bierabends* he did stammer and he was tipsy, though this was not the first meeting at which I had noted this. His secretary, who thought he was a great man, complained that he was "always drunk." Nevertheless he was not without ability in the crazy Nazi world. Like some of his roughneck colleagues, he got things done.

Son of a poor peasant, reared in oppressive poverty, Ley doggedly worked his way through high school and the university — a much more difficult feat in imperial Germany than in America — and gained a doctorate in chemistry. Wounded in the war, he taught briefly afterward at the University of Westphalia, served for a while as a chemist for the giant I. G. Farben Chemical Trust, joined the Nazi party in 1924, and soon thereafter quit his chemist's job to work full time for the party. Hitler named him *Gauleiter* of Cologne and shortly after coming to power gave him a formidable assignment: to destroy the powerful free trade unions, which had been the bulwark of the Weimar Republic.

To lull the unions before he struck, Hitler proclaimed May Day, 1933, three months after he had taken over the government, to be a national holiday and officially named it the "Day of National Labor." For half a century May Day had been the traditional day of celebration for the German — and European — worker. In every capital of the continent the Socialists, Communists and trade-union workers had staged gigantic May Day parades.

Though Hitler had just destroyed the Communist and Socialist parties and now secretly planned to destroy the unions, he promised the latter that the first May Day under National Socialism would be celebrated as never before. Actually, it was. But not in the manner expected by the lulled union leaders. They were flown to Berlin from all parts of Germany, along with big delegations of workers. And out at Tempelhof Field thousands of banners were unfurled acclaiming the Nazi regime's solidarity with the worker.

Before the massive rally Hitler received the workers' delegates in the ornate hall of the Chancellery in the Wilhelmstrasse.

"You will see how untrue and unjust," he said, "is the statement that the [Nazi] revolution is directed against the German workers. On the contrary!"

Later in his speech to more than a hundred thousand workers at the airfield, Hitler pronounced the motto of the day: "Honor work and respect the worker." He promised that May Day would be celebrated in honor of German labor "throughout the century."

The next morning, May 2, the trade-union offices throughout the country were occupied by the police, the S.S. and the S.A. All union funds were confiscated, the unions dissolved and the leaders arrested, beaten and carted off to concentration camp.

Ley, who had led the entire operation, tried to assure the workers with the customary Nazi double-talk.

> Workers! Your institutions are sacred to us National Socialists. I myself am a poor peasant's son and understand poverty.... I know the exploitation of anonymous capitalism. Workers! I swear to you, we will not only keep everything that exists, we will build up the protection and the rights of the workers still further.

Within three weeks the hollowness of such promises was exposed. Hitler decreed a law bringing an end to collective bargaining and outlawing strikes. Ley explained the decree to the country. It promised, he said, "to restore absolute leadership to the natural leader of a factory — that is, the employer." Henceforth, he added, the employer was to be "the master in the house."

That fall of my arrival in Berlin, 1934, Dr. Ley was busy setting up the so-called Labor Front to replace the dissolved unions. Like so much in Nazi land, the "Labor Front" was a swindle. It did not represent the workers. It took in not only wage and salary earners, but also the employers and members of the professions. All had to join. It was, I concluded after watching it in action for several years, in reality a vast propaganda organization and, as the workers soon found out, a gigantic fraud. Dr. Ley saw to it that it kept the German workers in line. There were no more demands for increased wages and the threat of a strike to obtain them. Workers, like everyone else under Nazism, did what they were told. As in the early days of industrialism, they took what the employers offered them.

Worse than that, they were bound by the state to their place of labor, like medieval serfs. A couple of months after I saw Ley at the Rosenberg evening, in February, 1935, he introduced the "work book," in which was kept a record of a worker's skills and employment. No worker could be hired unless he possessed one. The work book not only provided the state and the employers with up-to-date data on every employee in the nation, but was used to tie a worker to his bench. If he desired to leave for other employment, his employer could retain his work book, barring him from legal employment elsewhere. By 1938 the Nazis instituted labor conscription. It obliged every German to work where the state assigned him.

The German workers, like the Roman proletariat, were provided by the enterprising Dr. Ley with circuses to divert their attention from the lack of freedom and the scarcity of bread. Within the Labor Front Ley created a gigantic organization called Kraft durch Freude ("Strength Through Joy"), which provided the German worker with fun and games for his leisure at bargain rates. It offered, for instance, dirt-cheap vacation trips on land and sea. Dr. Ley built two 25,000-ton cruise ships (one of which he named for himself), and chartered ten others to handle ocean cruises for Kraft durch Freude. They were amazingly inexpensive. A cruise to Madeira cost twenty-five dollars for ten days. On land, vacations on the beaches in the summer and skiing excursions to the Alps in the winter cost eleven dollars a week. Hundreds of beach and lake resorts were taken over for the exclusive use of these worker vacations.

During the next few years I occasionally visited them and once was enticed by Dr. Ley to join a KDF ocean cruise — he wanted me to see, he said, how happy the German workers were in the Third Reich. I found life at the resorts and especially on the cruise ships excruciatingly organized. But the German workers and their families seemed to be having a fine time — Germans had always been great organizers, even of their leisure. Individuals I talked to expressed pride that for the first time ever a laboring man and his family could afford to take an ocean cruise or loll on the beaches for a week or go skiing in the mountains. Maybe in America, one coal miner said to me, a worker made enough to afford such vacations, but never in Europe, never in Germany.

By giving labor such circuses and, even more important, full employment after the weary, dreary years of unemployment after the war, Hitler, I would come to think, had won the cooperation of German labor despite destroying the unions, depressing wages and making the employer the complete master of his enterprise. The worker, it seemed to me, had been taken in less by Nazi propaganda than any other segment of German society. He was less Nazi. But he went along. He was thankful for a steady job. He enjoyed the new opportunities for leisure provided by KDF. Without his steady contribution as a skilled and dedicated worker, the great war machine which Hitler had started to fashion about the time I arrived in Berlin would never have reached the awesome proportions it did.

I found Robert Ley personally repulsive, though not so much so as Himmler, Ribbentrop, Goebbels and Rosenberg. He was tough, excitable, vulgar — a brawling roughneck. He seemed to me to have the instability, the sense of insecurity, that was common to most of the men around Hitler. University-educated though he was, he appeared incapable of making a coherent speech — and I must have heard at least a dozen — or even of carrying on a coherent conversation.

Probably in the years I bumped into him from 1934 on, when he was building up his incredible labor empire, Ley suffered from progressive brain damage. But I did not know this at the time. Had I known it I could have better comprehended his strange ways. At Nuremberg, after the war, Dr. Douglas M. Kelley, the American psychiatrist assigned to observe the accused major Nazi war criminals on trial there, found that Dr. Ley suffered from organic brain disease that had grown progressively worse over the last few years.

But the old drunk, who had wielded so much power in the Third Reich, was resourceful to the end. He cheated, as did Göring, the Allied hangman at Nuremberg. He hanged himself in his cell.

There were two other men around Hitler of whom mention should be made: Wilhelm Frick and Martin Bormann.

Frick was the perfect German bureaucrat, a colorless but competent civil servant all his life until Hitler, in recompense for past services to the Nazi party, made him minister of interior in his first government, a post Frick held until almost the end. His past services had included acting as one of Hitler's spies while he was an official at police headquarters in Munich before the 1923 Beer Hall Putsch. Hitler was particularly grateful for this early help. As minister of interior Frick, who had been trained in the law, drafted most of the so-called legislation of the Third Reich, including the Nuremberg Laws which doomed the Jews.

I ran into Frick occasionally. The world beyond Germany that I came from seemed to him so distant and different that he never, I believe, gave it a thought. He appeared to take me and my colleagues in the foreign press as if we were freak visitors from Mars. He knew only Germany and the narrow world of a German civil servant and Nazi party leader. He was the only bigwig Nazi at the Nuremberg war crimes trial, except for Hess, who declined to take the stand in his own defense. Only after being sentenced to death did he speak out. He had a clear conscience, he told the court. He had only done his duty.

Martin Bormann had not yet greatly distinguished himself, even as a Nazi, though he was a fanatical one, by the time I left Germany in 1940, in the second year of the war, and after more than six years as an American correspondent in Berlin. I note that I did not mention him in *Berlin Diary*, nor did my colleague Wallace Deuel in his *People Under Hitler*, both of which books were published after we left Germany at the end of 1940. But Bormann came to life in my *Rise and Fall of the Third Reich*, as he did in Nazi Germany after I left. His rise to power began after the strange flight to England in 1941 of Rudolf Hess, the deputy to the Führer and his immediate boss. Bormann took over Hess's office and soon made himself the secretary and confidant of the dictator. A molelike man who preferred to burrow in the dark recesses of political life to further his intrigues, he had once served a year in prison for complicity in a political murder. He was the type of German Hitler took to naturally. At the very end, when all was lost, Bormann had become the most powerful of all the men around Hitler, ahead even of Göring and Goebbels and Himmler.

Such were the men around Hitler in those first years of the Third Reich. In a normal, civilized society they surely would have stood out as a grotesque assortment of misfits. But that, as I had to keep reminding myself, was not how most Germans regarded them. The vast majority, so far as I could tell, gave these murderous louts not only the respect a German invariably accorded to high government officials, but held them in high esteem.

Above them all, towered Adolf Hitler. Tyrannical, brutal and emotionally unstable though he was, he was accorded an adulation by the people that no other figure in German history, I believe, had ever received. He was beloved by the populace, worshipped as a savior by many. Most were convinced that he was leading them out of the morass left by the defeat of 1918, the collapse of the currency and the economy in the 1920's, which had robbed them of their lifelong savings, and the Depression of the early 1930's, which had left so many millions hungry and unemployed. He was rescuing them from the political chaos and impotence of the Weimar Republic. He was beginning to thumb his nose at the Allied victors, who had imposed on Germany a shameful peace at Versailles. He was promising to liberate the Fatherland from the shackles of the despicable peace treaty. He was already beginning to make Germany strong again. In less than two years he had unified it for the first time ever.

For all these accomplishments or promises the German people were grateful. They threw themselves with astonishing unity behind the new Leader. And with great dedication and enthusiasm and confidence.

This was not yet realized abroad. But it was slowly, painfully becoming evident to me on the spot in Berlin as the year 1934, which had been so momentous in accomplishments for the dictator, came to an end.

That first fall of my arrival in Berlin I got a break that greatly helped me in my coverage of the news. I had found it very difficult, indeed almost impossible, to make any kind of contact in Nazi circles that would enable me to find out what was going on behind the scenes. I suppose it was the same in Stalin's Russia. In an absolute dictatorship the ruler and his minions knew how to keep party and state secrets. The minions risked their lives if they disclosed anything that displeased the dictator. What really happened behind the totalitarian façade remained mostly a mystery. As time went on my own anti-Nazi feelings made me even more suspect among Hitler and his aides than most of my colleagues, though God knows they learned precious little also of what the regime really was up to.

There was one exception. This was Norman Ebbutt of the *Times* of London. Though he was always hostile to the Nazis and eventually was expelled, he had certain contacts within the party and government which enabled him to know accurately and in detail and at once what went on in the highest and most secret places.

The trouble for Ebbutt was that his newspaper, the most esteemed in England, would not publish much of what he reported. The *Times* in those days was doing its best to appease Hitler and to induce the British government to do likewise. The unpleasant truths that Ebbutt telephoned nightly to London from Berlin were often kept out of the great newspaper.* Discouraged and frustrated, Ebbutt turned to giving me his information so that at least it would see the light of day. Since my dispatches were not published in England, he did not consider this disloyal to his newspaper. He never ceased submitting his reports first to the *Times*, which never ceased suppressing and cutting many of them. When it did, Ebbutt gave them to me, making me much more knowledgeable about what Hitler and his government were up to than I otherwise would have been.

With this fortunate development and with the background I was

---

* "I do my utmost, night after night, to keep out of the paper anything that might hurt their [Nazi German] susceptibilities," Geoffrey Dawson, the editor of the *Times* said at the time. "I can really think of nothing that has been printed now for many months past to which they could possibly take exception as unfair comment." (John Evelyn Wrench: *Geoffrey Dawson and Our Times*.) Ebbutt was expelled from Germany on August 16, 1937, at the moment when I was leaving, temporarily, on my own steam in a transfer to another medium of journalism.

acquiring as the months passed and my work brought me into contact with the barbarians who had seized control of this country and were making it over in their own image, and with the feel of it all beginning to penetrate my skin and bones, I felt fairly well equipped to report on the cascade of events that now began to fall upon us as 1935 got under way. Gathering a momentum of their own they began to hurl the Third Reich — and the rest of Europe with it — down the fateful road to war.

There was no mistaking that road. I think most of us American correspondents in Berlin instinctively felt, before 1935 was over, which road Hitler had chosen and what lay at the end of it.

I cannot say, though, that I yet felt sure of this as Tess and I, at the end of our first four months in the new land, joined a few colleagues on a wintry evening to greet the New Year with champagne. We sat up most of the night speculating about what the year might bring. We agreed that Hitler, having this past momentous year brutally and successfully consolidated his dictatorial hold on Germany, would next strike out in foreign affairs. He was determined, he had often said, to restore Germany to its rightful place in the sun.

But how?

We were pretty sure the answer would come in the next twelve months. The prospect excited me.

Rudolf Hess, Hitler and Hermann Göring

*Hitler with Neville Chamberlain; Joachim
von Ribbentrop is at the far left*

Hitler with Heinrich Himmler

Hitler with Joseph Goebbels

BELOW: *Hitler with Göring*

Hitler with Hess

BOOK THREE

The Road to Armageddon

1935–1938

CHAPTER 9

The First Stretch

1935-1936

On January 13, 1935, the inhabitants of the coal-rich Saar, occupied by the French since the end of the war, voted ten to one (477,000 to 48,000) to return to Germany. There had been some doubt that the Saarlanders, overwhelmingly Catholic and mostly miners or workers in industry, would choose to go back to a Germany run by a dictator who had crushed the free trade unions, harassed the Church, and destroyed the democratic republic. But the pull of the Fatherland, after years of hated French occupation, had been strong. Perhaps some were afraid to cast a ballot against Hitler for fear that if the vote returned them to Germany they might be found out and punished. Also, like most Germans, a lot of them had got the Nazi virus.

Hitler welcomed them back in a broadcast from Berlin. He took the occasion to assure the world that with the return of the Saar he had no further territorial claims on France. This was reassuring to the French because it meant that Germany had renounced its claim on Alsace and Lorraine, the bone of contention so long between the two countries, wrested from one country and then the other in bloody wars.

I flew down to Saarbrücken on March 1, when Germany formally took over the little land. I was a little surprised by the hysterical enthusiasm with which these Catholic workers greeted the arrival of Hitler and troops of the S.S. and the army. The rain, which fell all day, did not dampen their Nazi spirits. Hitler seemed pleased.

Before he arrived I stood in the reviewing stand next to bemono-cled General Werner von Fritsch, the commander-in-chief of the secretly growing army. Though he scarcely knew me — we had briefly met at one of Rosenberg's *Bierabends* — he made no attempt to hide his contempt for the Nazis, from Hitler on down, and for these simple Saar folk who had voted to join them. I was a little taken aback at his biting remarks about the S.S. and the party, and about each party leader as he arrived at the stand. How could the Führer, I wondered, depend on an army whose generals seemed to despise him? When Hitler's cavalcade arrived, the general grunted and went over and took his place directly behind the Leader. I kept an eye on him — in case he drew his revolver. He certainly was in an excellent position to bump off the dictator.

The peaceful return of the Saar and Hitler's renunciation of any more demands on France created an atmosphere of optimism and goodwill in the West as the new year got under way. In February the governments of France and Great Britain offered Hitler to free Germany from the military restrictions of the peace treaty and grant his demand for absolute equality of armaments if he would join in a general European settlement that included an Eastern Locarno Pact and thus provide the countries to the east of the Reich, especially Czechoslovakia, Poland and the Soviet Union, with the same security the Western nations enjoyed under the Locarno Treaty, and of course furnish Germany with the same guarantees of security.

This was a major concession by the Western Allies. Prodded by Britain, France had agreed most reluctantly to it. The French feared that once Germany, with its larger population and stronger heavy industry, was free to rearm, it would again be at their throats.

In our naïveté, all of us Western correspondents were sure Hitler would accept the Anglo-French offer. It appeared to give him all he wanted: freedom to rearm up to the levels of the others. At last, without fear of reprisal from the victors of 1918, he could make Germany militarily strong again. All in return for joining an Eastern Locarno.

I thought it a great bargain for Hitler. What democratic Britain and France had refused for years to concede to the democratic Weimar Republic they were giving on a silver platter to Nazi Germany. All they asked in return was that Germany give the same promises of peace in the East as she had given in the West. I was therefore surprised at Hitler's response on February 14. Vague and evasive, he welcomed the plan insofar as it left Germany free to rearm, but on the proposed Eastern Locarno, Hitler declined to commit himself. This omission should have alerted me, but it did not.

What I had not yet got through my thick skull was that Hitler would never agree to recognizing the status quo in the vast territory to the east. My ignorance — and I think it was shared by my journalistic and diplomatic colleagues, not to mention by the governments in London, Paris and Moscow — was inexcusable. Hitler had stated unequivocally in *Mein Kampf* what his goal was in the East: *Lebensraum* for Germany, more living space for Germans. And where was that space? *"Only in Russia,"* he wrote, *"and her vassal border states."* And how was it to be taken? "It is up to the fist to take," he added. By force then, if necessary.

Nothing could have been clearer. But like almost everyone else who had bothered to read the Nazi Bible, I had not taken the aims Hitler set down in that hodgepodge of a book seriously.

I have often thought subsequently that if more persons had digested *Mein Kampf* and seen it not only as a lot of Nazi gibberish, which it was, but also as a blueprint for action by Adolf Hitler if he ever gained power, then history might have taken a different course. But *Mein Kampf* was ignored, or forgotten or dismissed, and this later proved to be a boon to the author. It enabled him, when he became ruler, to disguise his aims until he was ready to strike.

He struck with lightning speed in Berlin on the morning of March 16, 1935, in the first of his "Saturday surprises." For me it turned out to be the beginning of a series of events that marked the path to war and that for the next four and a half years would absorb my time, attention, energies and abilities and dominate my life and work, leaving a strong imprint for the rest of my life.

That memorable day the once Austrian vagabond, now the sole ruler of Germany, by simple decree wiped out the military restrictions of the Versailles Treaty. He restored universal military service, which the treaty forbade, and proclaimed the formation of a conscript army of half a million men in defiance of the limit set at Versailles of one hundred thousand men. The peace treaty had also deprived the German army, small as it was, of tanks, heavy artillery and an air force. Now Hitler tore up those restrictions too.

The next day, Sunday, March 17, was one of rejoicing and celebration in the Third Reich. Hitler, in one bold move, had accomplished in a day what no republican government, over the long years of subjection to the peace treaty, had ever dared attempt. To most Germans, even to those who chafed at his savage rule, he had restored the nation's honor. The hated Treaty of Versailles lay in tatters.

Weary as I was from working through most of Saturday night dashing off my dispatches and telephoning them to our Paris office for relay to New York, I went over to the State Opera House at noon on Sunday to cover the main celebration. There I found a scene that had not been staged in Germany since 1914.

As it happened, that Sunday was *Heldengedenktag* (Heroes Memorial Day), the German equivalent of our Memorial Day, and Hitler and Goebbels skillfully blended its traditional celebration with that called for by the electrifying action of the previous day. The entire ground floor of the Opera House was a sea of military uniforms, the faded gray tunics and the spiked helmets of the old imperial army mingling with the brighter attire of the new army, including the sky-blue uniforms of the air force, which few had seen before since there was not supposed to be a Luftwaffe.

At Hitler's side in the royal box was Field Marshal von Mackensen, the last surviving field marshal of the Kaiser's army, in his uniform of the Death's Head Hussars and acting even more exuberant than I had seen him at Rosenberg's *Bierabend*. In the next box sat Crown Prince Wilhelm. He had a weak face — almost no chin. Had Hitler honored President Hindenburg's dying wish, a few months before, that the Hohenzollerns be restored to their throne, he might have been the center of attention on this occasion as king and emperor.

Strong lights played on the stage, where young officers stood like marble statues holding upright the nation's war flags. Above them on a vast curtain hung an immense silver and black Iron Cross. The ceremonies opened with the Berlin Philharmonic Orchestra playing the Funeral March from Beethoven's Third Symphony, a piece, I had noted, that seems to awaken the very soul of the German. It seemed to in this place once again. It suddenly occurred to me: what had been announced several days before as a ceremony to honor Germany's war dead was being turned into a celebration of the death of Versailles, the restoration of German honor and the rebirth of the conscript army, symbol of German might.

Hitler himself did not speak. He left that to General von Blomberg, minister of defense, who spoke Hitler's words. With them, I began to feel, as I listened, was being launched a brazen new Nazi propaganda campaign for peace to soften the blow of the Führer's surprise move, which that weekend threatened to upset the peace of Europe.

Said Blomberg, as the dictator looked on smugly:

. . . Europe has become too small for another world war. A future war would mean only self-mutilation for all. We want peace, with equal rights and security for all. We seek no more.

Hitler had echoed the theme in his Proclamation to the German People the day before. After reminding France that with the return of the Saar he had solemnly promised he would make no more territorial demands on her, he went on:

In this hour the German government renews before the German people and before the entire world its assurance . . . that it does not intend in rearming Germany to create an instrument for military aggression but, on the contrary, exclusively for defense and thereby for the maintenance of peace. In so doing the Reich government expresses the confident hope that the German people, having regained their honor, may be privileged in independent equality to make their contribution towards the pacification of the world in free and open cooperation with other nations.

Honeyed words!

It was not the last time Adolf Hitler would attempt to fool his own people and the rest of the world into believing that he was determined to keep the peace. He must have been astonished, I thought, how well his trickery worked. Every anti-Nazi German I talked to that weekend believed he meant it when he said he wanted peace. In London the Tory Sunday press hailed Hitler's professions of peace.

In my diary that Saturday night, I scribbled: *What will London and Paris do?*

Foolish question! They did nothing. The French army alone could have marched into Germany, and that would have brought the sudden end of Adolf Hitler and the Third Reich. The French were entitled to do so, once the peace treaty had been openly and defiantly broken.

Hitler, I was told, took due note of the spinelessness of Britain and France. I myself could scarcely believe that the Western Allies would not act while they enjoyed complete military superiority over Germany. It would take me some time, and several visits to London and Paris, to realize the extent of the rot that was paralyzing Britain and France. I began to suspect that Hitler already was aware of it — though I was not sure for a long time that he was right. It was that awareness, I later saw, that had encouraged him to act on that spring day in 1935.

The dictator now stepped up his feverish rearmament. It would take a lot of guns and tanks to equip overnight an army of half a million men, and a lot of money to pay for them and for the new air force and a bigger navy. The economic wizard, the good Dr. Schacht, minister of economics, was put in charge of finding the money. It would be necessary, he told his beloved Leader, to "use the printing press." But he had also obtained large sums of money, he confided, from the funds confiscated from the Jews and from blocked foreign accounts. "Thus," he cracked, "our armaments are partially financed with the credits of our political enemies."

To allay further uneasiness abroad, especially in London, Paris and Rome, about rearming for his new conscript army, Hitler decided to proclaim again his devotion to peace and even to disarmament and while doing so to see whether he couldn't divide the Allies. While not reacting belligerently to his fait accompli of March, they were by May threatening to unite against him. Britain, France and Italy had met in Stresa on April 11 and condemned him for breaking the peace treaty. They had also got the Council of the League of Nations in Geneva to chastise him and to duly appoint a committee to suggest means of taking some kind of action in the matter. France hastily signed a pact of mutual assistance with Russia, and Moscow concluded a similar treaty with Czechoslovakia.

Empty gestures, they appeared to me. Nevertheless, I noticed an increasing nervousness among political, diplomatic and military circles in Berlin. The generals, I gathered, though elated at the prospect of quickly building up a large army, were worried that the Allies might feel provoked into taking preventive military action against Germany. They knew that France, Italy, Poland, Czechoslovakia and the Soviet Union possessed the combined military means of utterly crushing the Reich even if Britain, with her powerful navy, remained aloof. The generals, I heard, were making their concerns known to the dictator. Discreetly, of course, The Foreign Office too, even more discreetly. And perhaps Göring, I judged from a brief talk I had with him.

He sometimes spoke wildly and irresponsibly in public, but in private and about foreign affairs he was prudent. He did not want to risk — yet — taking on a coalition of armies that could make mincemeat of the still relatively unarmed Reichswehr — and destroy the Luftwaffe that he was just getting airborne.

It was against this background that on the evening of May 21 Hitler delivered another "peace" speech to the rubber-stamp Reichstag. It turned out to be one of the most eloquent and certainly one of the cleverest and most misleading of his Reichstag orations that I, who was fated to squirm through most of them, ever heard. I had never before heard him speak with such passion for peace nor so movingly and persuasively. He was spellbinding and several times during his two-hour-long oration I found myself being carried away by his soaring words until I would catch myself up and think: *He doesn't mean it, it's all false, but it will wow the German people and impress world opinion, especially in Britain,* toward which some of his appeal was adroitly and specifically addressed.

What could be more reasonable — and convincing — than these words, spoken, I noted, in his beautifully modulated, low, resonant voice, his face, his eyes, his frown, his manner exuding sincerity as he recalled the history of the follies of warring mankind:

> The blood shed on the European continent in the course of the last three hundred years bears no proportion to the national results achieved. In the end France has remained France, Germany Germany, Poland Poland and Italy Italy. . . . The shedding of rivers of blood has not substantially altered their fundamental characters. If these nations had applied merely a fraction of their sacrifices to wiser purposes the success would certainly have been greater and more permanent.

Germany, Hitler went on, had not the slightest thought of conquering other peoples.

> Our racial theory regards every war for the subjection and domination of an alien people as a proceeding which sooner or later changes and weakens the victor internally and eventually brings about his defeat. . . .

This was just the opposite, I reflected, of what he had written in *Mein Kampf:* that the duty, indeed the obligation, of the German Master Race was to conquer *Lebensraum* in the East.

Now the Führer's voice started to rise and his gestures became more animated. "No!" he shouted.

> National Socialist Germany wants peace because of its fundamental convictions. And it wants peace also owing to the realization of the simple primitive fact that no war would be likely to alter the distress in Europe. . . . The principal effect of every war is to destroy the flower of the nation.

Hitler paused — his pauses could be terribly eloquent. Then he almost screamed it: "Germany needs peace and desires peace!"

And then came his proposals for a lasting peace in Europe — in thirteen points (how often had I heard him point to Wilson's "Thirteen points"!). As he enumerated them they seemed so admirable and reasonable that I had a feeling they would create a deep and favorable impression, not only in Germany but, what Hitler wanted even more, in the outside world. He prefaced them with some reminders and solemn promises, solemnly pronounced.

> Germany has . . . recognized and guaranteed France her frontiers as determined after the Saar plebiscite. . . . We thereby finally renounced all claims to Alsace-Lorraine, a land for which we have fought two great wars. . . .
>
> Without taking the past into account, Germany has concluded a non-aggression pact with Poland. . . . We shall adhere to it unconditionally. . . . We recognize Poland as the home of a great and nationally conscious people.

As for his native Austria:

> Germany neither intends nor wishes to interfere in the internal affairs of Austria, to annex Austria or to conclude an Anschluss.

Reassuring words for a Europe that feared Hitler's designs on Austria. But brazen all the same! Less than a year before, on June 25, 1934, a large contingent of outlawed Austrian Nazi S.S., which took its orders from Berlin, had seized the Chancellery in Vienna and murdered the Austrian chancellor, Engelbert Dollfuss, in cold blood. Hitler had been on the point of declaring an Anschluss when the coup failed. All of us in Berlin knew that Hitler was up to his neck in organizing Nazi terrorists to overthrow the Austrian government. I recalled the very first paragraph of *Mein Kampf*, in which Hitler had written that the reunion of Austria and Germany (i.e., the Anschluss) was a "task to be furthered with every means our lives long."

Hitler's thirteen-point proposal for peace struck me, I'm afraid, as quite a masterpiece — it sounded so reasonable. It was just what uneasy Europe hoped he would propose. How tolerant and conciliatory he sounded!

Though he had torn up the military clauses of the Versailles Treaty, Germany, Hitler said, would "unconditionally respect" the *non*military clauses of the treaty, "including the territorial provisions." In particular it would "uphold and fulfill all obligations of the Locarno Treaty" and would respect the demilitarized zone in the Rhineland, on which that treaty was based.

I wondered if many would notice that Hitler dodged answering the Allied demand that in return for agreeing to equality of armaments Germany join in an Eastern Locarno, which would provide for the same guarantees against aggression in Eastern Europe that the Locarno Treaty provided for the West. Instead, while claiming Germany was willing "at any time" to participate in "collective security," he proposed bilateral agreements. He was ready, he explained, to conclude nonaggression pacts with each of his neighboring states. How many outside of Germany, I wondered, knew that Russia was not a "neighboring" state? It did not directly border on Germany.

Then came Hitler's big pitch for disarmament. If he meant it, it was sensational.

> The German government is ready to agree to any limitation which leads to abolition of the heaviest arms, especially suited for aggression, such as the heaviest artillery and the heaviest tanks. . . . Germany declares herself ready to agree to any limitation whatsoever of the caliber of artillery, the size of warships and the tonnage of submarines, or even to the complete abolition of submarines. . . .

That was not all. Germany desired, said Hitler, the outlawing of weapons and methods of warfare contrary to the Geneva Red Cross Convention. He suggested the prohibition of dropping bombs of *any* kind outside a battle zone. He said he was willing to go even further: prohibit and outlaw *all* bombing.

Very cleverly, I thought, Hitler held out a special bait to Great Britain. He was willing, he said, to limit the new German navy to thirty-five percent of the British naval forces, which would still leave the Reich fifteen percent below the French naval tonnage. Very astutely, too, Hitler took note of objections raised "abroad" that this would be only the beginning of German naval demands.

"For Germany," he said, "this demand is final and abiding."

The Führer had now been speaking for more than two hours, and very effectively, I had to admit. A little after ten in the evening he came to his peroration.

> Whoever lights the torch of war in Europe can wish for nothing but chaos. We, however, live in the firm conviction that in our time will be fulfilled not the decline, but the renaissance of the West. That Ger-

many may make an imperishable contribution to this great work is our proud hope and our unshakable belief.

I would long remember Hitler's reasoned words of that May evening in 1935. They must have been burned indelibly in my memory for they would come back to me as the Nazi dictator began to make a terrible mockery of them.

But that evening I was impressed by the speech. At the Taverne, where many of us gathered after knocking out our dispatches, some of my British and French colleagues thought that Hitler's words might well help to pave the way for several years of peace. In London the esteemed *Times*, the most influential newspaper in the British Isles, welcomed them with almost hysterical joy.

> The speech [wrote the *Times*] turns out to be reasonable, straightforward and comprehensive. No one who reads it with an impartial mind can doubt that the points of policy laid down by Herr Hitler may fairly constitute the basis of a complete settlement with Germany — a free, equal and strong Germany instead of the prostrate Germany upon whom peace was imposed sixteen years ago. . . .
>
> It is to be hoped that the speech will be taken everywhere as a sincere and well-considered utterance meaning precisely what it says.

My own naïveté in regard to Hitler's designs, even after nine months in the Third Reich, was greater than I realized. This was recently brought back to me (forty-five years later!) by the finding of a long entry I made in my diary in Berlin the evening after the Führer's "peace" speech. It shows I was terribly taken in, as much as the *Times* of London, for whose growing appeasement of the Nazi dictator I would feel a growing contempt over the ensuing years.

> I begin to be impressed by him [I wrote of Hitler after remarking that it was by far the finest speech I have ever heard him make]. His detractors certainly underestimated the man, his mind, his skill, his ability. . . . His voice *sounds* tremendously sincere and convincing.
>
> Once and for all, as has never been done before with such completeness, Hitler summed up the whole German case. . . . And though certainly he is not completely "right," there *was* a case to present, and no one has ever presented it quite so well.

What seems so amazing to me today in the 1980's is that I left the Reichstag that evening convinced that Hitler, despite all my reservations about him, really wanted peace and had made the West, at

least, a serious offer. I had been derisive of the Germans for swallowing Hitler's propaganda. I should have included myself.

If only I had known what Hitler actually was *doing*, in contrast to
saying, that very day and a few days before!

One. On the morning of his great "peace" speech, Hitler had promulgated in the greatest secrecy the Reich Defense Law, which completely reorganized the armed forces and introduced a spartan war
economy. While *talking* peace to lull the outside world, he was going
to make ready for war as rapidly as he could.

Two. Nearly three weeks *before* pledging in this "peace" speech
that Germany would "unconditionally respect" the territorial provisions of the Versailles Treaty as well as the obligations she had freely
assumed at Locarno, including the demilitarization of the Rhineland,
*Hitler instructed the German High Command to prepare plans for the
military occupation of the Rhineland.*

The code name for the operation was *Schulung*. It was to be "executed by a surprise blow [at the French] with lightning speed" and
its planning was to be so secret that "only the smallest number of officers should be informed."

These secret moves came to light only after the war with the capture of the German confidential documents. I can see now how blind
we were in Berlin at the time to what was really going on behind the
ornamental façade of the Third Reich.

Hitler did not have to conceal one important aspect of his plans:
while dissipating the suspicions of the Western allies sufficiently so
that they would not unite against him in a preventive war, he would
strive to divide them definitely by holding out to one or another a
tempting bait. This proved easier than I'm sure he anticipated —
frighteningly so, it seemed to me. And first of all with the British,
whose weaknesses he was quite aware of.

In his peace speech of May 21 he had publicly offered them a
naval agreement that would limit the future German fleet (under the
restrictions of Versailles it was only a token force) to thirty-five percent of the British tonnage, thus guaranteeing British naval superiority over Germany. Hitler sent Ribbentrop to London to work out the
details. These were quickly agreed to and the naval treaty was signed
in London on June 18. Behind the backs of her principal allies,
France and Italy, which were also naval powers and much concerned
over German rearmament, the British government, for what it
thought was its private advantage, agreed to throw away the peace

treaty's naval restrictions and to give Hitler free rein to build up a navy as fast as he could, a navy that soon would rival those of France and Italy.

In Berlin we correspondents were dumbfounded at the British move. "It's beyond me," I scribbled in my diary. What seemed particularly amazing was that Britain agreed to Germany's building up to sixty percent of Britain's submarine tonnage, and even one hundred percent "in exceptional circumstances." "German submarines," I wrote in my diary, "almost beat the British in the last war, and may in the next."

I thought the deceit of the British toward their allies astounding. But it went further than I knew at the time. London refused to inform the French of the details of the naval accord — except for the submarine tonnage. Actually, as I found out only much later, the British agreed to the Germans' building a vast armada, including five battleships that would be heavier and more heavily gunned than anything the British — or any other nation — had afloat.

Mussolini, a cynic like Hitler, took due notice of England's cynicism. If London could join Hitler in flouting the peace treaty, whose terms were supposed to be enforced by the League of Nations, he too could defy the league's covenant. On October 3, 1935, he sent his armies into the ancient mountain kingdom of Abyssinia.

The next day, October 4, I spent several hours in the Wilhelmstrasse talking to government and party officials about Mussolini's move.

> The Wilhelmstrasse is delighted. Either Mussolini will stumble and get himself so heavily involved in Africa that he will be greatly weakened in Europe, whereupon Hitler will seize Austria, hitherto protected by the Duce; or he will win, defying France and Britain (which are asking for sanctions of the League) and thereupon be ripe for a tie-up with Hitler against the Western democracies. Either way Hitler wins.

Events now began rapidly to bear me out.

That summer of 1935 in Berlin we moved, and in September I paid a brief visit home, the first since 1929. Time raced by so fast it was difficult to realize that ten years had passed since I first set out at twenty-one from Iowa for Europe. By now I felt more at home on the old continent than in my native America. It was not that I had slipped into the role of an expatriate as so many Americans in Paris had done. It was simply that my work, which I loved, kept me abroad. Recently vague thoughts had crept into my mind that the time might not be too far off when I would want to return home for good. Say, when the story of Hitler's explosive Germany reached one conclusion or another. Say, when war came. Or when it ended. Or if we started to have children.

Perhaps now was a good time, I thought, to take three weeks off, go home and get the feel of our land: about living there and working. Rumors would not down that Universal might merge with INS or just fold, in which case I would again be out of a job. I could size that possibility up on the spot at our home office in New York and sound out Jimmy James, now managing editor of the *Times,* and Wilbur Forrest, recently made executive editor of the *Herald-Tribune,* both of whom I had known in Paris, about working for their esteemed journals.

The immediate purpose of my trip home, however, was to see my mother. She planned to come from Iowa to New York to be with my brother, with whom I would stay. She was sixty-four. I owed her much. And I loved her. I could not stand the idea of her possibly slipping away before we had been together once more. I had seen her only once since leaving home ten years before.

By using Germany's two crack liners, it would be possible to take the *Bremen* over, stay ten days in New York, and return on the *Europa* — all in three weeks. In 1935 there was no transatlantic plane service that could whisk you from one continent to the other in a few hours.

I had hoped to bring Tess over with me — she had never been in America — but we did not have the money, even for third-class fare. Tess decided to return to *her* native land for the three weeks and do some mountaineering in the Austrian Alps.

From the moment I stepped off the boat in New York I felt the enormous vitality of the teeming city. There was electricity in the clear, early autumn air. The place and the people seemed wonderfully alive. I felt it in the way people walked, talked, gestured, laughed and carried themselves.

The women looked most attractive. A surprisingly large number of them, compared to Berlin, had trim figures which their neat dresses showed off to good advantage. They had a graceful gait as they walked by. One noticed their shapely legs (after all the shapeless ones in Berlin) and a resplendent sheen to their hair. They talked animatedly, as if life was interesting and even exciting.

The men too. The intellectual curiosity of many I met delighted me, when I thought back to the dull, complacent Coolidge time that I had fled in 1925. Everywhere I went in the city people seemed to talk a lot about books, especially of the latest novels, and about the theater, sculpture and music and the paintings they were seeing in the galleries and museums.

On world affairs, though, I found them mostly rather naïve and uninformed and rather unconcerned. I expected, I guess, that people I knew or met would be anxious for firsthand impressions of Nazi Germany. Few were.

In the middle of my visit, in mid-September, the Reichstag, assembled in special session at Nuremberg, had, at Hitler's bidding, "passed" a number of laws virtually outlawing the Jews and further humiliating them by forbidding them to marry Aryans or have anything sexually or socially to do with "pure-blooded" Germans. No one, at least in New York, paid much attention. The news from Nuremberg depressed me, though I had known what was coming and for a year had watched with increasing horror the growing, brutal oppression of the Jews. But most Americans I talked to that fall, even Jews, did not grasp the enormity of Hitler's crimes; not only against the Jews, but against the human spirit. I kept getting the feeling that they thought I was a bit "emotional" and "sensational" on the subject.

Even two old friends who knew Europe well from long assignments there — Raymond Gram Swing, a veteran foreign correspondent who had first gone to Germany in the kaiser's time, and Nicholas Roosevelt, who had been our minister to Hungary and earlier also a foreign correspondent — surprised me by their apparent lack of interest in Europe. They were excited at being back in America and at trying to follow the swift unfolding of events of Franklin Roosevelt's New Deal — Swing with enthusiasm and approval, Roosevelt with growing apprehension and resentment.

The days of Swing's immense popularity as a radio commentator lay ahead. I was scarcely aware of radio in America during this stay and I do not recall that he even mentioned it. As an editor of the *Nation*, the only one who had had worldwide experience as a reporter, Swing was breathing new life into that somewhat moribund liberal weekly. He had recently done a dramatic series of pieces on Huey Long, the "Kingfish" dictator of Louisiana. As it happened, Senator Long had been assassinated in Baton Rouge the day before I arrived, and the newspapers were full of it. Swing had found him an unspeakably vulgar man but highly intelligent and with amazing vitality — rather like Adolf Hitler. We had not heard much of Huey Long in Europe and Swing's account, which he unfolded to me in an all-night talkfest, was fascinating. He believed that most Americans, like most Germans in the case of Hitler, had not taken Huey Long seriously enough or realized his threat to the American democracy.

Nick Roosevelt, who came from the "Teddy" Roosevelt branch of the family, lived near the ancestral home at Oyster Bay, and was a liberal Republican working now as an editorial writer for the staunchly Republican *New York Herald-Tribune.* I spent a weekend with him at his place on Long Island, and it was rather strange. A genial enough man, tolerant and civilized, he turned out to be an implacable foe of his cousin Franklin, whom he accused in the wildest terms of trying to set up a dictatorship in America. I was surprised at his paranoia, for Nick Roosevelt was the mildest of men. It was my first brush with American conservatives who, having recovered from the paralysis of the Depression, were convincing themselves that the energetic new President was the Devil himself, intent on leading the Republic to Bolshevik ruin. I could scarcely believe it. Indeed it seemed to me that Franklin Roosevelt had saved capitalism in America — despite the capitalists.

We sat up arguing through the night, my good friend looking at me more and more as if I were crazy.

"You've been in that Nazi cuckoo land too long!" he said.

"And you don't know how well off you are in this wonderful country!" I countered. "Thanks," I could not refrain from getting in, "to your cousin, FDR."

I was a little disturbed that autumn in New York to find myself feeling a stranger in my native land. It made me uncomfortable. But I could not deny that I felt much more at home in Europe than in America. I guess it had been true for a long time but I only realized it on rare visits home — just two in the last ten years. Now that I thought of it that fall of 1935 in New York, I had felt strange the first time I went back — in 1929, when I had returned to Chicago, the city of my birth, and then to Cedar Rapids, Iowa, where I had grown up after I was nine.

I had been happy in 1929 to get out of the country again and back to Paris. Now in 1935, after a fortnight in New York, I was restless to leave and to get back "home" — even if home had become Berlin. This feeling still puzzled me. Why was it, I wondered, that we

Americans were so rootless that after a few years abroad we felt strangers to our homeland? This could not be true of the English, French, Greeks and others. In due time I would come to feel that we Americans who worked abroad were really strangers in the countries in which we worked. We never quite mastered the language. We never quite slipped into the native way of life. We continued to be foreign *observers*. When that realization came, I knew what I would eventually do: go home. Before it was too late, I hoped.

Whatever strangeness I felt at being home, I was having a fine time in New York, getting reacquainted with my family, especially with my mother, seeing old friends returned for good from Europe, going to parties and meetings and prowling the fascinating city. Perhaps if I stayed a little longer, I thought, I might overcome my feeling of alienation.   But my editors insisted I return to Berlin as planned. They were afraid (as I was) that Mussolini might invade Abyssinia any day now. They were transferring Dosch-Fleurot to Rome so he could cover part of the story from there. I was to have the Universal bureau in Berlin.

This was a promotion that raised my spirits. Working with Dosch had been fine. I would greatly miss him. Just the same, it would be nice to be on my own again. Seymour Berkson, now head of Universal Service in New York, who had convinced me the last few days that the organization was not going to merge or fold, congratulated me on becoming "head of bureau" in Berlin. Comical! I would be head of a bureau consisting of myself!

Early in June that year we had moved out to Tempelhof. Through Knick we had run into Captain Hermann Köhl and his beautiful wife, who were anxious to sublet their apartment and get away from Berlin. The Köhls were Catholics. He had emerged from the war second only to Göring as a hero of the German air corps. In 1928, he, with two colleagues, had been the first to fly the Atlantic from east to west (Lindbergh had crossed the other way). Göring, an old friend from their flying days, had given him a key job with Lufthansa, but the captain had become increasingly apprehensive at the excesses of the Nazi regime, especially toward the Jews and the Catholics. Rather bluff and blunt in manner despite a warm heart, he had not been backward in expressing his views. This had cost him his job and some thought threatened his life. At any rate, he was retiring to a small farm he owned near Stuttgart. He planned in a year or two to resume flying for a Catholic missionary group in Africa.

Occasionally in the next few years the Köhls returned to Berlin for a few days and we became good friends. The course that Hitler (and his old friend Göring) were taking deeply depressed him. What drove him to despair and really broke his heart was the realization that Hitler was dragging Germany and Europe into war. Mercifully, he died shortly before the war began — a brokenhearted man.

We liked the new apartment. It was surrounded by a wooded little park and countless gardens. We needed the fresh air. And the quiet. We were far enough from the big Tempelhof airfield so that we could not hear planes approaching or taking off. We settled in easily.

But at the office I began to feel the strain of trying to report on the Nazi dictatorship. Toward the end of the year Goebbels was obviously in a foul mood, threatening the British and American correspondents with more expulsions. He was attacking Knickerbocker in articles and broadcasts as a "dirty liar." Knick had been told he would not be allowed back in Germany. Dorothy Thompson and Edgar Mower (of the *Chicago Daily News*) already had been expelled. Otto Tolischus of the *New York Times* was being threatened, as was Norman Ebbutt of the *Times* of London. John Elliott of the *New York Herald-Tribune* was moving on to Paris before Goebbels' axe fell on his neck.

When on the next to the last day of 1935, Ambassador Dodd called in the American correspondents for a talk with William Phillips, under-secretary of state, who was visiting the capital, we asked him what action Washington would take if the Nazis began expelling more of us.

"None," he said, with a smile that we did not much appreciate. "There is no law that would allow us to retaliate." He did not seem much interested.

Sooner than I expected I suddenly found myself in trouble.

Early on the morning of January 23, 1936, I was awakened by a telephone call from a fanatical hack at the Propaganda Ministry by the name of Wilfred Bade. He was on the telephone yelling at me for something I had written about the Winter Olympics, which were to open on February 6 at Garmisch-Partenkirchen in the Bavarian Alps. He charged that I had written a fake story about Garmisch and the Jews and that I was trying to torpedo the Winter Games. Six weeks or so earlier, I had written some stories about the Winter Olympics and the zeal with which the Germans, from Hitler on down, were preparing them as a prelude to the Summer Games in Berlin. The Führer meant to turn the Olympics into a huge propaganda triumph. I had therefore reported in the opening paragraph of the first of four pieces that Hitler was seeing to it that "the signs that last summer bellowed 'Jews Get Out' and 'Jews Unwanted' have been quietly removed from Garmisch.°

"All Jew baiting," I added, "is officially off in Germany during the Olympics."

For months government circles in Berlin had been in a tizzy over the threat of the United States to boycott the Olympics because of the Nazi persecution of the Jews. Actually the first of my dispatches had been published in newspapers from coast to coast on December 10, two days after the U.S. Amateur Athletic Union, in a stormy meeting in New York, had decided not to boycott the Olympic Games in Germany.†

It had taken Dr. Goebbels and the Propaganda Ministry nearly six weeks to react to my report, but he now laid on me with all the formidable propaganda tools he possessed. Bade, after fuming at me, finally hung up after I turned on him. I had learned early in the game that the best way to handle Germans when they attacked you was to counterattack immediately. If they shouted, shout back. If they threatened, dare them to carry out their threats. So, I had shouted back at him. But he had merely fired the first shot. Goebbels was bringing up his big guns.

At noon Tess, turning on the radio to catch the news, was greeted with a blast against me. I was accused of trying to torpedo the games at Garmisch by writing false stories about the treatment of the Jews in Germany. When I got to the office after lunch I found the front pages of the early editions of the afternoon papers given over to hysterical denunciations of me as a liar and a cheat and a "German-

---

° They were removed, not only from Garmisch and Berlin, site of the Winter and Summer Games, but from the rest of the country until the Olympics ended in August. One sign, at a sharp bend in the road near Ludwigshafen, read:

Drive Carefully!
Sharp Curve.
Jews 75 Kilometers an Hour!

† Nearly half a century later, in 1980, there was some agitation — though not nearly as much as in 1936 — against American participation in the summer Olympic Games in Russia, where they were being held for the first time. But the President, Jimmy Carter, angry and resentful at the Soviet Union's brazen invasion of Afghanistan, in effect decided on his own that the United States would boycott the Games in Russia. Though most of the American athletes, many of whom had been in training for three years, wanted to take part, Carter was able to pressure the U.S. Olympic Committee to go along with him. The U.S. Congress and press seemed uninterested but obedient.

It fascinated me to see how easily Americans in the last quarter of the twentieth century knuckled under to presidential authority. President Franklin Roosevelt, apparently, did not dare to insist on a boycott of the 1936 Games in Germany, despite his hatred of the Nazis and a much greater hold on the country than Carter ever had. Ironically, he made no move in that direction even after Hitler, as we shall see, just prior to the Summer Games in Berlin, carried out a daring act of aggression, in violation of solemn treaties freely signed by Germany — an act that paved the way for the outbreak of another world war.

hater." One forgot, until such moments arrived, how hysterical the Germans could get, though God knows I had seen it often enough, even in public. After all, Hitler, Goebbels and Göring rarely made a speech without at one point working themselves up to a fine fit of paranoiac hysteria.

Every time the office boy brought in a fresh batch of afternoon papers, with fresh attacks on me, I grew more hot under the collar. Most of my journalistic colleagues phoned to advise me to ignore the whole affair. They thought that if I tried to hit back I'd invite expulsion. I was determined, however, to have it out with Bade. I kept phoning him. Finally a secretary said he was out and would not be back. In a fine state of hysteria myself by that time, 9 P.M. or so, I rushed out of the office, down the Wilhelmstrasse, brushed by a guard at the Propaganda Ministry and burst into Bade's office. He was there. I pounded on his desk, yelled at the top of my voice, demanded an apology and a correction in the press. As I expected, he roared back. Our row must have echoed through the halls, for two or three times frightened flunkies would open the door and peer in — apparently to see if their boss was being harmed.

Finally — out of exhaustion, I guess — we quieted down. It had been foolish of me, I saw, to think that anyone in this regime would apologize for a lie or attempt to correct it. Bade was now mumbling something about it having been decided that despite my "lies" I would not be expelled. I dared him to expel me. But this too was foolish. It did not lie in his hands. It was Goebbels, the propaganda chief, who decided such things. Or Hitler. I also was told that the Nazi authorities believed they had thoroughly scared me, and that henceforth I would be more careful of what I wrote. If so, they were mistaken.

The Olympic Games were a dazzling success for Adolf Hitler. Both at Garmisch-Partenkirchen in the Bavarian Alps, where the Winter Games were held, and in Berlin, where the more important Summer Games took place, the Nazi hosts staged them on a scale more lavish than any other country had ever attempted. The athletes from around the world were delighted; the spectators, especially from America, were impressed. Never before, to my knowledge, had the Nazi bigwigs put on such extravagant parties, Göring, Ribbentrop and Goebbels each trying to outdo the others in their entertaining. The propaganda minister's "Italian Night" on the Pfaueninsel on Wannsee gathered more than a thousand guests (including even me) at dinner in a scene that resembled the Arabian Nights. While the best food and wine I had ever tasted in Nazi Germany were being served to the immense throng on a broad terrace overlooking the lake under a spreading canopy of five thousand Chinese lanterns, we listened to the Berlin Philharmonic Orchestra and stars from the State Opera and watched the dancers from the Opera ballet.

The Games themselves were not only beautifully organized and staged. Hitler saw to it that the country was on its best behavior: no persecution of the Jews. (They already had been outlawed by the Nuremberg Laws of the fall before.) No action against unruly Catholics and Protestants. No savage attacks against the "decadent" Western democracies and "Jewish-dominated" America. All was, for the moment, sweetness and light, except for an occasional diatribe in the press against the terrible Bolsheviks. The Russians had not yet been invited to the Olympics. They were still considered beyond the pale by the Olympic committees of Fascist Italy, Nazi Germany and democratic U.S.A., Britain and France.

The good Aryan German people struck most visitors from abroad as happy, content and united under the swastika dictatorship. The harassed Jews, shorn of their civil rights and the opportunity to earn a living, did not dare to approach the distinguished foreign visitors to enlighten them. At Garmisch I became so alarmed at the way some American businessmen were being taken in that I gave a luncheon for several of them and invited Douglas Miller, our commercial attaché in Berlin and one of the best-informed men on Germany we had at the embassy, to talk to them. He got nowhere. The genial tycoons told *him* what the situation in Nazi Germany was. They liked it, they said. The streets were clean and peaceful. Law and Order. No strikes, no trouble-making unions. No agitators. No Commies. Miller, a patient man, could scarcely get a word in.

In Berlin a group of American businessmen — Norman Chandler, the conservative owner and publisher of the *Los Angeles Times*, was one of them — invited me and Ralph Barnes of the *New York Herald-Tribune* to lunch in the Hotel Adlon bar. They were puzzled, they said, that the Germany they were seeing was quite different from what they had conceived from our reporting. They had never seen a people so happy and content, and so enthusiastic about their leaders. They had talked to Göring, they said, and he had told them that we American correspondents in Berlin peddled nothing but lies about National Socialist Germany.

For an hour, Barnes and I tried our best to tell them the truth. "I don't think," I noted in my diary that night, "that we convinced them."

I was rather puzzled that our American businessmen and our rich tended to sympathize with Fascist countries. I wondered if it was because the right-wing dictatorships claimed to be anti-Communist. (The ploy is still working in America in the 1980's, not only with our well-heeled men of affairs, but with our government.) I should have remembered how these well-off American types, who controlled our amateur athletics and our Olympic Committee, deliberately lied about conditions in Germany to get the United States not to boycott the Olympic Games that year.

In 1933, the year Hitler took power, both the American Athletic Union and the U.S. Olympic Committee had voted overwhelmingly to boycott the Games unless Jewish athletes were permitted on German teams. Our Olympic Committee had dispatched Avery Brundage, its president, to Germany the following year to check on whether Jews could try out for the German teams. He found that they could, and returned to New York to announce his recommendation that America not boycott the games.

The agitation for the boycott, however, continued, and in September, 1935, General Charles E. Sherrill, a member of both the American and International Olympic Committees, was sent back to Germany to make another check. While the general was touring the Third Reich, Hitler promulgated the Nuremberg Laws outlawing the Jews. General Sherrill took no notice. He returned to New York in October and announced: "I went to Germany for the purpose of getting at least one Jew on the German Olympic team, and I feel that my job is finished."

Actually, Sherrill had got *two* Jews on the German team, both of whom returned temporarily from exile to provide window-dressing for the Nazis. No Jewish athlete living in the country was allowed a tryout. But the minor Nazi concession of two token Jews satisfied the American Olympic Committee. In Berlin we could scarcely believe it when the *New York Times* quoted Frederick W. Rubien, secretary of the U.S. Olympic Committee:

> The Germans are not discriminating against Jews in their Olympic tryouts. The Jews are eliminated because they are not good enough as athletes. Why, there are not a dozen Jews in the world of Olympic caliber.*

* There were, in fact, nearly half that number of Jews, five, on the American team alone, and many more on teams from other countries. Two Jews, Sam Stoller and Marty Glickman, made up half of the American 400-meter relay team, which was expected to set an Olympic and possibly a world record in the event, which it did. But at the last minute, on the morning of the race, Stoller and Glickman were dropped from the team and replaced

On the basis of this brazen lie the Americans came to Germany that year to compete in the Olympic Games.

Our star that summer, one of the greatest in the history of the Olympics, was the sprinter Jesse Owens, who won four gold medals. Owens was black. Adolf Hitler, who was in the stands each day, refused to receive the American runner after his triumphs. Each time Owens trotted up the track after a smashing win the German spectators stood and gave him thunderous applause. But Hitler, I noticed from my seat in the press box a few feet away from him, turned his back to talk to some cronies. One of these was Baldur von Schirach, the Hitler Youth leader, who much later told what the Führer said when he turned away from Owens.

"The Americans ought to be ashamed of themselves," Hitler complained, "for letting their medals be won by Negroes. I myself would never shake hands with one of them."

When Schirach suggested that it would be good propaganda for the Führer to be photographed with Owens, Hitler screamed at the thought.°

During the Winter Games at Garmisch, I had run into an old colleague, Westbrook Pegler, and met a new friend, Paul Gallico, two of the best sports writers in America and both about to branch out into wider fields.

I had first noticed Pegler's talent when as sports editor of the *Cedar Rapids Republican* during my college years I had edited his copy as it came over the wires of the night service of the United Press. He had a lively style quite different from any other sports writer. He had later gone to the *Chicago Tribune* while I was on its European staff and I had seen a bit of him in Paris when he came over to France in 1926 to cover Gertrude Ederle's successful attempt that summer to be the first woman to swim the English channel. I liked his sardonic view of life and his way of deflating sacred cows. At that period, at least, he did not like fascism and he was offended by the Nazis and the Nazism he met in Garmisch.

---

by Owens and Foy Draper in order, the American coach claimed, to add speed to it. Owens certainly added speed, but Draper had never run a faster 100 meters than Stoller. I could not believe that the eleventh-hour elimination of the two Jewish sprinters from the American relay team was done, as some charged, to please Hitler. But it created a bad taste in many an American mouth.

° Owens, who behaved graciously and modestly throughout his unprecedented triumphs, believed he was being treated fairly and courteously by the Nazi hosts, including Hitler. Later he criticized American reporters for writing otherwise. "I think the writers showed bad taste," he was quoted as saying, "in criticizing the man of the hour in Germany."

Paul Gallico, less sardonic than Pegler but plenty cynical, had been partly educated in Berlin, spoke colloquial, if rusty, German, and could shout at policemen as well as any German. The three of us, with Tess, who was helping me cover the Games,* found plenty of opportunity to shout at Garmisch. At least twice a day we would be held up at the Olympic Stadium by big, bully S.S. guards. They would yell at us that the Führer was entering or departing, and we could not enter.

"Nuts to you, you so-and-so," Pegler would mutter in English and try to slip past the guards. And Gallico would begin yelling at them in mock hysteria with the German equivalent of four-letter words. It was a wonder we weren't arrested and carted off to jail. But the police, the S.S. and the army had been alerted to go easy on the barbarian visitors and we were merely held at bay, often missing parts of hockey games or the figure-skating. This infuriated Pegler and Gallico since hockey, with the American team in contention, and skating, with the incomparable Sonja Henie going for her third Olympic championship, furnished them with the best material for their columns.

Pegler used to come to my hotel room to phone his column in to his Paris office (he said he was sure the phones at the press camp were tapped) and it was amusing to an old Berlin hand to hear his biting, but also humorous, comments on his run-ins with the S.S. He himself began to fear that the Gestapo might pick him up and incarcerate him, but nothing so untoward happened.

Looking back, I can recall nothing at Garmisch in Pegler's talk or behavior that indicated he would soon start to make his name as a choleric right-wing commentator, albeit an eccentric, unpredictable one. Franklin Roosevelt had been in office nearly four years, yet I do not recall Pegler even mentioning him or Eleanor Roosevelt. His vituperation against them, the New Deal and everything else liberal in American life must have begun later, after I had lost touch with him. At Garmisch, as in Paris, he was warm, full of humor, rational. And he hated what he saw of Hitler and Nazi Germany.

Paul Gallico had arrived at an interesting crossroad in his life and work. He had just thrown up his job on the *New York Daily News,* where he was one of the finest and highest paid sports writers in the country. In fact, with the Olympic Games he was bidding farewell to sports. He had had enough of them, he said, and of the unsavory

* A fine Alpine skier herself, and an accomplished ice skater, she was invaluable in covering for me the main events in these fields.

characters who dominated them. He was going to settle down in the English countryside to see if he could make a living as a fiction writer. He was going to write a lot of short stories and begin a novel. It was an interesting decision to me — one that took a lot of guts, one that I vaguely knew I ought to make myself someday. With Gallico it paid off. After a slow and uncertain start and the usual setbacks and early discouragements of a budding writer, he began to make a very comfortable living from his writing.

Among the distinguished American visitors to the Olympic Games in Berlin that summer were Charles and Anne Lindbergh. I had not seen him since I covered his landing at Le Bourget, outside Paris, eight years before and the tumultuous welcome he had received for achieving the first flight over the Atlantic. He had gone home to an even greater reception and to fame such as no other American had had in our time, becoming the idol of the nation, its most publicized citizen, its one authentic hero.

And then, I gathered from afar, fame had turned into a curse. After bringing him so many honors and such unprecedented adulation, it had more recently brought him disillusionment, bitterness, tragedy, sorrow. The press had hounded him almost to death; it would not give him peace or quiet. And then his first child had been kidnapped and murdered. Finally, he had fled his homeland, first for England and then to France, where he and his wife had lived on a secluded island off the coast of Brittany with the Franco-American scientist and Nobel Prize laureate Dr. Alexis Carrel. I did not know that Carrel's sympathies for totalitarianism had begun to influence Lindbergh, but I began to suspect it shortly after the airman and his wife arrived in Berlin that summer.

They came a fortnight before the Games began, and Hermann Göring, the fat chief of the rapidly growing German air force, took them in hand, giving lavish parties for them and showing them enough of the budding Luftwaffe to impress them. Lindbergh had refused to meet with American correspondents in Berlin, but Lufthansa, the German state-owned airline, had invited some of us to a tea party on July 23 at Tempelhof in honor of the airman and his wife. I was surprised at how little he had changed in appearance; he still had a boyish air, though I noted that he had become more self-confident.

After tea, Lufthansa officials took us for a ride in the then world's largest airplane, the *Field Marshal von Hindenburg*, a huge, cumbersome eight-engined craft that the Germans hoped to put into service in the first transatlantic run. Göring turned over the controls to Lindbergh somewhere above the Wannsee and we were treated to some fancy rolls, steep banks and other maneuvers for which the Goliath machine was not designed. I thought for a few moments that the plane would be torn apart and that that would be the end not only of Göring and Lindbergh but of me. Cups of tea and coffee and liqueur glasses careened off our tables on to the laps of the distinguished guests. It was an unpleasant reminder of something I had heard about Lindbergh shortly after his arrival in Paris: that he was a terrible practical joker. Finally, Göring took back the controls and guided us smoothly back to Tempelhof.

I was somewhat puzzled that week by Lindbergh. On the one hand he delivered what I thought was a courageous speech at a luncheon given him by the Air Ministry, warning that the new bombers had become so deadly an instrument of destruction that unless mankind did something about outlawing them or at least restricting their number and size, they might make a wasteland of Europe. On the other hand I was disturbed by hearing in Nazi circles that they had made great progress in making the Lindberghs "understand" Nazi Germany.

"The talk is," I wrote in my diary that evening after the ride in the *Hindenburg,* "that the Lindberghs have been favorably impressed by what the Nazis have shown them."

Through Major Truman Smith, our American military attaché and a friend of the flyer, some of us American correspondents sought again to talk with Lindbergh in the hope of countering any Nazi propaganda he may have fallen for. But he refused anew to see us.

He changed his mind a fortnight or so later at Dr. Goebbels' glittering party on the Pfaueninsel during the Olympics. Apparently, the Nazi propaganda minister persuaded him to have a few words with us. Late that evening he sauntered over to our table and greeted us graciously enough. I thought it was a golden opportunity to enlighten the famous flyer about what lay hidden beneath the surface in Hitler's dictatorship. But like my American businessmen, Lindbergh proceeded to tell us what the situation was in Germany and to express his admiration for what had been achieved here. He, too, had found a happy, united people, he said. As an airman he was particularly impressed by the German air force and the progress of German aviation in general. Once again, we did not get a word in.

By this time, I was getting a little tired of bigwig American visitors to the Olympics telling me how it was in Nazi Germany. I thought I knew better than they. Far more important was a development that would have far-reaching and tragic consequences for Lindbergh. That summer in Berlin, the German Nazi leaders were able to sow in Lindbergh's mind, and in that of his attractive and gifted wife, seeds that, when they flowered, would poison their judgment about the course of history and of Western civilization.

As one who had felt so much admiration for Lindbergh's courage and modesty and, indeed, for his greatness in the heady days of his arrival in Paris in 1927, I was more saddened than surprised when two years after the 1936 visit, on October 18, 1938, Lindbergh accepted from Adolf Hitler the Service Cross of the German Eagle with Star, the highest German decoration that could be conferred on a foreigner, along with the citation that the recipient "deserved well of the Reich."

The timing could scarcely have been worse and showed, I thought, not only Lindbergh's insensitivity to man, but his ignorance of what was going on in the world. The evening Göring, on the Führer's behalf, hung the Service Cross around Lindbergh's neck at a ceremony in Berlin was just three weeks after Munich, when Hitler, by threatening war, had frightened Britain and France into abandoning Czechoslovakia to him and Europe trembled in fear of the mad dictator's next threats of aggression and war. It was just three weeks before *Kristall Nacht*, the Night of the Broken Glass, the worst pogrom Germany had ever experienced until the massacre of the Jews began in the Nazi extermination camps three years later.

While Adolf Hitler sat benignly in the stands watching the peaceful competition of the Winter Olympic Games at Garmisch that early February of 1936, his feverish mind was concentrating on a move that might turn out to be anything but peaceful and that, he recognized, was a dangerous gamble. If successful, it would be a turning point on the road toward Germany's triumphant comeback from the defeat of 1918. If it failed, it might well be the end of him and of his Nazi dictatorship.

We correspondents, of course, busy with our reporting, were blissfully ignorant of what the Führer was up to. We were ignorant of so much that was transpiring in secret those days behind the Nazi façade: that, for example, as far back as May 2 of the previous year, some nineteen days before Hitler's great "peace" speech of May 21, in which he had sworn he would respect not only the territorial clauses of the Versailles Treaty, which had been imposed on the defeated country, but the Locarno Pact, which Germany had freely signed, the dictator had ordered General von Blomberg, his minister of war, to issue to the armed services the first directive to plan for the occupation of the demilitarized zone of the Rhineland in violation of both Versailles and Locarno.

Occasionally during that time I heard rumors of clandestine German military activity in the Rhineland. They came mostly from the French embassy and had to do with reports of secret barracks, arms and munition depots, airfields, new roads and rail lines being built in the demilitarized zone.* And though, in my opinion, André François-Poncet, the French ambassador, was the best informed foreign envoy in Berlin, for some reason I did not take these rumors seriously. I kept after the American military attaché and his assistants on the matter. They detected no signs of the German army doing anything unusual about the Rhineland.

It should have occurred to me that Hitler's growing phobia about the Franco-Soviet Pact of Mutual Assistance, which had been hastily signed after Hitler's proclaiming of a new conscript army in violation of the peace treaty, in March of the previous year, might be merely an excuse for going into the Rhineland. In his great "peace" speech on May 21 he had mentioned that "an element of insecurity" had been brought into the Locarno Treaty as the result of France and Russia signing their pact. And I had noted that the German Foreign Office had sent a formal note to Paris protesting the agreement. But up to the end of the year and into 1936 the French Parliament had not yet ratified the pact with the Bolsheviks. It looked as if the Führer might have to find another excuse.

Still, the Nazi dictator knew how to bide his time. High-strung, emotional and even hysterical as he was, he had the willpower to be patient when it was necessary. And time and events that winter of 1935–36 were working in his favor. His organizing of the Winter Olympic Games and the picture of Nazi Germany he presented to foreign visitors had greatly impressed the ouside world. More important, Hitler took good note that France and Britain were busy all that winter trying — or seeming to try — through the League of Nations to stop Italy's aggression in Abyssinia. Their attention was diverted

---

* Actually, not only the embassy, but French consulates in the Rhineland, as I learned much later, had warned Paris for more than a year — since October, 1934 — of increasing German preparations to reoccupy the Rhineland. Unfortunately, the French government and, more unfortunately, the French army, insisted on ignoring the warnings. See the author's *Collapse of the Third Republic*, pp. 251–260.

from Berlin and from warnings that the Nazi ruler was cooking up something in the Rhineland.

Then on February 27, 1936, the French Chamber of Deputies, after a fortnight's debate, approved the Franco-Soviet Pact by an unexpectedly large majority, 353 to 164. Hitler had his excuse. I note from my diary that I at last began to wake up to what was afoot. On February 28 I wrote:

> The French Chamber has approved the Soviet Pact by a big majority. Much indignation in the Wilhelmstrasse.° Fred Oechsner [chief of the U.P. bureau] says that when he and Roy Howard [head of the Scripps-Howard newspapers] saw Hitler day before yesterday, he seemed to be very preoccupied about something.†

I still did not put two and two together, as my diary note makes clear. Not even five days later, though I was making slight progress.

> Berlin, March 5. Party circles say Hitler is convoking the Reichstag for March 13, the date they expect the French Senate to approve the Soviet Pact. Very ugly atmosphere in the Wilhelmstrasse today, but difficult to get to the bottom of it.

The atmosphere was not only ugly but confused. It was obvious that something very important was up, that we were in for another Hitler surprise. But my contacts in the party and government were not sure just what. Perhaps, I thought, Hitler was hesitating, as he sometimes did.

On this I was wrong. We know now, from the German secret documents captured after the war, that on March 1, two days after the vote in the French chamber, Hitler made his decision, much to the consternation of his top generals, most of whom were convinced that the French army would annihilate the small German forces gathered for the move into the demilitarized zone of the Rhineland. Disregarding them, Hitler had Blomberg issue formal orders the next day for the takeover. It was, Blomberg told his senior commanders, to be

---

° Traditionally, journalists, when they attributed anything to the "Wilhelmstrasse," meant the German Foreign Office, which was located on that short but famous street in Berlin. But Hitler's chancellery, as well as Goebbels' Propaganda Ministry and Rudolf Hess's party offices, were also in the Wilhelmstrasse. Hence, I sometimes attributed whatever I picked up from any of these places to the "Wilhelmstrasse."

† François-Poncet saw Hitler four days later, on March 2, and found him, as he reported to Paris, "nervous, excited and disturbed." The French ambassador had come to plead again with Hitler for a "peaceful rapprochement" between France and Germany. The Führer, the envoy noted, looked "very impatient, very much annoyed" at this. He asked his visitor to keep their meeting secret, which François-Poncet thought a little strange.

a "surprise move." The general said he expected it to be a "peaceful operation." If it turned out that the French, contrary to Hitler's opinion, would fight, the commander-in-chief reserved "the right to decide on any military countermeasures." I learned six days later what they were: a quick retreat back over the Rhine!

At midnight on Friday, March 6, after a hectic day scrambling around Berlin trying to find exactly what was going to happen, I scribbled in my diary: "This has been a day of the wildest rumors." However, I managed to pin down some facts.

Hitler had convoked the Reichstag for noon the next day and summoned the ambassadors of Britain, France, Italy and Belgium to the Foreign Office at 10 A.M. Since these were the other four Locarno powers it was obvious from that and from what I could pry out of party circles that Hitler intended to denounce the Locarno Treaty,* which exactly a year ago he had sworn to the Reichstag he would "scrupulously respect." My guess was that Hitler would proclaim an end to the demilitarized zone of the Rhineland, though the Foreign Office savagely denied this. Whether he would send in troops I simply could not ascertain for sure. Some informants said yes, others no. To me it seemed too big a risk, I noted in one of my dispatches that evening, "in view of the fact that the French army could easily drive them out." I also reported that there had been much opposition to Hitler from the generals, the Foreign Office and Dr. Schacht.

> Berlin tonight full of Nazi leaders hurriedly convoked for the Reichstag meeting [I wrote in my diary at the evening's end]. Saw a lot of them at the Kaiserhof and they seemed in a very cocky mood. Was on the phone to Dr. Aschmann, press chief of the Foreign Office, who kept giving the most categorical denials that German troops would march into the Rhineland tomorrow. That would mean war, he said. Wrote a dispatch which may have been a little on the careful side. But we shall know by tomorrow.

A little on the careful side was right!

At dawn the next morning, March 7, 1936, German troops began

---

* The Locarno Pact, signed in October, 1925, by the Big Four Western powers (Britain, France, Italy and Germany) and by Belgium guaranteed the frontiers of Belgium and France with Germany as fixed by the Versailles Treaty, including the demilitarized zone of the Rhineland. Articles 42 and 43 of the Versailles Treaty had stipulated that in the strip of German territory on the west bank of the Rhine and a zone 50 kilometers wide on the east bank Germany could not maintain troops nor build fortifications. It was part of the price paid to France in 1919 for abandoning Marshal Foch's demand that the territory on the west bank be awarded outright to France. The demilitarized zone gave France and Belgium some security against a repetition of the sudden German invasion of 1914.

marching into the demilitarized zone of the Rhineland. An hour or so later a small token force crossed the Rhine and made for the three main German towns on the demilitarized left bank, Aachen, Trier and Saarbrücken.* According to my local correspondent in Cologne, who began phoning in his eyewitness reports early that morning, it was a *parade*. The gray-clad Reichswehr troops simply marched in behind blaring bands — there was no battle order whatsoever. In Cologne and in other cities and towns delirious crowds of Germans greeted the soldiers, cheering them and throwing flowers into their ranks. There was no sign, my correspondent said, of any reaction from the French across the border.

This puzzled me. God knows I had seen the rot in France during my return to work there in 1934. Frenchmen were more concerned with fighting Frenchmen than Germans. Still. With their army so much more powerful than Hitler's it seemed incomprehensible that they would not march with so much at stake: not only the security of the northeast frontier, over which had come so many German invasions in the past, but perhaps the overthrow of the Nazi regime. Most of us in Berlin that fateful day of March 7, 1936, foreigners and Germans, realized that if the French army moved, as I noted in my diary that evening, *that* would be the "end of Hitler."

> He's staked all [I wrote] on the success of this move and cannot survive if the French humiliate him by occupying the West bank of the Rhine.

At 10 A.M., Hitler's compliant foreign minister, Constantin von Neurath, received the ambassadors of France, Britain, Belgium and Italy and handed them a long memorandum (written by Hitler) apprising them that because of the Franco-Soviet Pact, Germany no longer felt bound by the Locarno Treaty and was therefore, "as from today," occupying the demilitarized zone of the Rhineland.

Then came a typical Hitler stroke. Having just broken the treaty on which the peace of Western Europe had been established, he proposed new plans for peace — a seven-point program, no less. As

---

* According to the testimony of General Alfred Jodl at Nuremberg, only three German battalions crossed the Rhine, and only one division was employed in the occupation of the entire demilitarized zone on both banks of the Rhine. Allied Intelligence estimates, on which I based my own dispatches, werre much larger: some thirty-five thousand men or approximately three divisions. Hitler himself told his cronies later: "The fact was I had only four brigades." Whatever the figures, the German forces were no match for the French, either in numbers or armament or training.

François-Poncet would later quip: "Hitler struck his adversary in the face, and then declared: 'I bring you proposals for peace!' "*

They sounded fine — Hitler's "peace" proposals always did and always would, for he was a master propagandist. Actually, as I angrily confided to my diary that night after an exhausting day, they were "pure fraud,"

> and if I had any guts, or American journalism had any, I would have said so in my dispatch tonight. But I am not supposed to be "editorial."

Hitler offered to sign a twenty-five-year nonaggression pact with France and Belgium, to be guaranteed by Britain and Italy, but of what good was a new pact when the old one, which called for exactly the same terms, had just been broken? But Hitler's hypocrisy was even more brazen in a further proposal he made to demilitarize *both* sides of the western frontier. This would have forced France to scrap her Maginot Line, now, with the Rhine occupied, her last protection against another German invasion. It had taken nearly ten years and billions of dollars to build.

At noon that day I went over to the Kroll Opera† to hear Hitler address the Reichstag. He turned it into a spectacle I never forgot. It was fascinating, bizarre, gruesome and very German, or at least very Nazi German.

There was a good deal of tension on the floor, since most of the brown-shirted deputies (all hand-picked by Hitler) had not yet heard the news though they knew something was afoot. The French, British, Belgian and Polish ambassadors were absent from the diplomatic box, but the Italian was there and American Ambassador Dodd. General von Blomberg, the war minister, sitting with the cabinet on the left side of the stage, attracted my immediate attention. His face was as white as a sheet. He kept fumbling the top of the bench with his fingers. I had never seen him in such a nervous state.

Hitler began, as he nearly always did, with a long recitation of the injustices of Versailles and the peacefulness of the Germans. Then his voice, which had been low and hoarse, suddenly rose to a shrill, hysterical scream. He had arrived at another old and favorite subject,

---

* André François-Poncet: *The Fateful Years. Memoirs of a French Ambassador in Berlin. 1931–1938*, p. 193.

† After the fire in the Reichstag in 1933, Hitler had decided not to have the great building repaired, though only damage to the interior had occurred. Sessions of the Reichstag were held in the Kroll Opera House, an appropriate place for such theater, I always thought.

the horror of Bolshevism, with which the French had just made a hateful pact.

> I will not have the gruesome Communist international dictatorship of hate descend upon the German people! This destructive Asiatic *Weltanschauung* [view of life] strikes at all our values! I tremble for Europe at the thought of what could happen should this destructive Asiatic conception of life, this chaos of the Bolshevist revolution, prove successful!

The sausage-necked, fat-bellied, brown-clad deputies leaped to their feet and applauded. Hitler lowered his voice to explain that France's pact with the Soviet Union had invalidated the Locarno Treaty — a dubious argument since there was no connection. Then he paused (he was a master at pausing), cast his hypnotic eyes about the vast hall, and in a solemn, deep, resonant voice resumed:

> Germany therefore no longer feels bound by the Locarno Treaty. In the interest of the primitive rights of its people to the security of their frontier and the safeguarding of their defense, the German government has reestablished, as from today, the absolute and unrestricted sovereignty of the Reich in the demilitarized zone!

This was the news the deputies had been waiting for. The ensuing scene I got down as accurately as I could that night in my diary.

> Now the six hundred deputies, personal appointees all of Hitler, little men with big bodies and bulging necks and cropped hair and pouched bellies and brown uniforms and heavy boots, little men of clay in his fine hands, leap to their feet like automatons, their right arms upstretched in the Nazi salute, and scream "Heil's," the first two or three wildly, the next twenty-five in unison, like a college yell.
> Hitler raises his hand for silence. It comes slowly. Slowly the automatons sit down. Hitler now has them in his claws. He appears to sense it. He says in a deep, resonant voice:
> "Men of the German Reichstag!"
> The silence is utter.
> "In this historic hour, when in the Reich's western provinces German troops are at this minute marching into their future peace-time garrisons, we are all united in two sacred vows."
> He can go no further. It is news to this hysterical "parliamentary" mob that German soldiers are already on the move into the Rhineland. All the militarism in their German blood surges to their heads. They spring, yelling and crying, to their feet. . . . Their hands are raised in slavish salute, their eyes, burning with fanaticism, glued on the new

god, the Messiah. The Messiah plays his role superbly. His head lowered as if in all humbleness, he waits patiently for silence. Then, his voice still low, but choking with emotion, he utters his two vows:

"First, we swear to yield to no force whatever in the restoration of the honor of our people, preferring to succumb with honor to the severest hardships rather than to capitulate. [He's preparing the people for whatever happens if the French march, I thought. But nothing will save him if that happens.]

"Secondly, we pledge that now, more than ever, we shall strive for an understanding between European peoples, especially for one with our western neighbor nations. . . . We have no territorial demands to make in Europe! . . . Germany will never break the peace!"

It was a long time before the cheering stopped. Finally Göring, president of the Reichstag (among his many offices), pounded his gavel and declared the session over and the deputies streamed out to the lobby of the Opera House, still under the magic spell of their leader, acting as if they — or Nazi Germany — owned the earth. A few generals made their way out. Behind their smiles I thought I detected a distinct nervousness. It was 2 P.M., and they had been away from their offices for more than two hours. Perhaps while they were away, I thought, the French had marched.

I waited outside the Opera until Hitler and the other bigwigs had driven off and the burly S.S. guards would let us through. I walked through the Tiergarten with John Elliott, of the *New York Herald-Tribune*, to the Adlon, where we lunched. We were too taken aback to say much.

Before returning to the office to start writing my dispatch, I walked through the Branderburger Tor and out into the Tiergarten to breathe some fresh air and collect my thoughts. Near the Skagerakplatz I ran into General von Blomberg, walking along with two dogs on leashes. His face was still ashen, his cheeks twitching.

"Has anything gone wrong?" I wondered. Perhaps the French had finally begun to move? I was tempted to stop and ask him, but the general never spoke to correspondents except at a press conference or one of Rosenberg's evenings. He greeted me warmly enough; I nodded, and let him go.

The rest of the afternoon and early evening I was absorbed hammering out my dispatch. Because it was Saturday — Hitler's surprises seemed to be timed for Saturdays* — and American Sunday

---

* It did look as though Hitler timed his big gambles in foreign policy these first years for Saturdays, when, he had been told, British cabinet members and other high officials were away from London, scattered about in their country places for the British weekend, during

morning papers went to press early, I kept phoning my account in short takes to our Paris office for forwarding to New York. Each time, beginning that afternoon, I would inquire what the French were going to do.

"Nothing, so far," our Paris correspondent reported. But late in the evening, as I phoned in my last take, he said the French government, which he said had been meeting all day with the General Staff, had at least come to a decision.

"So they're going to march!" I said.

"No," came the answer. "They're not going to march. They're going to appeal to Geneva. To the League of Nations."

I could not believe it.

As I cleared my desk before going home I looked out the window, down the Wilhelmstrasse. Endless columns of storm troopers were parading down the street past the Führer's Chancellery in a torchlight procession, leaving a ribbon of light in the night. My German assistant, whom I had sent down to have a look, phoned that Hitler, apparently tireless and almost in a jovial mood, was taking the salute from his balcony.

"Hitler has got away with it!" I began my diary the next day. This was apparent not only in the news that began to come in over the wires from Paris and London, but from the smug smiles on the faces of Hitler and Göring, Generals von Blomberg and Fritsch, as they sat

---

which they stubbornly refused even to think of affairs of state. Just a year before, on March 16, 1935, also a Saturday, he had risked defying the peace treaty and decreed a new conscript army. Hitler, it was said, was confident that if the British government did not function on weekends, this would discourage the French from asking for British backing against Germany, without which France would not move.

Actually, in the Rhineland crisis that weekend, as I would later learn, that is what happened. Though the French ambassador in London, the veteran Charles Corbin, called on Anthony Eden, the British foreign minister, early Saturday morning, shortly after the German march into the demilitarized zone began, Eden put him off by making it clear that nothing could be decided in London until the following Monday, when the prime minister and his colleagues would be back from their weekend in the country. He would not listen to the Frenchman's plea that such a delay would give the Germans forty-eight hours to consolidate their hold on the Rhineland without interference. No English cabinet member, and especially the lethargic prime minister, Stanley Baldwin, was going to ruin the traditional English weekend.

Much later, from talking to Eden himself and from perusing his memoirs, I became convinced that the British foreign minister used the fact of the weekend off as an excuse to dampen the likelihood of the French marching. After that it would be too late. This was a time when British foreign policy made no sense to me. It seemed astonishingly suicidal. French foreign policy, as well. From my study of the French records much later, I am convinced that even if the British had been more encouraging France would not have marched that weekend. There was a complete paralysis of the French General Staff and almost as bad a one in the French government. This was a caretaker government presided over by Premier Albert Sarraut, a wheelhorse radical socialist politician, until the elections at the end of April.

in the royal box at the State Opera and for the second time in two years celebrated in this place Heroes Memorial Day, less for honoring the memory of the nation's war dead than for the Führer's boldness in again defying solemn treaties.

Again the ornate State Opera House seemed an appropriate setting for this Sunday's memorial celebration. Again there was a Wagnerian setting, a floodlit stage full of steel-helmeted soldiers bearing war flags. In the royal box sat Adolf Hitler, gracious and smiling, surrounded by Germany's past and present generals. His simple brown party uniform, his Iron Cross pinned over the left breast pocket, was quite a contrast to the glittering uniforms of the generals surrounding him. But, of course, I thought, this was deliberate, to emphasize to the public that he was at heart a modest leader, a man of the people, who had been a simple soldier in the Great War. No fancy uniforms for him, as there were, for example, for the strutting Mussolini.

Again, as last year, General von Blomberg delivered the Memorial Day address. For a man who looked frightened to death in the Reichstag twenty-four hours before and later that Saturday afternoon in the Tiergarten, the general was surprisingly defiant — even cocky. But then I remembered that he was merely uttering words prepared for him by his Master.

"We do not want an offensive war," he said. "But we do not fear a defensive war."

But, of course, he does, I reflected. On my way to the Opera I had learned from a source in the General Staff that the German troops that marched into the Rhineland the day before had strict orders to beat a hasty retreat if the French army moved against them. They were not prepared, or equipped, in the opinion of the General Staff, to fight the French regular army, which had been building up for eighteen years while Germany remained disarmed. Hitler had simply been bluffing.

After the ceremony at the Opera I called up our London office to check on what the British were going to do. My inquiry drew hearty laughter. The prime minister and the cabinet, I was told, had not yet returned from the weekend. Much of the Sunday press, especially Garvin's *Observer* and Lord Rothermere's *Dispatch*, actually welcomed Hitler's move, my London colleagues said. They had just got a copy of the lead editorial for tomorrow morning's *Times* of London. While deploring Hitler's precipitate action, this most influential of all British newspapers entitled its editorial: "A Chance to Rebuild."

The French, regardless of what the British did, had had a chance to stop Hitler and probably bring about his downfall. But by late that

Sunday afternoon, it became clear to me that they had let it slip by. The French army was not going to march. The French government was going to appeal to the League of Nations, which had just showed its spinelessness and helplessness by its failure to halt Mussolini's aggression in Abyssinia. I was sure that if the French army had budged it would easily have turned back the Germans in the Rhineland, and that that would have been the end of Hitler and of Nazi Germany. At 3 A.M. Sunday morning, I put down that feeling in my diary.

> Why it [the French army] doesn't march, I don't understand. Certainly it is more than a match for the Reichswehr. And if it does, that's the end of Hitler. He's staked all on the success of his move and cannot survive if the French humiliate him by occupying the west bank of the Rhine.

The next Sunday at noon, as I've mentioned, I learned that General von Blomberg had given strict orders to his contingents in the Rhineland to retreat if the French army moved against them. None knew better than the defense minister that the fledgling new German army, which Hitler had decreed barely a year ago, could not offer more than token resistance to a much larger and better-equipped and -trained French force.

For years some of my colleagues in Berlin and good friends in London and Paris disagreed with me that the French army could have easily disposed of the Reichswehr detachments in the Rhineland had it marched, and that this would have meant the fall of Adolf Hitler. But in time, confirmation of my conclusions came from the best possible sources — from Hitler and his generals themselves. At the Nuremberg trial in 1946 General Jodl testified that the German High Command, on learning that the French were concentrating thirteen divisions on the frontier, wanted to pull back.

"Considering the situation we were in," Jodl told the tribunal, "the French covering army could have blown us to pieces."*

Hitler, we now know, agreed: "If the French had marched into the Rhineland," he said, "we would have had to withdraw with our tails between our legs, for the military resources at our disposal would have been fully inadequate for even a moderate resistance."†

And what would have happened to him and his dictatorship if that had occurred? Hitler answered that question too.

---

* *TMWC. Trial of the Major War Criminals.* Nuremberg documents and testimony. Vol. XV, p. 352.
† Paul Schmidt: *Hitler's Interpreter,* p. 41.

"A retreat on our part," he conceded, "would have spelled collapse."*

The dictator was not so confident as he had seemed that Saturday morning in the Reichstag or on the Sunday morning at the ceremonies of Heroes Memorial Day. "The forty-eight hours after the march into the Rhineland," he later confessed, "were the most nerve-wracking in my life."†

Still, he stuck to his iron resolve to carry through the operation and to his gamble that the French would not move. He bluntly refused all requests of the generals to pull back. In fact, he later told General Gerd von Rundstedt, he regarded Blomberg's request to withdraw as nothing less than cowardice.‡

It was the first time, but not the last, that Hitler in the midst of a crisis of his own making would stand firm while his generals wavered.

The German people were highly pleased at Hitler's bold move. The Rhinelanders above all. Dosch-Fleurot had flown up from Rome to the Rhineland to help our coverage and that evening he came through with a story, which I forwarded by phone to Paris for New York. He said that Catholic priests met the German troops at the Rhine bridges and conferred blessings on them. In Cologne cathedral, he reported, Cardinal Schulte praised Hitler for "sending back our army." Very quickly, Dosch thought, the Rhineland Catholics had forgotten the Nazi persecution of the Church.

Very cleverly Hitler, as he had done on such occasions before, called for a national referendum on his move into the Rhineland. The result was a foregone conclusion. What German would oppose such a stirring act? Though we foreign correspondents found irregularities at some of the polling places we were able to check on election day, March 29, there is no doubt that the vote approving what Hitler had done was overwhelming. According to the official figures, some 99 percent of the 45,453,691 registered voters went to the polls, and 98.8 percent backed the dictator.§

In my dispatches and diary that weekend I wrote a great deal about the significance of Hitler's move into the demilitarized Rhine-

* *Hitler's Secret Conversations*, pp. 211-212.

† Schmidt, op. cit., p. 41.

‡ *TMWC.* Vol. XXI, p. 22.

§ Here and there Dr. Goebbels did overdo it. Dr. Hugo Eckener told me that on his new Zeppelin *Hindenburg,* which the propaganda minister had ordered to cruise over Berlin and other cities as an election stunt, the *Ja* vote, announced by Goebbels as forty-two, was two more than were aboard.

land and of France's failure to effectively react to it, but it was only years afterward that I could comprehend their true magnitude.

"And so goes the main pillar of the European peace structure, Locarno," I wrote in my diary the day German troops crossed the Rhine. This was a crushing blow to the rest of Europe, to be sure, but there were other consequences. By his bold action Adolf Hitler greatly strengthened his dictatorial grip on Germany and exposed the disarray and the supineness of the Western democracies. We can see now that the coup in the Rhineland was a milestone on the road to war. It brought about a fateful change in the military balance of power in Europe.

In retrospect I see that the Nazi dictator's successful gamble brought him a victory more staggering and more fatal in its immense consequences than I could possibly realize at the time. At home, as the vote in the referendum showed, it fortified his popularity and his power, raising them to heights that no German ruler of the past had ever achieved. It assured, finally, his ascendancy over his generals, who had hesitated and weakened at a moment of crisis when he had held firm. It taught them that in foreign politics and even in military affairs his judgment was better than theirs. They had feared that the French army might fight. He knew better.

And most important of all, as Hitler saw more clearly than any other statesman in Europe (with the possible exception of Winston Churchill in England, who was, in any case, out of power), the reoccupation of the Rhineland, small as it was as a military operation, had immense strategic consequences in Europe to the detriment of the Western democracies, especially France and her allies in the East, Czechoslovakia, Poland and the Soviet Union.

It is much clearer to me now that France's failure to repel the Reichswehr's battalions, and Britain's failure to back her in what would have been little more than a police action were disasters for the West, from which sprang all the later ones of even greater magnitude. In March, 1936, the two Western democracies were given their last chance to halt, without risk of serious war, the further rise of Germany and, in fact — as we have seen Hitler admitting — to bring the Nazi tyrant and his regime tumbling down. They let the chance — the last chance — slip by.

It took years for even Frenchmen to realize that for France it was the beginning of the end. That spring weekend in the Rhineland the whole structure of European peace and security set up at Versailles and strengthened by the Locarno Treaty collapsed. The French alliances with the countries to the east of Germany were rendered useless. If France would not fight to halt German aggression in the Rhineland when there were no fortifications or a strong German army to challenge her, she certainly would not budge when those fortifications were built and the Nazi armed forces greatly strengthened. Her Eastern allies, the Soviet Union, Poland, Czechoslovakia, Yugoslavia, Rumania, were suddenly forced to realize this. The basis of their security, the assurance of French help in the West if Germany attacked in the East, was destroyed over the weekend.

All this was succinctly put by the German foreign minister, Constantin von Neurath, to the U.S. ambassador to France, William C. Bullitt, who while vacationing in Germany paid a courtesy call on him in Berlin on May 18, five weeks after the coup in the Rhineland.

> Neurath [Bullitt reported to Washington] said that it was the policy of the German government to do nothing active in foreign affairs until "the Rhineland had been digested." He explained that he meant that until the German fortifications had been constructed on the French and Belgian frontiers, the German government would do everything possible to prevent rather than encourage an outbreak by the Nazis in Austria and would pursue a quiet line with Czechoslovakia. "As soon as our fortifications are constructed and the countries of Central Europe realize that France cannot enter German territory at will, all those countries will begin to feel very differently about their foreign policies and a new constellation will develop," he said.[*]

That development now began.

---

[*] NCA. Nazi Conspiracy and Aggression. Part of the Nuremburg documents. Vol. VII, p. 890. (Document L-150)

German troops crossing the Rhine, 1936

Deutsch ist die Saar

The opening of the Winter Olympics, Garmisch, 1936

Hitler turns away from the gold medal winner Jesse Owens as he applauds other athletes at the Summer Olympics

CHAPTER 10

Time Off to Live

1935-1937

In the midst of trying to report daily on so much current history and to interpret it and give it meaning, one attempted to lead some vestige of a personal life too. We were human beings, after all. Or at least we pretended to be.

Sometimes readers at home, judging by their letters, wondered. They would write to inquire whether the person behind the by-line on the dispatches crowding the front pages with tales of crises and calamities ever had any time off to live a normal life. We tried. We managed sometimes to push out of our minds for the moment what otherwise occupied them over a twelve-hour working day. We had wives and children, most of us, and we loved them, played with them and no doubt occasionally cursed them — and they us — just like normal persons elsewhere who were spared living and working in the Hitlerian madhouse. Now and then we stole off for an evening at the opera, the concert house, the theater. In Berlin, despite the idiotic and depressing Nazi banning of Jewish composers, musicians, playwrights and actors, all three houses of art could often be quite good. Since most of us in Berlin reported for morning newspapers at home and had to work nights, we did not often get to these places of entertainment. Or to cocktail or dinner parties. From about 5 to 9 P.M. was the busiest time for most of us. It was then that we made the final checkups of stories we had been working on all day, wrote them, and telephoned them to Paris or London for transmission to New York.

After work, which for me was usually any time between midnight and 2 A.M., a good many of us adjourned to the Taverne, where we had in the corner of the main room a large *Stammtisch,* reserved for British, French and American correspondents. There we would grab a bite to eat, have some wine or beer — or a schnapps, if you liked or needed it — and compare notes on the day's happenings, how we had reported them, and what authorities had tried to thwart us or deceive us. Sometimes a few top German reporters or editors would join us — invited or not — and though occasionally they could be helpful in tipping us off to something or in explaining the in-fighting going on around Hitler, we were always suspicious of them and their news. Three or four, we knew, would come to spy on us for Goebbels or Himmler or Göring or the big boss himself. In Nazi Germany you soon learned how to handle them and, what was also difficult, how to put up with them.

The proprietor of the place, Willy Lehman, called his tavern a *Ristorante Italiano* and the spaghetti and veal were good, but Willy was a big bluff German with nothing Italian about him, and his wife was a slim, timid, rather attractive Belgian woman. Whether it was because he did not kowtow to his Nazi customers or because he seemed too friendly to us foreign correspondents or because his wife was Belgian, Willy was often in hot water with the Nazi authorities, who would threaten to close him down and sometimes did — for good, I think, a year or two after the war came.

Usually presiding over our *Stammtisch* was Norman Ebbutt of the *Times* of London, who sat in the corner seat puffing an old pipe and holding forth in his rather high-pitched voice about the news of the day and how little of it his distinguished newspaper was publishing for fear of offending Hitler. The *Times*'s attitude toward the dispatches of its brilliant Berlin correspondent, the best informed of us all by far, had become, as I have mentioned, a boon to me. Ebbutt regularly fed me information his newspaper declined to print. This often took place in whispers around our big table or during a little walk outside in the dark, where no Nazi agent could see or hear us.

My other colleagues were a varied lot. Three from the *New York Times* were regulars. Guido Enderis, head of the *Times* bureau, was in his sixties and beginning to ail though he invariably sported a gaudy racetrack suit with a loud, bright red tie which made him look hearty and younger. A likable man, rather apolitical and not seeming to mind the Nazis, he had the distinction in the last war of working on as a correspondent in Berlin after America got into the war and his American colleagues were arrested and interned. This may have been because he might have had a Swiss passport — he was of Swiss-Italian origin. Maybe that was why Guido had a very Swiss feeling of neutrality.

He had little interest in, and no sympathy at all for, the hatred most of us felt for the Nazis. He thought we were too ideological — as bad as the Nazis in this. You couldn't work up any ill-feeling toward him for this if only because he had such a delightfully impish sense of humor. He took no one or thing very seriously.

Most of the *Times* copy from Berlin, I gathered, was written by Guido's two assistants. Otto Tolischus, who handled most of the big stories, was a complicated man of Baltic descent, in his forties, profound, studious, deadly serious and a conscientious reporter who dug deep for the news. Al Ross, the second assistant, was amiable, lethargic, extremely likable. From the United Press came Fred Oechsner, the chief of bureau, a quiet, unassuming, able Southerner, who was more troubled than his rival news agency heads about playing the game with the Nazis to get scoops and beats. A number of other U.P. men, most of them then in their twenties, ended up evenings at the Taverne. One was Ed Beattie, who had a moonfaced Churchillian countenance, a nimble wit and a fine store of funny stories and songs with which he often regaled us after a grueling day. The U.P. bureau in Berlin seemed to attract keen young men. Later came Howard K. Smith, who would ultimately make his mark in broadcast journalism, and Richard Helms, who would become a controversial head of the CIA, a post we could not faintly imagine him filling at that time. He gave no promise of being a secret cop. I remember young Helms as a rather innocent, naïve, gentle, charming young man.

One who did give promise of going far was a young embassy secretary who had been transferred from Moscow to Berlin shortly before the war came. This was George Kennan. He struck me as having too good a mind to be in the diplomatic service and, indeed, for a time he confided to me his doubts about remaining in it. He was attracted by the prospects of a literary career — he was already beginning to write short stories (influenced, as I recall, by Chekhov) and some criticism, and he was turning over in his mind a tremendous literary project of directing, editing and, in part doing, new translations of all the major Russian authors from Pushkin through Gogol, Tolstoy, Dostoevski, Turgenev, Chekhov to Gorki. Kennan told me something I had not realized before: that previous translations from the Russian, including those by Constance Garnett, which I had been raised on, were quite inadequate. No translations of any language convey the original completely, a fact that I had learned from my reading in German and French. But Russian, Kennan explained, was a complex language, extremely difficult to translate. Still, Kennan was convinced he could do and direct much better translations of the Russian classics than had been done.

Early in the war Kennan actually received an offer from a leading American book publisher to direct just such a project of Russian translations. He was to translate as many of the great novels as he could and supervise the translations of the others. He was sorely tempted, he said, to resign from the foreign service and devote a good part of the rest of his life to this exciting venture.

In the end, he elected to remain in the foreign service. It proved to be a wise decision. Eventually, after many frustrations, he played an important part in the negotiations in Lisbon for a separate peace with Italy after Mussolini's fall, went on to become our postwar ambassador in Moscow, the head of the planning bureau in the State Department and later, after he finally resigned from the service, a sort of elder statesman, author of several important and beautifully written books on foreign affairs and a luminary of the Institute of Advanced Studies at Princeton.

Other habitués of the Taverne were and remained two of my closest friends. Although unrelated, they had the same last name and both worked for the *New York Herald-Tribune*, one succeeding the other as Berlin correspondent. These were Ralph Barnes, whom I had met in my Paris days and who went on from Berlin to London; and Joseph Barnes, who came from the *Herald-Tribune*'s Moscow bureau to Berlin.

Ralph was a driving, high-strung fellow from Oregon with a catching and sometimes almost naïve enthusiasm for life, journalism and learning. In his Paris days he used to stagger around with a large armful of books, including two or three fat volumes of the Encyclopaedia Britannica. He had a beautiful wife of Armenian background, Esther, whom he had met at his small college in Oregon. They and their two young daughters became our close friends in Berlin, sharing with us Thanksgiving, Christmas and New Year celebrations. Since we were not direct competitors, Ralph and I often worked together on a story, usually helped out by Tess, whose knowledge of her native Europe and the German language proved invaluable to us.

Joe Barnes and I also worked together after he replaced Ralph Barnes. Joe was the most intellectual of all of us correspondents.

Educated at Harvard, where he majored in Chinese and Russian, he had lived and worked for a time in China and in the Soviet Union, where he worked on a collective farm and then in a factory to perfect his Russian. Somewhere along the line he had also picked up French and some German and had been an avid reader. Joe easily could have had a brilliant academic career, but he was not attracted to it, preferring the less intellectual field of journalism.

After his years abroad as a foreign correspondent, he became foreign editor of the *Herald-Tribune* and eventually editor of a short-lived New York daily, *The Star*, which was sort of a successor to the Marshall Field–financed *PM*. But somehow, partly because of the Joe McCarthy hysteria, Joe's career was thwarted in the end. He never quite reached the top in journalism, as I thought he deserved to. Or in book publishing, to which he transferred late in life. His fate kept reminding me of how our country wastes so many of its most talented sons.

Louis Lochner, the veteran head of the Associated Press bureau in Berlin and a Pulitzer Prize winner for his reporting from Germany, rarely came to the Taverne. Married to a German woman, and a close friend of the crown prince and other members of the fallen German royalty, and thoroughly at home in the language, Louis led pretty much of a German life outside the office. Despite his penchant for royalty Lochner did not strike one as snobbish. With his bald head, thick glasses and pedantic manners, he looked like an old-fashioned country schoolteacher.

Lochner had grown up in Milwaukee, where I presume he had learned his German, and he had been in his early days there a Social-Democrat, like so many citizens of this progressive German-American city, and also a pacifist. In 1916, during the Great War, he had sailed abroad on Henry Ford's ill-fated Peace Ship. But by the time I arrived in Berlin, Louis had become more conservative, though I never noted in him strong opinions or feelings about anything. He seemed to like to get along with everybody.

Also, he was a man in perpetual motion. One wondered if he ever paused to reflect. Well informed, with excellent contacts among the Germans, he continually spent his considerable energies in getting "scoops" and "beats," most of them of the most trivial nature, but which I am sure got him the headlines back home and the congratulations of the A.P. management. But he seemed so driven to getting these banal "exclusives" that when the big stories broke, as they did with increasing frequency, Louis seemed mentally unprepared to handle them — they were not "exclusives."

Since the departure of Dorothy Thompson, Sigrid Schultz of the *Chicago Tribune* was the only woman among us regular American correspondents. Like Lochner she was bilingual, having been educated in Germany, where her parents settled before the First World War. Though attractive Sigrid never married. After I came to know her well I had the feeling that she would have liked to but that the luck of life was against her on that. She was a good correspondent, well informed, hardworking, energetic. But, unfortunately, she was not a good writer. She had a passion for politics but no feeling for the American language. Despite — or perhaps because of — having spent most of her life in Germany, she took a dim view of the Germans and loathed the Nazis. Her postwar book was entitled *The Germans Will Do It Again.* She had personally seen them do it twice, in 1914 and in 1939, and saw no reason to doubt that there would be a third time.

Such were some of my colleagues, most of whom would end up evenings at the Taverne. The place became for us a momentary haven from the daily strains of living and working in the topsy-turvy, ugly Nazi world. It was a quiet, friendly place in which to gather after another day of battling against the insufferable Nazi hacks and feeling battered and drained by what we had to see and write. It sort of drew us together and gave us a collective spirit from which to draw encouragement and the strength to face the next uncertain day.

There were other distractions in our somewhat grim life in Berlin. I bought a sailboat for a hundred dollars from a broken-down German boxer Tess and I met in a bar. From the very beginning it provided my wife and me with a quick and inexpensive means of getting away, at least during the summer, from the tensions of Berlin. It proved to be a wonderful tonic to our frayed nerves and exhaustion. It was an eighteen-foot, gaff-rigged wooden sloop with a two-bunk cabin.

On a summer Saturday afternoon, if I felt fairly safe in taking the night off, we would take the streetcar out to our marina on the Havel, one of the larger lakes around Berlin, sail down it for eight or nine miles, anchor in a cove, swim off the boat for an hour, have a drink, fix up some dinner, wash it down with a bottle of wine, and hit the bunks for a good night's sleep after checking the news on the radio to see that nothing very sensational was breaking. (Had it been, we could have sailed or paddled to one of the many cafés dotting the shore, telephoned for a taxi and got back to work.)

Sunday mornings a launch would turn up hawking the newspapers, coffee and rolls. We would breakfast on the deck while thumbing through the newspapers. Though these Nazi or Nazified journals were dull and often insipid, a correspondent often found in them some hint of a story for Monday — usually a background story that might help to elucidate or illumine what was happening in the Third Reich. I would make a few notes from the newspapers for possible use that evening and then throw them all in a bag. Tess and I would have another swim, take an hour of sun stretched out on deck, and sail off, grabbing a sandwich and a beer from our stocks as we tacked back or coasted along with the wind to our mooring. Away from shore, on a sailboat, no matter how small the lake or the bay, you quickly shed your worries, leaving them behind on land. There is a magnificent silence, broken only by the swish of the water against the boat, a soothing feeling of peace and quietude I can get no other way.

And there were vacations, which enabled one to get away from it all — for a week or two or three, enough usually to restore one's sanity.

The first year, 1935, as I mentioned, I briefly returned to New York while Tess went mountaineering in the Alps of her native Austria. Next year, in June, we went to Dubrovnik, a charming old Adriatic port that had once belonged to Venice, then to Austria, which called it Ragusa, and now to Yugoslavia. A shy and attractive young woman with a soft Southern accent was staying at the little Russian-owned pension just outside the town along the rocky Adriatic shore. This was Katherine Anne Porter, whose first volume of short stories, *Flowering Judas*, I had read and admired. Politely but firmly she let it be known that she wished to be left alone, and we respected her wishes. Later, when she had become much more widely known, I got to know her somewhat, but I regretted that an acquaintanceship had not sprung up that June of 1936 at Dubrovnik.

We shared our Dalmatian holiday that year with the Knickerbockers. They were just back from Addis Ababa, where Knick had covered the Italian conquest of Abyssinia. It had not been a pretty story. The Italians had used mustard gas and indiscriminate bombing to augment the slaughter of the primitive Abyssinians, many of whom fought with spears and bow and arrow. The squalor of the Ethiopians was indescribable, Knick said, but so was their valor. It had been impossible to do much actual reporting from the disorganized Abyssinian side. An old friend and colleague of mine, Bill Barbour of the *Chicago Tribune*, Knick said, had tried but had died a miserable death from fever in the attempt to reach a battlefield and had been buried in Addis Ababa. He was one of the first fatal casualties among the American war correspondents.

One of the things that made these vacations away from Berlin so memorable was that my wife and I were deeply in love. Tess was twenty-six that summer and I was thirty-two, a wonderful age for married love and much too early for time and circumstance to take their toll. We felt lucky to have such a happy, exciting, harmonious marriage. The Knicks at that time were gloriously happy too, adding to the joys of us four being together. The next year the four of us would again get together for a vacation, the last holiday we would have before war came.

I find a diary entry from the early Berlin days that reveals what may have been another way of trying to escape from the depressing realities of Hitler's world.

> Have started, God help me, a novel. The scene: India. I was there twice, in 1930 and 1931, during Gandhi's Civil Disobedience movement, and I cannot get India out of my system.

My diary records that I finished the "Indian novel" a year later and that completing it brought "a great load off my mind." I don't doubt that it did. I had done the best I could, worked hard and thrown myself into it. But not to much avail. I have to say the novel was not very good. Fortunately, it was never published, though it almost was. Blanche Knopf agreed to bring it out if I would do some revising. But with the Hitler story becoming increasingly absorbing — and threatening — I did not have the time nor the stamina to do any further work on the book. My agent in New York, Berenice Baumgarten of Brandt & Brandt, wrote to say that she was sure she "could place it very satisfactorily elsewhere as it stands."

This was tempting. Almost every newspaperman and woman, it was said, and I believed, dreamed of writing a novel. I had not only written one, but seemed on the verge of having it published. Writing and publishing a book had freed many a journalist from the drudgery of newspapering and enabled them to devote full time to the muse. I had seen it happen to Hemingway in Paris with *The Sun Also Rises*. Sinclair Lewis had told me in Vienna how it had happened to him with *Main Street*. And now it had just happened to two of my closest friends and colleagues, both originally from Chicago like myself, Jimmy Sheean with *Personal History* and John Gunther with *Inside Europe*.

Unless you could break free, as they had, from dependency on journalism for a living to write books, you probably would never write them — unless you taught at some university.

But I did not want to abandon a job as exciting and, I thought, as important as covering Berlin for the newspapers in the Nazi time. It seemed to me more important and more rewarding than writing novels. Nothing that I, at least, could create in fiction could match the drama we were reporting in our dispatches.

In the end I counted myself lucky that the Indian novel was not published. The portrait of Gandhi, I believe, was good, but it belonged in a book of nonfiction, where eventually I would put it. My invented characters had the depth of cardboard. My women, Tess thought, were terrible.

But this failure did not mean that I had abandoned an ambition some day to write books or that I was not interested in writing novels. As a matter of fact, an idea had begun to sprout in my mind that perhaps in the end the likes of me could best get down the story of our time, insofar as we had lived it and felt it and understood it, in fiction. But not yet. I still lacked the maturity. I was far from sure that I would ever have the talent and the skill. In journalism I knew I had them, already.

I decided to stick to my last.

There were events elsewhere which had repercussions in Berlin, and we had to follow these closely too.

On May 2, 1936, Mussolini's legions entered Addis Ababa, completing the conquest of Abyssinia. It was a triumph of Il Duce not only over the primitive mountain kingdom, but over the League of Nations and the two great Western democracies, France and Great Britain, which had opposed his aggression.

Berlin was delighted. Mussolini's conquest doomed the league, which the Germans felt had been built on their defeat in 1918 and from which, under Hitler, they had withdrawn. The Italian victory also, Hitler was sure, made it certain the Mussolini would never become reconciled to Britain and France, which had orchestrated the league's weak sanctions against him. He was sure that instead Italy could fairly easily be drawn into his camp, helping to end Nazi Germany's isolation.

Hitler's infatuation with Mussolini, his tremendous admiration for him as a statesman and world leader, his absurd overestimate of Italy as a world power, were a mystery to me. At first I could scarcely believe that the Führer took the Duce so seriously. One could understand the German's admiration for the Italian who had been able to set up a Fascist dictatorship ten years before he did. Hitler obviously had learned something from Mussolini's experience. But that the Nazi chief, so astute in sizing up the character of men, could fail to see that the strutting Duce was really made of sawdust, astonished me.* More astonishing even was that Hitler, a realist in assessing the balance of power in Europe, could so far overestimate the strength of Italy and from this moment on court her as an ally, his only ally.

Another event that followed closely on Italy's subjugation of Ethiopia would speed this courtship and bring about an alliance, with consequences eventually fateful for both Fascist dictatorships. The event would prove fateful, too, for Great Britain and France, and would not leave the U.S.A. untouched.

On the evening of July 18, 1936, in Berlin, I noted in my diary:

> Trouble in Spain. A right-wing revolt. Fighting in Madrid, Barcelona and other places.

The day before, General Francisco Franco, retired chief of the General Staff, who had been banished to the Canary Islands, had staged a military revolt in the islands and Morocco which the next day spread to the mainland. The news we got in Berlin was at first sketchy. Both the rebel generals and the Republican government claimed victory. But on July 27 I wrote in my diary:

> The Spanish government seems to be getting the upper hand. Has quelled the revolt in Barcelona and Madrid, Spain's two most important cities. But it's a much more serious affair than it seemed a week ago. The Nazis are against the Spanish government, and party circles are beginning to talk of help for the rebels.

---

* He was not alone. In England George Bernard Shaw and Winston Churchill, who should have known better, publicly hailed Mussolini as a great statesman.

In the next few days it became obvious that this aid would be considerable. After all, a third Fascist country was more than welcome to Adolf Hitler. And on France's republican border to boot. That would stir up more strife and arouse further fears in France, against which the Führer still thirsted for revenge for the defeat of Germany in 1918.[*]

Actually, Hitler's decision to support the rebellion in Spain was taken on July 22, five days after it broke out. The Führer was taking a few days off at this time of year, as was his custom, to attend the Wagner Festival at Bayreuth. On the night of the twenty-second an urgent letter from Franco appealing for German aid was delivered to him after the evening's performance. Hitler called in Göring and General von Blomberg, who happened to be in Bayreuth, and that very evening the decision was taken to give military aid to the Spanish rebels.

Though it never equaled that of Italy, which dispatched more than fifty thousand troops as well as vast supplies of arms, tanks and planes, it was considerable. The Germans themselves estimated that they spent more than half a billion marks ($125,000,000) on the venture, much of it for, besides arms, thirty anti-tank companies it dispatched to Spain and the 6,000-man-strong Condor Legion, an air force unit, supported by armored ground troops, which distinguished itself by the obliteration of the Basque town of Guernica and its civilian inhabitants. Relative to Germany's own massive rearmament it was not much, but it paid handsome dividends to Hitler.

Besides helping to assure Franco's triumph and the destruction of another European democracy, thus gaining what he hoped would be another Fascist ally hostile to neighboring France and, probably, to Britain (despite London's pro-Franco slant), the Nazi dictator could count further benefits. The Spanish Civil War had begun to tear France apart, the Right working for Franco against its own government, the Left striving to save the Spanish Republic, each side accusing the other of treason. It caused further dissension between France and Britain, the former with its Left Popular Front government feeling that its own survival was threatened by a Franco victory, the latter, with its Tory government, sympathetic to the conservative, anti-Communist zeal of the rebel generals.

A victory for the Franco forces, Hitler saw, would also be a blow

[*] France, Hitler had written in *Mein Kampf*, was "the inexorable mortal enemy of the German People. . . . There must be a final active reckoning with France . . . a last decisive struggle. . . ."

to the Soviet Union, which alone among foreign nations had come to the aid of the Republic in Madrid, no doubt hoping that if the rebellion was put down, Spain might emerge Communist. Contrary to Nazi and other right-wing propaganda, the Spanish Republican government was not Communist and never had been.

Another dividend in supporting Franco was that it enabled Germany, as Göring later boasted, to test its new guns, tanks, war planes and troops in actual warfare in Spain.*

Much as I loathed Hitler's intervention against the Spanish Republic, I had to admire the cleverness of his policy. It was shrewd, calculated and farsighted.

Probably the greatest gain from the civil war in Spain for Hitler was that it brought Italy into Germany's camp.

In October that first year of the war (1936), before the two Fascist powers recognized Franco's rebels as the legitimate Spanish government, Galeazzo Ciano, the Duce's son-in-law and foreign minister, came to Berlin and signed with Foreign Minister Neurath a secret protocol creating a virtual alliance between Germany and Italy. A few days later Mussolini in a bombastic speech hailed it as an "Axis." Thus was born the celebrated "Rome-Berlin Axis," about which we foreign correspondents in those days wrote so much — too much, I can see now. The strutting Duce never failed to boast of it, and Hitler tried to convince the gullible that it was the foundation of a new order in Europe. Eventually, for Mussolini it would spell his destruction and that of his Fascist regime. It would cost Hitler dearly, especially toward the end when Italy hung like an albatross around the Third Reich's neck.

Despite all the tall talk of it in Berlin and Rome and the fears it provoked in London and especially in Paris, I could never take it seriously. It stood for an uneven, unequal partnership. The Italians were a splendid, civilized people with a glorious history and culture, but Italy did not have the natural resources and the industrial capacity to be truly a great power, even with Abyssinia added to its African possessions.

The Rome-Berlin Axis was a façade.

---

* At his trial for war crimes before the International Tribunal at Nuremberg on March 14, 1946, Göring spoke proudly of how the Spanish Civil War had enabled him to test his young air force: "With the permission of the Führer I·sent a large part of my transport fleet and a number of experimental fighter units, bombers and anti-aircraft guns; and in that way I had an opportunity to ascertain, under combat conditions, whether the material was equal to the task. In order that the personnel too might gather a certain experience, I saw to it that there was a continuous flow so that new people were constantly being sent and others recalled." (*Trial of the Major War Criminals.* IX, p. 281.)

❦ ❦ ❦

"April here and no Hitler surprise this spring yet," I had begun a diary entry in Berlin on the eighth of that month in 1937. I could scarcely believe it. It was my first spring in Nazi Germany after nearly three years that Hitler had not shocked Europe with a sudden, bold move.

In his address to the Reichstag on January 30 that year, the fourth anniversary of his taking power, Hitler had proclaimed: "The time of so-called surprises has been ended." For once he was as good as his word. So far, at least. We were already into April. Spring had come. One could almost relax.

A few days before I had been tempted to take advantage of the unusual calm and accept an offer from the Zeppelin Reederei for a free ride home on the new giant airship *Hindenburg,* scheduled to make its initial voyage of 1937 to Lakehurst, New Jersey the first week in May. I had written several stories about this aircraft, which could fly from Frankfurt to New York in two and a half days, half the time of the fastest ocean liners, and make the return trip in an even two days. It would be a new experience and it would get me home for a vacation, and back again, in record time.

But the New York office of Universal was uneasy about my leaving Berlin uncovered. A promised assistant had not arrived, because of a new economy wave at home. So I turned the offer down. Next day the press agent of the Zeppelin company called and offered a passage to Tess. He remembered that she had done much of the research for a series of my articles the year before on the launching of the airship at Friedrichshafen.

For some reason that is now obscure — I must have felt deep down a presentiment — I did not mention the offer to Tess, and politely turned it down on her behalf. Then I forgot about the matter. The transatlantic summer service of the *Hindenburg* was becoming rather routine. The dirigible had made ten regular ocean crossings the year before in its first regular commercial season without incident. They were no longer news.

The last time I had got any play about the airship in the newspapers at home was when the controversy arose over whether the United States would sell Dr. Hugo Eckener enough nonflammable helium to fill his new zeppelin. The previous spring he had told me he was off to Washington to ask his "good friend" President Roosevelt to give him enough helium to fill his balloon. Apparently, the United States was the only nation in the world that had any helium, the only gas that was not highly flammable. I gathered from Eckener later that Roosevelt had been willing enough but that Harold Ickes, the secretary of the interior and a stout anti-Nazi, had opposed giving it to the Germans. In the end Ickes had won out. So that first summer in 1936 of regular commercial flights between Frankfurt and Lakehurst, N.J., the airship had had to use hydrogen gas, which was highly flammable. Perhaps remembrance of that had had something to do with my not telling Tess of my turning down the offer of a free ticket for her on the zeppelin's first voyage of 1937 to America.

About 4 A.M. on May 7 in Berlin I was awakened by a telephone call from Bill Hillman, the head of our bureau in London, saying that the *Hindenburg* had crashed, caught fire and blown up on landing at Lakehurst, N.J., with a heavy loss of life.* New York wanted the German "reaction" — within an hour.

I immediately called Dr. Ludwig Duerr, the airship's chief designer and constructor. It was the first he had heard of it and he simply refused to believe me. I could not arouse anyone else at four o'clock in the morning, but I called back London and gave what German "reaction" was available, chiefly Dr. Duerr's disbelief.

Further sleep was impossible. I was not only in a state of shock about what had happened to the zeppelin and its passengers and crew, but I could not get out of my mind what a narrow escape Tess, and even I, had had. But for a stroke of luck, one of us would have been on that ill-fated airship. I felt better, though, about not having told my wife of the invitation.

Early that morning Claire Trask, the local representative of the Columbia Broadcasting System, called and asked me to do a broadcast about German reaction to the *Hindenburg* disaster. I turned her down — the very idea of talking into a microphone frightened me. And besides, it promised to be a busy day at the office. Cables from New York already had begun to arrive asking for further "reaction" from the Germans, specially from Dr. Eckener and his associates as to what could have been the cause of the *Hindenburg*'s catching fire and blowing up as it was being attached to the mooring mast at Lakehurst. New York also wanted more on the feelings of the Germans at not having been able to obtain from America helium for the dirigible.

Mrs. Trask refused to be cast aside. I finally agreed to do a fifteen-minute talk for CBS though, as I kept telling the lady, I had never done a broadcast in my life. Because of what happened to me subse-

* Eventually thirty-six lives.

quently, I remember some details of that first broadcast rather well. In the first place, the script had to be submitted for censorship to the Air Ministry. I had to turn out the text of the broadcast at intervals between getting off dispatches to Universal. After each page or two Mrs. Trask would rush off with it to the ministry.

Already as nervous as an old hen as the hour for going on the air approached — my stomach was churning — I arrived at the studio fifteen minutes before air time to find that Mrs. Trask, who was to introduce me and time me, had not yet arrived with the censored script. She finally arrived, out of breath, with less than five minutes to go. At least I had a script to read. But I objected to the Air Ministry's cutting out a paragraph saying the Nazi government suspected sabotage of the *Hindenburg* by anti-Nazis. I had already cabled it in a dispatch. An argument over the phone with the Air Ministry ensued, which I lost. When I hung up, a radio engineer had already begun to count down the final sixty seconds. I suddenly had a frog in my voice. What a lot of nerve-wracking commotion before you even began a simple broadcast!

I swallowed. I tried to clear my throat. I began, my quivering voice skipping up and down the scale, my lips feeling parched, my throat dry. After the first page I did begin to lose my fright. But it was a struggle to get through. An ordeal that left me limp at the end. Obviously, this sort of thing was not for me.

That night in my diary I confided: "Fear I will never make a broadcaster."

Tess holding Eileen a few days after her birth

CHAPTER 11

A New Job in a New Field

1937

All that spring and summer of 1937 rumors had been floating over from New York that Universal Service was about to fold. Apparently it had been losing money and Hearst was cutting his losses. This intelligence had spurred me, once again, to begin to look for a new job.

When Frank Knox, owner and publisher of the *Chicago Daily News*, showed up in Berlin in May he asked me if I would be interested in a job on his newspaper. His foreign editor, Caroll Binder, who for many years had been a foreign correspondent for the *News* and who knew me, would be over in July, Knox said, and he would instruct him to get in touch with me and work something out.

In the meantime I renewed my assault on the *New York Times*, which I had begun during the late twenties in Paris and in which I had never had any success. I could never understand why that esteemed newspaper persisted on turning me down for a job. I had first tackled Edwin L. (Jimmy) James ten years before in Paris, when he was head of the *Times* bureau there, and I had gone after him again in 1935, when I was briefly home on leave. James by then was the *Times* managing editor. In New York he was as amiable as ever, and as elusive.

Now, two years later, as the rumors of Universal's demise became more persistent, I once again approached the *Times*. This time I picked on Frederick T. Birchall, who had been an acting managing editor of the *Times* and on "retiring" recently had come to Europe as the journal's chief foreign correspondent. Enamored of a German woman, he spent most of his time in Berlin. Birchall, an Englishman bursting with energy despite his age, had retained his British citizenship throughout a lifetime in journalism in New York. He was friendly enough to me and during that summer, after many a talk (and a drink), we had finally, I thought, come to an understanding. The *Times* would take me on in the fall, probably in its Berlin bureau though I might be sent to Moscow, a prospect that excited me after three years in Berlin. Birchall and I even agreed on a salary, which was not large.

With this bright prospect of finally getting on a newspaper I had always wanted to work for, regardless of whether Universal shut down or not, Tess and I set out on our vacation early in July. We flew from Berlin to London, where we were going to see some old friends and also Caroll Binder, who, I thought, was going to offer me a job on the *Chicago Daily News*. With jobs on two of our best American newspapers practically assured me, I did not have to worry about again being out of work. After a couple of days in London we were going down to Devonshire with the Knickerbockers to stay with Paul Gallico, who since we had first met him at the Winter Olympics in Garmisch had made it as a free-lance writer. Paul was now living the life of an English squire in Devon, even to having a butler, of whom, he claimed, he was deathly afraid — an interesting turn for a tough former sports writer for the *New York Daily News*.

From Devonshire we were crossing over to Paris to see the Exposition and to confer with Seymour Berkson, head of Universal Service in New York, who was vacationing in France and wanted, he had written, to assure me that our news service was thriving and not going to fold. From Paris we planned to head south to the Riviera for some sun and swimming at Lavandou. I would have to return to Berlin after ten days there. But Tess was going to stay on with Agnes Knickerbocker until fall on account of — we were going to have a baby. Our first.

Things in London did not turn out quite as I expected. It felt good to join two of my oldest and closest friends, Knickerbocker and Jay Allen, both noted foreign correspondents, whom I had not seen for some time. We met one evening at Knick's house, where Caroll Binder was to join us. Binder, Jay said, would then and there offer me a job on the *Chicago Daily News*, as Colonel Knox had promised. Binder was cordial enough. We chewed the fat until 2 A.M., I expecting that at any moment Binder would take me aside, say I was hired and where. But he did not. He never faintly hinted at a job.

My diary for that day adds a note about a man I had never heard of.

> Jay also gave me a card to Ed Murrow, who, he said, was connected with CBS, but I shall not have time to see him as Knick and I leave tomorrow for Salcombe, where Tess and Agnes already are installed at Gallico's.

Jay Allen, in seeing us off at the station, had suggested I look up Murrow on my return to London. But this was not possible, as Tess and I were crossing from Plymouth to France without coming back to London. The broadcaster's name slipped out of my mind.

In Paris we marveled at the Van Goghs at the Exposition and I had a drink with Berkson, who assured me there was nothing to the rumors about Universal closing down. In fact, he said, for the first time in its existence it was making money.

Binder's apparent lack of interest had been a little discouraging, but Berkson's assurances bucked us up. So fortified with the knowledge that at least I would not soon find myself unemployed, we caught a train for the Riviera. At Lavandou we had a fine ten days of swimming and sunbathing and sampling various restaurants along the Riviera. And we talked a lot about our future with a new addition to the family. That future seemed bright enough. Hitler and Nazi Germany still pretty well dominated the news, so there was plenty to write about. I was determined to see the story through, if I could.

Berlin was not exactly the ideal place for an American to raise his children in, whether war came or not. For one thing, the young in Germany were being poisoned by Nazi indoctrination, their immature minds stuffed with the most awful nonsense, and they were being dulled by regimentation. It would be difficult to isolate one's children from them. Also there was the continuous tension, the witches' brew of stirred-up hatreds, the brutal suppression of the Jews and dissidents, the eternal sound of jackboots on the pavement, the screeching of Hitler, Göring and Goebbels over the air, all of which did not make for a healthy, sane atmosphere in which to raise one's children. And Tess, as an Austrian, continued to dislike Berlin — and the Germans — intensely, even more than I did.

Still, no job or life was perfect. Ours, we concluded, were pretty good. On that note, after nearly a fortnight in the sun, I returned to

Berlin at the beginning of August. Tess would rejoin me early in September.

The blow soon fell. My diary of August 14, in Berlin:

> Universal Service has folded after all. Hearst is cutting his losses. I am to remain here with INS, the chief Hearst wire service, but as second man, which I do not like.

It wasn't so much that I minded being number two in the bureau. With Dosch-Fleurot, who had brought me to Berlin, it had worked out well. He was a great and wonderful man. Pierre Huss, the INS correspondent, was neither. Besides, he was pro-Nazi and a favorite of the Nazis. He was always advising me to "watch my step" with them.

Huss and I clashed the second day of my transfer to INS. Norman Ebbutt of the London *Times* was departing that evening, having been expelled by Hitler. Since he was a good friend of mine and had been helpful to me in many ways, I intended to join my British and American colleagues in seeing him off at the Charlottenburg station, though we had been warned by Joseph Goebbels, the propaganda minister, that our presence there would be considered an unfriendly act. Huss came into my office and asked me to stay away from the sendoff for Ebbutt. It would embarrass INS, he said, which sold its news service to a chain of Nazi newspapers. It would get him and INS "in bad" with the authorities.

"I can't be that cowardly, Pierre," I told him. And I went.

About ten o'clock on the evening of August 24, a week later, I was in my office knocking out a dispatch. The German office boy came in with a cable. There was something about his face. I glanced at the wire. It was from New York. INS regretted it was unable to retain all the old Universal Service correspondents. I was getting the usual two weeks' notice.

I was a little stunned.

The folding of Universal should have been more of a warning. I guess INS's taking me on had reassured me — at least I would have a job. Things were not working out, though, as I had expected. Binder's coolness should have awakened me. And Birchall's procrastination. I had seen him the day that Universal had gone out of business and naïvely told him I could start working for the *Times* at once.

"It can't be before September first," he had said. "New York is stalling a little on us, I'm afraid." I was afraid it was Birchall who was stalling.

I finished my dispatch, put it on the wire, and went out for a breath of air, strolling along the river Spree down behind the Reichstag. It was a beautiful, warm, starlit August evening, and around the gentle curve in the river came a launch filled with noisy holiday-makers who seemed to have not a care in the world. I envied them.

I tried to think of what to do now. If the *Times* job didn't materialize, where would I turn next? Probably the best thing would be to head for New York as fast as I could, if I could borrow the money for the third-class boat fare. That was where an American had to find a newspaper job during this lingering Depression.

But I had few contacts there. I had been away from America for twelve years. I had never worked in New York. Jimmy James, the big-shot now at the *Times,* had given me the runaround there two years before. Another former Paris foreign correspondent I had known, Wilbur Forrest, was now executive-editor of the *New York Herald-Tribune.* But he had let me know there was nothing doing at the *Trib.*

Who else? I couldn't think of a soul. Maybe with the Depression continuing at home, I was out of luck.

Still in a daze and with the pit of my stomach feeling as if a heavy stone had lodged there, I turned back to the office.

On my desk I noticed a telegram that had come in a few minutes before the fatal wire from INS. I had put it aside until I finished my dispatch. I tore it open. It was from Salzburg.

CAN YOU MEET ME ADLON 8/27 FOR DINNER. . . .
MURROW COLUMBIA BROADCASTING.

He asked me to wire him in Vienna.

Jay Allen, I remembered, had suggested when I was in London that I look this Murrow up. But there had not been time. Jay had spoken vaguely about Murrow, who had recently arrived in London, needing an experienced foreign correspondent for CBS. He apparently, Jay said, had no experience as a journalist himself. He had been director of "talks" or education or something with CBS in New York.

I had never given much thought to radio. In Berlin I tuned in occasionally for spot news and the weather. And once in a while I snatched an hour to listen to a symphony concert or an opera. I had no idea of what radio was like at home. I had left America when it was in its infancy, before the rise of the networks. Doing that broadcast for CBS in May, I had been so nervous I could hardly speak and I had sworn that I would never attempt it again. The network had not asked me to.

As I made my way home that night of August 24, still in a funk at finding myself suddenly without a job, I pondered how to break the news to my pregnant wife on the Riviera.

And I wondered why Murrow had wired me. Proabably, like most visiting VIP's, I decided, he wanted to pick my brains. For some radio talk he must do from Berlin. Or could it be more than that?

I met Ed Murrow in the lobby of the Adlon in Berlin at seven o'clock on Friday, August 27, 1937. I was not in the best of moods. Birchall was still playing games. Several colleagues had congratulated me on the "new job." Birchall had told them that he was taking me on at the *Times.* But he had told me no such thing. I would have to be patient for another week, he had said when I saw him the day after the cable from INS. Jimmy James was arriving from New York over the weekend and Birchall would have to get his approval. This was more of a problem than it sounded. The two veteran *Times* men distrusted and disliked each other intensely. The hell with them both and their goddamn snooty paper, I thought.

As I walked across the Adlon lobby toward the man I took to be Murrow I was a little taken back by his handsome face. Black hair. Straight features. Fine chin. Flashing dark eyes. Just what you would expect from radio, I thought. Or even more, from Hollywood. His neat, freshly pressed dark suit, probably cut in London's Savile Row, contrasted with my crumpled gray flannel jacket and unpressed slacks. He had asked me for dinner, I was now almost certain, to pump me for material for a radio broadcast. Well, I would try to be as civil as possible. He was not the first.

But as we walked into the bar there was something in his manner that began disarming me. Something in his eyes and especially in his speech that was not Hollywood.

We sat down and ordered a couple of martinis. The cocktails came. I wondered why he had asked me. We began talking of mutual friends. I was surprised how many there were. Obviously, we liked the same kind of people: the more liberal and intelligent of the American foreign correspondents, the Labour party people in England, the New Deal crowd at home. We ordered another round of martinis. He spoke of his interest in getting Jewish and other intellectuals out of Nazi Germany. He had headed some university commission that had already placed several of them in jobs at home.

He asked me whether I thought the International Labor Office at Geneva, to which the U.S. belonged though it would have nothing to do with the League of Nations, was at all effective. He was a good friend, he said, of its head, John Winant, former governor of New Hampshire.

He went on about radio in America. The important thing, he said, was its potential. It was not living up to it yet, but it might someday.

"Are you tied up this weekend?" he asked.

"Hardly," I said. "I'll probably badger the *Times* people for the job they've apparently promised me. And I'll get in some sailing. Would you like to sail?"

"Very much," he said. He had a very warm smile. "Good place to talk. On a boat."

Murrow turned and gave me a rather quizzical look. He had a wonderful frown.

"How far are you tied up with the *Times*?" he asked.

"Not far at all," I said. "Birchall's promised me a job for some time now. But it has never quite materialized. He thinks it will next week. That's where it stands at the moment."

"I'm looking for an experienced foreign correspondent," Murrow began, "to open a CBS office on the Continent. I can't cover all of Europe from London."

It was the first good news I'd heard in months.

"Are you interested?" Murrow asked.

"Well, yes," I said, trying to stem the surge I felt.

"How much have you been making?"

I told him.

"Good. We can pay you the same — to start with."

I had hoped he might offer a little more — CBS and NBC had been making a lot of money and paid good salaries, I had heard — but I said nothing. Tess and I could continue to live all right on what I had been making: $125 a week. Even with an addition to the family. Birchall had balked a little at the *Times* paying even that. At any rate, I thought, this was not the time to quibble about salary. It felt good, after the uncertainty of the last few days, just to be offered a steady job.

I could feel Murrow trying to figure out my thoughts. I was taking my time — in case he wanted to raise the ante. Finally, his dark eyes narrowed.

"Is it a deal?" he asked.

"I ... I ... guess so," I said. "This is all rather sudden."

"No more for you than for me," he said, with a slight smile that helped to relieve the tension. "Anyway. Welcome to CBS!"

We had a good dinner. We had coffee. We had brandy. It was getting late.

"Oh, there's one little thing I forgot to mention," Murrow said. "The ... uh ... voice."

"The what?"

"Your voice."

"It's probably terrible. For radio."

"I doubt it. But, you see, in broadcasting it's a factor. And Bill Paley and his numerous vice-presidents will want to hear your voice first. We'll arrange a broadcast for next week. You give a fifteen-minute talk, say, on the coming Nazi party rally at Nuremberg."

My face must have begun to fall. The guy had offered me, in the nick of time, what looked like a good job in a new field. And then he had made it conditional on my voice sounding all right over the air. To someone called Bill Paley.

"Who's Bill Paley?" I asked.

"Bill's the president of CBS. Owns the damned network," Murrow said.

So all depended not on my qualities as a foreign correspondent, on my intelligence, my experience — but on the voice God had given me. What a wacky business! The hell with it, too!

Murrow, obviously, sensed my falling feelings.

"Don't worry about it," he said. "I'm sure it will work out all right."

I did my trial broadcast for CBS from Berlin on the early evening of Sunday, September 5. From the start almost everything went wrong that possibly could. I was terribly nervous, anyway. Even before the snafus began. More so, I felt, than that first (and only) time I had ever broadcast, the day the *Hindenburg* went down in flames and I had reported the reaction from Berlin.

This time there was much more at stake for me. And all depended upon what a microphone and an amplifier and the ether between Berlin and New York did to my voice. I kept thinking of Paley and all those CBS vice-presidents nodding their heads and grunting that the guy's voice was lousy, he would never do, no matter how good a foreign correspondent he was.

It was a wonder I ever got on the air at all. To begin with, Claire Trask, who was again to handle the broadcast, discovered fifteen minutes before air time that she had left the script of her introduction at a café. She dashed out of the studio to retrieve it, leaving me alone with the engineer. As the minutes ticked away, it began to look as if I would have to introduce myself.

The German engineer apologized for the squalor of the studio. It was a dusty, makeshift affair in a nondescript room in the government Post and Telegraph office cluttered with great packing boxes that obviously had been crates for upright pianos. Claire had explained that the studios of the German Broadcasting Company in Berlin were barred to CBS because of an arrangement that gave NBC exclusive use of them. NBC had a similar arrangement with the Vatican, which also refused all broadcasting facilities to CBS.

"One of the first things Bill Paley wants you to do," Murrow had told me, "is to break those two NBC monopolies."

Because the State Post and Telegraph Ministry owned and operated the shortwave transmitters that carried broadcasts to New York, it offered us this studio, which had only a stand-up microphone at one end of the littered room. CBS apparently was the only network that used it.

Claire finally returned, out of breath, with her script. We had a minute to go. At that point we discovered that the floor microphone, which apparently had been set for some eight-foot-tall giant, would not come down. It was stuck at seven feet or so above the floor.

"Sorry!" the German engineer said, advising me to point my head toward the ceiling. I tried, but it so constricted my vocal cords and my breath, that only a squeak came out when I tried to say a few words. A solution struck me suddenly. I motioned toward the piano packing case just behind the mike — it looked to be between five and a half and six feet high.

"*Bitte,*" I addressed the engineer, who had just given us the thirty-second signal. "Boost me up on this, will you please."

He seemed horrified at the idea. This had never happened before, he said. But I grabbed his shoulder and pulled myself up to the top of the box. With the engineer's reluctant help we also boosted Claire up by my side. Our mouths were now level with the microphone. We both began to laugh.

"Quiet, *bitte,*" the engineer called out. "Ten seconds!" There was no time now to get nervous again. My only worry was that I would begin this crucial broadcast with a giggle.

And then we were on the air, and with my spindly legs dangling down the side of the piano crate, I spoke into the microphone as clearly as I could, trying to remember the points Murrow had made in the previous weekend of coaching: to speak slowly, to pause frequently, to stress certain words and phrases, and to keep the talk on a relaxed, conversational tone — above all, *not* to sound as if I were reading a script.

But it was easier said than done. My voice kept jumping up an octave. My throat got dry, my lips parched. Try as I might, I could not contrive to sound as if I were not reading.

"You did awfully well, I think," Claire said, after we had adjourned to a sidewalk café and downed a double schnapps. I was sure I had done terribly.

I was glad I had accepted a last-minute urgent request of the United Press to cover the frenzied annual Nazi party congress at Nuremberg for them. It would relieve the strain of waiting for the verdict from the CBS management in New York. It would give me another week's salary, which I badly needed. And it might even end up getting me a job on U.P. in case the CBS thing fell through.

Murrow had promised to let me know definitely what CBS had decided by Tuesday, two days away. He asked me not to take any other job until I heard from him then. That would not be difficult, though Birchall had told me he would be seeing me in Nuremberg and hoped also to let me know, finally, about the place on the *Times*. By this time I did not take him very seriously. But still . . . it wouldn't do any harm to keep in touch with him this week that would decide my fate, one way or another.

As it turned out, there was not much doing at the party congress that year. There was not much to distract one, as I had hoped, or to make news.

The Jews already had been crushed and eliminated from German life. The so-called Nuremberg laws, proclaimed at the party rally two years before, in 1935, had legalized their suppression. The new conscript army, navy and air force, which Hitler had decreed that same year, were being rapidly built up and readied for war. Hitler's heart and mind, it was obvious, were tied up mostly with them. The party hacks and the S.A. and S.S. storm troopers, who had helped propel him to power, and for whom the annual party congress was the high point of the year, had to be strung along, to be sure, to keep up their spirit and determination. But the Führer found this easy to do with his customary palaver.

The year 1937 was turning out to be one of consolidation for Hitler and his dictatorship. His iron grip on the country was almost total. The once doubting generals were going along, helped by fast promotions, higher pay and the prospect of a vast military machine to run. Rearmament was humming. The churches, Protestant and Catholic, weary of struggle, had pretty well capitulated. The workers, their wages lowered, their unions busted, seemed content just to have jobs again.

We foreign correspondents had to admit that the vast majority of the people seemed squarely behind the Leader. They had enthused at his occupying the Rhineland the year before, humiliating the British and especially the French, who had not had the guts to oppose it. Now Hitler was feverishly fortifying the Rhineland so that the French could not march in from the west once he resumed the historic German march to the east.

There was no word from Murrow as the days in Nuremberg began to slip by. I kept running into Birchall, who kept saying it looked very good for me with the *Times*. In New York, he claimed, they were even considering me for the Moscow post, which I doubted, though the prospect was exciting.

Not hearing from Murrow, who had returned to his post in London, bothered me. When the Tuesday deadline came, all I heard out of him was a wire: EXPECT NEWYORK ANSWER TOMORROW CAN YOU DELAY OTHER DECISIONS WITHOUT JEOPARDIZING.

I did not answer. I figured the top CBS executives had had time enough — two full days — to make up their minds, and had made them up, but were stalling on telling me. When the next two days passed with no peep out of Murrow, I gave up. To hell with CBS, and to hell with the *Times*. As soon as I finished in Nuremberg, I would catch the first boat for New York and start job hunting there.

Friday, September 10, was turning out to be a rough day for a foreign correspondent at Nuremberg. I got back to my hotel dead tired at 6 P.M. after a long afternoon that began with having to listen to Hitler lecture ten thousand party women for two interminable hours about their duty of being good German wives and mothers. He had paid special tribute to the women's leader, a Frau Gertrude Scholz-Klink, a woman I had found particularly obnoxious and vapid. Then I had had to follow the Führer to his hotel, the Deutscher Hof, where he received the foreign diplomats. Though it was a state reception, Hitler could not refrain from making a speech to the foreign envoys, too. Getting back to my hotel there was just time to dash off a dispatch about the two meetings, put on a dry, clean shirt — it had been a stifling hot day — gobble down a sandwich and a glass of beer in my room before going down to hop a bus at 7 P.M. to the Zeppelin Meadow, where Hitler was going to wind up the day with still another long speech to a quarter of a million so-called political leaders of the party.

I had about had it for the day. It suddenly occurred to me, though, that it was Friday evening and I had not heard from Ed Murrow since Tuesday. Was he afraid to call me with the bad news? Surely the CBS brass had come to a decision about me by now. I decided to call Murrow. But there was scarcely time for that. The bus would be leaving in five minutes. I started to knock out a telegram, which I could leave at the desk as I left the hotel.

Just then my phone rang. It was a person-to-person call from London. Murrow was suddenly on the line. I could tell from the sound of his voice when he began to say "Bill, I'm terribly sorry to have kept you waiting so long" what his message was, even though the words themselves were rather ominous.

"The bastards in New York finally came through," he said.

"Yes?"

"They think you're terrific!"

"Really?"

"When can you start?" he asked.

"Any time you want."

"Shall we say October first?"

"Okay."

I dashed off a wire to my wife, who had just arrived in Paris and taken to bed there with some cramps from the expected baby or something. I was late for the press bus, but someone had kept it waiting. It had been raining on and off all week, spoiling the "Hitler weather" of other years, but on this evening, so exciting for me, the skies cleared and the searchlights around the Zeppelin Meadow shot their beams up miles toward the heavens and despite the grating of Adolf Hitler's voice, scratching out across the vast expanse in the night, I felt good.

As luck would have it, I sat next to Birchall at the stadium and I could not refrain from telling him my news. He started to say that the *Times* had really wanted me for the Moscow job. He couldn't quite believe that a journalist as intelligent as I would go over to radio, whose handling of the news was superficial and whose public, he said, wanted entertainment, not news. In radio I would be wasting my time and talent.

"In two or three years, Bill, I'll wager you'll be wanting to get back to newspaper work."

Well, maybe so, I thought. But maybe I'll never go back.

Murrow had fired me with a feeling that we might go places in this new-fangled radio-broadcasting business. We would have to feel our way. We might find a new dimension for reporting the news. Instantaneous transmission of news from the reporter to the listener, in his living room, of the event itself so that the listener could follow it just as it happened (as key speech by Hitler, for example) was utterly new. There was no time lag, no editing or rewriting, as in a newspaper. A listener got straight from a reporter, and instantly, what was taking place. The sound of a riot in Paris, of the pope bestowing an Easter blessing in Rome, or of Hitler and Mussolini haranguing their storm troopers might tell you more than all the written descriptions a newspaper reporter could devise. Going over to radio, I thought, was going to be challenging and exciting.

As we departed Berlin at the end of September, after three years among the Nazis, I noted in my diary:

> I leave Germany ... with the words of a Nazi marching song still dinning in my ears:
> *Today we own Germany.*
> *Tomorrow the whole world!*

Well, I would be coming back to see about that. Though I was moving to another place and was relieved to be getting away from Berlin, I knew I would be returning often. That was where the fate of Europe, and perhaps of the world, was being decided. I wanted to continue to be in on it and to write and now to broadcast about it as best I could. Not often, it seemed to me, in anyone's life, anywhere, in any time, had there been such an opportunity to watch at first hand a mighty surge of history approaching its climax and threatening to envelop the earth.

Though I was not in his class, I perceived that luckily I was roughly in the position of that great Greek historian, Thucydides, whose introductory words in his magnificent *History of the Peloponnesian War* came back to me.

I lived through the whole war, being of an age to comprehend events and giving my attention to them in order to know the exact truth about them.

The CBS foreign staff in 1938: Tom Grandin, the author and Ed Murrow in front of Le Bourget airport

(Left) *After the war began, the author was always checked by guards on entering Broadcasting House in Berlin to do his CBS broadcasts. The contraption under his elbow is a gas mask, which one was forced to lug around.* (Above) *The script was then checked by German censors.* (Right) *Broadcasting from Berlin.*

CHAPTER 12

Return to Vienna. Anschluss. The End of Austria. A Breakthrough in Broadcasting the News

1937-1938

The exciting prospect Ed Murrow had held out of our steering radio into serious broadcasting of the news, at least from Europe, was soon dashed.

After a week of conferring with him in London at the beginning of October, I confided to my diary:

> One disappointing thing about the job, though: Murrow and I are not supposed to do any talking on the radio ourselves. New York wants us to hire newspaper correspondents for that. We just arrange broadcasts. Since I know as much about Europe as most newspaper correspondents, and a bit more than the younger ones, who lack foreign languages and background, I don't get the point.

The point CBS made, Murrow said, was that for us to do the reporting ourselves on the air would commit CBS editorially. Commit the network to what? It made no sense to me.

So much for radio journalism! The idiocy of it staggered me. I felt let down by Murrow and the CBS brass led by William S. Paley. And I had thought — Murrow had told me — I had been hired because of my knowledge and experience of Europe as a veteran foreign correspondent! But since I had been jobless and broke, with a new addition to the family coming, I swallowed my bitter disappointment. I would stay on with this frustrating radio job until I could get back to newspaper reporting. Murrow himself, I quickly learned, would be a grand guy to work with. He was sensitive, serious, intelligent, with a warmth behind his reserve and a droll sense of humor.

We laughed about concocting a title for me that would impress the state-owned European broadcasting companies, whose facilities we would need, and came up with "Continental Representative of CBS" — my domain would include all the Continent except Scandinavia. Murrow, in London, would be the CBS "European Director." We discussed whether I should make my headquarters in Geneva or Vienna — they would have to be in a centrally located neutral country from which I could arrange broadcasts from all nations without censorship.

I knew Geneva from having covered the League of Nations and I did not particularly like the prospect of living and working there permanently. It was too stodgy Swiss. I preferred Vienna, which was more cosmopolitan, more centrally located and with better transportation and communication facilities. It had special charm and cultivation, and it was Tess's native city where we had met, married, and started life together. Ed agreed, and it was to Vienna we went.

In quick trips to Berlin and Rome I succeeded in breaking NBC's monopoly arrangements that had denied CBS broadcasting facilities from Germany and the Vatican. Though Doktor Goebbels, who ran the state-owned Reich Broadcasting Company, was not exactly pleased at my return, even for a few days — he thought I had been got rid of for good — he approved the new arrangement. In the face of foreign hostility and boycotts, it meant that another major American radio network would be broadcasting from Berlin. Because covering Nazi Germany would be one of my major jobs, it was extremely important to have the use of Germany's radio studios and other facilities for our broadcasts.

Breaking NBC's stranglehold on broadcasts from the Vatican had proved a little more difficult. It took only a day or two to strike a bargain with the monsignori who ran Vatican Radio. All they wanted was an initial lump payment of a few thousand lire (a few hundred dollars at the current rate of exchange) plus a modest annual contribution to their well-being. Like all the other foreign correspondents I had had a paid tipster in the Vatican when I worked as a newspaperman in Rome. That's the way it was in the Eternal City. But Bill Paley in New York objected. It smacked of a bribe, he said. CBS would never pay anyone a bribe. It took some days before I could get him to accept the facts of life in Rome.

There was a special reason why I was anxious to straighten things out with Vatican Radio, which had not only denied CBS use of its studios and its facilities for broadcasting from St. Peter's Square but had made it difficult for us to pick up the Vatican broadcasts. Radio had never covered a pope's death and the election of a successor. Pius XI had been on his papal throne since 1922, when radio was just coming in. He was getting along in years and was reported to be in ill health. I had a feeling that broadcasting his death, whenever it came, the elaborate funeral, the election of his successor and the colorful ceremonies of his installation would offer CBS a big breakthrough in covering world news. My diary says I made "elaborate arrangements for radio coverage" of these events before I left Rome.

Paley and Murrow became anxious for me to hurry to Munich to cover a story that was dear to Paley's heart. But my first real "news" assignment since going over to radio did not fire me with much enthusiasm. The Duke and Duchess of Windsor had come to Munich on a mission that seemed to me quite foolish. The duke, who as Edward VIII had given up the throne the previous December to marry a twice-divorced American, Wallis Simpson, was in Nazi Germany, he said, to study "labor conditions." What worse place could an Englishman study the working man! In Germany Hitler had destroyed the labor unions and stolen their funds. To make things worse, the duke and duchess were being taken around by a notorious Nazi ruffian, Dr. Robert Ley, the head of the German Labor Front, the phony organization concocted to replace the suppressed unions. The duke had embarked on this venture as a prelude to a much-advertised trip to America later that fall. That he had done so only reinforced an opinion I had first got in England when he was Prince of Wales — that he was a very stupid man. Paley instructed me to get acquainted with him, accompany him to New York, and arrange for him to broadcast for CBS when he got there.

Luckily it was not in the end necessary. There was such an outcry at home about the duke and duchess visiting America to study the labor situation after first going to Nazi Germany for the same purpose that the trip was called off. In Munich I noted in my diary that "Mrs. Simpson seemed quite pretty and attractive." But she certainly was not beautiful or, I thought, very glamorous. I wondered how she had been able to get such a hold on Edward. It was obvious that she dominated him — perhaps that was what he liked, for he seemed weak. In Berlin I had been told the previous year that she had Nazi sympathies and was a good friend of the then Nazi German ambassador, the nincompoop Ribbentrop. But in Munich, and much later in

America, where I saw the couple occasionally, she struck me as ignorant of politics and uninterested in them. But so, essentially, was the former king.

It was obvious those first months of our return to Vienna that beneath the drab surface of life there was a ferment that threatened to stir up not only Austria, but Europe. A good correspondent ought to be reporting it. But CBS policy forbade it. Paley and the rest of the brass in New York simply would not listen to the pleas of Ed Murrow and me to broadcast the news ourselves. It galled me to have to keep hiring newspaper correspondents to do it.

In Austria the Christian Fascist regime of Dr. Kurt Schuschnigg was crumbling, undermined by a surge of Nazism kindled from across the border in Germany, and by the revival of the Socialists, whom Schuschnigg's predecessor, Dollfuss, had put down so savagely and with so much bloodshed in 1934 before he was murdered by a Nazi gang. Hitler's interest was aroused, and there were rumors of another drastic housecleaning shaping up in Berlin before the Führer made his next move toward the country of his birth. Hitler had never made any secret of the ultimate move. As he had written in the opening lines of *Mein Kampf*, he wanted his native Austria joined to the German Reich.

Beautiful, stately, civilized, *gemütlich* Vienna had become a sad place in the years we had been away. The great baroque and neo-classical buildings were becoming dilapidated, the paint scaling from their walls. The city and the people, as I noted in my diary on Christmas Day of 1937, looked "terribly poor. . . . The workers are sullen, even those who have jobs, and one sees beggars on every street corner." As usual a few people seemed to have plenty of money. You could see them at the expensive nightclubs, the fashionable restaurants and the deluxe hotels. The great mistake of this clerical dictatorship, which was mild compared to the Nazi dictatorship in Berlin, was, as in America before Roosevelt, not to have a social program that would ease the lot of the unemployed, the poor, the ill and the old. Mussolini and Hitler had not made that mistake, but neither had Bismarck in Germany long before.

Tess and I were astonished at the amount of anti-Semitism in Vienna. There had always been a good deal. Hitler's first mentor, Karl Lüger, the Christian Social party leader who had once been mayor, had encouraged it long before the war. The Nazis now were heating it up from underground, promising that when they came to power they would settle with the Jews, as Hitler had done in Germany.

My diary of Christmas Day took notice of these things and also of some that were more personal. We had found a comfortable apartment in the Plösslgasse, next door to the Rothschild palace. The owners, being Jewish, had removed themselves to safer parts. Tess had liked the apartment, but it had one disadvantage. It was on the third floor and climbing the stairs was becoming increasingly difficult for her. Our baby was due in seven weeks. So far, all had gone well with Tess. Her pediatrician did not anticipate any complications.

Though I had left Germany, I was still supposed to cover it for CBS. But cover it how? Ed Murrow and I were busy putting kid choirs on the air for some children's program called "Columbia's American School of the Air." Still, I tried to follow the news, especially in Berlin and Vienna, which by early February, 1938, appeared to be on a collision course. In Berlin itself some kind of an internal struggle was going on that recalled the one in 1934 which led to the Blood Purge of June 30. I kept phoning my contacts in the German capital, mindful that one had to be careful over the phone. They knew something was "cooking," they said, but they were not sure just what. The meeting of the Reichstag called for January 30, the fifth anniversary of the Nazi takeover, had been postponed to February 20. This delay was most unusual.

On Saturday — another Saturday! — February 5, the news from Berlin burst upon us. Hitler had the night before cashiered the two men who had built up the German army from scratch, Field Marshal Werner von Blomberg, minister of war and commander-in-chief of the armed forces and General Freiherr Werner von Fritsch, commander-in-chief of the army. The Führer, a corporal in the Great War, named himself Supreme Commander of the Armed Services. The Ministry of War was abolished. Instead Hitler set up a "High Command of the Armed Forces," of which he was "Supreme Commander."

To make sure that the army accepted this drastic shakeup, Hitler relieved sixteen senior generals of their commands and transferred forty-four others. As a sop to Göring, who had hoped to replace Blomberg, Hitler made him a field marshal.

But that was not all. Neurath, the old-school but compliant foreign minister, was fired and replaced by Ribbentrop. Two veteran career diplomats, Ulrich von Hassell, the ambassador in Rome, and Herbert von Dirksen, the ambassador in Tokyo, were retired, and Franz von Papen, the Führer's minister in Vienna, was relieved of his post, which caused him to become, he later said, "speechless with astonishment." Papen had been zealous in furthering Hitler's interests in Vienna. But he had been somewhat taken aback at the beginning of February when he learned of a plan concocted by Rudolf Hess to stage a riot in front of the German legation in Vienna, have someone murder him, Papen, and the German military attaché, and thus give Hitler an excuse to march his troops into Austria "to restore order." I noted this down in my diary on February 7. I thought Papen, who had narrowly escaped with his life in the 1934 Blood Purge in Berlin, ought to have felt relieved, instead of astonished, to be fired from his post in Vienna. It probably meant that once again, like a cat with nine lives, he would be spared.

Finally, the old financial wizard, Dr. Hjalmar Horace Greeley Schacht, who had played such a key role in propelling Hitler to power and in keeping Nazi Germany from going bankrupt, was replaced as minister of economics by an oily cipher named Walther Funk. This was an extremely important development and I wanted to hurry to Berlin to report it for CBS radio. But Paley and the rest of the management in New York were not interested. I was to continue to put on the juvenile choirs for some kid program. I felt utterly frustrated.

Hitler's housecleaning marked a turning point in the evolution of the Third Reich. The last of the key conservatives in the army, Foreign Office and Economics Ministry, who stood in the way of Hitler's embarking on risky foreign adventures, had been swept away on a winter's weekend. Blomberg, Fritsch and Neurath had been put in office by Hindenburg and the old-school conservatives to act as a brake on Nazi excesses, and Schacht had joined them. Now they had been replaced by younger, more compliant men. Hitler had freed himself to embark on new conquests without being seriously opposed in the army or the Foreign Office or the Economics Ministry.

What provoked the downfall at this particular moment of Field Marshal von Blomberg and General von Fritsch we did not learn until much later. Of all things, matters pertaining to sex destroyed them and almost toppled General Walther von Brauchitsch, who succeeded Fritsch as army chief. Very briefly, this is what happened.

Field Marshal von Blomberg, a widower, had fallen in love with his secretary, one Fraülein Erna Gruhn, and toward the end of 1937 had proposed marriage. The haughty, aristocratic officers corps had

opposed it because the secretary was a commoner. But Hitler and
Göring approved — Göring even had a rival lover shipped off to
South America — and on January 12 the marriage took place, with
the Führer and Göring present as principal witnesses.

A few days later, while the couple began a honeymoon in Italy, a
Berlin police file was discovered. It showed that the bride had a police record as a prostitute and had once been convicted of posing for
pornographic photographs. The new Frau Field Marshal, in fact, had
grown up in a brothel run by her mother.

The officers corps was horrified. Hitler feigned horror himself and
on January 25, two weeks after the wedding, he dismissed his field
marshal. As General Ludwig Beck, chief of the army general staff,
put it: "One cannot tolerate the highest-ranking officer in the armed
forces marrying a whore."

Unsavory as the revelations of the past of Blomberg's bride were,
they were nothing compared to the accusations that now fell upon
General Werner von Fritsch, the commander-in-chief of the army, a
gifted and unbending officer of the old school. Fritsch never concealed his contempt for Hitler and his henchmen, and Heinrich
Himmler, head of the S.S. and Gestapo, had long determined to
"get" him. By the beginning of 1938, Himmler, assisted by his chief
aide, Reinhard Heydrich ("Hangman Heydrich," as he was later
known) and the resources of the Gestapo, had framed the general.
They had sent Hitler "documentary proof" that General von Fritsch
was guilty of homosexual offenses under Section 175 of the German
criminal code, and that he had been paying blackmail to an ex-con-
vict since 1935 to hush the matter up. Summoned by Hitler to answer the charge, the general was too outraged to speak and the
dictator fired him. Later Fritsch was completely exonerated by a military court of honor, which exposed the charge as a malicious frame-
up. But Fritsch was never restored to his post, nor were Himmler and
Heydrich demoted from theirs.

General von Brauchitsch very nearly lost his post at the very moment he was named to succeed Fritsch. Just as he reached the top,
Brauchitsch found his wife refusing to give him a divorce so that he
could marry a woman he had fallen in love with. The Prussian military aristocracy was opposed to divorce and it seems to have questioned the general's fitness to head the army if he persisted in
divorcing his wife. Even the new High Command spent hours pondering the matter. Fortunately for the love-struck general, the new
object of his devotion, unlike that of General von Blomberg, was not

only respectable, but was known in party circles, as Ambassador von Hassell wryly noted, to be "two-hundred-percent Nazi." Aware of this, Hitler and Göring themselves intervened for the troubled new army chief and persuaded his wife to free him.

In the meantime, as Tess and I waited rather anxiously in Vienna for the baby to come, events in Austria were reaching a climax. Adolf Hitler, who had spent most of his youth in this very capital, was now pushing the Austrian Nazis to take over. This was to be preliminary to the achievement of the very first goal of his life: Anschluss — the union of his native Austria with Germany. Having cleaned house in the army and Foreign Office of those who might oppose the venture as too risky, he now moved on Austria with great boldness and lightning speed.*

In his Alpine mountain retreat above Berchtesgaden on February 13, Hitler, in a scene probably unique in modern European history, had rudely threatened and badgered Schuschnigg to turn over Austria to the Nazis or face invasion of the German army. The forty-one-year-old Austrian leader, taken by surprise and overwhelmed by the Führer's threats and fury, had capitulated. He agreed to lift the ban against the Austrian Nazi party, to amnesty all Nazis in prison, including the murderers of Schuschnigg's predecessor, Dollfuss, and to appoint Austrian Nazis to key cabinet posts, giving them charge of the police, the army and the economy, the last of which was to be "assimilated" into the German economic system. As Schuschnigg later admitted, he was signing the death warrant of Austria.

Perhaps, I thought, I could interest CBS in the end of Austria. Its conquest would be Hitler's greatest triumph yet. I asked for fifteen minutes of air time to report on it. No interest. I had obtained a lot of inside information about the horrendous meeting of the two chancellors at Berchtesgaden that, so far as I knew, had not been published or broadcast. Nothing doing. I was told to continue to present my children's choirs — the next such broadcast was scheduled from Sofia on February 24. CBS, uninterested in the news, was especially pleased that I was arranging also to present the king of Bulgaria, no less. My superiors suggested I leave Vienna for the Bulgarian capital no later than February 22, so I would have plenty of time to prepare

---

* Publicly Hitler had continually promised that he would let Austria alone. On May 21, 1935, for instance, he told the Reichstag in his famous "peace speech" that "Germany neither intends nor wishes to interfere in the internal affairs of Austria, to annex Austria or to conclude an Anschluss." In an Austro-German Agreement signed on July 11, 1936, Germany reaffirmed its promise not to interfere in the internal affairs of Austria.

the program. I was reluctant to go. The story breaking in Vienna was really too important to leave uncovered — and I still hoped to convince the CBS brass to let me report it. Besides, our baby was due any moment.

But I went, spending my birthday, February 23, on the Orient Express as it puffed its way down through the snow-covered Balkans. No foreign correspondent let his personal life interfere with his assignments, however asinine. Despite having acquired a wife, and the both of us being young, I had had little personal life the last few years.

I returned from Sofia on the afternoon of February 26 to be greeted at the Vienna East Railroad Station by an old colleague with the news that that morning I had become the father of a baby girl. My good wife, after a last-minute emergency cesarean operation to save her life and that of her child, would, the doctors thought, survive. I hurried to the hospital.

Tess, it was obvious, had had a very narrow escape but she did not dwell on it. She wanted to show me what a beautiful child we had. I must say I thought it one of the most attractive babies I had ever seen. Fine color, well-shaped, already full of beans, with flashing blue eyes and a lovely face. But I was taken aback at Tess's appearance. She looked drained and was so weakened from her ordeal she could talk and breathe only with what seemed a desperate effort.

Neither her doctor nor the nurses who examined her on arrival at the hospital two days before had anticipated any complications. But the most simple one imaginable had developed. For forty-eight hours Tess was in labor, but nothing came of it. The child, though of normal size, would not squeeze through. Drugs to force it were tried but did not work. The obstetrician tried to pry it out with forceps but failed. This was a Catholic hospital and apparently the nurses, mostly nuns, kept insisting on a natural birth though every painful hour showed that this was improbable if not impossible. Finally, on the morning of the third day, the doctor, who was Jewish, in desperation to save the life of mother and child, had performed an emergency cesarean section. It had been a close thing, he told me. I wondered why he had waited so long, regardless of the nurses, to operate. But I did not ask him. For the moment I was immensely grateful that Tess and the baby were alive.

I spent most of the ensuing days and evenings at the hospital at Tess's side. Phlebitis set in in one leg. It threatened to cripple Tess if it did not kill her. I began to have a sickening feeling that care at the hospital was breaking down. No one seemed to know just how to treat the phlebitis. The best they could do was to apply a swarm of leeches to suck the blood. Everyone, doctors and nurses, was increasingly frightened by what was going on outside the hospital in Vienna. I had been trying to follow this in the hours I could break away from my young wife's bedside.

The Austrian government of Chancellor Schuschnigg was crumbling. The Nazis, whom Hitler had forced Schuschnigg to take into his cabinet, were fast undermining it. Nazi mobs in the streets, encouraged by the release from prison of their leaders and the legalization of their party, were on the rampage. On February 24, while I was doing my childish broadcast from Sofia, Schuschnigg, I learned, had attempted to answer in the Austrian Bundestag the boastful speech by Hitler to the German Reichstag of four days before. On that gloomy Sunday, February 20, in Vienna Tess and I had sat glumly around the radio and listened to the Führer's latest outburst. He had warned that Germany would know how to "protect" the ten million Germans living on its borders, seven million in Austria and three million in Czechoslovakia. Everyone knew what Hitler meant by "protect."

Schuschnigg's speech had been conciliatory to the Germans but he declared that Austria had gone to the limit of concessions "where we must call a halt and say: 'This far and no further.' " Austria, he concluded, would never voluntarily give up its independence, and he ended with a stirring call: "Red-White-Red [the Austrian national colors] until we're dead." (The expression also rhymes in German.)

The Austrian chancellor's speech set off a wild reaction in the provincial city of Graz, where twenty thousand crazed Austrian Nazis invaded the town square, tore down the loudspeakers carrying Schuschnigg's words, hauled down the Austrian flag, and raised the swastika banner of Germany. With the Austrian Nazi Seyss-Inquart, whom Hitler had forced Schuschnigg to make minister of interior, in charge of the police, no effort was made to curb this Nazi riot or others which began to break out throughout Austria.

In desperation, Schuschnigg turned for help to the Austrian workers, whose free trade unions and political party, the Social Democrats, he had kept suppressed after his colleague Dollfuss had brutally smashed them in 1934. These people represented forty-two percent of the Austrian electorate. Schuschnigg promised to restore their political party and release their leaders still in prison.

But it was too late.

Still, Schuschnigg made one last effort to save Austria from Hitler and the Nazis. In a speech at Innsbruck on the evening of March 9 he announced that a plebiscite would be held in Austria four days hence — on Sunday, March 13. The Austrian people would be asked whether they were for a "free, independent, social, Christian and united Austria — *Ja oder Nein?*"

I missed this sudden and fateful announcement. That evening I was on the overnight train to Ljubljana, the charming little capital of Slovenia in Yugoslavia, to do still another children's broadcast for "Columbia's American School of the Air." I still had been unable to interest anyone at CBS in letting me report at first hand on the fate of Austria. Ed Murrow had left London for Warsaw to arrange for a juvenile chorus to sing on this confounded School of the Air.

The sun was out and spring was in the air when my train from Ljubljana steamed into Vienna's Südbahnhof at eight o'clock on the morning of Friday, March 11. I felt good. In a few moments I would be seeing Tess and the baby. She was still in the hospital but had seemed these last few days to be getting better. The little Slovenian capital had turned out to be something of a tonic for me. A chorus of coalminers' children had sung magnificently for our program. After the broadcast, a group of miners and their priests had wined and dined me with much conviviality. For the moment I had forgotten Hitler and Schuschnigg and the Austrian crisis.

The taxi driver abruptly brought me down to earth. Overhead two planes were dropping leaflets.

"What are they all about?" I asked him.

"Plebiscite."

"What plebiscite?"

"The one Schuschnigg ordered for Sunday."

I climbed the stairs to our apartment, puzzled. I asked the maid. She handed me a stack of newspapers for the three days I had been away. The front-page headlines brought me up to date. Schuschnigg had called a plebiscite for Sunday. There was no mention of Hitler's reaction in the Vienna newspapers.

Breakfast over, I took the subway out to the hospital. Tess was running a fever and the doctor had not been able to halt the phlebitis in the left leg. He seemed to be worried over a possible blood clot. I comforted my wife as best I could and stayed with her until she dozed off. By this time it was 11 A.M. and I caught a taxi to the Schwarzenberg Café to catch up on the news.

Fodor, the Vienna correspondent of the *Manchester Guardian* and the *New York Post* and a walking encyclopedia of information about Austria, was there. With him was Ed Taylor, who had replaced me for the *Chicago Tribune*. Both were old friends. They were a little tense, but hopeful — even Fodor, who as a Jew had to fear for his life if the Nazis took over. The plebiscite would go off peacefully, he thought. And Schuschnigg would win it easily, now that he apparently had gained the support of the Socialists. That would be a blow to Hitler. Fodor made a special point of that.

I felt better. On the way into town I had tried to slough off some wishful thinking. Though to me Schuschnigg was certainly a lesser evil than Hitler, Schuschnigg's plebiscite was scarcely more free or democratic than those I had seen perpetrated by Hitler in Germany. There had been no free elections in Austria since 1933, so there were no up-to-date polling lists. And it was a farce to think that the four days' notice of the plebiscite would give Schuschnigg's opponents time to campaign. Also, only the chancellor's authoritarian Fatherland party had access to the radio.

All this I would point out in a broadcast — if CBS gave *me* access to the radio. Ed Murrow being away in Poland, I wrote out a cable to Paul White, the news director in New York, urging him to allow me to broadcast the results of the plebiscite Sunday evening. But before I could telephone it in, events on this Friday began to cascade.

Around 4 P.M. I dashed out to the hospital to see if Tess was feeling any better. As I crossed the Karlsplatz to catch the subway, I was stopped by a crowd of about a thousand people. Most of them wore Nazi swastika armbands on the right sleeve of their overcoats. But they were surprisingly docile. One lone policeman was yelling and gesticulating at them. And they were giving ground! If that's all the guts the Austrian Nazis have, I thought, Schuschnigg will have no trouble with his plebiscite. I hurried on to the hospital. Tess said she was feeling a little better. The baby was fine. Reassured, I headed back to town.

When I emerged from the subway at Karlsplatz about 6 P.M. I was amazed to find that the situation there had abruptly changed. A mob of several thousand shouting, hysterical Nazis was milling around the vast square in the gathering darkness. The lone policeman of two hours ago must have been captured by the crowd or gone home for supper.

I found myself being swept by this riotous, yelling throng out of the square past the Ring, past the Opera, into the Kärntnerstrasse and down this narrow street, where most of the fashionable shops were, to the offices of the German "Tourist" Bureau, which, with its immense flower-draped portrait of Adolf Hitler in the window, had been a rallying point, a veritable shrine, for the Austrian Nazis. Here the mob stopped to demonstrate and in the streetlights I noted the faces of some of the individuals who made up this churning herd: a familiar sight it was to an old veteran of Nazi Germany. I had seen those faces at the party rallies in Nuremberg: the fanatical popping eyes, the gaping mouths, the contorted expressions of hysteria and paranoia. And now they were screaming: *"Sieg Heil! Sieg Heil! Heil Hitler! Heil Hitler! Hang Schuschnigg! Hang Schuschnigg! Ein Volk, Ein Reich, Ein Führer!"* The Brownshirts at Nuremberg had never bellowed the Nazi slogans with such mania.

I had often seen the Vienna police break up Nazi demonstrations in this spot. But now they were standing with folded arms. And most of them were grinning. Some of the young women in the crowd began to take off their hooked-cross armbands and tie them on the sleeves of the police. More grins. Obviously, the Vienna police were going over to the Nazis. I wondered what the hell had happened so suddenly. I turned to some of those nearest to me. They were too excited to answer. Finally a middle-aged woman responded.

"The plebiscite," she yelled in my ear. "Called off! We think Hitler comes tomorrow. Isn't it wonderful!"

The calling off of the plebiscite was news to me. If true, I thought, Schuschnigg could scarcely survive this very night. He was already losing the streets and the police to the Nazis. I extricated myself from the swirling mob and fought my way back to the Hotel Bristol. Ed Taylor was in the lobby. He confirmed the news. Schuschnigg had called off his plebiscite. He had promised to broadcast an explanation shortly.

Ed and I caught a taxi to the American legation. John Wiley was standing before his desk, clutching his long cigarette holder and trying to smile — in the way one does after a terrible setback.

"It's all over, my friends," he said quietly. "There has been an ultimatum from Berlin. No plebiscite Sunday, or the German army marches in. Schuschnigg has capitulated."

Wiley advised us to keep the radio on. The chancellor might go on the air at any moment and explain the situation. Wiley invited us to stay for supper and listen in, but I had to get hold of Murrow in Poland and enlist his aid in getting New York to let me broadcast. I returned to our apartment in the Plösslgasse, in which was also my office, put in a long-distance call to Ed, and switched on the radio. It was playing a gay Strauss waltz. I could not reach Ed at a Warsaw number he had given me. I hung up. The waltz abruptly stopped.

"Attention! Attention!" an excited voice said. "In a few minutes you will hear an important announcement." Then came the familiar ticking of a metronome, the Austrian radio's identification signal. Maddening it sounded. Tick . . . tick . . . tick . . . I turned it down. Then a voice I knew well. It was Chancellor Schuschnigg. I took down his words.

> This day has placed us in a tragic and decisive situation. I have to give my Austrian fellow countrymen the details of the events of today.
>
> The German government today handed to President Miklas an ultimatum, with a time limit, ordering him to nominate as chancellor a person designated by the German government, and to appoint members of a cabinet on the orders of the German government. Otherwise German troops would invade Austria.
>
> I declare before the world that the reports launched in Germany concerning disorders by the workers, the shedding of streams of blood, and the creation of a situation beyond the control of the Austrian government are lies from A to Z. President Miklas has asked me to tell the people of Austria that we have yielded to force since we are not prepared even in this terrible situation to shed blood. We have decided to order the troops to offer no resistance.
>
> So I take leave of the Austrian people with a German word of farewell uttered from the depth of my heart:
>
> God Protect Austria!

Toward the end I thought his voice would break, that he would begin to sob. But he managed to control himself to the end. There was a moment of silence, as his voice fell away. Then the Austrian national anthem was played — it sounded as if it came off an old record. It was the familiar tune of *"Deutschland über Alles,"* only in the original and slightly different version as Haydn composed it. That was all.

A little later the rasping voice of the Judas came over the air. This was Dr. Arthur Seyss-Inquart, an early friend of Schuschnigg — they had served in the same regiment in the war — who announced that he was taking over power and felt himself responsible for law and order. He sounded confused but he made one important point. The Austrian army, he said, was to offer no resistance. This was the first I had heard of a German invasion. Hitler's ultimatum, Schuschnigg had said, was: capitulate *or* face invasion. Hitler had quickly broken the terms of his own ultimatum. He now had his Anschluss — the union of his native Austria with Germany. He might also have, it occurred to me, a war. This was the last time the old allies, Britain, France and Italy, assisted by Czechoslovakia, which had a well-armed military force, could act to stop Hitler.

At any rate, on the spot in Vienna, I had the most important story of my life. And I had it to myself so far as reporting firsthand on American radio was concerned. My sole rival, Max Jordan, of NBC, was not here.

My main problem was to get it on the air.

First, I had to convince CBS to put me on. Then I had to have facilities for the broadcast from whoever was in charge of RAVAG, the Austrian Broadcasting Company. I would need a studio, a microphone and a telephone line to a shortwave transmitter, preferably in Geneva, Switzerland, or London, where there would be no Nazi censorship. But I would take a Berlin transmitter if I had to and take a chance on getting the main story past the censor.

So far I had no word from CBS in New York whether they were interested in hearing from me. I had been unable to get in touch with Murrow, who had much more clout with the management in New York. Neither of us, I had to face it, had yet been allowed to report ourselves. Would CBS make an exception now? I forced myself to think that it would. I phoned the Austrian Broadcasting Company to set something up. No answer. Probably the Nazis had already taken over. Well, I had dealt with them in Berlin. I was sure I could handle them in Vienna. I hurried downtown to see.

In the Johannesgasse, before the RAVAG building, steel-helmeted soldiers in field-gray uniforms were standing guard with fixed bayonets. They must have been flown in from Germany. They were very businesslike. After some parleying they let me in. The vestibule and corridor, in contrast, was a scene of confusion. Young men in all sorts of Nazi uniforms were milling about, brandishing revolvers, playing with bayonets, and shouting continually. I tried to brush past them to the offices of Emil Czeja, the director-general, and Erich Kunsti, the program director, with whom I had worked on various broadcasts. At first they wouldn't let me through. But I barked at them and finally they allowed me to pass. In the hall outside their offices I found my two Austrian friends surrounded by excited storm troopers. They were obviously prisoners. I managed to get in a word with Kunsti.

"How soon can I get on the air?" I asked.

He shrugged his shoulders. "I've ceased to exist around here," he said, trying to laugh. He motioned to a scar-faced trooper.

"Ask him," Kunsti said. "He seems to be in charge."

I went up to the fellow and explained I wanted to set up a broadcast to New York. He had a blank look on his face that must have been permanent. It was obvious he knew nothing about radio broadcasting. I could make no impression on him. Finally, I said, raising my voice. "Let me talk to your chiefs in Berlin. I know them. I've worked with them. They'll want me to broadcast."

I had decided that getting a line through to a shortwave transmitter for Berlin to relay me through to New York was the only course left. I would have to use a little double-talk to get past the censor there.

"Can't get through to Berlin," the wooden-headed trooper said. "Lines all dead. Maybe later."

"Not a chance," Kunsti whispered to me.

A couple of guards, fingering their revolvers, nudged me away. Outside in the corridor I decided to stick around and wait for a chance to talk to the broadcasting people in Berlin as soon as the lines were restored. Time, though, was ticking away. I glanced at my watch. Midnight. A local news bulletin came through on the loudspeaker. It said a new government was being formed at the Ballhausplatz. I dashed over there in time to see Seyss-Inquart, standing on the balcony, naming himself head of a new National Socialist government.

On my way back to RAVAG, I stopped at the Café Louvre where the American correspondents hung out. Bob Best of United Press, who practically lived there, was dispensing the latest rumors. Martha Fodor, the beautiful Slovak Martha, was fighting to keep back the tears. This was the end of her world. Fodor was not there. He had gone home to try to telephone his story to London. John Wiley, she said, had already called saying he was going to take them in the morning to Bratislava, across the nearby frontier in Slovakia. So Fodor and his lovely wife would be safe!

My former assistant when I was the correspondent of the *Chicago Tribune* in Vienna, one Emil Maass, swaggered in. He had been a rather mousy man when he worked for me, a little retarded for his thirty years. He was half American, half Austrian, and had two passports. He came up to Best's table, where I was sitting with Martha and Major Goldschmidt, the monarchist leader, and two or three others.

"Well, *meine Damen und Herren*," he smirked, "it was about time."

He turned over his coat lapel, unpinned his hidden swastika party button, and ostentatiously pinned it on the outside over the button-hole. Martha shrieked "shame" at him. Bob Best got up as if to hit him (later, when Best changed, I would recall that) and the lout turned and left.

Martha, I knew, was worrying about what might happen to her husband. Fodor was Jewish. I assured her Wiley would get them out safely. He had been stationed in Berlin, where I first had met him. He knew the Germans. Also he was a tough Irishman.

Major Goldschmidt, whom I had taken a liking to, though he was head of a monarchist group working for the restoration of the Haps-burgs — a forlorn cause — rose quietly from the table. He had had a Jewish father but he was a practicing Catholic. Hitler, I thought, would never forgive him either for his racial mixture or his poli-tics — next to the Jews in Vienna he hated the Hapsburgs, as he made plain in *Mein Kampf.*

The major stood at the table for a moment.

"Thank you all for your friendship," he said quietly, "even if you didn't like what I was up to." He shook the hands of each of us around the table.

"You will please excuse me," he said. "I shall go home now and get my revolver."*

I hurried from the Louvre back to the Austrian Broadcasting House. Again a battle to get by the guards. My scar-faced trooper did not greet me warmly.

"You back?" he said. "Nothing doing. No lines. No broadcast. Will you please leave." And he beckoned a couple of storm troopers, one of whom took my arm none too gently and ushered me out to the street.

For several minutes I stood there in the chilly night, hating to admit defeat. I tried once more to get into the building. But this time the guards must have got word. "No admittance!" they shouted. "Get along with you."

As I walked home across the Karlsplatz I looked at my watch. It was 3 A.M. I had failed. I had been sitting on a great story all evening. And now I would never get it out. I felt crushed.

I headed toward home. The chilly night air began to clear my mind. How selfish and small-minded I was, I saw, to feel sorry for myself. What was my dismal failure to get the story out compared to the story itself: what had happened in a single night to this unlucky

---

* Later that night he shot and killed himself.

country — indeed to this strife-ridden continent? It was a milestone in the history we were living through in Europe, a great tragedy for Austria, a considerable triumph for Adolf Hitler. I had been lucky to witness it. Despite a personal frustration my life and work would go on. But for many Austrians this night's happenings meant the end. In a concentration camp, a prison. Or the ruin of a career or business. For the country's two hundred thousand Jews it meant worse.

Wearily I climbed the stairs to our apartment. It felt like I lived on the *fifteenth* floor instead of the third. Once inside I downed a beer. Despite the hour I did not feel sleepy. I had a second beer. I decided to write out the story anyway, if only for my diary.

The phone rang. It was Ed Murrow, finally, from Warsaw. I told him the news — and my bad news.

"Fly to London tomorrow morning, why don't you?" Ed suggested. "You can get there by tomorrow evening and give us the first uncensored eyewitness account. And I'll come down to Vienna."

Neither Ed nor I raised the question of whether I from London and he from Vienna would be allowed by CBS to broadcast. I guess we just took it for granted.

I phoned the airport at Aspern outside Vienna. All planes were fully booked tomorrow, though the airlines doubted if any would be allowed to take off. The German army had taken over the Austrian airfield. Only military planes were being cleared for landing or take-off. I decided to try anyway.

I phoned the hospital to leave a message for Tess explaining why probably she would not be seeing me for a few days and that I would be praying for her. But the telephonist declined to take any message. There seemed to be great confusion at the hospital like everywhere else. So I wrote down the message, with a note to our part-time maid, who would be coming in the morning, to take it out by taxi first thing.

Finally, at around 5 A.M., I lay down to catch an hour's sleep.

All that next day, Saturday, March 12, 1938, I struggled to get to London. When I arrived at the airport at 7 A.M. I found the German Gestapo had taken over the main building. A surly black-coated S.S. officer shouted at me that no planes were being allowed to take off. I soon found that actually Göring's Luftwaffe was running the airport. Military planes were landing every minute. An air force captain told me the ban on commercial flights might be lifted at any moment and advised me to try my luck with a British Airways plane leaving for London. No luck. It already was overbooked — mostly, I saw, by frightened Jews. I did not have the heart to try to replace one of them. I turned next to Lufthansa, the German airline. They had a plane for Berlin due out at 9 A.M. No Jews were applying to fly to Berlin. I got a seat on it. It would be stopping at Prague and Dresden, but should reach Berlin by noon. From there I had at least some chance of catching a plane to London. Unless — the thought occurred to me — Hitler banned all commercial flights from Berlin until the Anschluss crisis was over.

While waiting for takeoff, I ran into an Austrian police official I knew slightly. He, obviously, was not happy at being bossed around by arrogant Gestapo thugs from Berlin. He imparted an important piece of information. Schuschnigg had not fled after his resignation, as had been reported by the Germans. A plane had been kept waiting for him at Aspern all evening, but the fallen chancellor had refused to avail himself of it. Too bad, my police informant added, because Schuschnigg had been seized by the German Gestapo and taken to an unknown place. I was not surprised. But I was not prepared, I admit, for what followed.

At Tempelhof airfield in Berlin I made immediately for the offices of the Dutch airline. More luck. They had a plane leaving in an hour for Amsterdam and on to London. And they had one more seat, which I instantly bought. There was time for a lunch and a glance at Berlin's morning newspapers. I was taken aback by the headlines. Especially in Hitler's own newspaper, the *Völkische Beobachter*. Across the front page a banner-line in three-inch-high type: "GERMAN-AUSTRIA SAVED FROM CHAOS!"

Beneath was an incredible story, a tissue of lies no doubt concocted by Propaganda Minister Goebbels, describing violent "Red" disorders in the main streets of Vienna — "fighting, shooting, pillage," it said. It was accompanied by a DNB dispatch from Vienna saying that during the night Seyss-Inquart had wired Hitler to send in German troops to protect Austria from bloodshed provoked by "armed Socialists and Communists." Accustomed as I was from my years in Berlin to Hitler's lies, I could scarcely believe that he could perpetrate such a one as this. There had been no disorders in Vienna and I doubted that even a traitor like Seyss-Inquart had telegraphed Berlin saying there were, and asking for German troops. Hitler and his henchman, I was absolutely sure, had faked the telegram to justify his invasion.°

I tucked the newspapers into my briefcase — I intended to read

° This was confirmed by the secret German documents seized by the Allies at the end of World War II.

from them during my broadcast from London, if I ever got there. For a moment after lunch it looked as though I would not. There was a good deal of confusion at the airport, with priority being given to German planes taking off for Vienna. Our flight to Amsterdam kept being postponed. Finally, when I had about given up, it was called. I felt relieved when we had circled over Berlin and turned west. I was, at last, getting free of Nazi censorship. I began to scrawl a rough script for the broadcast from London. By the time we came down at Croydon it was almost finished. I phoned the office from the airfield. To my happy surprise the English secretary informed me that New York had arranged for me to go on the air for a fifteen-minute report at 11:30 that evening, 6:30 P.M. at home.

This was a breakthrough, the first time CBS had ever allowed one of its own staff to go on the air and report the news firsthand.* I could scarcely believe it, even hours later as I nervously watched the minute hand on the clock in the little BBC studio circle to 11:30 P.M., and over the feedback from New York heard the CBS announcer introduce me.

A little more than twenty-four hours ago, Nazi troops passed over the border into Austria.... At the time of the invasion yesterday, William L. Shirer, Columbia's Central European director, was in Vienna. This afternoon he flew to London to bring you an uncensored, eyewitness account of the move.... *We take you now to London.*

On that cue, facing a mike in a BBC studio, I began my first broadcast of the news since joining CBS.

Next day, a Sunday, there was a more important breakthrough. Ed Murrow and I, I think I can say, helped radio news broadcasting abruptly come of age. We arranged and put on the air the first world news roundup ever. From that hasty development sprang the principal format of broadcast news — first over the radio, then over television — as we have known it ever since.

Today in the age of television and satellite relays, the evening news roundup over the air looks easy and routine. The very first one

---

* So many persons who have read this section expressed disbelief that CBS would not up to this time allow a veteran foreign correspondent to report on the air himself that I feel I should cite the man who founded and ran CBS and owned most of it. William S. Paley in his memoirs *As It Happened*, p. 131, writing of this period, comments: "Shirer's regular assignment from a base in Vienna, like Murrow's from his base in London, was to arrange broadcasts and do interviews.... Neither of them at the time was really a broadcast newsman." It would have been more accurate to say that neither of us was *permitted* to be "a broadcast newsman."

on that evening of Sunday, March 13, 1938, took place only after we overcame considerable difficulties. In New York, CBS engineers told the management it couldn't be done. The main problems, to be sure, lay with us in Europe. All our engineers in New York had to do was to pick up the various European shortwave transmitters* we employed and feed them into the network, as they had been doing for years. Murrow in Vienna and I in London had, on short notice and on a Sunday evening when the offices of the European broadcasting companies were closed, to arrange for shortwave transmitters, studios, telephone lines linking them, and, of course, reporters in four or five countries, in which the officials we were dealing with spoke only foreign languages and, what is more, had never before been asked to handle such a thing, not to mention at such short notice and on their day off. This turned out to be more time-consuming than I had imagined.

Not until 5 P.M. on the day after my eyewitness report from London did CBS telephone from New York to ask if Murrow and I could arrange a news roundup from the chief European capitals for later that evening. It was only noon at home, but since the day was almost over in Europe it did not give us much time.

Paul W. White, Columbia's amiable news director, called that Sunday afternoon. "We want a European roundup tonight," he said, trying to make it sound routine. "One A.M., your time. We want you and some member of Parliament from London, Ed Murrow from Vienna, and we want you to line up American newspaper correspondents in Berlin, Paris and Rome. The show will run thirty minutes. Can you and Murrow do it?"

I said yes, and hung up. The truth was I didn't have the faintest idea how to do it. I put in a call to Murrow in Vienna and as I waited for him to call back I pondered what to do. I knew almost all the American foreign correspondents in the various capitals. It would be no problem to line up a good man in each capital, provided we could locate them on a Sunday evening, and had time to clear them with their employers in America.

Also Ed and I now knew the directors and chief engineers of the various European broadcasting systems whose technical facilities we would have to use as well as the key men in the ministries of post, telegraph and telephone, whose lines and transmitters we also needed. While waiting for Murrow, I put in long-distance calls to American correspondents in Paris, Rome and Berlin. I also called the directors and chief engineers of the French National Broadcasting

---

* Medium and longwave transmitters did not have the range to span the Atlantic.

Company and of the Ministry of PTT in Paris, the Ministry of Posts and the Reichs Rundfunk Gesellschaft (RRG) in Berlin and the Ente Italiano Audicioni Radiofoniche (EIAR) in Turin. I was thankful I had picked up French, German and Italian. Without them I don't know how I could have operated that Sunday afternoon.

Murrow came through from Vienna. He thought he could persuade the Germans to give him a telephone line to Berlin, where his broadcast could be relayed to New York by the shortwave transmitters there. He also gave me some tips about other technical problems. Rome had a good shortwave transmitter but if it was not available, we must order telephone lines from Rome to Geneva or London. Paris had no transmitters. I must book a telephone line from there to London through the French PTT. Before long my telephones were buzzing, and in four languages. In Turin I was unable to arouse any EIAR official or engineer who could help. I would have to book a telephone line through the Italian Ministry of Communications from Rome. Berlin came through. The RRG would give me a studio and a shortwave transmitter. They would also try to set up a line to Murrow in Vienna but warned me that the only good one between Vienna and Berlin was in the hands of the German army and, therefore, doubtful.

As the evening wore on, the broadcast began to take shape. White telephoned from New York with the exact times scheduled from each capital: London, Vienna, Berlin, Paris, Rome, with the cues that would get each talk on and off the air. I called the last four capitals with the time skeds and cues. I hoped the engineers would somehow understand our cues, which were in English.

My newspaper friends started to respond to the calls I had put in for them. Edgar Mowrer, Paris correspondent of the *Chicago Daily News*, was spending the weekend in the country, where I finally located him. It took some urging to persuade him to return to town to broadcast. But Mowrer had a passion for talking about anything connected with Hitler, who had booted him out of Berlin. No man, I knew, felt more deeply about what Hitler had just done to Austria. Frank Gervasi in Rome and Pierre Huss in Berlin came through. They would broadcast if their International News Service office in New York agreed. I called CBS in New York: Get INS to permit Gervasi and Huss to talk.

"Okay," Paul White said. "And while I've got you on the line, what transmitters on what wavelengths are Berlin and Rome using tonight?"

I had forgotten about that. We probably couldn't get the Rome transmitter, I told him. As for Berlin I'd have to phone there, and call him back, which I did. I was going to take Gervasi from Rome via a telephone line to Geneva, if I could set it up. I was having a hard time making contact with the Swiss and Italians on a Sunday evening.

"How about your own report from London?" White wanted to know. In the midst of arranging our pickups from the Continent I had forgotten that. "Remember," he said, "we've scheduled two of you from London: you and someone from Parliament. We want to know what Britain is going to do about Hitler's invasion of Austria."

"Okay," I said. "I'll call you back on that." I had been unable thus far to locate any member of Parliament; they were all weekending in the country. The same with officials from Downing Street, whom I had tried to call to find out what Britain was going to do in this crisis. I was pretty sure of the answer. The British weren't going to do anything. But I needed an official to confirm it.

While I was jotting down a few notes for my own broadcast, Ellen Wilkinson, the Labour M.P., came through on the phone. She, like everyone else, was in the country. It seemed to be an English custom that could not be altered, no matter how great a crisis suddenly broke on the continent of Europe.

"How long will it take you to get back to London?" I asked Miss Wilkinson.

"About an hour," she said.

It was 11 P.M. We had two hours to go.

"Okay," I told her. "We go on the air at one A.M. I'll meet you at the BBC shortly before that. That gives you two hours to compose some brilliant remarks about British reaction to Hitler's taking Austria this weekend. Or," Ellen was an old friend, "British lack of reaction."

Gervasi was on another line from Rome. "The Italians can't arrange it from here on such short notice," he said. "What shall I do?"

"We'll take you over Geneva," I finally said. "Tell EIAR to order the lines for you and to be sure to reserve a studio in Rome."

"I'll try," Gervasi said, but there was not much hope in his voice. He knew the Italians.

"I'll get after the Swiss," I said. "And if all fails, phone me back in an hour with your story and I'll read it over the air from here. New York," I added, "is very anxious to know what Mussolini is going to do."

"You know damned well what he's going to do, or rather not going to do, Bill," Gervasi said. We, too, were old friends.

"Sure. Same as Chamberlain here in London. Nothing," I said. "Right."

"But New York, Frank, wants to hear it from you, speaking from Rome. Sounds more effective than if I say it here from London."

The phones kept jangling and I kept chattering into them. Finally it was 12:45 A.M. I hurried up the street to BBC's broadcasting house. Ellen Wilkinson, flaunting her auburn hair, was just arriving breathlessly. We walked down the stairs to a studio. Soon New York came through on a feedback and I made a final checkup with Paul White. It looked as if we had clear sailing with Paris and Berlin and Vienna — Ed Murrow had become quite confident he would get through on a line to Berlin. We were bringing Paris in on a telephone line to London. Rome was out. I simply had been unable to get a line from Rome to Geneva. But Gervasi was on the phone this minute from Rome, dictating his story to a stenographer. White agreed to switch back to London toward the end so I could read it.

The last fifteen seconds ticked off to 1 A.M. London time, 8 P.M. in New York. Through my earphones I could hear the calm, smooth voice of Bob Trout introducing the show.

> ... To bring you the picture of Europe tonight Columbia now presents a special broadcast with pickups direct from London, from Paris and such other European capitals as have communication channels available.... Columbia begins its radio tour of Europe's capitals with a transoceanic pickup from London. *We take you now to London.*

I was on the air. All the fatigue of the last forty-eight hours disappeared. I felt a tinge of excitement. If we got through the next thirty minutes without too bad a hitch, this might be the start of something in radio. I spoke very briefly, expressing skepticism that the British government would do anything about Hitler's aggression except to protest. There would certainly be no war. Ellen Wilkinson, "who needs no introduction to American listeners," I said, turning over the microphone to her, thoroughly agreed. "The British," she said, "are *annoyed* at Hitler. But no one in Britain wants to go to war."

As disappointing as Britain's reaction was to me, I imagined that Miss Wilkinson's words probably were very reassuring to our American listeners, fearful of war, as so many were. And they must have been deeply moved by Edgar Mowrer from Paris and Ed Murrow from Vienna. Mowrer, who despised Hitler and had been trying to warn the world about him, was not sure that people everywhere would at last understand that he stood for "brutal, naked force" and was a menace to all of Europe. Ed presented a sad picture of the once gay Austrian capital now in the grip of the Nazis. Only Huss from Berlin was lacking, I thought. I should have got someone less sympathetic to the Nazis. He reported that "all classes in Germany believed *the fact* that Austria had come back to the German fold of its own will." The fact? Huss knew better.

Still, I thought, the roundup went very well, considering it was a first try. Berlin, Vienna, Paris came in on time and clearly. New York switched back to me so that I could read Gervasi's report from Rome. He stressed that Mussolini would not this time oppose Hitler in Austria, as he had been ready to do four years before. The Duce, he reminded us, had joined the Führer's camp.

Paul White came back to me on the feedback at the end of the broadcast. Everyone in New York, from Paley on down, he said, was elated.* They thought this first broadcast roundup had been a huge success.

"So much so," White said, "that we want another one tomorrow night — tonight, your time. Can you do it?"

I was awfully tired, but elated, too.

"No problem," I said.

Though I was anxious to return as soon as possible to Vienna to be with Tess, who was still in the hospital, and to see and report on what Adolf Hitler was going to do to his native land, New York asked me to stay on in London for the rest of the week to finish up the story from there. This would give Ed Murrow a well-deserved chance to cover Hitler's triumphant return to Austria. Ed was as pleased and excited as I at our having broken through, at last, as reporters on the CBS network and then having organized radio's first world news roundup.

Though, like me, he was working nearly twice around the clock daily, he had found time to visit Tess in the hospital and to phone me daily about her condition, which was not good. Her phlebitis, the doctor said, was still critical. The baby girl, whom we had not yet had time to name, was fine. Tess had survived the shock of Hitler taking over her country very well, Ed said. The worst strain, I gathered, had been the confusion and terror in the hospital the first cou-

* "For the time," Paley would write later of this first broadcast roundup, "it was an extraordinary feat of logistics and planning. Each correspondent reported live, some thousands of miles away from each other and each of their reports had to be scheduled precisely to the second. . . . In 1938 this technique was immediately recognized as an unusual event in the news. By bringing together in one program an anchorman at studio headquarters and correspondents on location, we were doing something that would become the important format of modern news broadcasting." (Paley, op. cit., p. 134.)

ple of days. Jewish patients, regardless of their condition, had fled in panic. And Tess's obstetrician, who was Jewish, had disappeared. All this worried me, but Ed assured me Tess had taken it in stride. Her chief complaint, he said, was the ear-splitting noise of Göring's bombers, which seemed to fly over the hospital's rooftops every hour and keep her from sleeping.

Back in London there was plenty to keep one busy. On Monday, I spent a good part of the day organizing our second news roundup scheduled for 3:30 A.M., our time, Tuesday, with pickups again from London, Berlin, Paris, Vienna and Rome. The second time it was a little easier.

I was more excited, and so was Murrow, at CBS's constantly putting us two on the air after having kept us off so long. At 4 P.M. on Monday, I broadcast a report on Prime Minister Chamberlain's statement to the Commons on Hitler's conquest. The immediacy of radio fascinated me. "Prime Minister Neville Chamberlain," I began, "arose to make a statement in the House of Commons a half-hour ago." It was still coming over the news ticker as I began to report.

What Chamberlain said did not surprise me, but it disturbed me, as had a statement to the Commons on the Austrian situation he made on March 2. Then he had pretended that "What happened [at Berchtesgaden] was merely that two statesmen [Hitler and Schuschnigg] had agreed upon certain measures for the improvement of relations between the two countries." In Vienna I had read that statement with astonishment. I knew that the British legation in Vienna had provided Chamberlain with the details of Hitler's Berchtesgaden ultimatum to Schuschnigg. The prime minister's deceit shocked me.

Now, as I read his statement over the air, I became skeptical of much that he was saying. He was telling the Commons that his new foreign secretary,* Lord Halifax, had told the new German foreign minister, Ribbentrop, in London twenty-four hours before Hitler's march into Austria "that the British government attached the greatest importance to all measures being taken to insure that the plebiscite in Austria was carried out without interference or intimidation from Germany." He himself, Chamberlain added, had made very earnest representations in the same sense.

---

* Anthony Eden had resigned as foreign secretary on February 20, a week after Schuschnigg capitulated at Berchtesgaden, principally because of his opposition to further appeasement of Hitler and Mussolini by Chamberlain. The resignation had greatly pleased Berlin and Rome.

I wondered.*

The prime minister finally got to the point of what he had to say: *"The hard fact is that nothing could have arrested what has actually happened [in Austria] unless this country and other countries had been prepared to use force."*

That was true enough. But I wondered what the future of Great Britain could be if it were unwilling to use force to counter Nazi force.

Winston Churchill, still out of power, still a lonely voice in the wilderness of British politics, touched on that subject in a speech that struck me as the most realistic and farsighted of any in the House that day.

> The gravity of the event of March 12 cannot be exaggerated. Europe is confronted with aggression, . . . and there is only one choice open . . . either to submit, like Austria, or else to take effective measures while time remains. . . .
>
> If we go on waiting upon events, how much shall we throw away of resources now available for our security and the maintenance of peace? How many friends will be alienated, how many potential allies shall we see go one by one down the grisly gulf? . . .

But few in Parliament were paying much attention to Churchill. His own Tory party was solidly behind Chamberlain's policy of appeasing the Fascist dictators.

Churchill said something else that reminded anyone who would listen of the staggering strategic victory Hitler had achieved by taking Austria.

> Vienna is the center of the communications of all the countries which formed the old Austro-Hungarian Empire, and of the countries lying to the southeast in Europe. A long stretch of the Danube is now in German hands. The mastery of Vienna gives to Nazi Germany military and economic control of the whole of the communications of Southeastern Europe, by road, by river and by rail. What is the effect of this on the structure of Europe?

It was a crucial question, but Chamberlain did not answer it. Some of my colleagues who had heard Churchill speak in the House told me that they had never heard him more eloquent. This gave me an

---

* After the war, in studying the captured secret papers of the Wilhelmstrasse, I came across a report of Ribbentrop's sent directly to Hitler on March 10 saying that after talking to Chamberlain and Halifax he was "convinced that England will do nothing in regard to Austria." (*Documents on German Foreign Policy*, I, p. 263.)

idea. Why not ask Churchill to talk over our network and speak the very eloquent words he had used in the House of Commons?

Paley, when I phoned him, liked the idea very much. Apparently, he knew Churchill.

"Call Winston immediately," Paley said, "and tell him I would like very much for him to do a fifteen-minute broadcast for CBS — preferably repeating what he said so well in the House of Commons."

"I'll phone him at once," I said. "How much do we offer him?"

"Fifty dollars," Paley said.

Fifty dollars? I could not believe it.

It just happened that I knew a little about Churchill's finances. Randolph, his son, had once discussed them with me, explaining that his father lived mainly from a syndicated weekly newspaper column sold around the world. There were over two hundred subscribers, he said, who paid a total of around $2,000 a week, of which Churchill received some £300, or $1,500, a fairly comfortable income. But not one that was making him really rich.

"Bill," I told Paley, "I don't think Churchill will do it for fifty dollars. That's only ten pounds."

"Explain to Winston," Paley countered, "that it will be a 'sustaining' program, that is, without commercials. Tell him fifty dollars is our standard fee for 'sustainers.' "

"But Churchill's a bit shot," I argued. "Couldn't we make it five hundred dollars — or at least two-fifty?"

"Fifty dollars," Paley said. I felt he was getting a little exasperated with me.

I phoned Churchill at the House of Commons. He would be delighted to talk for fifteen minutes over CBS, he said.

"What, may I ask, do you pay for such a talk?"

"Fifty dollars," I said. "Ten pounds."

My words apparently stunned him into silence.

"Fifty dollars?" he finally asked.

"Mr. Paley asked me to explain to you, sir," I said, "that that is the customary fee for a 'sustaining' program of fifteen minutes. That means there are no commercials, you see. We did not think you would like to be sponsored commercially, even if there was time to arrange it."

Mr. Churchill did not seem to appreciate the difference. Finally he said: "Tell your boss I'll be happy to do it for five hundred dollars — one hundred pounds, that is."

It was a very reasonable sum, I thought.

Paley, when I called him back, refused to pay it.

I left London at the end of that hectic week, depressed that Hitler had got away again with aggression and that the British and French had been so pusillanimous about it. No one in London, except Churchill, seemed to realize the significance of what had happened, that the Anschluss was just another step for Hitler toward domination of Europe. Chamberlain, at the end of his speech to the House, had announced that the government would *"review"* its rearmament program "in the light of events." What a paltry response to the German dictator!

As my plane lifted off from Croydon my lagging spirits began to revive. On a personal and professional level my whole life and work had been changed in the course of this dramatic week. I hated to admit it, but Hitler was mainly responsible for that. The Anschluss had overnight smashed all the barriers that had kept Murrow and me off the air. And Ed and I had achieved an even more significant breakthrough. We had put together the first broadcast news roundup. From now on millions of people would get their evening news that way — news that would not be in the newspapers until the following morning.

Murrow met me that evening at the Aspern airport. It was too late to gain admission to the hospital to see how Tess was, but Ed had just come from there and assured me that though Tess was still having a rough time, she would certainly pull through. It had been difficult in the confusion of the Nazi takeover. One Jewish woman across the hall from Tess had jumped out the window and killed herself and her baby. Others had fled. Tess's obstetrician had not yet returned, but another doctor had been found.

When Ed and I arrived before my house in the Plösslgasse, S.S. guards in steel helmets with fixed bayonets were standing at the door. What looked like a whole platoon of them stood guard before the Rothschild palace next to us. When we started to enter my home the S.S. men prodded us back.

"I *live* here!" I said.

"Makes no difference. You can't go in," one of the guards countered.

I tried to curb my rage. I had had so much experience with these Nazi roughnecks in Germany.

"Where can I find your commander?" I asked.

"In the Rothschild palace."

A towering S.S. man escorted us into the gardener's house, which adjoined our building and where Louis Rothschild had resided the last year. It was a big house, actually. As we entered we collided with some S.S. officers who were carting up silver and other loot from the basement. One, who appeared to be the commander of the unit, was loaded down with a heavy box of silver knives and forks. He put them down, not the least embarrassed, while I explained my business and our nationality. It struck him as rather funny, but he told the guard to escort us to my door.

"But you'll have to stay put there — at least for a while," he said, again chuckling — "until this little operation is finished."

From a window of my apartment, Ed and I, after a stiff drink, watched the S.S. men emerging from the Rothschild house and piling their booty in waiting trucks. I was anxious to see what the city, now that Hitler had taken it over, looked like. So we crept down the stairs, waited until our guards were away from the entryway, and sneaked out on tiptoe in the darkness. The streets were fairly quiet. Ed said all the Jews had pretty well been rounded up and arrested — several thousand of them — as well as several more thousand Socialists and followers of Schuschnigg. The former chancellor himself, Ed said, was under Gestapo arrest but no one knew exactly where.

We tramped around the inner city for an hour and then adjourned to a bar off the Kärntnerstrasse. By this time Ed had settled into a lugubrious mood — one I would get to know well. He was depressed by what he had lived through in Vienna all week: the hysteria of the crowds, the shouting and boasting of Hitler, the sadism of the Nazi bully boys in the streets. A few evenings before in this very bar, he said, he had seen a Jewish-looking man get drunk and slash his throat with an old-fashioned straight razor he had pulled from his pocket.

But Ed perked up a little when the talk turned to our work.

"I think we accomplished something," he said — I was getting used to his understatements, which I liked. "We've sort of become radio's first reporters, and we've found a format for rounding up the news. Maybe now, my friend, we can go places."

We had another drink on that, and next morning Murrow left for London. I myself hurried to the hospital to see Tess. Her condition, one of the doctors confided, was still critical. We still had to face the possibility, he said, of a blood clot from the phlebitis — only time would tell. I thought the physicians already had taken too much time on this case. Tess had gone to the hospital expecting to stay a week, at the most. She had been there now nearly a month.

I tried to put my worries aside by work. I did a special broadcast on how Vienna had changed over the week I was away. But I could not really give an accurate report. The Nazis had clamped down a temporary censorship of our broadcasts. It reminded me that I must move my headquarters to a neutral spot as soon as Tess was out of the hospital.

What one now saw in Vienna was almost unbelievable. The Viennese, usually so soft and sentimental, were behaving worse than the Germans, especially toward the Jews. Every time you went out you saw gangs of Jewish men and women, with jeering storm troopers standing over them and taunting crowds shouting insults, on their hands and knees, scrubbing Schuschnigg slogans off the sidewalks and curbs. I had never seen quite such humiliating scenes in Berlin or Nuremberg. Or such Nazi sadism. The S.A. and S.S. were picking hundreds of Jews off the streets or hauling them out of their homes to clean the latrines in the barracks and other buildings seized by them. Foreign Jews or foreigners whom the Nazi thugs fancied looked like Jews also were seized and put to work at menial tasks.

The wife of John Wiley, the American minister, happened to be a Polish Jewess. She dared not leave the legation for fear of being picked up and put to "scrubbing things." Gillie, an old friend of mine, who had been the correspondent of the London *Morning Post* in Berlin and was now covering the Anschluss, was halted by a band of storm troopers as we passed the cathedral. Though Gillie was the purest of Scots and looked it, they shouted anti-Semitic obscenities at him and started to rough him up. I looked around for a policeman and then realized that calling on the *Polizei* would be futile. Even those who were not Nazis were afraid to tangle with the S.A. Gillie finally produced his British passport and the Hitler bullies let him go.

I spent a good deal of my time those first days back in Vienna reconstructing the story of Hitler's triumphant return to his native land and mulling over the immense strategic gains he had achieved for Germany and what his next conquest would be. At his first stop in Linz, where he had spent his boyhood before going on to Vienna, he was carried away by the delirious reception he got from the huge crowds.

If Providence once called me forth from this town to be the leader of the Reich, it must in so doing have charged me with a mission, and that mission could only be to restore my dear homeland to the German Reich. I have believed in this mission, I have lived and fought for it, and I believe I have now fulfilled it.

The greatest moment of all for Hitler came on March 15 when, standing on the balcony of the Hofburg Palace in Vienna, from which the Hapsburg kings and emperors once had ruled, he shouted at the immense crowd assembled below: *"As the Führer and chancellor of the German nation and the Reich, I now declare before history the incorporation of my native land into the German Reich."*

Two days before at Linz, the day on which Schuschnigg's plebiscite was to have been held, Hitler had promulgated a so-called Anschluss law proclaiming the end of Austria. "Austria," it began, "is a province of the German Reich." Having decided this, Hitler, with his customary deceit, ordered "a free and secret plebiscite" in which "German Austrians" would decide on the union of their country with Germany. That he had already decided it and would announce it to the public two days hence in Vienna made no difference; he would go through with the sham of a "plebiscite" on April 10. On his return to Berlin a few days later Hitler announced that the Reich Germans would also have a plebiscite on April 10 to approve or disapprove the Anschluss and also, on the same day, there would be a new election for the Reichstag. Since Hitler appointed the deputies to the Reichstag and already had made the Nazis the sole political party in the country, this "election" was a further deceit.

Now that I was free to broadcast and could do some serious reporting, I covered the phony plebiscite. As if the people of Germany and Austria could really decide on the Anschluss, Hitler stormed up and down the length of Germany and Austria making bombastic political speeches exhorting the populace to vote *Ja*. As if Schuschnigg were still a political opponent, he heaped scorn and ridicule on the fallen, imprisoned Austrian chancellor. Schuschnigg, he kept reiterating, had "double-crossed" him by his "election forgery." I noticed though that he did not dare to tell the Germans and Austrians, or the outside world, that he had already put Schuschnigg under arrest. Such an outrage had not happened before in modern Europe.

During this outlandish campaign, Hitler seemed concerned at some of the points we foreign correspondents had made about his deceit — especially in annexing Austria before the plebiscite took place. In a speech broadcast from Königsberg he attacked the foreign press and gave a lame — if typical — excuse for his action.

"I have in the course of my political struggle," he said, "won much love from my people. But when I crossed the former frontier into Austria there met me such a stream of love as I have never experienced. . . . Under the force of this impression I decided not to wait until April tenth but to effect the unification forthwith. . . ."

If you believed that, as I felt sure millions upon millions of Germans and Austrians did, then you also believed anything else you were told.

Hitler wound up his election campaign in Vienna on April 9, on the eve of the polling. I must say he gave one of the most eloquent addresses that I had yet heard from him. But what impressed me most about the speech was that this man, who once had tramped the pavements of this beautiful imperial city as a vagabond, unwashed and empty-bellied, was speaking as Kaiser Wilhelm II and Emperor Franz Josef, the last reigning monarchs of the two Germanic empires,* had, as if he were in frequent communion with God, whose agent on earth he had become.

> I believe it was God's will to send a youth from here into the Reich, to let him grow up there, to raise him to be the leader of the nation so as to enable him to lead back his homeland into the Reich.
>
> There is a higher ordering, and we all are nothing else than its agents. When on March 9 Herr Schuschnigg broke his agreement, then in that second I felt that now the call of Providence had come to me. And that which then took place in three days was only conceivable as the fulfillment of the wish and the will of Providence. . . .
>
> I would now give thanks to Him who let me return to my homeland in order that I might now lead it into my German Reich! Tomorrow may every German recognize the hour and measure its import and bow in humility before the Almighty, who in a few weeks has wrought a miracle upon us!

That a majority of Austrians, who undoubtedly would have said *Ja* to Schuschnigg on March 13, would say the same to Hitler on April 10 was a foregone conclusion. Many of them sincerely believed that Austria, cut off from its Slavic and Hungarian hinterland in 1918, could survive only as a part of the German Reich. There were, of course, a large number of Austrians who had got the Nazi bug. Many Catholics in this overwhelmingly Catholic country were undoubtedly swayed by a widely publicized statement of

---

* Charles I reigned briefly — until the revolution of 1918 — on the death of Franz Josef in 1916 at the age of eighty-six after a record reign of sixty-eight years.

Cardinal Innitzer urging a *Ja* vote. Finally, there was the general feeling that a failure to cast an affirmative ballot might be found out and punished.

The afternoon of the plebiscite, Sunday, April 10, in Vienna I visited a polling station in the Hofburg. Inside one of the polling booths was a sample ballot showing you how to mark yours with a *Ja*. I noticed a fairly wide slit in the corner of the booth which gave the Nazi election committee sitting a few feet away a pretty good view of how one voted.

I broadcast at 7:30 that evening for fifteen minutes. Though the polls had just closed a Nazi official assured me just before I went on the air that the Austrians were voting ninety-nine percent for the Anschluss. And sure enough, the official figure turned out to be 99.75 percent *Ja*. In Germany the vote was given as 99.08 percent.

And so Austria, as Austria, passed for the moment out of history, its very name suppressed by the Austrian who apparently never forgave it for not recognizing his true worth. Vienna became just another city of the Reich, a provincial district administrative center, withering away. The former Austrian tramp, now the mighty German dictator, had wiped his native land off the map and deprived its once glittering capital, which he thought had rejected him, of its last shred of glory and importance.

No formal announcement of what had happened to Schuschnigg was ever made by the German government, so far as I know. The former Austrian chancellor simply disappeared into limbo. I spent some time ascertaining his fate.

On Hitler's orders Schuschnigg was arrested on the morning of March 12, a few hours after he had been forced to resign, and he was kept under house arrest until May 28. During those days I got some information from lukewarm Austrian Nazis that the Gestapo, which held him in custody, was employing a number of petty devices to deprive him of sleep, such as keeping the radio and lights on in his room twenty-four hours a day. He was then transferred to Gestapo headquarters at the Hotel Metropole in Vienna, where he was incarcerated in a small room on the fifth floor for the next seventeen months.

There, with one towel issued to him weekly ostensibly for his personal use, he was forced to clean the quarters, washbasins, slop buckets and latrines of his S.S. guards and to perform other degrading menial tasks. During his first year as Hitler's captive he lost fifty-eight pounds and became emaciated and ill, though an S.S. doctor who examined him claimed he was in excellent health. There followed more years of solitary confinement and then of life "among the living dead," as he described the ensuing years in concentration camps, mostly at Dachau and Sachsenhausen.

At Dachau, in his seventh year of imprisonment as the war neared its end, he was joined by some distinguished company — all, like himself, the victims of Hitler's wrath. Among his fellow inmates were Dr. Schacht, Léon Blum, the former French premier and a Jew, and Madame Blum, Pastor Niemöller, the former U-boat commander and later Lutheran minister, who from his pulpit in Berlin had dared to defy the dictator and who had been imprisoned for eight years, Prince Philip of Hesse, whose wife, Princess Mafalda, the daughter of the king of Italy, had been done to death at Buchenwald in 1944 as part of Hitler's revenge for Victor Emmanuel's desertion to the Allies, and a host of high-ranking German generals.

On May 1, 1945, this strange band of eminent prisoners, who had been hastily evacuated from Dachau and transported southward to keep them from being liberated by American troops advancing from the west, arrived at a village high in the mountains of southern Tyrol.

The Gestapo officer in charge of the prisoners showed Schuschnigg a list of those who, on Himmler's orders, were to be done away with before they fell into the hands of the Allies. Schuschnigg noted his own name, "neatly printed," as he later put it. His spirits fell. To have survived Hitler's brutality so long and then to be bumped off at the last minute!

His diary of May 4, 1945, however, noted a happy ending.

> At two o'clock this afternoon, alarm! The Americans! An American detachment takes over the hotel. We are free!

Not all the Austrian Jews perished in the Nazi camps and prisons. Many Jews were allowed to buy their way out of captivity and go abroad. Usually, it cost them their fortune. Baron Louis Rothschild, for instance, purchased freedom by turning over his steel mills to the Hermann Göring Works. Perhaps nearly half of Vienna's 180,000 Jews managed to purchase their freedom before the Holocaust began.

This lucrative trade in human freedom was handled by a special organization set up under the S.S. by Reinhard Heydrich and officially listed as the "Office for Jewish Emigration." It was the sole agency authorized to issue permits for Jews to leave the country. Later it would become an agency not of emigration but of extermination, and organize the systematic slaughter of more than four million Jews. It was administered from beginning to end by an Austrian Nazi, a native of Hitler's hometown of Linz, named Karl Adolf Eichmann.

No one, including myself, especially noted that name until long afterward.

Tess and the baby finally got home from the hospital on April 8. Because of the phlebitis in her leg Tess still could not walk. "The worst," I noted in my diary that evening, "is over." We felt an immense relief. But not for long.

Even though Tess's spirits rose at being home, her condition did not improve. The doctors were baffled. Finally one of them stumbled on what was wrong. New X-rays revealed that metal objects, apparently surgical instruments, had been left in her after the emergency cesarean operation. It would be best, the doctors advised, if they were removed by the obstetrician who had performed the operation. But being a Jew, he had gone into hiding since the Anschluss. I managed to locate him. He did not want to risk appearing at the hospital, for which I did not blame him. He agreed, however, to do it in a safe place.

I found a convent in the Wienerwald a mile or two down the Danube that had a clinic and whose good Sisters of Mercy agreed to accommodate us for the operation. In the dead of night we drove with our doctor out to the convent and the operation was performed. The doctor did find something that he had inadvertently left behind. From that day on Tess made a steady if slow improvement. In the excitement and confusion of her crises and of my professional ones, we had neglected to name our beautiful little daughter. We now corrected this. We named her Eileen Inga.

Murrow and I had agreed that as soon as Tess recovered enough to travel, I would move my headquarters to Geneva, where I would be free to broadcast and organize broadcasts without interference from Nazi officials. Now that Adolf Hitler was once again on the move, it was obvious that we would have a lot of news to broadcast from the Continent. It was also obvious *where* Hitler would strike next. I noted it down in my diary in Vienna on April 14, four days after Hitler's phony plebiscite.

Czechoslovakia will certain be next on Hitler's list. Militarily it is doomed now that Germany [by taking Austria] has flanked it on three sides.

I noted another point.

All our broadcasts from Prague now [after the Anschluss] must go by telephone line through Germany, even if we take them to Geneva for shortwave transmission. That will be bad in case of trouble. Must ask the Czechs about their new shortwave transmitter when I go to Prague tomorrow.

In Prague two days later, on April 16, I put on Eduard Beneš, president of the Republic, and Alice Masaryk, daughter of the sainted founder of the country, in a broadcast to America. The evening before, I had told Beneš, with whom I had become acquainted during the days I was covering the League of Nations, of which he was a dogged champion, that I hoped he would say something about the consequences of the Anschluss to his country, now surrounded on the north, west and south by a hostile German dictator.

He agreed to speak on "relations with Germany," but his language was exceedingly moderate and reasonable. No matter, as I learned when the broadcast was over. The Germans faded out his remarks about them. New York had booked a telephone line from Prague to the German transmitters at Zeesen, outside of Berlin. But even if we had used a line to a transmitter in neutral Geneva, it would have run through Germany and we could have been faded out.

Next day I got after the Czech Broadcasting Company to speed up its construction of a new shortwave transmitter so that we could get its side of the coming story. I was a little surprised that neither Beneš nor the chief engineer at the Prague Broadcasting House seemed unduly worried about Hitler's next step. Beneš was too experienced and wise a statesman not to know it would be directed against Czechoslovakia.

It was almost amusing how often CBS now put us on the air to report. On the evening of May 2 I found myself at a mike on the roof of the royal stables overlooking the entrance to the Quirinale Palace in Rome waiting for the king of Italy and Adolf Hitler to drive up in a gold carriage behind prancing horses. The experience on the roof that lovely Roman spring evening taught me some more about American broadcasting.

To tell the truth, I felt a little silly there. Hitler's official visit to Rome was an important event. He was coming to see how far the strutting Italian dictator would go in supporting his drive for European conquest, and what the price would be. I could have done a more thoughtful report, I felt, from a quiet studio. New York, however, liked the idea of doing the broadcast from the palace stables. It would sound more dramatic.

So I was scheduled to go on the air at the exact moment when the monarch and his guest were due to arrive. But suppose they did not appear on time? That raised a problem. It could easily have been solved by recording the event, whenever it happened, and broadcasting it later. But we were not allowed to record, as all European broadcasting reporters were. Everything we broadcast had to be live. A listener in America knew he was hearing events as they happened, the very second. This was the new dimension that radio gave, and it was exciting.

But the ban on our recording events for later broadcast could have dire consequences as I learned that evening waiting for the king of Italy and the Führer of Germany to appear.

They arrived six minutes *ahead* of schedule. By the time I went on the air they had driven up in their carriage, entered the palace, come out on a balcony, waved to the populace and disappeared. When my microphone opened there was nothing left to describe. Had I been allowed to record a few minutes before, New York would have had a firsthand description of the event while it was taking place and could have inserted it in the news program.

As Europe lurched down the road to war, Ed and I tried in vain to get Paley to allow us to record. There were two principal reasons why it was absolutely necessary in trying to report over radio from Europe.

The first had to do with atmospherics and their effect on shortwave radio transmissions across the ocean from Europe to America. These atmospherics differed from season to season, day to day, from hour to hour even. They were affected by many things, including sun spots and magnetic currents from the North Pole. And by light and darkness. Because of the difference in time, most American broadcasts from Europe originated at night but were received in New York while it was still daylight. As the crisis in Europe intensified and our broadcasts of its unfolding multiplied, a growing number of them failed to get through because CBS in New York insisted on having them live.

There were other handicaps to the ban on recording that hampered us in taking full advantage of this new medium in journalism. On any given day there might be several developments, each of which could have been recorded as it happened and then put together and edited for the evening broadcast. In Berlin, for example, there might be a bellicose proclamation, troop movements through the capital, sensational headlines in the newspapers, a protest by an angry ambassador, a fiery speech by Hitler, Göring or Goebbels threatening Nazi Germany's next victim — all in the course of the day. We could have recorded them at the moment they happened and put them together for a report in depth at the end of the day. Newspapers could not do this. Only radio could. But Paley forbade it.

Murrow and I tried to point out to him that the ban on recording was not only hampering our efforts to cover the crisis in Europe but would make it impossible to really cover the war, if war came. In order to broadcast live, we had to have a telephone line leading from our mike to a shortwave transmitter. You could not follow an advancing or retreating army dragging a telephone line along with you. You could not get your mike close enough to a battle to cover the sounds of combat. With a compact little recorder you could get into the thick of it and capture the awesome sounds of war.

In the coming conflict, if it came, there would be terrible bombing of the cities. But there would be lulls in the most savage attacks from the air. The broadcast time might easily come during the lulls. To let audiences *hear* a bombing we would have to start recording when the bombs began to drop and the anti-aircraft began firing and the sirens screeched and cries of the wounded pierced the air.

It seemed so simple, so logical. But Paley was adamant.

Our departure from Vienna to Geneva turned out to be more harrowing than we had counted on. All through the last ten days of May Europe had been jittery. The weekend which began on Friday, May 20, saw the governments in London, Paris, Prague and Moscow panicked into the belief that Europe stood on the brink of war. They had some reason. There were reliable reports of the movement of twelve German divisions up to the Czech frontier. The Czechs frantically called up one class of reserves and put their great fortress line on alert. I hurried up to Prague.

It looked there as if war was at hand. The cabinet met. The General Staff met. Conflicting intelligence poured in from the various capitals. Rumors were rife. Hastily called-up reserve troops embarked for the "front." I tried frantically to get the Czechs to put their new shortwave transmitter into action so we could broadcast directly to New York. The Germans refused us telephone lines through Germany, the only lines we could hook up with transmitters in Geneva or London.

By Monday, May 23, the crisis eased. Surprisingly, Hitler seemed to give in before diplomatic pressure from Russia, Britain and France and the quiet firmness of the Czechs. Though furious at being crossed, he ordered the Foreign Office in Berlin to inform the Czech government that the reports of German troop concentrations on their border were without foundation and that Germany had no aggressive intentions toward Czechoslovakia.

That was what he told the outside world. But to his generals, as we learned later, he spoke another language. In Berlin on May 28 he told them: "It is my unshakable will that Czechoslovakia shall be wiped off the map." He instructed them to complete plans for accomplishing this by October 1. It was a date to remember — over the next four months.

Relieved, like everyone else, though it had been an exciting weekend in Prague, I returned to Vienna and resumed preparations to move. We had to get to Geneva by June 10, since Tess's Swiss visa expired on that date. Tess still insisted on using her Austrian passport, which was no longer good.* She refused to apply for a German passport, which all Austrians who traveled abroad were now forced to have. With the help of the American legation I was able to obtain a special permit from the German authorities for her to leave.

My diary in Vienna for June 9, 1938:

> Leaving tomorrow. The Gestapo have been here for two days checking over my books and effects. . . . Tess in no shape to travel, all bound up in bandages still, but we are going by air.

She had had her second operation when I got back from Prague. Her recovery had been discouragingly slow. Still, we felt exhilarated at the prospect of escaping from this now Nazi land on the morrow.

I was on my guard, though. It was not so easy to leave Austria, now that Hitler had taken over. The Gestapo was on the prowl, not only for Jews and dissident Austrians, but for foreigners who might be trying to get out their money in violation of the strict currency laws. I myself had had a run-in with the Gestapo on my way to Italy to cover Hitler's visit there. At the border Gestapo agents had broken into my Pullman compartment in the middle of the night, seized all my foreign currency, which I needed for my expenses in Rome,† and threatened me with arrest. No doubt they had added my name to

---

* Foreign women who married Americans did not thereby acquire American citizenship.
† The German mark, which had replaced the Austrian schilling, had no exchange value. Not even the Italians would exchange marks for lire.

their little black book as one to keep tab on since my carrying foreign money across the frontiers looked suspicious.

I suppose I was a little nervous, then, when on the morning of our departure I called at the Vienna American Express office to collect five hundred marks owed me by the manager on a loan I had made in dollars. Technically we should have cleared the transaction through the Reichsbank, but the amount had seemed too small to bother. When I walked into his office, a German who had long posed as an anti-Nazi emigrant but who I was sure was a Nazi spy, stood grinning at me. I thought for a moment it was a trap. I did not know the manager, a young Englishman, well enough to trust him very far. We chatted for a while until the spy left. Even then I did not feel safe. Most of the Austrian employees at the American Express had turned out to be secret members of the outlawed Nazi party. Finally we walked down the Ring and he shoved the five hundred marks into my coat pocket. Only later did I realize how suspicious we must have looked. I had no intention, of course, of taking the five hundred marks out of the country. I could take out, legally, only fifty marks, about twelve dollars. The rest I had carefully calculated to pay last-minute bills.

About noon Tess, the baby, a young Austrian woman coming along as nurse, and I drove out to the airport at Aspern. Inside the building I explained to the Gestapo chief that Tess was too weak from recent operations to stand up, and that I would go over with him her exit permit and the inspection of her baggage. On entering the waiting room I had laid Tess out on a bench and asked her not to move until our plane was called.

The Gestapo head was not only skeptical but suspicious. If the woman was my wife, why did she not have an American passport? Patiently — I was determined to keep my cool until I got safely out of this country — I explained the American law. So the lady was Austrian! my tormenter cried. Then where was her German passport? All Austrians had to have German passports. I asked him to look closely at the exit permit, stamped by the chief Gestapo office in Vienna. This, thank God, impressed him. But then he reverted to character. Tess, he said, would have to stand up, like all the other passengers, to assist in the baggage inspection.

I started to protest. I regretted by this time I had not brought one of her doctors along to back me up, but it probably would not have made any difference. I began to raise my voice, whereupon my Gestapo man signaled a police inspector to take me away. I was led into a small room where two police officers went through my wallet and all my pockets, frisking me from top to bottom. They then led me to an adjacent small room. "Wait here," they said. When I started to say I had to get back to my invalid wife to help with her baggage inspection they closed the door in my face. I heard the lock turn. Five, ten, fifteen minutes. It seemed like hours. By now it was certainly time for our plane for Geneva to leave.

Just then I heard Tess cry: "Bill, they're taking me away! They're going to strip me! Where are you!"

I pounded the door. Through the window I could hear and see the Swiss racing the motors of their DC-3, impatient at being held up. After what seemed an age a plainclothesman unlocked my door and led me to a corridor connecting the waiting room with the airfield. I tried to get into the waiting room to find Tess, but the door was locked. Once again I heard the Swiss revving up their plane. Probably now they were leaving without us — I could not see the plane from the corridor.

Then a door opened. Out stepped my wife, the nurse supporting her with one arm and holding the baby in the other.

"Hurry!" snapped an official. "You've kept the plane waiting." I held my tongue and grabbed Tess.

She was gritting her teeth, trying to hold back her outrage. "They stripped me, the bastards!" she blurted out. "Tore off some of the bandages! The bitches!" I had never heard her curse before.

"Just hold on for a couple more minutes, darling," I whispered, "and we'll be out of this bloody place. . . . The bastards . . ."

I grabbed her other arm. We pushed through the door leading outside. We hurried as fast as we could across the grass. The plane stood there, fifty yards away, both motors humming. I wondered what more could possibly happen in the next few seconds before we could clamber up the steps into that blessed plane. Then we were in it and it was lurching across the field gathering speed for takeoff.*

We flew blind through thick storm clouds over the Alps all the way from Vienna to Zurich, the plane pitching and tossing in the turbulence. Tess was deathly sick. I thought four-month-old Eileen Inga would die. The nurse passed out. Then there was Zurich down there. Switzerland, sanity, civilization, freedom, after the barbarian Nazi nightmare. The sun came out as we continued on to Geneva.

By the time the doctor at the hotel had put fresh bandages on Tess and we had had drinks and dinner, we felt revived.

* European airfields in those days did not have concrete runways.

"Why in hell did they strip you, those Nazi bastards?" I asked Tess.

"Bitches," Tess corrected me. "At least they use women for such jobs. Tough little Hitler maidens from Germany."

"But why? I told them you were all bandaged up. From the operations."

"They were looking for money," Tess said. "They were sure we were smuggling a fortune out beneath the bandages. They didn't believe us. Until they saw the mess."

The next days, as we began to settle down, smug, staid, stodgy, Calvinist Geneva, which had bored me in the days when I had had to tear myself away from Paris to come down to cover the League of Nations, began to strike me as almost a paradise.

Ed Murrow flew down from London.

I remember a glorious June afternoon that summer when Tess, Ed and I took passage up the lake to Lausanne on a paddle-steamer, the calm water bright blue, like the Mediterranean, the shores splashing green, the Jura Mountains to the west a deep, smoky blue, the snows of Mont Blanc to the east pink in the waning sun. We sat on the deck after a late lunch, mellow from the mountain wine and the air's warmth, and talked and laughed and wondered. After what we three had been through during the Anschluss in Vienna, life looked good. We basked in the peace of it, the tranquility, the Alpine splendor, the freedom.

We stayed on in Lausanne by the lake a few days, Ed and I as American observers at a meeting of the European Broadcasting Union, of which CBS was an associate member. But there was not much work to do. Mostly we loafed, swimming, sailing, hiking up into foothills of the mountains, eating well, imbibing the local wines and gabbing through the balmy nights. How carefree we felt! How young!

They were the last days of peace and quiet, as it turned out, we would know for seven long years — until the three of us had slipped into middle age and gone through the wear and tear of constant threats of war, one after another, and in the end, like hundreds of millions of others, of war itself, this time more terrible in its horrors than any other in the life of the planet.

Hitler inspecting the first Nazi U-boat

Hitler and Mussolini

OVERLEAF:
*Vienna welcomes Hitler
after the Anschluss, 1938*

CHAPTER 13

Munich

1938

All that late summer and early fall of 1938 it looked as if war would come to Europe.

Having grabbed his native Austria, Adolf Hitler now turned to his next victim. He began provoking three million Sudeten Germans in Czechoslovakia to rebel, promising to come to their aid with all the might of the swiftly rearming Third Reich. As the summer progressed it was feared that the paranoiac Führer might attack Czechoslovakia any day.

The harassed Czech government, under the nation's co-founder, Eduard Beneš, was striving to keep its cool despite the hysterical Nazi provocation and what it suspected was British deceit in secretly backing Hitler's aims. It was prepared to grant the Sudeteners the autonomy they had asked for. But it was also determined to fight for the nation's survival.

The Anschluss had left Czechoslovakia in a terrible strategic plight. Hitler's armies now faced her on three sides — not only from the north and west, as before, but from the south, along two hundred miles of the old Austro-Czech border. Only one hundred twenty-five miles separated the German divisions in Silesia to the north from those in Austria on the south. Were they to meet halfway between, they would cut Czechoslovakia in two and complete the encirclement of Bohemia and Moravia, the heart of the nation. On the other hand Czechoslovakia had a well-armed, well-trained army of thirty-

five divisions, deployed behind the most formidable fortifications in
Europe outside of France's Maginot Line. It had the assurance that if
attacked, France was bound by treaty to come to her aid. If the
French moved, the Soviet Union was obligated to join her in defense
of their Czech ally.

The Führer's secret order in late spring to "wipe Czechoslovakia
off the map" by October 1 began to be evident as the summer wore
on. As the three million Sudeten Germans who lived on the frontiers
of Bohemia and Moravia and who had received arms and some military training from Himmler's S.S. began, at Berlin's instigation, a
virtual civil war against the government in Prague, the Führer insisted with increasing vehemence that the Sudeteners and their territory be handed over to the Reich.

To cede this land would destroy Czechoslovakia, depriving it not
only of its mining and industrial base and of a vital part of its transportation and communications complex, but of its formidable fortress line, without which it could not be defended against the
Germans. Nevertheless, in June I learned that Prime Minister Chamberlain had decided to support Hitler's claim to take over the Sudetenland. In May, Chamberlain had spoken "off the record" to a
group of American foreign correspondents at a luncheon at Lady
Astor's and frankly told them that Britain favored, "in the interest of
peace," turning over the Sudetenland to Germany. He had added
that in his opinion neither France nor probably Russia would honor
their treaty commitments to aid the Czechs in case of a German attack, and that Britain would certainly not get herself involved.

Whether the Czech government yet knew this, I was not sure,
though I thought it probable since its minister in London, the astute
Jan Masaryk, son of Thomas Masaryk, the co-founder and first president of Czechoslovakia, was a good friend of several of the American
reporters who had been at the luncheon. Berlin, I know, soon learned
of it from the German embassy in London.

And the whole world must have begun to suspect it after the *Times*
of London began to publish that summer its first leaders urging the
Czech government to grant "self-determination" to the Sudeteners
and its other minorities "even if it should mean their secession from
Czechoslovakia." The grapevine in London had it that the *Times*
leaders were inspired by the prime minister himself. My information
from Berlin was that the Germans knew it.

It was no surprise then that at the beginning of August Hitler
began to provoke a new crisis over the Sudeten Germans. On the

third I flew up to Prague to cover it. In the days that now seemed distant a threat of aggression by a power such as Germany would have brought the Council of the League of Nations in Geneva into special session to try to prevent it. But the League's failure to prevent Japan from overrunning Manchuria and Mussolini from attacking Abyssinia had doomed it. Now not even France, once the pillar of the League, bothered to ask it to intervene to halt Hitler. Nor did Czechoslovakia, whose president, Beneš, also had been a pillar of the League. It was now every country for itself. The League of Nations, that great dream of President Wilson — and of millions of others — who believed that it would, at last, prevent aggression and bring lasting peace with justice to mankind, was — one had to face it — dead.

My chief task those first days in Prague was to cover the so-called Runciman Mission, which Chamberlain, with more deceit than his own public probably was aware of, had dispatched to Czechoslovakia to "mediate" between the government and the Sudeten Germans. The deception of the British prime minister, I soon learned, had begun with his statement to the House of Commons on July 26 about the Runciman Mission. Chamberlain said he was sending Lord Runciman to Prague "in response to a request from the government of Czechoslovakia."

This was a lie. The truth was that Runciman had been forced on the Czechs by Chamberlain. He had warned Beneš himself, through the British minister in Prague, Sir Basil Newton, that if the Runciman Mission were not immediately accepted, dire consequences would result. Though shocked by the British proposal, the president finally agreed to it, probably because France, the supposed ally, had pressed him to do so. Beneš, I began to suspect, was losing faith in the French and in the value of their treaty obligation to help defend his country against German aggression. I suspected also that he already had given up on the British, though he was an experienced enough diplomat — he had been foreign minister until becoming president — to play along with them if only because he realized that Chamberlain was becoming the key figure in the diplomatic maneuvers that would determine his country's fate.

Viscount Runciman must have seemed to Beneš a rather incredible figure to suddenly appear on behalf of the British government. A shipping magnate and former president of the Board of Trade, he had no experience in foreign affairs and no knowledge of them either. Judging by his remarks and demeanor he viewed Central Europe as some out-of-the-way place to which stout Britishers journeyed only in line of duty to king and country. In truth, Runciman's "negotiations" with the Czech government and the Sudeteners were a hoax, since the Sudeten leaders, to whom he took a great personal liking and for whom he asked for more and more concessions from Beneš, were not free to negotiate. By this time they had become good Nazis, and they were taking their orders from Hitler in Berlin.

Still, all through August Runciman kept pressing the Czech government for more concessions to the Sudeteners. By the beginning of September, Beneš had offered them all they had ever asked for — complete autonomy and a more important role in the country's affairs. The Sudeten delegates were embarrassed. How could they turn down an offer of all they had asked? The question was put to Hitler.

By that time I was tired of the charade and had returned to Geneva for a few days to be with my wife and child before they departed for America, where Tess was going to try to get her citizenship. She needed an American passport to travel around. Her old Austrian passport was no good and, bless her, she refused to use a German passport. I also thought it well to get Tess and Eileen out of Europe until we knew whether there would be peace or war.

In Berlin, where I stopped off on my way home, Hitler seemed in a belligerent mood. On August 26 I watched him closely as he reviewed a big military parade he was putting on for the visiting Hungarian regent, Admiral Nicholas Horthy, but in reality to impress Britain, France, Russia and Czechoslovakia with Germany's new military might. When at one point tractors appeared hauling an enormous field-gun, the biggest piece of mobile artillery I had ever seen, Hitler turned to watch the reaction of the foreign military attachés. Most of the time in the reviewing stand he was surly, and party leaders told me he had been in an ugly mood, brooding about the despised Czechs. Most of my colleagues in Berlin believed he had decided to go to war if necessary to get his Sudeten Germans and their territory. Sadly I took note, but I was skeptical because, my diary reminds me, "First, the German army is not ready. Second, the German people are dead against war."

Still, I knew the dictator was unpredictable, especially when he was in a megalomaniacal mood, as he now seemed to be. In such a stew he might do anything. I also realized that the mood of the German people would not necessarily hold him back. He made the vital decisions. The German people obeyed.

But not all the German generals.

In fact, though I had no inkling of it, nor, I am certain, did Adolf Hitler, a conspiracy was afoot to overthrow him, led by no less a figure than the new chief of the army General Staff, the key military post that once had been occupied in Germany by the great Moltke and Schlieffen. This was General Franz Halder, who had succeeded General Ludwig Beck in August. The gifted Beck had failed to convince Hitler that to go to war before the army was ready would lead to disaster, and had resigned. Pro-Nazi, even before Hitler took power, General Beck had gradually seen the light. By 1938 he opposed his chief not only on military grounds, but because he had finally realized that the Nazi regime was a brutal, mindless tyranny that doomed Germany to destruction. His handpicked successor, Halder, shared these ideas.

Halder, fifty-four, was the first Bavarian and the first Roman Catholic ever to become chief of the General Staff — a severe break with the old Protestant Prussian tradition. Like Beck he was a man of wide intellectual interests. Also like Beck, he did not look like a typical arrogant, ramrod, bemonocled old Prussian officer. Rather gentle in manner, he struck me the first time I met him as resembling more a university professor of mathematics or physics.

Now as chief of the General Staff he not only was responsible for planning the assault on Czechoslovakia but had become the key figure in the first serious plot to overthrow the dictator of the Third Reich. Of that plot I learned only at the Nuremberg Trial that began in November, 1945. There Halder himself testified, as did some of the other surviving figures involved.

Their story briefly was this. A small number of army generals and colonels, in cahoots with a few civilians, the most prominent of whom were Dr. Schacht, now fallen from grace and resenting it, and Karl Gördeler, former mayor of Leipzig, planned to remove Hitler from power if he gave the order to attack Czechoslovakia. Their object was to prevent the mad dictator from plunging Germany into a war which they were sure would bring Britain, France and Russia in against it and would be lost. A few of the conspirators were genuinely concerned to depose Hitler not only to save the Fatherland from a lost war, but because they had come to view the Nazi regime as a criminal folly.

Only the army, it was recognized, possessed the physical power to overthrow the Führer, protected as he was by the considerable forces of the police, the S.S. and the S.A. General Halder himself, as General Staff chief, had no actual troops under his command. General

Walther von Brauchitsch, commander-in-chief of the army, disposed of all the forces needed, but Halder did not trust him. The General Staff chief therefore lined up a few trusted key generals who had troops at their disposal, especially at the most important strategic centers. Most important of these were General Erwin von Witzleben, commander of the all-important III Corps Area, which comprised Berlin and the surrounding territory; General Count Erich von Brockdorff-Ahlefeld, commander of the Potsdam garrison, made up of the 23rd Infantry Division; and General Erich Hoepner, who commanded the 1st Light Armored Division in Thuringia, which could block any S.S. troops attempting to relieve Berlin from Munich.

The 23rd Infantry Division was the key to the success of the plot. It would have to seize Hitler and his chief aides, especially Göring, Goebbels, and Himmler, and occupy the ministries and the communication and transportation centers in the capital.

There were three conditions necessary for the success of the coup. First, the conspirators had to have time enough after Hitler gave the order to attack Czechoslovakia to grab him and his cohorts and halt the troops before they moved across the frontier. Second, Hitler had to be physically present in Berlin. The plotters had no troops to seize him in his well-protected retreat at Berchtesgaden, where he was spending most of his time that late summer, despite the growing crisis. Third, the conspirators had to be sure that they were right in believing that France and Britain — and probably Russia — would back the Czechs militarily if they were attacked. For only then, with certain defeat facing Germany, could they justify the deposal of the dictator.

To make sure that they were correct in this, the conspirators sent confidential agents to London to sound out the British. They were also to inform them that Hitler was planning to attack Czechoslovakia at the end of September, but that if Britain and France held firm, a group of key military men, led by the chief of the General Staff himself, would overthrow Hitler before he could carry it out.

The first such envoy was Ewald von Kleist, a gentleman farmer and descendant of the great poet, who arrived in London on August 18. Though Britain's pro-Nazi ambassador in Berlin, Sir Nevile Henderson, asked the Foreign Office not to see Kleist, he was received by Sir Robert Vansittart, chief diplomatic adviser to the foreign secretary, and by Winston Churchill, still out of favor with the government. To both men the German emissary disclosed Hitler's plans and the plot to depose the dictator. He also stressed that further British appeasement of Hitler would abort the conspiracy. And he urged that the government or, even better, the prime minister himself issue a public warning that in case of German aggression against the Czechs, Britain would support France if it honored its treaty with Prague.

Vansittart and Churchill conveyed Kleist's message to both the prime minister and the foreign secretary, but as Chamberlain noted to Lord Halifax, he was inclined "to discount a good deal of what he [Kleist] says."

More warnings followed from various sources, and on September 2, General Halder, feeling that the British were still not taking them seriously, dispatched his own emissary, a retired army officer, to London to talk with the British War Office and Military Intelligence. But despite the fact that he spoke for the chief of the German General Staff, surely the first time the British had ever heard directly from this exalted military post, the officer apparently did not make much of an impression on his British colleagues.

Finally in desperation, the conspirators resorted to using the German Foreign Office and the embassy in London in a last effort to persuade the British to stand up to Hitler. They acted through Erich Kordt, chief of the Foreign Office Secretariat, and his older brother, Theodor, counselor of the embassy and chargé d'affaires in London, both of whom were in on the conspiracy. After consultations with Generals Beck and Halder, Erich Kordt relayed instructions to his brother Theodor in London to give a final secret warning to the British foreign secretary himself. This he did on the morning of September 7, after being spirited through a back door of the Foreign Office to the chambers of Lord Halifax. To that aristocrat, the second most important man in the British government, Kordt reiterated that Hitler had ordered an attack on Czechoslovakia to begin on October 1 at the latest, but that if Britain and France held firm against him the German army was prepared to overthrow the dictator the moment the final order to attack was given. He also urged the British government to broadcast a "final warning" to Hitler, saying bluntly what it would do in case of German aggression.

For a few days Chamberlain considered giving such a warning. He was acutely aware of the consequences of the failure of the British government to give Berlin such notice in the summer of 1914. But he was talked out of taking such a step by his ambassador in Berlin, Henderson, who by this time was clamoring for the prime minister to give Hitler what he wanted in Czechoslovakia. Instead of issuing the warning, as the German conspirators had urged, Chamberlain decided on another tack.

After the feverishness of Berlin and the growing fear in Prague of war, Geneva those last days of summer was a delight. Tess, Eileen and I would play most of the morning in a nearby park and all afternoon at a beach on the lake. Sometimes we took an excursion steamer up the lake and had a fine lunch and some excellent white mountain wine. The one hundred and second meeting of the League of Nations Council was about to be held as well as the nineteenth meeting of the League Assembly. But no one paid much attention. The Sudeten crisis in Czechoslovakia was not even on the agenda of either the Council or the Assembly, though it was the only issue that threatened the peace. Still, I noted, the official delegations were arriving in Geneva from all the nations in the world (except from the United States, which had never joined its own president's creation, or Japan, Germany and Italy, which had resigned).

One afternoon toward sunset Tess and I strolled along the shore of the lake with John Winant, a former governor of New Hampshire and now head of the International Labor Office at Geneva. He was a gaunt, awkward, Lincolnesque figure and I had taken a great liking to him. The vast white marble palace of the League came into view.

"A beautiful granite sepulchre!" Winant said, his resonant voice low, his craggy face sad. "Let us admire its beauty," Winant went on, "against the green hills and the mountains. There, my friends," he said, as we watched the lights going on in the sprawling building, "are buried the dead hopes of peace for our generation."

One day early in September I kissed Tess and Eileen goodbye, wished them well in their first visit to my native land, and once more caught a plane to Prague. Before this first month of autumn was out we would know whether there would be peace or war. I had tried to apprise the moguls of the Columbia Broadcasting System of the situation. As I departed the City of Peace I scribbled in my diary:

> Have almost convinced CBS they should let me talk five minutes daily [from Prague] — revolutionary in the broadcasting business.

Its main business, to be sure, remained the providing of popular entertainment. But the Anschluss had awakened CBS, at least, to the opportunities of also broadcasting the news. We now had the chance to report, as no other medium could, the worst crisis in Europe since the end of the Great War.

I can still feel in my bones, even after the lapse of nearly half a century, the almost unbearable tension that gripped Europe through the whole month of September. At the beginning its fate seemed to hang on what took place at the annual Nazi party rally, which began on September 6 at Nuremberg and was to culminate on September 12 when Hitler was scheduled to announce what he intended to do about the Sudeten Germans in Czechoslovakia.

Prague, to which I returned on the tenth, was calm but apprehensive. On the fifth, President Beneš, in a last desperate effort to save the peace, had called in the Sudeten negotiators and told them to write out their full demands. Whatever they were, he would accept them.

"My God!" the deputy Sudeten leader, Karl Hermann Frank, exclaimed to some of the correspondents the next day. "They have given us everything!" But that was the last thing Hitler wanted. The Sudeten Germans had been all along a pawn to conceal his real goal of destroying Czechoslovakia. On September 7 he ordered Henlein, the Sudeten leader, to break off all negotiations with the Czechs. A shabby excuse about alleged Czech police excesses at Moravska-Ostrava was invented.

On the tenth, the day of my arrival, Beneš broadcast to the world an appeal for calm and for peace. And in Nuremberg the bellicose Göring answered him. Beneš was sure, he said, that the crisis could be resolved with reason, goodwill and mutual trust on both sides.

Running into the president in the hall of Broadcasting House when he had finished, I wanted to rush up and say: "But Mr. President, you are dealing with gangsters, with Hitler and Göring! You think they are capable of reason, goodwill and trust?" But I did not have the nerve, and merely nodded a greeting; he smiled back and walked past.

As for Göring's speech at Nuremberg that same evening:

A petty segment of Europe is harassing human beings. . . . This miserable pygmy race [the Czechs] without culture — no one knows where it came from — is oppressing a cultured people [the Sudeten Germans] and behind it is Moscow and the eternal mask of the Jew devil. . . .

Next day, the eleventh, you could cut the tension in Prague with a knife. Rumors filled the air. One was that the Germans had massed two hundred thousand troops on the old Austro-Czech frontier. London reported continuous conferences in Downing Street. In Paris, Premier Daladier conferred anxiously with General Gamelin, commander-in-chief of the French armed forces. Everyone in Europe, it seemed, was anxiously awaiting Hitler's speech on the morrow.

My diary that day ended:

CBS finally okays a five-minute daily report from here, but asks me to cable beforehand when I think the news does not warrant my taking the time.

My God! Here was the old continent on the brink of war — Hitler might start it within twenty-four hours, Prague might be wiped off the map overnight by the big bombers — and the network was most reluctant to provide five minutes a day from here to report it!

To the surprise and relief of almost everyone in Europe, Hitler the next day, September 12, held back from war. In his speech to an audience of delirious Brownshirts on the final evening of the Nuremberg party rally he thundered against the Czechs, their nation, their president and their "brutal oppression" of the Sudeten Germans. But he stopped short of declaring war. I listened to the broadcast of the speech in the apartment of Bill Morrel of the *London Daily Express.* Though I had covered two annual party congresses at Nuremberg, I had never heard Hitler's voice so crackling with venom and spite, or heard this particular audience of party faithfuls quite so hysterical in its bedlam. He seemed to spew out poison as he assaulted and insulted the Czechs and especially President Beneš. But he did not demand, as many had expected, that the Sudeteners be turned over to him outright — or even after a plebiscite. He did insist, though, on "self-determination" for them.*

The relief in Prague, whose streets were deserted all evening because everyone was home listening to Hitler, was immense. I had spent a good part of the day, which was dark and dismal with a biting rain, roaming through the narrow streets trying to see how a people

* Three or four times during his lengthy and passionate harangue, Hitler, I noticed, paused to boast that this was "the first Nuremberg party rally of 'Greater Germany.' " "Germany" had become for him this year "Greater Germany" because of his acquisition of Austria.

It occurs to me as I write this that it was not only "the first . . . party rally of 'Greater Germany' " but also the last. In fact it was the last annual Nazi party congress, *ever.* Hitler billed the next one, to be held early in September, 1939, as "The Party Rally of Peace."

It never took place.

faced the imminence of invasion, war, bombing. To my surprise I found them going about their business, not gloomy, not frightened.

"Either these Czechs," I thought to myself, "haven't any nerves at all, or perhaps they're the people with the iron nerves."

The next day and night in Prague, September 13–14, I shall never forget.

"War very near," I began wearily in my diary at 3 A.M. on the fourteenth. "Since midnight waiting for the German bombers. Much shooting up in the Sudetenland. . . . The Czechs have declared martial law there."

The Sudeteners had been brought so near to hysteria by the prodding of Goebbels' propaganda machine that Hitler's speech, relatively restrained though I thought it had been, had touched off a violent outbreak among them. They had attacked Czech police stations and army barracks and public buildings, looted and burned. Prague had countered during the day by rushing troops to the area and proclaiming martial law.

About seven that evening we learned that Henlein had sent the Czech government an ultimatum. It was delivered at 6 P.M. and expired at midnight. By that hour, it said, the Czech government must repeal martial law, withdraw all state police from the Sudetenland, and confine all troops to their barracks. Otherwise all negotiations were off and the Czechs would be responsible for "further developments." Since Henlein was taking his orders directly from Hitler, we concluded that the ultimatum was backed by the Führer. The "further developments" threatened by Henlein surely meant war.

At that time, remember, the good people of Europe had had no experience of war for twenty years. Even in the Great War, murderous as it was, cities and homes outside the combat areas had been spared. Now, for the first time, they suddenly faced — in Prague, we believed we faced it this very night — a kind of war never before experienced by mankind: immediate bombing from the air that would overnight obliterate the cities and the homes and lives of many. Some of the bombs, people feared, might spew poison gas. The government had promised to distribute gas masks to the populace of the capital, but there had been no time, it said. I suspected there were no masks.

I kept making notes that night of how it felt when war came. Later, after some firsthand experience of war, especially of bombing by both sides, first in Berlin and then in London, the remembrance of that hectic night when we awaited Hitler's bombers somewhat paled for me. But as an account of how it felt the *first time,* it deserves perhaps a few words — from among those I hastily jotted down at the moment on the spot.

The tension and confusion this night in the lobby of the Ambassador Hotel, where the diplomats and correspondents gather, has been indescribable. Fascinating to watch the reactions of people suddenly seized by fear. Some can't take it. They let themselves go to a point of hysteria, and then in panic flee to — God knows where. Most take it, with various degrees of courage.

In the lobby tonight: the newspapermen milling around trying to get telephone calls through the hotel's one lone operator. Jews excitedly trying to book on the last plane or train. The wildest rumors coming in with every new person that steps through the revolving door from outside, all of us gathering around to listen, believing or disbelieving according to our feelings. Göring's bombers will come at midnight — unless the Czechs accept the ultimatum. They will use gas. How can a man get a gas mask? There are none. What do you do then? Beneš will accept the ultimatum. He must!

At one point in the evening an element of comedy breaks the tension. Alex Small, an old friend and colleague of mine from our days on the Paris edition of the *Chicago Tribune,* is sitting behind a large stein of Pilsen beer, frowning at a cable he has just received. It is from his boss, my old boss, the terrible Colonel McCormick, who owns most of the paper and runs all of it. He has cabled Alex on how to cover the war.

"Listen to this, boys and girls," Alex calls out, pausing to gulp down a big quaff of his beer. "Advice from the colonel." Alex starts to read the message. "Wars always start at dawn. Be there at dawn."

A chorus of laughs. At last something to laugh about, for a moment.

"Cable him you're already there," Reynolds Packard, a roughneck gem of a guy with a gravelly voice — he had recently returned from covering the war in Abyssinia — cries out. More laughs.

Alex Small crumples the cable, tosses it on the floor, and swallows more of his beer. We have long called him the "intellectual" among us. He is very learned, Harvard and all that. Few know, since he almost never talks about it, that after graduation from Harvard he enlisted in the army and served as a combat infantryman in the last war. He experienced much more actual fighting than Colonel McCormick, who was a battalion and regimental officer. Alex, I believe, is the only one of us who fought in the war. The rest of us were too young.

Toward midnight, when the ultimatum is to expire, we all grow a little apprehensive. We keep checking our watches. Finally an official from the Czech Foreign Office comes in, his face grave.

"*Abgelehnt,*" he says in German. "Turned down." The ultimatum is rejected by the government.

The correspondents fly to the telephone booths. Several Jews scurry out. The press agent of the Sudeten German party, a big jovial fellow who usually drops in to give us his party's news, comes in, as usual. This time he is not jovial.

"Have they turned it down?" he asks. He hardly waits for the answer. Grabbing a small bag, he vanishes through the door.

We all have put in calls to the Sudetenland, and finally one of them gets through. There is heavy fighting there between the Sudeten Germans and the Czech gendarmerie and army. Heavy casualties on both sides. It is war. Bill Morrell comes through on the phone from Haberbirk. Will I relay his story through to London? He is speaking from the police station there. Before him, he says, lie the bodies of four Czech gendarmes and one German. The Sudeteners had gained control of the town and then retreated when Czech army reinforcements arrived. Bill asks me to call up his wife, Mary, who is expecting, and tell her he is okay.

About 2 A.M. I raced up the street to Broadcasting House to do my piece. Out in the street, all was calm. No troops, no police, to be seen. Maybe we correspondents got too excited. Still, I had a good story, I thought. But it didn't get through. Atmospherics or sun spots, the Czech radio engineers suspected.

Next day I drove two hundred miles through the Sudetenland. The Czech army had crushed the Sudeten uprising. Many of the towns were in shambles. Both sides were counting their dead and wounded, which were considerable. I returned in the evening to Prague thinking that Hitler had suffered a serious rebuff. The Sudeten Germans were beaten, and the Nazi dictator had not moved to save them, despite all his bellowing. But a headline in the early edition of a morning paper caught me up: "CHAMBERLAIN TO FLY TO BERCHTESGADEN TOMORROW TO SEE HITLER!" The Czechs were dumbfounded. They suspected a sellout, and they were surely right. I broadcast my news soon after midnight, but again I did not get through.

Murrow called from London and suggested I get off to Berchtesgaden immediately to cover the talks between the Führer and the
prime minister. The prospect further depressed me. A telephone call
to the railway station: no trains were crossing the border into Germany for the present. I tried to rent a car but could find no Czech
driver who would risk the trip. When I called to report my difficulties to Murrow he said to forget it. Chamberlain was returning to
London in the morning. Ed, too, smelled a sellout.

Next day, September 16, the Czechs seemed to be sure of it. They
believed Hitler asked for, and Chamberlain agreed to, a plebiscite for
the Sudeteners. It probably sounded to the outside world like a reasonable proposal, and democratic (from Hitler, who destroyed democracy in Germany!) but what the British prime minister didn't
seem to realize, the Czechs feared, was that to cede the Sudetenland
was to cede the Czechs' mountain fortress line and therefore their
ability to defend themselves from a German attack. I wrote a broadcast saying that the Czechs would fight rather than give in on this
point. It was the only way they thought they could survive. I thought
it important at this confusing moment to let the American public
know this, but I felt frustrated at the thought that my broadcast
probably would not get through. For the third successive day CBS
had cabled that morning that they could not hear me.

This was becoming a sickening setback. If radio could not get
through regularly from Europe to America because of "atmospherics," then it had little future in the dissemination of the news from
abroad. The public at home would have to continue to depend on the
newspapers. I had probably made a big mistake in going over to
radio.

But later that night, after my broadcast, I could hear New York
perfectly on the feedback and they said they had heard me equally
well. I felt immensely relieved. And I felt better about the news. The
Czechs were standing up to Hitler.

On the eighteenth, we carried a broadcast of Premier Milan Hodža
from Prague. He said the proposal of a plebiscite, which Chamberlain and Hitler were said to have agreed on, was "unacceptable." He
implied the Czechs would fight rather than accept it. But when I saw
him at Broadcasting House after he had finished speaking, he seemed
very high-strung and nervous. The strain of the last few days was
showing, and I wondered about his resolve.

A late-night call from Murrow when I returned to the hotel shook
me up. He said he wanted me to proceed to Germany at once. The

British and French, Ed said, had decided they would not fight for Czechoslovakia and were asking Prague to surrender unconditionally to Hitler and turn over the Sudetenland to Germany. I protested to Ed that the Czechs wouldn't go along with that, that Premier Hodža had just said so on our broadcast. "They'll fight alone —"

Ed interrupted me. "Maybe so," he said. "I hope you're right. But in the meantime Mr. Chamberlain is meeting Hitler at Godesberg on Wednesday [three days hence] and we want you to cover that. If there's a war, you can go back to Prague."

I routed Maurice Hindus out of bed and asked him if he would broadcast for me while I was away. He, too, was taken aback at Murrow's news. He got up, threw some clothes on and proposed a walk — Hindus was a great walker. I phoned for a seat on the early plane to Berlin, surprised it was still flying. Then we went out to roam the streets and talk.

In Berlin the next day, I found Nazi circles jubilant over the Berchtesgaden meeting. Hitler, they said, had convinced Chamberlain that Czechoslovakia would have to turn over the Sudetenland to Germany.* The Foreign Office had sent out a confidential message to its embassies abroad to that effect. Long ago in Berlin I had learned to dissemble a little in my reporting, as I did that day in the capital by the closing words of my broadcast: "One thing is certain: Mr. Chamberlain will certainly get a warm welcome at Godesberg. In fact, I get the impression in Berlin today that Mr. Chamberlain is a pretty popular figure around here." In other words, which I hoped was understood in America, the British prime minister was backing Hitler against Czechoslovakia.

This was bad enough, but the propaganda lies about the Czech treatment of the Sudeten Germans, which Goebbels was perpetrat-

---

* Fooled, rather than convinced, I was sure, but I did not know until much later how far Hitler had succeeded in hoodwinking the aging prime minister. Chamberlain had gone to Berchtesgaden, we now know, intending to propose a compromise that would leave Czechoslovakia with her mountain fortifications virtually intact. But under Hitler's spell he had not even dared to bring it up. He had "personally" accepted Hitler's demand for the "detachment" of the Sudetenland. Hitler further had frightened the prime minister into believing that he was about to attack Czechoslovakia and had made a big concession to his visitor by saying that he would refrain from ordering the invasion "during the next few days." Actually, as we know from the German secret documents, the German army would not have been able to begin the attack before October 1 — two weeks hence — which was the target date all along. Perhaps Hitler fooled Chamberlain most of all in the personal impression he made on him at this first meeting. "In spite of the hardness and ruthlessness I thought I saw in his face," Chamberlain wrote his sister, "I got the impression that here was a man who could be relied on when he had given his word."

ing on the German people to whip them into a war fever, made me even more nauseated. I found the Nazi press — all the press there was in Germany — full of hysterical headlines that were pure and deliberate falsehoods. Some examples:

WOMEN AND CHILDREN MOWED DOWN BY CZECH ARMORED CARS
BLOODY REGIME! — NEW CZECH MURDERS OF GERMANS

The esteemed *Börsen Zeitung,* organ of the financial world, perhaps took the prize: "POISON GAS ATTACK ON AUSSIG?" The *Hamburg Zeitung* was pretty good: "EXTORTION, PLUNDERING, SHOOTING — CZECH TERROR IN SUDETEN GERMAN LAND GROWS WORSE FROM DAY TO DAY."

To one who had just come from the Sudetenland, these hysterical inventions of the sick minds of Goebbels and Hitler were revolting. Why hadn't Chamberlain at least mentioned them to Hitler and branded them for the lies they were? After all, he had had a man on the spot, Runciman.

CBS in New York, at last, was warming up to our radio reporting and its potential, despite the failure of several of my broadcasts from Prague to get through. The next evening, the twentieth, at 6 P.M., just as I was packing my bags for the overnight trip to Godesberg to cover the next meeting of Chamberlain and Hitler, Paul White phoned from New York. He suggested a broadcast from the train, interviewing the correspondents on the way to Godesberg on the chances for war or peace. I phoned the Reichs Rundfunk. It couldn't be done, they said. No facilities on the trains.

"Could you handle a broadcast from the Friedrichstrasse railway station [where we were to catch the train at 10:30 P.M.]?" I asked. Harold Diettrich, the amiable acting head of the German shortwave department, thought he could. I phoned back New York. White was delighted. I called several American and British correspondents and asked them to join me at the station by 10 P.M., when the broadcast began.

When I got to the station at five minutes before ten, there were no correspondents, but German radio engineers had set up a microphone on the platform. At the stroke of ten I found myself on the air, the mike all to myself. I soon exhausted whatever news I had picked up. Fortunately, I had brought along an armful of Berlin newspapers and I began to read the headlines. "CZECH SOLDIERS ATTACK GERMAN REICH!" one of them read. The usual lies, but if I said so, the Nazis would cut me off. Finally, the first of the correspondents sauntered up and before he knew it, I had him on the air. This was Pierre Huss of INS. Finally, some others appeared, Webb Miller of U.P., just in from London. Ralph Barnes of the *New York Herald-Tribune*, Sigrid Schultz of the *Chicago Tribune*. Philippo Boiano of the *Popolo d'Italia* motioned that he wanted to speak. Secretly, I knew, he hated the Nazis, but I was not sure of his English. It turned out to be a wonderful stage Italian-American. Then Jouve of Havas, the French news service, wanted to get into the act. Before I could ask him how his English was he was gabbing into the mike — in French. I started to translate as best I could when out of the corner of my eye I saw the train start to move. I signed off Jouve and myself rather abruptly and sprinted for the moving train.

"Fear the show was a flop," I jotted in my diary.

How little I knew American radio! Next day New York cabled me: "FRIEDRICHSTRASSEBAHNHOF SHOW LAST NIGHT A KNOCKOUT!"

In Godesberg, one of the loveliest towns on the Rhine, the drama being acted out by Chamberlain and Hitler, while all of Europe anxiously awaited the denouement, continued. Act One had been staged at Berchtesgaden the previous week. Here, where I arrived on Wednesday morning, September 21, the curtain was going up on Act Two. Hitler had put up at an old hangout of his, the Hotel Dreesen. I found him in an ugly and highly nervous mood. I was having breakfast on the terrace of the Dreesen, overlooking the Rhine, with a friend, an Austrian editor of a German magazine who, I knew, secretly loathed Hitler. Suddenly the dictator appeared, strode past us, and went down to the river's edge to inspect his yacht. My friend nudged me.

"Look at his walk!"

I had already noticed it. Every few steps Hitler cocked his right shoulder nervously, his left leg snapping up as he did so. I watched him closely as he came back past us. The same nervous tic. He had ugly black patches under his eyes. I thought to myself: "This man is on the edge of a nervous breakdown!"

And then I understood the meaning of an expression I had heard from some party hacks close to him since my return to Germany. They kept talking about the *Teppichfresser*, the "carpet chewer." At first I had not got it, and then someone had whispered to me. The Führer, he said, had been suffering one of his worst nervous crises, and it had taken a strange form. Whenever he went on a rampage about the Czechs or Beneš, as he had been doing almost daily for more than a week, he would fling himself to the floor and chew the edge of the carpet. I had been skeptical of the story, but after this morning on the Rhine terrace I could believe it.

Neville Chamberlain also seemed to me to be a little nervous and solemn, though less so than the German Leader, when he landed at the Cologne airport about noon and emerged from the plane scowling and clasping his umbrella, though the sun was out. Opposition to his appeasement of Hitler at the expense of Czechoslovakia, I knew, was growing in Parliament and in the press. However, he seemed to regain some of his jauntiness as he drove to Godesberg, whose streets were decorated with the Union Jack as well as the swastika, and up to his deluxe hotel on the Peterberg, on the east bank of the Rhine across from Godesberg.

Despite his mien, Chamberlain was in an optimistic mood as he prepared later that afternoon to cross the river and confer with Hitler. Members of his delegation stressed this as they set off. After all, he was bringing the raging Führer everything he had asked for at Berchtesgaden: agreement of the Czechs, extracted from them by Britain and France, to cede the Sudetenland to Germany.

"Do I understand," asked Hitler after the prime minister had spent an hour boasting of how he and the French had pressured the Czechs to give in, "that the British, French and Czech governments have agreed to the transfer of the Sudetenland from Czechoslovakia to Germany?"

"Yes," replied Chamberlain, beaming.

"I am terribly sorry," Hitler said, "but after the events of the last few days, this plan is no longer of any use."

Dr. Paul Schmidt, Hitler's interpreter, remembered later that Chamberlain sat up with a start, his owl-like face flushed with surprise and anger. But apparently the prime minister still could not face the reality that Adolf Hitler, like a common blackmailer, was upping his demands at the very moment they were being accepted. A few days later Chamberlain told the Commons:

> I do not want the House to think that Hitler was deliberately deceiving me — I do not think so for one moment — but, for me, I expected that when I got back to Godesberg I had only to discuss quietly with him the proposals that I had brought with me, and it was a profound shock to me when I was told . . . that these proposals were not acceptable.

Seeing his plans for peace at the expense of the Czechs collapsing like a house of cards, Chamberlain did summon up enough courage to reply to Hitler. He was "both disappointed and puzzled," he said. "He could rightly say that the Führer had got from him what he had demanded."

In order to achieve this [Dr. Schmidt's notes continue] he had risked his whole political career. . . . He was being accused by certain circles in Great Britain of having sold out and betrayed Czechoslovakia, of having yielded to the dictators, and on leaving England that morning he actually had been booed.

But the Nazi dictator does not seem to have been much moved by the plight of his British guest. He insisted on a German *military occupation* of the Sudetenland by October 1 — "at the latest." It was now September 22. Discouraged by the sudden failure of his appeasement of the Nazi dictator, Chamberlain returned with his aides to the hotel across the Rhine. He agreed to meet his host at 11:30 the next morning.

The two men, I must say, did not look as if they had had a falling-out when they emerged from their three-hour meeting. Just as I was about to broadcast from a makeshift studio in the porter's lodge off the lobby of the Dreesen hotel, Hitler and Chamberlain strode by, saying their farewells cordially enough. In fact the prime minister seem highly pleased, in his vain way, at some manufactured applause by a company of S.S. guards before the hotel entrance. This was surprising in view of what had happened, the details of which soon began to leak out. As a matter of fact, all the next day, Friday, until well into the evening Chamberlain sulked in his hotel. The meeting scheduled for the morning was canceled. Apparently, the talks had completely broken down.

"War seems very near after this strange day," I scribbled in my diary at 4 A.M. All the British and French correspondents, and Birchall of the *New York Times,* an Englishman, were preparing to scurry off for the nearest frontier. They did not want to be interned if war came.

Chamberlain did not give me the impression that he himself felt war was near. Hitler had invited him over for a meeting at 10:30 that Friday evening at the Dreesen. I did not learn much of what transpired until the next day. But it was plain from the gloom among the German officials and military officers in the lobby — Ribbentrop, Goebbels, Himmler, General Keitel and others kept popping in and out — that the meeting was going badly. Still, when it broke up at 1:30 A.M., and Hitler and Chamberlain strode by my porter's lodge while I was waiting to go on the air, I noted that neither seemed unduly strained. In fact, it seemed to me, they acted surprisingly cordial to each other. Dr. Schmidt, the official Nazi interpreter, took down the words which I could not actually hear through my glass door. Even this much later, after the lapse of nearly half a century, they astonish.

> Chamberlain bid a hearty farewell to the Führer. He said he had the feeling that a relationship of confidence had grown up between himself and the Führer as a result of the conversations of the last few days.... He did not cease to hope that the present difficult crisis would be overcome, and then he would be glad to discuss other problems still outstanding with the Führer in the same spirit.
>
> The Führer thanked Chamberlain for his words and told him that he had similar hopes. As he had already stated several times, *the Czech problem was the last territorial demand which he had to make in Europe.*

I was about to go on the air at 2 A.M. when Dr. Goebbels came rushing into my makeshift studio, grabbed my notes and excitedly forbade me to say anything except to read the official communiqué. He would not even let me quote what Chamberlain had said as he returned to his hotel. One of my friends had just phoned it in to me.

"Is the position hopeless, sir?" a British correspondent had asked him.

"I would not like to say that," the prime minister answered. "It is up to the Czechs now."

That was just what Hitler wanted — to shift responsibility on the Czechs. Chamberlain's crack was bad enough. But a further concession he had just made to Hitler was worse, it seemed to me. He had agreed, the communiqué said, to transmit Hitler's demands — that the German army begin occupying the Sudetenland on October 1, at the latest — to the Czech government. Why on earth? Why couldn't he let Hitler transmit his demands himself? By acting as messenger was not the prime minister in fact lending support to Hitler's demands?

About 2:30 A.M. I stumbled out of the Dreesen, drained. Just before leaving I overheard Goebbels say that according to the Czech radio President Beneš had ordered general mobilization. "It means war," he muttered.

That news cheered me up a little. It showed that the Czechs would fight. Despite all the belligerence of Hitler, Goebbels, Ribbentrop and the Nazi press and radio, I was not sure that the Germans wanted to fight. The German people, so far as I could tell, expected Hitler to get what he wanted without having to go to war, as in 1936 when he moved into the Rhineland and again just this previous spring into Austria.

I staggered down the street, bleary-eyed with fatigue, to my hotel. I found the British and French correspondents milling around in the lobby waiting to get away in their cars to the nearest border. I said goodbye to them. When I went up to my room I found it occupied by a German officer. I packed my things hurriedly, went down to the lobby and paid my bill, too tired to complain to the room clerk. It was now 5 A.M. I lay down on a table in the lobby and snatched an hour's sleep. At six I was off by taxi to Cologne to catch a seven o'clock plane to Berlin.

Back in the capital that warm, sunny weekend of September 24–25, probably the last bit of summer, I thought, we would see that year, I found a surprising optimism. No one seemed to think it would come to war. Half the population appeared to have taken the weekend off to flock to the nearby lakes or the forests of the Grünewald. I myself went for a sail and a swim on the Wannsee.

What impressed the Germans the most was the British prime minister's agreement to transmit Hitler's demands to Prague. This showed, they were sure, that Chamberlain was backing Hitler. The Nazi press that weekend took up a new propaganda cry: "With Hitler and Chamberlain for peace!"

The next day, Monday, September 26, the optimism in Berlin suddenly vanished. It became known that the Czech government had rejected Hitler's Godesberg demands, that France also had found them unacceptable and over the weekend had ordered partial mobilization, and that as a result the Führer was in one of the worst rages of his tumultuous life. He vented it at a speech at the Sportpalast that very evening.* Shouting and shrieking in the worst paroxysm I

---

* He gave it a preliminary venting that afternoon, when he received a special envoy of Chamberlain, Sir Horace Wilson, who had been hurriedly flown to Berlin to present an urgent letter pleading with the dictator to refrain from war and insisting that he could have the Sudetenland without war.

When Dr. Schmidt began to translate the letter, which opened with mention that the Czechs had rejected Hitler's Godesberg demands, the Führer, we later learned from Schmidt, jumped up and headed for the door, shouting: "There's no sense at all in negotiating further!"

Schmidt remembered it as a most painful scene. "For the first and last time in my presence," he wrote in his postwar memoirs, "Hitler completely lost his head. The dictator finally stamped back to his chair but continued to interrupt Schmidt's reading by screaming: "The Germans are being treated like niggers! . . . On October first I shall have Czechoslovakia where I want her! If France and England decide to strike, let them! I do not care a pfennig!"

Wilson had been instructed by Chamberlain to deliver a parting message if Hitler still

had ever seen him in, he hurled a torrent of insults against "Herr Beneš," denouncing him as the "father of lies." Trying to work up his audience of fifteen thousand party *Bonzen* into a suitable state for war, he grimly depicted the Sudetenland as "under a Czech reign of terror" where "whole stretches of the country were depopulated, villages burned down and attempts made to smoke out Germans with hand grenades and gas."

He was repeating the, by now, stale propaganda lies. I noticed as the Führer raved on that despite the crowd's hanging on to every venomous word, there was no war fever. The men and women in the vast audience were almost good-natured, as if they didn't realize what the Leader's words meant.

Hitler certainly made it plain enough. I was seated in the balcony of the Sportpalast just above the speaker's stand, translating as best I could the torrents of German words into a live microphone, through which they were being relayed by shortwave to New York and over the CBS network in the United States. Hitler twice asserted that this was his last territorial claim on Europe. "We want no Czechs!" he muttered contemptuously. But he must have the Sudetenland by October 1 — five days hence — he said. If "Herr Beneš" didn't turn it over to him by then, he would take it.

"It is now up to 'Herr Beneš'! He has the choice: peace or war!"

Toward the very end his shouting tapered off and he finished his speech in that low, resonant voice which was so moving to the German ear. Then he sank into his chair, utterly exhausted. From my seat in the balcony just above him I had noticed that he still had that nervous tic I had observed a few days before at Godesberg. He kept cocking a shoulder and, when he did, the opposite leg from the knee down would bounce up. Several times, when his face became horribly contorted, I thought he might have a stroke. I noted in my diary that night: "For the first time in all the years I've observed him, Hitler seemed tonight to have completely lost control of himself." And I described the Sportpalast rally's end.

When Hitler sat down, Goebbels sprang up and shouted: "One thing is sure: 1918 will never be repeated!" Hitler looked up to him, a wild, eager expression in his eyes, as if those were the words which he

---

threatened to go to war. He was to tell the Führer that if France, in fulfillment of her treaty obligations to Czechoslovakia, became engaged in hostilities, the United Kingdom would feel obliged to support France. But the inexperienced Wilson was too timid after Hitler's outbursts to deliver it.

had been searching for all evening and hadn't quite found. He leaped to his feet and with a fanatical fire in his eyes that I shall never forget brought his right hand, after a grand sweep, pounding down on the table and yelled with all the power in his mighty lungs: *"Ja!"* Then he slumped into his chair, exhausted.

One had to remember though — and I sometimes forgot — that Adolf Hitler was a consummate actor. By noon of the next day he seemed recovered from exhaustion when Sir Horace Wilson called on him again. The special British envoy had telephoned London after Hitler's speech, urging that he not deliver to the chancellor Chamberlain's warning that Britain would support France if she were drawn into war over Czechoslovakia. He had failed to deliver the message earlier that day in the face of a violent Hitler. He now suggested to London that it would be "neither necessary nor wise to deliver it tomorrow."

But Chamberlain insisted he deliver it, albeit "more in sorrow than in anger." The prime minister, inept as he was in dealing with Hitler, apparently had an eye on history, remembering that if Sir Edward Grey had warned Berlin in 1914 that Britain would support France, the Kaiser might never have gone to war.

Almost apologetically, Wilson read the British warning.

"I can only take note of this communication," Hitler replied. But he did not remain cool for very long. As if the reality of the situation were at last sinking in, he began to heat up. Denouncing the British and French for encouraging the Czechs to resist his terms, he suddenly shouted:

"I will smash Czechoslovakia! If France and England strike, let them do so! It's a matter of complete indifference to me. Today is Tuesday. By next Monday we shall be at war!"

That seemed plain enough, but apparently not to the wooden Wilson. According to Schmidt's notes of the meeting, the special envoy wanted to continue the discussion. But Ambassador Henderson, no mean appeaser himself, insisted he desist. That did not prevent the amateurish diplomat from getting in a parting word with the Führer as he shook hands to leave.

"I shall try to make these Czechs sensible," he assured Hitler, and the latter replied he "would welcome that." Hitler would also welcome, one can speculate, a means of crawling back off the limb. Late that afternoon he sat down and dictated a shrewdly worded letter to Chamberlain.

He had good reason to send it. Much had happened during this day of Tuesday, September 27, to give him pause. Toward dusk that day in Berlin I personally witnessed an event that surely must have made the Nazi dictator draw back from plunging into war.

A little earlier, soon after the departure of Wilson, Hitler had dashed off a "most secret" order directing the assault units — some seven divisions — to move forward to their jumping-off points on the Czech frontier. They were to be ready to attack on Friday, September 30, three days hence. Later that afternoon he ordered a further concealed mobilization of five divisions for the Western Front against the French. Of these highly secret moves we correspondents, of course, knew nothing. What we did know was that Hitler, apparently concerned about the populace's lack of enthusiasm for war, had ordered a parade through Berlin of a motorized division on the way to the Czech frontier. This, it was believed, would stir the people up. To make sure of a massive turnout, the Führer timed the parade to reach the center of the city at 5 P.M., when hundreds of thousands of Berliners would be pouring out of their offices into the streets.

Shortly before five, I went out to the corner of Unter den Linden where the column would be turning down the Wilhelmstrasse and past the Chancellery where from a balcony Hitler, presumably, would review the troops. I must admit I expected a repetition of the scenes I had read of in 1914 when down this same Unter den Linden the spike-helmeted German troops had paraded past Kaiser Wilhelm II, standing on the balcony of the Royal Palace, and the delirious crowds had tossed flowers at the marching soldiers and the girls had broken through the police lines to kiss them.

To my surprise, nothing of the kind occurred. Along the Linden the crowd was very thin. I walked farther down toward the Friedrichstrasse. Another surprise. The Berliners, streaming out of their offices, were ducking into the subways or buses or simply melting into the streets to make their way home on foot. The few who stood at the curb remained silent as the tanks and guns and trucks moved by.

I retraced my steps back to the Wilhelmstrasse. The columns were turning down the street past the government ministries, and a cop hurried up from the direction of the Chancellery and shouted to the few of us on the curb that the Führer had appeared on his balcony and was reviewing his troops.

Few of the pedestrians moved. I went down to have a look.

Hitler stood there (on the balcony) and there weren't two hundred people in the street or in the great square of the Wilhelmplatz [I noted in my diary that evening]. Hitler looked grim, then angry, and soon went inside, leaving his troops to parade by unreviewed. What I've seen tonight almost rekindles a little faith in the German people. They are dead set against war.

There were other developments during the rest of the day that were far from encouraging to Hitler.

A telegram from Budapest came in saying that Yugoslavia and Rumania had warned Hungary they would move against her militarily if she attacked Czechoslovakia. That would spread the war into the Balkans, the last thing Hitler wanted. He already lacked enough troops to seriously defend the Western Frontier against the French.

A telegram marked "Very Urgent" from the German military attaché in Paris warned that France's announced "partial" mobilization was actually "total." It informed Hitler that the French would complete the "deployment of the first sixty-five divisions on the German frontier by the sixth day of mobilization." Against such a force Hitler had only a dozen divisions, half of them reserve units of doubtful value. The German military attaché also stressed that the French army would attack "immediately — in the direction of Mainz."

Finally, this pessimistic German officer informed his leader that the Italians were doing "absolutely nothing" to pin down French troops on the Franco-Italian frontier.

Mussolini, at this stage a doubtful ally, wanted to know whether his fellow dictator was actually going to war three days hence. So far, Hitler had kept his Italian friend in the dark. A telegram came during the afternoon from the Duce suggesting an immediate meeting between the German and Italian foreign ministers to work out "military cooperation." Hitler, a little taken aback by the request but anxious to keep Mussolini behind him, accepted the proposal and added, as a sop, that military staff officers from both countries should also attend the meeting.

Even from Washington, which Hitler had totally ignored up to now, came a warning from the German ambassador, Hans Dieckhoff. A "Very Urgent" cable cautioned that if Hitler resorted to force against Czechoslovakia and Britain came in to support France, "The whole weight of the United States would be thrown into the scale on the side of Britain."

And finally that fateful Tuesday a wire came in from the German military attaché in Prague. It was factual, laconic. "Calm in Prague.

Last mobilization measures carried out . . . total estimated call-up is 1,000,000; field army 800,000."

That was as many men as Germany had for two fronts, and most of the Czechs were better trained. Together the Czechs and French outnumbered the Germans by more than two to one.

With such news, and mindful that his ultimatum to the Czechs to accept his Godesberg demands ran out at 2 P.M. on the morrow, Hitler got off a final letter to Chamberlain. It was nicely calculated to appeal to the prime minister and would show the British that he, Hitler, still held back from war. Moderate in tone, the letter argued that the German proposals for the "return" of the Sudetenland would not "rob Czechoslovakia of every guarantee of its existence." Hitler was willing to negotiate details of the takeover with the Czechs and to "give a formal guarantee for the remainder of Czechoslovakia." The Czechs, Hitler said, were holding out simply because they hoped to start a European war with the help of France and England.

> I must leave to your judgment [Hitler concluded] whether, in view of these facts, you consider that you should continue your effort . . . to spoil such maneuvers and bring the government in Prague to reason at the very last hour.

That evening in London, in a broadcast to the nation, Chamberlain had made clear his resolve "to continue his effort." This was before he received Hitler's communication. "I would not hesitate," he said, "to pay even a third visit to Germany if I thought it would do any good."

That must have pleased the Nazi dictator. And even more Chamberlain's further statement that "if we [British] have to fight it must be on larger issues than that" — i.e., over, as he put it, "a quarrel in a faraway country between people of whom we know nothing!"

Hitler's letter reached the prime minister at Downing Street at 10:30 P.M. It was a straw that Chamberlain grabbed desperately.

> After reading your letter [Chamberlain replied] I feel certain that you can get all essentials without war and without delay. I am ready to come to Berlin myself at once to discuss arrangements for transfer with you and representatives of the Czech Government, together with representatives of France and Italy, if you desire. . . . I cannot believe that you will take responsibility of starting a world war which may end civilization for the sake of a few days delay in settling this long-standing problem.

Thus the idea of a conference of the Big Four and Czechoslovakia to finally settle the conflict came first from Chamberlain. For some reason Chamberlain's reply did not reach Hitler until nearly noon the next day, Wednesday, September 28. A plea by the prime minister to Mussolini to urge Hitler to accept the proposal and to take part in the conference himself reached Rome a little earlier. It spurred the restless Duce to action.

The day had started badly, everywhere. Deep gloom hung over Berlin that morning, I remember, and the dispatches from London, Paris, Rome and Prague reported a similar despondency in those capitals. War seemed inevitable.

"A Great War can hardly be avoided any longer," Jodl quoted Göring as saying that morning.

In London, Ed Murrow phoned me, trenches were being dug in Hyde Park, schoolchildren were being evacuated from the city, hospitals were being emptied so that they could receive the war casualties. The evening before, at 8 P.M., Ed said, the order had gone out for the mobilization of the fleet, the backbone of Britain's armed forces, and it had been publicly announced on the BBC at 11:38.

"Have the German people been told of this step?" Ed asked. He thought it the most important move the British could make short of declaring war.

"No, they haven't," I said. There had been not a word about it over German radio or in the newspapers.

In Paris, Raymond Gram Swing called me to say there was a panicky scramble for the choked trains leaving the city, and motor traffic out of the capital was jammed with those fleeing the feared bombing. Raymond reported he had been able to fight his way through the frantic crowds at the Gare St. Lazare and get Tess and Eileen on a boat train to Cherbourg, but he was not sure if it would get as far as the port or that the liner for New York would sail. I worried about them all day. There were reports that morning of Germans on the western border also panicking. Thousands of them were fleeing from an expected French attack.

At 2 P.M., we knew, the time limit on Hitler's ultimatum ran out. Toward noon, I noticed rather frantic diplomats arriving at the Chancellery. It was evident that a desperate eleventh-hour effort to avoid Hitler's war was being made. You could sense that from the grim faces of the ambassadors of Italy, France and Britain — Bernardo Attolico, André François-Poncet and Sir Nevile Henderson — as they arrived. The faces of the Germans were no less grim: Göring, who I knew was urging peace; Ribbentrop, who was all out for war; Goebbels, who was on the fence; and the generals, led by Wilhelm Keitel, the toady chief of the High Command. General Franz Halder, chief of the army General Staff, was conspicuous by his absence from the Chancellery. I assumed he was busy making the last-minute preparations for the assault on Czechoslovakia, but, as I learned later, there was another reason. I had the feeling, strengthened subsequently by more knowledge, that this day marked a crucial turning point in the history of our times.

Two things happened. First, at midafternoon, as his ultimatum expired and at the instigation of Mussolini, frantically urged on by Chamberlain, Hitler postponed his attack on Czechoslovakia and agreed to meet with Mussolini, Chamberlain and Daladier on the morrow at Munich to settle the details of Germany's takeover of the Sudetenland. The Czechs were not invited. Second, the conspirators, led by General Halder, called off their plot to depose Hitler when they received word that there would be a conference the next day at Munich, which meant that there would be no war and therefore no need to seize the dictator.

In the Wilhelmstrasse and indeed in all of Germany, there was immense relief at the news, which was broadcast over the radio about 5 P.M. The sense of relief was probably even greater in Paris and London. The scene in the House of Commons that afternoon released pent-up feelings in Britain in a display of mass hysteria seldom witnessed on that chilly island. It had convened with the feeling among most members, some of them subsequently told me, that war was inevitable. By 4:15 Chamberlain had been addressing the body for an hour and twenty minutes, defending his appeasement of Hitler and praising Mussolini for having a few hours before persuaded Hitler to postpone his "mobilization" for twenty-four hours.* He paused to glance at a note which was handed to him as he spoke. He looked up, and smiled.

> That is not all. I have something further to say to the House. I have now been informed by Herr Hitler that he invites me to meet him at Munich tomorrow morning. He has also invited Signor Mussolini and Monsieur Daladier. Signor Mussolini has accepted, and I have no doubt Monsieur Daladier will accept.
>
> I need not say what my answer will be. . . .

---

* I never understood then, or later, all the talk about German "mobilization" being postponed. By this date the German armed forces were fully mobilized. The fact had not been publicly announced. But the prime minister could not have been unaware of it.

He did not have to say it. The ancient chamber burst out in a wild cry such as never had been heard in it. The honorable members shouted their joy at the top of their voices, hurled order papers into the air. A few sobbed. Some broke into tears. Above the tumult a shout was heard that seemed to express the deep feelings of all: "Thank God for the prime minister!"

No one asked the prime minister why Czechoslovakia had been excluded from the conference that was to decide its fate. That very morning, in his letter to Hitler, Chamberlain had proposed that it be represented. No one inquired why Russia, the co-guarantor of Czechoslovakia's integrity in case of a German attack, was left out. If it came to war after all, Britain would sorely need all the help it could get from the Soviet Union.*

Now, of course, it would not come to war.

And what of the Halder plot to depose Hitler?

The chief of the German General Staff and his confederates blamed Chamberlain for making them call it off! All was ready to seize Hitler in Berlin on that fateful Wednesday, General Halder claimed at Nuremberg eight years later. General von Witzleben had come to his office at noon to discuss final details.

> During this discussion the news came that the British prime minister and the French premier had agreed to come to Hitler for further talks. I therefore withdrew the order to carry out our plans. . . . The entire basis for action had been taken away. . . .
>
> We were firmly convinced we would be successful. But now came Mr. Chamberlain and with one stroke the danger of war was averted.

Gisevius, the police official involved, agreed with the generals when he took the stand at Nuremberg:

> The impossible had happened. Chamberlain and Daladier were flying to Munich. Our revolt was done for. . . . Chamberlain saved Hitler.

* Lord Halifax, the British foreign secretary, tried to console the Russians the next day, after Chamberlain had already taken a plane to Munich. He invited in the Soviet ambassador, Ivan Maisky, and explained that it had not been the British who wanted to exclude Russia from the conference.

"We all have to face facts," he said, "and one of these facts, as you well know, is that the heads of the German and Italian governments were not willing in present circumstances to sit in conference with Soviet representatives."

Maisky then asked Halifax if the Czechs would be represented at Munich. "This matter is one," the foreign minister replied, "that the prime minister has very clearly before him, and in regard to which he will do his best."

Such deceit!

Maybe so. But one remains skeptical. That there was a genuine plot there can be no doubt. But it was poorly and inadequately organized. And the leaders, especially the two top key generals, Halder and Witzleben, lacked clear and resolute leadership. Why, for example, did they wait *four days* after Hitler had finally returned to Berlin from Godesberg on September 24? By then all their conditions had been fulfilled: Hitler was in Berlin; he was determined to go to war; he had set the day for the attack on Czechoslovakia. Yet the conspirators hesitated.

Perhaps had they been more deeply motivated, they might have taken action in time. They did not plan to remove Hitler in order to bring an end to an evil tyranny, but only to avert a lost war. When Hitler called a conference at Munich to get what he wanted peacefully, the plotters saw no justification for deposing him.

The hastily called conference the next day was an anticlimax. The sorry spectacle it presented of France and Britain selling out the only democracy in Central Europe, the loyal ally of the French, and giving Hitler the greatest diplomatic triumph of his life, depressed me beyond words. Once I grasped what Hitler, Chamberlain, Mussolini and Daladier were up to, I felt too wretched to try adequately to report on their antics, a lapse that contributed to my being badly scooped by my arch radio rival, NBC.

I was conscious all through the miserable day that here in Munich, where Hitler had made his lowly start after the war, he was now playing the great conqueror, to whom the heads of other Western countries, frightened by his threats of war, deferred.

Incredible, I thought, how far he had come in so short a time!

Early that morning he had gone to greet Mussolini at Kufstein on the old Austro-German frontier, a few miles southeast of Munich. Aides said later he was in a belligerent mood despite knowing he was going to get what he wanted without having to go to war. Over maps he showed the Duce the dispositions of his troops and how they could easily "liquidate" the enemy. Either the talks that day must give him the Sudetenland immediately, he said, or he would resort to arms.

Besides, he told Mussolini, "the time will come when we shall have to fight side by side against France and England."

The strutting Duce heartily agreed.

On the train ride up to Munich and at lunch later in Hitler's private Munich residence, the two dictators discussed their strategy for the talks. Mussolini would start the ball rolling by introducing a "compromise plan," which in reality had been drafted in Berlin the evening before and telephoned to Rome. Together they would steamroller the British and French into accepting it.

That proved easier than even they must have thought. Unlike the two Fascist dictators, Chamberlain and Daladier made no attempt to get together to concert their strategy. I myself got the impression that this was deliberate on the part of the British prime minister. He had come to Munich to reach a quick agreement with Hitler and he was not going to let the French stand in his way. So far as I could determine, they never conferred privately during the entire conference. The premier, a man I personally got to like in Paris, went around the entire day in a funk.

The cant began as soon as the four leaders settled down in Hitler's private office at the Führerbau. Mussolini had brought with him from Rome, he said, "a definite proposal." Its German origin should have been evident to Chamberlain and Daladier since it closely followed Hitler's Godesberg demands, which the Czechs, the British and the French had rejected. But the premier, according to the German minutes of the meeting, "welcomed the Duce's proposal, which had been made in an objective and realistic spirit." The prime minister also "welcomed the Duce's proposal and declared that he himself had conceived of a solution on the lines of this proposal."

One could pardon Hitler if, after hearing these words, he concluded that it was easier to bamboozle the British and French statesmen than he had expected. "Little worms," he would call them later. And at luncheon with Mussolini after the first brief meeting of the four, he had confided that the British prime minister had impressed him as "an insignificant man" who was nutty about fishing on weekends. He, Hitler, had had to tell him: "I know no weekends, and I don't fish!" One can imagine the two Fascist dictators chuckling at that one.

As befitted an experienced politician and perhaps to soothe his conscience, Chamberlain went through the motions of trying to negotiate. The prime minister raised the question of who would compensate the Czech government for public property given up in the Sudetenland. There would be no compensation, Hitler replied angrily. What about the Czechs not being allowed even to take their cattle out of the Sudetenland with them? Chamberlain asked. At this Hitler exploded.

"Our time is too valuable," he shouted to Chamberlain, "to be wasted on such trivialities!" The prime minister desisted.

He did raise the point of the Czechs' being represented at a conference which concerned them most of all. Daladier gave him half-hearted support, but his words shock one when read today. This was an ally he was speaking about. The French government, Daladier said, "would in no wise tolerate procrastination . . . by the Czech government." But he thought "the presence of a Czech representative, who could be consulted, if necessary, would be an advantage."

But the Nazi dictator would not hear of it. Daladier meekly gave in, but Chamberlain won a small concession. He got agreement that a Czech representative might make himself available "in the next room."

And so at 4:30 that afternoon, while leaders of the four great Western powers were discussing details of Czechoslovakia's demise, two diplomats of that doomed country arrived in Munich by special plane from Prague. These were Dr. Hubert Masarik, from the Czech Foreign Office, and Dr. Vojtech Mastny, the unhappy Czech minister in Berlin.

They were treated hostilely by the Germans on their arrival, as if they were prisoners of war or, as Masarik put it, as "police suspects."

> We were taken in a police car [he subsequently related], accompanied by members of the Gestapo, to the Regina, where the British delegation was staying. We were forbidden to leave our rooms, which were guarded by policemen.

At 7 P.M., after the Big Four had agreed that the Germans would begin occupying the Sudetenland on October 1, just as Hitler had sworn in his Sportpalast speech that they would, and complete the occupation in stages by October 10, and there remained only the task of tidying up the details, a British delegate came to the Czechs' room to prepare them for the bad news. This was a Frank Ashton-Gwatkin, a Foreign Office official who had been a member of the Runciman Mission in Czechoslovakia in August. To the imprisoned Czech diplomats he appeared "nervous and very reserved."

A general agreement had been reached, he told them, but he could not yet give them the details. He *could* say that it was "much harsher than the Anglo-French proposals." When the Czechs protested the consequences of the accord — the destruction of their country — the Englishman answered icily, Masarik later reported, "that I did not seem to understand how difficult was the situation of the Great Powers and how hard it had been to negotiate with Hitler." The British diplomat, for his part, did not seem to realize how hard it might be for the Czechs.

At 10 P.M., during the British dinner-break, the two Czechs were taken to the room of Sir Horace Wilson for further bad news. Emphasizing that he was speaking for the prime minister, Wilson handed them a map showing the areas the Czechs must evacuate forthwith. When the Czech envoys attempted to object to what amounted to a dismantling of their country, the insufferable Wilson cut them short. He had nothing to add, he said, and left the room.

The Czechs were left alone for a moment with Ashton-Gwatkin, which was not much consolation. "If you do not accept," he told them, "you will have to settle your affairs with the Germans absolutely alone. Perhaps the French may tell you this more gently, but you can believe me that they share our views. They are disinterested."

Thirty minutes after midnight the translations of the Munich Accord were finally finished, and the four leaders sat down in the Führerbau to sign them. Hitler got all he had demanded at Godesberg and in his Sportpalast speech "except," I noted that evening, "he has to wait a few days longer for *all* of it."

German military occupation of the predominantly German territory in the Sudetenland was to begin on October 1 — one day hence — and be completed in three more stages by October 7. The remaining territory, after being delimited by the "International Commission," would be occupied by October 10. The Czechs were allowed a delegate on this commission, which also would arrange for plebiscites in those areas where the ethnographical makeup of the population was in doubt, and make the final determination of the new frontier.

Chamberlain and Daladier had asked that all four powers join in a common guarantee against unprovoked aggression toward the new rump Czechoslovakia. But Hitler, backed by Mussolini, would agree only to joining in the guarantee after "the question of Polish and Hungarian minorities" in Czechoslovakia had been settled. In the meantime, France and Britain solemnly declared that they "stood by their offer" of a guarantee against aggression toward the new Czech state.

It was a notable victory for Hitler, and he seemed to me far from unaware of it as I watched him leave the Führerbau surrounded by his faithful: Göring, Goebbels, Ribbentrop, Hess and General Keitel. His eyes were flashing. He had a positive swagger as he descended the steps. His tic was gone. Mussolini too looked cocky as a rooster as he left. Laced in a new Fascist militia uniform, his cap at a jaunty angle, he bounded down the steps, trying hard, it seemed to me, to appear to share in Hitler's triumph.

Daladier, on the other hand, I noted in my diary that night,

> looked a completely beaten and broken man. He came over to the Regina to say goodbye to Chamberlain. A bunch of us were waiting as he came down the stairs. Someone asked, or started to ask: "*Monsieur le President*, are you satisfied with the agreement . . ." He turned as if to say something, but he was too tired and defeated and the words did not come out and he stumbled out the door in silence.
>
> The French say he fears to return to Paris tomorrow, thinks a hostile mob will get him. . . . For France has sacrificed her whole continental position and lost her main prop in eastern Europe. For France this day has been disastrous.*

Chamberlain, in contrast to his French colleague, looked exceedingly pleased with himself as he strode into the lobby of the Regina after the end of the conference. He seemed a bit sleepy. He kept yawning and it was obvious that, unlike Daladier, he would enjoy a good night's untroubled sleep. There was still one more act for him to perform late that night, a most unpleasant one, I thought, though he did not seem to mind it. Dragging the members of the French delegation with him he went up to his room to speak briefly with the captive Czech envoys. Both he and Daladier made it clear to the Czechs that they were no longer to argue their plight but to accept promptly the dictates Hitler had frightened the Anglo-French statesmen into accepting.

It was now 2 A.M. The atmosphere, Masarik later noted, was "repressive; sentence was about to be passed."

> The French, obviously embarrassed, appeared to be aware of the consequences for French prestige. Mr. Chamberlain, in a short introduction, referred to the Agreement and gave the text to Dr. Mastny to read out. . . .

The Czechs began to ask several questions, but

> Mr. Chamberlain was yawning continuously, with no show of embarrassment. I asked MM. Daladier and Legér† whether they expected

---

* The premier need not have feared. Contrary to his expectation he was given a delirious and most friendly reception when his plane landed at Le Bourget. Hundreds of thousands of Parisians lined the streets to cheer him as he returned to the Ministry. It is said he could hardly believe it.

† Alexis Legér, born in Guadaloupe of French parents, had been secretary-general of the Quai D'Orsay since 1932 and was influential in shaping French foreign policy in the inter-

a declaration or answer to the Agreement from our government. M. Daladier, obviously embarrassed, did not reply. M. Legér replied that the four statesmen had not much time. He added hurriedly and with superficial casualness that no answer was required, that they regarded the plan as accepted, that our government had that very day, at the latest at 3 P.M., to send its representative to Berlin to the sitting of the Commission, and finally that the Czechoslovak official who was to be sent would have to be in Berlin on Saturday to fix the details for the evacuation of the first zone. The atmosphere, he said, was beginning to become dangerous for the whole world.

He spoke to us harshly enough. This was a Frenchman, saying that this was a sentence without right of appeal and without possibility of modification. Mr. Chamberlain did not conceal his weariness. They gave us a second slightly corrected map. Then they finished with us, and we could go. The Czechoslovak Republic as fixed by the frontiers of 1918 had ceased to exist.

I was exhausted and depressed by this long day. Hoping that a little fresh air might relieve my weariness, I walked back to the hotel breathing in the crisp night air. Calls from Ed Murrow in London and Paul White in New York had come in. When I called them back I found that I had been badly scooped this night by Max Jordan of NBC. I had gone on the air at 11 P.M., announced that an accord had been reached, and given the essential details. But Jordan, who because of NBC's special position in Germany had access to the Führerbau, from which I and the other correspondents were barred, had posed as a German official, received a copy of the agreement, rushed to the Führer's special radio studio, and at 1 A.M. read the text on the air, a half-hour before I could broadcast it. Both Murrow and White consoled me, insisting that I had done a good job. But this failure added to my dejection.

I didn't feel much better the next morning when I learned that Chamberlain, behind the back of Daladier, had gone to see Hitler at the latter's private apartment and induced him to sign a joint statement that the prime minister must have thought, with reason, would, so far as British public opinion was concerned, take the sting, or some of it, out of his sellout of Czechoslovakia the night before. It would also appeal to the deep pacifism of the British people.

No doubt I would have felt worse about this devious demarche had I known what Chamberlain said to Hitler to butter him up to sign his

---

war years. Under another name, St.-John Perse, he was a distinguished poet and eventually won a Nobel Prize for literature.

piece of paper, but that was revealed only much later by Dr. Schmidt, who interpreted for the two men. Rereading the prime minister's remarks a half-century later still gives me a feeling of nausea, especially the expression of his "hope that the Czechs would not be so unreasonable as to make difficulties," and that if they did, Hitler would not bomb Prague "with the dreadful losses among the civilian population which it would entail." To which the dictator replied that he would "always try to spare the civilian population and confine himself to military objectives — he hated the thought of little babies being killed by gas bombs."

Thus assured, Chamberlain, in one of his most jaunty moods, prattled on for an hour about every conceivable subject. The Führer, according to Schmidt, grew more and more morose. Finally Chamberlain pulled out of his pocket the statement he had composed and asked Hitler to join him in signing it.

> ... We regard the agreement signed last night and the Anglo-German Naval Agreement as symbolic of the desire of our two peoples never to go to war with one another again.
>
> We are resolved that the method of consultation shall be the method to deal with other questions that may concern our two countries, and we are determined to continue our efforts to remove possible sources of difference and thus to contribute to the peace of Europe.

Dr. Schmidt's impression was that Hitler signed the paper "with a certain reluctance ... only to please Chamberlain," who, he recounts, "thanked the Führer warmly ... and underlined the great psychological effect which he expected from this document."

Indeed the prime minister played it for all it was worth. Brandishing it in his hands as he addressed the happy crowd from a window at 10 Downing Street on his return that evening, he declared:

> My good friends! This is the second time in our history that there has come back from Germany to Downing Street peace with honor. I believe it is peace in our time.

Disraeli, of course, had returned from the Congress of Berlin in 1878 with a peace agreement.

The British press, Parliament and the people were jubilant, hailing the returning prime minister as a hero. The *Times* wrote that "no conqueror returning from the battlefield has come adorned with nobler laurels." Only Duff Cooper, the First Lord of the Admiralty, resigned from the cabinet in protest. And when in the ensuing House of Commons debate Churchill rose to brand Munich "as a total, unmitigated defeat," he was forced to pause until a storm of hostile shouting had subsided. The House backed Chamberlain by a resounding vote of 366 to 144.

The Germans, too, were happy. The Führer had won another bloodless victory, the third since he had gone into the demilitarized Rhineland and then taken Austria. He had increased his prestige with the people. He had won further ascendancy over the army, which had opposed his risking a lost war over the Sudetenland. Ironically enough, he himself was far from satisfied by his triumph over the West.

"That fellow [Chamberlain]," Dr. Schacht says he heard Hitler say on his return to Berlin, "has spoiled my entry into Prague!" And to his generals he later confided: "It was clear to me from the first moment that I could not be satisfied with the Sudeten-German territory. That was only a partial solution."

The immediate aftermath of Munich was, to me, as shabby and deceitful as the conference itself. The "International Commission" in Berlin was a farce. It sided with the Germans in every dispute over territory and in the final delimiting of frontiers. It never honored the Munich pledge to carry out plebiscites in areas where the makeup of the population was in doubt. Germany and Italy never honored their word to guarantee, once the question of Polish and Hungarian minorities was settled, what was left of Czechoslovakia against aggression. Britain and France, for their part, declined, when aggression occurred, to honor the guarantee they had solemnly given at Munich.

Such was Mr. Chamberlain's "Peace with Honor."*

His surrender to Hitler at Munich was not necessary. The Nazi dictator had put himself far out on a limb. The British prime minister rescued him from it. Not only that. He gave him a bloodless victory that not only strengthened his position in Germany, especially with the army, whose leaders had opposed him and been proved wrong, but also in Europe, whose powers henceforth would try to make the best accommodation they could with him, now that the Western democracies had so shamefully capitulated.

What if Hitler had attacked Czechoslovakia instead of being given

---

* "You were given the choice between war and dishonor," Churchill said to Chamberlain. "You chose dishonor and you will have war."

what he wanted at Munich? From covering the Czech crisis at first hand and even more from long study and reflection, I have come to certain conclusions that I believe will stand up in history.

Had it not been for Munich, most of his generals subsequently agreed, Hitler would have ordered the attack on Czechoslovakia for October 1, and one of two things would have happened. The Halder Plot would have succeeded and Hitler been overthrown or, if that failed and the aggression against Czechoslovakia began, it would have brought France, Britain and probably Russia into the war, which Germany would surely have lost. The chief of the General Staff and his colleagues, we have to remember, were opposed not to war but to a lost war.

The argument of those who supported Chamberlain and Daladier that Munich saved the Western democracies not only from war but from defeat in war, that it spared London and Paris from being wiped out by the Luftwaffe, and that it gave time — a whole year — to Britain and France at least partially to catch up with the Reich in rearming, has been effectively refuted, largely by those in the best position to know, the German generals.

The generals were not sure that the German army could even break through the Czech fortifications. They *were* sure that had the attempt been made, the French army, outnumbering the Germans in the West ten to one, would easily have broken through and occupied the Ruhr, the center of Hitler's arms industries.

On the stand at the Nuremberg Trial Field Marshal Fritz Erich von Manstein, who became one of the most successful of the German field commanders, told the tribunal:

> If war had broken out, neither our western border nor our Polish frontier could really have been effectively defended by us. And there is no doubt whatsoever that had Czechoslovakia defended herself, we would have been held up by her fortifications, for we did not have the means to break through.

Even the Nazi Warlord himself was impressed by what he saw of the Czech defenses. "When after Munich," Hitler told Dr. Carl Burckhardt, the League of Nations high commissioner in Danzig, "we were in a position to examine Czech military strength from within, what we saw of it greatly disturbed us; we had run a serious danger. . . . I now understand why my generals urged restraint."

One of the chief reasons that Chamberlain and Daladier surrendered at Munich was their fear, backed by their cabinets, military chiefs and large sections of the press and public, that if war came Paris and London and most other great cities of France and England would be obliterated by the German air force. The prime minister and the premier, it has been argued, spared their countries from such a terrible fate.

But, were such fears warranted?

Perhaps the chief instigator of such apprehension was an American, Charles Lindbergh, a civilian pilot of genius but with no real military training or knowledge. The Nazi Germans convinced this gullible young American, after a couple of visits to the Reich, that the Luftwaffe had become by the time of Munich superior to the combined air-fleets of Britain, France, Czechoslovakia and Russia, and capable of wiping out the great cities of Europe. Lindbergh's reputation as an airman was so immense in the West, despite his lack of military expertise, that his dire warnings to the French and British were taken very seriously and no doubt played a considerable part in inducing Chamberlain and Daladier to capitulate so shamefully at Munich.

Lindbergh was wrong. And it is difficult to excuse the French and British governments for believing his warnings of doom. Let us see how far the feared Luftwaffe at this time, the fall of 1938, fell short of the invincibility the "Lone Eagle" gave it.

On September 22, as Chamberlain arrived in Godesberg to see Hitler for the second time at the most crucial stage of the crisis over the Sudetenland, General Helmuth Felmy, commander of the 2nd Air Group in Brunswick, who in case of war would be responsible for Luftwaffe operations over the Low Countries and Britain, submitted a memorandum to the air force High Command about the prospects in the air against the British from German airfields.

It was far from optimistic. In fact, the general reported that unless and until the German army procured air bases along the coasts of the Netherlands, Belgium and Northern France opposite England, the Luftwaffe could not be effective against it. The distance from the nearest airfields in Germany to England was too great — three hundred miles (four hundred miles if the Luftwaffe did not violate the airspace of the Low Countries), necessitating round trips of six hundred or eight hundred miles. The range of German bombers with a thousand-pound bomb load was four hundred thirty miles. The range of fighter planes was even less. Besides, German crews were not trained for long-range strategic bombing. Their role was to support

German ground forces from the air. The Luftwaffe was a tactical air force, not a strategic one (a difference Lindbergh apparently did not comprehend). "With the means now at our disposal," the general had concluded, "a war of annihilation against England is out of the question."*

The Luftwaffe might have had more success against Paris and the cities of Northern France. They were within the range of German bombers and, in some cases, of fighters. But it must be remembered that in the first weeks at least of an invasion of Czechoslovakia the German air force would have been entirely concentrated in the East. It would have had its hands full supporting the ground troops as well as trying to destroy the Czech air force, which was not negligible and which might have been aided by Soviet warplanes operating from bases quickly reached in eastern Czechoslovakia from nearby Russia. The German generals say there were few planes available to attack the West. Probably the French air force, weak as it was, though it was strongest in fighter planes, could have pretty well protected Paris and the other cities in the North.

Finally, did the eleven months of peace which Munich gave France and Britain to speed up their armaments narrow the gap with Germany and thus put them in a better position to fight, as Chamberlain argued until his dying breath, when war came? Or were they actually worse off than in September, 1938?

It is a much debated question. I believe myself that with one exception — Britain's strengthening of its air defenses — the Western Allies did not gain on Germany in military strength. I believe they lost ground. Furthermore, their strategic position on September 1, 1939, when Hitler began his war, was much worse than it was at the time of Munich.

Winston Churchill summed it up: "The year's breathing space said to be 'gained' by Munich left Britain and France in a much worse position compared to Hitler's Germany than they had been at the Munich crisis."

The strategic position of the Western Allies worsened a great deal. Czechoslovakia, with its thirty-five well-trained, well-armed divisions deployed behind its formidable mountain fortifications, would have put up, as the German generals admitted, a stout and prolonged

---

* Friends who have read the above have asked how, two years later, the Germans were able to bomb Britain so savagely. The answer is that by July of 1940, the German army had occupied the channel ports of France and Belgium and the North Sea coast of Holland, from whose airfields England was but a short distance over an undefended waterway.

resistance to Hitler's forces. By holding down almost the entire German army and air force, the Czechs would have given France the time and opportunity to overrun Germany on its weakly defended borders in the west and to occupy its chief industrial district, the Ruhr, without which the Reich could not long continue fighting.

Poland, despite its foolish policy of also appeasing Hitler, almost certainly would have been drawn in against Germany. For beside the fact that it had a military alliance with France, its leaders, short-sighted and pig-headed as they were, knew that Poland's strategic position vis-à-vis Germany would become hopeless — she would be surrounded on three sides — if Germany overran Czechoslovakia.

It is difficult to say what the Soviet Union would have done. But I believe that despite Stalin's mistrust of the West and his resentment at being snubbed by Chamberlain and Halifax during the crisis, Russia would have given Czechoslovakia immediate help in the way of military supplies and that once Stalin saw that France and Britain would fight he would have dispatched important units of the Soviet air force to Czech airfields and in the end entered the war against Germany, which as long as Hitler, the great anti-Bolshevik, was alive would always be the principal threat to Russia.

So strategically, France and Great Britain were worse off in September, 1939, than in September, 1938.

But that was not all. As the last days of peace eked out in the summer of 1939, Germany began to receive large amounts of raw materials and oil from the Soviet Union. For Stalin, snubbed by the British and French who kept the Soviet Union away from Munich despite its treaty obligations to the Czechs, despite its value to the Allies as a major military and industrial power should war come, had come to the conclusion that others could play Chamberlain's game of appeasing the Nazi dictator. As a matter of fact, only four days after Munich an alert counselor of the German embassy in Moscow reported to Berlin a sudden change in the atmosphere as a consequence of the Munich Pact. He thought Stalin "would draw conclusions" and become "more positive" toward Germany. It was the first step in a turnabout that would have disastrous consequences for France and Britain.

But the calamitous consequences of their surrender to Hitler were scarcely, if at all, comprehended by Chamberlain and Daladier as they returned to their respective capitals in triumph. Indeed, the vain British prime minister (though not Daladier) would continue to boast of his accomplishment until the whole edifice of peace he thought he had built came crashing down on him. To do him credit, he did, finally, awake, prodded to be sure by some members of his cabinet who were more realistic than he.

By then it was very late.

For the first time in my life as a journalist I felt too sick at heart after Munich to work seriously at my profession. I followed the German army into the Sudetenland but military censorship was so stupid and severe that I made no broadcast reports. Finally Ed Murrow and I agreed to meet in Paris and, as I wrote in my diary, "drown our sorrows in champagne."

But the great, civilized city which I passionately loved now seemed, my diary reminds me, "a frightful place, completely surrendered to defeatism with no inkling of what has happened to France." The French were not only terribly relieved at being spared war, which was certainly understandable, but they had convinced themselves that it would have been a crime to get involved in war. Neither the newspaper editors, politicians or just plain people I talked to had the slightest conception of how disastrous Munich was to them. They did not realize that France's military position in Europe, secured after such terrible bloodletting in the 1914–1918 war, was destroyed. Because her population and industrial production were only a little more than half of those of Germany, France had laboriously built up alliances with the smaller powers in the East on the other flank of Germany: Czechoslovakia, Poland, Yugoslavia and Rumania, which together had the military potential of a Big Power. Now Czechoslovakia was lost. And after her surrender to Hitler, how could France's remaining allies in Eastern Europe have any confidence in her written word to come to their aid if attacked?

"France makes no sense to me anymore," I reluctantly concluded in my diary.

Champagne had little effect on Murrow and me, though we let it flow. Ed, naturally lugubrious, was more gloomy than I'd ever seen him. He was coming to love the British, and they had let him down. He did see one bright spot for us, personally and professionally. At home CBS seemed to have awakened to the opportunity for radio to present the news.

Ed had some statistics, cabled over by an enthusiastic Paley. In a scant three weeks CBS had done nearly five hundred broadcasts on the Czech crisis, over one hundred of them from pickups in Europe, including fourteen European roundups that Murrow and I had set up. No other network, Paley was sure, had approached CBS in its coverage of the story. In Paris Ed and I received cables from Paley: "Columbia's coverage of the European crisis is superior to its competitors and is probably the best job ever done in radio broadcasting."

I flew to Warsaw and on November 11 broadcast a program commemorating the twentieth anniversary of the Polish Republic. I was mainly interested in finding out whether the Poles, who, in cahoots with Nazi Germany, had just grabbed a small slice of Czechoslovakia, had sense enough to know that they were next on Hitler's list. It was obvious that the colonels, at least, who ran the country under a sort of military semidictatorship, did not have sense enough.

"The Poles [are] a delightful, utterly romantic people, and I've had much good food and drink and music with them," I concluded in my diary. "But they are horribly unrealistic. In their trust of Hitler, for instance."

Walter Duranty, the great Moscow correspondent of the *New York Times*, was in Warsaw on some kind of assignment, and one beautiful, blizzardy night we tossed aside our worries about the blindness of the Poles and the stupidity of mankind to make a night of it on vodka at numerous Russian cafés.

The pope, of all men, provided another distraction for me. I had gone to Belgrade to do a show on the twentieth anniversary of the birth of Yugoslavia when CBS phoned to say the pontiff was dying and asking me to rush to Rome. I caught young Cy Sulzberger, just breaking in on the *New York Times*, at a cocktail party and persuaded him to do my broadcast, after which I rushed to the station and caught the night train for Rome. As I have mentioned, no pope had ever died since radio began broadcasting news, and his death would bring a challenge to us that I personally was looking forward to. I spent a week arranging with the Vatican and the Italian Broadcasting Company for facilities, but Pius XI, despite his age (eighty-one) and another severe heart attack, refused to die.

Back in Paris again in early December to meet Tess and Eileen returning from America, I had to cover an unsavory event cooked up by the insufferable Georges Bonnet, the French foreign minister, who had boasted of pushing Daladier to sign the Munich Pact. He was as slippery as a snake. To be charitable about it, Bonnet was only doing that December day what Chamberlain had done the morning after the Munich Agreement: signing a "good neighbor" declaration with Germany, in the person of another insufferable foreign minister, Ribbentrop, stating that the two countries had no more territorial disputes to settle and that any future disagreements between the two countries, which so often had gone to war with each other, would be settled by consultation.

"What a farce!" I noted in my diary. Who but a fool like Bonnet would trust Hitler now to keep such a pledge?

Paris, I also noted, seemed to have recovered somewhat from its post-Munich defeatism. When Ribbentrop drove to various ceremonies, the streets were utterly deserted. The presidents of the two chambers of Parliament, several cabinet ministers and many leading figures in political, business, literary and social circles, ostentatiously refused to attend any of the numerous public functions accorded the Nazi foreign minister. I was relieved to see the French recovering their senses.

Relieved and happy too when Tess and Eileen arrived on the fifteenth from the States and we set off for home in Geneva. We had a fine Christmas reunion that year. At the year's end, as usual, Tess and I took stock of the eventful past twelve months. It had been quite a year: our first child, the Anschluss in Austria, our flight from her native Vienna to Geneva, and finally, the Sudeten crisis and the shame of Munich.

"As usual," I wrote in my diary, "Tess and I wonder what the new year will bring."

We were not hopeful — how could one be after the Anschluss and Munich? But we had no idea — nor, I believe, did anyone else on the planet — what terrible suffering for humanity it would usher in.

The author broadcasting from Friedrichstrasse Bahnhof,
Berlin, September 20, 1938

BELOW: *Chamberlain meeting with Hitler at Godesberg, 1938*

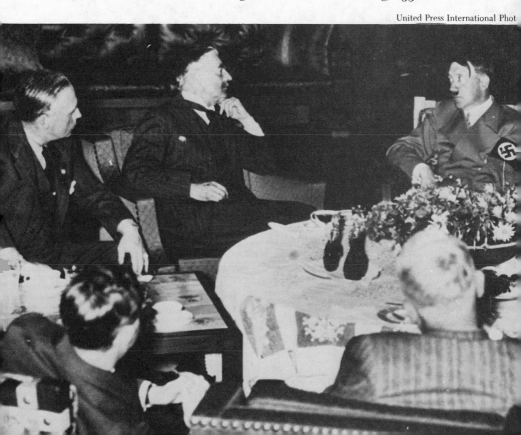

Germans entering the Sudetenland after Munich, 1938

BOOK FOUR

The Coming of World War II

1939–1940

CHAPTER 14

The Last Months
of Peace

1939

Early in the spring that year, Hitler struck again. At dawn on March 15, 1939, he sent in his troops to occupy the rest of Czechoslovakia and, as he had threatened to do, wiped it off the map. The splendid little democracy, the only one left in Central and Eastern Europe, ceased to exist. I should have rushed to Prague to report it firsthand. But I was too depressed. "I haven't the heart," I confessed in my diary in Geneva.

Also, I was worn out from covering the death of a pope and the election of a new one in Rome, and exhausted from trying to do it during nearly a month of the worst flu of my life. Besides, as I told Murrow when we discussed whether I should fly to Prague, German military censorship wouldn't have allowed me to say anything anyway about the takeover in Czechoslovakia. Even in Paris, which was as far as I eventually got, the insufferable French foreign minister, Georges Bonnet, had clamped down a censorship of my broadcasts. He was afraid of offending the Nazis.

Busy at the Vatican covering the change at the Holy See I had not followed developments in Prague and Berlin as closely as I should have. I did note in my diary in Rome on March 9: "A storm brewing in what is left of poor Czechoslovakia."

Dr. Hácha, the weak little president — successor to the great Masaryk and the able Beneš* — has proclaimed martial law in Slovakia and dismissed Father Tiso [the premier] and the Slovak cabinet. But Tiso, I know, is Berlin's man. . . .

Hitler, who had recently maneuvered Tiso into the top job, would not, I was sure, accept Prague throwing out the fat little Catholic prelate.

"Strange — maybe not? —" I mused, "that Germany and Italy have never given rump Czecho the guarantee they promised at Munich." I inquired at the Italian Foreign Office about that and was told that Hitler was holding the guarantee up.

"Hitler still considers Prague too Jewish and Bolshevik and democratic," one of Ciano's smart-aleck young henchmen had wisecracked to me. The truth was, as I had felt instinctively in Munich, Hitler would never give his guarantee. In Rome, Mussolini was snickering about his Axis partner's brazenness.

A few weeks before I had personally seen him snickering behind the back of Neville Chamberlain. This was on January 11, when Chamberlain and Halifax arrived in Rome to visit Mussolini. I was at the railroad station when the Duce and his son-in-law and foreign minister Ciano arrived to greet them. I noted the scene in my diary.

> . . . Chamberlain, looking more birdlike and vain than when I last saw him at Munich, walked, umbrella in hand, up and down the platform nodding to a motley crowd of British local residents whom Mussolini had slyly invited to greet him. Mussolini and Ciano, in black Fascist uniforms, sauntered along behind the two . . . Englishmen, Mussolini displaying a fine smirk on his face the whole time. When he passed me he was joking under his breath with his son-in-law, passing wisecracks.

Mussolini, I noted, looked "much older, much more vulgar, than he used to, his face having grown fat."

My local spies tell me he is much taken with a blond young lady of nineteen whom he has installed in a villa across the street from his res-

---

* Beneš had resigned as president on October 5, less than a week after Munich, under pressure from Berlin. At the insistence of his friends, who felt his very life was in danger, he had flown to London and exile. On November 30 Dr. Emil Hácha, the Chief Justice of the Supreme Court, a well-intentioned but weak and senile man of sixty-six, was elected by the National Assembly to replace him.

idence and that the old vigor and concentration on business is beginning to weaken.

This was the first I had heard of the Duce's latest mistress, Clara Petacci, a pretty and vivacious twenty-six-year-old daughter of a Vatican physician, with whom Mussolini had fallen in love six years before, and who would stick to him loyally to the bitter end. I do not believe that at this time I had yet identified Hitler's mistress. It was a pretty well kept secret — at least from the likes of me.

I got back to Geneva from Rome on March 14 and jotted down in my diary reports I picked up on the radio that Slovakia had declared its "independence," adding: "There goes the rest of Czechoslovakia." It was obvious that Hitler was pulling the strings for a takeover. I concluded my diary that evening:

The radio says [Czech President] Hácha and [Foreign Minister] Chvalkovsky arrived in Berlin tonight. To save the pieces?

Their savage ordeal that night at the brutal hands of Adolf Hitler ushered in the end, for the moment at least, of the Czechoslovak nation. From 1:15 A.M. until 4 A.M. Hitler, aided by Göring, Ribbentrop and General Keitel, hounded Hácha and Chvalkovsky with threats to bomb Prague into smithereens, wipe out Czechoslovakia, and "exterminate" the Czech people unless they surrendered their country to him forthwith. He had given the order, he said, for his troops to march into Bohemia and Moravia at 6 A.M. Czechoslovakia, he explained, was to be "incorporated in the Reich."

At this news, Dr. Paul Schmidt, who was interpreting, noted, Hácha and Chvalkovsky sat as though turned to stone. Only their eyes "showed that they were alive."

Further threats, hurled by Hitler, Göring and Ribbentrop, revived them. As Robert Coulondre, the new French ambassador in Berlin, who got it from one who was present, said, the Germans "were pitiless. They literally hunted Dr. Hácha and M. Chvalkovsky round the table on which the documents were lying, thrusting them continually before them, pushing pens into their hands, incessantly repeating that if they continued in their refusal half of Prague would lie in ruins from bombing within two hours. . . ."

At this point Dr. Schmidt says he heard Göring shout: "Hácha has fainted!"

For a moment, it seems, the Nazi bullies were afraid that the prostrate Czech president might expire in their hands and, as it occurred to Schmidt, "the whole world would say tomorrow that he had been murdered at the Chancellery."

Göring yelled for the doctor. This was Hitler's quack physician, Dr. Theodor Morell, whose specialty was injections — much later he would almost kill Hitler with them. In a jiffy he poked his needle into the arm of Hácha and brought him back to consciousness. A few minutes later the aging Czech guest fainted again and was again revived by Dr. Morell and his needle — revived enough, eyewitnesses say, to stumble back to the august presence of Hitler to sign his country's death warrant, the text of which had been dictated by the Nazi dictator before Hácha's arrival and hurriedly translated into Czech during the president's fainting spells.

It was one of the most brazen documents the shabby Nazi leader ever concocted. The Czechoslovak president declared, it said, that in order to restore "calm, order and peace in Central Europe he confidently placed the fate of the Czech people and country in the hands of the Führer of the German Reich. The Führer accepted this declaration and expressed his intention of taking the Czech people under the protection of the German Reich."

Despite all my experience of Nazi deceit, I was outraged when I heard these words being read over the Berlin radio the next day, as German troops poured into the stricken Czech land without resistance and Göring's bombers occupied the airfields of the conquered country. For sheer chicanery Hitler had reached a new height.

One of his secretaries later told how he rushed from the signing into his office, embraced all the women present (even at four o'clock in the morning!) and exclaimed: "Children! This is the greatest day of my life! I shall go down in history as the greatest German."

This was the first time that Hitler had invaded and occupied a non-German country. In the Sudetenland he had acquired three million people of Sudeten German blood, and the Anschluss brought him six million Austrian Germans. Now in Czechoslovakia he was taking his first Slavic country.

By nightfall on March 15 the German troops and air force completed their unopposed occupation of Bohemia and Moravia. That night Adolf Hitler, who as a youthful waif in Vienna had, like many Viennese, been contemptuous of the Czechs, slept in Hradschin Castle, the ancient seat of the kings of Bohemia, high above the River Moldau. Before leaving Berlin he had issued a grandiose proclamation to the German people, full of tiresome lies about the "wild excesses" and "terror" of the Czechs against the Germans which he had been forced to bring to an end. "Czechoslovakia," he proclaimed, "has ceased to exist!"

Next morning, from Hradschin Castle, Hitler proclaimed the "Protectorate of Bohemia and Moravia." And in words that set a new record for distortion of history he declared:

> For a thousand years the provinces of Bohemia and Moravia formed part of the Lebensraum of the German people. . . . Czechoslovakia showed its inherent inability to survive, and has therefore now fallen a victim to actual dissolution. The German Reich cannot tolerate continuous disturbances in these areas. . . . Therefore the German Reich, in keeping with the law of self-preservation, is now resolved to intervene decisively to rebuild the foundations of a reasonable order in Central Europe. For in the thousand years of its history it has already proved that, thanks to the greatness and the qualities of the German people, it alone is called upon to undertake this task.

Here you could see megalomania taking hold — not only in the Nazi dictator but in his people, who appeared to swell with pride at his silly boasts about their greatness. None of them spoke out against this naked aggression or the skulduggery with which it was done. For the Czechs a long night of German savagery now settled over their land.

On that day too, March 16, Hitler took Slovakia, whose phony "independence" he had concocted, under his "protection" — also in response to a "request," whose terms had been drafted in Berlin. He now had the whole of Czechoslovakia in his pocket, from which to mount his next military aggression.

Neither Great Britain nor France made the slightest effort to save it, despite their guarantee of it against aggression given at Munich. Chamberlain brazenly took the out Hitler had offered him. He told the House of Commons that "the proclamation of Slovakia's independence put an end by internal disruption to the State whose frontier we had proposed to guarantee. His Majesty's Government cannot accordingly hold themselves any longer bound by this obligation."

Not a word that, as he well knew, the "internal disruption" of Czechoslovakia had been engineered by Hitler. In fact, the prime minister told the Commons he would not go so far as even to say that Hitler had broken his word!

It is still difficult to believe that a British prime minister, after what had just happened, could stoop to say such a thing. But he went on. "I have so often heard charges of breach of faith bandied about," he said of Hitler, "that I do not wish to associate myself today with any charges of that character."

The prime minister did not even lodge a protest in Berlin, as the French at least did. He did have delivered a note which, in Geneva trying to broadcast a few sane remarks about what was unfolding, I found difficult to stomach:

> His Majesty's Government have no desire to interfere unnecessarily in a matter with which other Governments may be more directly concerned. They are however, as the German Government will surely appreciate, deeply concerned for the success of all efforts to restore confidence and a relaxation of tension in Europe. They would deplore any action in Central Europe which would cause a setback to the growth of general confidence. . . .

Not a word about what had taken place that day! To the prime minister, Hitler's military occupation of Czechoslovakia was a mere "matter."

And then, suddenly, to the surprise of friend and foe, Neville Chamberlain woke up. It took some prodding. He had been surprised that most of the British press (even the *Times*) and many members of the House had reacted violently to Hitler's latest aggression. Half his cabinet, led by Halifax, had turned against him.

The prime minister was scheduled to make a speech in his home city of Birmingham on March 17 — the eve of his seventieth birthday. Some days before he had drafted a speech, mostly about domestic affairs. At first not even Hitler's takeover of Czechoslovakia persuaded him to address a new subject. On the sixteenth, Sir John Simon, on behalf of the government, had made a speech so insensitive to what had occurred in Prague that, according to press dispatches I saw, the House had been roused to "a pitch of anger rarely seen."

But on the seventeenth, probably on the train going up to Birmingham, Chamberlain experienced his great awakening. He threw away his prepared speech and made rapid notes for a new one.* To

---

* Even Winston Churchill admitted that it surprised him. "I fully expected," he writes, "that he [Chamberlain] would accept what had happened with the best grace possible. This would have been in harmony with his statement to the House. . . . I therefore awaited the Birmingham declaration with anticipatory contempt. The Prime Minister's reaction surprised me." (Churchill: *The Gathering Storm*, pp. 343–344.)

his own country and others — his speech was broadcast (I caught it in Geneva) — he apologized for "the very restrained and cautious . . . somewhat cool and objective statement" that he had made to the Commons two days before.

"I hope to correct that statement tonight," he announced.

With that he began to reveal how the scales had fallen from his eyes. It dawned on him at last that Hitler had deceived him. He went over the times the Nazi dictator had assured him that the Sudeten-land was his last territorial demand in Europe and that he "wanted no Czechs." Now Hitler had gone back on his word — "he has taken the law into his own hands." Listening to the broadcast of the speech I began to sit up. Only two days before, in the Commons, Chamber-lain had refused to "associate" himself with any such charges "bandied about."

Now he hurled some questions at the man he had trusted so long. If there were disorders in Czechoslovakia, which Hitler cited as grounds for occupying the country, "were they not fomented from without?"

> Is this the end of an old adventure, or is it the beginning of a new one? Is this the last attack upon a small State or is it to be followed by others? Is this, in effect, a step in the direction of an attempt to domi-nate the world by force?

If it were, Chamberlain said, "no greater mistake could be made than to suppose that because it believes war to be a senseless and cruel thing, this nation has so lost its fiber that it will not take part to the utmost of its power in resisting such a challenge, if it ever were made."

This was a fateful turning point for Chamberlain and indeed for Hitler and for the history of these times. Herbert von Dirksen, the German ambassador in London, tried to warn the Führer of it. "It would be wrong," he wired Berlin the next day, "to cherish any illu-sions that a fundamental change has not taken place in Britain's atti-tude toward Germany."

Chamberlain made that even clearer a fortnight later. On March 31, sixteen days after Hitler entered Prague, the British leader rose in the House of Commons and made a fateful announcement.

> In the event of any action which clearly threatened Polish indepen-dence and which the Polish Government accordingly considered it vital to resist with their national forces, His Majesty's Government

would feel themselves bound at once to lend the Polish Government all support in their power. They have given the Polish Government an assurance to this effect. I may add that the French Government have authorized me to make it plain that they stand in the same position in this matter.

Neville Chamberlain, so blind so long, at last had recovered his sight. He knew very well which "small state," after Austria and Czechoslovakia, was next on Hitler's list.

Hitler was at first surprised and then enraged at Chamberlain's sudden guarantee of Poland. When the news reached him that Friday he was with Admiral Wilhelm Canaris, chief of the German counterintelligence, who later reported that the Führer stormed about the room, pounding his fists on the marble tabletop, his face contorted with fury, and shouting against the British: "I'll cook them a stew they'll choke on!"

I had flown up to Berlin to get the madman's reaction. He gave it publicly the next day, Saturday, April 1, in a speech at Wilhelmshaven, at the launching of the battleship *Tirpitz*. I had arranged with CBS to broadcast it live and was in a control room of the German Broadcasting Company in Berlin to introduce Hitler and check on the relay to New York of the broadcast. In Berlin it was being recorded for airing later to the nation, which surprised me since the Führer's speeches were always broadcast live.

The dictator had scarcely started speaking before he was cut off. This also had never happened before. But I could hear some excited official in Wilhelmshaven — it sounded like Goebbels — bellowing orders that the broadcast to CBS, on the Führer's orders, was to be immediately stopped. It could be carried later, he said, from the recording the Germans were making for their own broadcast.

I protested vehemently at being cut off, pointing out that it would give rise to suspicions in America that the Führer had been assassinated, cut down in the middle of a sentence. I knew I was wasting my breath. No one in Germany would risk his neck disobeying a command from the dictator. I suggested that the official in charge make an announcement, or allow me to make it, telling our American listeners that the speech had been cut off because of technical difficulties but that Hitler was actually continuing his speech — we could hear him shouting it over the telephone line feeding into the recorder. That would scotch any rumors. But the man rejected the idea. Everyone in the control room was getting hysterical.

Sure enough, within fifteen minutes Paul White, the CBS news director, was phoning me urgently from New York wanting to know why Hitler had been cut off and telling me that reports were spreading throughout the country that he had been assassinated.

"There's nothing in them, Paul," I said.

"How do you know?"

"Because I can hear him speaking on the telephone circuit from Wilhelmshaven."

"Can you cut me in on that circuit for a moment — so I can hear for myself?"

I consulted the harried officials. They shook their heads.

"No, I can't, Paul. But you can take my word for it. Hitler is alive. As I said, I can hear his voice, loud and clear. He's still speaking up there at Wilhelmshaven."

"Are you free to speak there?" White asked, suspiciously.

"Absolutely, Paul."

"Then please tell me why he was cut off."

"I don't know. I only know the order came from him."

It was beginning to dawn on me that Hitler, for the first time in my memory, perhaps did not trust himself in the heat of the moment in his reply to Chamberlain. You could always edit recordings. Probably he did not yet want to burn his bridge to the prime minister. But I could not say that to White over the telephone. I was tempted to tell him something else, but I decided it might not be prudent. This was that it would have been difficult to shoot Hitler that day at Wilhelmshaven. For the first time, I had learned, the Führer was speaking behind a bulletproof glass enclosure.

Actually, as I listened to most of Hitler's speech being piped into a recording machine, I took note that though the man was in a characteristically belligerent mood, he was fairly prudent in what he said. I had been tipped that morning that he would denounce the Anglo-German naval treaty. But all he said on that subject was that if the British no longer wished to adhere to it, Germany "would accept this very calmly." He harped on British perfidy, warned against an attempt of the Western powers and the "Bolsheviks" to try to encircle Germany, as they had in 1914, and repeated the shopworn slogans of Germany's might. Familiar also was the hypocritical plea at the end for peace.

"Germany," he claimed, "has no intention of attacking other people." (His troops had hardly consolidated their hold on Czechoslovakia.) "Out of this conviction," he went on, "I decided three weeks ago to name the coming party rally the 'Party Convention of Peace' " — a slogan that would increasingly haunt him and embarrass him as the summer of 1939 sped by.

All this malarkey, of course, was for public consumption — at home and abroad. Two days later, and in the greatest secrecy, as we later learned, the Nazi dictator gave his real answer to Chamberlain, and to the Poles. In a top-secret directive to the armed forces on April 3, he inaugurated *Case White*, the code name for the attack on his next victim.

Danzig was to be occupied and proclaimed a part of Germany. The task of the Wehrmacht was "to destroy the Polish armed forces. To this end a surprise attack is to be aimed at and prepared. . . ."

Date of the attack: "any time from September 1, 1939, onward."

A week in Poland, beginning on April 2, convinced me that the Poles were in no shape to withstand for long a German onslaught, but that valiant and headstrong as they were, they would try rather than to submit, as the Czechs had been betrayed and forced into doing. On the day of my arrival I attended an air force exercise. "Pitiful," I wrote in my diary, noting that the cumbersome bombers and the double-decker fighters were dreadfully obsolete. The army, so far as I could learn, was somewhat better off. But it lacked sufficient heavy tanks and artillery and a modern, sophisticated communications system. It no doubt outmatched the Germans in horse cavalry. But did its High Command intend to commit horses against tanks? The Polish troops I saw seemed confident — overconfident, I thought.

I found the officials and military attachés of the British embassy in Warsaw pessimistic about Poland's military strength. The British were concerned, since their government had just given Poland a guarantee against German aggression. Apparently, the ambassador, Sir Howard Kennard, and his military attachés regretted it. They were peppering London with reports about Poland's military deficiencies.

At our American embassy the military attachés took a more optimistic view, as did the always cheerful U.S. ambassador, Anthony J. Drexel Biddle. They thought the Polish armed forces would "give a good account of themselves." But there was one secretary at the embassy who tried forcefully to imprint on me another view. Landreth Harrison was very skeptical of the ability of the Poles to hold out long. They simply lacked the modern arms and organization to cope with a German offensive. Instead of heeding his view, I became exasperated with it. "He is a man of prejudices, though intelligent," I complained in my diary of this old friend and always sincere informant. This was silly. I suspected — against all my hopes — Harrison was right.

Of course, much depended, if war came, on how much fighting France and Britain did in the West to take some of the German heat off Poland — and on what the Soviet Union did. On April 6, the day before I left Warsaw, Beck, the Polish foreign minister, who had hastily flown to London, signed an agreement with Great Britain transforming the unilateral British guarantee into a temporary pact of mutual assistance. A permanent one would be signed, it was said, as soon as the details could be worked out. The Poles apparently wanted to know how many divisions and how many aircraft Britain could rush to the Western Front in aid of the French.

There was another question much on my mind which the British government did not raise and the Poles I saw in Warsaw simply would not face: Would Poland accept aid from hated Russia if it were offered? It was a question that remained crucial to the end. But the Poles evaded it, and the British government did likewise, until it was too late.

This astonished me from the beginning, even in Warsaw that first week. I understood well the fears in government circles, not only in Warsaw but in Bucharest and in Lithuania, Latvia and Estonia, that once the Red Army had entered their countries it might be slow to leave, and that Bolshevik propaganda among the peasants and workers might make their countries even harder to govern. But the fact remained that without Russia no sustained Eastern Front against Germany was possible, and Poland was doomed. I argued this all week in Warsaw: with members of the government and Parliament and the armed forces and the old Pilsudski legionnaires and the press and the universities. But to no avail. Poland didn't want and wouldn't need help from the Bolsheviks, they insisted.

The tragedy, at least in my mind, was that the British prime minister, who had so lightly given Poland his country's guarantee, was equally skeptical of the terrible Bolsheviks. To Moscow's proposals of March 18 for a solid front against Hitler, Chamberlain had been cold, and had let them drop. "I must confess," he wrote in a private letter on March 26, "to the most profound distrust of Russia. I have no belief whatever in her ability to maintain an offensive, even if she wanted to." This from the head of a nation that could field scarcely three army divisions talking about a country that could mobilize three *hundred!*

His ambassador in Warsaw tried his best to enlighten him. That very week, while Beck was still in London, Kennard, in a dispatch summing up his own views and those of his air and military attachés, stressed that because of their strategic situation (surrounded on three sides) and lack of modern equipment, the Poles could not defend the Corridor nor the western provinces but would have to fall back on the Vistula in the heart of Poland.

"A friendly Russia," he emphasized, "is thus of paramount importance to Poland."

In the House of Commons, Lloyd George, the great wartime leader, and Winston Churchill, still in the doghouse with the Tory leadership but not without political prestige, were trying to drum this into Chamberlain's head. On April 3, four days after the prime minister's unilateral guarantee of Poland, Lloyd George in the Commons had urged Chamberlain to make Warsaw's acceptance of Russian aid a condition of a British guarantee.

> If we are going in without the help of Russia we are walking into a trap. It is the only country whose armies can get into Poland. . . . I cannot understand why, before committing ourselves to this tremendous enterprise, we did not secure beforehand the adhesion of Russia. . . .

A month later Churchill warned the prime minister: "There is no means of maintaining an Eastern Front against Nazi aggression without the active aid of Russia."

This seemed self-evident to me. But obviously it was not to Chamberlain, nor to the Poles who, as I was beginning to learn in Warsaw, were too blinded by national prejudice to see it.

On Thursday, April 6, rumors began to mount of German troop movements on the Polish frontier. London seemed worried that Hitler, fuming at Beck's signing a mutual assistance agreement in the British capital that day, might invade Poland over the weekend. There were also rumors that Mussolini, not to be outdone by his Axis partner, was going into Albania this Easter weekend. But after talks with various contacts in Polish military and diplomatic circles I convinced myself that Hilter was not up to anything at the moment. Thus assured, I decided to go ahead with my plans to take the Nord Express on Good Friday morning from Warsaw via Berlin to Paris, where I was scheduled to do a broadcast Easter Sunday. The next day I planned to continue on to Geneva to get a glimpse of my family.

When my train pulled into the Schlesischebahnhof in Berlin on Friday evening I looked out the car window to see Pierre Huss grinning at me. I knew what that meant. Bad news. My London office, he said, had phoned and asked him to get me off the train. The British, it seemed, still feared Hitler would march against Poland that weekend.

"Besides," Pierre said, "they've got the jitters in London about the Italian thing."

"What Italian thing?" I asked.

"Mussolini went into Albania this morning. Sort of celebrated this Good Friday." (The Albanians were Moslem.)

It was a shabby little aggression but not unimportant in a Europe already jittery at what the Fascist dictators might do next. Occupation of little Albania would give the Duce a springboard against Greece and Yugoslavia. And a cheap victory.

I got off the train, checked into the Adlon, and telephoned around to see if the Germans were really going into another country this weekend. (I was getting to be something of an expert on the subject.) I had watched carefully from the train as it crossed the frontier. No sign of any German military activity. No troop trains. No trains bringing up tanks and guns. All my informants in Berlin denied that there would be anything doing over the weekend. Out in the streets I found the sidewalks full of soldiers on Easter leave, strolling up and down the Unter den Linden or filling up the vast sidewalk cafés along the Kurfürstendamm. I decided to fly to Paris in the morning, arriving there only an hour after the train I had left in Berlin was due.

I found France somewhat recovered from its jitters and defeatism of the Munich days. It was getting ready to celebrate when summer came the one hundred and fiftieth anniversary of the glorious revolution of 1789. Jean Zay, the minister of education, who was in charge of the lavish celebrations in Paris and Versailles, hoped, he said, that they would "symbolize all that was being menaced on our frontiers." I had been in Paris three weeks before, just after Hitler had taken Czechoslovakia. France, like Britain, had not lifted a finger to help its longtime ally, whose borders it, like Britain, had guaranteed against aggression.

My long love affair with Paris was souring. "How shoddy it has become in the last ten years!" I exclaimed in my diary. Some of my

French friends agreed. They would point to the neon signs, the gaudy movie palaces, the huge automobile sales windows, the cheap bars, which had begun to dominate the Champs Élysées, and say: "That is what America is doing to us." But I thought that that was what France was doing to herself. The country, it struck me sadly, had lost something she had fourteen years before when I had first arrived in Paris: her taste, part of her soul, the sense of her historical and cultural mission.

"Corruption everywhere," I noted, "class selfishness *partout* and political confusion complete." Most of my French friends had almost given up. *"Je m'en fous!"* (to hell with it), they said.

Now over this Easter weekend, two lovely spring days with the aroma of blooming chestnut trees along the broad avenues pervading the air, my spirits picked up. New York wanted me to broadcast France's reaction to Mussolini's aggression in Albania, and what would France do? Ed Murrow in London was to answer the same question about Britain. Our reports were similar. France, like Britain, was doing nothing. Still, I felt France becoming much firmer. It had mobilized over a million men without fuss. There was a feeling — though Bonnet was doing his best to poison it (he was a poisonous little man) — that this time, that is, when Hitler attacked Poland, France would fight. I noted in my diary that "France is clamoring for the British to adopt conscription and to line up with it with Russia."

I felt better for this Easter weekend in the still beautiful capital. I felt even better at the prospect of flying back to Geneva on the Easter Monday to see Tess and Eileen again. The year, 1939, which I was beginning to feel might turn out to be the most fateful I had ever experienced, had begun rather dismally for me — even before the spring aggressions of Hitler and Mussolini. In Geneva I had mourned the death of the Spanish Republic and, really, of the League of Nations, in both of which I had once had so much youthful faith.

"The League in its death throes has been a sorry sight the last four days," I had noted on January 19 in Geneva. Alvarez Vayo, Republican Spain's foreign minister, had made a dignified speech before the Council on the eighteenth, pleading for the League to continue its opposition to Franco and take some action against Germany and Italy, whose forces were enabling Franco to occupy most of Spain. He spoke moderately and from the heart. But Lord Halifax, the British foreign secretary, to show his contempt for the Spanish Republicans, had got up in the middle of Vayo's speech and ostentatiously walked out. That night over late drinks Vayo, an old friend of mine, was in the depths of despair. He said Barcelona was about to fall. On March 28, valiant Madrid, which had held out against all the odds for three years, surrendered to Franco. What was left of Republican Spain capitulated the next day. It was the tragic end of a decent and honorable attempt to give the Spanish people a democracy and to drag the backward country, with its terrible inequities, into the twentieth century. It was a triumph for Mussolini and Hitler, a setback for France and Britain, though they were too blind to fully realize it. France was now surrounded on three sides by Fascist adversaries, Germany, Italy and Spain. For the poor Spaniards, a long, black night in Spain's history began.

Early in February that year (on the tenth) Pope Pius XI had died in Rome and I had hurried there from Geneva to cover his funeral and the election and installation of his successor — the first time that opportunity had come for us in radio. For more than a year I had had frequent meetings with the people at Vatican Radio and the Italian Broadcasting Company, working out — discreetly, of course — plans for radio's first coverage of this event. We were handicapped, as usual, by the American networks' ban on using recordings. Often when our air time came, there was nothing very interesting to say. However, I did the best I could. Paley and Paul White cabled congratulations on our coverage — "miles ahead of the opposition," they said. All in all, CBS carried thirty-eight broadcasts for a total air time of twelve and three-quarters hours — more than any other network. I felt lucky that we did so well, for the final week I was down with the worst flu I had ever had, trying to direct our coverage from my bed in my hotel room.

Not being a Catholic and not knowing as much about the Vatican as I would have liked to, I secured various churchmen to assist in our broadcasts, the prize of them being an American Jesuit friend, Father John Delaney, born in Brooklyn and possessed of a golden voice and an Irish storyteller's genius. He was in charge of English-language broadcasts at Vatican Radio, but I persuaded him to do some special broadcasting for CBS, which his superiors, rather reluctantly, approved.

Late on the afternoon of the pope's funeral in St. Peter's, after broadcasting for several hours in the cold, dank Basilica, a hitch occurred that challenged Father Delaney's ingenuity. Stationed high up on a platform erected around a pillar facing the altar, Delaney was already hoarse from describing the long ceremony. I had been following him on earphones from my seat beneath the pillar. Suddenly he phoned me on a separate line we had.

"There's going to be a terrible delay," he said.

"Why?" I asked.

"Because the workmen who began to seal the Holy Father's casket before it is lowered to the vault below have run out of solder. They've sent for some in Rome but the workshops have closed for the day and they're having difficulty. It takes time to melt it. We may have two or three hours to fill before the ceremony resumes. What do I do?"

For a second I wondered myself. Father Delaney had already been on the air for several hours. He was obviously tired.

"John," I said, "you've been terrific. You'll just have to fill the time somehow."

"But how?" he persisted.

"You can say some more prayers," I suggested. "Tell some more of your wonderful Irish Catholic stories. Give us some more history of the Vatican, of St. Peter's, of the popes. And some more of your own experiences here. You know, the naïve kid from Brooklyn in Rome."

And Father Delaney did, eloquently, for several hours. He did it again a few weeks later, on March 2, when we scored a bit of a scoop on the election of a new pope. On this occasion we had installed Delaney atop the Bernini colonnade, close to the Basilica and with a view of the Sistine Chapel. Actually we had been tipped by friends in the hierarchy that contrary to long precedent, the cardinals in the chapel would probably pick the new pope on the first ballot. So we booked a broadcast from St. Peter's Square for 5 P.M. Just as Delaney was finishing speaking he got word through a special telephone line from inside the Vatican to stand by. We all knew what that meant. I passed on the word to New York, White kept us on the air, and soon the good Father Delaney was exclaiming that he saw white smoke coming out of the Sistine Chapel chimney, which denoted that a new pontiff had been chosen. Then we got word by telephone who it was, Eugenio Cardinal Pacelli. Delaney kept on talking, telling what he knew of the new pope. Then his name was formally announced from the balcony of St. Peter's, with fifty thousand Romans massed in the square shouting their approval and joy. In a few minutes the new pope appeared on the balcony and gave his famous blessing "to the city and to the world."

Finally there was the coronation service itself on Sunday, March 12, for which Delaney's running commentary continued for nearly five hours, from 8:30 A.M. to 1:10 P.M. In New York, because of the difference in time, it had begun at 2:30 A.M. and CBS had stayed on the air through the night to carry it.

I was tempted — but resisted the temptation — to discuss the politics of the Vatican in my broadcasts. I was fascinated by the intensity of the Romans' discussions of the politicking for the papal succession. Each cardinal candidate was discussed with the utmost frankness — often in language that was unprintable and certainly unbroadcastable in regard to his private life and his intrigues for election. I myself was interested in what attitude Pius XII would take toward Nazi Germany. His predecessor had quickly signed a concordat with Hitler and then regretted it in his famous encyclical four years later, *"Mit Brennender Sorge"* (With Burning Sorrow), which castigated the Nazi regime for its attacks on the Church and Christianity.

Pius XII, as Cardinal Pacelli, the papal secretary of state, had pushed for the concordat with Nazi Germany and had actually signed it for the Holy See. At that time I had wondered if he was pro-Nazi. As papal nuncio in Munich and then in Berlin for twelve years he had certainly become pro-German. But pro-Nazi? Much later, when he would be attacked for his failure to protest Hitler's massacre of the Jews, Pius XII would be the subject of much controversy. For the moment everyone in Rome believed he would make a brilliant pope. He had one of the most finely chiseled Roman faces I had ever seen and he was reputed to be a brilliant intellectual. Still, that slight cloud in my own mind was not dissipated when I learned that the veteran German ambassador to the Holy See was expressing his pleasure that "at last" there was a pope who was a "Germanophile."

My job in radio was now keeping me on the road most of the time. I loved the life and the work, though I did wish I could contrive to be with my family more, especially now that we had a young child. When did a family life start? I was thirty-five. But one had to face it: a roving foreign correspondent over these last years of crisis in Europe had little personal life.

Geneva, since the Anschluss, had become my permanent post and home. But except for an occasional broadcast about the expiring League of Nations or the International Labor Office, which continued to thrive, the beautiful Calvinist city by the lake, rimmed by the Juras and the Alps, was little more than a jumping-off place for assignments up and down Europe.

On April 20 I was back in Berlin for Hitler's fiftieth birthday — just in case he used the occasion to spring something. From there I flew on to London to touch base with Murrow about our increasingly heavy schedule, to do a joint broadcast with him, and, very important to me, to try to find out from my English friends in Parliament if the British would stand up to Hitler during this Polish crisis and, if necessary, fight. And with what. (Very late in the day, it seemed to me, Parliament was debating whether to adopt conscription and my best friends, who were Labour, were strenuously opposing it.)

And then it was back to Berlin again to cover what turned out to be, in my estimation, Hitler's greatest feat of oratory in his life — his reply in the Reichstag on April 28 to Roosevelt's plea to him not to go to war. On April 30 I was once more in Warsaw, broadcasting a report on how well the Poles were holding out against Hitler's increasing pressure. Early in May, by scheduling some broadcasts from Geneva, I was able to snatch a few days at home with Tess and Eileen before they departed again for America, where this time Tess hoped a federal court in Virginia would grant her American citizenship.

The United States, alone among nations, still refused to grant citizenship to wives of its nationals. On her previous trip she had brought an action in federal court to have the five-year residency requirement eased by giving her credit for the years she resided with an American husband in Europe. The State Department, suspicious of foreigners, was opposing us in court but Tess thought she had a good chance of winning. It had been difficult for her to travel without a passport.

In mid-June I was back in London, mainly to take ship on the maiden voyage of the new *Mauretania* to New York, from which CBS wanted to experiment with some ship-to-shore broadcasts en route. It would give me a chance to talk about plans to cover the war, if it came, with the CBS brass and, above all, to retrieve my family in Washington.

Adolf Hitler used the occasion of his fiftieth birthday on April 20 to stage in Berlin what I described in my diary as "the greatest display of German military might we've yet seen." Obviously, it was meant to impress Poland, Britain and France, and, for different reasons, the Soviet Union. I must confess it impressed me. I had never seen such an awesome display of weapons: overhead swarms of bombers, fighters and the new Stuka dive bombers; clattering past on the pavement an array of heavy tanks, big anti-tank and anti-aircraft guns and a motorized artillery piece it took five trucks to haul. At the sight of it, the German spectators gasped and broke into frenzied applause, always causing me to wonder: Why did Germans applaud inanimate things like guns and tanks?

I wondered as I watched a happy but imperious Hitler, standing for hours at the reviewing stand saluting unit after unit, whether at fifty he had not become acutely aware that he was now at the height of his powers, personal and political, and that he had decided for this crucial year of 1939 to act boldly even at considerable risk. Chamberlain had revealed that at Godesberg, during the Czech crisis, Hitler had remarked to him that he was forty-nine years old and that if Germany were to become involved in world war, he wished to lead his country while he was in the full strength of manhood.

Not only he but his great creation, the Wehrmacht, as this birthday parade showed, was also reaching its "full strength." And the feeling was now growing in me that Hitler was the kind of German who would not stand idly by while the strength of the armed forces and his own strength began to ebb after reaching a peak.° He would strike while he felt at his strongest — if not this summer, then the next. Unless Poland and the West abjectly capitulated to him in a second "Munich."

In a broadcast from London on April 23, I tried to sum up the aims of Nazi Germany and how the German people felt about them and Hitler. I had to keep in mind that whatever I said abroad about the Third Reich and its impetuous leader quickly got back to Berlin and that if Hitler and Goebbels disapproved too strongly they might not let me return. In that case my somewhat long career of covering Nazi Germany would be terminated — something I wanted to avoid if I honorably and decently could, since this was the biggest and most important continuing story there was in the world. On its outcome depended whether there would be peace or war. By this time, I had learned what all correspondents became aware of after working in the totalitarian lands: that you could say a great deal if you were not too careless in how you said it. This talk from London, over which I

° A year and a half before, on November 5, 1937, in a highly secret meeting with the chiefs of the armed services and the foreign minister, Hitler had warned them of the "danger" of the Wehrmacht's arms becoming obsolescent unless they were used in time. This could be as early as 1938 "to settle the Czech and Austrian questions," and, at the latest, between 1943 and 1945 for a larger war against Poland, France, Britain and Russia. Hitler made one thing absolutely clear to his military chiefs. "Germany's problem — getting more living space — can be solved," he said, "only by means of force." We learned of this meeting only after the capture of the German secret documents. In my opinion it was the decisive turning point in the life of the Third Reich. Hitler had communicated his irrevocable decision to go to war.

had given much thought all that spring, expressed accurately my thinking on the subject. I could not have broadcast it from Berlin. I could from London, and hope to get away with it.

The German people, I said, believed in a number of things, most or all of which might surprise Americans.

1. That Great Britain, backed by France, and Soviet Union and the United States, was forging an encirclement of Germany designed to crush it.

2. That, in view of the German experience in the Great War, Hitler was right to attempt to break that encirclement before it was completed.

3. That Eastern and Southeastern Europe were a natural part of Germany's *Lebensraum*, literally "living space," the domination of which was necessary for its existence, and that neither Britain nor any other country, including America, had any right to interfere with Germany's action there.

4. That Hitler would get what he wanted in Eastern Europe, and get it, as he got Austria and Czechoslovakia, without war.

5. That there would therefore be no war, and that they, the German people, at any rate did not want war. War could only come if the "encirclement powers," jealous of Germany's success, attacked the Reich, in which case they would gladly fight and this time would win.

6. That Hitler had outsmarted the "foreign tyrants" who were trying to keep Germany down and that he had restored it to its proper place in the world. And done it without a single shot being fired, nor the life of one German soldier sacrificed.

> Now naturally these views of the situation which the German people hold have been largely hammered into them by a controlled press and radio — they rarely have the chance to get the news as it is presented elsewhere. But that does not alter the fact that those views are held — and stubbornly held, too.

I ventured to comment on Nazi Germany's *goal.*

> Neither Germans nor foreigners in Berlin believe for one second that Hitler will stop now. . . . The goal is the domination of Eastern Europe down to the Black Sea. If it reaches it, Germany will not only be the most powerful country in Europe, but it will be invulnerable to the blockade which lost it the last war. The raw materials and food so necessary for its existence will be available in its own backyard.

The time factor was important, I thought.

> Because Germany must hurry to complete its tasks while it can still
> bear the tremendous economic, financial and psychological strains.
> The Nazi economic machine is now at its peak. So is the military ma-
> chine.

Peace?

> Yes, [I concluded,] the German people wanted peace. [But] a *German
> Peace* [and one] ensured by the German army. Hitler's own newspa-
> per, the *Völkische Beobachter*, the day after his big military birthday
> parade, put it this way: "This army is for us the shield and the security
> for Peace, which admittedly is a German Peace, that will provide for a
> powerful people its necessary rights."

In the Nazi dictatorship, I had learned, there was nothing more
effective than quoting Hitler's own newspaper to buttress your views
and expose his.

But in London in the spring and early summer that year, and in
Washington and New York in July, people would scoff at my views.
Still, I could not shake them. Hitler's speech to the Reichstag on
April 28 in reply to Roosevelt left little room, I thought, for opti-
mism about peace. Perhaps one had to be there to hear it, as I had, to
fully comprehend this.

It was the longest major speech, I believe, he had ever made —
two and a half hours. And I believe it was the greatest — certainly
the greatest I had ever heard from him. "For sheer eloquence, crafti-
ness, irony, sarcasm and hypocrisy," I wrote, "it reached a new level
that he was never to approach again." It also reached the largest audience he ever had. It was broadcast not only over all German radio
stations, but over hundreds in Europe. In America the major networks carried it. Never before or afterward, I have calculated, did
Adolf Hitler have such an immense audience.[*] I thought he made the
most of the opportunity.

On April 15, one week after Mussolini sent his troops into Albania
and it was feared that Hitler might send his into Poland, Roosevelt

---

[*] Since Hitler was replying to Roosevelt and had been assured — erroneously, I was
sure — that he had many sympathizers in the United States, the German Foreign Office ordered its chargé in Washington to give the Führer's speech the widest possible publicity in
America. Two days after the address, Hans Thomsen, the chargé, wired Berlin: "Interest in
speech surpasses anything so far known. I have therefore directed that the English text
printed here is to be sent ... to tens of thousands of addressees of all classes and call-
ings. ... Claim for costs to follow."

had got off telegrams to the two Fascist dictators pleading for peace
and posing a sharp question.

Are you willing to give assurance that your armed forces will not attack or invade the territory of the following independent nations?

There were thirty-one countries on the president's list, including
Poland, the Baltic and Balkan states, the Soviet Union, Denmark, the
Netherlands, Belgium, France and Britain.

Roosevelt's cable arrived in Berlin and Rome late on April 15. The
Duce, according to Ciano, at first refused even to read it. Göring,
who happened to be visiting Mussolini in Rome, suggested that it
was not worth answering, that the American president "was suffering from an incipient mental disease." The Duce said he was inclined to the belief that Roosevelt's strange behavior was "the result
of his infantile paralysis."

Whatever his own inclinations, Adolf Hitler decided to give a resounding answer. He called the Reichstag into special session for
April 28 to hear it. To be able to ridicule Roosevelt for his question,
Hitler had shrewdly had the German Foreign Office ask the governments of each of the countries listed by the president whether they
felt themselves threatened by Germany and whether they had asked
Roosevelt to include them in his list. If any country hesitated to give
the answer Hitler wanted, a little threatening was to be employed.
The Führer well knew what fear he had aroused in the small countries, none of which wanted to be his next victim. The Wilhelmstrasse was especially pleased to hear from Belgium, the Netherlands,
Luxembourg, Norway, Denmark and Yugoslavia that none of them
considered themselves threatened by Nazi Germany — which to my
mind showed either a terrible naïveté or a terrible fear. These countries and most of the rest, some of them only after considerable prodding, provided replies that gave Hitler potent ammunition to fire at
the American president.

As he stepped to the podium of the Reichstag in the old Kroll
Opera House at twelve noon on April 28, 1939, his very first words
struck a new note in hypocrisy. He had called the Reichstag into
special session, he said, so that the members could hear his answer to
Roosevelt and "either accept it or reject it." I had never heard him
say that in the Reichstag before. After all, he had handpicked the
deputies himself. Not a single member would dare to "reject" him;

that would guarantee a deputy a swift trip to a concentration camp and probably a swift end there.

Then, as always in a Hitler speech, came a long rehearsal of the iniquities of the Versailles Treaty, the injustices and suffering it had inflicted on the German people and how, with God's help, he had freed them from this terrible yoke. More briefly, but with amazing aplomb, he justified his aggression against Austria and Czechoslovakia on the grounds that Germany had only taken back into the Fatherland ten million Germans who had yearned to return, along with twelve million Czechs, who until Versailles had always lived happily under German rule. He turned to a new subject. Before answering Roosevelt, he had answers to give to Britain and Poland for the way they had been treating Germany.

The man's technique was fascinating, though not new. After proclaiming again his admiration and friendship for England, he attacked it for its "new policy of encirclement of Germany," which forced him, he said, to denounce the Anglo-German naval treaty of 1935.

"The basis for it," he intoned solemnly, "has been removed."

He used the same argument with Poland. He had made the most "generous offer" to the Polish government, he claimed: the return of Danzig to Germany and an extraterritorial road through the Polish Corridor to East Prussia in return for his agreeing to a new nonaggression pact with Poland that would be good for twenty-five years. (The 1934 nonaggression pact still had five years to run.) He regretted that Poland had rejected his "one and only offer" which he insisted was "the greatest imaginable concession in the interest of European peace," though of course it was no concession at all on his part.

Then more lies.

I have regretted this incomprehensible attitude of the Polish government. . . . The worst is that now Poland, like Czechoslovakia a year ago, believes that under pressure of a lying international campaign, it must call up troops, although Germany has not called up a single man and has not thought of proceeding against Poland in any way.

This was so brazen I winced a little. Everyone knew that for weeks the Germans had been calling up troops secretly, and planned by summer's end to be fully mobilized. Already Hitler was building up an overwhelming force on the frontiers that surrounded Poland on three sides. But there was no limit to the dictator's brazenness. For next he was insisting that reports that Germany intended to attack Poland "were mere inventions of the international press." This from a man who had given orders three weeks before, on April 3, to his generals to make plans to begin the destruction of Poland by September 1, *"at the latest."*

By making a mutual assistance pact with Britain, Poland, said Hitler, had broken the Polish-German nonaggression pact of 1934.

"Therefore I consider the agreement as having been unilaterally infringed by Poland and thereby no longer in existence."

As well as I thought I knew Hitler, I was surprised that he would tear up these two treaties. I recalled how bitterly in *Mein Kampf* he had criticized Kaiser Wilhelm II for his anti-British stand before 1914 and for attempting a naval race with Britain. As for dropping the nonaggression treaty with Poland, was he not alerting Europe to what he intended to do? It also occurred to me that he was alerting the German people to prepare themselves for war.

Finally, after more than an hour, Hitler turned to what was supposed to be the chief subject of his oration: the reply to Roosevelt. Here his oratory took wing. His audience had never heard such ridicule heaped upon a foreign leader, and it seemed to delight them, at least the ones in the Reichstag. They rocked with raucous laughter at his endless taunts of the American president. I must say I had never seen him before perform so superbly as an actor, silly or deceitful as many of his words were, especially to an American.

He would answer, he said, all twenty-one points raised by Roosevelt. One by one he paraphrased them, paused, half smiled, and then, like a schoolmaster, said in a low voice one word: *"Answer,"* and after another perfectly timed interval gave it. I can still see him hesitating, looking with his magnetic eyes over the audience, his face all seriousness, then saying quietly, *"Antwort."* Above the rostrum in the president's chair Göring, I noticed, would try to stifle a snicker and you could feel the deputies on the floor holding back until the *Antwort* was given, at which point they broke into thunderous guffaws.

A sample of what went on for an hour:

> Herr Roosevelt declares that it is clear to him that all international problems can be solved at the council table.
> *Answer:* . . . I would be very happy if these problems could really find their solution at the council table. My skepticism, however, is based on the fact that it was America herself who gave sharpest ex-

pression to her mistrust in the effectiveness of conferences. For the greatest conference of all time was the League of Nations . . . created in accordance with the will of an American president. The first state, however, that shrank from the endeavor was the United States. . . . It was not until after years of purposeless participation that I resolved to follow the example of America.

The freedom of North America was not achieved at the conference table any more than the conflict between the North and the South was decided there. I will say nothing about the innumerable struggles which finally led to the subjugation of the North American continent.

I mention all this only in order to show that your view, Herr Roosevelt . . . finds no confirmation in the history of your own country or of the rest of the world.

After further lessons to the president Hitler got to the core of Roosevelt's telegram, that he give assurances he would not attack any of thirty-one countries. As he slowly, solemnly intoned the name of each of the nations, laughter built up in the Reichstag. He had taken the trouble, he explained, to ask each of the countries whether it felt threatened by Germany.

The reply was in all cases negative. . . . It is true that I could not cause inquiries to be made of certain of the states because they themselves — as for example, Syria — are at present not in possession of their freedom but are occupied and consequently deprived of their rights by the military agents of the democratic states.

Apart from this fact, however, all states bordering on Germany have received much more binding assurances . . . than Herr Roosevelt asked from me in his curious telegram.

Now the sarcasm of his voice, looks, words reached a climax.

I must draw Herr Roosevelt's attention to one or two historical errors. He mentioned Ireland, for instance, and asks for a statement that Germany will not attack Ireland. Now, I have just read a speech by De Valera, the Irish *Taiiseach* [how clever, I thought, to use the Gaelic word for prime minister] in which, strangely enough and contrary to Herr Roosevelt's opinion, he does not charge Germany with oppressing Ireland but he reproaches England with subjecting Ireland to continuous aggression. . . .

Laughter and applause. Nevertheless, Hitler said, he was prepared "to give each of the states named an assurance of the kind desired by

resident." The dictator paused, his eyes lighting up, a slight
smile breaking over his face. He was ready to give more than that!

I should not like to let this opportunity pass without giving above
all to the president of the United States an assurance regarding those
territories which would, after all, give him most cause for apprehension, namely the United States itself and the other states of the
American continent.

I hereby solemnly declare that all the assertions which have been
circulated in any way concerning an intended attack or invasion on or
in American territory are rank frauds and gross untruths. . . .

The Reichstag rocked with laughter. Hitler, superb actor that he
was, did not crack a smile.

And then came the peroration, perhaps the most eloquent at least
for German ears, I had ever heard him make. Yet to me it revealed
more clearly than ever before Hitler's half-baked, distorted view of
history — not only of his own country, but of mine — and how paro-
chial was this man, in whom was burning a desire to conquer the
world.

Herr Roosevelt! I fully understand that the vastness of your nation
and the immense wealth of your country allow you to feel responsible
for the history of the whole world and for the history of all nations. I,
sir, am placed in a much more modest and small sphere. . . .

I took over a state which was faced by complete ruin, thanks to its
trust in the promises of the rest of the world and to the bad regime of
democratic governments. . . . I have conquered chaos in Germany,
reestablished order and enormously increased production. . . .

I have succeeded in finding useful work once more for the whole of
the seven million unemployed.* Not only have I united the German
people politically, but I have also rearmed them. I have also endeavored to destroy, sheet by sheet, that treaty which in its four hundred
and forty-eight articles contains the vilest oppression which peoples
and human beings have ever been expected to put up with.

I have brought back to the Reich provinces stolen from us in 1919. I
have led back to their native land millions of Germans who were torn
away from us and were in misery . . . and, Herr Roosevelt, without
spilling blood and without bringing to my people, or to others, the
misery of war. . . .

You, Herr Roosevelt, have a much easier task in comparison. You
became president of the United States in 1933, when I became chan-

* The Nazi press constantly reminded its readers that in America there were twelve million
unemployed — "despite the New Deal."

cellor of the Reich. From the very outset you stepped to the head of one of the largest and wealthiest states in the world. . . . Conditions prevailing in your country are on such a large scale that you can find time and leisure to give your attention to universal problems. . . . Your concerns and suggestions cover a much larger area than mine because my world, Herr Roosevelt, . . . is unfortunately much smaller, although for me it is more precious than anything else, for it is limited to my people!

I believe however that this is the way in which I can be of the most service to that for which we are all concerned, namely, the justice, well-being, progress and peace of the whole world community.

"In the hoodwinking of the German people," I would later write of my experience in the Reichstag that day, "this speech was Hitler's greatest masterpiece." But as one traveled about Europe in the proceeding days, I noted, it was easy to see that, unlike a number of Hitler's previous orations, this one no longer fooled the people or the governments abroad. "In contrast to the Germans," I reported, "they were able to see through the maze of deceptions. And they realized that the German Führer, for all his masterful oratory, though scoring off Roosevelt, had not really answered the president's fundamental questions: Had he finished with aggression? Would he attack Poland?

"As it turned out," I concluded, "this was the last great peacetime public speech of Hitler's life."

But I could not know this that late April day in Berlin. Like almost everyone else I still clung to the hope for peace — despite what Hitler had said; despite what he had done, tearing up two more treaties; despite all his deceit.

If I had known what Hitler would tell his generals in the greatest of secrecy less than a month later and if I had learned of the direction a new wind was beginning to blow in Moscow, I would not have entertained such illusions.

For on May 23 that year, Adolf Hitler, as he himself said, burned his boats. Convoking in his study in the Chancellery in Berlin the chiefs of the three armed services and their top aides, the Führer told them bluntly that war was now inevitable. The notes of the meeting, jotted down this time by the Leader's adjutant, Lieutenant-Colonel Rudolf Schmundt, make up one of the most revealing documents of the Third Reich's road to war. Hitler himself regarded them as so confidential that he forbade a single copy being made. The one we have, from the captured German papers, is the original in

Schmundt's own handwriting. What is especially remarkable about this harangue is that Hitler cut through the deceit of his own propaganda and diplomacy, and to this inner circle spoke the truth about why he must attack Poland "at the first suitable opportunity," take on Britain and France in the West, and occupy neutral Belgium and Holland in order to obtain air and naval bases for an all-out attack on England.

"Declarations of neutrality can be ignored," Hitler said. There is nothing in the record to indicate that any German officer raised any question of ethics or honor. Their country, as before 1914, had given its solemn word to respect the neutrality of the Low Countries.

At a moment when the Nazi-controlled German press was clamoring for the return of Danzig and Hitler was believed to be ready to go to war with Poland to reclaim it, the dictator put his military chieftains straight.

"Danzig is not the subject of the dispute at all," he explained. "It is a question of expanding our living space in the East." Germany had to have more room in the East if it was finally to settle with the West. In the midst of war it would need the foodstuffs and labor of the East.

Hitler cautioned his generals about counting on another Munich. "We cannot expect a repetition of the Czech affair," he said. "There will be war. Poland will be attacked at the first opportunity. . . . Further successes can no longer be attained without the shedding of blood.

"The war with England and France," he warned, "will be a war of life and death. The idea that we can get off cheaply is dangerous; there is no such possibility." He planned to seize the air bases and channel ports of Belgium and Holland preliminary to the attack on England. "Considerations of right and wrong, or of treaties, do not enter into the matter," he admonished — in case some of the generals had qualms. "If we succeed in occupying Holland and Belgium as well as defeating France, the basis for a successful war against England has been created."

So there would be war. Poland would be attacked in the East, and England, France and the Low Countries in the West. No general could have had any doubts as to the Führer's intentions at the end of this diatribe.

"We must burn our boats!" the dictator declared. "It is no longer a question of right or wrong but of to be or not to be for eighty million [German] people!"

☙ ☙ ☙

As I look back on the summer of 1939, I see that I remained woefully ignorant of the secret rapprochement of Nazi Germany and Communist Russia that made a second world war inevitable.* There were public hints from Moscow that should have made us aware that the Soviet Union was not going to automatically side with France and Great Britain against Nazi Germany, though it never occurred to me that such mortal ideological enemies as Hitler and Stalin might ever make up.

Yet the Bolshevik dictator had publicly warned the West — and sent a signal to Berlin — as early as March 10 that spring, five days before Hitler's entry into Prague.

In a lengthy speech to the Eighteenth Party Congress in Moscow, the text of which was published in the Soviet press, Stalin castigated Britain and France for their failure to stand up to Hitler. He accused them of encouraging Nazi Germany to expand eastward in order to embroil it in war with the Soviet Union. (Since Munich I was sure this was Chamberlain's aim.) Russia, Stalin concluded, would be guided by two principles.

1. To continue to pursue a policy of peace and consolidation of economic relations with *all* countries.

2. . . . Not to let our country be drawn into conflict by warmongers, whose custom it is to let others pull their chestnuts out of the fire.

The astute Nazi German ambassador in Moscow, Friedrich Werner Count von der Schulenburg, took note of Stalin's speech, wiring extracts to Berlin.†

Despite his warning to the West, Stalin, shocked by Hitler's entry into Prague on March 15, promptly (on March 18) had his foreign minister, Maxim Litvinov, propose to London and Paris an immediate conference in Bucharest of Britain, France, Poland, Rumania, Turkey and Russia to form a common front against Hitler.

Chamberlain found the proposal "premature" and rejected it. But

---

* I was not even alert enough to notice that in his speech on April 28 Hitler had failed to deliver his customary onslaught against the Soviet Union. Only much later, when I went back to try to trace the course of Nazi-Soviet relations that summer, did I realize that for the first time in a major publicized speech, so far as I was aware, Hitler did not utter a single word about Russia.

† Göring also brought up the Stalin speech with Mussolini during their talk. He said he "would ask the Führer whether it would not be possible to put out feelers cautiously to Russia . . . with a view to rapprochement."

The Duce, according to Göring, warmly welcomed the idea. He thought a rapprochement could be "effected with comparative ease." This was a fateful turn in Axis policy.

frivolously! Lord Halifax told Ivan Maisky, the Soviet ambassador in London, that no minister of the Crown could be spared for the moment to go to Bucharest! This flimsy excuse did not go down well in Moscow.

Maxim Litvinov, the longtime Soviet commissar for foreign affairs, had staked his reputation and career on building up collective security against Nazi Germany. He thought a united front of the two Western powers and the Soviet Union, joined, if possible, by the lesser powers in the threatened East (Poland, Rumania and Turkey), was the only means of deterring Hitler and, if this failed, successfully opposing him in war. Undaunted by Chamberlain's rejection of Russia's March 18 proposal, Litvinov called in the British ambassador in Moscow on April 16 and made a formal proposal for a triple pact of mutual assistance among Great Britain, France and the Soviet Union. It called for a military convention to enforce the pact and a guarantee by the signatories, joined by Poland if it desired, of all nations in Central and Eastern Europe which felt themselves menaced by Germany.

It was Litvinov's last bid to the West to join Russia in stopping Hitler. Churchill urged British acceptance in a stirring speech in the Commons. Later, in his memoirs, he speculated that if "Mr. Chamberlain on receipt of the Russian offer had replied: 'Yes. Let us three band together and break Hitler's neck,' Parliament would have approved. Stalin would have understood, and history might have taken a different course. At least it could not have taken a worse."

But Chamberlain stalled, and this was fatal to Litvinov. On May 3, almost hidden in the back pages of the Soviet newspapers, a short item appeared. "M. Litvinov has been released from the Office of Foreign Commissar at his own request." It added that he had been replaced by Vyacheslav Molotov, chairman of the Council of the People's Commissars.

The significance of Litvinov's abrupt dismissal was obvious to all. It woke me from my apparent slumbers. For Stalin, Litvinov's attempt to build up an alliance with the West to halt Hitler had failed. Since Munich, from which the Soviet Union was excluded, Stalin, I guessed, had been coming to the conclusion that the aim of Chamberlain and of Bonnet, the French foreign minister, was to encourage Hitler's drive eastward until Germany found itself in a conflict with Russia. Stalin had publicly warned that the Soviet Union would not be caught in such a trap. Privately he must have concluded that two could play at appeasing Hitler.

The ouster of Litvinov carried a strong message to Berlin. And it was acted upon, with a resoluteness that was lacking in London and Paris.

London made little sense to me. I was in and out of it three or four times in May and June but I could not understand why the British government stubbornly resisted recognizing reality. True, Chamberlain had given Poland a unilateral guarantee against Nazi aggression. Welcome as this crucial change was, it made no sense unless the prime minister got it into his head that Russia, as Moscow had proposed, had to be included in any guarantee of Poland if that country was to be saved.

In London on May 19 in the Commons Lloyd George and Winston Churchill had severely criticized Chamberlain for his failure to respond to the Soviet offer of a triple alliance against Germany. Churchill, I thought, was particularly effective.

> What is wrong with this simple proposal? . . . I beg His Majesty's Government to get some brutal truths into their heads. Without an effective Eastern front, there can be no satisfactory defense of our interests in the West, and without Russia there can be no effective Eastern front.

Although Churchill was still in the political doghouse, this speech, I felt, made a strong impression on the House. There was growing criticism, even on the Tory benches, of Chamberlain's failure to do something to line up Russia with the West. Bowing to this criticism, the prime minister on May 27 finally agreed to instruct the British ambassador in Moscow, in association with the French ambassador, to begin discussions of a mutual assistance pact, a military convention, and guarantees to the countries threatened by Hitler. But he took the step, as the astute German ambassador in London, Herbert von Dirksen, reported to Berlin, "with the greatest reluctance."

In Moscow the hard-boiled Molotov was not fooled. On May 31, in his first public speech on foreign affairs to the Supreme Council of the U.S.S.R., he lambasted the two Western democracies for their hesitation. If they were serious in wanting to join Russia to halt aggression, they must agree on three things: a mutual assistance pact, a military accord stating exactly what each power would do in case of war, and guarantees by the three powers of the smaller states of Eastern Europe.

But the French and especially the British dragged their heels. And there was a complete deadlock over guarantees to Poland, Rumania and the Baltic states, none of which wanted one from Russia.

To break out of the impasse Molotov suggested at the beginning of June that Chamberlain send his foreign secretary to Moscow to conclude the negotiations. Apparently the Kremlin felt that this would be a sign that the British really wished to find agreement with Moscow. But Lord Halifax told Ambassador Maisky in London that "it was really impossible to get away." Anthony Eden, who had been foreign secretary and who had made valuable contacts with Stalin, offered to go in his place, but Chamberlain would not hear of it. Instead, on June 12, he dispatched William Strang, a competent career official in the Foreign Office, who previously had served in the Moscow embassy and spoke Russian. But he was little known even in his own country, and his appointment was interpreted by the suspicious men in the Kremlin as indicating that the British were not very serious about forging an effective alliance against Hitler.

The Germans, we now know, were beginning to strike the Bolsheviks as perhaps more serious in wanting to come to an understanding with them.

The first moves between Moscow and Berlin had been very cautious, and completely secret. We may date them as beginning four days after Munich. On October 3, 1938, the counselor of the German embassy in Moscow informed Berlin that one result of Stalin's exclusion from Munich was the likelihood that he would become "more positive" toward Germany. The ambassador, Friedrich Werner Count von der Schulenburg, a month later informed Berlin that he intended to approach Molotov "in an attempt to reach a settlement of the questions disturbing German-Soviet relations." This new tack in Nazi foreign policy would not have been taken by the ambassador without some hint from Hitler himself. Schulenburg, I knew, was not entirely in the good graces of the Führer. He was one of the last survivors of a small group of German generals and diplomats who had insisted on close relations with Soviet Russia after 1919 and had achieved it at Rapallo in 1923. This had remained a cornerstone of German foreign policy throughout the life of the Weimar Republic, but Hitler had abandoned it on taking power in 1933. For him the "Bolshevik-Jewish regime" in Moscow remained the mortal enemy. But after Munich this view began to mellow.

At Berlin's suggestion trade talks were quietly resumed. Then each nation's ambassador began to do a little probing. At the beginning of

1939 Alexei Merekalov, the Soviet envoy in Berlin, drove to the Foreign Office and informed it "of the Soviet Union's desire to begin a new era in German-Soviet economic relations." Three months later, on April 17, he called for the first time on Ernst von Weizsäcker, the permanent state secretary of the Foreign Office, and went further, stressing that "ideological differences need not disturb relations between their two countries."

On May 20, in Moscow, Molotov called in the German ambassador, spoke with him "in a most friendly mood," as the latter reported, and informed him that economic negotiations, which had been temporarily halted, could be resumed if the *necessary political bases* for them were created.

This was a new line from the Kremlin. It wanted not only to establish better economic relations with Nazi Germany but establish them on a solid *political* basis. Berlin was interested. Talks were resumed. They did not escape the attention of the new French ambassador in Berlin, Robert Coulondre, who had come there from the embassy in Moscow. Twice in early May he warned his government that Germany had begun to talk with Russia "about a fourth partition of Poland."

All through May, we now know, Hitler blew hot and cold, fearing one day that Russia would come to an agreement with the West and make his efforts to work out a deal with Moscow look ridiculous. On other days he would give a go-ahead for further talks. On May 25, two days after he had decided definitely to attack Poland, he ordered the Foreign Office to move ahead with the talks with Russia. New instructions to Ambassador Schulenburg in Moscow were drawn up. He was to point out to Molotov that there was no conflict of interests in foreign affairs between Germany and the Soviet Union, that the time had come to "normalize" their relations, and that in case of "hostilities" against Poland, Germany "would take Russian interests into account as far as possible." This last point may have been leaked to Coulondre and led him to conclude that the two powers were considering another partition of Poland. These instructions, in a somewhat toned down form, were telegraphed from Berlin on May 30.

Of these highly secret goings-on between Berlin and Moscow I was of course ignorant as I set sail from Liverpool on June 7 on the maiden voyage of the *Mauretania* to New York. I had found England depressingly complacent. From the debates in the Commons, it was evident that the negotiations with Moscow for a solid anti-Hitler front were not going well.

Chamberlain had finally announced on April 27 that conscription for military service would be introduced, and the House had approved. Both the Liberal and Labour parties had opposed it. For days I had argued in vain with some of my young Labour friends in the House that conscription was the fairest and most democratic way of providing manpower for an army. It made service compulsory for the rich as well as the poor. Beyond that, and even more important, I argued, was the fact that conscription was the only way you could raise a large army quickly. As it was, in the summer of 1939, Britain could put only two divisions in the field if war came. France planned to mobilize one hundred divisions.

My good friends in England also did not appreciate my pessimism about the chances for peace. They thought Hitler was bluffing. They inclined to agree with Chamberlain that it was not very important whether Russia was lined up on their side. They thought Poland could stand by itself.

There was one piece of good news for me personally. Just as I embarked on the *Mauretania* Tess cabled that the U.S. court in Virginia had granted her American citizenship.

I found my native land that hot summer of 1939 even more complacent than Britain. But of course the United States did not have so much at stake. It would not become directly and immediately involved if Hitler struck. Senator Borah, veteran member of the Foreign Relations Committee, issued a public statement while I was in Washington saying there would be no war. Almost everyone in the capital agreed. I was appalled.

I found Congress, I noted in my diary, "in a hopeless muddle, dominated by the Ham Fishes, Borahs, Hiram Johnsons, who stand for no foreign policy at all." I was surprised to find the president so powerless.

> Roosevelt's hands absolutely tied by Congress. . . . He sees the European situation correctly, but because he does, because he sees the danger, the Borahs and Fishes call him a warmonger.

Even though I was home, I felt lost. It is depressing and bewildering to feel yourself a stranger in your native land. It was now exactly fourteen years since I had gone abroad at twenty-one, and I had only been back twice, both times briefly, in 1929 and 1935. Europe had become my home. Berlin, Paris, London and Vienna were much more familiar to me than Washington, New York and Chicago. I could not get my bearings, either in Washington or New York, but nevertheless much that I saw and experienced was exciting. One felt the electricity in the air, especially in New York. The electricity and the dynamism: in the great rebuilding of our cities, in the plans for the future (as the World's Fair and its Futurama out in Flushing showed), in the pace of people's lives and work, though there seemed to me to be little direction.

Where were we Americans going? No one knew. We were racing hell-bent to somewhere. That, to most people, seemed enough.

President Franklin Roosevelt had gradually rescued the country from the devastating Depression, but there were still ten million unemployed. The figure took my breath away. I could not comprehend how this could happen in the greatest and the richest industrial nation on earth. The relatively poorer countries in Europe had done much better. The brutal dictatorships had solved the problem. In Nazi Germany and, I believe, in Soviet Russia, there had been no unemployment for the last three years.

I did not spend all my time in Washington moping over the problems of the universe. We had a wonderful family reunion at the home of my brother, John, in McLean, Virginia, where Tess had stayed while she was battling in the federal court for American citizenship. We uncorked a bottle of champagne to celebrate her becoming an American. Now she could return to her native Vienna or accompany me to Germany without having to worry about being apprehended by the Gestapo for not having proper German papers.

My brother, John, had reached nearly the top of the civil service, at the moment assigned as an economist to the Securities and Exchange Commission. This was a much-needed agency, which President Roosevelt had set up to correct some of the abuses of the New York Stock Exchange and to see that there was less skulduggery in the floating of securities. I heard John highly praised at the office for his pioneer contributions to the commission's work. A few years before John had married a German woman, a Berliner, whom he met in New York. So oddly enough, we were both married to German-speaking women, though John, I believe, never learned the language. His wife spoke excellent American.

Not so our daughter Eileen. As yet, she spoke only French, which she was picking up in Geneva and which we spoke at the table for the benefit of our Swiss nurse. I was sure Eileen was learning a good deal of English, if only from listening to Tess and me around the house. But she would not speak a word of it, and this puzzled my mother, who had braved the heat that summer to come by train from Iowa to join us. It seemed strange to her, she said, that a granddaughter of hers did not speak our family's language. A little exasperated sometimes, despite her utter devotion to her granddaughter, Mother would carefully enunciate very slowly her English words, pausing to draw out each syllable so it would sink in on Eileen. But that young lady, with great glee, would act as if she did not understand a word, and in reply pour out a torrent of French.

"I can't quite get it into my poor head, Will," Mother would say, "that my own granddaughter can't speak English." Mother had completely forgotten her college French.

I loved seeing her again. Timid and modest as she was, she exuded, as during all the days we were growing up, a marvelous wisdom. About life in general and her own in particular, which I felt had been thwarted by her long widowhood — it was twenty-six years since my father had died in Chicago in 1913 when both were forty-two, his brilliant career at the bar abruptly ended by early unexpected death. But she did not curse her fate. She had made her peace with it.

Mother was puzzled that I had stayed on so long in Europe. But she had taken a certain pride in my career, such as it was. She had felt we were keeping in touch, she said, during my newspaper years through my dispatches in the *Chicago Tribune,* which she read avidly, and then, during the last two years, through listening to my broadcasts from Europe over CBS. She felt like I was talking to her.

She seemed a little apprehensive when we departed that I might be going back to a war. But I assured her, as I suppose all sons have assured their mothers, that if war came Tess, Eileen and I would be all right.

She was sixty-eight that summer and in wonderful shape. Fortunately I would see her once more. During a brief leave six years later while CBS decided whether I was to return to Germany to cover the imminent collapse of the Third Reich or the founding of the United Nations in San Francisco, I happened to be in Cedar Rapids, Iowa, on April 12, 1945, the day Franklin D. Roosevelt died at Warm Springs, Georgia. I had spoken in Omaha the night before and was on my way back to New York for reassignment. Mother met me at the door. She was in tears — at my coming to say goodbye, I thought.

"He's dead," she said.

"Who?"

"The president." She began to sob.

We turned on the radio to learn more. Then CBS phoned from New York and asked me to get down to the studio of a local radio station to do some commentary. Toward midnight I finished my last broadcast and went out to Mother's apartment to say goodbye.

"What'll we do now?" she kept saying. Roosevelt's death was such a personal loss to her, as it must have been for millions of citizens. She seemed very tired, and depressed, and there was no use in talking of family matters, as we originally had planned.

"We'll leave them for the next time," I said.

We kissed and said goodbye, and I phoned for a taxi and caught the night train to Chicago.

There was not to be a next time. Some seven months later, on November 26, in Cedar Rapids, when she was seventy-four, she fainted while talking to a neighbor, did not waken again, and died twenty minutes later — "swiftly, painlessly," Tess cabled me from New York. The war had ended that summer, Adolf Hitler was dead, and I was in Nuremberg covering the trial of the surviving Nazi war criminals. There was no way of getting home in time for the funeral. There was no way I could express my loss. But I felt it, and I knew it.

In New York that summer of 1939 I met for the first time the top brass of CBS. And I learned a little about radio in general, and about the Columbia Broadcasting System in particular, whose rise under William S. Paley was one of the spectacular success stories of the 1930's.

Paley, son of a prosperous Philadelphia cigar maker of Russian Jewish background, had bought an ailing network known as the United Independent Broadcasters and sometimes as the Columbia Phonograph Broadcasting system in 1928, when he was twenty-six, for some half-million dollars of his and his family's cigar fortune. It had fifteen affiliate stations, compared to NBC's fifty, it was losing money, and apparently to everyone but the obstreperous young Paley it had no future. Bill Paley, by hard work and imagination and drive and an instinctive feeling for the possibilities of a new medium, gave it a future. More than any other single figure, I think, he created and dominated American broadcasting, first in radio and then in television, and made it such a vital part of life in our country as well as an immensely profitable business.

When I first met him in July, 1939, CBS was still way behind NBC, with its two networks, the Red and the Blue. But Columbia was closing the gap fast, and in public affairs and especially news, I think, it had already achieved first place, and this gave it a certain prestige that its arch rival lacked. For this development Paley was largely responsible, as he was for the growing popularity of Columbia's entertainment programs, which of course were the core of broadcasting, its chief source of revenue.

It was not that Paley himself knew much about the news. I could see that after out first conversation or two. But he had a feeling for its importance in broadcasting (which the powers-that-be at NBC, I think, lacked) and he was shrewd enough to pick a few men who were professional newsmen and give them free rein to develop the fledgling medium as a new and exciting form of journalism.

The three key men who were beginning to shape radio news at CBS were Ed Klauber and Paul White in New York and Ed Murrow in Europe. Klauber in 1939 was the most important. In the first place, he was an experienced newspaperman, having been long with the *New York Times* in various editorial posts. Second, he was quick to grasp the potential of radio as a purveyor of news. Paley hired him in 1930. I found Klauber a dour, difficult man, inclined to be autocratic and even tyrannical — Paul White was deathly scared of him. But I quickly saw that he was a fine professional newsman who set, and insisted on, the highest standards of truth, accuracy and responsibility in broadcasting the news. In a medium that tended to be preoccupied, like Hollywood, with the tinsel, the trivial and inane, Klauber impressed me as a man who meant to make news broadcasting a serious business. I took a liking to him because he was tremendously concerned with the state of the world and was interested in its history and complexities and uncertainties. I was happy that here at headquarters Ed Murrow and I had a man who understood what we were trying to do.

And Paley, I saw, would be interested in it and encouraging. He was most friendly when we met and talked for the first time. He was overgenerous in his praise of Murrow and me for our reporting from Europe. Unlike almost everyone I met in Washington and New York, he wanted to know how imminent I thought war was and what ideas Ed and I had for covering it. He would be sending over Paul White in a week or two to discuss further with us plans for radio coverage of the war, if it came.

Genial as he was, Paley, I also saw, could be tough. He could not have survived the savage jungle of broadcasting if he had not been. And behind the youthful charm I thought I detected something cold — as if he would not let any personal relations affect his business judgments and decisions. He was also a man who, though he would amiably discuss anything with you, did not like to be crossed once he had made up his mind — something I would duly learn.

In those days Paley was very accessible, friendly and informal. Murrow and I, when we were in New York, could drop in on him in his office for his advice any time something bothered us. Later, when CBS, with the coming of television, became a far bigger corporation, I believe this accessibility faded away.

Paul White, our news director, was a rather happy-go-lucky fellow whom Paley had brought over from the United Press. He had a good nose for news and an instinctive feeling for developing radio as a medium for purveying it. He was, as was natural for a man trained in a wire news service, more interested in spot news, in which radio left newspapers far behind, than he was in the sort of interpretive news that Murrow and I were trying to give. He sometimes struck me as a little superficial and occasionally a little silly in his enthusiasm for "stunts." But I felt good at having him, as well as Klauber, to work with. Like most American newspapermen who had never worked abroad, he was somewhat ignorant of Europe, and he could be occasionally a little insensitive to our problems of handling the news from there. But on the whole I found him very supportive.

The day after the Fourth of July, 1939, joined at last by Tess and Eileen, I sailed back to my job in Europe on the *Queen Mary*. I was happy about that job, now that I had seen something of CBS in New York and experienced the impact of radio news on the people of America. But I had a sinking feeling that I was returning to a Europe that would soon be at war. It would be a tremendous story to cover — and in a new medium. I had missed being old enough to participate in the Great War in 1917, and had cursed what I thought was my bad luck. Now, at thirty-five, I was more mature. No person in his right mind could look forward to being caught up in another world war. It would be an abomination. Perhaps, though, I was too pessimistic about the prospects of avoiding it. In New York, our star commentator, Hans Kaltenborn, had kept assuring our listeners that there would be no war.

"I'm so sure of it, Bill," he had said to me, "that I'm sending my son and his bride off to Europe for their honeymoon."

✿ ✿ ✿

Constantine Oumansky, the Soviet ambassador in Washington, was a fellow passenger on the *Queen Mary,* and he pretty much agreed. I had heard in Washington that Oumansky was shrewd and highly intelligent and our talks during the voyage confirmed it. He was also, like most Soviet diplomats I had known in Europe, extremely cynical. With a straight face he had gone down to Third Class to address a group of American and European university students on "Soviet Democracy." But no doubt, I mused, you had to be like that to survive (even with your life) in the jungle that Stalin had created. So many Soviet diplomats I had known had been liquidated by the maniac in the Kremlin.

Still, at least in his conversations with me, Oumansky seemed optimistic about the chances for peace. If France and Britain could forge a military alliance with Russia, Hitler, he believed, would be afraid to start a new European war. He thought, I noted in my diary, that the Soviet Union would "line up with Britain and France in a democratic front against Fascist aggression." (How I could write "democratic" without a question mark or at least an exclamation, I no longer remember.) The ambassador, it is true, always attached an "if" to it. "*If,*" he would add, "Paris and London show they mean business, and are not merely trying to maneuver Russia into a war alone against Germany."

I myself doubted, as I'm sure he did, that Chamberlain and Daladier "meant business." In London in mid-July when Columbia's "European Staff" (which was made up entirely of Ed Murrow, Tom Grandin in Paris and myself) conferred with Paul White on plans to cover the war, Murrow also was sure that Chamberlain was stalling in the talks at Moscow. From that he concluded that the prime minister would try to pull another Munich. He said he smelled another deal. It was possible, I argued, but not probable. Hitler, it seemed to me, was determined this time to go to war, unless Poland surrendered completely to him, which it surely would not do. So there would be war, and we should plan how to cover it. Murrow disagreed. What we were facing here, he thought, was another crisis like the one the year before, but it would not come to a war either.*

To improve our coverage of "the crisis," we took on one more foreign correspondent, bringing the number up to four. Ed and I

---

* In his memoirs, *As It Happened,* p. 136, Paley quotes a letter from Murrow to Klauber from London on July 26, 1939: "I think that such plans as can be made have been made for covering the next crisis, which I remain convinced will not result in war."

crossed over to Paris and had lunch with a young American newspaperman I had heard nothing but good about. This was Eric Sevareid, who was literally working day and night in the French capital, during the day as city editor of the Paris *Herald* and then as night editor of the United Press. Before lunch was over young Sevareid had a new job in a new field, that would give him more sleep and on which he would make an indelible mark.

In New York CBS took on two more journalists to help at home. These were Major George Fielding Eliot, a veteran of both the Australian and American armies in the Great War and the author of several books on military affairs; and Elmer Davis, the amiable, civilized, gravelly voiced journalist and author from Indiana, a Rhodes scholar and a delightful man. His dry, Hoosier humor, which readers of his books knew well, would shortly become familiar to millions of radio listeners. Eliot and Davis would soon become good friends of mine.

Despite my feelings that war was almost inevitable, I blew hot and cold that late summer, like Ed Murrow and almost everyone else. My diary corrects a faulty memory I've cherished for years that unlike a lot of others *I knew* that war would come when the harvest in Europe was in. Perhaps it was merely that most of us grasped desperately for straws. We clung to the hope that somehow, unlike in 1914, Germany and Russia and the Western democracies would find some way of preserving the peace. After all, Europe had enjoyed peace only since 1918, a bare twenty-one years ago. It was much too soon for the Europeans to go to war again. They were still exhausted from the last one.

On July 16, in a broadcast from Geneva a week after I arrived back, I said there seemed to be less tension on the Continent than when I had left three weeks before. A week later, in another broadcast from Geneva, I began:

> The days of this fateful summer tick off, one after another, and the five hundred million inhabitants of this part of the world go on hoping — each day — that the inevitable showdown will yet turn out to be a peaceful one.

I went on hoping with them. One reason, selfish I suppose, was that I was getting acquainted with my family again and cherishing every minute of our new life together in the old Swiss city. We spent hours on the beach along the lake. We took off on the little steamers churning up Lake Geneva to Lausanne and back. We hiked up into the mountains — the Alps one day, the Juras the next. "From a personal point of view," I concluded my diary on August 3, "it will be nice if there's no war. But I must get off to Danzig next week to see."

I stopped off in Berlin en route. I had not been there since Hitler's Reichstag speech three months before. I was struck by how completely isolated a world the Germans lived in. Whereas all the rest of the world feared that Germany would attack Poland over Danzig, in the crazy world the Nazi-run press and radio made in Germany just the opposite was believed. After three months away in saner places, I found the headlines almost unbelievable. On the train coming up from Switzerland I had bought a copy of *Der Führer*, the daily Nazi paper of Karlsruhe. Splashed all over its front page were these headlines:

WARSAW THREATENS BOMBARDMENT OF DANZIG!
UNBELIEVABLE AGITATION OF
POLISH ARCH-MADNESS

In the station in Berlin I picked up a copy of the *Börsen Zeitung*, organ of the financial community and usually a little less hysterical than the party press; it had a flaming headline: "POLAND AGAINST PEACE AND RIGHT IN EUROPE."

Noting that the German press and radio made Danzig the main bone of contention with Poland, I scribbled in my diary as I left Berlin that evening for Danzig: "Will the Germans keep their real designs under cover until later? Any fool knows they don't give a damn about Danzig. It's just a pretext."

What Hitler wanted was to humiliate and destroy Poland, as he had Czechoslovakia the year before, and push eastward, reviving the old German *Drang nach Osten* of the Hohenzollerns.

My nerves, after a couple of days back in Nazi Germany, were getting more frayed than I realized. They were conjuring up images of how unattractive the Germans were. I cannot remember what led me to conclude my diary that evening with this quip:

> Struck by the ugliness of the German women on the streets and in restaurants and cafés. As a race they are certainly the least attractive in Europe. They have no ankles. They walk badly. They dress worse than English women used to. Off to Danzig tonight.

Did such observations relieve the tension of the buildup for war, perhaps? Noting the shapeless ankles of German women?

Danzig, where I arrived for the weekend of August 11, did not strike me as the place where a new European war was going to break out. True, it was being rapidly militarized and fortified by regular German army units, whose officers and men scarcely bothered to disguise themselves or their purpose. German military cars and trucks — with Danzig license plates — raced through the streets. My hotel, the Danziger Hof, was full of Wehrmacht officers. The roads leading in from Poland were blocked with tank traps and log-barriers. And you only had to look about you to see that the Germans had brought in a large supply of machine guns, anti-tank and anti-aircraft guns, and light artillery.

Yet, the local inhabitants did not believe it would come to war. Completely Nazified, and with the gullible Nazi faith in the genius of Adolf Hitler, they were sure he would bring about their return to the Reich without war. For two decades they had deeply resented the detachment of Danzig from Germany as a part of the provisions of Versailles that had given Poland access to the sea through a corridor to the Baltic. The Allies had made Danzig a "Free City" under the supervision of the League of Nations, but dominated economically by Poland, for which it was the main port. The Danzigers, I found, wanted to continue to have the Polish business. They wanted their city returned to Germany. But they were not in as much of a hurry as Hitler pretended.

The summer was winding down, the weather was warm and sultry, and Danzig's numerous cafés, beer and wine gardens, were filled with Germans enjoying themselves despite all the talk of imminent war. I saw little uneasiness in their faces. Zoppot, near by, the Baltic's leading summer resort and a part of Danzig's territory, was jammed with bathers on the beach and, as evening came, with vacationers crowding the casino. It was difficult to conceive such folks going to war or causing war to break out over them.

"I have more and more the feeling," I jotted down in my diary after two days there, "that Danzig is not the issue and that I'm wasting my time here. The issue is the independence of Poland. I must push on to Warsaw."

"All in all," I concluded on August 20, after a week in the Polish capital, "the Poles are calm and confident." But so had the Czechs been the year before — until Chamberlain sold them down the river. In Warsaw the Poles did not believe that the British prime minister would — or could — do that to them. I must say I admired them for their cool self-confidence. But I was taken aback by their blindness to reality. I questioned them, in the army, the Foreign Office, the university, the business offices, the trade-union headquarters, about the refusal of their government, despite the apparent urging of France and Britain, to agree to bringing in the Soviet Union in a grand military alliance to save Poland from German aggression. It was the only way, I argued, citing Churchill and Lloyd George, to forge an Eastern Front that could hold back the Germans while France and Britain attacked in the West. But the Poles would not listen. They would not join Moscow any way, in anything.

Before the week was up I began to feel that there was a terrible self-destructiveness in the Polish character. Had it not been largely responsible, I wondered, for their nation being destroyed and partitioned by Russia, Germany and Austria in the eighteenth century? I could understand the historic distrust of the Poles for the Russians, who had treated them so badly in the past when they ruled in Warsaw. But to survive in this world you had to make compromises. Without Russian help they were doomed. That's what the British and French, who at last had begun to negotiate a military alliance with the Soviet Union, tried to tell them. Poland had to cooperate in its own vital national interest. But it would not.

Faced with threats from the Russians to call off the negotiations with the Allies in Moscow over a treaty of mutual assistance unless talks began immediately to achieve a military accord to back it up, and badgered by the French, who believed this would be a disaster, Chamberlain had reluctantly agreed on July 23 to the Soviet proposal that military staff talks between the three countries get under way, though he stalled on announcing it until July 31. Before the Russians committed themselves politically to a pact to stop Hitler, as Molotov had insisted all along, they wanted to know exactly how much military help they could expect from the West. This seemed to the French as well as to men like Churchill and Lloyd George a reasonable request, but Chamberlain did not like it. As the confidential papers of the British government made clear, his strategy was to string out the talks in Moscow until after it became too late in the autumn for Hitler to attack Poland.

The British military mission named to negotiate in Moscow at least was more prestigious than the political team Chamberlain had sent earlier. It consisted of Admiral Sir Reginald Plunkett-Ernle-Erle

Drax, Air Marshal Sir Charles Burnett and Major General Heywood. Not the cream of the British military establishment, but certainly high level. The Russians, as a gauge of their seriousness, had appointed their top men: Marshal Kliment E. Voroshilov, commissar for defense, General Boris M. Shaposhnikov, chief of the General Staff of the Red Army, and the commanders-in-chief of the navy and air force.

We now know from the prime minister's instructions that his military negotiators were admonished to go slow. They were to prolong the talks, as the British ambassador to Moscow, Sir William Seeds, put it, "sufficiently to tide over the next dangerous few months." Not only were they told to go slow, but Chamberlain dispatched them to Russia on a slow boat. A plane would have got them there in a day, but they were sent on a passenger-cargo vessel that took five days. By the time they reached Moscow on August 11 it was almost certainly too late.

Adolf Hitler had beaten them to it.

The next day, August 12, Hitler, conferring with Ciano, the Italian foreign minister, informed him that he would settle with Poland, "one way or the other, by the end of August." Because of the autumn rains, he explained, which would render useless his armored and motorized divisions in a country that had few paved roads, he could not wait longer than that.

Toward the end of the meeting a telegram was handed to the Führer. It turned out to be a message from the German Foreign Office in Berlin informing the Führer of a call from the Soviet chargé d'affaires the day before. Molotov, he had informed the Germans, was now ready to talk with them, "even about Poland," and he suggested Moscow as the place for the discussions. There was only one condition: the talks would have to proceed "by degrees."

But Hitler could not wait for such a slow process. He had set the date for the attack on Poland as September 1, "at the latest." If he were to sabotage the Anglo-French negotiations in Moscow, which apparently at last had taken a serious turn with the arrival of the Allied military delegations, and swing a deal of his own with Stalin, it must be done at once.

Monday, August 14, the day I arrived in Warsaw from Danzig, was a crucial day for all the parties: the Western Allies, the Germans and the Russians. In Moscow Marshal Voroshilov had fired questions at the British and French. What exactly was the military contribution that each nation would make to confront Germany if it attacked Poland? How many divisions would the French put on the Western Front? How many British divisions would there be to reinforce them? What would Belgium do? For its part, the Soviet Union, he said, would be ready to deploy one hundred twenty divisions at the outbreak of hostilities. Voroshilov pressed for an answer to one more question. Would Poland allow Soviet troops to enter her territory to meet the Germans?

This was the key question. Ambassador Seeds tried to stress this to his own government. "The Russians," he wired London, "have now raised the fundamental problem." But his government's instructions were to evade it and, if the Russians persisted, to say they must "refer home." Which is what the British did, though at the end of the session Voroshilov warned that "without an exact and unequivocal answer . . . the continuance of the military conversations would be useless."

Time was running out for the Allied negotiators. They do not seem to have realized it. But Voroshilov did. He was close to Stalin. The Soviet dictator was beginning to listen to surprising and unexpected signals from Berlin. On August 14 they grew urgent and tempting — quite a contrast to the exasperating temporizing of the Allies. On that day Hitler made his great bid.

Later that evening he instructed Ambassador Schulenburg in Moscow to call on Molotov and read him a lengthy communication which proposed that Ribbentrop himself make a short visit to Moscow "to set forth the Führer's views to Stalin." Germany, he added, was ready to work out with the Soviet Union an agreement on all "territorial questions in Eastern Europe. There is no question between the Baltic and the Black Sea which cannot be settled to the complete satisfaction of both countries."

To make sure that Stalin understood exactly what Hitler had in mind the telegram specified that he meant particularly Poland and the Baltic states. The Russian dictator could hardly not understand. What Hitler was proposing out of the blue was nothing less than a dividing up of Eastern Europe, including Poland, with the Soviet Union. This was strong bait, one Hitler knew the Allies could not match. Great as the enmity had been between the two dictatorships of opposing ideologies, the Nazi dictator apparently was confident that his opposite number in Moscow would not turn him down. That same day, August 14, he again convoked his military chiefs and told them he was sure Great Britain and France would not fight. So Poland probably could be confronted alone. It would be conquered in a fortnight. The generals need no longer worry about Russia. He was in contact with Moscow. The Bolsheviks were not interested in saving Poland.

When, on August 15, Ambassador Schulenburg read Molotov Ribbentrop's urgent telegram proposing that the Reich foreign minister come to Moscow to quickly settle German-Soviet relations, the Soviet premier was greatly interested. In fact, the ambassador reported to an anxious Berlin, Molotov had asked whether the German government would be interested in a nonaggression pact between the two countries.

The Soviet Union then, not Germany, was the first to suggest a nonaggression pact. And at the very moment it was negotiating a military alliance against the Reich. Hitler had not yet dared to go that far. But he was delighted. A nonaggression pact would keep Russia out of the war, frighten Britain and France into staying out, and enable him to take Poland alone.

But there was one catch. Molotov had insisted that talks with Ribbentrop in Moscow would require "adequate preparation." That would take time. With August running out Hitler had little time left if he was to strike at Poland by the end of the month. The next day, the sixteenth, another urgent telegram to Moscow went out. Hitler, the message said, agreed to a nonaggression pact. Only, time was short because of increasing "Polish provocation." The Germans therefore urged that Ribbentrop be received in Moscow "at any time after August 18 [three days hence] to deal on the basis of full powers from the Führer with the entire complex of German-Russian relations and, if the occasion arises, to sign the appropriate treaties."

Hitler waited impatiently and anxiously in his mountain retreat on the Obersalzburg for Moscow's response. It came on the seventeenth. And it was disappointing — and frustrating. Molotov, sensing German impatience, was beginning to play cat and mouse with Hitler. This time he gave a written reply to the German proposals. If the Soviet Union and Germany were to come to an agreement, after years of hostility, it must be "by serious and practical steps." The first step was conclusion of a trade and credit agreement. After that they would discuss a nonaggression pact. Again Hitler could not wait for that. Another urgent wire went off to Moscow on the eighteenth. "Quick results" were necessary. A conflict with Poland might break out any moment. There was no time to lose. Ribbentrop proposed "his immediate departure for Moscow." He would come, he said, "with full powers from the Führer" authorizing him to settle fully and conclusively the total complex of problems. This would include, he added, signing a special protocol, as the Russians had asked, settling their "spheres of interest." In delivering this message the German ambassador was told he must not take any more Russian "no's."

August 19 turned out to be the decisive day. The tension in Berlin and at Berchtesgaden was great. Orders for the navy's twenty-one submarines and two pocket-battleships to sail for British waters were being held up until word came from Moscow. The warships would have to get off at once to reach their appointed stations athwart British shipping lanes by Hitler's date for beginning the war — September 1, only thirteen days away. The two great army groups, designated for the attack on Poland, had to begin their complicated deployment immediately.

Finally at 7:10 P.M. an urgent telegram from Schulenburg arrived. The Soviet government agreed to Ribbentrop's coming to Moscow on August 26 or 27. Hitler was relieved that Moscow finally had agreed to receive his foreign minister. But the date was too late. It did not give him time to launch his attack on Poland on September 1. Swallowing his pride Hitler now intervened directly. He begged the Soviet dictator to receive his foreign minister at once. His first telegram, rushed off to Moscow on the evening of August 20, urged Stalin to receive Ribbentrop "on Tuesday, August 22, or at the latest on Wednesday, August 23." He had given his foreign minister, he advised, "the fullest powers to draw up and sign the nonaggression pact as well as the protocol. . . . I should be glad," he concluded, "to receive your early answer."

Aides said later that during the next twenty-four hours they feared Hitler might suffer a nervous breakdown. He seemed about to collapse. He could not sleep. In the middle of the night he telephoned Göring in Berlin to complain of the delays in Moscow. He did not feel any better when a telegram, received at 3 A.M. on the twenty-first, was read to him in the early morning hours. Ambassador Schulenburg, who had been apprised by phone of Hitler's telegram to Stalin, reported that it had not yet been received. At 10.15 A.M. on Monday, August 21, the Führer had the anxious Ribbentrop get off another telegram to the embassy in Moscow. "Please do your utmost," it admonished the ambassador, "to ensure that the journey materializes."

But the day passed, and there was no answer. Finally, at 10:30 that evening, Stalin's reply came over the wire to Hitler at Berchtesgaden.

To the Chancellor of the German Reich,
A. Hitler:

I thank you for your letter. I hope that the German-Soviet non-aggression pact will bring about a decided turn for the better in the political relations between our countries. . . . [It] provides the foundation . . . for the establishment of peace and collaboration between our countries.

The Soviet Government has instructed me to inform you that they agree to Herr von Ribbentrop's arriving in Moscow on August 23.

J. Stalin

Hitler lost no time in putting the news out to the public. Scarcely half an hour after receiving Stalin's message a musical program on the German radio network was suddenly interrupted and an excited voice came on to announce: "The Reich government and the Soviet government have agreed to conclude a pact of nonaggression with each other. The Reich minister for foreign affairs will arrive in Moscow on Wednesday, August 23, for the conclusion of the negotiations."

I missed the broadcast. I had returned to Berlin that morning. That evening I dropped by the *New York Herald-Tribune* office to catch up with Joe Barnes on what had been going on during my ten-day absence in Poland. I left his office at five minutes to eleven, walked back to the Adlon Hotel to pick up some notes and was about to leave for Broadcasting House when Ed Murrow phoned from London with the news. At first I could scarcely believe it. There had been no inkling that such an amazing deal was in the works. Ed was as flabbergasted as I was. He thought the news might sweep Chamberlain from office.

I rushed out to Broadcasting House, trying to figure out what must have happened to bring these two dictatorships, such deadly enemies up to now, together. They had fought it out in Spain and on a hundred propaganda fronts. On the way out to the Rundfunk, I wondered how much I could say in my broadcast. I need not have worried. Strict orders had come "from above," I was told. I would not be allowed to broadcast. Not even the Nazi German commentators would be heard this night. Obviously Hitler and Goebbels had not yet had time to figure out how to handle this abrupt reversal of everything they had said for a dozen years. In the meantime they were not going to allow any foreign broadcaster like myself to muddy up the waters.

Next day the German press was something to behold. Goebbels' *Angriff*, the most ferocious anti-Bolshevik sheet of them all, wrote in big black type on the front page: "The world stands before a towering fact: two peoples have placed themselves on the basis of a common foreign policy which during a long and traditional friendship produced a foundation for a common understanding. . . ."

So that was to be the official line. Ribbentrop had hit upon it in his telegram of August 14 which he asked Schulenburg to read "verbatim" to Molotov: "There exist no real conflicts between the interests of Germany and Russia. It has gone well with both countries previously when they were friends and badly when they were enemies."

The day after the announcement, Hitler, assured now that he had maneuvered the Soviet Union out of the Allied camp, again convoked his top military commanders to give them a final pep talk before they led the assault on Poland. Stalin had made that aggression possible.

Hitler's monologue is almost unbelievable, even for him, but his words were taken down by an admiral and by General Halder. First there was a word about his own greatness.

> Essentially all depends on me, on my existence, because of my political talents. Furthermore, the fact that probably no one will ever again have the confidence of the whole German people as I have. There will probably never again in the future be a man with more authority than I have. My existence is therefore a factor of great value. . . . No one knows how long I shall live. Therefore a showdown had better take place now.

The attack on Poland, he told his military chiefs, would probably begin on August 26, six days ahead of schedule. That is, if Chamberlain did not pull another Munich on him. "I am only afraid," he said, "that some *Schweinehund* will make a proposal for mediation."

In conclusion Hitler admonished his generals how to fight the campaign in Poland. To the more civilized, old-fashioned Prussian officers he must have sounded like a wild Hun. The rough notes of some of the participants gave the flavor.

> The most iron determination on our part. No shrinking back from anything. A life-and-death struggle. . . . The destruction of Poland has priority. . . . A quick decision, in view of the season.

How was he to justify his aggression in the eyes of his own people and the world?

I shall give a propaganda reason for starting the war. Never mind whether it is plausible or not. The victor will not be asked afterward whether he told the truth or not. In starting and waging a war it is not right that matters, but victory.

And then a final exhortation.

Close your hearts to pity! Act brutally! Eighty million people must obtain what is their right. . . . Be hard and remorseless! Be steeled against all signs of compassion! . . . Whoever has pondered over this world order knows that its meaning lies in the success of the best by means of force. . . .

Adolf Hitler had never put his view of life more clearly.

Wednesday, August 23, in Berlin was sultry and hot. Everyone seemed on edge. Troop convoys continued to pour through the capital. There were the usual rumors. A German friend at the War Office tipped me that Hitler might go into Poland on the morrow. Another contact at the Foreign Office was sure he wouldn't. The Nazi-Soviet nonaggression pact, he said, probably would be signed in Moscow this very night. That would frighten Britain and France from fulfilling their guarantees to Poland. The Poles themselves, he added, would see the light. And give back Danzig. The odds, he wanted me to report, were against war. I couldn't tell which depressed me more: the prospect of another Franco-British betrayal of a country whose destruction Hitler was bent on, or the prospect of war, which might destroy what was left of Western civilization, slaughtering millions of people, obliterating their cities.

Shortly after lunch I went out to Tempelhof to meet Hans Kaltenborn, who was flying in from London. He had become our star commentator since the Munich crisis, when he had broadcast day after day around the clock. It had given him an immense following. Now he was in Europe on a three-week tour to see if there would be war. Before leaving New York he had asked me to ascertain in official circles in Berlin whether he would be allowed to enter Nazi Germany. Some of his broadcasts, apparently, had not been sparing of Adolf Hitler. At the Propaganda Ministry, I was informed that there was no objection to Kaltenborn visiting the country, but that he could not broadcast or call on any officials. Goebbels himself, I gathered, had made the ruling.

I don't know why I trusted Goebbels, who never had much regard for the truth. But I was surprised when the German passport officials at the airport continued to hold Hans after all the other passengers from London had been cleared. His German-born wife, who had come ahead a few days earlier and was waiting for him, along with half a dozen of her German relatives, became uneasy.

"Why do you suppose they are holding him up?" she asked.

"Maybe we've been double-crossed," I said. I explained to her the clearance I had got for Hans.

Standing in the humid heat behind the brass railing which separated us from him, waiting, became almost unbearable. I finally complained to a Gestapo officer and after a heated argument — one got so used to them in Nazi Germany! — he finally agreed to allow Hans to join us on the terrace of the airport café, where I ordered cold beer while Hans was embracing his wife and relatives.

Hans, who could remain as cool as a cucumber in a broadcasting studio during the height of a crisis, was flustered.

"I told them," he said, "that you had got assurances from Dr. Goebbels himself that I would be free to come here."

"They assured me of it, Hans."

Now and then he would be called back to talk to the officials, who apparently were waiting for a decision from downtown. We sat at the table drinking beer for what seemed an age. I was getting anxious to get back to town. The story of the signing of the Nazi-Soviet non-aggression pact might break at any moment and I would have to go immediately on the air. It had been a quarter to four when we sat down. It was now a quarter to six.

Just then a Gestapo officer approached, and told Hans he would be catching the six o'clock plane back to London.

Hans spoke up. "May I ask why?" He was fighting to keep cool. But beads of sweat formed on his forehead.

Somewhat to my surprise, the Gestapo man started to leaf through a notebook. He turned to Hans.

"Herr Kaltenborn, on June 24 in Oklahoma City, U.S.A., you made a speech insulting the Führer."

"I do not remember that," Hans said. "May I see your note?"

But the man closed his notebook. "You will come with me, please," he said. He led Hans out through the gate to a waiting plane. But soon he was back. There was no seat for him on the plane. Hans had another beer. I noticed the Gestapo officials were engaged in a heated discussion, all the time directing unpleasant looks at us. Finally one came striding toward us. There was *doch* a place on the plane to London. Obviously they had thrown someone off. The plainclothesman motioned to Hans to follow him. As he passed beyond the railing he remembered that his coat pockets were stuffed with American pipe tobacco for me. For weeks I had been smoking an ill-smelling German weed. Hans pulled out four packages of Edgeworth and tossed them to me.

"Verboten!" cried a German officer — perhaps he belonged to the customs service. He picked up the tobacco packs and pocketed them himself.

It must have been nearly 2 A.M. when Joe Barnes and I got to the Taverne that night. We had waited all evening at his office for some word about the signing of the Soviet-Nazi treaty in Moscow. The announcement Monday night that it would be signed had devastated Joe. He had come to Berlin only recently from a long tour of duty for the *Herald-Tribune* in Moscow. Fluent in Russian, Joe had come to know the Soviet Union as well as I thought I knew Nazi Germany. Like me he had been absolutely astounded at Monday's news. True, he had often pointed out to me that the Kremlin distrusted Chamberlain, believed he would try to embroil Germany in a war against the Soviet Union, and was determined not to be caught in that trap. Still, the last few days he had believed that Russia would get a military pact with Britain and France that would make Hitler hesitate to attack Poland. He could not imagine Stalin, the arch-foe of fascism, making a deal with Hitler.

Shortly after 2 A.M. we got the terms of the deal. They were a further blow to me — and to Barnes and the rest of the Anglo-American correspondents gathered at the Taverne. The published terms contained a pledge that the two countries would refrain from attacking the other, that in case one was attacked by a third power, the other party would in no manner lend its support to this third power. Nor would Germany and Russia "participate in any grouping of powers whatsoever which is aimed directly or indirectly against the other party."

Thus, for all to see, Hitler got from Stalin what he needed immediately: an agreement of the Soviet Union not to join France and Britain if they honored their obligations to Poland in case of an attack.

We did not know until after the war the price Hitler paid for this green light to attack Poland. By the terms of a "Secret Protocol" the two dictators literally divided up Eastern Europe. In the Baltic the northern frontier of Lithuania was the dividing line. To the north was Russia's "sphere of interest"; to the south, Germany's. As for Poland — and this was the most important part of the secret agreement for Hitler — the dividing line, "in the event of a territorial and political transformation of the territories of the Polish State," was along the Narew, Vistula and San rivers. To the west of them was Germany's "sphere of interest"; to the east, Russia's.

Finally, there was this sinister concluding paragraph to the secret protocol.

> The question whether the interest of both Parties make the maintenance of an independent Polish State appear desirable and how the frontiers of this state should be drawn can be determined only in the course of further political developments.
>
> In any case, both Governments will resolve this question by means of a friendly understanding.

"This Secret Protocol" the document concluded, "will be treated by both Parties as strictly secret." And it was.

As Joe Barnes and I walked home through the Tiergarten as dawn began to break at the end of that night of August 23, we had the feeling that war was now inevitable.

Not CBS in New York, however. For two or three weeks Paul White had been nagging Murrow and me to set up a program he called "Europe Dances." We were to broadcast from night spots in London, Paris and Hamburg an evening of entertainment and dance music. I had opposed the idea in the beginning, as had Ed, but White had persisted and I had lined up a program from a joint in Hamburg's St. Pauli nightclub district, from which I would broadcast the last Sunday in August. To give American listeners an impression that Europe was dancing while gliding swiftly into war was cruelly misleading, and on August 25 I called Murrow and again asked him to urge New York to call off the program. Paul White insisted that we go through with it. Apparently he thought Ed and I were being much too pessimistic about the chances for peace.

The day before, August 24, I had jotted down in my diary at 7 P.M.: "It looks like war tonight."

> Across the street from my room [in the Adlon] they're installing an anti-aircraft gun on the roof of I.G. Farben. . . . German bombers have been flying over the city all day.

The British ambassador, Sir Nevile Henderson, had flown down to Berchtesgaden that day to stress to Hitler that Britain would stand by its guarantee to Poland despite the Nazi-Soviet pact, and Hitler in a rage had replied that this was immaterial to him. He was, he told the ambassador, fifty years old; he preferred war now to when he would be fifty-five or sixty. The talk in the Wilhelmstrasse was that Hitler might send his troops into Poland at dawn. The remaining British correspondents had been impressed enough by the reports to pull out hastily that evening for the nearest frontier.

We now know that on the evening of August 23, Hitler, despite what the ambassador had told him about Britain honoring its pledge to Poland, moved up the date of the attack from September 1 to August 26, at 4:30 A.M. Carried away by his coup with the Russians, Hitler simply couldn't believe that the British meant what they said. But the next day he came down to earth.

All day long on the twenty-fifth you could feel the tension building up in Berlin. Since early afternoon all communication with the outside world by radio, telegraph and telephone had been cut off. The American newspaper correspondents could not get their dispatches off. I was told I could not broadcast. I tried to phone Murrow in London, White in New York. I could not get through. The cutting off of all contact with the outside reinforced the tips we were getting that the German army would push off at dawn the next day, as indeed it had been ordered to do.

Shortly after 6 P.M., though, the tension began to ease. Only later did we learn the reason for it. That afternoon in London the British and Poles had signed a Treaty of Mutual Assistance, to replace the unilateral guarantee Chamberlain had given in March. News of its signing reached Hitler in Berlin about six. Dr. Schmidt hastily translated the terms of the agreement to him. Thereafter, Schmidt noted, the Führer sat at his desk brooding. A very few minutes later a long letter from Mussolini was brought to the Chancellery by the Italian ambassador. In it the Duce informed the Führer that despite the Pact of Steel, if Germany attacked Poland, Italy would have to stay out.

"Führer considerably shaken," General Halder noted in his diary at 7:30 P.M. He was so shaken in fact that he ordered his chief of staff to postpone the Polish invasion. At 8:35 telephone restrictions were lifted.

I happened to be the first journalist to benefit from this reopening of communications with the outside world. Though I had been told I would not be allowed to broadcast because of the ban, I went out to the Rundfunkhaus anyway for my usual 1 A.M. broadcast. None of the officials said anything, one way or another, about my going on the air. I went down to the studio. An engineer appeared to be setting up my broadcast. At 1 A.M. he waved to me to begin speaking. At the end of the feedback Paul White, to my surprise, congratulated me. Mine was the first word America had had from Berlin all day. With communications cut, there had been the wildest rumors. He said they were surprised but relieved to hear from me that all was calm in Berlin and that war had not yet come.

"Radio has a role to play, I think," I noted in my diary. If a news-paperman's dispatch had got through from Berlin, the public would not know until they read the next morning's paper that Hitler would not be going to war at dawn. But with radio we informed the public of it at once — at 8 P.M., New York time. Our good people could go to bed, assured of at least another twenty-four hours of peace in Europe. In Washington our government would know it had another day to do what it could to dissuade Hitler from going to war.

The weekend of August 26 and 27 in Berlin was hot and sultry, which made the tension in the air even harder to bear. The signs in Berlin were ominous. A big Nazi rally set for Sunday at Tannenberg, scene of Hindenburg's great victory over the Russians in East Prussia in 1914, at which Hitler was to have spoken, was called off Saturday because, said the official announcement, "of the gravity of the situation." Later in the evening Hitler called off the annual party rally at Nuremberg the first week in September. He himself had earlier designated it as the "Party Rally of Peace."

In view of these developments our embassy issued a warning urging all Americans whose presence was not absolutely necessary to leave the country forthwith. Most of the correspondents and businessmen already had sent out their wives and children. In my case, Tess and Eileen were safe in Geneva. Just before I went on the air at 1:30 A.M. Saturday night, the German news bureau informed me that rationing of food, soap, shoes, textiles and coal would be instituted Monday, August 28. The fact that the official German news agency called me with the news — it had never done that before — just before my broadcast to America made me think that the government was anxious to impress public opinion abroad that it was not bluffing. Somewhat to my surprise none of the officials at Broadcasting House objected to the opening lines of my broadcast.

I don't know [I said] whether we're going to have war or not. But I can tell you that in Berlin tonight the feeling is that it will be war unless Germany's demands against Poland are fulfilled.

Sunday afternoon, August 27, Hitler addressed the members of the Reichstag in an informal meeting at the Chancellery. "He outlined the gravity of the situation," an official announcement said. Despite all my efforts I could not get a coherent account of what the dictator said.

Much later I got it from General Halder's crisp diary.

Conference at the Reich Chancellery. 5:30 P.M. Reichstag . . . Situation very grave. Determined to solve Eastern question one way or another. . . . If minimum demands not satisfied, then war. Brutal! He himself will be on front line. . . .

General Halder noted the applause for the Führer "on proper cues." He thought it a bit "thin."

Personal impression of Führer: exhausted, croaking voice, preoccupied. Keeps himself completely surrounded now by his S.S. advisers.

Hitler's press was also speaking in a croaking voice that last week of peace. It was trying to whip up the people to a frenzy for war. Any shabby lie would do. Thus, on Saturday, August 26, the *Börsen Zeitung* proclaimed:

COMPLETE CHAOS IN POLAND — GERMAN FAMILIES FLEE — POLISH SOLDIERS PUSH TO EDGE OF GERMAN BORDER!

Next day, the Sunday edition of Hitler's own newspaper, the *Völkische Beobachter,* splashed across the front page this headline:

WHOLE OF POLAND IN WAR FEVER! 1,500,000 MEN MOBILIZED! UNINTERRUPTED TROOP TRANSPORT TOWARD THE FRONTIER! CHAOS IN UPPER SILESIA!

There was no mention, of course, that the Germans had been mobilizing for a fortnight. By now, in the midst of so much hysteria and war fever, it was almost impossible to cling to some shred of reality. I myself had a feeling of floundering in a sea that was about to engulf me.

There were all the eleventh-hour peace appeals. On August 24, President Roosevelt had sent urgent telegrams to Hitler and to the president of Poland urging them to settle their differences without resort to arms. In Berlin, at least, there seemed something absurd in the appeal, for the president of Poland was not threatening war; only the Nazi dictator was. Nevertheless, the Pole replied. Hitler did not. So the American president got off another urgent message to the Führer. No response either. On the twenty-fourth the pope, broadcasting to the world, also had urgently called for peace, beseeching "by the blood of Christ . . . the strong [to] hear that they may not become weak through injustice." At least more publicly courageous than the American president, the pope was pointing the finger at Hitler. There had been other passionate appeals for peace. On August 23 there had been a moving one from the king of the Belgians on behalf of Belgium, the Netherlands, Luxembourg, Finland and the three Scandinavian states.

Noble in form and intent as these appeals were, I noted in Berlin, there was something unreal and pathetic about them. It was as if President Roosevelt and the pope and the rulers of the splendid little democracies in the north lived on a different planet from the frenzied Third Reich and had no more conception of what was going on in Berlin than on Mars. They simply could not conceive of Adolf Hitler as he really was, nor the German people as the Führer had shaped them over six frenetic years. Even Premier Edouard Daladier of France, who, like Hitler, had fought for four years in the trenches on the Western Front, had no comprehension of his opposite number in Berlin. He too appealed to the Führer for peace in perhaps the most eloquent message of all.

> Unless you attribute to the French people [Daladier wrote] a conception of national honor less high than that which I myself recognize in the German people, you cannot doubt that France will be true to her solemn promises to other nations such as Poland. . . .
>
> If the blood of France and of Germany flows again, as it did twenty-five years ago, in a longer and even more murderous war, each of the two people will fight with confidence in its own victory, but the most certain victors will be the forces of destruction and barbarism.

That was the last diplomatic contact in Berlin between Germany and France. Though it would be France that would put an army of over a million men on his western frontier — against a paltry ten British divisions — if war came, Hitler seemed concerned now only with Great Britain. As he had told Göring on the evening of August 25, when he postponed jumping off against Poland, he had to see whether he could "eliminate British intervention." The canny Nazi dictator, whose political instincts had been so sure, now began to cling to this illusion! An entry in General Halder's diary for Saturday, August 26, conveys Hitler's thinking.

On that Saturday the Führer suddenly recovered his nerve and rescheduled the date for the attack on Poland. The chief of the German General Staff noted it at 3:22 that afternoon.

> Führer very calm and clear. Get everything ready for morning of 7th Mobilization Day. Attack starts September 1.

Hitler telephoned the order to the army High Command. He now had five days to try to talk and bluff the British out of intervention. General Halder's diary clues us in on the strategy of the Nazi Warlord.

> Rumor has it that England is disposed to consider comprehensive proposal.*
>
> *Plan:* We demand Danzig, corridor through Corridor, and plebiscite on the same basis as Saar. England perhaps will accept. Poland probably not. *Wedge between them.*

Halder himself underlined the last three words. They give the key to Hitler's mind that weekend. The dictator would try to drive a wedge between Poland and Britain and give Chamberlain an excuse for ditching Poland as he had Czechoslovakia.

On Monday, August 28, I had a long talk on the telephone with Ed Murrow in London. His view had abruptly changed. He believed now that Chamberlain would not sell out Poland. He thought Ambassador Henderson, who was returning to Berlin from London later in the afternoon, would bring an answer to Hitler "that will shock him." This, to me, was good news.

Henderson arrived back at 8:30 P.M. and after dinner at the embassy drove the hundred yards or so down the Wilhelmstrasse to the Chancellery. He looked debonair as always as he alighted from his car and strode past an S.S. Guard of Honor, which presented arms and rolled its drums. The formal diplomatic pretensions, I noted, were being preserved to the very end.

* A reference to a preposterous proposal which Hitler made to England on August 25 to "guarantee" the British Empire.

The British reply was firm. Hitler's offer to "guarantee" the British Empire was gently declined. The British government "could not, for any advantage offered to Great Britain, acquiesce in a settlement which put in jeopardy the independence of a State to whom they had given their guarantee." The guarantee to Poland would be honored. But Britain still hoped for a peaceful settlement. It suggested a way out for Hitler. The government in London had received "a definite assurance" that the government in Warsaw was prepared to enter into direct discussions with Berlin. Britain was now asking Germany "to agree to this course."

"A just settlement," the British note concluded, "between Germany and Poland may open the way to world peace."

Neither we American correspondents nor the British government realized that such talk — and indeed all these eleventh hour negotiations to save the peace — had by now become irrelevant. We did not know that Hitler had set the date of the army's jump-off against Poland for September 1, four days off. The "just settlement," which Chamberlain was still seeking, was no longer possible.

Despite what the British had told Hitler about honoring their commitments to Poland, the Führer made one last effort to keep Britain out of the war. If he could no longer talk Chamberlain out of letting Poland down, perhaps he could trick him into doing so.

On the early evening of Tuesday, August 29, there was a stormy meeting at the Chancellery between Hitler and Henderson. The ambassador, arriving to receive Germany's written answer to the British note of the previous day, found the Nazi dictator in an ugly mood. Germany, Hitler said, could no longer tolerate the "barbaric actions" of the Poles against Germans, "which cry to heaven." To eliminate such horrors, he went on, "there no longer remain days . . . but perhaps only hours." In the written reply Hitler also upped his demands on Poland. It must now return not only Danzig but the Corridor and agree "to safeguard" the Germans in Poland.

And then he sprang a trap.

"Solely" to please the British government, Hitler agreed to enter direct negotiations with the Poles. But a Polish emissary, with full powers to conclude negotiations, must arrive in Berlin the next day.

"That sounds like an ultimatum," Henderson remarked. He probably had in mind Hitler's brutal treatment of Austrian Chancellor Schuschnigg and Czech President Hácha before their countries were taken over. There followed, the ambassador later reported, a shouting match with Hitler in which Henderson claimed to have, "at the top of his voice," outshouted Hitler. The British envoy at last was waking up.

Not entirely though. He does not seem to have realized the extent of Hitler's trickery until the following day, when another trap was sprung.

Obviously, though apparently it was not obvious to Henderson, the Polish government could not have produced an emissary in Berlin on such short notice. It was late evening by the time Henderson got the text of the German note off to London and informed the Polish ambassador in Berlin unofficially of its contents. Henderson urged him to have his government nominate a plenipotentiary "without delay." Cooler heads prevailed in London. Halifax wired Henderson at 2 A.M. that it was "of course unreasonable to expect that we can produce a Polish representative in Berlin today, and the German government must not expect it."

I doubt if the German government for one moment "expected" it. The whole offer was a hoax. But if by any chance a Polish emissary did show up, Hitler, we know, was prepared to demand so much from him that the Poles would turn him down. Then, he was sure, Poland would be blamed for not being willing to negotiate "a peaceful settlement." The British might well fall for that, and reconsider their guarantee to Poland.

Once again Halder put the game succinctly in a diary entry that evening of the twenty-ninth.

> Führer hopes to drive wedge between British, French and Poles. Strategy: Raise a barrage of demographic and democratic demands. . . . The Poles will come to Berlin on August 30. On August 31 the negotiations will blow up. On September 1, start to use force.

At midnight the next evening, August 30–31, Henderson had another stormy meeting in the Wilhelmstrasse. This time he met with the German foreign minister to deliver Britain's latest reply to Hitler. While again urging direct conversations between the two governments, London considered that "it would be impracticable to establish contact so early as today." But Ribbentrop was not interested in the contents of the British reply. He obviously had been ordered to stage a scene. It turned out to be, Dr. Schmidt, the only observer present, later wrote, "the stormiest I have ever experienced during my twenty-three years as interpreter."

Henderson readily confirmed this. "I must tell you," he wired Halifax, "that Ribbentrop's whole demeanor — was aping Hitler at his worst." Later in his *Final Report* the ambassador recalled the minister's "intense hostility, which increased in violence as I made each communication to him."

He kept leaping from his chair in a state of great excitement and asking if I had anything more to say.
I kept replying that I had.

As Schmidt remembered it, Henderson was also aroused to leap from his chair. At one point, Schmidt says, the two men both jumped up from their seats, glared at each other angrily, and almost came to blows. The two men finally settled down long enough for the ambassador to ask Ribbentrop for the German proposals for a Polish settlement, which Hitler had promised the night before to give him. It was now too late to produce them, the foreign minister answered, since the Polish emissary had not arrived in Berlin by midnight. Nevertheless Hitler had drawn up sixteen proposals and Ribbentrop proceeded to read them.

"But in German at top speed," the ambassador reported to London, "or rather gabbled to me as fast as he could in a tone of utmost annoyance. When he had finished I accordingly asked him to let me see the text. Ribbentrop refused categorically, threw the document with a contemptuous gesture on the table and said that it was now out of date."

Out of date? But the proposals were never meant to be taken seriously. They were never presented to the Poles, who had not yet even heard of them. They were a sham to fool the German people and, if possible, world opinion into believing that Hitler, at the last moment, in an attempt to reach a reasonable settlement had made a fair offer to Poland and that the Polish government would not even send an emissary to Berlin to discuss it.

Later the dictator would admit this. "I needed an alibi," Dr. Schmidt heard him say, "especially with the German people, to show them that I had done everything possible to maintain the peace. This explains my generous offer about Danzig and the Corridor."

Actually his sixteen proposals *were* generous. They astonished me when I first heard them. This was twenty-four hours later, at 9 P.M. on the last night of August. I was about to go on the air with a broadcast to New York when the German radio interrupted a program and an announcer read them. All Hitler asked for was the return of Danzig. Two days before he had demanded the Corridor.

Now, in his latest proposals, he asked that the question of the Corridor be settled by a plebiscite a year hence, after tempers had cooled. The Polish port of Gydnia was to remain Polish if the Corridor was voted back to Germany.

In the rush to get Hitler's proposals on the air I was fooled completely. After enumerating them I ventured to call them reasonable. I did not know they were never meant seriously, and never even shown the Poles. I swallowed the Nazi line that the Poles had refused to send an emissary to Berlin even to discuss them.

Despite his experience with Ribbentrop at their stormy midnight meeting, Henderson too had begun to swallow that line through most of the next day, August 31. His education, contrary to what I thought, was not quite complete, after all. On that last day of August he tried to convince his government that the Polish government ought to send an emissary to Berlin immediately, as Hitler had ordered, and that in view of the "German offer" war "would be completely unjustifiable."

"The terms sound moderate to me," the ambassador wired his foreign secretary in London. "This is no Munich. . . . Poland will never get such good terms again."

Early that day I went out into the streets of Berlin to try to get a feeling of how the German people were facing the imminence of war.

> Everybody against the war [I noted in my diary]. People talking openly. How can a country go into a major war with a population so dead against it?

Despite all my years in the Third Reich, I asked such a question! Maybe like the British ambassador's, my education too was not quite complete. Coming back up the Wilhelmstrasse to the Adlon, I stopped by the British embassy. The halls were full of baggage. Henderson had not seen either Hitler or Ribbentrop and had no engagement to. He had had a talk with his French colleague, Coulondre. And he was seeing the Polish ambassador again, to urge him anew to get his government to dispatch a plenipotentiary to Berlin immediately. At the Polish embassy the bags were packed too. I got the feeling that all the desperate last-minute diplomatic moves had come to an end. An ominous calm hung over the capital.

"The situation tonight is very critical," I said in a broadcast to America at 7:30 P.M. "Hitler has not yet answered the British note of last night. . . . An answer may not be necessary." (I hoped our listeners would catch the meaning of that.) I noted there had been no contact between the German and British governments all day. But that there *had* been "between Russia and Germany. Berlin expects the Soviets to ratify the Russo-German pact this evening." Of course, that was a mere formality. Something else was up between the two dictatorships, one felt from talking with Germans in the Wilhelmstrasse, but I could not find exactly what.

Toward evening we learned that Josef Lipsky, the Polish ambassador, was being received by Ribbentrop at the Foreign Office at 6:15. I knew the Germans had kept him cooling his heels since 1 P.M., when he had asked for an interview. What I did not know was that the German foreign minister dismissed the ambassador icily as soon as he learned that he had not come with full powers to accept the German proposals. And that when Lipsky got back to his embassy he found his telephone lines cut. He could no longer communicate with his government at Warsaw.

It made no difference now. Neither Lipsky nor Henderson nor we of the press knew that at thirty minutes past noon Hitler had issued, in the greatest secrecy, his Directive No. 1 for the Conduct of the War. Poland was to be attacked at 4:45 A.M. on the morrow, September 1, 1939. In the west, German troops were to remain on the defensive. Having taken the plunge, Hitler was in a state of euphoria the rest of the day. At 6 P.M. General Halder scribbled a shorthand note in his diary: "Führer calm; has slept well. . . ."

I remember that last night of August in Berlin how shut off we felt from the outside world. My broadcasts and the press dispatches of the newspaper correspondents via wireless to America were getting through. But when I attempted to telephone London, Paris and Warsaw I was told communications with those capitals had been cut. Driving to and from my broadcasts that night I noted that Berlin seemed quite normal. There had been no evacuation of women and children as we had heard there was in London and Paris, not even any sandbagging of storefront windows.

Shortly after 4 A.M., as soon as I had done my last broadcast, I drove back down the broad highway from Adolf Hitler Platz through the Tiergarten to the Adlon Hotel just beyond the Brandenburg Gate in the German-built Ford which Selkirk Patton of the *London Daily Express* had left me when he pulled out hastily a few days before. He had been confident he would be back shortly.

The hours of darkness had cooled off the night a bit. There was no traffic up or down the broad allée. Not even military trucks, which had been pouring through eastward toward Poland all week. I had the street to myself. The houses and office buildings off to one side of the Tiergarten were dark. As was their habit, the Berliners probably had gone to bed fairly early. No one appeared to have stayed up, as my work had forced me to, to see if there would be peace or war. So far as I could see, the Berliners that day had been apprehensive but still hopeful. They did not want war.

I was so exhausted from all the tension of the last days and from broadcasting daily around the clock that I stumbled to my bed, lay down without trying to undress, and fell almost instantly into a heavy sleep.

It seemed only a moment later that the ring of my bedside telephone awakened me. As I fumbled for the receiver I noticed it was getting light beyond the window shades. I glanced at my alarm clock. 6 A.M. Sigrid Schultz, an old colleague of mine from the *Chicago Tribune*, was on the line.

"It's happened!" Sigrid said.

My mind and body were so numb from fatigue and lack of sleep it took me a few seconds to grasp what she was saying. Suddenly I got it.

"Thanks, Sigrid," I mumbled, and tore myself out of bed.

It had come at last. War!

The author broadcasting from St. Peter's Square in Rome during the election of Pope Pius XII, 1939

Hitler, Raeder and Göring

Hitler with General Keitel (left) and Göring (behind) during the Battle of France

---

CHAPTER 15

War!
The Conquest of Poland, Sitzkrieg in the West. The Overrunning of Denmark and Norway

1939-1940

"A counterattack!"

That was what Adolf Hitler and the German High Command called their onslaught on Poland that got under way at daybreak on Friday, September 1, 1939, the very date the Nazi dictator had set for the invasion back in April.

As the German troops, led by their armored divisions of several thousand tanks, poured across the frontier and drove rapidly into Poland, hundreds of German bombers and dive-bombers rained destruction from the skies, not only on military targets, but on millions of civilians in the cities and towns. It was the first taste of sudden death and ruination from above, I reflected, ever experienced on a great and murderous scale.

In Berlin we woke to a gray, somewhat sultry morning, with clouds hanging low over the city. A good protection against Polish bombers, I thought. All day long and into the night I expected to hear them overhead. But they never came, not that day or night — or ever.

I gobbled down some breakfast and went out into the streets to see how the German people were taking the coming of war. They struck me as apathetic. They were not snatching up the Extras, which the newsboys were loudly hawking. They were going about their morning business as usual, tramping toward the bus stops and subway stations on their way to work.

Across the Unter den Linden from the Adlon Hotel the morning shift of construction laborers had gone to work on the new I. G. Farben headquarters building just as I'd seen them do all summer long. Newsboys stopped to try to sell them their Extras but they were not buying them. No doubt they had heard the news on the radio before coming to work. Perhaps they were still dazed by it. Like most other Germans I had talked to in recent days, they had been sure Hitler could humble Poland, as he had Austria and Czechoslovakia, without resorting to war. They could not quite believe it had come.

What a contrast, I imagined, between this gray apathy and the way it had been here the day the war started in 1914. Then, from all I had read, there had been a wild enthusiasm for the war. The streets had filled up with delirious crowds. They had tossed flowers at the marching troops, shouted their support and frantically cheered the Kaiser, Wilhelm II, when he appeared on the balcony of the palace.

I walked down the Wilhelmstrasse to the Chancellery to see if such scenes were being reenacted in front of Hitler appearing on *his* balcony as the troops marched by. But the Nazi Warlord, as I supposed we would have to call him now, did not make an appearance. No soldiers paraded by — they were already all galavanting into Poland, I imagined — and the street was almost deserted.

I hurried out to Broadcasting House on Adolf Hitler Platz to do my first broadcast of the war. I decided to skip the Reichstag, which Hitler was to address at 10 A.M. I would have liked to witness the scene. But we were carrying the speech live over CBS and the only facilities available for handling the broadcast were at the nerve center of the German radio. There I would be able to hear him plainly enough, translate the speech as he went along, and throw in a few comments. It was an historic occasion, after all: another great war, assuming the British and French honored their commitments to Poland, and the first such war radio would cover.

I assumed Hitler would be in great form — to match the occasion. But he was not. To my surprise he was hesitant and unsure of himself and strangely on the defensive, as if (I noted in my diary) he was "dazed at the fix he had got himself into and felt a little desperate about it."

There was far less cheering than on previous and less important sessions of the Reichstag. The party hacks Hitler had appointed to the Assembly seemed strangely lacking in enthusiasm. He did not appear to be getting through to them, for the first time in my experience. It was almost uncanny. In a brief pause, Max Jordan of NBC, with whom I was doing a joint broadcast of the speech, turned to me and whispered: "Sounds like his swan song."

Hitler seemed to struggle to explain why Italy, which by the "Pact of Steel" was obligated to come to Germany's aid militarily if war came, would be staying out.

"You will understand," he said, "that for the carrying out of this struggle we do not intend to appeal for foreign help. We will carry out this task ourselves."

In boasting that he had spent "ninety billion" on building up the Wehrmacht, Hitler seemed to be saying, lamely, that for that money it ought to be good, and indeed was — "the best armed in the world, far better than in 1914," he assured the nation.

The dictator seemed to stumble over the question of his successor, should anything happen to him. After announcing that Göring was first in line to succeed him, and then Rudolf Hess, he continued: "Should anything happen to Hess, then by law the Senate will be called to choose from its midst the most worthy — that is to say, the bravest — successor."

What law? I wondered. What Senate? Neither existed!

How often in this very Reichstag I had heard Hitler spew out one grotesque lie after another, and sometimes I would marvel at how completely the gullible German people swallowed them. But on this morning he seemed to be outdoing himself. He stumbled on and on concocting his shabby prevarications to justify his wanton act of aggression. I took down a few examples.

> You know the endless attempts I made for a peaceful clarification and understanding of the problem of Austria, and later of the problem of the Sudetenland. It was all in vain. . . .

> In my talks with Polish statesmen . . . I formulated at last the German proposals . . . there is nothing more modest than they were, for in making them I brought myself into opposition to millions of Germans. These proposals have been rejected. . . .

> For two whole days I sat with my government and waited to see whether it was convenient for the Polish government to send a plenipotentiary. . . . But I am wrongly judged if my love of peace and my patience are mistaken for weakness or even cowardice. . . . I have therefore resolved to speak to Poland in the same language that Poland for months past has used toward us.

> This past night for the first time Polish regular soldiers fired on our territory. Since 5:45 A.M. we have been returning the fire, and from now on bombs will be met with bombs.

Neither "regular" Polish troops nor any other kind, as we shall see, fired on German territory, nor did Polish war planes drop a single bomb on Germany.

A little earlier in his speech and also in his grandiose Proclamation to the Wehrmacht, Hitler had insisted that the Poles had fired first and that the previous night Polish forces had launched twelve "border violations, of which three were very serious." During the day Baron Ernst von Weizsäcker, the permanent secretary of the Foreign Office, got off a circular telegram to all German diplomatic missions abroad laying down the line they should take in confirming Hitler's lies:

> In defense against Polish attacks, German troops moved into action against Poland at dawn today. This action is for the present not to be described as war, but merely as engagements which have been brought about by Polish attacks.

Even the British ambassador, whom I thought had been thoroughly awakened by the events of the last few days, fell for this lie. At 10:30 that morning Henderson telephoned a message to Lord Halifax at the Foreign Office in London:

> I understand that the Poles blew up the Dirschau bridge during the night.* And that fighting took place with the Danzigers. On receipt of this news, Hitler gave orders for the Poles to be driven back from the border line and to Göring for the destruction of the Polish Air Force along the frontier.

Only at the end of his dispatch did Henderson admit that Göring "himself" was the source of this information. Still it is astounding that he swallowed it. The ambassador attached a final sentence to this dispatch. "Hitler," he apprised London, "may ask to see me after Reichstag as a last effort to save the peace." Hitler did not send for the ambassador, who obligingly had passed along to his government the Nazi propaganda about the Poles having started the fighting. But, even accounting for Henderson's limitations, one wonders what peace he thought a last effort might save. For six hours Germany had been waging violent war.†

---

* The Germans had long planned to seize the Dirschau bridge over the Vistula near Danzig before the Poles could blow it up. Helped by early morning fog Polish army engineers on September 1 succeeded in blowing it up before German paratroopers could seize it.
† I have tried to be as objective as possible about Sir Nevile Henderson, but it has been difficult. From the moment of his arrival in Berlin he struck me as being not only sympathetic

❦ ❦ ❦

Neither in his speech to the Reichstag nor in his proclamation to the armed services did Hitler name any specific "attack" by "regular" Polish troops. He just said the "attacks" had occurred. But during the night, I remembered, DNB had issued a bulletin recounting an attack by Polish troops on the radio station at Gleiwitz, a German town on the Polish frontier. I had been suspicious of the report, and did not use it in my broadcasts that night, though I later learned that the A.P. and U.P. had routinely forwarded it to New York, where the *Times*, as well as other American newspapers, published it.

Not until six years later at Nuremberg did we learn what actually had happened. The Germans themselves organized a fake attack on the German radio station at Gleiwitz and went to extraordinary lengths to make it look as if the assault had been carried out by the Polish army.

Early in August, Hitler ordered Admiral Wilhelm Canaris, chief of counterintelligence of the High Command, to furnish Himmler and Heydrich, the latter the head of the S.S. Security Service, with 150 Polish army uniforms and some Polish small arms. The man picked by Himmler to carry out the operation at Gleiwitz was one Alfred Helmut Naujocks, who typified a species of intellectual gangster who rose to important assignments in the Gestapo. University educated, Naujocks had earlier distinguished himself by provoking armed "incidents" in Slovakia during the Sudeten crisis. At Gleiwitz he was to make it appear, he said, "that the attacking force consisted of Poles."

"We need practical proof," he quoted Heydrich as telling him, "of these attacks by the Poles for the foreign press as well as for German propaganda."

So the young S.S. ruffian spent the last fortnight of August carrying out his orders. He was to be given by the Gestapo "twelve to thirteen condemned concentration camp criminals, who were to be dressed in Polish uniforms and left dead on the ground of the scene to show they had been killed while attacking." And how were they to be "left dead"?

---

to Nazism, but to Nazism's aims. The ambassador did not try to hide his personal approval of Hitler's taking Austria and then Czechoslovakia — he seemed to loathe the Czechs as much as Hitler did.

But worse than Henderson's personal prejudices were his personal limitations. Sir L. B. Namier, the British historian, summed them up: "Conceited, vain, self-opinionated, rigidly adhering to his pre-conceived ideas, he poured out telegrams, dispatches and letters in unbelievable numbers and of formidable length, repeating a hundred times the same ill-founded views and ideas. Obtuse enough to be a menace and not stupid enough to be innocuous, he proved *un homme néfaste.*"

"They were to be given," Naujocks said, "fatal injections by a doctor employed by Heydrich. Then they were also to be given gunshot wounds."

The Nazi thugs even had a code word for these hapless victims from Hitler's concentration camps: *"Canned Goods."*

While they were being "left dead," S.S. troopers in Polish uniforms would fire shots in the air, "seize" the radio station, and have a Polish-speaking Nazi agent broadcast an inflammatory speech announcing that Poland's attack on Germany had begun. Then Naujocks was to call in the press, he said, and show the reporters the "proof" of the Polish attack.

This is more or less what happened at Gleiwitz and certain other places on the evening of August 31. The S.S. men who put on Polish uniforms and simulated "Polish attacks" that evening did not long survive the "canned goods." According to the testimony at Nuremberg of General Erwin Lahousen of military counterintelligence, "all of them eventually were put out of the way." Hitler wanted no telltale traces left. Naujocks himself saved his skin by deserting to the Americans on the Western Front in 1944.

This was the first day and night of the first war I was to experience and I made notes from hour to hour for my broadcasts on how it was. The blackout of the great city was eerie. Initially, in the darkness you could make out nothing. Then gradually your eyes adjusted and you could see vaguely a few objects: the great buildings looming behind the sidewalks, the whitewashed curbs along the streets, even sometimes a lamppost.

At 7 P.M., when it was still light, we had our first air-raid alarm. At last the Poles had arrived, I thought. I had wondered why their bombers had not come, since the Luftwaffe had been busy all day, according to the communiqués, strafing and bombing deep into Poland. I was at Broadcasting House when the sirens sounded for the first time. A melancholy wail. The lights in the building went out. S.S. guards with flashlights ordered everyone to grab his gas mask and hurry to the cellar. But I wanted to go out in the street and see the first bombing of Berlin. That would be something to see! A surly S.S. guard, poking his rifle at me, herded me toward the stairs. But in the darkness and confusion I escaped him, and made my way up to the street-level studios, where I found a small room, in which a candle was burning on the table. By its light I scribbled a few notes for the next broadcast. Then I went out into the broad courtyard to watch the skies. An S.S. guard joined me — a decent one this time, for he said nothing against my being there. We watched the German searchlights switching their beams back and forth. There was not even the sound of a plane above.

"False alarm!" my guard muttered, as if we had missed a good show.

I finished my last broadcast at 1:30 A.M. As I groped my way in the blackout down the Kaiserdamm hoping to find a taxi that would take me back to the Adlon I had an empty feeling in my stomach that had little to do with fatigue or lack of food. How will it be, I wondered, night after night of this, staggering around in the utter darkness, especially when the long, cold winter nights come, and the shrill of the sirens piercing the night air, and being herded like sheep into the shelters, especially after the bombs begin to fall? How will one's nerves stand that for long?

Half a mile down the Kaiserdamm I espied a taxi and started to get in. But another pedestrian hopped into it from the other side and growled at me to get lost. Finally I quieted him and we shared the ride to the Adlon, he very drunk and the driver drunker, both cursing the darkness and the war.

For a long time I could not get to sleep. It was more than the excitement of the first day of war. I felt a burning resentment against Hitler for so irresponsibly and deviously plunging this country and Poland, and no doubt tomorrow the rest of Europe, into a war which, with the big bombers and the big bombs, would be much more murderous than the last.

And then there was the feeling of isolation, of being cut off from so much that was familiar and desirable in life: from a world that had managed to be at peace since I was a youngster; from the rest of Europe, which had become my home during all my adult time, even during the years I was in Berlin; from my young family in Geneva that I had seen so little of since our first child arrived amidst the Anschluss. The feeling of isolation was enhanced by a decree that had been issued that very evening. It forbade listening to foreign broadcasts — on the pain of death. For years in Berlin, ever since Hitler and Goebbels had closed down the independent newspapers and turned the radio into a Nazi propaganda machine, one depended on the broadcasts of the BBC from London for news of what was really going on in the world.

Now you would risk getting your head chopped off if you continued to listen to them. Beheading with the axe was still the customary form of execution in this country.

My diary for Saturday, September 2, in Berlin:

The German attack on Poland has now been going on for two days and Britain and France haven't yet honored their promises. Can it be that Chamberlain and Bonnet are going to try to sneak out of them? . . . No air-raid tonight. Where are the Poles?

And where were the French and British?

With their capitals cut off, we didn't know. All we knew in Berlin as Saturday passed was that Hitler had not deigned to answer the Anglo-French ultimatums of the evening before saying that unless the Germans suspended their attacks on Poland and withdrew their troops, the two countries would fulfill their obligations to the Polish government. Every moment that weekend that the Western Allies continued to do nothing strengthened the conviction in Berlin that in the end they would give in and allow Hitler to get by with his conquest of Poland.

After two days of fighting the German army had advanced much farther into Poland than the High Command publicly admitted in its communiqués. By Saturday evening my contacts in the military were hinting — though not for broadcast — that the German armored columns were racing through Poland. They told me the Polish air force had already been destroyed — there would be no bombing of Berlin or any other city in Germany. I took all this with several grains of salt.

We heard vaguely during Saturday that the British and French were stalling because Mussolini had intervened at the last moment with a proposal for another Munich. France, or at least Georges Bonnet, was believed by the Germans to be interested; Britain less so. The evening before, Hitler had let Mussolini off the hook by publicly releasing Italy from its obligations under the military alliance. Rome had hastily assured Paris and London that it would remain neutral. But the Duce feared that the British and French might attack him anyway, while Germany was busy in Poland. So he was rather frantically striving for a settlement that would give Hitler what he wanted in Poland and still keep the French and British out of the war. He proposed a conference of the Munich powers and Poland for September 6. Bonnet in Paris wanted to accept it, but the government in London would have none of it.

Neither would Hitler, though he would later claim, falsely, to have agreed to it. He was determined to destroy Poland. The first two days of his attack were going even better than expected. I couldn't believe

it, but some of my friends in the military by late Saturday were talking of it all being over in Poland in another two or three weeks.
Apparently, Ribbentrop had convinced Hitler that the British and
French were looking for an excuse to stay out of the war. This much
seemed clear to me: if they didn't act by the end of this week — by
tomorrow, Sunday — it might be too late.

Sunday, September 3, was another lovely summer day. The sun
warm and bright, the sky a deep blue, the air balmy. Ordinarily I
would have been out on my boat sailing on the Havel.

It was not long that morning before the situation began to clear
up. At 9 A.M. Ambassador Nevile Henderson walked determinedly
down the Wilhelmstrasse from the British embassy to the Foreign
Office. He had been told that Ribbentrop would not be available so
early in the morning — though on most days, one knew, the Nazi foreign minister was already at his desk at that hour. The British government had told its wavering ambassador that the message he was
bringing had to be delivered at precisely nine o'clock. The Germans
had told him that in that case he could leave it with Dr. Schmidt, the
official interpreter.

But on this historic day, the genial interpreter, fatigued like everyone else in Berlin by the last few days, overslept. Grabbing a taxi in
front of his residence, he sped to the Foreign Office to see the British
ambassador already mounting the steps. Schmidt ducked in by a side
door and managed to slip into Ribbentrop's office on the stroke of
nine o'clock, just as Henderson was being ushered in. The ambassador declined Schmidt's invitation to be seated and read him a solemn
declaration from his government.

The British note of September 1, it reminded the German government, had clearly stated Britain's intention of fulfilling its obligations
to Poland unless German troops were promptly withdrawn.

> Although this communication was made more than 24 hours ago, no
> reply has been received, but German attacks upon Poland have been
> continued and intensified. I have accordingly the honour to inform
> you that unless not later than 11 A.M., British summer time, today Sep-
> tember 3, satisfactory assurances to the above effect have been given
> by the German Government and have reached His Majesty's Govern-
> ment in London, a state of war will exist between the two countries as
> from that hour.

Henderson handed Schmidt a copy, bade him goodbye, and left.
The official interpreter hastened down the Wilhelmstrasse to the

Chancellery to inform Hitler. Outside the Führer's office he found several members of the cabinet and the party hierarchy standing about "anxiously waiting" his news. But first he had to give it to the dictator.

> Hitler was sitting at his desk [Schmidt later recounted] and Ribbentrop stood by the window. . . . I stopped at some distance from Hitler's desk and then slowly translated the British ultimatum. When I finished there was complete silence.
> Hitler sat immobile, gazing before him. . . . After an interval which seemed an age, he turned to Ribbentrop, who had remained standing by the window.
> "What now?" asked Hitler, with a savage look, as though implying that his Foreign Minister had misled him about England's probable reaction.
> Ribbentrop answered quietly: "I assume that the French will hand in a similar ultimatum within the hour."

Dr. Schmidt, after leaving Hitler, stopped in the outer room to inform the others of Britain's ultimatum. The news reduced them to silence. Then Göring turned to him and said: "If we lose this war, may God have mercy on us!" Dr. Goebbels, the rabble-rousing minister of propaganda, also observed an unaccustomed silence. He "stood in a corner by himself, downcast and self-absorbed," Schmidt later recalled. "Everywhere in the room I saw looks of grave concern."

Thus did the Nazi dictator and his cohorts in Berlin see the German "counterattack" on Poland become a European war. Hastily Hitler and Ribbentrop prepared an answer to the British government and shortly before noon the Nazi foreign minister, who had declined to see the British ambassador at 9 A.M., sent for him and handed him Germany's reply.

It was a shabby document designed principally to fool the German people. It blamed the British for the breakdown of peace and accused the London government of "preaching the destruction and extermination of the German people." It refused "to receive or accept, let alone to fulfill," the British ultimatum.

Henderson read the document. Later he would characterize it as a "completely false representation of events." But to Ribbentrop, on this last meeting between them, he merely remarked that "it would be left to history to judge where the blame really lay."

Ribbentrop, vain and pompous to the end, answered that "history has already proved the facts."

❦ ❦ ❦

I was standing in the bright sunshine in the Wilhelmstrasse before the Reich Chancellery about noon when the loudspeakers suddenly announced that Great Britain had declared war on Germany. Some 250 people — no more — stood about me. They listened attentively to the announcement. When it was finished, there was not a murmur. The handful of people just stood there, silently, in the midday sun. You could see it was still incomprehensible to them that Hitler had led them into a European war.

They lingered on a few minutes in the hope (I heard several say) that the Führer would appear on the balcony, but he did not show himself — I did not expect that he would — before only 250 undemonstrative people. Quickly the tiny group melted away.

As I went up the Wilhelmstrasse, newsboys came around the corner at Unter den Linden shouting their extras. They were giving the papers away. I took one, the *Deutsche Allgemeine Zeitung*. Its headlines, in the biggest type I had ever seen, marched across the page.

BRITISH ULTIMATUM TURNED DOWN

ENGLAND DECLARES A STATE OF WAR
WITH GERMANY

BRITISH NOTE DEMANDS WITHDRAWAL
OF OUR TROOPS IN THE EAST

THE FÜHRER LEAVING TODAY FOR THE FRONT

One column was devoted to the text of a German memorandum, which Hitler had affixed to the German reply. Ribbentrop must have suggested the headline — it sounded so much like him.

GERMAN MEMORANDUM PROVES
ENGLAND'S GUILT

Even if the German people were convinced of the "proof," they certainly displayed no hostility toward the English or the French. There was no echo of the 1914 war cry: *Gott straff England!* When I passed the British and French embassies the sidewalk in front of each was deserted. The Germans in the street weren't even curious. A lone Schupo, pacing up and down before each, stood guard.

The French did not present their ultimatum until noon, when Ambassador Coulondre arrived at the Foreign Office. Ribbentrop was not available to see him either, despite the later hour. Actually, the Nazi foreign minister was busy partaking in a strange little ceremony at the Chancellery, where the new Soviet ambassador was being cordially received by the Führer. Until his pact with Stalin, Hitler had never received a Soviet ambassador nor had one scarcely ever set foot in the Wilhelmstrasse. So this was a unique occasion and not even a declaration of war by France, after that declared by Great Britain, could keep Ribbentrop from attending it.

To this bizarre note was added another. In the absence of Ribbentrop, the French ambassador was received by Weizsäcker, who when asked by Coulondre if he, the state secretary, was empowered to give a "satisfactory" answer to the French ultimatum, replied that he was not in a position to give him "any kind of reply." When the Frenchman tried to hand over France's formal ultimatum, the state secretary rudely declined to accept it. He asked the ambassador "to be good enough to be patient a little longer and see the foreign minister personally." So Coulondre cooled his heels for another thirty minutes, when he was told he could see Ribbentrop.

Coulondre, one of the most intelligent of the diplomats in Berlin, I always thought, was treated to one of Ribbentrop's customary harangues, but not for long. He broke in to ask if Germany's answer to France's note was negative.

"*Ja*," replied Ribbentrop.

Coulondre then handed him his country's ultimatum, in words similar to that of the British, adding that "for the last time" he must emphasize Germany's "heavy responsibility" for war.

"Then France will be the aggressor," Ribbentrop snapped.

"History will be the judge of that," Coulondre replied, and got up to leave. All the leading figures in the final act of the drama that Sunday in Berlin kept calling on the judgment of history. Alone the insufferable Ribbentrop tried to give history's judgment himself.

At last the French government had honored its word to Poland. But the Wilhelmstrasse, I observed that historic Sunday afternoon, took due note of the lack of harmony of the Western Allies in timing their ultimatum. Though I did not know it, the German High Command had already concluded that the French army did not intend seriously to attack on the Western Front to help the hard-pressed Poles. I did note that in his two proclamations later that day, one to the German army, the other to the German people, Hitler blamed only Great Britain for landing Germany into a war. There was not a word about France.

In the West the first action came not on the Western Front but at sea. That Sunday evening, ten hours after Great Britain declared it was at war with Germany, the German submarine U-30 torpedoed and sank without warning the British liner *Athenia* two hundred miles west of the Hebrides as it was en route from Liverpool to Montreal with fourteen hundred passengers, of whom one hundred and twelve, including twenty-eight Americans, lost their lives.

I learned of it late the next evening on the feedback from New York. The government denied that a German U-boat was involved. Goebbels' propaganda ministry claimed the British had sunk the ship in order to curry sympathy in America — a phony line it would adhere to for months.

I must say I felt lousy having to give the German explanation. On my next broadcast that evening I went out of the way to explain that I had been assigned to give the news from Germany, that official denials such as that a German U-boat had torpedoed the *Athenia* were part of the news, that I was in no position myself to confirm or deny the story, and that my orders from CBS were to refrain from expressing my personal opinions. I did not say that I intended to get around such orders as best I could, regardless of what CBS or the Germans thought. I resurrected a stern rule I had laid down for myself when I first came to Nazi Germany five years before: that I would remain in Berlin only as long as I could fairly depict what was going on. Naturally there were limits imposed by censorship, especially military censorship. Ed Murrow in London and Tom Grandin and Eric Sevareid in Paris were subject to censorship of their radio scripts too. You could not say anything that might jeopardize a military operation or give the other side military information. If within those limits I could not broadcast a true picture of the situation I would go home. I told the Germans that. And CBS.

On September 8 NBC and Mutual halted all network broadcasts from Europe, leaving the field to CBS alone. Apparently — and unbelievably! — they thought it was unneutral for them to report on the war! It may also have been because the two networks had failed to line up their own war correspondents, as we had done. Ed Klauber cabled from New York that we would continue alone. I felt relieved that this new medium of radio would not give up covering war for the first time — without a try.

But in one way its American managers — in our case Bill Paley and Ed Klauber — were its own worst enemies. Those first weeks of the war both of them were generous in their praise of what we were doing from London, Paris and Berlin. But they did not understand our main problem. During the very first week of the war RRG, the German broadcasting company, informed me they would give us facilities to make radio recordings from the battlefield for later broadcast to New York. It was the only way radio could really cover the war. It was obvious from the first days of fighting in Poland that there would be no "front," as there had been in the First World War, which was fought in the trenches. The panzer divisions were racing forward several miles a day with the motorized infantry closely following to mop up. You could record the awesome sounds of modern battle — the deafening thunder of a thousand tanks in action, of a massive dive-bomber attack — with a small mobile unit carried in your jeep. You could not take a telephone line up to them for instant, direct broadcast. But CBS turned me down flatly, as it did Murrow in London. No recordings! Every broadcast must be live. It was an idiotic ruling that prevented American radio from doing the job it should have done covering World War II.

Each day's news of the German onslaught on Poland astonished and bewildered us. Within a week we began to comprehend that the Germans had instituted a new kind of warfare such as the world had had no inkling of. They called it the *Blitzkrieg*. By September 5 — in five days — the Germans had smashed through the Polish Corridor, General von Kluge's Fourth Army from the west, General von Küchler's Third Army from East Prussia. We began to hear that General Heinz Guderian, the great advocate of armored warfare, had easily broken through the Polish defenses with the tanks of his Panzer Korps. At one point, while racing east across the Corridor, an armored division of Guderian's had been attacked by the famous Polish Pomorska Brigade of horse cavalry. A few days later I saw what mincemeat he had made of it. The bodies of a thousand horses or so were still rotting along the roadside and across the adjoining fields. The remains of hundreds of dismounted men had been hastily buried near by.

Horses against tanks! Only the Poles, with their incredible bravery and foolhardiness, would have pitted the old horse cavalry against the new cavalry of steel.

On September 6, six days into the war, the Germans captured Cracow, second city of Poland.

The High Command also states that Kielce has fallen . . . almost due south of Warsaw. Nobody had any idea the German army had got that far. In one week the Germans have pushed far beyond their 1914 frontiers. It begins to look like a rout for the Poles.

September 7. It's just a week since the "counterattack" began, and tonight I learn from an army friend that the Germans are within twenty miles of Warsaw. . . .

September 8. The German High Command announced that at 5:15 P.M. today German troops reached Warsaw. . . . Even our military attachés were astonished at the news.

I added this: "And while Poland is being overrun, not a shot yet — so the Germans say — on the Western Front!" The inaction in the West was as astonishing as the action in the East. My own puzzlement kept cropping up in my diary.

September 9. . . . Apparently the war in Poland is all over. . . . Britain and France have done nothing on the Western Front to relieve the tremendous pressure on Poland.

It seemed to me in Berlin that the French were missing a golden opportunity to shatter the Germans in the West while they were completely preoccupied in Poland and perhaps even win the war by occupying the Ruhr and Rhineland. Could they have done it? The German generals thought so.

"They have missed their opportunity!" exclaimed a relieved General Halder at the end of September. At Nuremberg after the war he was more specific. "If the French," he said, "had used the opportunity presented by the engagement of nearly all our forces in Poland they would have been able to cross the Rhine without our being able to prevent it and would have threatened the Ruhr, which was decisive for the German conduct of the war."

General Siegfried Westphal, who served on the Western Front that fall, believed the French could have advanced to the Rhine in two weeks, had they tried.

During September [he later wrote] there was not a single tank on the German western front. . . . All the flying units of the Luftwaffe were in service in Poland, leaving only a few reconnaissance planes and obsolescent fighters available for the West. . . . It was incomprehensible that the appalling weakness of the German defense should be unknown to the French leaders. . . . The German forces were much too weak to block the path of a French assault. . . . Yet nothing happened.

The failure of the French to act, when action might have quickly won the war, made, I believe, a lasting impression on Hitler. He knew that when he had finished liquidating Poland he could turn on France with little fear that they — the French of the Marne and of Verdun in the last war! — this time would seriously fight.

In the meantime he would lull them, and the British, with proposals for peace.

After the serious fighting in Poland was over the Germans invited the American correspondents to visit the "front." We saw very little — some bitter but small-scale fighting for Gydinia and the Hela peninsula, west of Danzig, where the Poles continued to hold out. More important, we happened to be in Danzig to hear Hitler launch his first proposal for peace. "Happened" is probably the wrong word. It is more likely that the dictator, master propagandist that he was, arranged for us to be in Danzig.

His speech punctuated by the boom of the eleven-inch guns of the old battleship *Schleswig-Holstein* firing at Gydinia from the port of Danzig, Hitler spoke on the afternoon of September 19 in the lovely old Gothic Guild Hall.

He was in an ugly mood. I had a seat on the aisle, and as he strode past me toward the platform I could not help but note his rage. This surprised me, since he was appearing as a conqueror. Later a Nazi acquaintance explained to me the reason for his black mood. He was in a terrible temper because he had counted on making this speech in conquered Warsaw. But the surrounded Polish garrison there had refused to surrender, and the conqueror had been forced to move his platform to Danzig. Despite his frustration, he seized on this meeting at Danzig to launch a political offensive for peace in the West.

"I have no war aims against Britain and France," he said. And he called upon the Almighty "who now has blessed our arms, to give other peoples comprehension of how useless this war will be . . . and to cause reflection on the blessings of peace."

From this hypocrite, who had just demolished Poland by war!

To make sure that we got the message out to America, Hitler lent us one of his thirty-two passenger junker planes to speed us back to Berlin, where transmission facilities were much better than in battered Danzig. Next day in the capital the orchestrated Nazi press took up the Führer's propaganda "for peace."

"Why should England and France," asked the *Frankfurter Zeitung*, "waste their blood against our West wall? Since the Polish state has ceased to exist, the treaties of alliance with it have no more sense."

This was a shrewd propaganda line, designed to appeal especially to the strong antiwar sentiment in France. It got a boost from the Bolsheviks in Moscow, which caused me less surprise than it would have a week before. For Stalin in the meantime had moved boldly to take advantage of his pact with Hitler.

At 6 A.M. on September 17, the Red Army began *its* invasion of Poland. The Poles, already beaten by the Germans, could offer little resistance. The next day Soviet troops met the Germans at Brest Litovsk, where just twenty-one years before the Bolshevik government, abandoning its Western allies, had made a separate peace with Germany on terms so harsh that, had they been carried out, they might well have destroyed the Russian nation.

In Berlin that morning I felt nauseated at the news from Moscow. How many times had I sat in Geneva and heard Soviet statesmen talk about common fronts against the aggressor! The Germans had urged the Russians to move in. Though the Nazis could not publicly say so, they felt that Stalin's move took some of the onus of Nazi aggression in Poland off Germany and placed it on the Soviet Union.

Thick as thieves, the two dictatorships now sat down together to divide up the spoils of conquest. Ribbentrop journeyed again to Moscow to complete the new deal. It is clear from the captured German archives that it was Stalin, rather than Hitler, who insisted that Poland must disappear from the map. To mollify world opinion the Führer had toyed with the idea of leaving a small Polish state — on the order of Napoleon's Grand Duchy of Warsaw. But he was not unhappy to accede to Stalin's insistence that the two nations gobble up all of Poland and divide it between them. This was done on September 28 after a day of talks between Stalin and Ribbentrop in Moscow.

As in the original Nazi-Soviet pact, there were "secret protocols." The most nefarious was worded as follows:

> Both parties will tolerate . . . no Polish agitation which affects the territories of the other party. They will suppress in their territories all beginnings of such agitation. . . .

It was the signal for regimes of terror designed to brutally suppress Polish freedom, culture and national life.

Finally, as part of the bargain, Stalin joined in furthering Hitler's peace offensive. A statement concocted by Ribbentrop and Molotov

was issued on September 28, along with the announcement of a
Russo-German accord on the disposal of Poland.

> The governments of Germany and the U.S.S.R., after having defi-
> nitely settled the problems arising from the disintegration of the Po-
> lish state and created a firm foundation for a lasting peace in Eastern
> Europe [sic!], mutually express their conviction that it would serve
> the true interests of all peoples to put an end to the state of war be-
> tween Germany and England and France. Both governments will
> therefore direct their common efforts . . . toward attaining this goal as
> soon as possible.
> Should, however, the efforts remain fruitless, this would demon-
> strate the fact that England and France are responsible for continuing
> the war.

In this revolting exercise in hypocrisy and deceit Stalin had
thrown his weight solidly behind Hitler against the West — the
West which a few weeks before he was beseeching to join him in a
common front against Hitler.

Such are the weird twists of history!

Eight days later, on October 6, in the Reichstag, Hitler delivered
his long-awaited appeal for peace. As I sat in the ornate chamber of
the Kroll Opera listening to him I had the impression of hearing an
old scratchy gramophone record being replayed for the fifth or sixth
time. How often before I had heard him from this same rostrum,
after his latest conquest, and in the same dripping earnestness of
voice and of manner, propose what sounded like a fair and decent
peace — if you forgot his last victim.

> Germany [he said] has no further claims against France. . . . I be-
> lieve that there can only be real peace in Europe and throughout the
> world if Germany and England come to an understanding.
> Why should this war in the West be fought? For restoration of Po-
> land? Poland of the Versailles Treaty will never rise again. . . . It
> would be senseless to annihilate millions of men . . . in order to recon-
> struct a state which at its very birth was termed an abortion. . . . No,
> this war in the West cannot settle any problems. . . .

There were problems. But he suggested they be solved at a conference of "the leading European nations."

It was a shrewdly conceived speech, and I had no doubt, as I made
my way back to the Adlon on a crisp, sunny, autumn afternoon, that

it would impress the German people, who wanted peace, and probably the French, who had no heart for this war, but I had no doubt either that the British would easily see through it.

On my way to Broadcasting House that evening I picked up an early edition of Hitler's own newspaper, the *Völkischer Beobachter.* The headlines were in large type and stretched across most of the front page.

GERMANY'S WILL FOR PEACE — NO WAR AIMS AGAINST FRANCE AND ENGLAND — NO MORE REVISION CLAIMS EXCEPT COLONIES — REDUCTION OF ARMAMENTS — COOPERATION WITH ALL NATIONS OF EUROPE — PROPOSALS FOR A CONFERENCE

It sounded so reasonable. At the Rundfunkhaus, as I prepared my own broadcast, the Germans milled about excitedly. They were sure peace had come.

Chamberlain's reply was picked up in Berlin six days later. It came in the form of an address to the Commons. "No reliance," the prime minister said, "could be put on the promises of the present German government." The wrongs done to Poland and Czechoslovakia would first have to be righted. The Man of Munich, I was relieved to see, could no longer be fooled by Hitler's promises.

On October 9, I left Berlin briefly for Geneva to see my family, to fetch some winter clothing and, my diary says, "to recover my senses." Only those who did long stretches of time in Nazi Germany, especially in wartime, probably can appreciate the sense of relief one felt in getting out of Berlin. I had left Geneva just two months ago. In that flicker of time a familiar world had disappeared, the world of peace I had grown up in, come of age in, and that, despite its faults, was essentially a decent one. It was gone now. Another world, born in war, was in the making. I did not look forward to it.

My train arrived in Geneva after darkness had fallen. I could not get used to the lights. They blinded me, after six weeks in blacked-out Berlin. I had never much liked this Calvinist Swiss city. But now, as I romped about with Tess and Eileen, it seemed a beautiful and civilized place. All too soon my three and a half days there were over.

Along the Rhine from Karlsruhe to Basel on the way to and from Berlin I skirted the Franco-German border for a hundred miles, and it was plain to see that all was quiet on the Western Front despite the French claims of mighty battles being fought there. The German train crews, who made the trip daily, said not a shot had been fired on this sector since the war began. Where the train ran along the east bank of the Rhine, as it did in stretches for miles, you could see the French bunkers on the far shore and French soldiers idling about outside them. At one place they were playing a soccer match, and on our side of the river German troops stood about watching it, sometimes cheering when one side scored a goal. French *poilus* waved back. Sometimes they would wave at our train. They looked bored. This was war?

All through that autumn and the rest of 1939 the Sitzkrieg, the sit-down, phony, *drôle-de-guerre* continued. There was a little action at sea, but no fighting on land or in the air. When British planes ventured over Berlin it was to drop not bombs, but leaflets — and in bad German! There was very little to occupy an American reporter except to survive in the Nazi madhouse with one's sanity somewhat intact.

One got used to things: the blackout, which with the short days of the northern winter began around five in the afternoon; the shortages of food and clothing, the monotonous, largely vegetarian meals, the shrill exhortations of Goebbels and the controlled press and radio.

Some things you could never get used to: the continual announcements of executions — in the occupied lands and in Germany. They crept into my diary. "November 9. The Germans announce they've shot . . . the Polish mayor of Bromberg . . . implicated in the murder of Germans and the theft of city funds. . . . November 18. Yesterday nine young Czech students at the University of Prague were lined up before a German firing squad and executed. . . . Here in Germany three youths were executed yesterday for 'treason.' " Every day or two the newspapers announced a few beheadings: for listening to the BBC, for "endangering the defensive power of the German people," and so on.

Occasionally we would have a word or two with a big shot. On November 7, four or five of us American correspondents had a talk with Göring at — of all places — the Soviet embassy, to which we had repaired for the annual reception on the anniversary of the Bolshevik revolution — and also, frankly, for the opportunity of getting some good food and drink: caviar, sturgeon, vodka. Standing in front of a portrait of Lenin smiling down on us, Göring held forth as he quaffed beer and puffed away at a long stogie. He was, as usual, in an expansive mood. His fighters and bombers, especially the Stuka dive-bombers, had done a good job in Poland. I wanted to know how the marshal felt about Congress's repeal of the American neutrality law and about the boasts of some in Washington that soon America would be selling thousands of planes to the Allies to help beat Germany. He knew very well about our backwardness in producing war planes. "Your planes are good," he said. "But you don't make enough of them fast enough." He was not worried, he said, at the possibility of the United States supplying the Western Allies with planes, tanks, guns.

"Despite what happened the last time?" I asked.

"*Ja.* Despite that," he said, and chortled.

I got the impression he had given the matter little thought. Unlike Hitler and Goebbels and Himmler, Göring obviously had no dislike of us American correspondents, no matter what our country did. He didn't seem to care. He could not take America seriously as a military power. But wasn't that the same mistake, I wondered, the Germans had made in the first war? In their arrogance they remained ignorant of the rest of the world.

German arrogance! In December that year it took a tumble.

On the evening of December 14 the newspapers and radio in Berlin celebrated what they called a great victory at sea of the pocket-battleship *Graf Spee* over three British cruisers off Montevideo. The British warships had been put out of action, said the Germans, while the *Graf Spee* had suffered only "superficial damage." For two days the press and radio gloated over the victory. Then on December 18 they announced briefly that the victorious battleship had scuttled itself in the Plate estuary just outside the Uruguayan capital. Three days later the navy announced that the ship's commander, Captain Hans Langsdorff, had "followed his ship" and thus "fulfilled like a fighter and hero the expectations of his Führer, the German people and the navy."

The wretched German people were not told that Captain Langsdorff did not "follow his ship" but committed suicide by putting a revolver shot through his head in a lonely hotel room in Buenos Aires. Nor were they told, as I was, that the Führer, enraged that the *Graf Spee* had been scuttled instead of fighting to the last, personally ordered the hapless Langsdorff to kill himself.

A good many of my broadcasts that fall and early winter were about action at sea, since after the fall of Poland there was no serious fighting anywhere else. The only German "offensives" were on the ocean with submarines.

At midnight on September 28 I put the commander of one of those submarines on the air. There had been an angry exchange between the British and the Germans over the radio concerning the torpedo-ing of a British ship, *Royal Sceptre*. London claimed it had been sunk without warning and that the crew and passengers, numbering sixty, presumably had perished. Berlin denied it.

A day or two later Winston Churchill, then Lord of the Admiralty, admitted to the House of Commons that the U-boat skipper had ra-dioed him a message advising him of the location of the ship he had just sunk so that the British might save the passengers and crew. That commander, Churchill added with obvious glee, had been captured and was now a prisoner of His Majesty's Government. Berlin denied that, too.

I was sure the British were telling the truth. I had had too many lies from the Germans.

When I questioned the German navy about it, a testy admiral obligingly produced the commander of the submarine and said I could question him on one of my broadcasts. This was Captain Her-bert Schultze, who swore to me that though he had sunk the *Royal Sceptre*, he had radioed another British vessel, the *Browning*, telling it where it could pick up the survivors, and that he learned from the latter's radio signals that it had picked them up. This the British con-tinued to deny.

Captain Schultze also told me that in a moment of impishness he had radioed a saucy message to Winston Churchill, apprising him too of the spot where the survivors of the torpedoed ship could be found. I must say that as we worked over our script at the Ministry of Ma-rine I began to feel that the young naval officer was telling the truth.

If he had radioed Churchill, I said, still trying to be skeptical, surely he had the text in his U-boat log.

"Indeed I do," he said. "But it's in Kiel."

Would he mind telephoning Kiel and try to get a member of his crew to read back the exact words he had radioed Churchill?

"I'll try," he said, and picked up a phone. The logbook was found. The message was read back. And when we went on the air that eve-ning I had him read the text.

As we were leaving the Ministry of Marine for the broadcast, I got another break. A press officer came running after us with a bulletin from Reuter, the British news agency. It said the *Browning* had just landed at Bahia, Brazil, with the crew and passengers of the *Royal Sceptre,* all safe.

Who in London fooled Churchill into announcing to the Commons that Captain Schultze had been captured I never found out. Later, after our broadcast, the British Admiralty confirmed the captain's version and admitted that he had not been captured.

Schultze, when I interviewed him, was one of those instant heroes the Germans were making of their U-boat commanders. An even greater hero surfaced on October 15 when the German press and radio, with much fanfare, announced a staggering U-boat victory that was so sensational I could not believe it until I picked up a BBC broadcast admitting that it was true. On the previous day the submarine U-47 had penetrated the seemingly impenetrable defenses of Scapa Flow, the great British naval base, and sank the battleship *Royal Oak* as it lay at anchor, with a loss of 786 officers and men. The commander, Öberleutnant Günther Prien, who was promptly promoted to captain, was paraded before us at the Propaganda Ministry on October 18, along with his crew of young sailors, most of them eighteen to twenty, I judged. I noted in my diary:

> Prien told us little of how he did it. He said he had no trouble getting past the boom protecting the bay. I got the impression that he must have followed a British craft, perhaps a mine-sweeper, into the base. British negligence must have been something terrific.

A German friend, a World War I submarine skipper, told me that German U-boats had tried twice to get into Scapa Flow during the first war and that both submarines were lost in the attempt. It was something to crow about. It helped to keep up war spirits among a people who certainly were doing their duty, but without the early enthusiasm for war they had shown in 1914.

Was it to buck up their sagging war spirits that on the evening of November 8, twelve minutes after Adolf Hitler had finished making his annual speech at the Bürgerbräukeller in Munich in celebration of the 1923 Beer Hall Putsch, and, with all the big party leaders, had hurriedly left the hall, that a bomb went off behind the rostrum, killing seven persons and injuring sixty-three others? Himmler blamed the "British Secret Service" and even Chamberlain for the crime.

The thing sounded fishy to me. Hitler, I learned, made a much shorter speech than usual on this anniversary. He and his entourage of the most important party leaders, Göring, Goebbels, Himmler, Hess, quickly left the premises as soon as the address was over, though in other years, I knew, they had lingered over their beer and sausage to reminisce with old party comrades. Also Hitler's own newspaper, the *Völkischer Beobachter*, was the only newspaper in Berlin to carry the story the next day. Why didn't the other journals mention it? A friend had telephoned me the news at Broadcasting House just as I finished my midnight broadcast. But German radio officials and my censors pooh-poohed the story, and would not let me return to the air to give it.

> What Himmler and his gang are up to [I wrote in my diary] obviously is to convince the gullible German people that the British government tried to win the war by murdering Hitler and his chief aides.

It smacked of the Reichstag Fire.

On November 21 Himmler announced that he had found and arrested the culprit, one Georg Elser, a carpenter and a Communist, who formerly had resided in Munich but lately in a concentration camp. Elser had been aided and abetted, Himmler said, by two British secret agents, Captain S. Payne Best and Major R. H. Stevens, who the day after the Munich explosion had been arrested at the German-Dutch frontier. Actually, we would learn later, they had been kidnapped at the Dutch border town of Venlo by a gang of S.D. (Security Service) ruffians led by Alfred Naujocks, he who had staged the faked "Polish attack" on the German radio station at Gleiwitz, which Hitler had used as his excuse for beginning the "counterattack" that destroyed Poland.

The mystery of the bombing, like that of the Reichstag Fire, was never completely cleared up. Elser pleaded guilty but was never brought to trial, though one was continually scheduled and then "postponed." Elser himself told fellow inmates at Dachau concentration camp, where he had been incarcerated previous and subsequent to the bombing, that certain men, posing as enemies of Hitler, had arranged for him to make the bomb and place it in a pillar behind the rostrum where the Führer made his annual speech. He was promised freedom and a large sum of money. Later he was coached, he said, to implicate Best and Stevens, of whom he had never heard.

After the war I learned that Elser was made a privileged inmate of both Dachau and the Sachsenhausen concentration camps and treated very well. But Himmler kept his eye on him. It would never do to let the carpenter survive, if the war were lost, to tell his tale. When it became irretrievably lost, the Gestapo chief acted. On April 16, 1945, as the end of the Third Reich neared, it was announced that Elser had been killed in an Allied bombing attack. Actually, Himmler had him murdered by the Gestapo.

December came, and with it, on its very first day, some more depressing news. The Soviet Union, having occupied Eastern Poland in cahoots with Hitler and begun to digest the Baltic states that had belonged to Russia in czarist times, invaded Finland. Soviet bombers attacked Helsinki, killing seventy-five civilians and wounding several hundred. The Red Army crossed the frontier and began a drive on the Finnish capital.

I was on a brief leave in Geneva when the news came in. I felt the same outrage as when Hitler went into Czechoslovakia and then Poland. I fumed in my diary.

> The great champion of the working class, the mighty preacher against "Fascist Aggression," the righteous stander-up for the "scrupulous and punctilious observance of treaties" (to quote Molotov as of a month ago), has fallen upon the most decent and workable little democracy in Europe in violation of a dozen solemn treaties. . . .
>
> I have raged for 30 hours; could not sleep last night, though I got little chance.

I had worked through the day and night, continually on the phone to Helsinki, Stockholm, Berlin, Bern, Amsterdam and London trying to arrange for broadcasts to get through from Finland to America. It proved hard going.

The Germans refused to give me either a transmitter or transit telephone lines through Germany. They said frankly they had orders not to offend Russia. I called Amsterdam and begged the Dutch for one of their shortwave transmitters to carry our broadcasts to New York, but they were frightened that this would jeopardize their neutrality and turned me down. Finally, Ed Murrow, with whom I was on the phone through the twenty-four hours, solved our problem. He got the BBC to pick up the Swedish medium-wave transmitters, which could relay our Helsinki broadcasts piped through by telephone to Stockholm.

Having found a way of getting our broadcasts out I then had to find someone to do the broadcasting from Finland and the front. I finally located Bill White, son of William Allen White, with whom I had become acquainted when he arrived in Berlin a few weeks before. Bill was an elusive one. In Berlin he was constantly disappearing. After many a telephone call and some detective work I now found him in Stockholm and got him off to cover the Russo-Finnish war.

He proved a happy choice. His broadcasts, especially from the front, where the outmanned and outgunned Finns were stopping the Russians cold, were very moving, and one on Christmas Eve from the frozen, snow-covered Finnish trenches was memorable. So much so that it inspired Robert Sherwood, who was listening to it in New York, to write his play *There Shall Be No Night.*

I broadcast Christmas Eve from Berlin and Christmas night from Kiel, the great German naval base.

It was the first Christmas of the war, and in Berlin it was rather grim. It rained, turned to snow and back to a drizzle. On many a Christmas Eve I had wandered through the streets of this city. There was not a home in the poorest quarter that did not have its candlelit Christmas tree sparkling merrily through the uncurtained, unshaded windows. Usually it snowed. People hurried home through the whitened streets from their offices, factories or shopping, full of the Christmas spirit. This afternoon it grew dark in the rain by four o'clock and you could make out people only dimly, stumbling dismally through the wet, blacked-out streets, making their way sullenly home. Perhaps there were lighted Christmas trees behind the blackout curtains, but you could not see.

Perhaps there was some cheer and warmth within, but I wondered. People had looked so glum as Christmas, a very sentimental time for most Germans (and I must confess, for me), approached. There was little in the shops for presents; even less food, which in any case was severely rationed. Hitler, I heard, was the glummest of all. He had pulled out of Berlin on the twenty-first in a black mood and boarded his special train for the Western Front, though there had been no action there, skipping his traditional Christmas party at the Chancellery, though a big celebration, I knew, had been planned.

I celebrated part of Christmas Eve with American friends. The wives of most of the correspondents had left, but two or three had remained and there were a few single young women from the embassy. There was some cheer, I guess, but I had the feeling that we were all a little too desperate to forget the war and the Germans and enjoy the holy eve.

I had to leave our host's home at midnight for my broadcast. At the Rundfunk the Germans had set up a Christmas tree in one of the larger offices and when I arrived they were dancing and trying to make merry with champagne. My broadcast, my diary says, "was inexcusably sentimental," though I do not remember it. I do remember thinking of a number of Christmas Eves at home — in Chicago before my father died; in Cedar Rapids, Iowa, where my mother finished rearing us youngsters. It invariably snowed in those places and it was cold and there was a fire in the fireplace, from whose mantel hung three stockings. And outside in the snow those nights before Christmas there was the tinkle of sleighbells. Friends and relatives came in from the cold laden with presents, stamping the snow off their boots, hovering over the fire to get warm, munching nuts and cookies my mother proffered. They were full of Christmas cheer.

I left the Rundfunk around 3 A.M., snatched some sleep at the Adlon, and was off at 5 A.M. by car to Kiel in the rain of Christmas Day. This was the first visit of a foreign correspondent to the German fleet since the war began. A couple of days before, one of our U.S. naval attachés, whom I suspected of being head of our military intelligence on the Continent — such as it was — had coached me on how to identify the various German warships by their silhouettes. He wanted to know, he said, where the hell the German fleet was, particularly the two new battle-cruisers, *Scharhorst* and *Gneisenau,* which he believed had just been commissioned, and the battleship *Bismarck*, which he said was by all odds the most powerful battleship afloat, but probably not yet finished. I suspected he was anxious to tip the British off about them, if he could.

At Hamburg, where we stopped first, in the early morning of Christmas Day, the rain was coming down in sheets. We finally found the naval yard and waded through foot-deep puddles to where the warships were. The first vessel we visited was the new cruiser *Admiral Hipper,* which was tied up at a dock undergoing last-minute construction work. The officers assured me it would soon be able to put to sea.

I had always got along well with German naval people. When I asked the *Hipper's* skipper about a report from London that a British submarine had torpedoed and sunk a German cruiser — a report categorically denied in Berlin — he winked and led me up a narrow ladder to the ship's battle-tower.

"Look over there," he said slyly. A hundred yards away a somewhat smaller cruiser was propped up in dry dock, a gaping hole that
must have been fifty feet in diameter torn in its side exactly amid-
ships.

"The British hit her," he said. "But contrary to what they said,
they did not sink her."

My captain obligingly identified the ship as the cruiser *Leipzig*.
Since he was so obliging, I asked him what the huge ship I could see
farther down the river was.

"The *Bismarck*," he smiled with pride.

So this was the mighty *Bismarck*! The British would have liked to
have my view, I mused. The *Bismarck* looked almost completed. A
swarm of workers were hammering away on its decks.*

As we drove on to Kiel in the waning afternoon, the rain turned to
snow and we had difficulty getting over the hills because of the ice.
At the great naval base some officious official from the Propaganda
Ministry welcomed me with a little speech.

"I understand," he said, "that you have stopped at Hamburg and
seen some of our warships there. Did you see the cruiser *Leipzig*,
Herr Shirer?"

"Yes, sir, and —"

"Those British liars, they say they have sunk the *Leipzig*, Herr
Shirer."

"It didn't look sunk to me, but —"

He cut me off again. "Herr Shirer, that's fine. You will answer this
dastardly English lie, isn't it? You will tell the truth to the great
American people. Tell them you have seen the *Leipzig* with your
own eyes, isn't it — and that the ship has not been scratched."

Before I could interrupt *him* he was pushing me down a gangplank
toward a naval launch. My naval guide, a bemonocled officer from
the High Command who I judged was a veteran of the first war, was
wincing from the fool's talk. Wolf Mittler, a German broadcaster and
a friend, who had been assigned to help out on the technical aspects
of my broadcast, grinned sheepishly.

Out in Kiel harbor, as our naval launch began a tour, I was surprised to see that almost the entire German navy was concentrated
here for the holidays. My briefing by our naval attaché began to pay

* The sinking of the *Bismarck* a year and a half later climaxed the greatest naval battle in
the Atlantic of the Second World War. In the running engagement that lasted an entire
week, with the *Bismarck* most of that time pitted alone against the bulk of the British home
fleet, the 42,000-ton battle-cruiser *Hood*, the largest and most powerful vessel in the British
navy, was sunk in the first engagement.

off. I could make out and identify most of the ships: the pocket-battleship *Deutschland,* two cruisers of the *Cologne* class, both 26,000-ton battle-cruisers, *Scharnhorst* and *Gneisenau,* a number of destroyers and some fifteen submarines. If the British only knew, I could not help thinking, they could come over this night, which would see almost a full moon, and wipe out almost the entire German fleet with a few bombers. Could, but wouldn't!

Our launch stopped at an immense dry dock. A swarm of workers was just leaving the big ship in it, which my hosts soon confirmed was the battle-cruiser *Gneisenau.* The captain sent word he would be happy to show me over his vessel. He quickly explained that the big ship was in dry dock not because it had been hit but because it was in need of overhaul. He invited me to inspect the sides of the vessel. I could detect no holes.

The spirit of camaraderie between officers and men on the battle-ship surprised me, as it did my German military escort, who said he had never seen anything like it in Germany during the first war. Four or five senior officers accompanied me through the ship and when we entered some of the crew's quarters, there was no snapping to attention, not even for the vessel's commander. The captain, a genial fellow, apparently noticed our surprise.

"We have a new spirit in the German navy," he said, and obviously he was proud of it. He explained that in this war officers and men aboard all German naval ships got the same food and the same amount. This had not been true in the last war, he said, and he quoted a naval proverb that the same good food for officers and men puts an end to discontent. I remembered — as I'm sure he did — that the German revolution in 1918 started here in Kiel among the discontented sailors.

When we returned to shore in the launch, a magnificent nearly full moon was rising behind the snow-banked hills, spreading a silvery light over the water and making the ships stand out in outline. What a target for the R.A.F.!, I again could not keep from thinking. I went back to the hotel to work out the details of the Christmas night broadcast. I planned to begin the program from the deck of a U-boat tender and then slide down a hatch to the hold, where the crew of a submarine just back from British waters was having Christmas dinner.

The view from the deck as we waited to go on the air was breathtaking. The moon over the vast harbor was now well up, lighting the waters, the ships, the snow-covered hills beyond. For a few seconds I had a terrible temptation to blurt out that practically the whole damned German fleet lay there before me, knowing that the British would be picking up, as they always did, my broadcast from the German shortwave transmitter. It was that dizzy feeling you get when you stand atop a skyscraper and have a momentary urge to jump off. But I quickly recovered my senses. I had no desire to have my head chopped off. Britain was not my country, though I ardently hoped she would somehow, someday, defeat the Germans, and anyway I knew the British would do nothing about it, even if I tipped them off.

I said a few words describing the Kiel naval base on this moonlit Christmas night, slid down the hatch with my microphone to the hold, in my awkwardness ripping a sleeve and smashing the face of my stopwatch, on which I depended to get off the air on the split second required by American broadcasting.

The U-boat sailors — mere boys in their late teens most of them looked to me — greeted me with a Christmas song. They had made the rather crude room very festive. A large Christmas tree, gaily decorated, shone with electric candles in one corner. Red bunting reached across the ceiling. On one side the men had rigged up a number of amazing exhibits. One was a miniature ice-skating rink in the midst of a snowy mountain resort, on which skaters moved about on the ice. Another showed the coastline of England. A man turned on a switch and a naval battle off the coast began. Three or four of the young men knew a little English and I introduced them. They described what it was like to live and fight in a small submarine against the British. They seemed content enough with their lot though it occurred to me that none of them probably had very long to live, the toll on the U-boats being what it was.

With my stopwatch broken I had no idea when my fifteen minutes was up. When I judged it was, I closed the broadcast with the men singing *Stille Nacht* to the accompaniment of an accordion. Afterward the U-boat commander served rum and tea, and then good Munich beer, of which he seemed to have put in several cases. Both officers and men wanted to continue our talk. Their questions were rather touching.

"The English, why do they want to fight us?" they kept asking. But I saw no point in trying to get into that subject. The crew, it was plain, had swallowed Hitler's propaganda. I bid the men a Merry Christmas and thanked them for sharing it with me. Mittler, my officer escort, and I walked back several miles to the hotel in the moonlight. We had a bottle of champagne in the bar. The radio was on, and someone was reading a batch of Christmas proclamations from the Nazi big fry. One was particularly inane, and I noted it down. It was from Dr. Robert Ley, boss of the phony Labor Front.

"The Führer is always right," he said. "Obey the Führer!"

And so to bed at 3 A.M. after my first Christmas of the war.

The German radio continued the next day to air the endless Christmas proclamations and messages. Among the latter I noted a warm exchange between Hitler and Stalin. The German dictator wired the Soviet dictator: "Best wishes for your personal well-being as well as for the prosperous future of the peoples of the friendly Soviet Union." To which Stalin replied: "The friendship of the peoples of Germany and the Soviet Union, cemented by blood, has every reason to be lasting and firm."

How long would the hokum last? I wondered.

Then came the torrent of New Year's proclamations. I was interested that Hitler should go to great length to justify his war. The maniac assured the German people that the war was started by "Jewish reactionary warmongers in the capitalist democracies."

> He says [I noted in my diary] "the German people did not want this war." (True) "I tried up to the last minute to keep the peace with England." (False) "But the Jewish reactionary warmongers waited for this minute to carry out their plans to destroy Germany." (False)

I had little doubt that the majority of the German people would swallow these idiotic lies. After all my time in this Nazi cuckooland, I still found it profoundly depressing to see a people so easily deceived. A diary entry for January 25, 1940, gives an example.

> Dined alone at Habel's. . . . I was about to leave when an old duffer sat down at my table. . . .
> "Who will win the war?" he asked.
> "I don't know," I said.

Though he didn't look like a Gestapo man, you never could tell for sure, so you were on your guard.

> "Why, selbstverstandlich, Germany," he laughed. He argued that in 1914 Germany had the whole world against her; now only Great Britain and France, and Russia was friendly.

"Each side thinks it will win," I said. "In all the wars."

He looked at me with pity in his old eyes. "Germany will win," he said, "It is certain. The Führer has said so."

Evenings like that depressed me, and there were more than one that dark, bitterly cold winter. Perhaps it was the cold, the lack of anything substantial in the war to report, the boredom. On February 23, 1940, I noted in my diary:

> My birthday. Thought of being 36 now, and nothing accomplished, and how fast the middle years fleet by.

My depression had been relieved by a fortnight off with my family at Villars-sur-Ollon in Switzerland, where Tess and I got in some skiing and began to teach Eileen, now all of two, how to ski. But it returned, as it invariably did, on my return to Berlin on the twenty-second. I resented being separated from my family, missing the growing up of what might be our only child, since Tess had had such a bad time with the first, missing too the normal life with Tess — we had really never been together more than a few days or weeks at a time since our marriage. I did not let these feelings dominate me, or last for long. After all, millions of men in uniform in this war were separated from their families. I was a noncombatant. I had a good chance to survive. Millions of men had been torn from their jobs. I had a job I still liked.

As spring approached it looked as if the war would warm up and perhaps spread. In that case hundreds of thousands, perhaps millions of people might get killed, like the last time. I probably would be spared. What had I to be sorry about?

From January through most of March, 1940, we had the coldest winter in German history. It was made worse for the people by the lack of coal for heating. The rivers and canals, which carried most of the coal, were frozen over solid for nearly three months. The coal barges became stuck in the thick ice. Coal stocks in the cities, particularly Berlin, became exhausted and offices and homes went unheated for days at a time. Plumbing froze and burst. Life became a struggle to keep warm — and dry.

The war was almost forgotten. There was no fighting on land. The bombers of both sides were still dropping mostly leaflets. Only at sea was there still a little action. German submarines continued to sink Allied shipping.

Only in another war, on the Russo-Finnish front, was there fighting on land. It was taking place in the snows and intense cold behind the old frontier northwest of Leningrad. The whole Western World was applauding the heroic Finns for stopping the Russian colossus. Two days after Christmas the Finns began a counteroffensive, cutting up four divisions of the Soviet Eighth and Ninth armies. But they lacked the men, the tanks, heavy guns and planes to score a breakthrough. By this time the Russians had concentrated 1,200,000 men on the front. The Finns, with their tiny population, could mount only 200,000. The British and French promised to send an expeditionary force to help them if Norway and Sweden would allow them transit, which they continued to refuse to do.

The Finnish offensive petered out on January 6, and two days later, after the Soviet Union's leading general, S. K. Timoshenko, took personal command, the Russians went over to the offensive, throwing in masses of fresh troops and thousands of tanks, guns, planes. By the beginning of March the Finns realized they faced defeat and began secretly to negotiate for peace. On March 12 they signed a peace agreement with the Russians. It was harsh enough. It gave the Soviet Union Vyborg, Finland's second city, northwest of Leningrad, and a number of Finnish island fortresses in the Gulf of Finland.°

In Berlin the men around Hitler did not hide their relief. Germany was freed of its unpopular support of Russia against the gallant Finns. It counted now on the Soviet Union's resuming shipment of badly needed raw materials, especially oil and food. It also made it less likely that Hitler would have to occupy Scandinavia to prevent the Allies from taking it over under cover of supporting their line of communications through Norway and Sweden for an expeditionary corps in Finland. "Conclusion of peace between Finland and Russia," Colonel Jodl of OKW† noted in his diary, "deprives England, but us too, of any political basis to occupy Norway."

That was true. But there were other considerations. In fact, all winter long it had looked to me that the war would spread to Scandinavia. I find mention of it as early as January 3 in my diary.

> The press is beginning to harp about "Britain's aggressive designs in Scandinavia." Hitler, we hear, has told the army, navy and air force to

---

° Finnish losses were 25,000 dead and 45,000 wounded, out of a force of 200,000, a grievous toll for so small a country. Russian losses were heavier, but smaller in comparison with the population and the number of troops involved: 48,000 dead, 158,000 wounded, out of a force of 1,200,000.

† Oberkommando der Wehrmacht — High Command of the Armed Forces.

rush plans for heading off the Allies in Scandinavia should they go in there to help Finland against Russia. The army and navy are very pro-Finnish, but realize they must protect their trade routes to the Swedish iron-ore fields. If Germany loses these, she is sunk.

Germany's very existence, now that it was blockaded by the British, depended upon the import of iron ore from Sweden. During the warm-weather months this ore was transported from northern Sweden by sea down the Gulf of Bothnia and across the Baltic to Germany. But in the wintertime this shipping route could not be used because of the thick ice in the shallow gulf. During the cold months the Swedish ore had to be shipped by rail to the Norwegian port of Narvik and brought down the Norwegian coast by ship to Germany. As spring approached the British showed signs of taking action in Norwegian waters to cut off this lifeline of Germany's. Churchill, the First Lord of the Admiralty, had proposed at the beginning of the war to mine Norwegian territorial waters to stop the German ore traffic. But Chamberlain had turned him down.

Russia's attack on Finland radically changed the situation in Scandinavia. The Germans learned early of Allied plans to send an army to Finland by way of Norway and Sweden. They realized that once Britain and France had landed their troops in Norway, no matter how many might continue on through Sweden to Finland, some would remain to cut off their iron ore shipping route down from Narvik. This would be a disaster that Hitler was determined to avoid at all costs. An incident that occurred in Norwegian waters on the night of February 17 seems to have been the last straw for the Nazi dictator.

An auxiliary supply ship, the *Altmark*, of the lost *Graf Spee* had managed to slip back through the British blockade and was discovered by a British scouting plane sailing southward in Norwegian waters toward Germany. The British government knew that aboard it were three hundred captured British seamen from the merchant ships sunk by the *Graf Spee* in the South Atlantic. The Norwegian navy claimed to have inspected the German vessel and found no British prisoners aboard. But Churchill was not satisfied. He personally ordered a British destroyer flotilla to go into Norwegian waters, board the German ship, and liberate the British prisoners. This the destroyer *Cossack* did on the night of February 16–17. After a scuffle in which four Germans were killed and five wounded, the British boarding party liberated two hundred ninety-nine seamen, who had been locked in storerooms and an empty oil tank to avoid detection by the Norwegians.

Hitler was furious. Two days later, on the nineteenth, he told OKW to complete plans for *Weserübung* (Weser Exercise, the code name for the plan for German occupation of Norway).

"Equip ships. Put units in readiness," he told Colonel Jodl, at OKW. An element of comedy now entered an otherwise serious business. Jodl reminded the Führer that he had not yet appointed a general to lead the Scandinavian campaign. At the suggestion of General Keitel, chief of OKW, Hitler named General Nikolaus von Falkenhorst, who commanded an army corps on the Western Front, for the job. Falkenhorst had never met the Führer and had never even heard of the plan for war in the north. Hitler called him into the Chancellery on February 21, told him he had information that the British were going to land in Norway, fumed about the *Altmark* incident, and told him to report back in five hours with plans to invade Norway. Hitler did not inform him of the plan already drawn up by OKW, so the general had to start from scratch. He knew absolutely nothing, he later said, about Norway.

> I went out [he explained at Nuremberg] and bought a Baedeker travel guide in order to find out just what Norway was like. I didn't have any idea. . . . Then I went back to my hotel room and I worked on this Baedeker. . . . At 5 P.M. I went back to the Führer.

Hitler approved the "Baedeker" plan and on March 1 issued his formal Directive for Weser Exercise, "the occupation of Denmark and Norway" — Denmark had been hastily added to the list of Hitler's next victims.

The British and French, we now know, were making their own plans to intervene in Norway. All through the winter and early spring Churchill had pressed Chamberlain to allow the navy to mine Norwegian waters to cut off the German iron ore traffic. Finally he wangled approval to mine the Norwegian Leeds on April 8. Hurriedly, preparations were made for the dispatch of small Anglo-French contingents, backed by strong naval support, to occupy and defend the Norwegian ports of Narvik, Trondheim, Bergen and Stavanger in case the Germans reacted. This last operation was known as "Plan R-4."

Thus that first week of April as "Plan R-4" and "Weser Exercise" were beginning to be carried out, German troops were being secretly loaded on transports in the Baltic ports while on the Clyde and in the Forth in northern Britain French and British troops, though in smaller numbers, were being secretly embarked on Allied ships.

Both sides, though, had a pretty good idea of what the other was up to. The Scandinavians too. By the beginning of April they were getting plenty of notice of German intentions and preparations. Only, they failed to heed them. Somehow it was beyond the comprehension of these decent, peaceful Nordics that Hitler could do such a thing to them.

On April 2, the military censors in Berlin let me broadcast what was no longer a secret in the capital:

> Germany is now waiting to see what the Allies intend to do in stopping shipments of Swedish iron ore down the Norwegian coast to the Reich. It's accepted here as a foregone conclusion that the British will go into Scandinavian territorial waters to halt this traffic. It's also accepted as a foregone conclusion here that the Germans will react. . . . Germany cannot afford to see these shipments of iron stopped without fighting to prevent it.

Never before since the war began had the Nazis permitted me to be so frank in what I broadcast. True, they did not allow me to air my information that German troops were concentrated at the Baltic ports. I remember feeling rather relieved that evening at the thought that at last the British, who were still fighting the phony war on the so-called Western Front, would have a chance to deal the Germans a devastating blow in Norway. I had no doubt the British navy would have little trouble in doing that. The German navy was still no match for it.

On the afternoon of April 2, after a long confab with Göring, Admiral Raeder and General von Falkenhorst, Hitler issued a formal directive ordering "Weser Exercise" to begin at 5:15 A.M. on April 9. The first naval forces, those earmarked for Narvik, were ordered to sea. The others were to follow in the ensuing days and be in position on April 9 to occupy Copenhagen and Norway's five main ports, from Oslo in the south to Narvik in the far north.

There were further directives. In the first, Hitler ordered that "the escape of the kings of Denmark and Norway from their countries at the time of the occupation must be prevented by all means." He did not want them setting up troublesome governments-in-exile, as two of his previous victims, Czechoslovakia and Poland, had begun to do. In the second, the High Command instructed the German Foreign Office to prepare diplomatic measures for inducing Denmark and Norway to capitulate without a fight and to concoct some kind of justification for Hitler's latest aggression.

The third directive, from the navy, I did not see until the Nuremberg trials. The German navy was going to slip warships and transports with troops hidden in their holds past the British into Norwegian harbors by deceit! They were instructed to pass as British craft when challenged by the Norwegians!

My Berlin diary:

> April 8. The British announce they have mined Norwegian territorial waters in order to stop the German iron ships coming down from Narvik. The Wilhelmstrasse says: "Germany will know how to react." . . .
>
> April 9. Hitler this spring day has occupied a couple more countries. At dawn Nazi forces invaded the two neutral states of Denmark and Norway in order, as an official statement piously puts it, "to protect their freedom and independence."
>
> After twelve swift hours it seems all but over. Denmark, with whom Hitler signed a ten-year nonaggression pact only a year ago, has been completely overrun, and all important military points in Norway, including the capital, are now in Nazi hands.
>
> The news is stupefying. Copenhagen occupied this morning, Oslo this afternoon, Kristiansand this evening. All the great Norwegian ports, Narvik, Trondheim, Bergen, Stavanger, captured.

We were urgently convoked to a special press conference at the Foreign Office at 10:30 A.M. We waited for half an hour. Then Ribbentrop strutted in, dressed in a flashy field-gray Foreign Office uniform. The insufferable man acted as if he owned the earth. With a straight face he insisted that the Germans had occupied Denmark and Norway to "protect these countries from the Allies" and "to defend their true neutrality until the end of the war."

Before reading his absurd statement, he had introduced his press chief, a fat cipher named Schmidt, to read the text of the German memorandum, which had been thrust upon the two surprised Scandinavian governments at dawn as German troops began to occupy their capitals.

I thought it one of the most brazen diplomatic documents yet concocted by Hitler and Ribbentrop. After declaring that Germany had come to the aid of Denmark and Norway to protect them against an Anglo-French occupation, it went on:

> The German troops therefore do not set foot on Norwegian soil as enemies. The German High Command does not intend to make use of

the points occupied by German troops as bases for operations against England as long as it is not forced to. . . . On the contrary, German military operations aim exclusively at protecting the north against the proposed occupation of Norwegian bases by Anglo-French forces.

. . . In the spirit of the good relations between Germany and Norway which have existed hitherto, the Reich government declares to the Royal Norwegian Government that Germany has no intention of infringing by her measures the territorial integrity and political independence of the Kingdom of Norway now or in the future. . . .

The Reich Government therefore expects that the Norwegian Government and the Norwegian people will . . . offer no resistance to it. Any resistance would have to be, and would be, broken by all possible means . . . and would therefore lead only to absolutely useless bloodshed. . . .

After such a blatant display of deceit, I felt the need of fresh air. I walked up the Wilhelmstrasse and then through the Tiergarten. The walk cooled me off and restored my senses.* At noon I drove out to the Rundfunk to do my regular broadcast. From a score of rooms Goebbels' unpleasant voice came roaring over the radio loudspeakers. He was reading the various memorandums, proclamations and news bulletins with his customary vehemence. I started to check the war communiqués telling of the military action so far. I must admit they stunned me. Everything apparently had gone according to plan — or better. Copenhagen and the rest of Denmark occupied by noon with hardly a shot. No Danish resistance at all. In Norway there had been a little, but all the major objectives had been attained: occupation of Oslo and the five other major ports. It was incredible. Where had the British navy been? I transmitted the German claims on the broadcast though I could scarcely believe them, and drove back to the Adlon, dispirited, for lunch.

When I returned to Broadcasting House in the evening, I found the atmosphere decidedly changed. The cockiness of the Germans at noon had evaporated. One of the naval censors, who had assured me that some slight scattered resistance in Norway would be over by nightfall, now admitted that he might have been premature.

Here briefly is what happened in Norway, as we would eventually

---

* But not for long. Later I would get the proofs of the early editions of the morning newspapers. I noted down some of the front-page headlines and editorials in my diary.

The *Börsen Zeitung:* "England goes cold-bloodedly over the dead bodies of the small peoples. Germany protects the weak states from the English highway robbers. . . . Norway ought to see the righteousness of Germany's action, which was taken to ensure the freedom of the Norwegian people."

The *Völkische Beobachter:* "GERMANY SAVES SCANDINAVIA!"

learn. In Denmark it had been a breeze. The Danes realized their island kingdom was defenseless. It was too small, too flat, and the largest part, Jutland, lay open to Hitler's tanks. There were no mountains for the king and government to flee to, as there were in Norway. Nor, as in Norway, could any help be expected from the British.

Still the Danish army commander-in-chief wanted to fight. He was overruled by the king and the government. Only a scattered few shots were fired. The navy itself, whose ships and shore batteries might have repelled the weak German force landing at Copenhagen to occupy the capital, never fired a single gun. The German freighter *Hansestadt Danzig*, with one battalion of troops hidden in its hold, arrived off Copenhagen shortly before dawn, passed without challenge the guns of the fort guarding the harbor (which could have blown it to bits), proceeded past several Danish gunboats, and tied up neatly at Langelinie Pier in the heart of the city and but a short distance from the Amalienborg Royal Palace. Within a few minutes the king's palace was seized by the lone battalion of Germans.

In Norway's capital of Oslo that morning it had gone differently.

All through the chilly night of April 8–9 a gay welcoming party from the German legation had stood at the quayside in Oslo Harbor waiting for the arrival of a German fleet and troop transports. It was the strongest naval force sent to Norway, led by the pocket-battleship *Lützow* (its name changed from *Deutschland* because Hitler had not wished to risk losing a ship of that name), with six eleven-inch guns, and the new 10,000-ton heavy cruiser *Blücher*, flagship of the squadron, carrying eight eight-inch guns.

The happy little party from the legation waited in vain. The big ships never arrived. They had been challenged at the very entrance to Oslo Fjord, where the Norwegian mine-layer *Olav Trygverson* sank a German torpedo-boat and damaged the light cruiser *Emden*. The rest of the fleet continued up the fjord. Fifteen miles south of Oslo, where the waters narrowed to fifteen miles, stood the ancient fortress of Oskarsborg. An alert garrison opened fire with the fort's old twenty-eight-centimeter Krupp guns and also launched torpedoes. Direct hits were scored on the *Blücher* which, ablaze and torn by the explosions in its ammunition holds, soon sank, with the loss of sixteen hundred men, including many Gestapo and administrative officials on their way to arrest the king and government and take over in the capital. The *Lützow* was also hit several times and badly damaged. The battered naval force turned back.

Elsewhere, the Germans had had better luck. In Narvik, so important to both the Germans and British, the Norwegian army commander surrendered without firing a shot. The naval commander was of sterner stuff. He fired warning shots from an ancient iron-clad at a squadron of ten German destroyers that had slipped into the harbor through the British blockade, but then fell victim to German treachery. Asked to withhold his fire until a German naval launch reached him to discuss the situation, his ship was blown up by torpedoes from the German destroyers, which in the meantime had surrounded him. A second Norwegian iron-clad, which then had opened fire, was similarly dispatched. By 8 A.M. the Germans were in complete command of the port and railhead of the iron ore line from Sweden.

Farther south along the long Norwegian coast, the Germans were equally — and as easily — successful. By noon or shortly afterward on that early spring day, the Germans had captured the five principal Norwegian port cities and the one big airfield along the west and south coasts. They had accomplished this with a handful of troops conveyed by a navy vastly inferior to that of the British. Daring, deceit and surprise had brought Hitler a staggering victory at relatively little cost.

The setback at Oslo when the strongest of his naval squadrons was turned back was quickly compensated for by a surprisingly easy victory in the air. Where the navy failed, the air force succeeded. And with what I can only describe as a phantom force.

The capital's airport at Fornebu was for some reason not defended, though there had been plenty of warning from the naval engagement fought during the night down the fjord. A few cars parked in the field could have made it impossible for the Germans to land. But even this precaution was not taken. By noon some five companies of parachutists and airborne infantry had been *landed* by the Germans. As they were lightly armed, a small force of Norwegian troops with a tank or two, a piece or two of artillery, could have wiped them out. But it failed to develop. So shortly after noon, behind a makeshift military band, the German force *paraded* from the airport into the capital.

They arrived too late, however, to achieve one of Hitler's main objectives: the capture of the king and the government. These, along with all but five of the two hundred members of the Parliament, had fled the capital by special train at 9:30 A.M. for Hamar, eighty miles to the north. Twenty-three motor trucks had proceeded north also, laden with the gold of the Bank of Norway and secret papers of the Foreign Office. The German minister eventually caught up with the king and sought to persuade him to surrender and return to Oslo. But King Haakon VII, the only monarch in the twentieth century who had been elected to his throne by popular vote and the first king Norway had had for five centuries, refused. So did his government.

Hitler was furious. The Luftwaffe was ordered to wipe out the village of Nybergsund, the temporary headquarters of the Norwegian government and king. This was done on April 11. The Germans at first were sure they had destroyed the monarch and his government. The diary of a captured German airman had the following entry for April 11: "Nybergsund. *Oslo Regierung. Alles vernichtet.*" (Oslo government. Completely wiped out.)

Actually King Haakon and the members of his government had fled to the nearby woods. Standing in snow up to their knees they had watched the German bombers reduce the village to ashes.

Serious resistance to the Germans in Norway now depended on the British. The Norwegian army, such as it was, had been nearly wiped out when its scattered garrisons at the port cities surrendered. Colonel Ruge, inspector general of infantry, had managed to round up four or five battalions of infantry to protect the retreating king and government. This force now began to make its way up the rugged Gudbrandsdal Valley to Andalsnes on the western coast, a hundred miles south of Trondheim. At Andalsnes, the British were reported to be landing troops to come to Norway's aid.

But there, as elsewhere along the long Norwegian coast, the British action was timid, slow, late. The Western Allies had built up over the winter an Anglo-French expeditionary corps of fifty-seven thousand men for service on the Finnish front. This force, which it had planned to land at Narvik, Trondheim, Bergen and Stavanger, was assembled in ports in northern Britain the morning the Germans went into Norway. Several sizable units were on their ships. But instead of being rushed to Norway, where they would have greatly outnumbered the German invasion forces, they were hurriedly *disembarked.* The Anglo-French High Command wanted to see what the situation was before risking its expeditionary force in Norway.

It seems to have been the British army that held back. In Narvik, for instance, the navy quickly gained the initiative. One day after the Nazis had taken the port, a flotilla of British destroyers entered the harbor and wiped out most of the German naval vessels. Three days later, on April 13, another British squadron, this time led by the battleship *Warspite*, destroyed the remaining German war vessels. Vice-Admiral W. J. Whitworth, the British commanding officer, urged the army to occupy Narvik at once — the two Nazi battalions had taken to the hills out of gun range of the British ships. But the British army commander, General P. J. Mackesy, instead timidly landed them at Harstad, thirty-five miles to the north, which was still held by the Norwegians. This was a costly error.

More followed.

Not until April 20, eleven days after the initial German landings, did a force of one British infantry brigade and three battalions of French Chasseurs Alpins land at Namsos, a small port eighty miles northeast of German-held Trondheim, while another contingent of one British infantry brigade was put ashore at an equally small port of Andalsnes, one hundred miles southwest of Trondheim, which thus was to be attacked from north and south. But lacking field artillery, anti-aircraft guns and air support, their small bases pounded night and day by German bombers operating from captured Norwegian airfields, neither Allied force ever seriously threatened Trondheim. The British brigade at Andalsnes abandoned the proposed attack on Trondheim and headed southeast down the Gudbrandsdal Valley to help the Norwegian troops, which had been slowing the main German drive coming up the valley from Oslo.

I remember in Berlin hearing that Hitler was furious at the slow pace of this most important land action of the campaign. On April 21 the first engagement of the war between British and German troops took place at Lillehammer. But it was not much of a battle. The ship carrying the British brigade's artillery had been sunk by German bombers. Its men had only machine guns and rifles to oppose a German force well supplied with light artillery and light tanks and supported by bombers which pounded the brigade. The engagement did last twenty-four hours, after which the British and Norwegians resumed a retreat a further hundred and forty miles up the valley to Andalsnes, halting now and then to fight a rear-guard action that slowed the Germans somewhat but never stopped them.

On the nights of April 30 and May 1, the Anglo-Norwegian forces were evacuated from Andalsnes, and on May 2 the Anglo-French contingent from Namsos. It was a wonder that anyone got away. Both ports were pounded into shambles by Luftwaffe bombing. But King Haakon and his government were safely got out and put aboard the cruiser *Glasgow*, which conveyed them to Tromsö, far above the Arctic Circle, where the provisional Norwegian capital was set up.

The southern half of Norway, comprising all the main cities and ports, was now in German hands, but the northern half seemed secure for the British-backed king. On May 28 — at last! — an Allied force of twenty-five thousand men, including two brigades of Norwegians, a brigade of Poles and two battalions of the French Foreign Legion, drove the greatly outnumbered German garrison out of Narvik. Hitler would get no more Swedish iron ore through this port. Or so it seemed. But not for long.

By this time, the end of May, Hitler had struck on a new front, with stunning force, and every available Allied soldier was suddenly needed to try to stop him. Narvik was hastily abandoned, and the German troops, who had held out in a wild, mountainous tract near the Swedish border, reoccupied Narvik on June 8, there to remain for the duration of the war. With the British pulling out, the rest of Norway north of Narvik now lay open to the Germans. On June 7 at Tromsö the British took King Haakon and his government aboard the cruiser *Devonshire*, which conveyed them to London and five bitter years of exile.

In Berlin I followed the campaign in Norway, as outlined above, with a heavy heart. Apparently, Hitler was unstoppable; the British and the French paralyzed. My friends in the German army, navy and air force pointed out to me the important lessons being learned in Norway. The chief one was that for the first time in the history of warfare, land-based *air* power had triumphed over *sea* power. The British navy had been unable to use its superiority to drive the Germans out of the Norwegian ports and secure the bases from which British troops tried to operate. These bases had been pounded to smithereens by German bombers, making it impossible to land artillery and tanks and even suitable stores. For fear of land-based bombing the British had pulled back their ships that they had counted on to regain the German-occupied harbors. Only in Narvik, which was out of range of German land-based bombers, had they dared to risk their naval vessels.

Air power had revolutionized modern warfare.

The Nazi conquest of Norway, incidentally, gave the languages of the Western World a new word for a traitor: *quisling*. This was the name of a former Norwegian army officer and minister of war who tried to sell out his country to the Nazi Germans.

Major Vidkun Quisling had started out honorably enough. Born in 1887 of peasant stock, he had graduated first in his class at the Norwegian Military Academy, and while still in his twenties had been sent to Petrograd as military attaché. There he had witnessed the Bolshevik revolution and had sympathized with it. So much so, that when he returned to Oslo he offered his services to the Labor party, proposing to resign from the army and set up a "Red Guard," modeled after that of the Russian Bolshevik party. But the Labor party turned him down. Then after serving as minister of war from 1931 to 1933 he seems to have changed his early enthusiasm for communism to one for Nazism. Seeing it triumph in Germany in 1933 encouraged him to form a Norwegian Nazi party called Nasjonal Samling, or National Union. But Nazism did not thrive in the democratic soil of Norway. Quisling could not even get himself elected to Parliament. Defeated at the polls by his own people, he turned to Nazi Germany for support.

There he got in touch with Alfred Rosenberg, the muddled official philosopher of Hitler's party. The two hit it off and began to dream up the idea of a Nordic Empire, a union of the "Jew-free" Scandinavian peoples, which would join Nazi Germany to dominate the world. Rosenberg helped out Quisling in various minor ways until 1939, when the coming of war opened up possibilities for more important collaboration. During that first winter of the war Quisling visited Berlin and presented a plan that interested Hitler. He would seize power in Oslo with his storm troopers and ask for military help from Germany.

This was the old Anschluss plan, with Quisling playing the part of the Austrian traitor Seyss-Inquart. It appealed to Hitler, who saw Quisling in the greatest of secrecy three times in mid-December of 1939. The Norwegian warned him that the British, in the guise of sending troops to Finland, might occupy Norway at any moment. Hitler gave him a sizable sum of money and a promise of more to finance a coup and arranged for the training of some Norwegian storm troopers in Germany.

Thus it was that on the evening of April 9, once the capital was firmly in German hands, Quisling stormed into the Oslo radio station and broadcast a grandiose proclamation naming himself the head of a new Norwegian government and ordering all Norwegian resistance to the Germans to cease. This shameful act of treachery aroused a public that had been stunned by the lightning occupation of their country. It would lead shortly to a considerable resistance.

Quisling did not last long in his first attempt to govern Norway for the Germans. Six days after he had proclaimed himself prime minister, the Germans kicked him out. They tried for a time to enlist the cooperation of more important Norwegians, but the attempt failed. The chief justice, Paal Berg, and the fifteen other judges of the Supreme Court resigned rather than carry out German orders. (Berg soon became the secret head of the resistance.) The Lutheran Church also resisted German demands. On April 23 Hitler, exasperated by the defiance of the Norwegians, appointed Josef Terboven, a tough young Nazi *Gauleiter,* to be Reich commissar for Norway, and he ran the occupied country with increasing brutality. He reinstated Quisling as prime minister in 1942 but gave him no real power.

The contemptible little traitor, "a pig-eyed little man," I described him after seeing him one day in the Reichstag in Berlin, was captured at the end of the war and tried for treason by his fellow countrymen. After an exhaustive trial he was sentenced to death and executed on October 24, 1945.

To my dismay, one very distinguished Norwegian got the Nazi bug. This was the great novelist Knut Hamsun, winner of the Nobel Prize for literature in 1920. I had read his *Growth of the Soil* while in college and later *Hunger* and had been deeply moved by them. Like Maxim Gorki he had started life as a laborer; in one stretch he worked as a streetcar conductor in Chicago. In his writing he had taken a tragic view of man's struggle with the land, the sea, with society. I could not believe it when articles by him sympathetic to Nazism began to appear in the German press and later when reports came in from Norway that he was collaborating with the Nazi German occupiers. At the end of the war he too, like Quisling, was indicted for treason, but the charges were eventually dropped on the grounds of his old age and senility (he was in his eighties), though he was later tried and convicted for "profiting from the Nazi regime" and fined $65,000, a considerable sum in Norway in those days. Hamsun died in 1952 at the age of ninety-three.*

Toward the end of April I took four or five days off to represent CBS at a meeting of the International Broadcasting Union at Lau-

---

* The two Germans who ran Norway for Hitler during the war, Commissar Terboven and General von Falkenhorst, met separate fates. Terboven killed himself rather than face capture. General von Falkenhorst was apprehended, tried by a mixed British-Norwegian court for having handed over captured Allied commandos to the S.S. for execution, and sentenced to death. But the sentence was commuted to life imprisonment and he was ultimately released.

sanne and to get a glimpse of my family at Geneva, a few miles down the lake. The meeting of the European broadcasters, including French, British and Germans, in neutral Switzerland and a look I had that week at part of the Western Front along the Rhine below Basel reminded me of the strangeness of this war. At Lausanne the supposed enemies, while no longer convivial, as I had seen them at other such conferences, acted in a civilized manner toward each other. Despite their countries being at war, they knew they had to continue to respect each other's radio wavelengths lest broadcasting come to an end in Europe. This they did, without recriminations.

Along the Rhine two great armies were dug in on opposite banks in plain sight of each other. Neither fired a shot. Back in Berlin I got the impression that this uncanny situation was about to change. The eight-month phony war along the Franco-German border was coming to an end. With Norway in the bag the Nazi Warlord had decided to strike in the West.

All through that first week of May the German press, obviously on orders from on high, stepped up its campaign to convince the people that the Allies, having failed in Norway, were about to become aggressors in the West. On May 7 there was a choice headline in one of the morning newspapers: "CHAMBERLAIN, THE AGGRESSOR. ALLIED PLANS FOR NEW AGGRESSION."

The next day, Wednesday, May 8, I noted in my diary:

> Could not help noticing a feeling of tension in the Wilhelmstrasse today. Something is up. . . .

Ralph Barnes, my old friend and colleague from the *New York Herald-Tribune*, who had gone from Berlin to be the newspaper's chief correspondent in London, had returned here the day before by way of Holland. He told me that guards on his train had pulled down the window blinds for the first twenty-five miles of the journey from the Dutch-German frontier. He assumed this was to prevent passengers such as he from seeing German troop movements toward the border. I checked at the Dutch and Belgian legations. At both places everyone seemed on edge. I checked in the Wilhelmstrasse. The Foreign Office was furious at an A.P. report that two German armies were moving up to the Dutch frontier.

Next day, Thursday, May 9, Berlin seemed even more tense. The scare headlines continued. "BRITAIN PLOTS TO SPREAD THE WAR!" said one. "It may well be," I said in my broadcast that evening, "that the war will be fought and decided before the summer is over." Increasingly in the last few days my censors had let me get by with ever stronger hints that war in the West, where the big armies were, was imminent. I didn't know yet the exact date. All I knew was that it could not be far off.

I was sound asleep when the phone in my room at the Adlon rang at 7 A.M. the next morning, Friday, May 10. It was one of the young women at the Rundfunk. "It has started on the Western Front," she said. "You want to go on the air soon?"

"As soon as I can get there," I said, trying to arouse myself. "Please book me a shortwave sender — for, say, in about thirty minutes."

I turned on the radio. Bulletins were being read.

At dawn Hitler had struck in the West. His troops, comprising probably the most powerful army ever assembled on one front, were invading the three little countries he had promised not to touch: Holland, Belgium and Luxembourg. They were driving through them toward France. The showdown with the Western Allies had begun.

The author with his daughter in Geneva

CHAPTER 16

Conquest of the West

1940

Once again, on the fine spring day of May 10, 1940, the ambassadors in Berlin of three more small countries were called to the Foreign Office shortly after dawn and told that German troops were pouring into their lands to protect them against imminent attack by the British and French — the same shabby excuse Hitler used a month before with Denmark and Norway. And once more the hapless envoys, this time of Belgium, the Netherlands and Luxembourg, were told any opposition would be crushed, and responsibility for the bloodshed would be borne exclusively by them.*

In his press conference at the Foreign Office at 8 A.M. Ribbentrop said he had presented the ambassadors of the Low Countries with "incontrovertible evidence" that Britain and France were about to invade Germany through Holland and Belgium and that Germany

---

* In Brussels, where, as in The Hague, the German ambassador arrived shortly after dawn at the Foreign Office to deliver the same message, the Belgian foreign minister, Paul-Henri Spaak, stopped him short.

"I beg your pardon, Mr. Ambassador. I will speak first."

They could hear the roar of German bombers overhead and the explosion of their bombs on nearby airfields, which rattled the windows of the office.

"The German army has just attacked our country. This is the second time in twenty-five years that Germany has committed a criminal aggression against a neutral and loyal Belgium. What has happened is perhaps even more odious than the aggression of 1914. No ultimatum, no note, no protest of any kind has ever been placed before the Belgian government. It is through the attack itself that Belgium has learned that Germany has violated the undertakings given by her. . . . The German Reich will be held responsible by history. Belgium is resolved to defend herself."

When the German diplomat then began to read his message, Spaak again interrupted. "Hand me the document," he said. "I should like to spare you so painful a task."

therefore deemed it necessary to send in its own troops "to safeguard the neutrality of Belgium and Holland." He said the German High Command had "proof" that Allied forces were about to march into the Low Countries in an effort to seize the Ruhr.

German insolence went further that day. When later in the morning the Belgian and Dutch envoys returned to the Wilhelmstrasse to ask for their passports and to lodge protests at the violation of their neutrality, "an official on duty," a communiqué informed us, "after reading the contents, which were arrogant and stupid, refused to accept them and asked the two ministers to request for their passports in the usual manner." That afternoon the Berlin newspapers carried large headlines dubbing as "shameful" the protests of Belgium and Holland against being invaded.

What was truly shameful, of course, was that Germany, as in 1914, had broken her solemn word to respect the neutrality of Belgium. Was there no honor among these Germans, I kept muttering, whether under Wilhelm II or Adolf Hitler? Couldn't they ever keep their word?

As far back as 1839, Germany had joined the other great powers of Europe in guaranteeing "perpetually" the neutrality of Belgium, which had just gained its independence. But in 1914, as German troops poured through Belgium to catch the French army in the rear, the chancellor, Bethman-Hollweg, had declared that for Germany the guarantee was "merely a scrap of paper," an admission that had shocked most of the outside world. After the war the Weimar Republic had sworn never to take up arms against Belgium, and Adolf Hitler had given Belgium (and the Netherlands) similar assurances. But the captured German secret papers reveal, from 1938 on, a familiar counterpoint in Hitler's public assurances to the Low Countries and his private admonitions to his generals.

On August 24, 1938, for instance, after he had publicly sworn that his demand for the return of the Czech Sudetenland was his very last territorial demand in Europe, he was pointing out to his generals the "extraordinary advantage" to Germany if Belgium and Holland were occupied. On April 28, 1939, in the Reichstag, Hitler stressed the "binding declarations" he had given to the Low Countries. Less than a month later, on May 23, we find him telling his generals that "the Dutch and Belgian air bases must be occupied by armed force . . . with lightning speed. *Declarations of neutrality must be ignored.*"

On August 22, a week before attacking Poland, Hitler conferred with his generals about the "possibility" of violating Dutch and Belgian neutrality, pointing out the advantage to Germany because England and France would not violate it. Four days later, on August 25, Hitler ordered his envoys in Brussels and The Hague to inform their governments that in the event of war, "Germany will in no circumstances impair the inviolability of Belgium and Holland," an assurance he publicly repeated on October 6 after the completion of the Polish campaign. The very next day, on October 7, he had his army chief, General von Brauchitsch, advise his group commanders "to make all preparations for immediate invasions of Dutch and Belgian territory, if the political situation so demands."

Two days after that, on October 9, in Directive No. 6, Hitler ordered:

> Preparations are to be made for an attacking operation . . . through Luxembourg, Belgium and Holland. This attack must be carried out as soon and as forcefully as possible. . . . The object of this attack is to acquire as great an area of Holland, Belgium and northern France as possible.

He made it plain he was thinking of November, "between the 12th and the 20th, at the latest."

On November 23, having postponed the attack in the West because of unfavorable weather, Hitler again summoned his generals and told them:

> My decision is unchangeable. I shall attack France and England at the most favorable and earliest moment. Breach of the neutrality of Belgium and Holland is of no importance. No one will question that when we have won. We shall not justify the breach of neutrality as idiotically as in 1914.

All that fall, we now know, Hitler's generals had opposed striking in the West through Holland and Belgium — not on any moral grounds but because they felt the army was not yet ready. There was one exception, so far as the confidential papers show. On October 11, the day after Hitler had first told his generals to plan to attack in the West through neutral Belgium and Holland, General Wilhelm Ritter von Leeb, commander of Army Group C on the Western Front, dashed off an angry memo to General von Brauchitsch protesting the Führer's orders. "The whole world," General von Leeb wrote, "would turn against Germany, which for the second time in twenty-five years assaults neutral Belgium! Germany, whose government solemnly vouched for and promised the preservation and respect for this neutrality only a few weeks before."

Not one other German general, so far as I can ascertain from the secret records, dared to support Leeb's stand — despite all the talk you heard among German officers, as I have mentioned before, about honor.

At the Rundfunk that morning the German military censors told me I could not say in my first broadcast that there had been "an invasion" of Belgium and Holland. They kept denying there was any such thing. At first I thought of canceling all my broadcasts that day. But since the censors had overlooked the word "invasion" three times in the heart of my script I changed my lead to say the Germans had "marched in." I regretted having to make the compromise, but I finally concluded that when the Germans "marched into" a country everyone but they recognized it was an "invasion."

And what one had to stress, even more than that the Germans again had violated the neutrality of Belgium, was that at last Hitler had struck in the West. The phony war was over. Once more on the battlefields of Belgium and northern France the fate of the Reich — and of Belgium, Britain and France — probably would be decided before the summer was out. It looked as if there would be the greatest series of battles ever fought on earth — with more men and guns and tanks and planes than ever before.

In his Order of the Day made public that morning Hitler seemed to recognize what was at stake.

"The hour of the decisive battle for the future of Germany has come," he said, and concluded: "The battle beginning today will decide the future of the German nation for the next thousand years."

First German reports from the front that evening seemed too optimistic, and I put them down mostly as propaganda. The army claimed to have crossed the river Meuse and captured Maastricht, which lay in a tongue of Dutch territory that stretched south into Belgium. It said its troops had driven through Luxembourg into Belgium. As in the first August days of 1914, the German army lay before Liège, the Belgian fortified area which in the first war had held out for twelve days against Ludendorff's juggernaut.

This time, I felt, Liège would hold out even longer. I had had a look at the terrain there a year before and had been impressed by the way the Belgians seemed to have strengthened the defenses of the area, especially with the completion of Fort Eben Emael, which commanded the junction of the Meuse River and the Albert Canal. With its series of steel and concrete galleries deep underground, its gun turrets protected by heavy armor and manned by a force of twelve hundred men, it was regarded by both the Allies and the Germans, I had heard, as the most impregnable fortress in Europe. The Belgians thought it could hold out indefinitely.

So though I was alarmed by the German claims that first evening — there were many more, such as that their attacks on scores of airfields in Holland, Belgium and France had destroyed hundreds of enemy planes on the ground — I nursed a sort of inner confidence that maybe now Hitler at last had met his match, that the Belgians would hold Liège and Namur until the British and French had come to their rescue, that the Dutch might halt the Huns along their reputedly well-fortified water lines, and that the mighty French army, helped by a British Expeditionary Corps of ten divisions, would stop the Germans, as they had on the Marne a quarter of a century before.

My secret hopes collapsed the next day. The news from the Western Front that came in to Berlin was unbelievable. And each new day it became worse, and utterly incredible. My diary recalls what happened, day by stunning day.

> Berlin, May 11. The German steamroller sweeps on through Holland and Belgium. Tonight the Germans claim to have captured Fort Eben Emael.

In a special communiqué that evening announcing the swift capture of the supposedly impregnable fort, OKW declared that it had been taken "by a new method of attack." This caused Berlin to fill with rumors. Some of the military men I talked with hinted that the German army had a deadly new "secret weapon," perhaps a nerve gas that at Fort Eban Emael had temporarily paralyzed the defenders and enabled the attackers to take the fort in thirty hours.*

---

* The truth was more prosaic. Fort Eben Emael was quickly captured by eighty German soldiers under the command of a sergeant who landed in nine gliders on its roof. There they placed "hollow" explosives in the armored gun turrets, which put them out of action and spread flames and gas in the chambers below. Portable flame-throwers were also used at the gun portals and observation grills. Within an hour the attackers were able to penetrate the upper galleries, render most of the fort's guns useless, and blind its observation posts. Belgian infantry behind Eben Emael tried to dislodge the small band of Germans but were driven off by Stuka dive-bombers and by reinforcements of parachutists. Within the smoking galleries there was some hand-to-hand fighting, but not for long. At noon on May 11, a little more than twenty-four hours after the attack began, the defenders hoisted a white flag and twelve hundred dazed Belgians filed out and surrendered. The Germans lost six dead and nineteen wounded.

With Fort Eban Emael fallen, how could Liège hold out? I wondered.

By evening of the next day, May 12, the Germans claimed to have occupied all of Holland east of the Zuider Zee and to have broken through the first and second water defense lines in the heart of the Netherlands. Broadcasts I picked up from the BBC said the Germans had landed thousands of parachutists and glider troops behind the Dutch water lines and tried to seize the airfields around The Hague and key bridges over the Maas (Meuse) River south of Rotterdam. At most places they had been turned back, London claimed, by Dutch forces. In Berlin OKW kept mum about any troops landed behind the Dutch lines and my military censor forbade me to mention the subject. With that residue of complacency which still clung to me I concluded that things were going badly in Holland for German airborne troops or they wouldn't be so secretive about it. So the bulletins the next couple of days were hard to take.

> Berlin, May 13. Astounding news. The headlines at five P.M.: "LIÈGE FALLEN! GERMAN LAND FORCES BREAK THROUGH AND ESTABLISH CONTACT WITH AIR FORCE TROOPS NEAR ROTTERDAM!" . . .
>
> Berlin, May 14. We're all a little dazed tonight by the news.
> The Dutch army has capitulated — after only five days of fighting. . . .
> Having broken through at Liège, the Germans claimed tonight to have pierced the second line of Belgian defenses northwest of Namur. They must be very close to Brussels. . . .

The news of the Dutch surrender was bad enough. But the German claim about the fighting in Belgium was worse. It suddenly dawned on me, from what I had learned from German military sources and from listening to the BBC broadcasts from London, that if the Germans had really pierced the Belgian defense line northwest of Namur, as they claimed — and by now I grudgingly had to admit that most of the High Command's claims had turned out to be all too true — then it meant that the largest and most powerful forces the Allies had assembled in the West were in trouble. This force comprised the cream of the French army, the First, Seventh and Ninth armies and nine out of ten divisions of the British Expeditionary Corps. They had rushed into Belgium as soon as the German attack began and established, with the Belgians, a line of defense along the Dyle River, from Antwerp through Louvain to Wavre and thence across the Gembloux Gap to Namur and south along the Meuse to Sedan.

Apparently, that had been the Allied plan, based on the anticipation that the Germans, as in 1914, would concentrate their strength on their right wing in a new attempt to sweep around the flanks of the main French armies farther south. And the violence of the offensive of General von Reichenau's Sixth Army against Liège and then Namur along the same road the Kaiser's main armies under von Moltke had taken in 1914 must have convinced the French and British commands that they were right. What I did not know, nor, as it turned out, did the Allies, was that the wheeling of the principal Allied armies into Belgium was just what the German High Command wanted. The Germans were now in a position to do what they had not done the last time: hit the French in the center around Sedan, of disastrous memory to France, with the most formidable army Europe probably had ever seen, break through, race to the Channel, and trap the main Allied armies in the north.

Next day, on May 15, we got the first news of disaster for the Allies.

> Berlin, May 15. Very long, stunned faces among the foreign correspondents and diplomats today. The High Command claims to have broken through the Maginot Line near Sedan and that German forces have crossed the Meuse River both at Sedan and between Namur and Givet, farther north.

I was among the stunned. From my years in Paris I knew what a humiliation the mere mention of Sedan was for the French, who never forgot that it was this forlorn town that had been the scene of Napoleon III's surrender to Moltke in 1870 and the end of the French Third Empire. And now catastrophe had happened there again.

"To anyone who has seen that deep, heavily wooded Meuse Valley [around Sedan]," I scribbled in my diary, "it seems almost incredible that the Germans could get across it so quickly."

But I had to admit that everything that had happened since the Germans began their drive less than a week before had seemed absolutely unbelievable. In my diary I put on a stiff upper lip that shows how foolish I could be. (No consolation that I probably had company.)

> Almost all my friends [the diary for May 15 continues] have given up hope; not I, yet. It must have looked even darker in Paris in August 1914, when nothing appeared to stand in the way of the German army and the capital.

I may not have given up hope, but my diary reminds me that I began to worry about Tess and the baby in Switzerland. On May 16 I learned that Italy might come into the war any day, cutting off escape for my family in that direction. Later that day Tess phoned from Geneva that every available man was being called up because the Swiss feared the Germans might attack in an effort to launch an army through Switzerland to catch the French from the south. She said the U.S. legation in Berne had advised Americans in Switzerland to leave immediately for Bordeaux, where they would be picked up by American ships. I urged her to go — the next day, if possible — but she said the French had stopped issuing transit visas. Next day, May 17, I phoned her and pressed her to get off with Eileen this very day.

"Just take the car and drive through France to Spain," I pleaded. "I'm sure the French won't stop you, especially with a baby."

The news that day had overwhelmed me. My diary:

> Berlin, May 17. What a day! What news! At 3 P.M. the High Command came out with its daily communiqué. I would not have believed it except that the German army has seldom misled us. . . .
>
> It says today its armies have broken the Belgian Dyle defense line south of Wavre and have taken the fortress of Namur. More important still — it claims its forces have broken through the Maginot Line on a one-hundred-kilometer (63-mile) front (!) stretching from Maubeuge to Carignan, southeast of Sedan.

This news was almost too staggering to grasp. The great Maginot Line pierced on a sixty-mile front!* The Germans at Maubeuge, halfway to Paris. And at Rethel, halfway to Reims from Sedan. At the Rundfunk, to which I hastened to broadcast the news, the military people for the first time spoke of a "French rout."

> I returned to the embassy, where I found everyone dazed at events. . . . Hell, this offensive is only eight days old. And the Germans have overrun Holland and half of Belgium and are now halfway from the French border to Reims!
>
> LATER. The High Command late tonight announced that German troops entered Brussels at sundown. During the day they had pierced the Allied lines north and south of Louvain. . . . In 1914 it took sixteen days for the Germans to reach Brussels. This time, eight days.

* OKW's communiqué was in error. There was no Maginot Line between Maubeuge and Carignan. The line, stretching westward from the Rhine, ended at Longwy, twenty-five miles southeast of Carignan.

Berlin, May 18. Antwerp fell today. And while the German army is rolling back the Allied forces in Belgium toward the sea, the southern army . . . is driving rapidly toward Paris.

Going to the front tomorrow. At last will get a chance — maybe — to see how this German army colossus has been doing it. . . .

It was years actually before I got straight exactly what had happened up to this point, only the ninth day of the German offensive. A good deal of research after the war and talks with some who were there shed much light on how it developed into such a tremendous victory for the Germans and such an unexpected and unmitigated disaster for the Western Allies, especially the French, whose army, I had thought, would be the equal of the German, as it had been in 1914.*

The reasons for the catastrophe for the Allies go back, one can see now, to the rival plans for the war in the West.†

The original German plan, drawn up in October, 1939, had been a variant of the famous Schlieffen plan of 1914. It provided for the main German drive to be carried out by the right wing on a sweep through Belgium and northern France to the Channel ports, thus cutting off France from Britain. This would also give the Germans sea and air bases on the coast from which to harass and blockade the British Isles. In the face of such a defeat, the Allies, Hitler was sure, would sue for peace, and leave him free to turn on Russia in the East.

The German plan was anticipated by the Western Allies. On November 17 in Paris the Allied Supreme War Council adopted "Plan D," which called for the French First and Ninth armies and the British Expeditionary Corps to rush forward to meet the Germans on the main Belgian defense line along the Dyle and Meuse rivers from Antwerp through Louvain, Namur and Givet to Mezieres. At the end of November, alarmed at signs that Hitler would also attack through the Netherlands as well as through Belgium, the Allied command decided to send the French Seventh Army up the Channel coast to

---

* I had gathered from talks with German generals the last couple of years that they had a healthy respect for the French army. Later General Heinz Guderian, the genius of the German panzer armies, would say that he and his fellow officers believed that "France possessed the strongest land army in Western Europe and the numerically strongest tank force," and that "French tanks were superior to the German both in armor and gun caliber." (General Heinz Guderian: *Panzer Leader* (paperback), p. 73.)

† In a deeper sense they go back much further: to the failure of the British in the 1930's to rearm, especially in the air, and to the failure of the French to strengthen their lagging air force, modernize their conception of armored warfare, and rid themselves of their defensive Maginot Line complex.

help the Dutch. Thus a very powerful force would confront what the Allies believed would be the principal German thrust in the north — some sixty-seven divisions in all: twenty-six divisions of the three French armies, nine divisions of the B.E.F., twenty-two divisions of the Belgians, ten divisions of the Dutch. They would considerably outnumber the Germans.

It was, I think, to avoid such a clash in the north, which might bring a stalemate, and, even more important, to trap the cream of the Anglo-French armies which would thrust northeast to come to the aid of the Dutch and the Belgians, that the Germans began to consider changing their plan. This may also have been partly because on January 10, 1940, the main features of that plan fell into the hands of the enemy. A German courier plane had been forced by bad weather to make an emergency landing on the Belgian side of the frontier and a Luftwaffe major, carrying a good many details of the plan in his briefcase, had been seized by Belgian troops.

But mainly, I judge from the secret German records, it was because a daring new plan, proposed by General Erich von Manstein, a gifted staff officer though of relative junior rank, caught the fancy of Hitler. Manstein proposed that the main German assault be carried out not on the northern flank through Belgium but farther south in the *center*, through the Ardennes Forest with a massive armored force of seven of the army's ten panzer divisions. It would cross the Meuse at Sedan and just north of it, break through the French defenders into the open country, and race to the Channel at Abbeville, not only cutting off France from Britain but trapping the main Anglo-French-Belgian forces to the north. Manstein, opposed at first by Brauchitsch, the army chief, and by Halder, the chief of the army General Staff, was removed by them to a minor corps command. But he contrived to see Hitler personally to argue his plan. On February 24 it was formally adopted and a vast redeployment of troops was begun.

That redeployment did not escape the notice of the Allies. But because of some mysterious paralysis of intelligence and will — it still baffles me — they did nothing about it. Later I found in the French military papers that as early as December 5, 1939, when the new German plan was still in the discussion stage, General Alphonse Georges, commander-in-chief of the Allied Forces on the Western Front, had warned his chief, Generalissimo Maurice Gamelin, of the risk of committing the major part of their armies in Holland and Belgium. The German offensive in the north, he suggested, might be "merely a diversion." The "main enemy attack might come in our *center*" (he himself underlined the word) ". . . between the Meuse and the Moselle." In that case, he pointed out, the Allies, with their principal forces committed in Belgium and Holland, would be "deprived of the necessary means to repel it."

General Georges's warning went unheeded. To hit the French Ninth and Second armies at Sedan, Gamelin held, the Germans would first have to drive through the Ardennes Forest. Had not the great Marshal Pétain, the hero of Verdun, assured the French Parliament that the Ardennes was *"impenetrable"*? Both generals were absolutely sure that the rugged, wooded hills and narrow winding roads of that sector made it impossible for any large forces, especially of tanks, to get through it. Gamelin made no special plans to defend it.

Yet all through the late winter and early spring there were increasing signs that the Germans were concentrating their strength for a main blow in the center, where Allied intelligence counted an increase of enemy infantry divisions from twenty-five to fifty-seven. By March, seven of the ten German panzer divisions had been located assembling to strike *south* of Liège. On March 8 the Belgian king, although he still stubbornly refused to cooperate with the Allies in working out plans to come to the aid of his country — he was afraid of offending Hitler — did inform General Gamelin that he had information pointing to the main German attack coming "through the Ardennes." Moreover, he added, he had "documentary evidence that the principal axis of the enemy maneuver would be oriented perpendicularly on the Longwy-Givet front." This was just to the northwest of the Maginot Line, which ended at Longwy and which was defended, above Sedan, by the French Ninth Army, regarded as probably the weakest of the French armies. King Leopold repeated his warning on April 14, saying he was now certain that the Germans hoped to draw the main Franco-British armies into Belgium and there destroy them from the south by "armies coming through Luxembourg."

Allied intelligence continued to confirm the king's warnings. Message after message came in, yet the Allied High Command did nothing. Not even when on the last day of April, after a mass movement of enemy troops, tanks, artillery and ammunition up to the front made it obvious that an all-out attack was imminent, the French military attaché in Berne, Switzerland, one of the best sources of Allied intelligence, warned the French High Command not only of the new date set for the German offensive, but exactly where its strong point would be. The attack, he said, was set for May 8–10, and Sedan would be "its center of gravity." This gave Gamelin and Georges ten days to correct their strategy. They declined to use it.

When the Germans struck at dawn on May 10, the French and British, as planned, moved rapidly into Belgium. As I would learn later, the German High Command, General Franz Halder particularly, could hardly believe that the Allies had fallen so easily and completely in its trap. It only remained for the Germans to spring it.*

Actually the French and British thought the first couple of days of the German attack had gone fairly well for them.

Returning to Paris on May 12 from a meeting of the Allied High Command with the king of the Belgians, Daladier, the French minister of defense, told his colleagues that "everything is going well." He said the powerful French First Army was well established in the Gembloux Gap between Wavre and Namur, where the Allies expected the Germans would attempt their principal breakthrough. To Winston Churchill in London — he had succeeded Chamberlain as prime minister two days before, on May 10 — "there was no reason to suppose [as he later put it] up to the night of the 12th that the operations were not going well." Generalissimo Gamelin was pleased and complacent and he left military operations entirely to General Georges.

Georges himself was pleased with the way things had gone the first two days. The British Expeditionary Force, under Lord Gort, and the French First and Ninth armies had wheeled into position on the Dyle-Meuse line and were containing the first powerful attacks of General von Reichenau's German Sixth Army. General Giraud's Seventh French Army, largely motorized, had sped up the Channel coast and reached southwest Holland. On the sixty-mile front between Antwerp and Namur, both powerful fortresses, there were now thirty-six Belgian, British and French divisions against the twenty divisions of the German Sixth Army. As late as the afternoon of May 15, the sixth day of battle, the Allied positions on the Dyle and in the Gembloux Gap had held. At 5 P.M. that day, in fact, General von Reichenau suspended the Sixth Army's attack, which was getting nowhere. Lord Gort and General Blanchard, whose troops

---

* At army headquarters Colonel Heusinger could not contain his joy. "They have poured into Belgium," he exulted, "and are falling into the trap!" (The author's *The Collapse of the Third Republic*, p. 638.)

had borne the brunt of the German attacks, had every reason to be pleased.

Then to their south, around Sedan, the dam burst. Suddenly they found themselves entrapped. That very day, May 15, though they did not know it, Premier Reynaud in Paris had rung up Churchill in London.

"We have been defeated! We have lost the battle!"

"Impossible!" Churchill had retorted. He could not believe him. The great French army defeated on the fifth day of battle? Impossible.

What on earth, he wondered, had happened?

May 14, the fifth day of battle, was the fatal day. Disaster came faster than the French could comprehend.

In three days a German armored spearhead of seven panzer divisions, the greatest concentration of armored forces the world had ever seen, swept through the "impenetrable" Ardennes Forest, and on the afternoon of May 12 reached the Meuse River on an eighty-mile front from Sedan to Dinant. The French Command had estimated that it would take the Germans fifteen days to bring up strong enough forces to make a serious attack on such a front. They had not considered tanks. General Halder, of course, had, and he had estimated it would take nine days for the huge armored army to penetrate the Ardennes to the Meuse. At one juncture it had stretched back in three columns for one hundred miles, well beyond the Rhine, highly vulnerable on the narrow, twisting roads to bombing and harassing attacks from the wooded hills. But Allied planes had not disturbed it. They were being employed farther north where the French and British believed the main attack would come. The French Ninth and Second armies had sent ahead their five light armored divisions to slow up the Germans and if possible stop them, and already on the scene were the two divisions of Belgian Chasseurs Ardennais, whose whole training had been to defend the forest. But the Belgians had not fought after blowing the bridges. Instead, they had quickly fallen back — on the orders of King Leopold, the French believed — and the French light tanks were overwhelmed by the German heavy armor.

At 4 P.M. on May 13 the German assault across the Meuse on both sides of Sedan began. Before the armored divisions could move tanks across the river, bridgeheads first had to be established on the far shore with infantry and combat engineers. The first ground troops crossed over on rubber boats. Ordinarily they would have been sitting ducks for French artillery. But the French gunners were pinned down by incessant attacks of German Stuka dive-bombers. German artillery and tanks, firing their guns point blank across the river, helped. Soon the Germans were over the river, and by nightfall General Guderian's three panzer divisions had established bridgeheads across the Meuse, penetrating as far as five miles and occupying the heights on the west bank.

To General Grandsard, the commander of the French Tenth Corps of the Second Army, which was defending against the enemy's three tank divisions, the situation was serious, he later said, but "no more than that." German infantry had got across the Meuse and established a small bridgehead. But they had not been able to bring over a single tank or piece of artillery. He had tanks and artillery with which to counterattack. He felt fairly confident.

Then, as darkness approached, the troops of one of his two infantry divisions, the 55th, suddenly panicked. Artillery spotters saw the infantry falling back before the Germans. They imagined German tanks were leading the assault. Soon there was a general cry: "The Boche tanks are coming!" Two colonels, commanding the division's heavy artillery, abandoned their posts, followed by their frightened men. French infantrymen got wind that their artillery was leaving them in the lurch, turned and ran to join the retreating gunners, throwing away their rifles and machine guns. Within thirty minutes between 6 and 6:30 P.M. that early evening, the roads were suddenly jammed with hordes of terrified troops in wild flight. Soon the whole division, two infantry and two artillery regiments, was fleeing pell-mell down the roads in utter disorder toward Reims, sixty miles away. The 55th Division had ceased to exist.

Later officers and men of the dissolved unit swore they had seen swarms of German tanks bearing down on them. Actually not one German tank was across the river as night fell. Or one piece of artillery. Or even one anti-tank gun. The first pontoon bridge, on which German army engineers were working, was far from finished. At German headquarters there was worry that a spirited French counterattack with tanks might push the attackers back to the river and wipe out their bridgehead. Their infantry would be no match for the reinforcements they knew the French were rushing to the scene: the powerful 3rd Armored Division with heavy tanks, and the 3rd Motorized Division.

But the French counterattacks were put off — until it was too late.

By dawn German engineers had completed their first pontoon bridge over the Meuse, and at 6 A.M. one brigade of tanks began to cross over. In the meantime that morning, the French 71st Division, which had successfully stopped the 10th Panzer at the river crossing, found its left flank exposed by the collapse of the 55th. Here it was the divisional commander who first panicked. He hastily removed his command post seven miles to the rear, his troops followed him, and soon there was a second scene of wild disorder, as French infantrymen and artillerymen abandoned their weapons and fled down the roads in terror. And this without being attacked!

That evening of May 14 General Charles Huntziger, commander of the French Second Army, hastily moved his headquarters from behind Sedan all the way to Verdun, fifty miles south. Apparently Huntziger was not yet aware that around three that afternoon General Guderian, having got two of his three panzer divisions across the river, decided to drive not south against the rest of Huntziger's Second Army, but west across the Bar River and the Ardennes Canal toward Rethel, thirty-two miles southwest of Sedan. It was a gamble. It left his southern flank dangerously exposed. But if he succeeded he would reach Rethel in a day or two and would rupture the front between the French Second and Ninth armies. Once at Rethel, the way to Paris, little more than one hundred miles away, would be open. Or the way to the sea, as the Manstein plan had calculated. Only weak French forces, he believed, lay ahead of him. The main Allied armies were already to his north in Belgium. His thrust would cut them off. It would also help to destroy one of those armies, the French Ninth Army, which already was in deep trouble. The Second Army's failure around Sedan had sealed its fate.

The Ninth Army was the southernmost of the Allied forces that had wheeled into Belgium on May 10. And it was one of the weakest of the French armies. The High Command, in sandwiching it in on the Meuse between the crack First Army north of Namur and the Second Army at Sedan, had not expected it to be involved in heavy fighting. Yet, weak as it was, it was given the widest front to defend. Confronting it on the evening of May 12 was a German force even more powerful than the one that had struck with such deadly effect just to the south at Sedan. It was made up of the German Fourth and Twelfth armies, each with an armored corps of two panzer divisions. One of them, the 7th Panzer, was commanded by a daring young general, Erwin Rommel.

Rommel got some ground troops across the Meuse near Dinant

during the night of May 12 and though French resistance was fierce he was able to establish a small bridgehead by noon the next day. The French Command ordered counterattacks to drive the German riflemen down to the river (no German tanks had crossed here either). Their units were led by tanks and seemed strong enough to do it. But once again, as at Sedan, the counterattacks came either too late or, as in most cases, were postponed so often that they never came off at all.

May 14, only the fifth day of the campaign, brought disaster to the French Ninth Army as it had that very day to the Second Army below it at Sedan. It was the same story. Behind the small bridgeheads obtained by the infantry on May 13, the Germans were able to construct pontoon bridges over the Meuse during the night. At dawn their four panzer divisions struck. By afternoon the French began to panic. The generals began ordering retreats as they moved their own headquarters rapidly farther and farther to the rear. The Luftwaffe attacked the retreating troops incessantly — no Allied planes showed up to challenge them. By evening the Germans had a bridgehead beyond the Meuse west of Dinant some thirty miles wide and ten miles deep. The Ninth Army was rapidly disintegrating.

On the morning of May 15, the French threw in its crack 1st Armored Division to try to stem the tide. But it had been hopelessly dispersed during the first days of the German offensive. By the time it could be assembled and thrust into battle, its tanks had run out of gas and most of its gasoline trucks had, in the confusion, been left far to the rear. Had this powerful force been thrown into the battle on May 12, or even the thirteenth, it might well have prevented the German armor from crossing the Meuse. As it was, at 9:30 A.M. on May 15, two panzer divisions, Rommel's 7th and General Walsporn's 5th, supported by swarms of bombers and a full complement of artillery, fell on the French 1st Armored Division while it was refueling its tanks. A furious but uneven battle ensued. Both sides suffered heavy losses in tanks, but the Germans prevailed. Three of the four tank battalions of the 1st Armored were decimated. What was left of the battered Ninth Army fell back in great disorder toward the French frontier. General Giraud, who replaced General Corap that day as commander of the Ninth, rushed to headquarters at Vervin to rally the stricken army. He could not find it. No wonder. It had ceased to exist.*

* In the case of General Touchon, who on May 14 was charged with plugging the gap on the Meuse between the disintegrating Ninth and Second armies with his "Sixth Reserve Army," this force had never existed!

❀ ❀ ❀

On the morning of the fateful May 15, Premier Paul Reynaud, as we have seen, had rung up Winston Churchill in London and told him: "We have been defeated! We have lost the battle!" Churchill had been unable to believe him. At seven o'clock that evening Reynaud got off another message to Churchill.

> We lost the battle last night. The route to Paris is open. Please send all the planes and troops you can.

Sometime after midnight General Gamelin alerted the government that it must prepare to leave Paris.

Next day, Winston Churchill flew to Paris and found the situation, he later admitted, worse than he had expected. In the courtyard below the room in the Quai d'Orsay where he met with General Gamelin and Reynaud, employees were hastily burning Foreign Office papers. This looked to the prime minister as if the French government was preparing to abandon the capital. Gamelin informed him that nothing stood in the way of the Germans' driving on Paris after the breakthrough over the Meuse.

"But where is the strategic reserve?" Churchill asked.

"There is none," the general responded.

"I was dumbfounded," Churchill later wrote. It had never occurred to him, he confessed, that a great army, when attacked on a five-hundred-mile front, would not have held back troops in reserve. "I admit this was one of the greatest surprises I have had in my life."

This led the prime minister to proffer some military advice which he later regretted. He stoutly opposed pulling back the Allied armies in the north, which were now being dangerously outflanked on the south and soon might be entrapped.

The French minutes of the meeting disclose a second miscalculation Churchill made. He refused to believe, he told the French, that the thrust of the German armor toward the sea — or toward Paris — represented "a serious menace."

> Unless the tanks are supported by infantry, they represent a limited force. They will not be able to maintain themselves. They will have to be refueled, resupplied. . . .

A scattering of men from the debris of the Ninth Army finally was rounded up and ordered to take up positions on the "fortified sector of Maubeuge," along the French border. But the troops found the casemates locked! When the original occupants had set off on May 10 with the Ninth Army for the Meuse they had padlocked their blockhouses and turned the keys over to the local mayors. But the mayors had fled with the approach of the Germans. No keys. The doors had to be blasted open with dynamite.

And in *his* confusion, according to the French minutes, Churchill urged both that the B.E.F. and the French First Army "dig in where they are" in Belgium, *and* that they vigorously attack the advancing Germans on their flank. Obviously, you could not do the second if you did the first.

Not until May 17, three days after the debacle on the Meuse, was the first order given by the Allied High Command for its troops to begin pulling back from Belgium. This was a disastrous delay. By the night of May 16, German armored units had smashed through the feebly defended French frontier positions south of Maubeuge and sped westward toward the sea or toward Paris — the French were not sure which. By the morning of May 19 seven panzer divisions, driving relentlessly along the Somme past the storied scenes of battle of the First World War, were only fifty miles from the English Channel. Next day, the twentieth, the 2nd Panzer Division reached the sea at Abbeville, closing the trap on the Belgians, the B.E.F. and three French armies.

On that day I myself finally got to the front. I caught up with the German Sixth Army, pushing the surrounded Allied forces, British, Belgian and French, west and southwest of Brussels, toward the panzer divisions that had just reached the sea behind them.

The initial sight of the destruction of modern war appalled me.

> What guns and bombs [I wrote in my diary that night] do to houses and people . . . , to towns, cities, bridges, railroad stations and tracks and trains, to universities and ancient noble buildings, to enemy soldiers, trucks, tanks, and horses caught along the way!
>
> It is not pretty. . . . Take Louvain, that lovely old university town, burned in 1914 by the Germans in their fury, and rebuilt — partly by American aid.

In shambles it was. The great library of the ancient Belgian university, rebuilt by the donations of American schools and universities after the first war, was completely gutted — a sickening sight. We poked through the still-smoldering ruins. I noted down the inscriptions on some of the stones. UNIVERSITY OF ROCHESTER. PHILLIPS ACADEMY, ANDOVER. UNIVERSITY OF ILLINOIS. They were among the many who helped rebuild the university's library, now once again destroyed.

There was not much left of the town. Block on block of smashed-in buildings were still smoking. Some forty thousand people lived in Louvain until the morning Hitler attacked in the West. A week later, a German officer told me, when the first invading troops entered the town, not a single Belgian civilian was there. Though the officer did not say so, I imagined the good people had remembered what happened in 1914 when the Germans came to Louvain. Then two hundred of the leading citizens had been shot in reprisal for alleged sniping.

As we left Louvain and pushed on to Brussels the first residents were filtering back along the dusty road jammed with German troops and guns moving westward. They looked dazed, bitter, resentful. And yet somehow they had a dignity in their bearing — dignity, I thought, masking suffering and adding up to a certain nobility. It was something I would see often in the forlorn refugees in Belgium and France before their ordeal was over. It kept reminding me of the immense fortitude of human beings on this sorry earth.

We had taken off at dawn that morning from Aachen (Aix-la-Chapelle), driving across a narrow shoulder of Dutch territory to Maastricht on the Maas, as the Dutch called the Meuse River here. There was little evidence that the Dutch had done much fighting. Almost all the buildings and bridges were intact. Two or three miles south, as we arrived at the Albert Canal and Fort Eben Emael in Belgium, it was a different story. Though the Belgians, like the Dutch, had been taken by surprise, they had evidently quickly recovered and begun to fight. Blocks of pulverized houses along the roads to Brussels showed that the Germans had had to battle for them. At Tongres, St. Trond and Tirlemont the British and French had joined in the defense. Little was left standing in these towns; they were merely mounds of debris and rubble. One thing was becoming clear to me: this war, unlike the last one, was being fought along the roads. Most of the fields on both sides of the highways looked untouched. The armies did not deploy on wide fronts as they had the last time. The Germans simply smashed down the roads with their tanks, preceded by Stuka dive-bombers which pinned down the defenders and destroyed tank obstacles, and followed by motorized infantry, which held the positions against flank attacks after the panzers passed on. That explained how the Germans had moved with such incredible speed.

Just before we got to Brussels we came across, along a dusty road, a medieval castle at Steenockerzeel. Recalling who the distinguished residents were, I asked the officer in charge of our caravan if we could stop and have a look. Years before when I was stationed in Vienna I had written these residents for an interview. They were Zita, former empress of Austria-Hungary, and her son Otto, heir to the Hapsburg throne. There were constant reports in those days that Otto might try to return to Vienna to regain his throne. As little likely as this seemed to me, I had wanted to talk to the young Hapsburg heir about his intentions.

The castle had been bombed, part of the roof had been blown off and most of the windows shattered. But the bridge over the moat leading to it was intact, and we drove in and entered the house. It had been plundered, though not thoroughly. In what I took to be Zita's bedroom, clothes were lying helter-skelter on the floor, on the bed, on chairs. Evidently the former empress had felt pressed to get out before there was time to pack her clothes. Her wardrobe obviously had been extensive. The closets were filled with dresses and robes, hanging neatly from hangers. Otto, too, I judged from the look of his room had been in a hurry. Jackets, books, gramophone records and golf clubs were scattered about. In what I took to be his study, more books in French, German, English lay about in disorder. I stopped to examine them. On his desk was a book in French entitled *The Coming War.*

Castle though it was, it was a far cry from the splendor of the Hofburg in Vienna, where the House of Hapsburg had reigned over the centuries. The furnishings looked rather shabby; the interior a little dilapidated; the whole place run-down. On the young man's desk, I noticed a notebook of English composition, and remembered Otto's recent visit to America. A German officer handed me Otto's student cap, which he had picked up from a dresser. Sheepishly I took it, and then when his back was turned, tossed it back. I did pocket a few of Zita's personal calling cards, feeling like a plunderer. They read: *L'Imperatrice d'Autriche et Reine de Hongrie.*

West of Brussels the next day, May 21, we finally caught up with the "front." Or at least with the German Sixth Army, which was relentlessly pushing the retreating Allied forces back toward the sea, where the panzer divisions lay in wait for them. At a château near Enghien, not far from Waterloo, we met the commander of the Sixth Army, General Walter von Reichenau, with whom I had a passing acquaintance from Berlin. He was as amiable as ever, his face tanned, his step springy, his invariable monocle squeezed over one eye. My impression was that he was frank and thorough in his briefing of us, but later I concluded this was not quite so. He kept insisting, for instance, that despite early successes the decisive battle in the West had yet to take place. He did not tell us that the day before, a panzer division had reached Abbeville, entrapping the Allied armies in front of him.

Reichenau did express surprise at the lack of Allied activity in the air. "I ride a hundred and fifty miles a day along the front," he said, "and I haven't seen an air fight yet. We've certainly been surprised that the enemy didn't try at least to bomb our bridges over the Maas River and the Albert Canal. The British tried it only once during the daytime. We shot down eighteen of their planes."

Obviously, he said, the British were holding back their air force. I asked him why. He said it puzzled him. Actually Reichenau was in a jaunty mood. He showed no sign of being tense, worried, rushed.

Later in the war I remembered that spring day with General von Reichenau at the temporary headquarters near Waterloo of the great German Sixth Army, which was marching and fighting its way triumphantly through Belgium. Its morale was terrific. The general was immensely proud of it. I could not forget that it was this same Sixth Army which two and a half years later perished in the cold and snow at Stalingrad, deep in Russia. By that time the dashing Reichenau was no longer its commander. He had died of a stroke the year before, on January 17, 1942, after the German armies finally had met their match in Russia and been pushed back from Moscow and Rostov. Pushed back and forced to retreat — for the first time in the war. It was a fatal turning point and the German generals knew it. Several of them suffered nervous breakdowns, as did Hitler. For Reichenau the strain was more serious.

If one had told me that day that such would be the fate of this crack army and its brilliant commander, I would have thought him crazy. I had not yet learned that in war, as in other aspects of life, early success can turn into failure, and that little in war is certain or predictable.

"I've now given you permission to go up to the front," Reichenau said, as he bid us goodbye. "You may be under fire. But you'll have to take your chances." He need not have worried, if he did.

I believe it was called the Battle of the Scheldt, but it certainly did not go down in history as one of the decisive battles on the Western Front that spring. These already had taken place along the Meuse.

As we drove down toward the Scheldt between Audenarde and Tournai, the British, with the Belgians to the north of them and the

French First Army to the south, were fighting a delaying action so that they could get their troops, artillery and supplies over the river, and continue their retreat to the sea, which lay only forty-two miles away at Dunkirk. Later I would wonder, as did many military historians, why the Allied armies had not withdrawn more quickly and turned south to attack the flank of the thin German lines to the sea, break through them and reestablish themselves on the southern bank of the Somme, where General Weygand was trying to organize fresh forces. By such a move they could have broken out of the trap and lived to fight another day. But the chief of the Allied High Command, first General Gamelin and then General Weygand,* who had succeeded him on May 19, the day I left for the front, had not seized the opportunity. They had let things drift. They had taken no drastic action.

So the leaderless Allied forces were belatedly and slowly falling back, and the German Sixth Army was keeping the pressure on them, but not too much pressure. The German strategy was to make the retreat difficult enough so that the Allied armies could not easily strike south against an overextended line. But no more than that, since they preferred to back the enemy into the waiting armored divisions, where it would be easier to dispose of him.

As we approached the Scheldt the British were withdrawing across the river, but still held fairly strong positions on the east bank. It was these the Germans were trying to dislodge before an assault across the river. The rumble of artillery increased as we reached Ath, a small town behind the Scheldt. There was evidence of battle. German Red Cross ambulances passed us more frequently. Dead horses lay along the roads, by the side of abandoned British and French guns. In the fields immediately off the roads cattle lay motionless, felled by bombs or shells. A gaping hole in the pavement made by a land mine forced us to detour down a country lane. Suddenly there was a very pungent odor. We came across all that was left of what must have been a retreating French column a day or two before. Along the path were the bodies of a dozen horses stinking in the hot noonday sun. Close by were an abandoned six-inch gun and an old French 75, two light French tanks, their feeble armor pierced like tissue paper, and a dozen trucks obviously abandoned in great haste, for scattered about them were cooking utensils, coats, shirts, over-

---

* General Weygand, who had preceded Gamelin as commander-in-chief of the French army in the early 1930's, had been a brilliant staff officer, a valued aide to Marshal Foch in the first war. But he had never commanded a sizable unit in battle.

coats, helmets, tins of food and — letters to wives and mothers and sweethearts back home.

Just off the lane were freshly dug graves, marked by a stick on which hung a single French helmet. I picked up some of the scattered letters, thinking that the next time I went out to Switzerland I could mail them to their destinations, along with a note describing where the end had come. But there were no envelopes, no addresses, no last names. Just the scrawled letters there had been no time to mail: *"Ma chère Jacqueline," "Chère Maman."* I glanced through two or three. They must have been written before the German offensive began and the men were rushed pell-mell into Belgium. They told of the boredom of army life during the *drôle-de-guerre* and how they were waiting for the next leave home.

We pushed on. We passed a tiny village. Half a dozen farmhouses at a crossroads. Their roofs smashed in. In the pastures cattle grazed. Pigs squealed in the barnyards. All seemed thirsty, for the farmhouses were deserted. The cows had not been milked for two or three days; their udders were swollen.

As we came closer to the Scheldt at Leuze, we entered the German artillery zone. Their 88's and bigger guns were pounding away relentlessly with a deafening roar. Now the road was choked with columns of trucks carrying troops, ammunition, oil drums, and often hauling more guns. The square in the village, most of its houses pulverized, was jammed with infantry and combat engineers with their bridge equipment waiting to take off. The school in the square, fairly intact, was being used as a Red Cross station. Seven ambulances were drawn up before it, waiting to discharge the wounded. Inside army medics were busy bandaging. In one room an emergency operating room was already functioning. It was scarcely a scene of anguish though, as I had expected. The wounded were not groaning or crying out. Everything was quiet, efficient, sanitized.

Finally, we got near the Scheldt below the town of Renaix. An occasional shell, apparently British, exploded not far off. No one paid much attention. An officer warned us to look out for the approach of British planes. But we saw none. Now infantry on foot, the first we had seen away from their trucks, were deploying down various paths toward the river. We stopped to watch a battery of six-inch guns, concealed under trees in an orchard just off the road, pound away. We now had a view over the valley of the Scheldt and could see the slopes on the other side, where the British had dug in. An artillery officer showed us how through glasses we could follow his barrage as it climbed a road on the far shore. The road looked deserted to me, but the officer swore it was choked with British vehicles. Shortly an engineering unit passed us. Tractors were lugging huge rubber boats down to the river. Trucks were carrying some steel girders. We were told the last of the British were making it across the river and that by evening, with the near shore cleared, the German engineers would start building a pontoon bridge across it. Artillery spotters claimed they could see the British already pulling back toward the nearby French frontier. "Or maybe they're making for the Channel," one said, with a grin. "It's not too far away."

Maybe so. But even with glasses and German military guidance I could see very little. It was not that there was chaos. There was not. Everything on the German side seemed to be going smoothly. The Sixth Army was a mammoth, well-oiled, efficient machine. I was sure the movements of the tanks, the infantry, the combat engineers, the artillery, made sense to the commanders directly involved. They knew where each unit was going and what its objective was. But to a lone observer, there was no picture at all of what was going on. You saw too small a segment of the battle. And what you saw made little sense. It did not fit into anything.

In my frustration I remembered from my Paris days what Stendahl had written of the Battle of Waterloo in *La Chartreuse de Parme*. Hemingway had told me that it was a classic description of one of the decisive battles in modern history. But I remembered it differently this day on the Scheldt, a few miles away from where it had been fought. So far as I recalled, Fabrice, the hero of the novel, had wandered about the battlefield at Waterloo utterly confused, understanding nothing. No one he talked to, officers or common soldiers, seemed to understand either. Tolstoy, I remembered, had taken the same attitude in his great novel *War and Peace*. Didn't Pierre Bezukhov in that novel wander about the battlefield of Borodino during Napoleon's march into Russia in 1812, thinking that he would see the engagement at first hand as clearly as historians had seen great battles in the past, only to find utter confusion and chaos? To Tolstoy, if I remembered his masterpiece correctly, not even the generals understood what was going on, not even Napoleon.

But if I could not follow the actual battle, I was immensely impressed by the German army in action. It was very hard-hitting, led by gifted, dedicated officers who had invented a new kind of modern warfare, the *Blitzkrieg*. It was being fought and won down the roads of Western Europe by German panzer divisions, motorized infantry and artillery, and battalions of bridge-building combat engineers. And by swarms of Stuka dive-bombers, which softened up the defenders before the phalanxes of tanks ever hit them. Again that day we did not see a single Allied plane over the battlefield. The air belonged to the Luftwaffe.

Somewhere between Brussels and the German frontier on our return we had an experience which saddened me — but which helped explain why the war in the West was going as it was. We ran across a batch of British prisoners-of-war. They were herded together in the brick-paved yard of an abandoned factory. We stopped and went over to talk with them. I had not yet had enough experience of war to realize, as I later would, that P.O.W.'s always look forlorn immediately after capture, before the shock has worn off. Some obviously were still in a state of shock; many wore bandages over their heads, faces or arms. All were dead tired.

But what troubled me most about them were their physiques. They were hollow-chested, skinny, round-shouldered. A third of them wore glasses. Their teeth were yellow, their complexions sallow. Typical, I guessed, of the youth that England had neglected in the twenty-two postwar years, when Germany, despite its defeat and crippling inflation and six million unemployed, was raising its youth in the open air and the sun.

I asked the young men where they were from and what they did at home. They came from offices, they said, in London and Liverpool. They had never got much exercise or fresh air until they were called up, when the war began. I judged from their looks that they had never had a proper diet either. As for military training, they had had just the nine months since the war began the previous September.

Along the road outside the yard where they were huddled, a long column of German infantry was marching by toward the West, the men singing lustily. What a contrast with the British youngsters. The German soldiers were tanned, clean-cut, robust, their bodies fully developed, their teeth white, healthy-looking as lions.

Some of the young Tommies were standing apart, and Fred Oechsner of the U.P. and I went over to them. They were all that was left, they said, of a company that had gone into battle at Louvain.

"We didn't have a chance," one of them said. "We were simply overwhelmed. Especially by those dive-bombers and tanks."

"What about your own?" I asked.

"Didn't see a bloody one," he said. The others nodded agreement.

One skinny fellow grinned. "I'm from Liverpool," he said. "Funny thing. You're the first Yanks I've ever seen. Funny place to meet, ain't it!"

We laughed. But inside I wasn't feeling much better than these poor P.O.W.'s were. Fred and I gave them our cigarettes and went away.

Back in Berlin on May 24, I tried in my diary to sum up the situation.

> Two weeks ago today Hitler unloosed his *Blitzkrieg* in the West. Since then . . . Holland overrun; four-fifths of Belgium occupied; the French army hurled back toward Paris; and Allied army believed to number a million men, and including the elite of the Franco-British forces, trapped and encircled on the Channel.

I tried to figure out from a few days with the German army what had happened and why. For one thing:

> It has absolute air superiority. . . . I did not see a single Allied plane over the front during daytime.

Stuka dive-bombers wrecked Allied communications in the rear, bombed tanks, guns, trucks, troops along the road, wiped out strategic railroad junctions and stations. German reconnaissance planes gave German commanders a bird's-eye view of the battlefield. They spotted for the artillery. The Allies, with no observation planes, were blinded. The Germans were able to bring up supplies on a vast scale without hinderance from the air. "What magnificent targets," I exclaimed, "these endless German columns would make if the Allies had any planes!" The German army in the field had struck me as "run as coolly and efficiently as our automobile industry in Detroit. . . . Morale of the German troops fantastically good."

On my return to Berlin I had caught a BBC broadcast from London contending that the flying panzer columns that had broken through to the sea were weak forces which could not possibly hold. This is what I had thought at first. And, as we have seen, so did Churchill. But it was not true. The Germans raced forward not only with tanks and a few motorized infantry units, but with everything. By now, I felt, their lines to the Channel, long as they were, were strong enough to withstand any counterattacks the Belgians, French and British might attempt.

Back in Berlin my diary grew more ominous.

May 25. German military circles here tonight put it flatly. They said the fate of the great Allied army bottled up in Flanders is sealed.

May 26. Calais has fallen. Britain is now cut off from the Continent.

May 28. King Leopold has quit on the Allies. At dawn the Belgian army . . . laid down its arms.

In Brussels old Belgian friends, whom I had managed to see secretly, warned that this might happen. For them King Leopold had long been a problem. We know now that there had been a showdown between the Belgian government and the king on the morning of May 25. At 5 A.M. that day the three leading members of the cabinet, Premier Hubert Pierlot, Foreign Minister Paul-Henri Spaak and the minister of war, General H. Denis, called on Leopold at his headquarters at the Château de Wynendaele near Bruges and urged him not to let himself be captured by the Germans. If the army was forced to give up, he himself must heed the advice of his government, as he was obliged to do by the constitution, and follow it into exile, as the monarchs of Norway and the Netherlands had done. If he gave himself up to the tender mercies of Hitler, they warned, he would be humiliated, as Hácha of Czechoslovakia and Schuschnigg of Austria had been. His conduct would be treated in Belgium and among the Allies as treason.

But they could not move the young ruler, who received them coolly and kept them standing.

"I have decided to stay," Leopold told them. "The cause of the Allies is lost. There is no more reason for us to continue in the war."

On May 26 the king asked for surrender terms. The answer came from Hitler himself. Unconditional surrender. This Leopold accepted and a cease-fire at 4 A.M. on May 28 was agreed upon. The Germans demanded free passage for its columns through the Belgian lines to the sea.

What this meant to the B.E.F., Lord Gort, its commander, later revealed. "I now found myself," he reported, "suddenly faced with an open gap of twenty miles between Ypres and the sea, through which enemy armored forces might reach the beaches."

In Berlin there was great exultation. For the first time since the war began communiqués came pouring out to us not from OKW but from the "Führer's Headquarters." They sounded to me as if the demonic dictator was dictating them himself. In one of them he tried to sound magnanimous, even chivalrous.

Führer's Headquarters, May 28. The Führer has ordered that the king of the Belgians and his army be given treatment worthy of the brave, fighting soldiers which they proved to be. As the king of the Belgians expressed no personal wishes for himself, he will be given a castle in Belgium until his final living-place is decided upon.

And then:

The king of the Belgians, in order to put an end to the further shedding of blood and to the completely pointless devastation of his country, reached his decision to lay down arms against the wishes of the majority of his cabinet. This cabinet, which is mainly responsible for the catastrophe which has broken over Belgium. . . .

So the Belgian cabinet, not Hitler, who had ordered his armies to attack a country whose neutrality he had sworn a dozen times to honor, was responsible for the terrible devastation the Germans had wrought in Belgium. I surely should have been used to such outrageous declarations in Berlin by now. Nonetheless, I raged when I read those lines. Was there no honor, I kept muttering, no decency, no truthfulness at all among Germans!?*

The controlled, sycophantic press compounded my sense of outrage. One particularly obnoxious headline I noted in my diary:

CHURCHILL AND REYNAUD INSULT KING LEOPOLD! — THE COWARDS IN LONDON AND PARIS ORDER THE CONTINUATION OF THE SUICIDE IN FLANDERS.†

My diary in Berlin the next few days chronicled the climactic sealing of the fate of the encircled Allied armies.

May 29. Lille, Bruges, Ostend captured! Ypres stormed! Dunkirk bombarded . . . the incredible headlines went on today without a let-up. . . . The German High Command told the story at the beginning of its communiqué today.

---

* Against my better judgment I went that evening to the Propaganda Ministry to see a full-length newsreel, with sound effects, of the destruction the Germans had carried out in Belgium. Town after town, city after city, was shown going up in flames as the Germans bombed and bombarded them. The German commentator's enthusiasm for pure destruction seemed to wax with each new ugly scene. He had a cruel, rasping voice: "Look at the destruction, the houses going up in flames," he cried. "That is what happens to those who oppose Germany's might!"

† Premier Reynaud, in a bitter broadcast in Paris that morning, had called the king's action "treason."

"The fate of the French army in Artois is sealed. The British army, which has been compressed into the territory around Dixmude, Armentières, Balleul, Bergues, west of Dunkirk, is also going to its destruction before our concentric attack."

May 30. The great battle in Flanders and Artois neared its end today. It's a terrific German victory. Yesterday, according to the German High Command, the British made a great bid to rescue what is left of the B.E.F. by sea.

This was the first mention by OKW that the British were trying to get away by sea. It went on to say that the British sent over fifty transports to fetch their troops along the coast around Dunkirk, but that "two Luftwaffe corps" sank sixteen of the transports and three "warships" and hit and damaged, or set on fire, twenty-one transports and ten "warships" and shot down sixty-eight British planes.

These British shipping losses struck me as vastly exaggerated, as did the German claim to have shot down sixty-eight British planes. Still, they indicated that the British must have committed a large number of ships and planes at Dunkirk. That might mean that the British were making a serious effort to evacuate large numbers of troops from the French port. I questioned some German military sources about that. They claimed the British didn't have a chance to rescue more than a few men on the Channel. The Luftwaffe would see to that.

Next day, May 31, there was no mention of Dunkirk in the OKW communiqués, which seemed strange. The day after that, a friend of mine on the High Command explained that "God" had given the British "a break." Two days of fog on the Channel, he said, had prevented the Luftwaffe from attacking the transports off the Dunkirk beaches, and considerable numbers of British troops were getting away.

June 2. Those British Tommies at Dunkirk are still fighting like bulldogs. The German High Command admits it.

"In hard fighting," it said, "the strip of coast on both sides of Dunkirk, which yesterday also was stubbornly defended by the British, was further narrowed."

It made the usual claims for the Luftwaffe. "Altogether four warships [what kind, it did not say] and eleven transports were sunk by our bombers. Fourteen warships, including two cruisers, two light cruisers, an anti-aircraft cruiser, six destroyers, two torpedo boats as well as 38 transports were damaged by bombs. Numberless small boats, tugs, rafts were capsized."

I wondered why after four days, "hard fighting" was still going on at Dunkirk. Why hadn't the panzer divisions, with the overwhelming power that had brought them from the Meuse to the sea in a week, finished off the much weaker and nearly armorless British army, trapped at Dunkirk, long before this?

There was something strange about it. What is beyond dispute — and beyond the understanding of many generals and historians — is that on May 24, the German panzer divisions, within sight of Dunkirk and poised for the final kill, received from Hitler a strange, and to most of their commanders inexplicable, order to halt their advance. It was, as it turned out, the first major blunder made by the German High Command in World War II — "one of the great turning points," as General von Rundstedt, who was partly responsible for it, said he later realized.

At the moment it seemed to Hitler and Rundstedt justified enough. Despite what they contended afterward, some of the panzer commanders on the spot had suggested a temporary halt. The armored divisions had lost half of their tanks on the dash across France. They needed to refit them for the offensive south across the Somme toward Paris and the rest of France. The entrapped British and French armies, they were sure, were done for anyway. They could be disposed of with infantry. General Guderian, commanding the 19th Armored Corps of three tank divisions — the ones that had broken through at Sedan — though he would later rail against the order to halt, had actually advised OKW that "a tank attack is pointless in the marshy country [around Dunkirk] . . . and that infantry forces are more suitable than tanks for fighting in this sort of a country." The area, he pointed out, was crisscrossed with canals, which were natural tank barriers.

There were other reasons for the stop order. Neither Hitler nor his generals, being ignorant of the sea, had the faintest idea that the naval-minded British could improvise a big enough armada to evacuate any sizable number of troops. They thought they had plenty of time to wipe out the battered British and French troops falling back on Dunkirk.

Actually they delayed only two days — until May 26. But it was long enough for the British and French to strengthen the Dunkirk perimeter with three divisions and to begin the evacuation on a major scale.

General Halder in his diary raged against Hitler's stop order:

May 24. Our left wing, consisting of armor and motorized forces, which has no enemy before it, will thus be stopped dead in its tracks upon direct orders of the Führer! Finishing off the encircled enemy is to be left to the air force!*

May 26 . . . These orders from the top just make no sense. . . . The tanks are stopped as if they were paralyzed.

May 30. [Halder was still fuming!] Brauchitsch is angry. . . . The pocket would have been closed at the coast if only our armor had not been held back. The bad weather has grounded the Luftwaffe and we must now stand by and watch countless thousands of the enemy get away to England right under our noses.

That was precisely what they watched. Some 338,226 troops got away — under their noses. Of these, 120,000 were French.

Dunkirk was a great deliverance for the British. But as Churchill reminded the relieved House of Commons on June 4, the day it finally fell, "wars are not won by evacuations."† Dunkirk, in fact, it looked to me in Berlin, marked the culmination of a disastrous defeat for the Allied armies and of a tremendous victory for the Germans. It would go down in history, said the OKW communiqué that day in words that could only have come from Hitler, "as the greatest battle of destruction of all time." Britain somehow, behind the natural defenses of the sea, might survive. In my own mind I refused to believe it would not. But its predicament was grim, the worst since the last

* General Halder believed that Göring himself intervened with Hitler to let the air force finish the job. In a letter to the author on July 19, 1957, in response to a request for elucidation on this whole affair, Halder wrote:
". . . Hitler's decision [to halt the advance] was mainly influenced by Göring. To the dictator the rapid movement of the army, whose risks and prospects of success he did not understand because of his lack of military schooling, became almost sinister. He was constantly oppressed by a feeling of anxiety that a reversal loomed. . . .
"Göring, who knew his Führer well, took advantage of this anxiety. He offered to fight the rest of the great battle of encirclement alone with his Luftwaffe."
Halder was sure Göring had an ulterior motive.
"He made his proposal . . . for a reason which was characteristic of the unscrupulously ambitious Göring. He wanted to secure for *his* air force, after the surprisingly smooth operations of the army up to then, the decisive final act in the great battle and thus gain the glory of success before the whole world."
† It was in this speech that Churchill delivered his most eloquent lines of the war.
"Even though large tracts of Europe and many old and famous States have fallen or may fall into the grip of the Gestapo and all the odious apparatus of Nazi rule, we shall not flag or fail. We shall go on to the end. We shall fight in France, we shall fight on the seas and oceans, we shall fight with growing confidence and growing strength in the air, we shall defend our island, . . . we shall fight on the beaches, we shall fight on the landing grounds, we shall fight in the fields and in the streets, we shall fight in the hills; we shall never surrender. . . ."

invasion of its isles by the Normans a millennium before. Its army had been shattered in Flanders, its air force greatly diluted. Only the British navy remained to defend the land, and the Norwegian campaign had shown how vulnerable its ships were to German land-based aircraft. Now Hitler had air bases on the coast of northern France, Belgium and Holland from which to bomb Britain. Still, I thought, there was hope. But for the French it surely was the end. All their main armies had been destroyed. Paris now lay open to the Germans. On June 6, two days after German troops finally got into Dunkirk, Hitler announced that a new offensive had just begun in France.

For the next three days there was not a word in Berlin about it, though from the BBC in London we heard that it was launched on a two-hundred-kilometer front from Abbeville to Soissons, with the greatest pressure along the Somme-Aisne Canal. Only on June 9 did the German High Command break its silence. It said the French south of the Somme and in the Oise area had been beaten all along the line. It claimed that German units were now driving toward the lower Seine. Later in the day OKW announced that the offensive had been extended farther east on a new front from Reims to the Argonne.

> The Germans are now hurling themselves [I noted in my diary on June 9] forward on a two-hundred-mile front from the sea to the Argonne. No drive in World War I was on this scale!

Next day, on June 10:

> Italy is in the war.
> She has stabbed France in the back at the moment when the Germans are at the gates of Paris, and France appears to be down.*

The news did not exactly surprise me. On May 31 I had noted in my journal: "Italy seems to be drawing near to the day of decision — to go in on Germany's side. Today Alfieri, the Italian ambassador, saw Hitler at his headquarters." I had no doubt about what they talked of.

On June 11 I had lunch at the Adlon with Karl von Wiegand, the veteran Hearst correspondent, who was just back from interviewing

---

* President Roosevelt put it more eloquently. Speaking at the University of Virginia at Charlottesville that evening, a broadcast of which I picked up in Berlin the next morning, he said: "On this tenth day of June, 1940, the hand that held the dagger has plunged it into the back of its neighbor."

Hitler at the front. The dictator had told him France would be finished by the middle of the month — four days from now! — and Great Britain by the middle of August — two months hence. Karl, an old hand with the Germans (he covered Germany during the First World War) said Hitler acted as if he had the world at his feet. The generals, although highly pleased with the military successes, were a little apprehensive, Karl thought, of the future under such a wild and fanatical man.

On the afternoon of June 12 I had a bad scare. I was listening to a BBC broadcast from London when the announcer suddenly reported that Geneva had been bombed the previous night and that several people had been killed and wounded in our suburb, where Tess and Eileen were. It took hours to get through on the phone to Tess. But when I heard her voice, I knew that at least she was alive. The bombs *did* fall near by, she said, hitting a hotel down the street where we had lived our first weeks in the city, killing five or six and wounding a score or more. She and the baby had taken refuge in the cellar. In my despair I urged her to come with Eileen to Berlin and join me. This was the safest place to be. *

Events were now moving fast. On June 12 it became clear that Paris was about to fall. The Berlin press played up a CBS broadcast from Eric Sevareid in the French capital. It quoted him: "If in the next days anyone talks to America from Paris, it won't be under the control of the French government."

> I suppose I'm nominated for the job [I wrote in my diary]. I will be the saddest assignment of my life. . . . Though the High Command does not mention it, the truth is the Germans are at the gates of Paris tonight. Thank God, the city will not be destroyed. Wisely the French are declaring it an open city and will not defend it. . . . The taking of Paris will be a terrific blow to the French and the Allies.

To me too, personally, I reflected. For I loved it — passionately. To me it was more home than any other city in the world.

> Berlin, June 14. Paris has fallen.
> The hooked-cross flag of Hitler flutters from the Eiffel Tower there by the Seine. . . . This morning German troops entered the city.

---

* I assumed, as did Tess, that it was the Germans who bombed Geneva. Actually, as I learned later, it was the British. The R.A.F., prevented by French defeatists from launching their bombers from Marseilles for an attack on Genoa, Turin and Milan, had dispatched a squadron from England. The British bombers on a long and unfamiliar flight mistook Geneva for Turin, 120 miles farther southwest over the mountains.

We got the news on the radio at 1 P.M., after loud fanfares had blazed away for a quarter of an hour, calling the faithful to hear the news but causing me excruciating pain. An announcer read the communiqué from OKW:

> The complete collapse of the entire French front from the Channel to the Maginot Line at Montmédy destroyed the original intention of the French leaders to defend the capital of France. Paris therefore has been declared an open city. The victorious troops are just beginning to march into Paris.

I was having lunch in the courtyard of the Adlon. It was a superb, warm, sun-filled summer day. Most of the guests had crowded around the radio loudspeaker. They returned to their tables with wide smiles on their faces, but I had to admit there was no undue excitement, no gloating, as I had rather expected. It reminded me that the Berliners had taken all the good news since the offensive began on the Western Front quite phlegmatically. Outside in the streets, only a few people, I noticed, bought Extras despite their headlines: *PARIS FALLEN!* Later, at a beach out in Halensee, I talked to a number of Germans and gathered that despite the calm with which they took the news, it had nevertheless stirred something very deep in most of them. For a German army to capture Paris — after coming so near to it in 1914 — must have seemed the fulfillment of an unconscious wish-dream for millions in this country. Today, I felt, helped wipe out the bitter memories of defeat in 1918.

If the Germans in the streets, restaurants and beaches took the news of the fall of Paris in stride, the same could not be said of the fanatical party hacks. Hitler's own newspaper, the *Völkische Beobachter* was typical of these. "Paris," it said in a front-page editorial, "was a city of frivolity and corruption, of democracy and capitalism, where Jews had entry to the court, and niggers to the salons. That Paris will never rise again."

I did my broadcasts that day in Berlin with a heavy heart. I wept for Paris. Late that night the High Command announced:

> The second phase of the campaign is over with the capture of Paris. The third phase has begun. It is the pursuit and final destruction of the enemy.

As I was leaving the Rundfunk at 1 A.M., after my last broadcast, Dr. Harald Diettrich, director of the Shortwave Transmitters section, a decent German and one I got along with well, asked me if I'd like to go to Paris. My first impulse was to say no. I did not want to see German jackboots tramping down the streets I loved. But then it hit me with a thud. I was slipping, in my work. My burning hatred for these people, their Leader and what they were up to — and had been for so long — was getting the best of me. I recovered quickly. I told the good Doktor I would like to go. I knew he was including me in even though he knew the Propaganda Ministry, which arranged these tours to the front, detested me and wanted to leave me out. Diettrich had done me this good turn before — on the trip to Kiel on Christmas night, and on the recent visit to the front in Belgium.

Our Mercedes broke down six miles out of Berlin on the way to Potsdam, costing us several hours' delay until a new one could be brought out from the capital. That evening, June 15, in a hostelry near Magdeburg we listened to the war communiqués.

Verdun taken! [I jotted down in my diary.]
Verdun, that cost the Germans six hundred thousand dead the last time they tried to take it. This time they take it in a day. . . . What has happened to the French?

In Paris, in a day or two, perhaps I could find out.

We spent the next evening at Maubeuge, on the Franco-Belgian border, a town of twenty-five thousand inhabitants that had been completely destroyed. The local German commandant, a middle-aged reserve officer and former businessman, told us that a Luftwaffe bomb scored a direct hit on the church in the center of the place, burying five hundred civilians in the air-raid shelter underneath. "Buried air-tight," I scribbled in my notebook, "because on this warm, starlit summer night there is no smell."

The good-natured major, businessman that he was, was trying to revive life in the town. Some ten thousand inhabitants had either returned, he said, or had remained and ridden out the bombing and bombardment. The wounded he had already been able to evacuate to hospitals; the dead he had buried. He was getting in some bread from Germany, he said, and the day before he had discovered a cache of wheat, which he was getting ground into flour.

"One business," he said with a grin, "apparently didn't close up shop at any time, during the battle or since. The local *bordel.*" This offered some comedy, he thought, to offset the suffering.

"I finally closed it down," he explained, but then, the day before, the army High Command had ordered the reopening of all houses of prostitution in occupied France.

"I must send for the madam," the major chuckled. "She will be pleased to hear it."

We spent the night in an abandoned house on the edge of Maubeuge. From the furnishings and papers lying around we established that it was occupied by one of the leading local bankers. His clothes hung neatly in the armoire of the big bedroom. Obviously, the family had departed in a great hurry. There was no time to pack anything. Breakfast dishes were still on the dining-room table. It was a meal never finished.

I let myself speculate a little.

What a break in his comfortable bourgeois life this must have been, this hasty flight before the town was blown up! Here in this house — until last month — solidity, a certain comfort, respectability; the odds and ends collected for a house during a lifetime. This house one's life, such as it is. Then boom! The Stukas. The shells. And that life, like the houses all around, blown to bits; the solidity, the respectability, the hopes gone in a jiffy. And you and your wife and maybe your children along the roads now, hungry, craving for a drink of water. . . .

Coming into Paris that splendid summer day of June 17 was no fun for me. As we drove down the familiar streets, where I had spent the golden years of my mid-twenties (in the mid-twenties) I felt a gnawing ache in the pit of my stomach, and I wished I had not come. To make it worse, my German companions were in high spirits at the sight of the beautiful city.

It was noon when we reached the outskirts. It was one of those lovely June days which Paris always had at this season of the year and which, if there had been peace, the Parisians would have spent at the races at Longchamp, or the tennis at Roland Garros, or idling along the boulevards under the chestnut trees, or on the cool terraces of a café.

The streets, which would have been so teeming at this hour on another summer day, were utterly deserted, the shops closed, the shutters down tight over all the windows. The emptiness got me. Coming in past Le Bourget (remembering sentimentally that May night in 1927, thirteen years before, when I was twenty-three, and I had run all the way from the airfield to Paris to write the story of

Lindbergh's landing), our car drove down the rue Lafayette. German army vehicles sped past us, their horns tooting as if it were a holiday. On the sidewalks not a man or a woman or a child to be seen. Then we were passing the various corner cafés along Lafayette which I knew so well. The tables and chairs had been taken inside behind the drawn shutters. There on the corner, the Petit Journal building, in which I had worked for the *Chicago Tribune* when I first came to Paris in 1925. Across from it, the Trois Portes — how many hours I had idled away in that café with my *Trib* colleagues and often with my great love, Yvonne! Where was she now? I wondered.

At the Place de l'Opéra, for the first time in my experience, there was no traffic tie-up, no French cops shouting futilely at cars hopelessly blocked. The façade of the opera house was hidden behind stacked sandbags. The Café de la Paix at the corner showed signs of reopening. A lone *garçon* was bringing out some tables and chairs. German soldiers stood on the terrace grabbing them. At last! They could have a drink on the terrace of the famous café.

We drove up the boulevard, turning down the rue Royale at the Madeleine. Larue's and Weber's, I noted, were closed. And then before us suddenly the unforgettable view. The Place de la Concorde, the Seine, the Chambre des Députés beyond it, over which a huge swastika flag fluttered, and in the distance the golden dome of the Invalides, where the body of Napoleon must be turning over in his tomb.

We stopped at the Hotel Crillon, German military headquarters, to inquire about where we could stay. The Hotel Scribe, of course, said a monocled officer. At that venerable hotel just beyond the Café de la Paix at the corner of the boulevard and the rue Scribe where I had sometimes stayed, we were greeted warmly in German by the old hotel porter whom I knew well — he was, among other things, a distinguished linguist. He knew every language you could think of.

"*Wilkommen! Wilkommen!*" he cried in his best Frenchified German. "*Kommen Sie herein, meine Herren! Bitte. Bitte.*"*

Two old friends, Demaree Bess, of the *Saturday Evening Post*, and Walter Kerr, of the *New York Herald-Tribune*, were in the lobby — the only American correspondents who had not followed the French government in its flight to Bordeaux.

---

* He would greet the American correspondents equally warmly in English when they arrived at the Scribe four years later on a summer day. "Welcome! Welcome!" he cried out then. "Please come in. Very glad again to see Americans."

Demaree says the panic in Paris was indescribable [I noted in my journal]. Everyone lost his head. The government gave no lead. People were told to scoot, and at least three million out of the five million in the city ran, without baggage, literally ran on their feet toward the south. . . .

The inhabitants are bitter at their government, which in the last days . . . completely collapsed. It even forgot to tell the people until too late that Paris would not be defended. The French police and fire departments remained. . . .

After listening to my friends and then walking about the streets talking to the few French who began to emerge from behind the shutters of their homes I concluded:

What we're seeing here in Paris is the complete breakdown of French society — a collapse of the army, of government, of the morale of the people. It is almost too tremendous to believe.

No newspapers had yet appeared and the French state radio had closed down, so it was difficult to find out what was happening to the French government in Bordeaux. There were rumors that Reynaud had resigned and been replaced by Marshal Pétain, the hero of Verdun. If true, that must mean, I thought, that French resistance would continue to the end, and that though what was left of the shattered army would have to surrender, the French government, and as many troops as possible, would move to North Africa to continue the struggle. The French navy was still intact. It could probably prevent the Germans from reaching French Tunisia, Algeria and Morocco. The considerable French garrisons in North Africa could easily handle the Italians if they tried to attack from Libya.

I was, therefore, surprised by what happened the next day, June 18. Shortly before noon I was standing in the middle of the Place de la Concorde chatting with a group of French men and women. Suddenly from loudspeakers, which German army engineers were just finishing erecting about the square, a voice came on announcing that Marshal Pétain was about to speak. A hush came over the crowd. First the aging marshal — he was eighty-four, I recalled — announced in a quivering voice that he had assumed the heavy responsibilities of premier. "I have made a gift of my person to France," he put it — strangely, it seemed to me. Then came the blow. He had asked the Germans for an armistice, he said. *"With a heavy heart I tell you today that it is necessary to stop the fighting."*

The French about me, some fifty men and women, were stunned.

They were speechless. They could not believe that their great war hero, whom Verdun had made the symbol of resistance to the Germans, was as his first act in office caving in to the eternal enemy. Finally, when the truth dawned on them, they began a discussion that became so animated that a pair of German military police asked them to disperse. Their main argument was over why Pétain asked for the fighting to be stopped before any armistice talks had even begun. The troops who were left, they said, surely would not continue resisting after they heard the marshal's message.*

"Why should they?" one man, with only a stub for one arm, said. He claimed he had fought four years in the trenches the last time. "Why get killed when the war's over?" he kept muttering. Some agreed. Some did not. And then the M.P.'s moved in and dispersed us.

There was another broadcast that day by another French general. This was from a relatively unknown officer named Charles de Gaulle, who had flown to London from Bordeaux with a British liaison officer, General Edward L. Spears, aflame with a burning passion of somehow making France continue in the war. As a colonel he had commanded the hastily formed 4th Armored Division and given a good account of himself west of the Meuse; for years he had pled with French governments, parliaments and the General Staff to build up an armored force, as the Germans were doing. Recently promoted, temporarily, to brigadier-general, he had served for a few days (from June 5 to 16) as Premier Reynaud's under-secretary of defense. Both Pétain and Weygand, who loathed him, had opposed the appointment. Now they were livid that de Gaulle had flown from France to consort with the British. They ordered him to return immediately, on pain of court-martial for desertion.

But the stubborn, rebellious tank general intended to stay. At 6 P.M. on June 18, sitting alone in a BBC studio in London, de Gaulle began to speak:

The [French] government, alleging the defeat of our armies, has made contact with the enemy to put an end to the fighting. . . .

* They were correct. Researching the events of this day for my book on the fall of France I found that many French units, hearing the broadcast, quickly laid down their arms and surrendered. The German army not only arranged the broadcast of Pétain's message over all of occupied France, but hastily printed leaflets and dropped them by plane over large parts of still unoccupied France. General Rommel, closing in on Cherbourg with his 7th Panzer Division, personally helped spread the news. He drove through several villages in a tank, waving a white flag, and shouting in three languages through a portable loudspeaker: "*Guerre finie! Krieg fertig!* War's over!"

But has the last word been said? Is all hope gone? Is the defeat final? No!

For France is not alone. . . . She has a vast empire behind her. She can form a bloc with the British Empire, which holds the seas and continues to struggle.

As he launched into his speech, de Gaulle remembered later: "I felt in myself the termination of a life, one which I had led within the framework of a solid France and an indivisible army. At 49 I plunged into an adventure, like a man whom destiny was casting off from all previous connections."

He tried to convey to his countrymen a world view of the war, one which was beyond the comprehension of Pétain, Weygand, Laval and the other defeatists who had grabbed control of the French government.

This war has not been decided by the Battle of France. This war is a world war. All our mistakes, all our delays, all our suffering, do not alter the fact that there is in the universe all the means needed to crush our enemies one day. . . . The destiny of the world is there.

Historic words! But very few persons in France heard them. With electricity cut off in most cities and towns and villages, not many French radio sets were in operation that day and most of those that were, it seems, were tuned in on Bordeaux, where the decisions for peace or continued war were being made.

Even in England no one seems to have taken it seriously. The BBC, to its later embarrassment, did not think it important enough to record. I heard not a word about it from anyone during those June days in Paris.

I walked over to the Crillon to see if I could pick up any news from the German army people there. Cars raced up unloading gold-braided, heel-clicking German officers. They were in a jubilant mood. Sure, there would quickly be an armistice, they said. What else could Pétain do? One of my friends on OKW said he might have some definite information for me the next day. I began my diary that evening, June 19, with it.

The Armistice is to be signed at Compiègne!

In the same *wagon-lit* coach of Marshal Foch that witnessed the signing of that other armistice on November 11, 1918, in Compiègne

Forest. The French don't know it yet. The Germans are keeping it secret.

At 4:30 P.M., thanks to my friend, the military rushed me out to
Compiègne. Driving out I recalled that the day before, I had asked a
Foreign Office official, half-jokingly, if Hitler, as rumor had it, would
insist on the armistice being signed at Compiègne. He had not liked
my question and had replied icily: "Certainly not!" But when we arrived on the scene at 6 P.M. the answer was obvious. German army
engineers, working with pneumatic drills, were feverishly tearing out
the wall of the museum where Foch's private car, in which the armistice had been signed, had been preserved.

The plan was, the German officers volunteered, to place the car in
exactly the same spot it had occupied in the little clearing in Compiègne Forest that morning at 5 A.M. on November 11, 1918, and
make the French sign *this* armistice there. So the Nazi dictator was
taking his sweet revenge. It would make a spectacular broadcast, if
we could watch the proceedings and get through to New York from
this forest. I took a colonel aside to probe him about setting up a telephone line back to Berlin. He said he would work on it. He had been
friendly enough to show me through the armistice car. Place cards
indicated where each had sat at the historic meeting in 1918. Marshal Foch had sat in the center. I had no doubt that was where Hitler
would sit, if he took part.

Returning to Paris at dusk — toward nine o'clock — we stopped
on the road that winds over the wooded hills between Compiègne
and Senlis. A retreating French column had been bombed there.
Scattered along a quarter of a mile of the road were some twenty
hastily dug soldiers' graves, with a steel helmet resting on each. The
dead horses had not been buried very deep and still stank. An abandoned 75 stood near the road along with other debris a retreating
army leaves: guns, ammunition, shoes, blankets, etc. I looked at the
date of the cannon. 1918! So here the French defended the most important road to the capital with World War I guns!

Later that evening back in Paris I attended a briefing by General
Glaise von Horstenau, whom Hitler had appointed to be one of the
official military historians of this war. I had always disliked and distrusted Horstenau since my Vienna days, when he, an Austrian, had
shamelessly betrayed Schuschnigg. But he was not an unintelligent
man and he took the long, historical view. He thought Germany had
caught the Western Allies at one of those rare moments in military

history when, for a few weeks or months or years, offensive weapons are superior to those of defense. He explained that this particular campaign, with its results, could have taken place only in this early summer of 1940. Had it been delayed until next year, he suggested, the Allies would have had the defensive weapons — anti-tank and anti-aircraft guns and a sufficient number of tanks and fighter-planes — to offset the offensive arms of Germany. There then would have ensued, he thought, the kind of stalemate which developed on the Western Front from 1914 to 1918, when the powers of offense and defense were about equal.

That was why Hitler struck in the West, he said, when he did.

As long as I live I shall never forget that afternoon of June 21 when I stood in a little clearing in the Forest of Compiègne to observe the latest and greatest of Hitler's triumphs, of which I had seen so many over the last turbulent years. As with Austria, which he felt had rejected him as a youth, and then Czechoslovakia, whose people he hated, the messianic Nazi dictator was again taking revenge — revenge this time for the German defeat that had been sealed in this very clearing in 1918.

It was a perfectly lovely summer day. A warm June sun beat down on the stately trees, elms, oaks, cypresses and pines, casting pleasant shadows on the wooded avenues that led out from the little circular clearing of Rethondes. In the middle of it stood the old *wagon-lit* of Marshal Foch. The stage was set for Hitler to savor his greatest hour.

Precisely at 3:15 P.M., by my watch, I watched the dictator and his minions arrive in a caravan of black Mercedeses and alight in front of the French monument to Alsace-Lorraine. I noted down their dress: Hitler in a double-breasted gray military uniform (in contrast to the brown Nazi party uniform he had always worn until the war came); Göring, by the grace of the Führer the only field marshal of the Reich, in a special, fancy sky-blue uniform of the Luftwaffe, fiddling with his marshal's baton; General Keitel, the toady chief of the Supreme Command, and General von Brauchitsch, commander-in-chief of the army, in field-gray uniforms; Dr. Raeder, Grand Admiral of the Fleet, in a dark blue naval uniform; the faithful Rudolf Hess, Hitler's deputy, dressed in a uniform similar to that of his boss; and last the foreign minister, Ribbentrop, in his ornate field-gray Foreign Office uniform.

I did not see Goebbels. He must have been left behind in Berlin to tend the shop. I could imagine him cursing that he had been cheated out of appearing by the side of his beloved Führer on this crowning occasion.

The party stopped to look at the Alsace-Lorraine statue. I noticed that it had been covered with large German war flags, undoubtedly so that Hitler could not see its sculptured work nor read its inscription. But I remembered them from previous visits when I had lived and worked in Paris. The sculpture, I recalled, showed a large Allied sword sticking into a limp eagle representing the German Reich. And the inscription read: "TO THE HEROIC SOLDIERS OF FRANCE . . . DEFENDERS OF THE COUNTRY AND OF RIGHT . . . GLORIOUS LIBERATORS OF ALSACE-LORRAINE."

Hitler turned away from the monument and followed by his party started to stroll the two hundred yards toward us, standing by the *wagon-lit.*

Through my binoculars I observed his face. It was grave, solemn, yet brimming with revenge. There was also in it, as in his springy step, a note of the triumphant conqueror, the defier of the world. There was something else . . . a sort of scornful, inner joy at being present at this great reversal of fate — a reversal he himself had wrought.

The Führer paused for a moment in the center of the clearing while his personal standard was run up on a pole. Then noticing nearby a great granite block that stood some three feet above the ground he strode over to take a look at it. I wondered as he stepped up on it how he would react when the inscription (in French) was read to him and translated.

I myself remembered it very well. Its simple words had always deeply moved me, no matter how often I read them.

"HERE ON THE ELEVENTH OF NOVEMBER 1918 SUCCUMBED THE CRIMINAL PRIDE OF THE GERMAN EMPIRE — VANQUISHED BY THE FREE PEOPLES WHICH IT TRIED TO ENSLAVE."

Hitler reads it, and Göring reads it. [I quote again from my diary.] They all read it, standing there in the June sun and the silence. I look for the expression on Hitler's face. I am but fifty yards from him and see him through my glasses as though he were directly in front of me. I have seen that face many times at the great moments of his life. But today! It is afire with scorn, anger, hate, revenge, triumph.

He steps off the monument and contrives to make even this gesture a masterpiece of contempt. He glances back at it, contemptuous, angry — angry, you almost feel, because he cannot wipe out the awful, provoking lettering with one sweep of his high Prussian boot.°

He glances slowly around the clearing, and now, as his eyes meet ours, you grasp the depth of his hatred. But there is triumph there too — revengeful, triumphant hate. Suddenly, as though his face were not giving quite complete expression to his feelings, he throws his whole body into harmony with his mood. He swiftly snaps his hands on his hips, arches his shoulders, plants his feet wide apart. It is a magnificent gesture of defiance, of burning contempt for this place now and all that it has stood for in the twenty-two years since it witnessed the humbling of the German Empire.

In this mood he led his delegation into the armistice car and quickly sat himself down in Marshal Foch's old place in the middle of the table. Five minutes later the distraught French plenipotentiaries arrived, led by General Charles Huntziger, who, as we have seen, commanded the hapless Second Army at Sedan. The others were a little-known vice-admiral and an air force general, and Léon Noël, who as French ambassador at Warsaw had seen at first hand what the German army did to a country. The Frenchmen looked shattered, but they retained a certain dignity. They had been purposely humiliated by Hitler. General Halder noted it in his diary.

The French had no warning that they would be handed the terms at the very site of the negotiations in 1918. They apparently were shaken by this arrangement and at first inclined to be sullen.

Even a German as decent and as cultivated as General Halder did not seem to know the difference between human dignity and sullenness.

As soon as the members of the French delegation were seated General Keitel opened the proceedings by reading a statement that obviously was drafted by Hitler, for it was full of the tiresome distortions of history I had heard from him in his speeches a hundred times.† He began by stating that Germany had laid down her arms here in November, 1918, because of "the assurances of the American

---

° He had it blown up three days later.

† Through the windows of the railroad car I could follow the proceedings. The Germans had placed microphones about and recorded all that was spoken. When I discovered where the army communications van doing the recordings was located, I myself was able to listen in and take notes. I did this especially with the last dramatic session the second day. By a miracle of engineering plus some luck the Germans succeeded in setting up a telephone line right through the battle lines between the armistice car and the French government in Bordeaux. Thus I could also overhear some of the telephone conversations between Huntziger and General Weygand and other members of the French government.

President Wilson. Thus there came an end to a war which the German people and government had never wanted and in which the enemy had never succeeded in defeating the German army, navy and air force in any decisive way." Then had followed the terrible Allied oppression of Germany which had brought so much suffering to its people. Finally, he said: "On September 3, 1939, twenty-five years after the outbreak of the World War, England and France again without any justification declared war on Germany." God! How many times had I heard these lies!

He could not end without attempting to justify his choosing this place as the scene of another armistice. "The historic forest of Compiègne has been chosen in order to efface once and for all by an act of reparative justice a memory, which was not for France a glorious page in her history and which was resented by the German people as the greatest shame of all time."

This was vintage Hitler. And Keitel read it, Ambassador Noël remembered, "with vehemence, insolence and brutality." Hitler then left with his entourage. He had admonished Keitel, who remained to talk with the French, that his terms were not to be altered in any way. Keitel's only job was to "explain them." The demands struck General Huntziger as "hard and merciless — much worse than the Allied terms in 1918." He tried over the rest of the day and all through the next to soften them. But in vain.

The most crucial clause concerned the disposal of the French fleet — this was of the utmost importance also to the British, who did not intend to surrender, and to the U.S.A., whose president, Roosevelt, was especially sensitive to the naval balance in Europe. If the French navy were to pass into the hands of the Germans intact, Britain would be in an even more terrible predicament than it was already. Mindful of this, Churchill, as France tottered, had offered to release her from her pledge not to make a separate peace if the French fleet were directed to sail for British ports.

Hitler was determined to prevent this. He had discussed it with Mussolini on June 18 and said he would have to make some kind of a concession to France. The German armistice terms stipulated that the French fleet would be demobilized and disarmed under German or Italian supervision and the ships laid up in their home ports. In return Hitler gave a solemn promise — another!

> The German government solemnly declares to the French government that it does not intend to use for its own purposes in the war the French fleet which is in ports under German supervision. Further-

more, they solemnly and expressly declare that they have no intention of raising any claim to the French war fleet at the conclusion of peace.

Apparently the French still had trust in Hitler's promises, for they accepted this one. Not so Churchill in London.

"What is the value of that?" he said of it in a speech on June 25. "Ask half a dozen countries."*

The most odious of the German demands — at least to me — required the French to turn over all anti-Nazi German refugees, thousands of whom had fled Hitler's tyranny and settled in France. Even General Weygand, who was now running affairs under Pétain in Bordeaux, protested that such a demand was "contrary to honor" and requested its deletion. But the Germans, of course, refused.

Later Weygand apparently forgot that he had first considered the stipulation as dishonorable, for he would contend that there was "nothing dishonorable" in the German armistice conditions. Unfortunately, as two French ambassadors, Léon Noël and Kammerer, later testified, this article was carried out by the Pétain government in a manner "even more odious." The French Ministry of Interior and the French Secret Police became relentless in tracking down the German refugees and handing them over to Hitler. Among them were two old and honored German Socialist leaders, long retired from politics, Breitscheid and Hilferding. They were brought to Berlin and axed.

Not very honorable either, I thought, was another article under which the French government undertook to forbid its nationals to fight against Germany in the service of other states. Those who did so would be treated as *franc-tireurs* — that is, shot upon capture. The article was of course aimed at General de Gaulle, who was trying to organize a Free French force in Britain. Pétain and Weygand, I am sure, as well as Hitler and Keitel, knew that to treat Frenchmen in such service as *franc-tireurs* was a crude violation of the rules of war. Bordeaux did not protest this article. So far as I could find out, it also did not protest Article 20, which provided that French prisoners-of-war, of whom there were now nearly a million and a half, would remain in German custody until the conclusion of peace. This puzzled

---

* Admiral Jean Darlan, commander-in-chief of the French navy, seemed more concerned with keeping his ships out of the hands of the British than of the Germans. On June 23, the day after the armistice was signed, he signaled all French warships that the British were "trying to get their hands on the French fleet." Next day he radioed all ships: "Disembark immediately all British liaison officers and personnel. . . . *Watch out for possible British attacks!*"

me until I later learned that Pétain, Weygand and Darlan were sure that the British would be defeated or would give up in a matter of weeks, after which peace would be made and the P.O.W.'s released.

The other clauses of the German armistice terms provided for German military occupation of three-fifths of the country, most of which in the north and west was already captured, including the entire Atlantic coast. This was the most industrialized part of France. Paris would remain occupied, though the French government could have its seat there if it desired. The French Empire, of which North Africa was the most important part, was left intact and unoccupied, though its armed forces, except for small units necessary for internal order and defense, were to be demobilized.

The next day, June 22, I went out to Compiègne early. My friend on the High Command tipped me that almost certainly the Franco-German armistice taking France out of the war would be signed during the day. There was another reason for getting out to the scene early. At breakfast at the Hotel Scribe I learned that Hitler had ordered all the correspondents, foreign and German, flown back to Berlin, where he himself was going. If and when the armistice was signed, he would release the news from Berlin. All the American newspaper correspondents I talked to were going to follow orders and take the press plane back to the capital. I decided to stay. I wanted to see the climactic scene in the armistice car. Perhaps the French would refuse to sign. Either way it would be a good story to cover personally. And I wanted to broadcast an eyewitness account from the scene.

So before I could be rounded up that morning at the Scribe and flown back to Berlin, I hooked a ride to Compiègne with Diettrich, who was handling the coverage for the German shortwave transmitters, and with my army friend. They did not seem to worry about helping me to evade an order of the dictator himself. Diettrich thought it applied only to the *newspaper* correspondents. My officer friend was pleased that I was defying Hitler, whom he despised. But he warned me that the Führer had ordered that all broadcasts this day from Compiègne be automatically recorded in Berlin. They could be retransmitted to America only when Hitler himself gave the word.

That was fair enough. At least, unlike the newspaper correspondents, I would have an eyewitness story, and it would get out of Berlin at the same time as the newspaper dispatches. And being instantaneous it would beat them by hours before their stories could appear in print.

As the day progressed I noted from what I picked up from the army communications truck that there was a good deal of bickering between the two sides. The French delegation kept asking for concessions — minor ones, it seemed to me, except on the question of turning over the German refugees — and the Germans kept refusing them. At one point Weygand insisted that at least the French requests and the German responses be attached to the armistice treaty as part of the "protocol," but the Germans turned him down.

Toward the end of the afternoon General Huntziger made a curt demand of General Weygand in Bordeaux. He insisted, he told him on the telephone, on not merely an "authorization" to sign the agreement but an "order" from the French government to do so. He did not himself intend to share the government's responsibilities for the capitulation. The fiery little Weygand did not like the request from a subordinate general but Huntziger was adamant.

By that time, late afternoon, the Germans were becoming impatient. At 5:30 P.M. General Keitel handed General Huntziger a written ultimatum. The French must accept or reject the German armistice terms within an hour — by 6:30 to be exact. Otherwise the talks were off. For the next half hour or so, in my naïveté, I envisaged the negotiations breaking down, the French walking out and the government in Bordeaux beating it to North Africa, as I had heard that Churchill and de Gaulle and Roosevelt were urging, and continuing the war from there. I did not yet realize the depths of the defeatism in Bordeaux. Weygand was directed to give Huntziger what the latter had insisted on, an *order* to sign, not merely an authorization. He dictated it over the phone. "No. 43/DN. Order is given to the French delegation . . . to sign the armistice convention with Germany."

At 6:42 P.M., by my watch, the two delegations assembled in Marshal Foch's old railroad coach for the signing. Through the windows I could see General Huntziger's drawn, ashen face. He fought to keep back the tears. Before signing the treaty, he said, he had a personal statement to make. I took it down in French, as he spoke, his quivering words echoing through the communications van.

I declare that the French government has ordered me to sign these terms of armistice. . . .

Forced by the fate of arms to cease the struggle in which we were engaged on the side of the Allies, France sees imposed on her very hard conditions. France has the right to expect in the future negotiations that Germany show a spirit which will permit the two great neighboring countries to live and work peacefully.

He believes Hitler will have the grace to permit that? I muttered to myself. We knew already from the examples of Czechoslovakia and Poland what Hitler had in store for France.

We could hear the scratching of pens as the armistice agreement was signed. It was 6:50 P.M. There were muffled remarks from the French that I could not catch. Then the deep voice of General Keitel:

> I request all members of the German and French delegations to rise in order to fulfill a duty which the brave German and French soldiers have merited. Let us honor . . . all those who have bled for their Fatherland and all those who have died for their country.

A minute of silence ensued, and then the members of the two delegations filed out. The French set off for Paris, where the next day they would be flown in a German plane to Rome to submit to Mussolini's armistice demands, a meeting the very thought of which embittered the French.* But Article 23 of the agreement they had just signed stipulated that it would not come into effect until six hours after the French had concluded an armistice with Italy.

I went on the air at 8:15 P.M., when the army and the German Broadcasting Company cleared the line to Berlin for us. I spoke ad lib from my notes for nearly half an hour on the conclusion of the armistice. Since I was broadcasting blind — we had no "feedback" during which I could talk to New York — I kept calling CBS and NBC† for four or five minutes before I began to speak, but I had no idea whether they were listening and would pick up the broadcast. In the excitement, I obviously forgot that we were not supposed to be broadcasting live but only for a recording in Berlin that would be

---

* Particularly embittered was Huntziger, who at one stage told Keitel: "Although Italy declared war on France, she has not waged war. France in fact does not have to ask Italy for an armistice because an armistice has actually existed since the day of the declaration of war." On the Riviera on the road to Nice the small French forces had easily repulsed a much larger Italian army. The farthest Italian advance, after ten days of fighting, had amounted to a few hundred yards.

† At the request of the German army and the Reichs Rundfunk, I agreed to make it a joint broadcast to CBS and NBC. The army, the government and the German broadcasting company, it was explained to me, badly needed the telephone line for their own messages and broadcasts. Diettrich and my OKW friend assured me that I would speak first, since NBC had sent only a stringer, Bill Kerker, without much journalistic experience. I spoke, as I recall, for about twenty minutes and Kerker, using mostly my unused notes, for the last ten minutes. It may well have been the first joint broadcast the two rival networks ever made.

transmitted to America when Hitler gave the word. Or did I have a premonition that maybe, somehow, we might be getting through directly and instantaneously? I cannot now remember.

As it turned out, it was extremely important that I did keep calling New York before beginning to narrate the story.

As I finished speaking into the mike, which I had set up just outside the army communications van about thirty yards from the armistice car, it began to rain lightly. Down the road, as I wrote in my diary that evening,

> through the woods, I could see the refugees, slowly, tiredly, filing by — on weary feet, on bicycles, on carts, a few on trucks — an endless line. They were exhausted and dazed, those walking were footsore and many limped, and they did not know yet that an armistice had been signed and that the fighting would be over very soon now.
>
> I walked out to the center of the clearing. The sky was overcast and the rain was coming down a little heavier. An army of German engineers, shouting lustily, had already started to move the armistice car.
>
> "Where to?" I asked.
>
> "To Berlin," they said.°

I slept late the next morning, which was a Sunday, savoring the first full night's sleep since we left Berlin a week before. I was still sound asleep when I heard a banging on the door and noticed by my watch that it was nearly noon. It was Walter Kerr.

"You scooped the world yesterday," he said. "Congratulations!"

"You have to be kidding," I said, trying to shed my drowsiness.

Walter, having no press credentials with the Germans, had not been able to go out to Compiègne. He had sat up in the *New York Herald-Tribune* office, he said, listening to shortwave rebroadcasts from New York, mostly from CBS. (The Germans had not yet removed the antenna on the roof of the building.) For several hours, he said, my announcement of the signing of the armistice and a detailed description of the proceedings from Compiègne Forest were the only news America had of the event. Not until nearly midnight, our time, had the dispatches of the newspaper correspondents in Berlin begun coming through. (Hitler had released the news at 11:30 P.M.)

Elmer Davis and some of the other commentators at CBS, Walter went on, began to be somewhat embarrassed and then disturbed when no confirmation of my broadcast came through from any other

---

° It arrived there July 8, and went on exhibition in Berlin shortly afterward. Ironically, it was destroyed in an Allied bombing later in the war.

source. After an hour or so, Davis, though sticking by my story, began to point out that it had not been confirmed from any other source — whatsoever.

"On the other hand," Walter said Elmer would say, "Mr. Shirer is a very experienced correspondent and an extremely conscientious one. We expect confirmation from other sources shortly. In the meantime, stay tuned. . . ."*

Probably Elmer Davis, a good friend and a great broadcaster, was thinking of the premature United Press story announcing the armistice on November 7, 1918 — four days before it was signed. The mistake had almost cost the U.P., then a fledgling news service, its life.

In good time I found what had happened that had enabled me to score probably the greatest scoop of my journalist life. What occurred was very simple, and a very lucky break for me — most scoops are largely a matter of luck. The German radio engineers at the Berlin end of our military telephone line from Compiègne threw the wrong switch. Instead of steering my broadcast to a recording machine at the Reichs Rundfunk for recording, they channeled it into a shortwave transmitter at Zossen, which sent it out automatically and instantly to New York. Thus CBS in New York (and NBC, if they picked it up) got the news of the signing of the armistice exactly an hour and twenty-five minutes after it took place. American newspapers and wire services did not get it from their Berlin correspondents until nearly six hours later.†

* Ed Murrow picked up my broadcast in London. He could get the Berlin shortwave transmitters on his office radio. He told me later he immediately telephoned Churchill at Chequers in the country, it being a Saturday, with the news — in case he hadn't heard it. According to Ed, he hadn't, and, what is more, he didn't believe it — the British government, it was explained, had its own sources of news and it knew nothing of the Franco-German armistice being signed.

Indeed on the front page of the *New York Times* for Sunday, June 23, under a three-line banner headline, the newspaper inserted in the United Press dispatch on the armistice from Berlin a note from London saying: "Authoritative British quarters said there was no confirmation in London that the French have signed an armistice, as reported by American and German sources. These quarters said they understood the French had presented counterproposals."

So hours after the armistice had been signed and we had reported it from the spot, London "quarters," including the prime minister, apparently still did not believe it.

† Thus the afternoon newspapers at home had only our broadcast from Compiègne to go on. Press dispatches from Berlin did not reach them in time even for their late editions. Probably my hometown newspaper in Iowa, the esteemed *Cedar Rapids Gazette*, an afternoon journal, was typical. Under a two-line banner headline on page one it ran a story in large boldface type which began:

New York (UP) — A French-German armistice, to become effective upon conclusion of a similar agreement between France and Italy, was signed at 6:50 P.M. Saturday (10:50 A.M. Central Standard Time) Columbia Broadcasting System and

I must say I was glad I had had the gumption to keep calling New York for four or five minutes before I began to broadcast, though it is a monotonous chore to keep repeating the banal words and never know whether anyone is picking you up. I kept chanting: "Hello CBS, New York. Hello NBC, New York. This is William L. Shirer in Compiègne, scene of the Franco-German armistice talks. In exactly five minutes from now [and four and three, etc.] we shall begin broadcasting from here on the results of the armistice talks. . . . Hello CBS, New York . . ."

Paul White, our news director in New York, told me later they had not heard my signal at first. It was Saturday, and only a skeleton staff was manning the CBS listening post. Someone finally picked up my call only a minute before I said I would begin to speak. An announcer to introduce the broadcast was found only at the last second, and Elmer Davis had to be yanked from a restaurant below on 52nd Street, to come and offer his commentary.

The day after the broadcast I learned from my army friends that Hitler, in Berlin, was furious at my having, as he thought, broken the release time on the armistice story. It must have been the first time — and probably the last, I thought — that he, the absolute dictator of Germany, was scooped — and by an obscure foreign journalist for whom he had nothing but contempt. He had ordered, I was told, an immediate investigation of who — in the army and Rundfunk — were responsible for switching my broadcast through. The culprits, he had stormed, would pay for the lapse.

Was it a lapse? I never learned. Questioned by the army and

---

the National Broadcasting Company reported in a joint broadcast from Compiègne forest.
    William Shirer, CBS correspondent, said that the Franco-German armistice had been signed for the Germans by Gen. Wilhelm Keitel, chief of the German High Command, and for the French by Gen. Charles Huntziger. . . .

The *Gazette* published the entire text of my broadcast. As perhaps might have been expected, it puffed up the hometown boy, who for a time had been its college correspondent. Above a photograph of me sitting behind a CBS microphone it had a caption:

Flashes 1st Report
of Armistice To
America

and under the photograph: "William L. 'Bill' Shirer, formerly of Cedar Rapids and now chief of the Columbia Broadcasting System's central European staff, Saturday reached a pinnacle in his career as a radio correspondent when he flashed the first word to America that the German-French armistice had been signed. Shirer spoke jointly over the NBC and CBS networks from the Compiègne forest.
"Shirer . . . is a former Coe college reporter for the Cedar Rapids Gazette."

Rundfunk brass and the Propaganda Ministry, I replied that though I was grateful for what happened I had no part in it. But some of my friends in the army High Command, after the matter had blown over — scoops are very ephemeral — hinted that perhaps there had not been a lapse, that the army had deliberately let my broadcast go through because it wanted the news of the armistice out as soon as possible and resented Hitler's holding it up in Berlin so that he could build up a lot of publicity for himself. Actually, as I learned when I returned to Berlin, Hitler and Goebbels concocted a dramatic radio ceremony for the official announcement of the armistice.

It was distaste for just such a propaganda stunt, my friends at OKW said, that may have led the army to see to it that my broadcast from Compiègne carried instantly to the world the news of the signing of the armistice. The army, after all, they argued, by its incredible campaign in the West, had brought about the French capitulation. The army did not intend to let Hitler take all the credit. There had been much more friction between the High Command and the Führer during the campaign than any of us knew. General Halder, the chief of the General Staff, would tell me of some of it later and reveal more in his diaries. Letting my broadcast of the armistice through, against Hitler's express orders, was perhaps another act of defiance by the army brass.

I wondered, though, when I returned to Berlin whether I would be expelled.

I lingered on a bit in Paris. The last days of June along the Seine were lovely: warm, sunny, the air fresh, the sky blue, but despite that, despite revisiting old haunts and old friends and acquaintances from the golden years, I grew more and more depressed.

I could no longer understand the French, whom I had come to admire and like when I had lived and worked in Paris. I could not understand why they had not fought, as their fathers had in the last war against the German invaders. I could not fathom why they welcomed the armistice, as most of them did, and why they would not see what was in store for them under the Nazi German yoke.

"Better Hitler than Blum," the reactionaries said when the Socialist leader, who happened to be a Jew, had tried to make a go of it with his Popular Front government. They had forced Blum out, and now they had Hitler, but they refused to face what this meant for them.

They also had the old, doddering Marshal Pétain, as head of what was left of the French government after the armistice that the marshal had insisted on asking for and accepting. Though it shocked me, I reluctantly had to admit that most French men and women were behind Pétain in taking France out of the war and capitulating to Hitler. I could understand, of course, how relieved the French were that the killing had stopped — the killing at least of Frenchmen. But the situation was not that simple, not black and white. Could not have France continued in the war from her empire, as a majority of the Reynaud government had first proposed? French forces in North Africa had more than enough strength to repulse any German-Italian attempt to take it. True, as some of my friends argued, if the government had fled to North Africa, as it first intended to do, that would have left all of metropolitan France at the mercy of the Nazis. But all of France, regardless of the armistice terms, I argued, would in reality be at the mercy of Hitler. The Pétain government would not be free, would have no real independence.

Churchill in announcing "with sadness and stupefaction" the armistice to the Commons had said: "A victory of Great Britain constitutes the only hope for the restoration of the grandeur of France and the freedom of her people."

That seemed self-evident. But not to my French friends or to Pétain, who believed the British, like the French, ought to know when they were beaten.

"The French will be saved by their own efforts," Pétain said in a response to the British prime minister. "Monsieur Churchill should know this."

I scarcely could believe it, but so far as I could tell almost all the French agreed. "The fact was," de Gaulle would remind his fellow countrymen later, "that not a single public figure [in France] raised his voice to condemn the armistice." In a broadcast on June 24 he expressed his shame "at France and the French being delivered hand and foot to the enemy" by the armistice terms.

"De Gaulle? Who on earth is he?" I remember French acquaintances saying. Very few French had heard of him.*

* Even in England, from which he was broadcasting his urgent appeals to the French, he was snubbed by most of his fellow countrymen, military and civilian. Alexis Léger, the former permanent head of the Foreign Office, André Maurois, the writer, Jean Monnet, the economist, and many other prominent Frenchmen who had fled to London, refused to join him. All but a handful of several thousand French troops evacuated from Narvik, including three generals and most of the officers, declined to join de Gaulle's Free French forces and asked to be repatriated to their subjected motherland. A sizable French fleet, which had taken refuge in the British ports of Portsmouth and Plymouth, and consisted of two battleships, four cruisers, eight destroyers, several submarines and two hundred smaller craft, also

They would hear, of course, in time as his cause, so hopeless in those June days of 1940, prospered, and he, with the Allies, became the only hope of liberation. And they would, finally, transfer to him the adulation they first had felt for Pétain. Take Paul Claudel, the poet-diplomat, who just after the armistice wrote an impassioned ode in praise of Pétain. Four years later, when de Gaulle reentered Paris, Claudel wrote an equally impassioned ode to the Free French leader. As I recalled it, it was in almost the identical words. François Mauriac, the eminent novelist and member of the Académie Française (Pétain and Weygand also were members), was just as bad. In an article in *Le Figaro* on July 3, he went into ecstasies at the sound of the voice of the hero-marshal calling on the country to accept defeat and to get back to work.

> The words of Marshal Pétain . . . had a sound that was almost intemporal. It was not a man who spoke to us, but something out of the profound depths of our history. This old man was delegated to us by the dead of Verdun. . . .*

Later, when the tide had turned, Mauriac, like Claudel, became just as ecstatic over General de Gaulle. Paul Valéry, the celebrated poet, and like Mauriac a member of the Academy, exulted that Pétain "has offered himself in order to maintain in the midst of a disorder without example the unity, indeed the existence of the country." André Gide kept up with his fellow writers. He thought Pétain's first broadcast, which had called on the French to cease fighting even before the Germans had agreed to discuss an armistice, "simply admirable." On July 10 he confided to his journal — he was a great diarist — that he "would accept a dictatorship, which alone, I fear, can save us from decomposition." He would soon get his wish — in a double dose: a French dictatorship under Pétain and Laval under the heel of the Nazi dictatorship of Hitler. The day before, on July 9, he said he thought that "if the German domination assured us abundance, nine out of ten French would accept it." Fi-

---

declined to join de Gaulle. A good many of these resisted British boarding parties when they took over this fleet and interned it on July 3. Only nine hundred sailors agreed to join de Gaulle. The rest, some nineteen thousand men, including two admirals and most of the officers, opted to be sent home, and were.

* The words of the marshal had another sound for de Gaulle. In a broadcast from London directed to Pétain, after charging him with having "reduced the country, the government, you yourself, to servitude," he concluded: "Ah! to obtain and accept such an enslavement, we did not need the Conqueror of Vedun. Anyone else would have sufficed."

nally by the middle of July this eminent writer, who had been a sort of conscience of the French people, could write that he had "almost come to believe that France did not merit victory." Rehashing the spurious lines of Pétain, Weygand and Laval he added: "It appears she [France] threw herself into the adventure, or rather, let herself be drawn into it, with a perilous imprudence."

From André Gide! He had been one of my idols in my earlier days in Paris. Now he had joined the claque of defeatists who had taken over the country.

There were a few in Paris I saw who kept their heads. They would quote, for example, the words of the German philosopher Fichte after Jena, where Napoleon had humbled the Germans:

"A cowardly surrender will not save you from destruction!"

Some recalled a famous exchange between General Ducrot and Thiers in 1870 when the general had advised defending Paris against the approaching Germans (after the first debacle at Sedan) even though final victory seemed improbable.

"General," Thiers had said, "you speak like a soldier, and that's good. But you do not speak like a political man."

"Monsieur," the general had replied, "I believe I also speak as a political man because a great nation such as ours rises always from her material ruins, but it will never rise from her moral ruins."

I wondered those June days in German-occupied Paris whether the French, wallowing in their defeat, would ever rise from their moral morass. I hoped so because I loved that country and its civilization. But I cannot say that I was very hopeful. In another place I recalled something Thucydides had written about a people who refused to surrender no matter what the odds.

I myself in that bleak summer thought of the reply of the Melian delegates to the Athenians of Pericles, who had sent an ultimatum demanding surrender of the island state of Melos.

The Athenians had behaved a good deal like Hitler, telling the Melians: "You know as well as we do that right, as the world goes, is only in question between equals in power, while the strong do what they can and the weak suffer what they must."

Thucydides had given the Melian answer:

". . . It were surely great baseness and cowardice in us who are still free not to try everything that can be tried before submitting to your yoke. . . . We know that the fortune of war is sometimes more impartial than the disproportion of numbers might lead one to suppose; to submit is to give ourselves over to despair, while action will preserve for us a hope that we may stand erect."*

Back in Berlin on June 27 I still felt stunned by the fall of France — and in the unbelievable interval of six weeks. With nothing else to do I tried to sum up what had happened and how and why. Perhaps it was too early to tell. But from what little one correspondent could see I drew a few preliminary conclusions.

France did not fight. Its armies were overwhelmed on the Meuse from Sedan to Namur on the fifth day of the war in the West, and offered little resistance thereafter. Why had this happened in 1940 and not in 1914, when the French, with less aid from the British than now, had stopped the Germans at the Marne — and held out for four years to win in the end? I did not know the answer.

Was it that the German *Blitzkrieg* — the thrust with armor and Stuka bombers down the roads — caught the French by surprise? Impossible. The Germans had used it in Poland eight months before. Had the French and British High Commands not heard of it? Most unlikely. There was nothing secret about it.

I remembered hearing — I think from Ralph Barnes — that only a few weeks before the onslaught in the West General Sir Edmund Ironside, chief of the British Imperial General Staff, had boasted to American correspondents in London of the great advantage he had in possessing several generals in France who had been division commanders in the Great War, whereas the German generals were too young to have had that combat experience.

It was an idle boast. The German generals *were* younger — a few not yet forty, most of them in their forties, a few at the very top in their early fifties. But that gave them the qualities of youth: dash, daring, imagination, flexibility, initiative and physical prowess. General von Reichenau was the first in his army to cross the Vistula River

---

* Some forty-two years later, on a chilly, sunny afternoon, Sunday, October 31, 1982, in the Piskaryovskoye Memorial Cemetery in Leningrad, my mind again, as so often in the intervening years, went back to those lovely June days of 1940 in Paris when the French, to preserve their beautiful city, surrendered it without a fight to the Germans. Leningrad also was a beautiful city, the loveliest in Russia, but when the Germans approached it a year later, in September of 1941, the Russians were determined to defend it. This they did during a siege of nine hundred days, through three of the coldest winters in living memory, when the inhabitants died like flies of starvation and cold. Some half a million of them lie buried in the Piskaryovskoye Memorial Cemetery. As I walked through its grounds past the mass graves that chilling Sunday in Leningrad I kept thinking: What other people would have submitted to such a hell for three years, refusing to surrender; who else among the people on this earth would have shown such incredible bravery and fortitude? Not the French I had seen in Paris that June of 1940. My own countrymen? Say, in New York? I wondered.

in the Polish campaign. He swam it. Guderian, Rommel and the other commanders of the panzer divisions led many of their attacks in person. They did not remain, as the French were inclined to do, in the safety of divisional command posts far to the rear.

I guess another reason for the incredible German victory in the West was the fantastically good morale of the German army. Few people who had not seen it in action realized how different this army was from the one the Kaiser sent hurtling into Belgium and France in 1914. I first discovered this entirely new esprit in the German armed services when I visited the navy at Kiel over Christmas. It was based on a camaraderie between officers and men that would have shocked the old Prussian generals and surprised the French, the British and even, I think, the American military of today. I felt it in the army, to my surprise, from the first day at the front. For one thing, officers and men were often eating the same food from the same soup kitchen. Officers listened attentively to the reports of enlisted men. The man in charge of the capture of Fort Eben Emael was a sergeant. When we got to Paris I noticed officers and men off duty sitting at the same table and exchanging talk. In one instance there was a colonel treating a dozen privates to an excellent luncheon in a little Basque restaurant off the Opéra. During the repast he discussed with them over a Baedeker the sites of Paris he thought would interest them. Hitler himself, I was also surprised to learn, had drawn up detailed instructions for officers about taking an interest in the personal problems of their men.

One thing about all this puzzled me. These soldiers came from a country that had ruthlessly stamped out human freedom, savagely turned on its opponents, persecuted its Jews, whom it was planning to exterminate — a country, a dictatorship, finally, that, like a gangster, without provocation, attacked and occupied one neighboring country after another that it had sworn not to attack and that it was now enslaving.

How could these soldiers fight so enthusiastically for such a barbarous regime? I could not understand it.

Next day, June 28, I remembered, was the twenty-first anniversary of the signing of the Treaty of Versailles. The world it created, which the victors thought would last indefinitely, appeared now to be gasping its last breath. That day German troops moving down from Bordeaux reached the Spanish border, and Soviet contingents marched into Bessarabia and Bukovina, which the peace treaty in 1919 had awarded to Rumania. The Wilhelmstrasse, I noted, did not like this latest Russian move — the Red Army was the last few days already taking over the three Baltic states — but what could Hitler do? The Bolsheviks were cashing in on their deal with him. He had to be especially circumspect about Rumania, from which the Reich got most of its imported oils.

"What next?" I asked a friend of mine on the High Command on my return to Berlin.

"England," he smiled.

The army was not keen about it, he said, in fact did not know how it could get across the Channel. But the Führer was insisting.

"It's bound to be your next assignment," he chided me. I was less keen about it than he said the army was. If I had to cover the invasion of Britain I hoped I would see the German army drowned in the Channel in the attempt. Here I was — I stopped myself — getting paranoid again. I needed to get away from the Germans. I cabled New York I was taking a week's holiday in Geneva with my family over July 4. After my armistice scoop, I figured, CBS would not begrudge me a few days off.

For a few days over our national holiday I lolled on the beach along the lake, listening to the joyous screams of Eileen as I tried to teach her how to swim, talking with Tess about our uncertain future, dining with them in a quiet place along the water, from which we could see Mont Blanc, its snows pink in the summer late afternoon's lingering sun. On the afternoon of the Fourth of July the American consul-general entertained the dwindling American colony at his place above the lake. Cows grazed in the adjoining pastures. Sailboats tacked lazily in the quiet waters below. On an immense grill we roasted frankfurters, hamburgers and sweet corn, tossed them down with good Swiss beer and fine local wines, and my fellow countrymen talked nostalgically of home, which seemed so far away from war.

Each day we would pass the vast marble edifice of the League of Nations, which I had covered as a young foreign correspondent coming down from Paris. For countless millions it had offered the prospect of world peace.

> This evening in the sunset [I wrote in my diary on July 5] the great white marble of the League building showed through the trees. It had a noble look, and the League has stood in the minds of many as a noble hope. But it has not tried to fulfill it. Tonight it was a shell, the building, the institution, the hope — dead.

Back in Berlin on July 8, I noted in my journal another death, that of democratic France. Pierre Laval had announced that the French Chamber and Senate, the pillars of parliamentary democracy in the Third Republic, were going to vote themselves out of existence. The aged, senile Marshal Pétain would take over all power in unoccupied, authoritarian France. I had no doubt that the sinister Laval would be behind him, pulling the strings.

The Nazis in Berlin were mildly amused at this belated attempt of the French to emulate Hitler's Third Reich. But officials in the Wilhelmstrasse stressed to me that it would not get them easier or better peace terms. In fact, the Foreign Office put out a statement:

> The change of the former regime in France to an authoritarian form of government will not influence in any way the political liquidation of the war. The fact is that Germany does not consider the Franco-German accounts as settled yet. Later they will be settled with historical realism.

It never pays to cringe, especially before the bullying Germans. It was a lesson the French would learn.

On my return to Berlin from Geneva, I found a distinct cooling in relations between Germany and the Soviet Union. Hitler was in a rage at Stalin's taking over the three Baltic countries, Estonia, Latvia and Lithuania, while the Führer was engaged in conquering France. This extended the frontiers of the Soviet Union hundreds of miles down the Baltic to the borders of East Prussia and threatened Germany's position there. And as June ended, Stalin had grabbed two oil-rich provinces of Rumania. But Hitler was liking it less and less. And now that he had conquered the West he was thinking, we heard, especially if he could make peace with Britain, of turning on Russia.

But we were not allowed to say so. Two or three times I had tried to slip past the censors a story of the new crisis in Russo-German relations but they had cut it out. It became obvious to all of us correspondents that it was a touchy subject and that Hitler wanted nothing written about it — yet. Ralph Barnes, who had returned from his post as chief correspondent of the *New York Herald-Tribune* in London to cover the campaign in the West from the German side, decided nonetheless to cable a story about Hitler and Stalin beginning to fall out. Ralph had been the *Herald-Tribune*'s correspondent in Moscow before coming to Berlin, knew Russia and the Russians well, and got his story mostly, I suspect, from contacts in the Soviet embassy in Berlin. Hitler was furious. He ordered Ralph's immediate expulsion. I had got back to Berlin from Geneva in time to see Ralph off. We were old and close friends. We had met first in Paris when we both were young reporters and our families had seen a great deal of each other when we both ended up in Berlin. Tess and Esther Barnes had become bosom friends. We loved their two daughters. We invariably spent the holidays together — Thanksgiving, Christmas, New Year's, Easter. I hated to see Ralph go.

The day before his forced departure Ralph and I had a long walk in the Tiergarten, the last of many we had taken in that green refuge over the years. He was depressed at being kicked out, not being sure his newspaper would understand it, and resentful that he was being ousted for writing what he was certain was the truth. I tried to console him. He had more guts than the rest of us in trying to get a big story through. The threatened breakup of the collaboration between Hitler and Stalin, who we were sure hated each other's guts, was important news. It would affect the course of this war. In the meantime, I reminded Ralph, he could go back to London and cover the biggest story he had ever had: the German invasion of England. I probably would have to be reporting it from the hated German side.

We adjourned to the Adlon bar, as so often before, and had a farewell drink. The next day Ralph was off. Four months later he was killed in a British bomber returning over the fog-shrouded mountains to a base in Greece after a raid on the Italian lines in Albania. Mussolini, not to be outdone by Hitler, had attacked a new country, Greece, on October 28.

On July 15 in Berlin came the first public announcement that Hitler was now ready to invade Britain. "German troops of all arms," it said, "now stand ready for the attack on Britain. The date of the attack will be decided by the Führer alone."*

But first, I was advised in the Wilhelmstrasse, Hitler would offer the British "a most generous" peace. And peace he did offer them in a speech to the Reichstag on July 19. It was, as I have noted elsewhere, the last of Hitler's great Reichstag orations and the last in this place that I would hear. It was also, I thought, one of his best, one of his cleverest, very eloquent and as usual full of deceit.

I noted my impressions of it later that evening.

> The Hitler we saw in the Reichstag tonight was the conqueror, and conscious of it, and yet so wonderful an actor, so magnificent a handler of the German mind, that he mixed superbly the full confidence of the conqueror with the humbleness which always goes down

---

* This was a bluff. We now know, from the secret German records, that there was no possibility of the troops being ready before mid-August, if then.

so well with the masses when they know a man is on top. His voice was lower tonight; he rarely shouted as he usually does; and he did not once cry out hysterically as I've seen him do so often from this rostrum.

His lengthy speech, to be sure, was full of his usual distortions and outright lies. He could not refrain from more personal insults hurled at Churchill, who, I mused, really had his goat. But the address was moderate in tone, considering that he was celebrating an astonishing military victory. And it was shrewdly calculated, I thought, to appeal to his own people, to those in the still neutral lands and to give the British people, bracing with the few means they still had, after the debacle in France, to meet an invasion of their island, something to ponder. I had no doubt as I listened that he believed (falsely, I was sure) he might well succeed in separating the masses of Britain from their government.

From Britain I now hear only a single cry — not of the people but of the politicians — that the war must go on! I do not know whether these politicians already have a correct idea of what the continuation of this struggle will be like. They do, it is true, declare they will carry on the war and that even if Great Britain should perish, they would carry on from Canada.

Hitler now loosed his sarcasm.

I can hardly believe that they mean that the people of Britain are to go to Canada. Presumably only those gentlemen interested in the continuation of their war will go there. The people, I'm afraid, will have to remain in Britain and . . . will certainly regard the war with other eyes than their so-called leaders in Canada.

Believe me, gentlemen, I feel a deep disgust for this type of unscrupulous politician who wrecks whole nations. It almost causes me pain to think that I should have been selected by fate to deal the final blow to the structure which these men have already set tottering. . . . Mr. Churchill . . . no doubt will already be in Canada. . . . For millions of other people, however, great suffering will begin. Mr. Churchill ought perhaps, for once, to believe me when I prophesy that a great Empire will be destroyed — an Empire which it was never my intention to destroy or even to harm. . . .

Harmless Hitler! His mien took on the angelic look of a choirboy. He paused, looked over the audience in the ornate old Kroll Opera

House, the paunchy Reichstag deputies in brown party or gray military uniforms directly in front of him, some fifty or so gold-braided generals assembled in the first balcony, their chests heaving with decorations, and continued in a low, resonant voice. He had reached the main point of his speech. He was contriving to make it a most solemn moment.

In this hour I feel it to be my duty before my own conscience to appeal once more to reason and common sense in Great Britain as well as elsewhere. I consider myself in a position to make this appeal since I am not the vanquished begging favors, but the victor speaking in the name of reason.

Another pause.

I can see no reason why this war must go on.

There was no applause, no cheering, no stamping of heavy boots. There was silence. And it was eloquent.

I am grieved to think of the sacrifices which it will claim. I should like to avert them, also for my own people.

He looked as solemn as a bishop.

The shabby deputies and the bemedaled generals seemed deeply moved. I thought of the millions of Germans listening to the broadcast of the speech on the radio that evening. It was to them — as well as to the British — that the speech was addressed. They, too, must be moved. This appeal to them was a masterpiece. For now they would say, I was sure, that the Führer had offered England peace, with no conditions attached. He had said himself he saw no reason why this war must go on. If it did, why it was England's fault.

But most of his hearers were convinced that the British would accept Hitler's "generous" offer of peace. I chatted with some of them, deputies and army officers, as the Reichstag session was breaking up. They seemed to take it for granted that the British would be grateful for the opportunity the Führer was giving them to get out of the war. They thought Hitler had been most magnanimous. How could the British turn him down?

At the Rundfunk where I arrived to do a broadcast on the speech the optimism was even greater. Junior officers from the High Command and junior officials from the Foreign Office were even more optimistic. The war in the West was as good as over, they said. The British were a sensible people. They knew a good thing when they got it. They would opt for peace.

Someone in the room turned on the radio to pick up a BBC broadcast in German from London. Perhaps it would give us the first inkling of British reaction to Hitler's "peace" speech. Not much more than an hour had passed since Hitler ceased speaking and it was probably, I thought, too early to expect any reaction from London.

But now came the calm voice of a BBC announcer giving a resounding *no* to Hitler's proposal. Great Britain, he said, utterly rejected it. My German associates in the room were struck dumb. They were dazed. They couldn't believe their ears. "The British, they are crazy!" one naval officer kept muttering.[*]

Hitler couldn't believe the swift British reaction either. On July 21, three days later, he reminded his confidants that thus far only the British press and radio had made statements and that one must await definite word from the Churchill government. It came the next day. Lord Halifax, the foreign secretary, in a broadcast from London made the British rejection official.

My diary reminds me that I found many "angry faces" in the Wilhelmstrasse that afternoon following the Halifax broadcast. The official spokesman of the Foreign Office told us: "Lord Halifax has refused to accept the peace offer of the Führer. Gentlemen, there will be war!"

But how? Where? With what? Obviously the next logical step was the invasion of Britain. But, so far as I could ascertain, the German High Command, for all its brilliance, had not given this much thought. It did not know how to further exploit its glittering summer's success in overrunning France and the Low Countries.

This is one of the great paradoxes of the Third Reich, though I cannot say I was much aware of it at the time. At the moment when Hitler believed he had achieved the greatest military victory in the history of his soldiering nation, when his armies occupied most of Europe, from the Arctic Circle to the Pyrenees, from the Atlantic to beyond the Vistula, he had no idea how to go on and bring the war to a victorious conclusion.

---

[*] Listening to the BBC broadcast I assumed that the announcer was simply the mouthpiece of the British government, but I wondered how Downing Street could have reacted so swiftly. Churchill later declared that the brusque and prompt rejection of Hitler's peace offering was made "by the BBC without any prompting from H.M. Government as soon as Hitler's speech was heard over the radio." Obviously, the prime minister did not think any *official* statement was necessary.

In retrospect I can see it was because the Germans, despite all their military talents, lacked a grand strategic concept. Their horizons were limited — they had always been limited — to *war on land* against neighboring countries on the European continent. Hitler admitted he had a horror of the sea ("On land I am a hero, but on water I am a coward," he had said once) and his generals suffered almost a total ignorance of it. They were *land*-minded, not *sea*-minded, as the British were.[*]

Now in July they hesitated. Their triumphant armies could easily crush the weakened forces in Britain, survivors of Dunkirk mostly, if only they could get over the Channel — so narrow between Calais and Dover that on a fair day you could see across to the opposite shore. It was an obstacle that baffled them — hence their hesitation.

Was it to stir them up that Hitler had made a dramatic break in the midst of his peace speech in the Reichstag to promote a dozen of his generals to the rank of field marshal? I had watched the scene, unprecedented in German history, with considerable amazement.

Suddenly, while praising his generals for leading their armies to the stupendous victories in the West, Hitler paused and began to name twelve of them field marshals. For Hermann Göring, the Luftwaffe chief and, incidentally, president of the Reichstag, who already was a field marshal, Hitler created a new title: Reich Marshal of the

---

[*] The German navy, sea-minded as *it* was, also appeared baffled by the problem of a landing in England. Admiral Erich Raeder, the naval commander-in-chief, conferred with Hitler on July 11 and was exceedingly cool to the idea of an invasion. He urgently advised that it be attempted "only as a last resort." In his own confidential report of the meeting, he noted that he had told the Führer: "The C. in C., Navy, [Raeder] cannot for his part advocate an invasion of Britain as he did in the case of Norway."

At the end of July in another confab with the Führer, who pressed the admiral to give him a definite date for the crossing, Raeder replied that September 15 — six weeks hence — would be the "earliest possible date" and that would depend on the weather. When Hitler inquired about the weather on the Channel at that time of year Raeder replied that it was terrible and proceeded to give his chief a long lecture on the subject. There was the constant likelihood of fog and heavy seas.

"The operation," he said, "can be carried out only if the sea is *calm*," which it almost never was. If the water was rough, he warned, the barges, on which most of the troops, tanks and supplies in the first waves would have to be ferried, would sink, and even the big ships would be helpless, since they could not unload supplies. Raeder became gloomier as he droned on. "Even if the first wave crosses successfully under favorable weather conditions, there is *no* guarantee that the same favorable weather will carry through the second and third waves. . . . As a matter of fact we must realize that no traffic worth mentioning will be able to cross for several days until certain harbors can be utilized."

That would leave the army in a fine pickle, stranded on the beaches without supplies and reinforcements, and the army brass — Brauchitsch, Keitel, Halder and Jodl were at the meeting — was not pleased to hear it. Raeder had been trying for a month to make the Warlord forget the whole business. Now he came to his conclusion.

"All things considered," he said, "the best time for the operation would be May, 1941" — ten months hence.

Greater German Reich, which put him above all the others. Not content with this, Hitler created a new decoration for him: the Grand Cross of the Iron Cross, the only one given in the entire war, or ever.

Göring was delighted. Sitting up on the dais of the Speaker in all his bulk he acted like a happy child playing with his toys on Christmas morning. When Hitler handed him a small box with the new decoration, Göring fingered it with boyish pride, grinning from ear to ear, and as soon as the Leader had returned to the rostrum he pried open the lid enough to sneak a glance at the glittering medal.

That Hitler would name so many field marshals seemed to me to debase the value of what had hitherto been the highest grade a great commander could reach in the Prussian-German army. Nine army generals, Brauchitsch, Keitel, Rundstedt, Bock, Leeb, List, Kluge, Witzleben and Reichenau were promoted to field marshal; as were three air force generals, Milch, Kesselring and Sperrle. During the Great War, I recalled, Kaiser Wilhelm II had named only five new field marshals — not even General Ludendorff, second in importance to Hindenburg, had been made one.

This time, I noted, General Franz Halder, the brilliant chief of the army General Staff and believed by many to be the brains of the German army, was passed over, being promoted merely one grade, from lieutenant- to colonel-general. It must have been, I speculated, because General Halder was one of the few generals to speak up to the dictator. Halder, it will be remembered, had led the generals' plot to overthrow Hitler at the time of Munich. Had Hitler learned of this? I watched Halder warmly congratulating his younger generals who would now, as field marshals, outrank him. His classically intellectual face, unusual for a general, seemed to be masking a weariness and a sadness.

There were two other characters, both foreigners, whom I remember watching that evening of Hitler's speech to the Reichstag. One was Count Ciano, Mussolini's son-in-law and foreign minister, who had been flown up from Rome to put the seal of Axis authority on the Führer's offer of peace to Britain. I had met him in Rome and had rather liked him despite his pompousness and clowning. There was something human and decent in him underneath all his foolish Fascist strutting. But on this evening in the Reichstag Ciano cut a sorry figure. In his gray and black Fascist militia uniform and seated in the first row of the diplomatic box in the first balcony, Ciano kept jumping up constantly like a jack-in-the-box every time Hitler paused for breath and snapping out the Fascist salute with his right arm. It was ludicrous. Even, I think, to the Germans.

Toward the back of the diplomatic box I espied a pig-eyed little man, crouching in a corner seat. This was Quisling, who, someone told me, had come down to Berlin from Oslo to beg Hitler to reinstate him in power in Norway.*

* Hitler did, on September 25, naming him head of a new government. The same day the Nazi Warlord formally "deposed" the king of Norway, now a refugee in England.

The author (extreme left) with other correspondents being briefed by General von Reicheman (center right) during the battle of the Scheldt in Belgium, May, 1940

The author with the German army passing a typical scene on the road west of Brussels, 1940

*A piece of German heavy artille
during the Battle of France, 19*

*German infantry crossing
Rhine, 1940*

*German machine-gun units, B
tle of France, 1940*

*A giant 72-ton French tank ca
tured by the Germans, 1940*

The bombing of Dunkirk

British soldiers wading out to ships at Dunkirk, June, 1940

The evacuation of Dunkirk, June, 1940

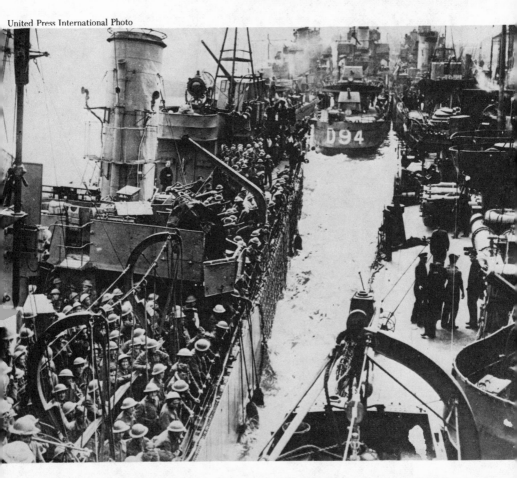

A Nazi swastika covers the Alsace-Lorraine monument at Compiègne commemorating the German defeat in World War I. German war flags covered the lettering the day Hitler viewed it.

RIGHT: *The author preparing his broadcast on the armistice from Compiègne, June 22, 1940*

In Marshal Foch's old armistice car, General Keitel reading Hitler's conditions in the presence of the Führer. Hess in center, at table; French delegation at right. June 21, 1940

CHAPTER 17

Sea Lion *and the Battle of Britain*

1940

We know now from the German secret military records that on July 16, three days before his "peace" speech, Hitler issued "Directive No. 16 on the Preparation of a Landing Operation Against England." He was riled that the British didn't have the sense to know they were beaten.

> Since England, despite her militarily hopeless situation, still shows no sign of willingness to come to terms, I have decided to prepare a landing operation against England, and if necessary to carry it out.
> The aim of this operation is to eliminate the English homeland as a base for the carrying on of the war against Germany, and if it should become necessary, to occupy it completely.

The code name for the assault was to be *Sea Lion.* Preparations for it were to be completed by mid-August. But the Nazi Warlord had not really made up his mind. Five days later, on July 21, as he gathered his generals about him in Berlin, he admitted that it was not clear what on earth "was going on in England." He was clear though on one thing:

> England's situation is hopeless. The war has been won by us. A reversal of the prospects of success is impossible.

England's situation might be hopeless — it seemed so to everyone but the English — but that did not mean that Hitler could ferry his troops across the Channel and take advantage of the enemy's "hope-lessness." He, his admirals, his generals, had not yet figured out how to get across that narrow body of water. On July 29 the Naval War Staff drew up another memorandum advising "against undertaking the operation this year." Instead it proposed that "it be considered in May, 1941, or thereafter."

But Hitler insisted it be "considered" now. On July 31, again con-voking his military chiefs, he urged them to get on with the job and to come up with a date for the invasion. Raeder, repeating that "the best time for the operation" would be in the following spring, was overruled. The navy, Hitler declared, would not be any stronger, compared to the British navy, by spring. The British army, which after Dunkirk was now in poor shape, might become a formidable force of thirty to forty-five divisions if it were given eight to ten months to rebuild. Therefore, he said, he had come to a decision, which Halder noted down.

> Diversions in Africa should be studied. But the decisive result can be achieved only by an attack on England. An attempt must therefore be made to prepare the operation for September 15, 1940. . . . The decision as to whether the operation is to take place in September or is to be delayed until May 1941, will be made after the Luftwaffe has made concentrated attacks on southern England for one week. If the effect of the air attacks is such that the enemy air force, harbors, naval forces, etc., are heavily damaged, Operation *Sea Lion* will be carried out in 1940. Otherwise it is to be postponed until May 1941.

So all now depended on the Luftwaffe.

Throughout July and the first week of August the German air force had gradually stepped up its attacks on British shipping in the Channel and on Britain's southern ports, causing considerable damage, though at some cost. A total of 296 German aircraft, mostly bombers, were lost and 136 damaged. The R.A.F. lost 148 fighters. On August 11, I noted in my diary, the German air attacks had in-creased in intensity. German bombers in large numbers, protected by swarms of Messerschmitt 109 fighters, attacked all along the south-ern coast.

On August 12, Göring gave orders to launch Operation *Eagle* (*Adler-angriffe*) the next day. This was to be a massive assault on Brit-ain with the largest air force ever assembled. It would be carried out by three great air fleets, comprising most of the planes the Germans had. Airfleet No. 2 under Field Marshal Kesselring operated from captured air bases in the Low Countries and northern France, while

Airfleet No. 3 under Field Marshal Sperrle was based on French air-fields in northern France. Together the two had a total of 929 fighters, 875 bombers and 316 dive-bombers. Airfleet No. 5 under General Stumpff operated from bases acquired in Denmark and Norway. It had 123 bombers and 34 twin-engined Messerschmitt 110 fighters. Against this array Britain had some eight hundred fighters, Hurricanes and Spitfires, to defend the island.

One day after *Adler* began, on August 14, I flew from Berlin to the Channel to watch what soon would be called the Battle of Britain, one of the most decisive battles in history and the first such in the air. If the Luftwaffe were successful — and Göring was boasting it would destroy the R.A.F. in a few days — I would then cross over with the German army and cover the invasion of Britain, the first since the Norman Conquest of William the Conqueror in 1066. It would be a tremendous story, but as with the attack on France I did not look forward to it. Not that I believed it would be successful. Making my rounds in the Wilhelmstrasse on August 1, I had taken two bets from Nazi officials: one, that the swastika would be flying over Trafalgar Square by August 15; the other, by September 7. I bet no.

Before leaving Berlin I had once more gone for a briefing to my naval friend at the American embassy, the one who had coached me the previous Christmas on how to identify the German warships at Kiel. He now instructed me on how to tell if the Germans were actually going to invade across the Channel.

"If they're serious," he said, "they will have to have assembled in Antwerp and the Channel ports an immense amount of shipping. Not only all the warships they've got left after their heavy losses in Norway — to protect their invasion fleet against superior British naval forces and the R.A.F. But more important, the ships to carry over their troops, ammunition, supplies, artillery, tanks. Just to convey ten to twelve divisions, an absolute minimum for the first wave, and to keep their supplies coming until they establish a secure beachhead will take at least fifty transport ships, a thousand seagoing barges and five hundred sea-going tugboats to haul the barges."*

He doubted that the Germans had the barges or even the tugboats. They could scare up a lot from the inland waterways, but these small craft would be of little use in the choppy waters of the Channel, which would swamp most of them.

Of course, he pointed out, even if the Germans could assemble the

---

* Specially designed landing craft had not yet been developed.

shipping, their invasion could not succeed until they had wiped the R.A.F. from the skies. You could not land a large body of troops on hostile beaches defended by strafing fighter planes and bombers blasting at your troops going ashore. And the Germans could not really land any sizable forces in England until the British navy was first disposed of. From what my friend had heard in German naval circles, British warships were patroling the south coast in considerable strength. Göring had boasted his Luftwaffe would soon destroy them all, as well as the R.A.F. But the German navy was most skeptical.

There was another piece of intelligence he had picked up from German naval circles. The R.A.F was already pounding the Channel ports, making it difficult for the Germans to assemble their landing craft in them. This surprised me. OKW had not admitted the existence of such attacks.

"So keep your eye on these night attacks on German shipping in the Channel ports — not only from British bombers, but from British warships," he went on. "It is very important to know if they are preventing the Germans from concentrating their shipping for the jump-off.

"More important, try to estimate as accurately as you can the number of transports, barges and tugs being assembled. Look for them not only in the ports, Antwerp, Ostend, Calais, Boulogne, Havre, Cherbourg, but in the rivers and canals back of these ports. And try to see if they have crews ready. If you find they've got the shipping," he warned, "and the surface warships and submarines to protect it, and that they've cleared the Channel of British warships and the R.A.F. overhead, they'll probably invade. If not, not — no matter what they tell you."

I told him I realized the Germans might try to use us to help bluff the British into thinking they were about to invade.

"That's why this assignment of yours is so important," he said as he escorted me to the door of his office. "Keep your eyes open. Aside from the battle in the air, which no one can predict, it all depends on whether they've got the shipping. That's what you must look for!"

We had a bit of a scare coming in to land at a Belgian military airfield outside of Ghent. We had flown low, between five hundred and a thousand feet, all the way from Berlin so that trigger-happy anti-aircraft crews would recognize us as friendly — they had shot down too many of their own planes, the pilot said. Suddenly, south of Antwerp two fighters dove at us out of the clouds. Our pilot dove too at the sight of them, as steeply as he could in a clumsy JU-52 transport plane. I must say the fighters looked to me like British Spitfires, and I remembered hearing of a German general who was shot down by a Spitfire between Paris and Brussels a few days before. But as we lurched toward the landing field, the two fighters veered off. For the first time in my life I was happy to see the German cross painted on a plane. They were Messerschmitt 109's.

Late that afternoon we took off in cars for the coast, skirting around Bruges, a lovely Gothic town in which I had spent my first night on the Continent exactly fifteen years ago. Driving into Ostend I kept my eyes open for the invasion ships, but I could make out very few craft of any kind. The vessels in the harbor were mostly Belgian fishing ships. In the canals behind the town there were only a few barges. No tugs to haul them. The Germans were certainly not going to launch much of an invasion from Ostend. Our German military guides put us up at a Belgian hotel called the Piccadilly. Was that supposed to be a portent?

Next morning, August 15, driving down the Channel coast to Dunkirk and Calais, what impressed me were the *defensive* measures of the Germans, and this puzzled me greatly. Here we were being taken on a trip along the Channel that might lead to our covering a German invasion of Britain, and all around us were signs that the Germans were preparing to meet a British landing in France. A line of trenches, dugouts and machine-gun nests, strongly manned, stretched along the sand dunes a hundred yards from the water's edge all the way down to Dunkirk. Immediately behind them were anti-aircraft batteries and a quarter of a mile farther to the rear, clusters of artillery.

What about the jumping-off places for the invasion? Surely the Germans would be concentrating troops, guns, tanks, ammunition, supplies here by now. "No evidence at any place along the coast so far of German preparations for an invasion," I jotted down in my notebook.

The sight of the famed beaches around Dunkirk cheered me as I thought of all the British troops who had got away. Probably they were already deployed on the beaches on the far shore. But did they have anything to fight with? For here, stretched along the Dunkirk beaches as far as the eye could see, were mountains of arms they had had to leave behind. German army mechanics were working on them, stripping off the rubber tires from the trucks, the guns from the tanks, and trying to get both to run so they could remove them from the coast. I had never seen such a vast amount of military hardware in my life.

We had scarcely sat down to lunch on the terrace of our hotel in Calais, before we heard a wave of German bombers roaring overhead toward the cliffs of Dover. They were flying high — at least twelve thousand feet, I estimated — but I could make out twenty-three of them, with a swarm of Messerschmitt 109 fighters above. Already excitement among our military guides was mounting. Coming into Calais from Dunkirk they had begun dropping hints that this day, Thursday, August 15, 1940, might be an historic one. The Luftwaffe might be carrying out, if the weather held, its most murderous attack yet against Britain.

As it turned out, August 15 saw the biggest engagement of the Battle of Britain, with more planes in action than had ever been seen before. The Luftwaffe flew 1,950 sorties, the R.A.F. nearly a thousand, as they joined battle over a front of five hundred miles. It was one of the decisive battles of history and, along with a similar one exactly a month later, on September 15, determined the fate of Britain and indeed of Nazi Germany.*

The battle this crucial day was far from over as we set off after lunch and drove along the coast to Cap Gris-Nez, the nearest point to England. Passing the harbor in Calais I noted that here, too, there was no concentration of shipping for an invasion. All I could see were a few small ships, a dozen or so barges and three torpedo boats. Could the Germans be bluffing about their invasion of Britain? In the fifty-mile stretch of coast from Ostend to Calais I had seen nothing to indicate that the Germans were ready, or even preparing, to cross the Channel. I understood well enough that until they wiped the Royal Air Force from the skies they could not risk an assault on the British beaches. But supposing the Luftwaffe succeeded in making good Göring's boast to destroy the R.A.F. in a few days? It seemed strange to me that the German army and navy were not yet in any position at all to take immediate advantage of that, if it happened, and launch the invasion. But first things first. At the moment the Germans were concentrating on eliminating the R.A.F., and we were here to witness it.

On the road to Cap Gris-Nez the air overhead was almost choked

* Two dates "of supreme consequence," Winston Churchill later called them. "August 15," he wrote, "was the largest air battle of this period of the war; five major actions were fought, on a front of five hundred miles. It was indeed a crucial day." (Churchill: *The Second World War.* Vol. II, *Their Finest Hour*, pp. 321, 325.)

by German bombers and fighters roaring toward England or limping back. We halted to watch a large squadron of Heinkel bombers returning. Three or four were having a hard time. One, nearly out of control, just managed to reach a wheat field behind the sea cliffs. Messerschmitt 109 fighters dashed about at 350 miles an hour to see that the crippled bombers landed safely, and then turned and headed across the Channel to help protect another wave of bombers on their way back.

Peasants were at work in the lush fields harvesting the brown-ripe wheat. They did not look up to watch the roaring machines, but sat on their horse-drawn mowers and watched the swath of grain they were cutting. The thought popped into my head: *Who's being civilized now?*

We passed a big German naval gun on a railroad carriage; it had been firing on Dover. We had heard it from miles away — the sound had become more deafening as we approached. It was answering a big British gun that had been firing from Dover. We had heard the thuds of the shells exploding, but so far they had not come near us.

As we turned down a road that lead to Cap Gris-Nez and the beaches below the cliffs I was once again struck by the German *defensive* measures: gangs of French laborers, some of them prisoners-of-war, for they were still in uniform, were at work digging trenches, pillboxes and artillery emplacements.

"Isn't that against the Geneva Convention, making P.O.W.'s work on your military installations?" I asked a German army officer in our car.

He did not reply. Perhaps he did not hear. A swarm of bombers and fighters had just passed overhead. When the roar had died down I asked him: "Why all these defensive measures? You don't expect the British to invade, do you? I thought you brought us up here to watch *you* invade."

"A good army takes no chances," he said. He pointed across the Channel — "Please be patient. You'll get your trip over soon enough. I guarantee you that."

We climbed back up the cliff behind the beach. The din of the bombers and fighters going and coming was now almost continuous. They crossed over rather high on the way out, some fifteen thousand feet I estimated, and were soon lost in the skies. Through field glasses we could see the cliffs of Dover and occasionally even spot a sausage balloon protecting the harbor.

The sea directly below us had become as smooth as glass. German patrol boats darted about, hugging the coast. With the sea so calm, German seaplanes with big Red Cross signs painted on their wings were lighting on the water and taxiing to the beach to discharge what I took to be German flyers, some of them wounded. Then the planes would take off and head to sea. This sight surprised me. We had seen no dog-fights over the Channel. In fact, we had not seen a single Spitfire or Hurricane all day.

"How come the wounded?" I asked a Luftwaffe captain in our party. "We haven't seen any British planes all day."

"You can't see them from here," he explained. "The air battles are almost entirely over the land, beyond the Channel. Some of our planes that are hit try to make it for home. . . . Not all make it. Some come down in the water. We try to rescue the crews. That's why you're seeing these Red Cross rescue planes."

His face darkened.

"I think it my duty to add something to what I told you," he said. "It is very serious. The British are violating the Geneva Convention. They are firing on our Red Cross planes! It is a criminal act! I hope, gentlemen, you will report it."

Aside from the hypocrisy, I didn't believe the man. When I had followed the German army across Belgium and France in June I had noted that many huge gasoline trucks, which the Germans were using to fuel their tanks, had large Red Cross signs painted on them to ward off British flyers. They abused the Red Cross designation at will. As to the captain's accusations, I doubted whether the British were firing on these German Red Cross planes.

But they were, as I would learn much later from Churchill, who not only admitted it, but justified it.

> German transport planes, marked with the Red Cross, began to ap-
> pear in some numbers over the Channel in July and August whenever
> there was an air fight. We did not recognize this means of rescuing
> enemy pilots who had been shot down in action, in order that they
> might come and bomb our civil population again. We rescued them
> ourselves whenever it was possible, and made them prisoners of war.
> But all German air ambulances were forced or shot down by our fight-
> ers on definite orders approved by the War Cabinet. The German
> crews and doctors on these machines professed astonishment at being
> treated in this way, and protested that it was contrary to the Geneva
> Convention. There was no mention of such a contingency in the Ge-
> neva Convention, which had not contemplated this form of warfare.
> The Germans were not in a strong position to complain, in view of all

the treaties, laws of war, and solemn agreements which they had violated without compunction whenever it suited them. They soon abandoned the experiment, and the work of sea rescue for both sides was carried out by our small craft, on which, of course, the Germans fired on every occasion.°

About 6 P.M. we saw sixty bombers — Heinkels and Junker 82's — protected by a hundred Messerschmitt fighters wing high overhead toward Dover. It was the biggest attacking squadron we had seen all day. In three or four minutes we could hear the British anti-aircraft guns around Dover going into action. Judging by the deep roar, the British had a number of heavy flak guns, probably the equivalent of the German 88's. Another deeper thud came from their bombs falling farther inland. An hour later what looked to us like the same bombing squadron returned. We could count only eighteen bombers from the original sixty. Had the British shot down the rest? I realized our count was far from conclusive. German bomber pilots often had orders to return to other fields than those from which they had taken off. For one thing it prevented the airmen at the takeoff field from knowing what the losses really were.

I was surprised at the pounding Calais harbor took that night from British bombers. Were the Germans moving ships into the port under cover of darkness? There had not been too much to bomb when we passed the harbor that afternoon. But it now was being severely pummeled.

"It is 3 A.M. now," I noted in my diary, and German flak has been firing at top speed since 11:30 P.M., shortly after dark." As I listened to the din of anti-aircraft fire and exploding bombs I thought of Hitler's recent speech assuring the German people that the R.A.F. was not attacking German military objectives but only civilians in the cities.

After the Germans in our party had gone to bed, we sat in the back room with the French proprietor of the hotel and drank *vin rouge* to each British bomb that we could hear crashing.

Next day, August 16, the great battle in the air seemed to taper slightly.† Perhaps both sides were licking their wounds. The Germans had been hurt more than they admitted. In fact, it was only much later I learned that while they had done quite well in the south of England, opposite to where on the French coast we had been

---

° Churchill: *Their Finest Hour*, pp. 322–323.

† Postwar official figures showed the Germans flew 1,715 sorties; the British, 776.

watching all day, they had suffered a crushing defeat in the air off the northeast coast of Britain in the region of the Tyneside.

Believing that the British had concentrated all their fighter planes for the defense of southern England, the Germans struck north of the Wash with one hundred Heinkel III bombers, protected by thirty-four twin-engined Messerschmitt 110 fighters from Airfleet No. 5, based in Denmark and Norway. To their surprise, as they approached the coast they were met head-on by seven squadrons of Hurricanes and Spitfires, which had been withdrawn from the intense fighting in the south for a rest and also to guard against just such an attack. Thirty of the one hundred bombers were shot down with no loss to the British except two fighter pilots wounded. That was the end of Airfleet No. 5 in the Battle of Britain.

In the south of England, from the outskirts of London to the Channel, the Luftwaffe had had better luck. They had mounted four massive attacks, one of which was able to penetrate almost to London. Four aircraft factories near the civil airfield at Croydon were hit and five R.A.F. fighter fields damaged.

We kept asking the German officers who led our little party for permission to talk to some of the returning bomber and fighter pilots, either on or off the record, but Göring, apparently directing the Luftwaffe from his luxurious palace of Karinhall outside Berlin, would not allow it. This was a setback. I had heard from one of the airmen that the great German fighter ace Major Adolf Galland was in the vicinity and I had asked specifically if we could talk to him. He was said to be an extremely intelligent and sensitive young pilot and I felt that we could get a much better picture of how it looked to the German airmen over England if we could talk to him. I was turned down.

Had I been able to talk to Galland, I might have learned of a serious tactical error that Göring made at the end of the day's battles on August 15 that would profoundly affect the outcome of the Battle of Britain. He might have revealed, as he did later, because it was directly concerned with Göring's decision, a secret of Britain's air defenses which already was having a decisive effect on the world's first great battle in the air.

The skill of British Fighter Command in committing its planes to battle against superior attacking forces was based on its shrewd use of radar. From the moment they took off the German craft were spotted on British radar screens, and their course so accurately plotted that Fighter Command knew exactly where and when they could best be attacked. This was something new in air warfare and it puzzled the Germans, who were far behind the British in its development.

"We realized," Major Galland later told the Allies,

> that the R.A.F. fighter squadrons must be controlled from the ground by some new procedure because we heard [on our radios] commands skillfully and accurately directing Spitfires and Hurricanes on to German formations. . . . For us this radar and fighter control was a surprise, and a very bitter one.

Nonetheless that night of August 15 back in Berlin Göring made a strange decision. He called off the attacks on British radar stations. No doubt he had no inkling that on August 12 the Luftwaffe's attacks against R.A.F. radar stations in the south of England had been disastrous to the British. Five of the radar stations were hit and damaged; a sixth was completely knocked out. If this continued the R.A.F. fighter defense of England would be fatally handicapped. But the day we watched from the French side of the Channel they were abruptly called off.

"It is doubtful," Göring explained in his order, "whether there is any point in continuing the attacks on radar stations, since not one of those attacked so far has been put out of action."

The British were reprieved.

On the morning of August 16 we continued down the coast to Boulogne. On the way we passed three airfields, beautifully camouflaged, stuffed with German bombers. At intervals they would take off and head toward the British coast. It was difficult for us to appraise how the great battle in the air was going. Obviously, the Germans had not yet achieved two conditions for the invasion of Britain. They had not yet cleared the skies over southern England of the R.A.F. And so far as I could see they had not assembled the shipping necessary to carry an invasion force over the Channel. In the harbor at Boulogne I could make out only a few barges, half a dozen tugs and the same number of torpedo boats. There was considerable damage around the port, as there was at Calais, from the British night bombing. German army engineers were busy clearing it up. But where was the shipping?, I kept wondering. Perhaps we would see it that afternoon on our way back to Brussels. We were returning via St. Omer, in the vicinity of which, I recalled, were a number of canals, rivers and streams — the ones that had held up the German tanks before Dunkirk.

There was considerable shipping backed up in these waterways, and I saw what under the camouflage looked like barges and pontoons loaded with artillery and tanks; but certainly not enough, I noted in my notebook, "to begin an invasion of England with."

I began to grow suspicious.

Why did the officers in charge of our little party halt the bus so we could peek at these craft loaded with artillery and tanks? They were the first such we had seen. And why did our military guides start hinting that we were seeing only the tip of the iceberg? There was much more, they kept implying, that they could not show us.

"Maybe," I jotted down in my notebook, as we drove along through battered Lille and Tournai, "but I'm suspicious. I think the Germans want us to launch a scare story about an imminent invasion of Britain."

My suspicions, I guess, had first been aroused that morning when our military guides had abruptly announced that they were taking us late that afternoon back to Brussels, where the newspaper correspondents would find good telephone lines to Berlin and I would have at my disposal a special line of high quality for radio broadcasting. Why were the Germans being so accommodating?

The answer became apparent when we arrived in Brussels early that evening. At military headquarters we were briefed by some general, who said in effect: "Gentlemen, you have seen for yourselves. The Luftwaffe has gained mastery of the skies over Britain. That was the one requirement for our invasion. In a few days the R.A.F. will be completely eliminated. Then we can begin. We naturally cannot tell you the invasion date. But we are relaxing military censorship in order to allow you to report what you have seen the past few days on the Channel."

I asked the general about the shipping. We had not seen very much — certainly not enough for an invasion.

The general smiled. I wondered if he was an official in disguise from Goebbels' Propaganda Ministry.

"Admittedly," he said smoothly, "there are things we cannot show the press. But I believe you have seen enough to convince you that we are ready to invade."

I had certainly not seen enough.

We were taken to our hotel, where special rooms had been set up for us with direct telephone lines to Berlin. I did not intend to use the special one reserved for me. I had decided that the Germans were not going to invade — at least not now. Regardless of how the great battle in the air was going — and I could not say yet as to that —

they simply had not assembled enough shipping to launch an invasion. And what little shipping they had in the Channel ports was being pummeled every night by R.A.F. bombers.

I knew the Germans would not permit me to say that. It was quite understandable in the midst of war, and I had no quarrel with it. Their game at the moment obviously was to bluff the British into believing that invasion was imminent and that it would be wise for them to accept Hitler's offer to end the war. Then the Nazi dictator could turn on Russia. That was becoming all too clear. But I would have no part of it. To broadcast now and say that the Germans were all set to invade would be not only to lie, but to do the beleaguered British a terrible disservice that could be fatal. Our responsibility was all the greater because as Americans we were neutral and therefore considered to be fair and objective. The British would not believe a German boast that Hitler was about to invade their isle. But they might believe neutral American observers. It suddenly occurred to me that we American correspondents, representatives of the three wire services, the A.P., the U.P. and INS and myself for CBS radio, were faced with a decision that had consequences far more serious than we had ever experienced. The decision was not difficult for me. I would not broadcast.

With no script to prepare, no work to do except in my diary, which could wait, I went down to the bar, had a drink, and then moved on to the restaurant, where I had a hearty dinner — for the food was still quite good in Brussels despite the German occupation.

Soon after I returned to my room about 10 P.M., there was a knock on the door. An official from the German Broadcasting Company, whom I knew, and one of the military guides to our little party came in.

"We've got an excellent line for you to Berlin," the radio man said. "When do you want to broadcast?"

"And no censorship this time," the army captain said. "You are free to tell what you've seen the past few days."

"I'm not broadcasting," I said.

They seemed stunned. Before they could regain their voices, I added: "Gentlemen, I appreciate your setting up the line to Berlin. But I cannot use it. I won't be broadcasting. . . ."

"And why not?" the radio official broke in to ask.

"Because I do not believe, from what I've seen, you're going to invade, at least for now."

The two Germans made some noises, but found no words.

"I do not expect you to allow me to say that," I said. "That would be a military secret. But you must not expect me to broadcast what I don't believe."

Later that evening, Fred Oechsner, head of the United Press bureau in Berlin, and a correspondent whose integrity I had always respected, came by. In his hands was a sheaf of cablegrams. From his New York office, he said.

The A.P. and INS were clobbering U.P. and grabbing all the headlines in the afternoon papers with their eyewitness stories that the Germans were all set to invade Britain. The New York office wanted to know what had happened to its correspondent.

"I guess this will finish me," Fred said. "But I honestly couldn't say they were set to invade when obviously they are not."

Fred and I had not actually discussed it. He had come to his own conclusion, as I had.

"How did you handle it in your broadcast?" Fred asked.

"I didn't broadcast," I said. "For the same reason you didn't cable anything."

"How do you account for Louis and Pierre doing it?" Fred asked. Louis Lochner was head of the A.P. bureau in Berlin; Pierre Huss was the INS correspondent there. Pierre, it seemed to me, had always played the Nazi game a little. Louis too, if only to get a beat, a scoop. I did not envy them. There were things more important to a journalist than scoops. The truth. And at this moment and place, when so much depended on it, especially for the British.

We now know, from the confidential records of both sides, what the status of the invasion was at that moment and during the following four weeks, what the Germans were planning and doing to launch it, and the British to repel it.

Nearly a month before our trip to the Channel, on July 17, the day after Hitler had issued Directive No. 16 to prepare the invasion (and two days before his "peace" speech), the army High Command ordered thirteen picked divisions to the jumping-off places on the Channel for the first wave of Operation *Sea Lion*. On that day the army High Command had finally completed a detailed plan for a landing on a broad front on the south coast of England.*

---

* Surprisingly, the British expected the main German attack to come on the east coast and had concentrated most of their depleted forces there. Later, when they discovered where the Germans were concentrating their divisions, they changed their dispositions, moving the bulk of their troops from the east to the south coast.

As in the Battle of France, Army Group A, under the command of Field Marshal von Rundstedt (as he would be titled on July 19) constituted the principal invasion force. Six of its infantry divisions were to embark from the Pas de Calais and hit the beaches between Ramsgate and Bexhill. Four divisions would cross the Channel from the area of Le Havre and land between Brighton and the Isle of Wight. Further to the west three divisions of Field Marshal von Reichenau's Sixth Army (which I had followed through Belgium), embarking from the Cherbourg peninsula, would be put ashore in Lyme Bay, between Weymouth and Lyme Regis. There would be altogether some ninety thousand men in the first wave whose objective it was to secure a beachhead. Reinforcements would pour in beginning with the third day so that within two weeks the Germans would have ashore some thirty-nine divisions, or two hundred sixty thousand men — a formidable force, which would include six panzer divisions and three motorized divisions. For good measure the German plan called for two divisions of airborne troops to be dropped at Lyme Bay and other places behind the British defenses to disrupt them.

The German plan also laid down the immediate objectives of the invading armies. After the beaches had been secured — a matter of three days at the most, the Germans thought — Army Group A in the southeast would push forward to its first objective, a line running from Gravesend to Southampton. Farther west Reichenau's Sixth Army would advance north from Lyme Bay to Bristol, cutting off Devon and Cornwall. Their second objective would be to reach a line between Maldon on the east coast north of the Thames estuary to the Severn River, surrounding London and blocking off Wales.

The German army High Command did not expect that it would be easy going the first few days. "Heavy battles with strong British forces," it warned, would develop. But they would be quickly won, London would be enveloped, and the drive northward resumed. The German generals, who had been so skeptical of the invasion, now seemed to have been encouraged by the very act of issuing their plan. Field Marshal von Brauchitsch, commander-in-chief of the army, told Admiral Raeder that very day that the whole operation would be finished in a month and would be relatively easy.

Raeder and his fellow admirals were not so sure. In fact, they realized the German navy could not transport, land, and protect such a large force on so extensive a front. Raeder so informed OKW a couple of days later and repeated it at a meeting in Berlin on July 21 with Hitler and the army and air force brass. On July 29 the naval War Staff put it in writing, advising Hitler and the army "against undertaking the operation this year." It proposed instead that "it be considered in May, 1941, or thereafter."

But the Nazi Warlord did not want to wait that long. He believed he had won the war. He had offered the British peace. They had turned him down. So he would finish them off now. On July 31, he insisted that preparations to invade on September 15 continue. Next day, he put it in writing in Directive No. 17 "for the Conduct of the Air and Naval Warfare against England." He also had Field Marshal Keitel, chief of OKW, issue a similar directive, settling the dispute between the army and navy about the length of the proposed landing front on the south coast of England.

> In spite of the navy's warning that it can guarantee only the defense of a narrow strip of coast (as far west as Eastbourne), preparations are to be continued for the attack on a broad basis, as originally planned. . . .

This decision only inflamed the feud between the two services. The naval War Staff already had estimated that to fulfill the demands of the army for landing a hundred thousand men with equipment and supplies in the first wave along a two-hundred-mile front from Ramsgate to Lyme Bay would necessitate rounding up 1,722 barges, 1,161 motorboats, 471 tugs and 155 transports. Even if it could be done, Admiral Raeder told Hitler, taking away so much shipping from the rivers and canals would wreck the German economy, destroying the inland-waterway transportation system on which the economic life of the country largely depended. At any rate, Raeder repeated again, supporting a landing on such a wide front in the teeth of "certain" attacks by the British navy and air force was beyond the powers of the German navy. He backed his position with a new warning he had received from the naval War Staff that if the army insisted on a broad front, the navy might lose *all* its ships. The implication was that the entire invading force might go down with *all* the ships.

But the army persisted. Overestimating British strength, it maintained that to land on a narrow front would confront the German attackers with a "superior" British land force. On August 7 there was a showdown between the two services when General Halder met his opposite number, Admiral Schniewind, the chief of the naval War

Staff. The clash was sharp and dramatic. The general, usually a rather taciturn man, was beside himself.

"I utterly reject the navy proposal," he fumed. "From the point of view of the army I regard it as complete suicide. I might as well put the troops that have landed through a sausage machine!"

But the admiral stuck to his position. "It would be equally suicidal," he said, "in view of British naval supremacy" to go along with the army plan.

The controversy continued as Field Marshal Brauchitsch, the army chief, informed OKW on August 10 that he "could not accept" a landing on the shorter front. But the fears of the navy were now taking root in OKW. On August 13, General Jodl, the brains of the Wehrmacht High Command, drafted an "appreciation of the situation," saying that no invasion should be attempted before the British navy had been "eliminated" from the south coast and the R.A.F. from the skies above it. The navy's fear and Jodl's hesitation now began to have an effect on Hitler. I had already concluded that the Nazi Warlord leaned much more heavily on Jodl than on Keitel at OKW. On August 13 and 14 Hitler again listened to the arguments of his naval and army commanders and on the sixteenth finally made a decision. The proposed invasion front was to be shortened by abandoning the landing in Lyme Bay. But as sop to his generals the Führer stipulated that while the main crossing was to be on a narrow front, as the navy wished, the army could carry out "a simultaneous landing of four to five thousand troops at Brighton by motorboats and the same number of airborne troops at Deal-Ramsgate."

General Halder, chief of the army General Staff, was not pleased. "An attack on this basis," he wrote, "has no chance of success this year." But he was addressing his diary, not his Warlord.

Not until September 1 did OKW order the movement of all available shipping from Germany's North Sea ports toward the embarkation harbors on the Channel. It was rather late for a vast landing operation which had been set to begin September 15. So on September 3 a directive from OKW postponed the landings six days — to September 21. It was the first of many postponements, revealing further uncertainties in the minds of Hitler and his military chiefs.

On September 6 Raeder had another long session with Hitler. "The Führer's decision to land in England," the admiral recorded in the Naval Staff War Diary that night, "is still by no means settled, as he is firmly convinced that Britain's defeat will be achieved even without the 'landing.' "

The uneasy admiral seems to have breathed a sigh of relief at Hitler's indecision. But to the generals it must have seemed incredible. Here was a vast amphibious military undertaking, the first attempt to invade England in nearly a thousand years, subject to a series of postponements. And the Nazi Warlord was "firmly convinced" that a landing was not necessary to ensure Britain's defeat.

When on September 3 it was put off from the fifteenth to the twenty-first, OKW had stipulated that the final order for it would be forthcoming on September 11, giving the three armed services ten days to make final preparations. But on September 10 Hitler decided to postpone his decision until the fourteenth. There seem to have been two reasons for the delay. One, it was believed at OKW that the bombing of London was causing so much destruction, both to property and to British morale, that an invasion might not be necessary.

Second, the German navy was experiencing more difficulties than it had anticipated. Besides being hampered by the weather, which naval authorities complained on September 10 was "completely abnormal and unstable," it found that the British air force, which Göring had promised to destroy by now, and the British navy, which he also had promised to put out of action, at least on the southern coast, was increasingly interfering with the concentration of the invasion fleet. The nightly bombing of the Channel ports, which we had first seen in mid-August, had now become much more devastating — "undoubtedly successful" as the naval War Staff reported that day. On September 12, two days later, Naval Group West, in immediate charge of the invasion fleet, sent an ominous warning to Berlin.

> Interruptions caused by the enemy's air forces, long-range artillery and light naval forces have, for the first time, assumed major significance. The harbors of Ostend, Dunkirk, Calais and Boulogne [the very four we had visited in August] cannot be used at night as anchorages for shipping because of the danger of English bombings and shelling. Units of the British fleet are now able to operate almost unmolested in the Channel. Owing to these difficulties further delays are expected in the assembly of the invasion fleet.

The next day was no better. British naval forces bombarded the main Channel invasion ports, Ostend, Calais, Boulogne and Cherbourg. In Ostend harbor the R.A.F. sank eighty barges. In Berlin that day and the next, September 14, Hitler again met with his military chiefs. The records we have of these meetings show amazing confusion among the participants. General Jodl got the impression, as he noted in his diary, that Hitler "apparently has decided to abandon *Sea Lion* completely." That was not quite the impression received by General Halder and Admiral Raeder. Raeder complained that the Führer would give neither the final order to launch the invasion nor the final order to call it off, despite the admiral's urging the latter. General Halder, reporting to his diary, could not quite follow the Leader's train of thought. On the one hand Hitler declared that the navy had "achieved the necessary conditions for the invasion," which astonished the General Staff chief, who knew better, and that the Luftwaffe's operations were "above all praise," which astonished the general even more. Hitler, on the other hand, conceded, according to Halder's notes:

> The enemy recovers again and again. . . . Enemy fighters have not yet been completely eliminated. Our own reports of successes do not give a completely reliable picture.

Finally Hitler came to a decision that was decidedly negative, and Halder scribbled it down.

> On the whole, then, in spite of all our successes the prerequisite conditions for Operation *Sea Lion* have not yet been realized. . . . Decision therefore: The operation will not be renounced — yet.

A new date would be given on September 17. Hitler would give the air force a few days more to knock out the R.A.F. But, as the navy continued to complain, it was the R.A.F. that was knocking out its efforts to assemble the invasion fleet.

September 17 was the decisive date.

Most of our information about that crucial day comes from the German navy. That night there was a full moon — the one the Germans had intended to take advantage of if their invasion had begun on September 15, as planned — and British night bombers made the most of it. The navy reported "very considerable losses" of shipping in the invasion ports. At Dunkirk eighty-four barges were sunk or damaged, and from Cherbourg to Den Helder in Holland the naval staff listed further losses: a 500-ton ammunition dump blown up, a rations depot burned out, various steamers, barges and torpedo boats sunk, and many casualties to personnel sustained. The severe bombings and bombardments, continued the naval staff, made it necessary to disperse the naval and transport vessels already concentrated on the Channel and to stop further movement of shipping to the invasion ports.

> Otherwise [the report concluded] with energetic enemy action such casualties will occur in the course of time that the execution of the operation on the scale previously envisaged will in any case be problematic.*

It already had become more than problematic. We owe it to the German Naval War Diary for giving us this climactic information. On the evening of September 17 some officer made a laconic entry in it.

> The enemy air force is still by no means defeated. On the contrary, it shows increasing activity. The weather situation as a whole does not permit us to expect a period of calm. . . . *The Führer therefore decides to postpone "Sea Lion" indefinitely.*

The navy diarist, obviously with great relief, underlined the last sentence.

At last, after so many years of stunning successes, the Nazi dictator had met failure. The invasion of Britain, which Hitler had been sure would end the victorious war, was called off — indefinitely. The war would go on. For a month, in order to keep up the pressure on the British, a pretense would be made that the invasion might still be launched that autumn.

---

* On September 16, according to a German authority on the Luftwaffe, R.A.F. bombers surprised a large German training exercise for the invasion off the French coast and inflicted heavy losses in men and landing craft.

This gave rise to reports in Germany and elsewhere on the Continent that the Germans had actually attempted a landing on the English coast and been repulsed. (Georg W. Feuchter: *Geschichte des Luftkriegs*, p. 176.)

I heard such a report on the night of September 16 in Geneva, Switzerland, where I was taking a few days off with my family. My diary says I took it "with a grain of salt."

Nevertheless, on September 18 and again on the next day in Berlin, to which I had returned, I saw two long ambulance trains unloading wounded soldiers. Judging by their bandages I concluded most of them were suffering burns. There had been no fighting anywhere since the fall of France three months before.

Churchill later recounted that the corpses "of about forty German soldiers were washed up at scattered points along the coast." He gives the date as August, which might have been an error. "The Germans," he writes, "had been practising embarkations in the barges along the French coast. Some of these barges put to sea in order to escape British bombing and were sunk, either by bombing or bad weather. This was the source of a widespread rumour that the Germans had attempted an invasion and had suffered very heavy losses either by drowning or by being burnt in patches of sea covered with flaming oil."

The British, the prime minister adds, "took no steps to contradict such tales." (Churchill: *Their Finest Hour*, p. 311.)

On September 19 Hitler formally ordered the further assembling of the invasion fleet to be halted, and the shipping already in the Channel ports to be dispersed, but he would not consent to dispersing the troops that had been assembled for the landings. General Halder fumed in his diary that "this state of affairs is unbearable." To Hitler he complained that holding the troops on the Channel "under constant British air attacks led to continual casualties." The army and navy wanted *Sea Lion* called off altogether.

Finally on October 12 Hitler gave in to them.

> Führer's Headquarters
> October 12, 1940
>
> TOP SECRET
>
> The Führer has decided that from now on until the spring, preparations for *Sea Lion* shall be continued solely for the purpose of maintaining political and military pressure on England.
>
> Should the invasion be reconsidered in the spring or early summer of 1941, orders for a renewal of operational readiness will be issued later. . . .

What made Hitler finally abandon the invasion of Britain that fall? Three things, it seems obvious to me.

The turning of his thoughts once more eastward, to Russia.

The inability of the German navy to provide shipping to transport the German army over the Channel to England.

And above all, the fatal course of the Battle of Britain in the air.

Let us return briefly to that engagement, the first major battle ever fought in the skies and one of the most decisive battles in history. Up to and through August 17, when our little party of American correspondents left the Channel, the Battle of Britain appeared to be going well for the British. Their Spitfires and Hurricanes were taking such a heavy toll of German bombers that Göring's aerial offensive could not long be sustained. From August 24 to September 6, after a week's lull, the Germans sent over an average of a thousand planes a day in an all-out effort to wipe out Britain's fighter defense.

The Battle of Britain entered its decisive stage. The German preponderance in sheer numbers began to tell. Five forward R.A.F. fighter fields in the south of England were badly damaged. Worse, six of the seven key sector stations were so nearly knocked out that the whole defensive communications system of the R.A.F. was on the verge of being destroyed. This threatened disaster as the sector stations, along with radar, had been the key to Britain's successful aerial defense up to now. These were the underground nerve centers from which the Hurricanes and Spitfires were guided by radiotelephone into battle on the basis of the latest intelligence from radar, from ground observation posts and from pilots in the air.

"The scales," Churchill revealed later, "had tilted against Fighter Command. In the life-and-death struggle of the two air forces, this was a decisive phase."

And then suddenly Göring, directing the battle from Karinhall, made his second tactical mistake, akin to the first when he had called off the assaults on the British radar stations. Just when he had the R.A.F. reeling, suffering losses in the air and on the ground that it could not for long sustain, he switched his air assault on September 7 to massive *night* bombings of London. The R.A.F. Fighter Command was reprieved.

Three years later, in 1943, when I returned to Britain for the first time during the war, Londoners still vividly recalled that Saturday evening, September 7, when the greatest bombing of a city ever carried out up to then reached its full fury. The onslaught began toward the end of the day, shortly after 5 P.M., when the first wave of three hundred twenty German bombers — no one had ever before seen such a huge formation of the heavy planes — escorted by every fighter the Germans could scrape up, appeared over the Thames estuary, flew up the river, and began dropping bombs on Woolwich Arsenal, various gas works, power stations, depots and on miles of docks of the port of London. In a few minutes, people remembered, the whole vast river area was a mass of flames. At one place, Silvertown, the population was surrounded by fire and had to be evacuated by water.

A little after 8 P.M., at dusk, a second wave of two hundred fifty bombers arrived to resume the attack, to be followed by more waves throughout the night to 4:30 A.M. on Sunday, when the skies began to lighten and the great assault ceased. It was renewed at dusk and continued through Sunday night. British civilian casualties for the two nights were 842 killed and 2,347 wounded and a staggering amount of damage was inflicted on the sprawling city. Some of the American correspondents who covered that flaming initiation in saturation bombing of a city told me they wondered how long the British people could take it. Hitler and Göring were encouraged by reports from the German embassy in Washington, which relayed alleged opinions from American military attachés in London that Britain could not hold up much longer in the face of such deadly bombing. According to one officer in OKW, Hitler seriously expected a revolution to break out in Britain.* Undoubtedly this erroneous impression helped persuade the Führer to keep postponing *Sea Lion*, in the belief that it might not be necessary.

The great aerial assault on the British capital went on night after night through the following week. Then, buoyed by its success, the Germans decided to carry out an immense *daylight* bombing of London. This led on Sunday, September 15, to the decisive battle in the air and to a turning point in the fortunes of war. Churchill followed it from the underground Operations Room of Number 11 Fighter Group at Uxbridge.

"We must take September 15 as the culminating date," Churchill later observed. "On this date the Luftwaffe, after two heavy attacks on the 14th, made the greatest concentrated effort in a resumed daylight attack on London. It was one of the decisive battles of the war."†

About midday two hundred German bombers, escorted by six hundred fighters, appeared over the Channel, headed for London. R.A.F.'s Fighter Command had watched on its radar screens the assembling of the attackers and was ready. Most of the bombers were intercepted before they could reach the capital and several shot down and more damaged and forced to turn back. New waves of attackers appeared and were routed. Though the British triumphantly announced they had shot down one hundred eighty-five German planes, the actual figure, as determined from Luftwaffe records after the war, was fifty-six. But thirty-four of these were bombers. The R.A.F. lost only twenty-six aircraft.

The crucial day had shown that Göring's squadrons could not, for the moment, anyway, carry out a successful major daylight attack on London. Despite a six-week all-out attempt, they still had not gained mastery of the skies over southern England. An invasion therefore was not yet possible. Two days later, on September 17, Hitler, as we have seen, postponed *Sea Lion* indefinitely. Churchill later concluded that "September 15 may stand as the date of its demise."

It could stand, too, I would soon come to think, as a vital turning point in Hitler's war. It was his first setback, after so many glittering victories. He would have more military triumphs, to be sure,

* Lt.-Col. Bernhard von Lossberg in *Im Wehrmacht Fuehrungsstab*, p. 91.
† Churchill, op. cit., p. 332.

but the tide of war, which had been running so strongly in his favor, now slackened, and before another year was out would turn against him.

The British nation was saved — to fight another day. For nearly a millennium it had successfully defended itself by sea power. Just in time, a very few of its leaders, Churchill above all, had recognized that air power would become decisive in the mid-twentieth century, and they had prevailed against a skeptical House of Commons and a lagging government, but not by very much. They had made the little fighter plane and its pilot (I had seen the prototype of the Spitfire at the Schneider Cup Races in England in 1928) the chief shield for defense.

With his usual eloquence Churchill had noted the consequence in a speech to the Commons on August 20, when the Battle of Britain still raged, with its outcome very much in doubt. "Never in the field of human conflict," he said, "was so much owed by so many to so few."

In the meantime, even before the Nazi Warlord gave up on the invasion of Britain, there had been in Berlin a sort of turning point in the war.

On the night of August 25, 1940, the British bombed the German city for the first time. Their bombers had come over the capital perhaps half a dozen times during the previous winter, but they had dropped only leaflets. Now they were letting fall the real thing. Actually, this first attack did not amount to much. Because of a high thick cloud cover, only about half of the eighty-one R.A.F. bombers dispatched found the target. Material damage, so far as I could ascertain, was negligible, and no one was killed. But the effect on German morale was great. *This was the first time that bombs had ever fallen on Berlin.*

The Berliners are stunned [I wrote in my diary the next day]. They did not think it could happen. When this war began, Göring assured them it couldn't. . . . They believed him. Their disillusionment today, therefore, is all the greater. You have to see their faces to measure it.

The British came back in greater force on the night of August 28–29 and, as I noted in my diary, *"for the first time killed Germans in the capital of the Reich."* The official count was ten killed and twenty-nine wounded. Most of the American foreign correspondents and our embassy military attachés estimated the casualties, judging by the apartment houses hit, at four or five times that. Even so, compared to what the British were beginning to get in London and to what the Germans in the ensuing years would experience, the figure was modest. But again the effect on the morale of the Berliners was tremendous. On the Nazi government too.

Its bigwigs were enraged. Goebbels, who had ordered the press to play down the first bombing, giving it only a few lines, now gave instructions to pull out all stops in condemning the "brutality" of the British flyers in attacking the defenseless women and children of Berlin. Most of the newspapers used the same flaming headline: "COWARDLY BRITISH ATTACK." And the propaganda minister made them concoct stories that while the German planes over England were attacking only military objectives, the "British pirates, on the personal orders of Churchill," dropped their bombs only on "non-military objectives." Though God knows I was used to Goebbels' lies by this time, I was depressed at the thought that the gullible Germans would believe them.°

One thing I realized that night as I drove back to my hotel about 3 A.M. after my broadcast and the "all-clear." You could see the lights in the sky from several fires. *There was no defense against the night bombers.* No doubt my colleague Ed Murrow was learning that in London. During the last two raids I had stood on a balcony out at the Rundfunkhaus watching the fireworks in the sky — the German flak, mostly 88's, blasting away and the giant searchlights trying to catch the British planes in their beams. None ever did, nor did I see a single British bomber fall in flames. There was nothing you could do against the night bomber but pray that its bombs would not fall on you.

I remember uttering that prayer the last night of August. I had been in the bathroom and had not heard the sirens sound the alert. When I emerged, the anti-aircraft guns nearby were thundering away. Since the Adlon Hotel was on the corner of Unter den Linden

---

° A few evenings later, while laid up with the flu, I fell into a conversation with the chambermaid who looked after my room in the Adlon Hotel. My diary recalls it.

"Will the British come over tonight?" I asked.

"For certain," she sighed. All her confidence, all the confidence that the five million Berliners had, that the capital was safe from air attack, was gone.

"Why do they do it?" she asked.

"Because you bomb London," I said.

"Yes, but we hit military objectives, while the British, they bomb our homes. . . ."

"Maybe you bomb their homes too," I said.

"Our papers say not," she said.

She believed them.

and the Wilhelmstrasse, down which street were several ministries and Hitler's Chancellery, there was a great concentration of flak around us, especially in the adjoining Tiergarten. Still a little dopey from the flu I soon fell asleep, to be awakened a few minutes later by the thud of two bombs exploding very near the hotel.

Next morning OKW announced that the only bombs dropped fell outside the city limits. Hitler and Goebbels must be editing the High Command's communiqués, it occurred to me, because I found the nearby Tiergarten roped off, and even the afternoon newspapers reported several bomb craters in the park.

Since this day, September 1, was the first anniversary of Hitler's launching the war, I dragged myself out to the Rundfunk to do a special broadcast on the occasion.

> A year ago today [I wrote] the great "counterattack" against Poland began. In this year German arms have achieved victories never equaled even in the brilliant military history of this aggressive, militaristic nation. And yet the war is not yet over, or won.

The censor cut out the word "counterattack." He said it sounded too sarcastic.

"It was the very word OKW used in its first official communiqué a year ago today," I reminded him.

"It does not sound right today," he said. "Find another word. And you can't call Germany 'aggressive and militaristic.' Please remember it was Poland which attacked us first."

Scribbling in my diary that night I felt a resentment not only at the cuts the censor had made in my broadcast, but at the thought that more and more the censorship was clamping down on me. I could not broadcast a tenth of what I was putting down nightly in my diary. From that night it began to dawn on me that my usefulness as a correspondent in Berlin was drawing to an end. I had sworn when I arrived six years ago that I would stay only as long as I could report the essential truth. Now, with the restrictions of wartime censorship, it seemed to me that state of affairs had come to an end. I decided to broach the matter with CBS in New York.

A few days later, however, on September 4, I found I still could do a fair job as a reporter. There was another chance to see the terrible dictator and to observe his mood now that his victorious armies were poised, as we still thought, for the invasion of Britain. Perhaps I could also get a clue as to how he thought the Battle of Britain was really going.

The occasion was the opening of the annual Winter Help campaign at the Sportpalast in Berlin before an audience of mostly women nurses and social service workers. I had rarely seen Hitler so hypocritical or sarcastic, though I knew from years of experience that he was a master of both. He also tried to provide his audience with what Germans regarded as humor. All this I found instructive. He obviously meant to convey the impression that all was going well — in the great air battle over Britain and with his preparations to invade it. No need to be too solemn about another easy victory. The occasion called for a little irony and humor.

He referred to Churchill as "that noted war correspondent." For "a character like Duff Cooper," he said, "there is no word in conventional German."

> The babbling of Mr. Churchill or of Mr. Eden — reverence for old age forbids the mention of Mr. Chamberlain — doesn't mean a thing to the German people. At best, it makes us laugh.

Still, I thought, as I settled down to listen to still another Hitler speech, he has to answer three questions which are uppermost in the minds of Germans:

1. How was the Battle of Britain, which Göring had boasted would be over by now, going?

2. When would England be invaded?

3. What was he doing about the night bombings of Berlin (which Göring had solemnly declared could never happen) and other German cities?

As to the invasion, he disposed of it with little more than a quip.

> In England they're filled with curiosity and keep asking: "Why doesn't he come?" Be calm. Be calm. He's coming! He's coming! They shouldn't always be so curious!

His listeners, I noted, found this very funny. They roared with laughter. In regard to the bombings of Berlin, Hitler began by a typical falsification and ended with a dire threat.

> In recent days Mr. Churchill has been demonstrating his new brainchild, the night air attack. Mr. Churchill is carrying out these attacks not because they promise to be especially effective, but because his air force cannot fly over Germany in daylight — whereas German planes fly over English soil day after day. . . . Wherever a British pilot

sees a light, he drops a bomb — on residential districts, farms and villages.

As I listened to that I wondered how many, if any, in the vast audience realized that the Germans flew over England by day because it was only a few miles from German bases in France and Belgium, and they could protect their bombers with fighters. Germany was too far from Britain to enable the British to accompany their bombers with fighters. This was the reason the British came over under cover of the night.

Now he hurled his threat.

For three months I did not answer because I believed such madness would be stopped. Mr. Churchill took this for a sign of weakness. We are now answering night for night.

His voice rose.

When the British air force drops two or three or four thousand kilograms of bombs, then we will, in one night, drop 150, 250, 300, or 400 thousand kilograms!

At this point, according to my diary, Hitler had to pause because of the hysterical applause of his women listeners. It was a reminder to me that German women did not really differ from their men.

"When they declare that they will increase their attacks on our cities then I say we will *raze their* cities to the ground!" At this, the young ladies were quite beside themselves. They leaped to their feet and, their breasts heaving, screamed their approval.

"The hour will come," Hitler shouted, coming at last to his conclusion, "when one of us will break, and it will not be National Socialist Germany!"

At this, the raving maidens kept their heads sufficiently to break their wild shouts with a chorus of "Never! Never!"

So in the end he had lost his temper. Was it because as so often before, he was carried away by his audience? Or was it mainly because the Battle of Britain was not going as well as Göring had promised, and that this kept forcing him to postpone the invasion? At any rate, I later concluded that his frustrations, plus his hysterical reaction to the British bombing of Berlin, were both factors in switching the Luftwaffe's daylight attacks on the R.A.F. to massive night bombings of London which began three days after his Sportpalast speech, on September 7. Hitler considered them a retaliation.*

If the Battle of Britain was heating up as the middle of September approached, so was German propaganda. The government, the High Command, the press, let forth a torrent of lies about the bombing here and in Britain; lies that became shriller with each passing day. Some of the ravings were so inane that they made rather good copy, and I sometimes would quote them in my broadcasts. I assumed my listeners at home would clearly comprehend the sort of lies the German people were being fed. What I could not add in my broadcast I put down in my diary: that the bombing on the night of September 7 was "the biggest and most effective" yet.

> The British were aiming better last night. When I returned from the Rundfunk shortly after 3 A.M. the sky over the north-central part of Berlin was lit by two great fires. The biggest was in the Lehrter railroad station. Another railroad station in the Schussendorfstrasse was also hit. A rubber factory, I was told, was set afire. . . .

More and more that frenzied September I felt myself being caught up in the Nazi propaganda war. When I went down to the studio to do my broadcast on the night of September 5 I found that the German Broadcasting Company had installed a lip microphone, which you had to hold to your lips in order to be heard. This special mike did not pick up the roar of the anti-aircraft batteries ringing Broadcast House nor the thuds of bombs exploding near by. I had already been warned that I could no longer mention a British bombing while it was taking place. In vain I argued that Ed Murrow in London not only mentioned much severer attacks, but vividly described them as they went on. A night or two before, Elmer Davis in New York had made one of his wry comments after I had finished my broadcast, and the Germans had heard it. I had made no mention of an air attack then in progress, though the thunder of the flak guns and the sound of

---

* On September 7, obviously taking its cue from Hitler, the German High Command issued a special communiqué. "The enemy again attacked the German capital last night, causing some damage to persons and property as a result of his indiscriminate dropping of bombs on nonmilitary targets in the middle of the city. The German air force, as reprisal, has therefore begun to attack London with strong forces." Next day all of Berlin's Sunday morning newspapers carried the same headline, dictated by Goebbels: "BIG ATTACK ON LONDON AS REPRISAL." The German people were not told that for a fortnight the Luftwaffe had been dropping bombs on a far larger scale on the center of London. In fact, an OKW communiqué issued later that evening said London had been attacked "for the first time." As a result, it added, "one great cloud of smoke stretches from the middle of London to the mouth of the Thames." This description, at least, was true.

exploding bombs was so great that I could hardly hear my own voice. Elmer, with his dry Hoosier irony, had remarked that though I did not mention that Berlin was being bombed the sounds coming over the ocean spoke louder than words. My regular mike had picked them up. It was replaced by the lip microphone the following evening. As the days passed there were further attempts at restricting me. On several nights during a bombing I was ordered to the air-raid shelter in the basement so that I could not watch from my balcony what was happening in the skies.

Finally, on the evening of September 9, the Nazis played a trick on me that hastened my resolve to depart. By now three censors had to approve my script: one from the military (who gave me the least trouble); one from the Foreign Office; and a third from the Propaganda Ministry. That evening I had a royal fight with the last two. They charged me with undue irony in saying the Germans insisted that the new all-out night bombing of London was a "reprisal" for the bombing of Berlin. I fought them tooth and nail. By the time they finally decided, reluctantly, to let me go on the air with what was left of my script, my five minutes of air time had passed. Next evening Tess rang me up from Geneva to say that Paul White, CBS news director in New York, had telephoned asking why I had not broadcast. CBS had received a cable, he told her, from the director of the German Broadcasting Company: "Regret Shirer arrived too late tonight to broadcast."

Ever since the war started I had made my position clear both to the Germans and to the Columbia Broadcasting System. I would cease broadcasting and pull out of Germany if the censorship made it impossible to report from Berlin truthfully and reasonably completely. God knows I had had constant difficulties with the Germans. But I was surprised to meet with a considerable lack of understanding at CBS. When I had complained in April during the Nazi conquest of Norway about the censorship making it difficult for me to report enough to make it worthwhile to continue broadcasting from Berlin, Paul White had sent me a cable that I could not accept.

BILL, WE THOROUGHLY UNDERSTAND, SYMPATHIZE CONDITION IN BERLIN BUT FEEL WE MUST CARRY ON WITH BROADCASTS EVEN IF ONLY READING OFFICIAL STATEMENTS AND NEWSPAPER TEXTS.

CBS would have to get someone else for that menial chore. I replied to White that I could hire a pro-Nazi American student for $50 a week "and no expenses" to read that crap.

Then in May Hitler had attacked in the West, and because everything had gone amazingly well for the Germans, the censorship had been relaxed. I was able to do some honest reporting of the war, culminating in the scoop at Compiègne on the Franco-German armistice. Now with the air war reaching a new intensity, Hitler hysterical over the British bombing of Germany and apparently wavering about his invasion of Britain, censorship had again become impossible. I cabled White, and on September 10 received a reply, relayed by Tess on the phone from Geneva, asking me to return to Geneva "as soon as possible" to "talk on the telephone."

Berlin, September 12, 1940.
Off to Geneva for a few days so that I can talk some matters over with New York on the telephone without being overheard by the Nazis. . . .
The rumor is that the big invasion hop against England is planned for the night of September 15, when there will be a full moon and the proper tide in the Channel.
I'll chance this trip anyway.

I knew what I would tell CBS: that unless the Germans relaxed the censorship in Berlin I was getting out. Tess and I had pretty well agreed that she and Eileen would leave for America by the end of October. I had been reliably informed in Berlin that if Hitler had to call off his invasion, he might take out his frustrations with the British by going into Spain and taking Gibraltar. From there he could close the Mediterranean and cut Britain's lifeline to Egypt, the Near East and India. That would also, incidentally, cut off the last avenue of escape for my family in Geneva. The only way you could get to America now was through unoccupied France to Spain and then through Portugal to Lisbon, the last port on the Continent from which you could catch a plane or a boat to New York. Reluctantly, Tess agreed that perhaps she and the child should get out while there were still means to do so. I tried to encourage her by swearing that it would not be long before I followed them — say, by Christmas, or New Year's.
It was wonderful to be back with them again, if only for four days. Switzerland had never been my favorite country — it was too stodgy — but now, after wartime Germany, I loved it. It seemed wonderfully civilized and sane. My family never looked better. Some day, I swore, when this bloody war was over, I would find a job that

enabled me to spend more time with them — perhaps we would have an addition or two by then. Tess and I sat up late each night talking it over. She had mixed feelings about leaving Europe, where she had been born and raised. She was sure she would like life in America. But she was a European and would miss Europe. She also found it difficult to face the prospect of an ocean separating us. Ed Murrow had his wife, Janet, with him in London, she pointed out.

"And unlike you," she reminded me, "they are working with, and sharing life and the bombing with, a people they admire and love."

When I got Paul White in New York on the phone, I first asked him to arrange passage for Tess and Eileen on the clipper from Lisbon, which he said he would do, though it would take time.

"We'll get them over here by Christmas, for sure," he promised.

"I may be with them," I said.

"Bill, we understand your feelings," White said. "But we want you to stay in Berlin. We think you're doing a wonderful job."

I found it difficult to make him understand. Paul White was very capable in his job. He had helped make CBS preeminent in the news. He had a natural instinct for radio as a news medium. But he had little understanding of Europe. He could not see that my situation in Berlin was very much different from Ed Murrow's in London. He had not the slightest inkling of what trying to work in the Nazi madhouse was like.

Despite several hours on the transatlantic telephone over three days White and I did not quite solve our differences. We finally left it as I put it in a long letter to confirm what I had said on the phone:

> I realize that the next few weeks may decide the issue of the war, and that it is not the best time to pull out because of censorship. If Germany should win, you will naturally want coverage of the events to follow that victory — a coverage which would largely come from the German side.
>
> For that reason I'm going back to Berlin to have another crack at the job. But if there is a stalemate this winter and the censorship is not relaxed, I personally cannot remain there and do Nazi propaganda.

I added a postscript.

> By the time you get this Hitler will either have tried his invasion of Britain or given it up at least until spring.

I lingered on in Geneva until September 17. September 15 came and went, and there was no word of Hitler's invasion. Whether the postponement had any effect on my feelings, I cannot remember. But I find in my diary for those fleeting days in Geneva that I was talking about "Hitler's defeat" and "if Britain wins." On the sixteenth I had lunch with John Winant, the American head of the International Labor Office, who was trying valiantly to keep his institution from becoming a casualty of the war, as the League of Nations, I felt, already had become.

> We talked about the job to be done after the war if Britain wins and if the mistakes of 1919 are not to be repeated. He spoke of his own ideas about reconstruction.... Personally I cannot look that far ahead. I cannot see beyond Hitler's defeat....

I returned to Berlin on September 18, and my diary for the next few days echoes familiar themes: the British bombings; the angry outbursts of the German press against them and the increasing tightening of the censorship. This I took to be the result of growing frustration in the capital over the failure thus far to destroy the R.A.F. in the Battle of Britain, to launch the invasion and to prevent the nightly bombings of Berlin and other German cities.

My diary:

> Berlin, September 18. Somewhere near Frankfurt on the train from Basel last night the porter shouted: *"Flieger-Alarm,"* and there was a distant sound of gunfire, but nothing hit us....
>
> Berlin, September 19.... Not since the war started has the German press been so indignant against the British as today. According to it, the British last night bombed the Bodelschwingh hospital for mentally deficient children at Bethel in western Germany, killing nine youngsters, wounding twelve.*

---

* An interesting sequel to this piece of news appears in my diary of September 21. "X came up to my room in the Adlon today, and after we had disconnected my telephone and made sure that no one was listening through the crack of the door to the next room he told me a weird story. He says the Gestapo is now systematically bumping off the mentally deficient people.... The Nazis call them 'mercy deaths.' He relates that Pastor Bodelschwingh, who runs a large hospital for feeble-minded children at Bethel, was arrested a few days ago because he refused to deliver up some of his more serious mental cases to the secret police. Shortly after this, his hospital is bombed. By the 'British'..."

It was not the first time the Germans bombed one of their own places to stir up feeling against the British. On the first day of the attack in the West, on May 10, the Germans fumed about a British bombing of Freiburg, which killed twenty-four civilians. It was later established the Germans did it.

I cited some of the choice headlines in the Berlin newspapers:

Nachtausgabe: "NIGHT CRIME OF BRITISH AGAINST 21 GERMAN CHILDREN — THIS BLOODY ACT CRIES FOR REVENGE."
Deutsche Allgemeine Zeitung: "MURDER OF CHILDREN AT BETHEL; REVOLTING CRIME."
B.Z. am Mittag: "ASSASSINS' MURDER IS NO LONGER WAR, HERR WINSTON CHURCHILL! — THE BRITISH ISLAND OF MURDERERS WILL HAVE TO TAKE THE CONSEQUENCES OF ITS MALICIOUS BOMBINGS."

Things must be going worse for the Germans than they admit, I concluded. Only this could explain such insane outbursts. And the worse things became, the stronger the censorship. My gripes about it increased in intensity.

September 19: Censorship . . . growing more impossible. I had a royal scrap with one Nazi censor tonight. He wouldn't let me read the newspaper headlines quoted above. He said it gave America a "wrong impression." . . .

Next day, September 20, the longest gripe I had yet written. I mentioned in the script of my broadcast that the German press and radio were making the most of a report from New York that the British censor had forbidden American radio correspondents in London to mention air-raids while they were on. America, said the Germans, was thus deprived of trustworthy news from Britain. So far so good — my censors loved my report. But when I added that the authorities in Berlin had clamped the same restriction on me weeks ago, my censors would not allow me to say any such thing.

I ask myself why I stay on here. Censorship . . . has become increasingly worse. For the last few months I've been trying to get by on my wits, such as they are: to indicate a truth or an official lie by the tone and inflection of the voice, by a pause held longer than is natural, by the use of an Americanism which most Germans, who learned their English in England, will not fully grasp. . . . But the Nazis are on to me.

The Propaganda Ministry had sprung on me two new censors who knew American English, a professor who had long taught at an American university and a financier who had been a partner in a Wall Street bank.

And the Foreign Office and Propaganda Ministry keep receiving reports from the United States — not only from the embassy at Washington, but from their intelligence services throughout our country — that I'm getting by with murder and must be sat upon. . . .°

The British bombings of Berlin went on. Noting them in my diary began to become monotonous.

September 24. The British really went to work on Berlin last night. They bombed heavily and with excellent aim for four hours. They hit some important factories in the north of the city, one big gas works and the railroad yards north of the Stettiner and Lehrter stations.

But we couldn't tell the story. The authorities said no damage of military importance was done. . . .

September 26. We had the longest air-raid of the war last night, from 11 P.M. to 4 o'clock this morning.

As soon as I had finished my broadcast that evening the Nazi air-wardens forced me to the air-raid cellar. I usually had avoided them, but this time they nabbed me. I soon looked for a way to escape. "Lord Haw-Haw," the British radio traitor, and his wife joined me. We slipped past the S.S. guards and found an unfrequented tunnel, where we paused to imbibe from a liter bottle of schnapps, which "Lady Haw-Haw" had thoughtfully brought. Though "Haw-Haw's" selling out to Nazi Germany made me contemptuous of him, I must say that I found him amusing and even intelligent. On many a night he joined me in evading being herded into the air-raid shelter when the bombing began. This night we ended up in his office-room, where after watching the fireworks in the sky through the window, we had another long talk.

He was pleased and flattered that the British press had dubbed him "Lord Haw-Haw" and had conceded that he had a large listening audience in Britain.† It was almost the first recognition, I concluded, he had ever got at home. Though he assumed the name of Froehlich (which in German meant "joyful") when he got to Germany the week the war began, his real name was William Joyce — a leading brawler in Mosley's British Union of Fascists.

° A German informant kept me up to date on these reports from Washington.

† This audience, which in the dull first eight months of the war had found him droll and amusing, dwindled drastically when the phony war ended in April, and it disappeared when the fall of France, the heavy bombings, the threat of invasion and the Battle of Britain brought the war home to the British. Joyce, cut off from his native land and with nothing but Nazi propaganda to feed upon, did not yet realize it.

"Doesn't the treason thing bother you?" I asked him, not for the first time.

It didn't, he said, because he had renounced his British nationality and become a German citizen.

"I consider myself no more a traitor than those thousands of Americans who renounced their citizenship to become comrades in the Soviet Union," he said, "or than those Germans who gave up their nationality after 1848 and fled to America to become Americans."

Why a man betrays his country was a subject that had always fascinated me. And in the long evenings of the bombings, when you couldn't go home, I often probed Joyce about why he had done it. He had hated the British, with all the fury of a fanatical Irishman. He had failed to become much of anything in Britain, where he grew up, and he was a man who obviously craved recognition. I noted he had two hatreds which partially explained, at least, why he had fled to Berlin.

He loathed the Jews. And, to my surprise, he loathed the capitalists. I came to feel that had it not been for his hysteria about the Jews, he might easily have made his mark in the British Communist party — and perhaps have fled to Moscow instead of Berlin. Night after night he inveighed against the evils of capitalism. Somehow, he had convinced himself that the Nazi movement was primarily proletarian and was freeing the world from the "plutocratic capitalists." He considered himself a toiler for the working class.

"Then you're in the wrong place," I would taunt him. I confess I had a sneaking liking for the man. And I was not surprised when at the war's end, during his trial for treason in London, he made no apologies for what he had done, and showed great courage to the end, when he was found guilty and on January 3, 1946, hanged on the gallows in Wandsworth Prison in London.

There were three Americans in Berlin that winter broadcasting Nazi propaganda for the Germans over their shortwave transmitters. We were not yet in the war, so there was no question in their case of treason. That would come later after Hitler declared war on us, and among others, an old friend from Vienna, Bob Best, the United Press correspondent there, would become involved — to the amazement of all of us who had known and liked him. In the end, Bob, like "Haw-Haw," paid for it, though he got off with life imprisonment and died behind bars at Leavenworth.

None of the American broadcasters hired by the Nazis ever gained the kind of following at home that Joyce achieved for a time in Britain. This was also true later of Bob Best, who, with his gentle Carolinian accent, spoke rather well on the air; and of Donald Day, a former colleague of mine on the *Chicago Tribune* who began to broadcast for Hitler the last year of the war because of his fury over the Bolsheviks. It was also true, I believe, of Ezra Pound, whom I had so admired in my youthful days in Paris, and who broadcast the most utter nonsense from Fascist Italy during the war. To me Pound was the saddest case of all. He had been such a fine poet.

My diary:

> Zürich, October 18. Flew down from Berlin this afternoon. . . . I sit here in the Bahnhof waiting for my Geneva train . . . and sad at the farewell that must be said, and at the realization that still another home we tried to make will be broken up.

At dawn on October 23 in Geneva I saw Tess and Eileen off on a Swiss bus that was scheduled to take them in two days and nights of hard driving across unoccupied France to Barcelona, from where they planned to travel by train to Madrid and on to Lisbon, and from Lisbon to New York by boat. Tess and I had been too busy closing up the rented apartment to become very depressed at another separation, another house-closing, though I felt low and drained after they had gone.

We were lucky enough as it was, because there were more than a thousand refugees clamoring to get out on the two buses that set off once a week for Spain. The American Express would not allow its bus to leave that week because of reports of floods in the Pyrenees that had washed out the roads between France and Spain, but the people in charge of the Swiss bus on which we had booked decided to chance it. Most of Tess's baggage consisted of food and water sufficient for two days, as there were no provisions en route in France. No gasoline either, apparently, for the bus had a couple of small tanks strapped to the front fenders.

Young Eileen's excitement at the adventure — she was bubbling over — helped to lighten our farewells, and I felt grateful that she was much too young to notice or feel the tragedy in that busload of human beings. Most of them were German Jews trying to distance themselves still further from Hitler. As they crowded into the bus they were nervous and jittery to a point of hysteria, and I did not blame them. Almost every day in Geneva, Tess had told me, there were reports of the French turning over German Jews to the Gestapo, and I had overheard several of them waiting for the bus express their fears that the French might take them off it and hand them over to Himmler's torturers, or that Franco's pro-German Spaniards would hold them up at the frontier.*

It was all I could do to get myself off to return to Germany the next day. I remember on the train up to Bern gazing with leaden heart through the window of my compartment at the Swiss, Lake Geneva, the mountains, Mont Blanc in the distance, the hills and pastures still green, the marble palace of the defunct League of Nations. I kept wishing I had taken that bus with Tess and Eileen.

I had felt for some time that I had used up all my chances in Nazi Germany. I could no longer get by reporting the truth from there. But that was not all. I had had the feeling in the past few weeks that the German authorities were closing in on me. This was not a paranoid reaction. I was not imagining it. A close German friend at Broadcasting House had access to cables about me from the German embassy in Washington and to the reaction they caused in Berlin. Even before my trip to Geneva to see my family off, she had warned me that I was in deeper water than I realized.

I saw her on my return to Berlin toward the end of October. She was worried. The Gestapo, the Propaganda Ministry, the Foreign Office and even the military, she said, were beginning to build a case of espionage against me. For the first time, she suggested I ought to consider leaving, soon — while there was still time. Specifically, she said, the German embassy in Washington and especially the military attaché there, were cabling that they were convinced I was a spy and that I was getting out secret intelligence by use of code words in my broadcasts. She also told me that the Gestapo was increasing its surveillance of me, and that I should be careful whom I saw, including her.

I trusted her — one of the few Germans I did. All the more reason I dared not confide her warnings to my New York office or even to my diary, for fear of jeopardizing her very life. But they made it easier for me to overcome my hesitations about leaving. Ordinarily — and I was very conscious of this — you do not desert your post, especially in wartime. But I had no intention of letting the Nazis frame me as a spy.

As daylight that northern winter grew shorter and the nights longer, the British bombers visited us nearly every evening in Berlin. The damage was never very great, but the attacks killed a few people each time, damaged factories, rail yards, streets, buildings, houses,

* Most of them, Tess told me later, were turned back at the Spanish frontier.

and robbed the populace of its night's sleep, cutting down war production and keeping everyone's nerves on edge.

Sometimes, thank God, there was a humorous side to it all, as happened when Vyacheslav M. Molotov, the Soviet premier, foreign minister, and right-hand man of Stalin, arrived in the German capital on November 12 for a friendly visit with the Germans.

It was a dark, drizzling, chilly day and Molotov, I thought, looked anything but humorous as he drove from the Anhalter Bahnhof to the Soviet embassy in the Unter den Linden, a stone's throw down the street from the Adlon. I watched him as he drove by. His face had little expression, but what there was seemed rather dour. He looked like a provincial schoolmaster. But I realized that his looks belied him. He must be, in fact, a man of considerable ability and especially toughness to have survived in Stalin's Kremlin jungle. He must, I mused, be almost the last of the old Bolsheviks who had made the revolution with Lenin. The rest were dead — murdered by Stalin.

I wondered how Molotov would handle the Germans on this first visit to them; and how the Germans would handle him. I hoped the British flyers would not fail to pay us a visit in Berlin. To my disappointment they did not show up the first night, when Göring and Ribbentrop were hosts at a formal state banquet. But they came the second night, while Molotov was entertaining his hosts at the Soviet embassy.*

It got dark at that time of year in Berlin about 4 P.M., and I remember the British came over early that evening. Shortly after nine o'clock the air-raid sirens began to whine and soon you could hear the thunder of the flak guns and, in between, the hum of the bombers overhead. According to Dr. Paul Schmidt, the interpreter at the banquet, Molotov had just proposed a friendly toast and Ribbentrop had risen to his feet to reply, when the sirens went off and the guests began to scatter. There was no proper air-raid shelter in the embassy, so Ribbentrop hastily proposed that they make for the deep shelters beneath the Foreign Ministry. Since the official automobiles had taken cover, it was necessary for the eminent officials to stumble the six hundred yards or so through the blackout and the falling shrapnel (and perhaps bombs — you never knew) down the Linden and then into the Wilhelmstrasse.

There was considerable hurrying and scurrying, I remember, as the Germans and Russians came pell-mell down the street and made

---

* The air attack, says Churchill, was timed for this occasion. "We had heard of the conference beforehand," he later wrote, "and though not invited to join in the discussion did not wish to be entirely left out of the proceedings." *Their Finest Hour*, p. 584.

for the Foreign Ministry. In the dark some of them missed the turn at
the corner of the Wilhelmstrasse — a great burst of anti-aircraft fire
at the moment was certainly disconcerting — and reaching the
Adlon, in front of which I was standing, ducked into the hotel. I noticed Dr. Schmidt among them. Apparently, they had departed the
embassy in such haste that it was not clear where the meeting was to
resume — Schmidt thought it was to be in the Adlon's shelter, to
which he and his colleagues and a stray Russian or two repaired.
Thus Schmidt, who had kept the minutes of two days of talks of
Hitler and Ribbentrop with Molotov, missed the impromptu meeting
of the two foreign ministers that continued far into the night — until
the British left — in the underground depths of the Foreign Office.
But Gustav Hilger, counselor of the German embassy in Moscow,
who had managed to make it, acted as interpreter and made notes of
what was said.

Mostly Ribbentrop repeated what he and Hitler had been telling
Molotov for two days: that Britain was beaten and that it was time
now for Germany and Russia to divide up the British Empire, as they
had Poland, except that now Japan and Italy would have to be invited in to share the spoils.

> He could only repeat again and again and again [the German min-
> utes quote Ribbentrop as saying] that the decisive question was
> whether the Soviet Union was prepared to cooperate with us in the
> great liquidation of the British Empire.

Molotov's response was duly noted by Hilger.

> In his reply Molotov stated that the Germans were assuming that
> the war against England had already actually been won. If, therefore,
> as had been said in another connection, Germany was waging a life-
> and-death struggle against England [Hitler had used those words to
> him in a talk earlier in the day], he could only construe this as mean-
> ing that Germany was fighting "for life" and England "for death."

The sarcasm may have gone over the head of Ribbentrop, a man of
monumental denseness, but the Bolshevik foreign commissar took no
chances. To the Germans' constant reiteration that Britain was finished, Molotov finally replied:

*"If that is so, why are we in this shelter, and whose are the bombs
which fall?"*

The two days of talks with the obdurate Molotov had been a
wearing, wearying experience for the Führer, frustrated by his fail-

ure to invade Britain, which, as his Bolshevik visitor could see, remained very much in the war. Hitler, we know now, drew his final conclusions.

A month later, on December 18, 1940, he issued the most fateful war directive of his life, No. 21. It began:

> The German armed forces must be prepared to *crush Soviet Russia in a quick campaign* before the end of the war against England.* . . . Preparations . . . are to be completed by May 15, 1941. . . .

The code word for the operation was *Barbarossa.*

By that date I was on my way home, looking forward to the first Christmas in my native land in sixteen years. It would be the first there, ever, for Tess and Eileen.

I had worried about their crossing unoccupied France and Franco's Spain on their way to Lisbon. For a week I heard nothing from them. There had been such a breakdown of normal life in both countries I knew that anything could happen. Finally, at the beginning of November, I received word through our embassy that they had arrived safely in Portugal. In Lisbon they had met our old friends, John Carter Vincent, the American consul-general in Geneva, and his wife, Betty, and their two children, all of whom would be taking the ship with them from there to New York. I felt immensely relieved.

My high spirits held up. On November 5 in Berlin I confided to my diary some more good news:

> If all goes well, I shall leave here a month from today, flying all the way to New York — by Lufthansa plane from here to Lisbon, by Clipper from there to New York.

And November 20:

> I am definitely getting away from here by plane to Lisbon on December 5, if I can get all the necessary papers in time. The Foreign Office, the police, the secret police, and so on must approve my exit visa before I can leave.

Getting Spanish and Portuguese transit visas, I noted, was "proving no easy job." The German authorities were being sticky about my

---

* The italics are Hitler's.

exit visa. But all of this I expected. Somehow I felt confident that all
the difficulties would be overcome. I had still a fortnight to work on
them, and Harry Flannery, my replacement from a CBS radio station
in St. Louis, had arrived.

Those last days that winter in Berlin I could not help thinking
back over the years I had spent abroad since leaving college in Iowa
in June, 1925.

Fifteen and a half years! I had been twenty-one then. Now I was
nearly thirty-seven, downright middle-aged, in fact. The time had
passed so swiftly: through the first exciting golden years in Paris; the
assignments in Italy, the wonders of Rome, Florence and Venice; the
job in Vienna, where I had met and married Tess; the interlude in
India with Gandhi; the fishing village in Spain just before the civil
war broke out; and finally the long nightmare in Nazi Germany.
What luck I had had, in my life and in my work!

The last years in Berlin among the Germans had not been pleasant.
But they were not dull either, and I had no regrets at having come
here and stayed so long. The Third Reich had given me a tremendous
story to report, a vital chunk of history to recount. And it had deepened my comprehension of life on this earth: its brutality, violence,
chicanery, repression, hypocrisy, deceit, intolerance, senselessness. I
had learned this not from books, but from experience. But I had also
seen some beauty and meaning and fulfillment in men's lives, some
courage and fortitude in people, even some decency and honesty and
goodwill and tolerance in their relations to one another. I had attained, I thought, something that had eluded so many of us in the
West: a tragic sense of life. But also, I hoped, a sense of humor, and
enough self-knowledge not to take myself too seriously. Gandhi,
among others, had helped to teach me that.

So it was here, on the old continent, through a decade and a half,
that I had really grown up and come to feel at home.

Yet deep down, those dark, dreary November days in Berlin, I
knew that this was a farewell — not only to Germany, but to the rest
of Europe where I had found so much personal happiness in my life
and work.

I would return to Europe to continue covering the war, though not
from Germany. Here, as long as Hitler lived, I was finished. But when
the war was over, I had made up my mind, I would go home — for
good. Much as I loved the Old World and felt at home in it, I would
not stay on. I would not become an expatriate.

An American abroad, I had found, was always a foreigner, however long he had lived and worked in these European lands. No mat-

ter how well he spoke their languages, absorbed their cultures, knew their peoples, adapted to their great cities, he was forever a stranger. It was not a role I intended to play to the end of my days. Eventually — whether now or when the war was finished — I had to return to where my roots were, embedded in the American earth.

My Berlin diary for December 2 was limited to four words. "Only three more days!"

Next day, December 3: ". . . The Foreign Office still holding up my passport and exit visa, which worries me. Did my last broadcast from Berlin tonight."

"Berlin, December 4: Got my passport and official permission to leave tomorrow. Nothing to do now but pack."

There was one other thing to do. For weeks I had mulled over how to get my diaries safely out of Berlin. At some moments I had thought I ought to destroy them before leaving. There was enough in them to get me hanged — if the Gestapo ever discovered them. A couple of weeks before I had entrusted some of the most damaging pages to a friend in the Swedish embassy, who promised to get them out to Lisbon, where I could pick them up. Another friend in the U.S. embassy also had helped. He would take a small batch out to Spain when he went on leave a few days before I did. But the U.S. chargé d'affaires, an otherwise decent fellow, had put his foot down on any of his attachés taking out a sizable package of my papers. I was not surprised. The embassy had been rather sticky with us American correspondents.

The morning I got my passport and exit visa I realized I had less than twenty-four hours to figure out a way of getting the bulk of my Berlin diaries out. I again thought of destroying them, but I wanted very much to preserve them, if I could. Suddenly, later that morning, the solution became clear. It was risky, but life in the Third Reich had always been risky. It was worth a try.

I laid out the diaries in two big steel suitcases I had bought. Over them I placed a number of my broadcast scripts, each page of which had been stamped by the military and civilian censors as passed for broadcast. On top I put a few General Staff maps I had picked up from friends on the General Staff or the High Command (OKW). Then I phoned the Gestapo Headquarters in the Alexanderplatz. I had a couple of suitcases full of my dispatches, broadcasts and notes that I wanted to take out of the country, I said. As I was flying off at dawn from Tempelhof the next day, there would be no time for Gestapo officials at the airfield to go over the contents. Could they take a look now, if I brought them over; and if they approved, put a Gestapo seal on the suitcases so I wouldn't be held up at the airport?

"Bring them over, and we'll take a look," the official said.

After I hung up, I had some more doubts. Wasn't I tempting fate? How could these hard-nosed Nazi sleuths help but sniff out the diaries beneath my broadcasts? That would be the end of me. Maybe I had just better begin to flush them down the can. On the other hand . . . I calculated that the secret police would, of course, seize the General Staff maps. You couldn't take out such military maps, especially in wartime. That's why I had put them there on top. Customs officials always felt better if they found something in your bags to seize, and so would these Gestapo characters.

Then they would look at the layers of my broadcast scripts and I would ostentatiously point to the censors' stamps of approval on each page. Nothing impressed German cops more than official stamps, especially by the military. "Approved by So-and-So for OKW" — for the Supreme Command of the German Armed Forces! That would make a Gestapo official sit up and take notice. It would give me prestige in his eyes, or at least make me less suspect, foreigner though I was. I was going to gamble on their inspection ending there, before they dug deeper to my diaries beneath the radio scripts. I was going to gamble too that they were not high enough up to be aware of exactly who I was, and that when they learned, I would be out of the country, out of their reach. The feared Gestapo, I knew, was really not very efficient.

Once again I was lucky. Everything at Gestapo Headquarters worked out as I had planned. The two officials who handled me seized at once my General Staff maps. I apologized. I had forgotten, I said, that I had put them in at the last moment. They had been very valuable to me in reporting the Wehrmacht's great victories in the field. I realized I shouldn't take out General Staff maps.

"What else you got here?" one of the men said, putting his paw on the pile of papers.

"The texts of my broadcasts," I said, ". . . every page, as you can see, stamped for approval by the High Command and two ministries."

Both men studied the censors' stamps. I could see they were impressed. They poked a little deeper, each man now working a suitcase. Soon they would reach the diaries. I now wished I had not

come. I felt myself beginning to perspire. I had deliberately got myself into this jam. What a fool!

"You reported on the German army?" one of the agents looked up
to ask.

"All the way to Paris, and to the armistice at Compiègne," I said.
"A great army it was, and a great story for me. It will go down in
history!"

That apparently clinched it.

"Okay," one of them said, obviously proud of his one word of
English.

One of the officials brought some kind of metal tape, tied up my
two bags with it, and affixed half a dozen Gestapo seals. I tried not to
be too effusive in my thanks. Outside I hailed a taxi, drove to Tempelhof, and checked the suitcases in the luggage room. I had not yet
got my papers out of Germany, but so far, so good.

The last entry I would ever make in my diary from Hitler's Berlin
began:

> December 5. — It was still dark and a blizzard was blowing when I
> left the Adlon for the airport at Tempelhof this morning. . . .

As my taxi skidded through the familiar route to Tempelhof I
wondered if my plane could take off in such weather. If the flight was
canceled it might mean I would be stuck here for weeks. The plane
to Madrid and Lisbon was booked for weeks ahead.

At the airport I first got my two bags out of the luggage room, the
porter piling them on a cart with a couple of suitcases containing the
rest of the worldly goods I was taking out of this country: a few
clothes and a dozen German books. At the customs there was literally
a herd of officials. I opened the two bags with my personal belongings, and after pawing through them two officials chalked a sign of
approval on them. I noticed from their insignia they were from the
Gestapo. They pointed to the two bags full of my diaries.

"Open them up!" one of them said gruffly.

"I can't," I said. "They're sealed — by the Gestapo."

I felt grateful that my good friends at the Alexanderplatz had affixed at least a half-dozen seals. The two officials conferred in whispers for a moment.

"Where were those bags sealed?" one of them snapped.

"At Gestapo Headquarters at the Alexanderplatz," I said.

This information impressed them. But still they seemed suspicious.

"Just a minute," one said. I had seen his colleague pick up the phone at a table behind them. Obviously he was checking the Alexanderplatz. The man hung up, walked over to me, and without a word chalked the two bags. I was free at last to get to the ticket counter to check my luggage. A Lufthansa man weighed the bags. I told him I wanted to check the large ones.

"Where to?" he asked.

"To Lisbon," I said.

The thought of the German airline delivering my diaries to me safely in Portugal, beyond the reach of the last German official who could seize them, bucked me up.

The tower kept postponing the departure of our plane. The visibility was zero over Tempelhof. I went to the restaurant and had a second breakfast. I really was not hungry. But I had to do something to relieve the tension. I started to glance at the morning papers I had bought automatically on arriving at the airport. I usually picked up first Hitler's own paper, the *Völkische Beobachter*, full of propaganda though devoid of news. It gave the Nazi line, as the Führer himself probably determined it. I glanced at the front page. The usual bullshit. I tossed it down on the table.

"I don't have to read it," I thought. "I don't have to read any of this trash anymore!"

Before the end of this day, when we would arrive in Barcelona, I wouldn't have to put up with anything anymore in the great Third Reich. The sense of relief I felt was tremendous. I had only to hold out this one more day, and the whole nightmare for me would be over, though it would go on and on for millions of others — well, the millions of Germans didn't seem to mind it, at least not yet.

Finally they called out the plane to Barcelona. As I walked out to it I could see the workers loading my luggage. We cleared the field and zoomed over the house where Tess and I had spent most of our time in Berlin. We had had a pretty good life there together and we had survived the Nazi horror and its mindless suppression of the human spirit. But many others, I felt sadly, had not survived — the Jews above all, but also the Czechs and now the Poles. Even for the great mass of Germans who supported Hitler, who were now basking in his conquest of most of Europe, I felt a sort of sorrow. They did not seem to realize what the poison of Nazism was doing to them.

Estoril, near Lisbon, December 7.
Lisbon and light and freedom and sanity at last! . . .

No matter that the Portuguese passport authorities held me up at the airport because I could not show a ticket for New York. I was so full of euphoria, so relieved to be free of Germany, that I didn't mind.

"You have only transit visa," the head passport man said in English. "That means you pass through. You cannot stay. You have to have ticket to America. Show me ticket."

I told him I intended to get out on the first plane, and that a ticket to New York was undoubtedly waiting for me at the Pan Am offices in town. Apparently, he had heard such talk before.

"Show me ticket!" he kept saying.

I finally persuaded him to let me check with the Pan Am counter. After much telephoning to the office in town, it was established that I indeed had a ticket. CBS had cabled it from New York. I was let go.

I stopped at the Lufthansa counter and showed my tabs for the two suitcases full of my diaries which the airline had been good enough to fly from Berlin to Lisbon. The bags had, in fact, accompanied me. The German clerk was much impressed by the Gestapo seals. In fact, he seemed awed by them. He offered to deliver my diaries to my hotel in Lisbon. But I thought I had played my luck far enough. I claimed them, hailed a taxi, and drove with them into town.

I still had to pick up the diaries waiting for me at the Swedish legation. In Barcelona I had collected those I had sent out through a friend in the U.S. embassy in Berlin.

In Lisbon the hotels were full. Refugees, the room clerks said, had swamped them. Ordinarily this would have annoyed me. I had no place to stay, and evening was already coming on. But again, I didn't mind. I called a taxi and drove out to Estoril, a resort and gambling center north of Lisbon on the sea. I found a room in one of the big hotels there. I still felt so elated I would have gladly slept on the beach. I washed up, changed my shirt, had a good dinner — a local wine the waiter recommended was excellent — and spent the evening strolling through the town and along the beach, staring at the lights. They seemed so blinding — and beautiful — after a year and a half in blacked-out Berlin.

When I got back to my room the telephone was ringing. It was Ed Murrow in London. He had been trying to get me, he said, in every hotel in Portugal. He had wangled a seat on a plane that would be arriving the next afternoon. "We need to talk," he said, "and toss down a few, before you go. And New York wants us to do another broadcast together — you know, how the war looks from Berlin and London. But not so cut-and-dried this time.* The Portuguese probably won't let us do it. They're afraid of offending either side. But see if you can fix it up. If not, what the hell! We'll have some fun."

I drove into Lisbon the next afternoon to meet Ed's plane, which didn't come in until shortly before midnight. We spent the rest of the night talking ourselves out, swapping stories, getting caught up and comparing notes on how the war was going. Considering the bombing he had taken in London — much worse than what I had gone through in Berlin — and the killing pace of his job, Ed looked surprisingly fit. He was naturally high-strung, but the strain of the war had made him no more so. He was still, I noticed, a chain cigarette smoker, and when I chided him about it he retorted that he had never seen me without a foul-smelling pipe in my mouth. It was just our usual banter.

What concerned me was that one of these days a bomb might have his number. He was leading a charmed life, it seemed to me, braving the German bombs night after night in order to give his eyewitness accounts of the tremendous pounding London was taking. Three days after his arrival in Portugal, he received a wire from London that his new office had been demolished the previous night. His old one had been destroyed by a direct hit two months before. Luckily he had been out in the street watching the battle.

Now in Lisbon for a fleeting moment, we tried to relax together, sauntering along the beach, watching the churning waves roll in and break into fountains of foam, sitting on the terrace of a café overlooking the sea sipping the local white wine, and in the evening trying our luck in the gaming rooms of the casino, fascinated by the sight of the British and German secret agents, male and female, spying on each other even as they gambled together.

We hammered out a script for our joint broadcast. But the Portuguese government, wary of displeasing London and Berlin, kept stalling on approving it until the time for a 2 A.M. broadcast on the thirteenth and then for its reschedule at 4 A.M. had passed.

* After weeks of negotiating with the British and German governments, we had done a broadcast together the winter before, Ed from London, I from Berlin. It was the first and last time, I believe, a direct conversation was allowed between the two belligerent capitals. But it came off very stilted, we thought. We had had to write out our questions and answers beforehand, submit them to the censors, and stick to them word for word when we broadcast.

In the meantime, Pan American had informed me that its planes to New York were being held up by ground swells at Horta — the flying boats needed a smooth sea to take off — and that if I wanted to get home by Christmas I had better try to book on the weekly Export Line ship leaving December 13.

Thousands of refugees were clamoring for a place on the small vessels, which had accommodation for only one hundred fifty passengers each, but the line's local manager promised he would get me on the *Excambion* sailing this week, though I might have to sleep on a couch in the lounge.* I couldn't have cared less.

All day that Friday the thirteenth in Lisbon I felt depressed at parting from Murrow, and he apparently felt the same about saying goodbye to me. In the last three years we had become very close to each other, both in our work and as friends; and, as I wrote in my diary that night, "a bond grew that was very real, a kind you make only a few times in your life, and somehow, absurdly no doubt, sentimentally perhaps, we had a presentiment that the fortunes of war, maybe just a little bomb, would make this reunion the last."

Ed was not returning to London until the following day. He drove into Lisbon with me. It was dusk when we arrived at the docks, and after we found my ship and I had checked in with my baggage, we strolled around the wharf in the gathering darkness. There was, I remember, a makeshift open-air bar for the stevedores presided over by a wonderfully frowzy, plump Portuguese blonde.

"It ain't natural, that bundle of blond hair — on a Portuguese," Ed quipped.

We were trying to be lighthearted at the end. We crowded up to the little bar and had some drinks. We fell silent. It got dark. I could no longer make out his face. It had been clouding up, taking on a familiar frown. A loudspeaker blared a warning that all should be on ship. The crew started to pull up the gangplank. I shook hands with Ed. We found no words. I climbed aboard. I turned around. Ed had disappeared into the night.

Five American foreign correspondents, old colleagues, some of whom I had not seen for years, showed up in the ship's bar as tugs

---

* The Duke and Duchess of Windsor, I found, had departed Lisbon four months before on the sister ship *Excalibur*. We now know, from the Nazi secret papers, that the Germans made a considerable effort to get the duke to come over to them, suggesting that they would be interested in putting him back on the throne he had given up for the duchess as soon as they had conquered Britain. The Germans, in cahoots with the Franco Spaniards, were even prepared to kidnap the duke and have him interned in Spain so that he would have plenty of time to think it over. But he and his consort slipped out of town on the *Excalibur*. For the whole fantastic story, see my *Rise and Fall of the Third Reich*, pp. 785–792.

pulled us away from the dock. They were going home from France, Germany, England. We quickly renewed old ties. We ordered drinks; but I was too restless to stay, glad as I was to see them. I went up on deck. A full moon was rising over the Tagus, and up and down the broad river millions of lights sparkled from both shores and from the hills that rose beyond them. For how long? I wondered. They had gone out over most of this wonderful, ancient continent and over Britain. Would the Nazi gangsters come here too, and despoil and enslave it? I knew they were planning to move through neighboring Spain to drive the British out of Gibraltar. The Portuguese could not stop them, as the Austrians had not been able to, and the Czechs and the Poles and the Danes and the Norwegians and the Dutch and the Belgians and the French.

I stood for a long time at the rail, watching the lights recede on the Europe that for more than fifteen years had been my home and place of work and where I had found so much personal happiness and fulfillment. A long, dark, savage night had now settled over it. For years, mostly from Berlin, but also from Paris, London, Vienna, Rome, Geneva, Spain, I had watched it come, and tried to describe it, though it was beyond expression in words. Now, through luck, simply because I was a stranger, I was escaping it. The people I was leaving behind could not get away. Amid the slaughter of the bombs and the murderous persecutions of the Nazi conquerors they sought only to survive until a more decent time returned. They were in a predicament I had not faintly imagined when I had first arrived, unbelievably innocent and ignorant. The good people of Europe were then just beginning to recover from the devastation of the war that had ended only seven years before. They had a right, they believed, to look forward to a long stretch of peace in which they could rebuild their lives and their countries. Many had hoped the League of Nations would, at last, provide it. But it had not. No nation would give up an iota of its selfish sovereignty for the common good. Perhaps no nation ever would.

My own country, no more than any other. Still, I felt excited that I was going back to it. I had been so restless to get away as soon as I finished college that June of 1925. But now, like myself, it had grown up a bit. Surely it had now shed much of that shallowness, superficiality, mindlessness, and provincialism of the 1920's, with its Prohibition, its mad rush for a buck, its bloodless Coolidge in the White House, its isolationism, its Babbitty culture dominated by the Rotary and the Chambers of Commerce. Certainly, like me, it had come a long way in fifteen years. But even if it had not, I would take my chances in it, as I had for so long in Europe and Asia. And when the war was over, for good.

I remained glued to the rail of the ship for what must have been hours — until the last dim lights ashore faded into the darkness, and Europe was gone. I was glad to have been alone. I could not have shared my thoughts, my feelings, with anyone. Finally, I pulled myself away. My colleagues had returned from dinner and were having a nightcap in the bar. They were in high spirits, laughing and talking about making it home for Christmas for the first time in ages. I joined them.

The End of the Third Reich—
Judgment at Nuremberg

1945-1946

Five years later, at the war's end in 1945, I went back to Germany. The Thousand-Year Reich had ceased to exist. Adolf Hitler was dead. The war, which he had launched in Berlin on that gray morning of September 1, 1939, and which had brought him so many conquests, had been lost. The country lay in ruins. The people wandered around in a daze, cold and hungry. Those of their Nazi leaders who had not committed suicide, as Hitler and Heinrich Himmler had done, were in prison at Nuremberg, waiting trial for crimes against humanity. Justice, at long last, had caught up with them.

In Berlin, where I had watched them rule so arrogantly and savagely, I prowled through the mountains of debris past the bombed-out buildings, mile upon mile of them as far as the eye could see, dazed myself at the sight of such utter desolation.

On Sunday, November 5, I did my first broadcast since returning to the city. It sounded strange hearing myself begin: "This is Berlin!" The last time I had said those words was on December 3, 1940 — nearly five years before. How much had happened, I reflected, in that fateful interval!

The war had expanded after I left Berlin in December, 1940, until it engulfed all the major nations of the planet. On June 22, 1941, Hitler had turned on Russia and brought the Soviet Union into the war. On December 7 that year our turn had come. The Japanese attacked us at Pearl Harbor. Four days later, on December 11, Hitler declared war on the United States, as did Mussolini.

The blows to Russia and the United States in the beginning were grievous, and in the case of the Soviet Union they threatened the nation's very survival. Caught by surprise despite ample warnings given Moscow by Britain and the United States, the Russians had suffered a debacle in the early weeks of the great German offensive. By the end of September 1941 three great German armies, advancing on a thousand-mile front from the Baltic to the Black Sea, had penetrated so far into Russia that Hitler instructed the High Command to disband forty infantry divisions, which he believed would no longer be needed. In the north his armies were surrounding Leningrad. In the center they were only two hundred miles from Moscow. In the south they had taken Kiev, occupied most of the Ukraine, the breadbasket of the U.S.S.R., and were driving on the Caucasus and its rich oil fields.

On October 3 at the CBS listening post in New York I had picked up Hitler proclaiming from Berlin the collapse of the Soviet Union. "I declare today without reservation," he said, "that the enemy in the East has been struck down and will never rise again."

Five days later when Orel, a key city south of Moscow, fell, the Nazi Warlord sent his press chief, Otto Dietrich, flying back to Berlin to tell the correspondents that the final blows had been struck. "For all military purposes," Dietrich concluded, "Soviet Russia is done with. The British dream of a two-front war is dead."

These were dark days for those of us who had hoped that Hitler would meet his match in Russia. Now it looked as though he had achieved his greatest conquest. I remember that within a couple of weeks of the German onslaught our own U.S. Army General Staff was confidentially informing us reporters that the collapse of the Soviet Union was only a matter of weeks. It hoped we would not mislead our listeners or readers by holding out false hopes.

The turn of the tide in Russia came on a blizzardy, sub-zero day, December 6. Four days before, a reconnaissance battalion of the 285th German Infantry Division had reached Khimki, a suburb of Moscow. Through field glasses the men could see the spires of the Kremlin. But not for long. The Russians, despite their tremendous early losses, had amassed in great secrecy before their capital a force more formidable than the Germans could possibly imagine: seven armies and two cavalry tank corps — one hundred divisions in all of fresh troops equipped for fighting in the bitter cold and deep snow. It hit the Germans on a two-hundred-mile front in front of Moscow on the morning of December 6, drove them back with heavy losses, and doomed their chances of knocking Russia out of the war.

The next day, at the other end of the world, the United States, caught by surprise as the Soviet Union had been on June 22, suffered the destruction of its Pacific Fleet at Pearl Harbor. The undefended west coast of America suddenly lay open to Japanese attack and invasion. That Sunday we were too shocked by our own staggering losses and by the danger suddenly confronting us to take much note that the tide had turned in Russia. Nonetheless, we found ourselves that week in the war on the side of the Bolsheviks, a development fraught with consequences for both peoples.

Gradually the tide began to turn in our favor too. We started to drive the Japanese northward from island after island in the Western Pacific. Across the Atlantic on November 8, 1942, an Anglo-American force under General Eisenhower landed on the beaches of Morocco and Algeria and doomed the Italo-German armies, retreating headlong westward from Egypt, in North Africa. On the last day of January, 1943, the German Sixth Army, the one I had followed in its triumphal advance through Belgium and northern France in 1940, surrendered at Stalingrad. It was one of the worst military defeats in Germany's history.

By the middle of the next year the Third Reich itself, which had launched so many attacks on other countries, faced for the first time attack from east and west. Its one ally, Fascist Italy, had been largely overrun by Anglo-American forces coming up from liberated North Africa. Mussolini had been deposed in July of 1943 and Italy had surrendered to the Allies in September. On June 5, 1944, American and British forces made a triumphal entry into Rome. The Germans, who had taken over in Italy and given ground only grudgingly, fell back from the Eternal City and resumed their retreat northward.

Next day, on June 6, a large Anglo-American force under General Eisenhower landed on the beaches of Normandy and rapidly drove the Germans back through northern France and Belgium to their own frontier. I caught up with the U.S. First Army on November 8 at the German frontier city of Aachen, from which four and a half years before I had set out to cover the German advance through Belgium and northern France. In the battered streets of Aachen, I reported in a column I wrote for the *New York Herald-Tribune*, one could "see Nazism dead among the ruins." All through that bitterly cold winter, however, the Germans fought on doggedly: against us on their western borders and against the Russians, who had arrived on their eastern frontiers.

The next spring I was back in my hometown, Cedar Rapids, Iowa, visiting my ailing mother when word came on April 12, 1945, that

Franklin Roosevelt had died. In the Midwest and back in the East I saw and felt the grief of the nation. The loss to the country seemed irreparable. A week later I was assigned by CBS, not to return to Europe to report the last months of the war, as I had hoped, but to San Francisco to cover the founding of the United Nations, which in our naïveté in the heady days of that final summer of world war we believed might preserve the peace of the planet forevermore. Our hopes for it were so high!

But not for long. At San Francisco disillusionment soon set in. Reading over my diary of that time I see that one thread dominates the account of the birth of the United Nations: the sharp rivalry of the United States and the Soviet Union, which were emerging from the war as the two superpowers that would largely determine the nature of the postwar world. Their delegates in San Francisco, I noted, started to quarrel on the day the conference opened, April 25, and continued to disagree until it ended on June 26, when nevertheless the Charter of the U.N. was signed by all the nations present. The constant hostility between the representatives of the two Big Powers, their total lack of trust in the other, depressed me. In a CBS broadcast I made from San Francisco on Sunday, May 13, I noted that

> The United States and Russia have no great historical conflicting interests. They never have had. But if we don't get together, Russia and ourselves, there will not be a peace for very long.

Tremendous news broke elsewhere while I was reporting the birth-pangs of the United Nations in San Francisco.

Nazi Germany was expiring. The Russians were in Berlin, fighting their way toward the Chancellery in the Wilhelmstrasse where Adolf Hitler was reported making a last stand. They had met up at the Elbe with the Americans, who with the British were mopping up western and southern Germany. The U.S. Seventh Army was pushing into Austria toward a link-up with the Russians in Vienna.

On Sunday, April 29, we got word in San Francisco that Benito Mussolini was dead. He and his mistress, Clara Petacci, had been caught by the partisans at Como and executed along with seventeen of his Fascist henchmen. The bodies had been trucked to Milan, strung up in the Piazza Loreto, reviled by a joyous mob, struck down and left in the gutter.

Next day my diary began:

San Francisco, Monday, April 30. The Russians are in the heart of Berlin. They've taken the gutted old Reichstag building. They've captured the Kroll Opera, where the Reichstag (later) met . . . and where Hitler announced to the world that gray morning of September 1, 1939, the opening shots in his war.

Berlin is finished, and Germany, and Nazism! The war is just about over. . . .

Next day, Tuesday, May 1, came word that Adolf Hitler was dead. As was befitting, he died with what I was sure was a lie. The German radio reported that "our Führer, Adolf Hitler, fighting to the last breath against Bolshevism, fell for Germany this afternoon at his headquarters in the Reich Chancellery in Berlin." "A hero's death," Admiral Karl Doenitz, his successor, called it in a broadcast that immediately followed. I doubted that Hitler had died a hero's death. Shortly, I hoped to get back to Berlin to check that one out.

With Hitler dead, it was obvious what the next news from Germany would be. It came on May 7. An A.P. bulletin flashed:

Reims, France, May 7. — Germany surrendered unconditionally to the Western Allies and Russia at 2:41 A.M., French time, today.

It took me all day to grasp it. This was it. This was the end of the story I had spent so much of my life recounting. The barbarian conquerors had themselves been conquered.

And then, out of the blue, on August 6, 1945, came the news of the most important event of the war, of the century, of our lives. We dropped an atomic bomb on Hiroshima, Japan, killing eighty thousand persons, injuring tens of thousands more, most of them for life, and wiping out sixty percent of the city. At last, man had unlocked the terrible force of the tiny atom. Overnight this hot summer we had entered a new age, leaving behind the old one that had lasted since the emergence of man on this earth. We had found a weapon that could blow up our world.

It took some time to realize it. I stared at the three-line banner headline in the *New York Times* in disbelief.

FIRST ATOMIC BOMB DROPPED ON JAPAN
MISSILE IS EQUAL TO 20,000 TONS OF TNT
TRUMAN WARNS FOE OF A "RAIN OF RUIN"

There was a subhead over the main story.

NEW AGE USHERED

HIROSHIMA IS TARGET

There was a fiery statement from President Truman.

Sixteen hours ago an American airplane dropped one bomb on Hiroshima, an important Japanese army base. That bomb had more power than 20,000 tons of TNT. . . .

The Japanese began the war from the air at Pearl Harbor. They have been repaid manyfold. And the end is not yet. . . .

It is an atomic bomb. It is a harnessing of the basic power of the universe. The force from which the sun draws its powers has been loosed against those who brought war to the Far East. . . .

We are now prepared to obliterate more rapidly and completely. . . . Let there be no mistake. We shall completely destroy. . . . If they [the Japanese leaders] do not now accept our terms they may expect a rain of ruin from the air, the like of which has never been seen on this earth. . . .

After the dire threats came the olive branch.

The fact that we can release atomic energy ushers in a new era in man's understanding of nature's forces. Atomic energy may, in the future, supplement the power that now comes from coal, oil and falling water. . . .

He promised to give "further consideration as to how atomic power can become a powerful and forceful influence toward world peace."

Winston Churchill, I felt, was more thoughtful — and eloquent.

This revelation of the secrets of nature long mercifully withheld from man should arouse the most solemn reflections in the mind and conscience of every human being.

I liked, too, Hanson Baldwin, the military correspondent of the *Times.*

Yesterday we clinched victory in the Pacific, but we sowed the whirlwind. . . .

"We may reap it," he thought.

A quick end for Japan, one way or another, was now inevitable. A week later, on August 14, it surrendered, unconditionally. The news of the surrender broke a few seconds after 7 P.M. I was in the CBS newsroom in New York when we got the word on a direct line Paul White had set up to the White House. Bob Trout was standing by with a microphone in hand and immediately broke the news.

From the newsroom on the seventeenth floor you could soon hear on this warm August evening the tugs and ships in the Hudson and East rivers tooting their horns. In between broadcasts I looked down on the streets of the great city. They were teeming with happy people, moving toward Radio City and Times Square to celebrate. CBS kept a team of us broadcasting through most of the night. When, dead tired but happy, I stumbled down 51st Street toward home, the summer's sun was coming up beyond the East River, rising on this first day of peace.

World War II was over!

London, Wednesday, October 10. The great, grimy city in the Indian summer of the last few days. . . .

The lights were on again at night and the people in the street seemed in high spirits after six years of blackout and war. It was strange to see so many of my old friends in the Labour party, whom I had first known when I was a young reporter in London and they had just entered Parliament, now ministers in the new Labour government. (The voters, to the surprise of everyone, had thrown out Churchill, the indomitable, the great victor, in the very first days of the Peace.) My fiery Welsh friend, Ny Bevan, was minister of health, Russell Strauss was minister of something, Jennie Lee, the beautiful Scottish lass who had been elected to the House in 1929 when she was scarcely of age, was now married to Ny and herself slated for a high post, as was Dick Crossman.

Paris, Thursday, October 19. The wonderful, magic city again! . . .

That first day back I wandered for hours through the familiar streets in which I had grown up in the mid-twenties. Somehow I felt a wonderful loneliness. This day was, I ended my diary, "one of the freest and happiest of my life."

Paris, Thursday, October 25. Yvonne dropped by today and insisted on our lunching at Knam, a little Russian place in the Latin Quarter where we had often gone in our great days. . . . We had, I fear, a very sentimental time.

Yvonne had been my first great love in Paris. We had remained friends. My diary is punctured with items about joyous reunions with old friends on my return to this place I still passionately loved.

> ... To lunch at the little bistro in Levallois with Eve and Philippe after they had put *Paris Presse,* their afternoon newspaper, to bed.

Eve Curie and Philippe Barrès. Each of them the child of famous parents. I had seen a good deal of them during the war. There is a note in the diary of driving out with Dos Passos to Barbizon to see Drue, an American actress, who had remained in France after the Germans came and hidden British and American flyers in her country place, passing them along to the next underground station on their way to freedom.

> ... At dinner at the British embassy tonight, much droll talk with Lady Diana. ...

Diana Cooper had also been a beautiful woman on the stage. Duff Cooper, her husband, was now British ambassador in Paris.

Obviously I was enjoying coming back to Paris.

> ... Forgot to note: in the Scribe bar Monday evening when we got back from Barbizon, Hadley, the first Mrs. Hemingway, and Martha, the third (just in from Berlin), having a wonderful time over their aperitifs discussing the fourth. ...

I got back to Berlin on October 30.

> Berlin, Saturday, November 3. So this is the end of Hitler's Thousand-Year Reich. ... It is something to see — here where it ended. And it is indescribable.
>
> How can you find words to convey the picture of a great capital destroyed almost beyond recognition; of a once mighty nation that has ceased to exist; of a conquering people who were so brutally arrogant and so blindly sure of their mission as the master race when I departed from here five years ago, and whom you now see poking about their ruins, broken, dazed, shivering, hungry human beings without will or purpose or direction, reduced like animals to foraging for food and seeking shelter in order to cling to life for another day.

Day after day I wandered through the rubble of the city. Already from the air that first moment coming in on the plane I had gotten a general view. The center of the capital around the Leipzigerstrasse and the Friedrichstrasse was completely wiped out. All the smaller streets nearby were gone, simply erased. The principal railroad stations — Potsdamerbahnhof, Anhalterbahnhof, Lehrterbahnhof — were gaunt shells. The Imperial Palace of the Hohenzollern kings and emperors at the eastern end of the Linden was roofless, some of its wings were pulverized and here and there the outer walls battered in. The Tiergarten, that lovely park in the very heart of Berlin, in which I had found so much relief from the pressures of life under Hitler, looked like any other battlefield, pockmarked with shell-and-bomb holes, the stout old trees I knew so well, bare stumps. As far as you could see in all directions from the plane there stretched a great wasteland of debris, dotted with roofless, burnt-out buildings with the low autumn sun shining through holes where windows had been.

The next days, on foot or in a U.S. Army jeep, I sought out familiar places. The building in the Tauentzienstrasse, between the Wittenbergplatz and the Gedächtniskirche, where on our arrival in Berlin in 1934 Tess and I had rented on the top two floors a spacious studio from a Jewish couple, he a sculptor and she an art-historian, had been bombed to the ground level. They had got out of Germany forthwith and we had helped them survive in London by paying the rent to them there in sterling. We had also given shelter here to hunted Jews until they escaped, but this, we realized, had only been a drop in the bucket.

The great square of the Wittenbergplatz had been so thoroughly pulverized by British and American bombing that you could no longer tell where it began and ended. The huge K.D.W. department store on the west side had disappeared in the rubble. I looked for a little pub on the south side of the platz, where occasionally, before the war started, I had had a beer. I had gone there because of the proprietor, one Alois Hitler, half brother of the Nazi dictator of Germany. I remembered Alois Hitler as a harmless-enough fellow, grown portly on good beer, whose chief fear was that his half brother would fly into a rage and order him to close shop, since the Führer did not like to have people reminded of the lower-middle-class origins of the Hitler family. The ground floor of the building was still habitable and, in fact, the pub was open for business. I went inside, had a beer, and asked what had happened to Alois Hitler. No one seemed to know. The answers were vague. Perhaps this was because I was still in uniform. No one was going to admit to an American in uniform any connection with a Hitler. In fact, after a few days I was getting used to the good Berliners telling me how much they had opposed the dictator. As I left the pub I noticed above the window a freshly painted sign: "FENT." But alongside it, if faintly, were the smeared letters I remembered: "*A. Hitler.*"

Most days I went out prowling with Howard K. Smith, whom I had hired away from United Press before I left Berlin. He had done a fine job here for CBS and then elsewhere as a war correspondent.*
Once, after a long day climbing over the ruins, Howard had looked back at the vast wasteland and cracked, in German: "*Das ist einmalig in der Geschichte!*" (That happens once in history!) It had been a favorite Nazi expression to describe one of Hitler's triumphs. Now it had another connotation.

We had started out that morning at the ruins of Berlin's great Protestant church, the Gedächtniskirche — the Kaiser Wilhelm Memorial Church — where the Kurfürstendamm turns half-right into the Tauentzienstrasse, my old street. The battered columns of the old church stood forlornly above the rubble.† Howard, too, had lived for a time near by and we were curious to see what had happened to our old quarter.

The Romanisches Café, where the artists and writers used to gather before the Nazis stamped the good ones out, was largely rubble. The Eden Hotel, down the Budapesterstrasse, where the racy girls hung out, was entirely rubble. How had the light-hearted damsels, Howard and I speculated, taken the horrors of the Allied bombing and the Russian bombardment? Opposite the façade of the church the Gloria Palast, the city's leading movie house, was just a mound of broken bricks and stone. It had had its great moments. I remembered two of them, when Hitler joined Leni Riefenstahl to watch her two great propaganda films, *The Triumph of Will* and *The Olympic Games.* Now German women, some of whom looked — from their fur jackets — as though they had come from that smug middle class that had been the backbone of Hitler's support, formed a chain gang, passing jagged broken bricks to one another.

The Kurfürstendamm, that broad avenue that stretched westward from the Memorial Church, had expressed the strivings, the showy pretentiousness, of the German middle class. Along it had been concentrated the great sidewalk cafés, the big restaurants, the nightclubs, the fashionable shops. Up and down the tree-lined avenue the

---

* Howard had got out of Berlin just in time — a few hours before Hitler declared war on the United States and interned our diplomats and correspondents for several months. Hence the title of his excellent book: *Last Train From Berlin.*

† The ruins were left intact, as a sort of memorial to the destruction of the war.

smart people had paraded, to see and to be seen. Now bulldozers were clearing a path through the rubble. All the buildings, all the café and restaurant fronts I remembered, had been smashed in. You could not distinguish one from the other.

We drove over to the East-West Axis, the triumphal boulevard that Hitler had widened from the old Charlottenburger Chausée into a sort of Via Triumphale down which his goose-stepping supermen used to parade in the brief hours of Nazi glory. In line of duty as a reporter I had often stood for hours on the reviewing stand behind the Führer and watched them pass by. There the Nazi Warlord had first shown the world the new tanks, the huge self-propelled guns, as Göring's new bombers and fighters roared overhead — a sight of the new German might that provoked immense enthusiasm among the good people massed along the curbs. They had cheered wildly.

Hitler, I was told, later regretted widening that boulevard, which cut a great swath through the wooded Tiergarten. Apparently, it became a fine landmark for British and American pilots, who took their bearings from it on their bombing runs. I now learned that Hitler, enraged, had had the boulevard covered at great expense with wire netting to camouflage it. One night, however, a fierce wind from the east had blown the covering down. The Berliners, who had more of a sense of humor than other Germans, had chuckled.

We were surprised to see the Siegessaule, the great Victory Column built to commemorate Prussia's victory over France in 1871, still standing in the middle of the Grosser Stern. Neither Anglo-American bombs nor Russian shells had toppled it. High on its top a French flag was flying, which reminded one of how in history the tables were so often turned. There was another reminder of that a few hundred yards down the avenue toward the Brandenburger Tor. A swarm of workmen were putting the finishing touches to a large monument. Though it was in the sector of the city taken over by the Western Allies it was, Smith explained to me, being hastily constructed by the Russians to honor their soldiers killed in the Battle of Berlin. Against all the odds and all the predictions, Soviet troops had got to Berlin but German troops had failed to reach Moscow. The Russian workmen seemed in great haste. The monument had to be finished in a few days, by November 7 in fact, the anniversary of the Bolshevik revolution.

We continued on through the Brandenburg Gate, its Grecian columns nicked by shrapnel, a couple of sculptured horses atop it wounded by shell fire. The Pariserplatz just beyond the gate had been pretty much the center of my life during the last years in Berlin. Around it was the Adlon Hotel, where I lived, the American embassy that I often frequented and the French embassy, where, until the war came and it was closed, I had good friends and informants. The platz was obliterated. The two embassies were no more. The Adlon, too, was in ruins. But a sign on the battered door announced that "Five O'Clock Tea" was being served. I wondered where. We crawled over the debris. A stairway led down to the old air-raid shelter. There I found two of the veteran waiters I had known and Jimmy the barman — all three dressed in tattered dinner jackets, and as friendly as ever, as if the war that had demolished this famous hostelry had never happened. They welcomed us back heartily.

After tea we walked down the Wilhelmstrasse, where so much of our work as correspondents had centered, since it contained the Foreign Office, the Propaganda Ministry and Hitler's Chancellery, from which we collected much of our news. It was from this little but famous street that first Prussia and then the German Reich had been ruled with an iron hand. No longer. We looked down the street. As far as you could see not a single building was standing. Debris was piled high on the broad sidewalks and spilled over on most of the street. Men and bulldozers were still working to clear a path wide enough for two cars to pass.

On the right we paused to look for President Hindenburg's old presidential palace which Ribbentrop had taken over for his official residence the first year of the war and remodeled at great expense — despite the shortage of labor and materials. It was a catacomb of rubble. Likewise the Foreign Office down the street. How often had we been convoked there to hear that Germany had attacked another neighbor. I felt relieved that he was now locked up in Nuremberg, along with the other surviving Nazi thugs. Even Rudolf Hess had been brought back from Great Britain, to which he had flown in the midst of the war to try to convince the British to give in so Hitler could turn on Russia. At Nuremberg, we heard, he was feigning madness. For such a fanatic this would not be difficult. I had always thought him a little mad. We paused to look at his office across the street. It, too, was gone. Farther down was what was left of the Propaganda Ministry, which was not much — a few blackened walls, twisted girders and piles of rubble. Howard and I had spent a lot of time there, much as we disliked it and its boss, Dr. Goebbels, the propaganda minister. What a pack of lies we had had to listen to there!

I was anxious to press on, across the street, to the Chancellery, where Adolf Hitler had lived and worked — and died. There was not much left of it either. Some girders, some bare walls poking out of a mountain of rubble. A rather forlorn looking Red Army sentry stood guard over the door to the shelter underneath, where I now knew that Hitler had not, as the expiring Nazi propaganda line had broadcast, "died a hero's death . . . fighting to the last breath against Bolshevism." I had already begun to check that one out.

As Howard and I climbed about the ruins I recalled how often I had stood on the curb opposite this Chancellery and watched the comings and goings of the great. As I put it in my diary that evening:

> They would drive up in their black Mercedes cars, the fat bemedaled Göring, the snakelike little Goebbels, though he lived just across the street, the arrogant, stupid Ribbentrop, though he lived a mere hundred yards down the street — these and Hess and the drunkard Ley and the debauched-looking little Funk with the small eyes of a pig and the sadist Himmler (though he looked like a mild schoolmaster) and the other swashbuckling party hacks and then the generals, their necks stiff even when they dismounted from a car, one eye inevitably squeezing a monocle, their uniforms immaculately pressed. They would come, be saluted by the guard of honor, and pass within this building to plot their wars and their conquests.

Well, I mused, as we stood back to get a good look at the ruins, they were all dead or in jail. This stately building, too, in whose gilded rooms they had worked out so cold-bloodedly their obscene designs, was, like them, smashed forever. Germany, too, I thought, though this was premature. Conservative Americans were already talking about rebuilding the country.

Still, it was difficult in this wasteland to remember that these wretched Germans I had watched scarcely five years before come to this Chancellery to help the dictator concoct his inhuman plans, were heroes in this nightmarish land. Crowds in the Wilhelmstrasse cheered them as they arrived and departed. The whole German nation followed them not only obediently but with enthusiasm.

Howard and I were tired. We did not wait for a guided tour of the bunker that some Russian officers were preparing. I would do that in a day or two. In the meantime I continued my little investigation of Hitler's end in this place.

Briefly this was the way it was.

Adolf Hitler killed himself, dying in the bunker at the side of his longtime mistress and now bride of twenty-four hours, Eva Braun, who took poison. He committed suicide by shooting himself in the mouth with his service revolver as Soviet troops closed in on the Chancellery, bouncing their artillery shells against it at point-blank range. It was 3:30 P.M. on Monday, April 30, 1945, ten days after his fifty-sixth birthday and twelve years and three months to a day after he became chancellor of Germany. He ended his life rather than risk capture by the Russians, whose land he came close to destroying.

> I shall not fall into the hands of the enemy [he said in a last will and testament], who require a new spectacle presented by the Jews, to divert their hysterical masses.

After all his experience, all his conquests and, in the end, all the bitter defeats, Adolf Hitler, his last testament shows, had learned nothing. He still believed that the Jews alone were responsible for all the ills of this earth, including the defeat and destruction of the Third Reich. The Jews bore "sole responsibility," he wrote in the last hours of his life, not only for the millions of deaths on the battlefield and in the bombed cities but for their own terrible end at his hands.

Joseph Goebbels, loyal to the end, next day emulated his Master, but in a gruesome way. Early on the evening of May 1 he had his six children — ages twelve to three — poisoned by lethal injections and then had himself and his wife Magda dispatched by an S.S. orderly shooting them in the back of the head. Their children, Frau Goebbels had explained to a friend the day before, "belong to the Third Reich and to the Führer, and if these two cease to exist there can be no further place for them." The children had not been asked to decide for themselves. "They were too young" for that, Goebbels had written in a brief "Appendix" to Hitler's testament. "If they were old enough they would unreservedly agree with this decision."

Thus passed Adolf Hitler and one of his chief henchmen, Dr. Goebbels. Just before he ended his life the Führer "expelled" his other two closest associates, Hermann Göring and Heinrich Himmler, from the party for treason to him and Germany. He also stripped them of all their government posts, and in the case of Göring revoked his decree of June 20, 1941, naming him as his successor. Himmler already had killed himself by swallowing a vial of poison soon after his capture by the British. Göring was among the rest of the surviving leaders waiting trial by an Allied court in Nuremberg.

On November 16 I left Berlin, I hoped for the last time, and set out for Nuremberg. Howard and I drove all night. Though the war had been over for six months the sight of its destruction along the way still staggered me.

> Frankfurt Am Main, Saturday, November 17.
> The stench of the dead under the ghastly ruins of Kassel last night beneath the winter's full moon! . . . the first sight, in the early morning moonlit fog of the rubble of this once great German city of Frankfurt, the birthplace of Goethe, the seat of election of the German kings, the capital of the German Confederation, a stronghold of the nineteenth century German liberalism . . . and a bulwark of Nazism. . . . Dead it is, in the cold ruins. . . .

> Nuremberg, Sunday, November 18.
> It is gone! The lovely medieval town behind the moat is utterly destroyed. It is a vast heap of rubble. . . . As the prosaic U.S. Army puts it, Nuremberg is "91 percent dead."

I crawled for hours in the debris that Sabbath looking for familiar landmarks. The old town, the Nuremberg of Dürer and Hans Sachs and the Meistersingers and the venerable churches of St. Lorenz and St. Sebald and Our Lady and the old Rathaus and my favorite inn, the Bratwurstglöcklein, was "99 percent dead." Half of the wonderful old frame dwellings along the river Pegnitz had caved into the stream. The Deutscher Hof, where Hitler had always stayed during the annual Nazi party rallies — I had caught my first glimpse of him there one September evening nine years before standing on the balcony acknowledging the acclaim of the delirious crowd — I could not find at all. The whole city block, which also contained the Wurttemberger Hof down the street where correspondents had stayed, was gone.

I stopped to ask some of the local citizens, who had come out from their cellars to catch the unexpected sun of this November afternoon, what had happened. The first big bombings had come in October, 1943, they said. They had scarcely ever let up after that. Then the day after New Year's in 1945 had come the biggest attack of all. A thousand planes or more, all day and all the following night, had finished the destruction of the medieval city, burying it in its ruins.

Justice caught up with the Nazi war criminals at 9:30 A.M. on Tuesday, November 20, 1945, when their trial began in the Palace of Justice in Nuremberg before the International Military Tribunal. I had never thought I would live to see it. Such a thing had never occurred before. The last time we had triumphed over the Germans and ordered the trial of their war criminals, the whole thing had ended in a farce. In 1919 the Allies had drawn up a list of three thousand Germans accused of war crimes, and then quickly reduced it to 892. Of these, only *twelve* were finally brought to justice — before a German court at Leipzig. But the Germans never took it seriously. Three of the twelve defied the court by not bothering to show up, charges against three others were dropped, and the six remaining men, all minor offenders, got off with light sentences. To most Germans, I recalled reading at the time, the whole affair was a joke, just another example of how dumb the victors could be.

This time the Allies, the United States, Great Britain, the Soviet Union and France, meant business. Yet there had been much criticism of the trial at home and in Britain, especially in legal circles. A good many lawyers were against it for several reasons, but chiefly because of our trying the Nazi leaders by *ex post facto* law, that is, making them liable for crimes that were not punishable — at least by an international court of the victors — when they were committed.

I was too emotional about these Nazi barbarians to put much credence in such objections. I did have doubts about prosecuting on one of the four indictments,* which considered it a crime to have started a war of aggression. If you went back in history there would be a legion of men guilty of this charge. And I believed there would be more in the future — man had not yet progressed far enough from savagery to abandon making aggressive war. Justice Robert H. Jackson of the U.S. Supreme Court and the chief American prosecutor, I knew from talks with him, believed very strongly that he could make a case that might set a tremendous precedent in history: that a war of aggression is a crime and that those who plot it and wage it are liable to be prosecuted, and convicted and punished after due process. God knows that as one of the few persons at Nuremberg who had seen Hitler and his henchmen in Berlin deliberately start the war, I felt that it was a crime and that the perpetrators should be held responsible. But this was, I realized, an emotional reaction. Justice had to be more than that.

On those other charges, though, war crimes and crimes against humanity — especially those of the massacre of the Jews and of the Poles and Russians — I felt grateful that they had been brought. To

---

* There were four counts in the general indictment: 1, the charge of conspiracy to seize power, establish a totalitarian regime, prepare and wage a war of aggression; 2, the charge of waging wars of aggression; 3, the charge of violation of the laws of war; 4, the charge of crimes against humanity, which included the slaughter of the Jews.

those legal hair-splitters at home and in Britain who argued that you couldn't try men for acts that were not specifically crimes on the statute books when they were committed — however horrible they might have been — there was, I thought, a sufficient answer. Massacre, murder, torture, even enslavement, had long been recognized by all civilizations as crimes and embodied in their laws. As Justice Jackson argued:

> We propose to punish acts which have been regarded as criminal since the time of Cain and have been so written in every civilized code.

There was also a good argument, I thought, against those who held that the Nazis should not be tried for deeds for which they had no reason to believe they would be held accountable. The fact was that on November 1, 1943, two years before, the Allies had given the Germans fair warning that they would be held responsible for the atrocities, massacres and cold-blooded mass executions, which were just then beginning to come to light. The warning had been given in a formal declaration by Roosevelt, Churchill and Stalin.

> Let those who have hitherto not stained their hands with innocent blood [the warning surely was written by Churchill] beware lest they join the ranks of the guilty, for most assuredly the three Allied powers will pursue them to the uttermost ends of the earth and will deliver them to their accusers in order that justice may be done.

None of the twenty-one Nazi leaders, Göring at their head, who were already seated in the dock when I arrived shortly after 9 A.M. that first day at the courthouse, could say they hadn't been warned.

I was shocked at my first sight of them. How the mighty had fallen! Shorn of the power and the trappings of Nazism, how common and mediocre they looked. Was it possible, I asked myself, that these nondescript, little men, fidgeting nervously in their shabby garb, were the ones who when last you saw them wielded such monstrous power? How could *they,* so measly of countenance as they slumped in their seats, have conquered a great nation and then all of Western Europe? They no longer looked like conquerors, like chieftains of the Master Race. Gone was the arrogance, the insolence, the truculence.

"Broken, miserable little men!" I jotted down in my running notes. I began noting how each of the defendants looked and behaved as the first day of the trial proceeded.

This is Göring. He sits in the first seat of the two rows that compose the dock. It is the number-one place. At last he has achieved his ambition of being number-one . . . though not precisely as he had once dreamed. At first glance I scarcely recognize him. He has lost much weight — eighty pounds, a U.S. Army doctor whispers to me. . . . His faded air force uniform, shorn of the insignia and of the medals he loved so childishly, hangs loosely on him. . . . And gone is his old burliness, his old arrogance, his flamboyant air.

How a twist of fate, I marveled, could reduce a man to size. It had reduced the next man in the dock to even less than size.

This was Rudolf Hess, for long the closest of all the Nazi aides to Hitler and at one time his heir-apparent, and still number-three when he set out on his ridiculous flight to Scotland in 1941. Now in the dock he struck me as a broken man, his face so emaciated it looked like a skeleton. His mouth kept twitching nervously, his once bright eyes stared vacantly about the courtroom. It was the first time I had ever seen Hess out of uniform. In the brown shirt of the S.A. or the black coat of the S.S. he had always seemed a strapping fellow. Now in a threadbare civilian suit he looked small and wizened. He was claiming, we knew, to have lost his memory while a prisoner of the British the last four years of the war. Rather ostentatiously, I thought, he declined to follow the proceedings of the court. For the most part he sat reading a book, oblivious of what was going on.

Next to him sat Joachim von Ribbentrop. He was an evil, pompous little ignoramus and even most of Hitler's cohorts — Göring especially — wondered why the Führer had taken him on, and kept him on. Like most of the others, he too was bent and broken and had aged beyond belief.

On his left sat Wilhelm Keitel in an army officer's faded uniform stripped of all insignia and decorations. I had last seen this field marshal and chief of the Supreme Command at close quarters at Compiègne where on Hitler's behalf in the sad June days of 1940 he sat in Marshal Foch's old 1918 *wagon-lit* and dictated armistice terms to France. I remembered how jaunty and cocky he was then. Now he looks subdued, but not broken. The monstrous Nazi crimes do not seem to weigh on him unduly. You can see his appetite is good. He keeps munching crackers — from an American army K-ration kit.

Next to him is Alfred Rosenberg, the phony "philosopher" and once the mentor of Hitler and the Nazi movement. He too has lost weight, the puffiness on the sallow, square Baltic face is gone.

Dressed in a dark-brown suit, this dull, confused, but dangerous Balt, who contributed so much to the Nazis' race hatreds, who masterminded the loot of art objects from the conquered lands and who finally helped direct the extermination of the Slav people in the conquered Russian territories, is nervous in the dock, lurching forward to catch every word, his hands shaking.

At his side was Hans Frank, the Nazi's great legal light, who as Hitler's governor-general of occupied Poland decimated the Polish people and the Jews. Like Himmler, Frank struck me as sort of a refined murderer, who could kill and kill without becoming excited or appearing especially brutal. He was the most self-assured Nazi in the dock.

Wilhelm Frick, next to him, was also a cold and ruthless man behind his rather modest exterior. He was one of Hitler's oldest comrades, dating from Munich days when, though a member of the Barvarian police, he had connived with the Führer in the Beer Hall Putsch. He was a bureaucrat through and through. In his checkered sport jacket, he seemed a forlorn figure in the dock. But I could not forget the cold brutality he had shown as Hitler's longtime minister of the interior and, in the end, as "Protector" of Bohemia and Moravia.

It is difficult to recognize the next man in the dock, Julius Streicher. The former undisputed master of this town, who strode through its ancient streets brandishing a whip and waxed fat on pornography and Jew-baiting, has rather wilted away. He sits there, an obscene, bald, decrepit old man, perspiring profusely. Occasionally the old scowl comes back as he glares at the judges. The guards tell me Streicher is convinced they are all Jews. It fortifies your belief in ultimate justice to see this repulsive German at last brought to judgment.

Walter Funk, who shouldered Dr. Schacht out of the presidency of the Reichsbank and of the ministership of economics, is next. He still looks like a toad, coarse, greasy, and shifty eyed. Next to him, and the last one in the prestigious first row, was a man who would not speak to Funk for ten years, until today — the inimitable Dr. Hjalmar Horace Greeley Schacht. It is obvious that this wily financier, who in my opinion did more than any other individual in Germany except Papen to bring Hitler to power, is furious at having to stand trial with men he now, belatedly, considers to be thugs.

Sitting erect, his head separated from the rest of his body by his invariable high choker collar, he folds his arms defiantly across his chest.

Knowing English, he follows the reading of the indictment without earphones and with rapt attention. . . . I'm told Schacht is sure he will be acquitted.

The defendants in the second row in the dock were less interesting to me. The first two were Nazi Germany's only Grand Admirals, Karl Doenitz and Erich Raeder. Doenitz, an able naval officer and for most of his career a submarine man — he worked out the wolf-pack technique for German U-boats — until he succeeded Raeder as commander-in-chief of the navy, sits erect in a civilian suit, looking for all the world like a grocery clerk. I found it hard to imagine him as the successor of Hitler, which he had been for a brief moment after the Führer killed himself. Raeder, still in uniform, still wearing his high turned-up collar (I had never seen him without it) had aged, I thought, beyond his considerable years. He had had the energy and the imagination to build up the German navy after the first war. In the dock he looked like a tired and bewildered old man.

At his side sat the most personable-looking and the youngest of the defendants. This was Baldur von Schirach, leader of the Hitler Youth and, during the war, the hated *Gauleiter* of Vienna. He looked more American than German, his mother and one grandmother and one grandfather having been American. Young Schirach had actually believed in the Nazi nonsense and had done a brilliant job of building up the *Hitler Jugend* into a formidable force. On this first day of the trial he seemed a bit dazed at finding himself in this place.

Fritz Sauckel, next to him, had been the tough boss of slave labor in the Third Reich, a coarse and brutal man who looked like a pig, with his narrow little slit-eyes. If Germany in our time had been a normal land, Sauckel, an ex-sailor and construction worker, would have found his place in life, say, running a butcher shop. I was surprised at how nervous such a roughneck could be as a prisoner — he who had carried out the enslavement of millions of workers seized from the conquered countries. He swayed to and fro.

There was no sway in the man next to him, Colonel-General Alfred Jodl, who sat there stiff as a ramrod in his faded army uniform. As the number-two officer, after Keitel and much more intelligent, on OKW, he had become the closest general to Hitler and had served him loyally to the end.

Next to him was Franz von Papen, the intriguer more responsible than any other for getting Hitler the chancellorship in 1933, though this had not saved him later from more than once being nearly bumped off by the Führer. He had been a great survivor, but you could see he was not happy now to have outlasted the dictator only to find himself imprisoned by the Allies. I found him incredibly aged, his once jaunty eyes sunk in, the skin taut over his wizened face, his shoulders stooped. Not much was left of this sly old fox.

On the other hand, Arthur Seyss-Inquart, the contemptible Austrian traitor and, during the war, the brutal oppressor of the Dutch as Nazi governor of the Netherlands, seemed unchanged — still cool and businesslike. Albert Speer, Hitler's architect and also minister of armaments in the last years of the war, the next in the row, seemed strangely earnest. He had always struck me as one of the more decent Nazis but he had been too ambitious to risk ruining his dazzling success by opposing until the very end the barbarous tyrant who alone had made his career possible. Hitler had been very fond of him and had given him opportunities for building that were beyond an architect's fondest dreams. Later in the trial Speer would distinguish himself by being the only defendant to show remorse for his crimes.

Next to the last in the dock was Baron Konstantin von Neurath, the typical example of an upper-class career diplomat without convictions and integrity, who had served Hitler well first as foreign minister and then later as "Protector" for what was left of the Czech nation, a sort of front man for Nazi butchery there. He sat in the dock on this opening day a broken old man, apparently dazed by the discovery that one could come to the end of the road of compromise and accommodation with evil, on which this conservative from an old German family had traveled so long. Last in the dock was Hans Fritzsche, a talented but unscrupulous Nazi radio commentator and journalist, who had also been chief of German broadcasting at the Propaganda Ministry. Since Goebbels was dead and could not be tried, Fritzsche, I gathered, had been hauled in as his substitute. He appeared taken aback by the importance attached to him, as if he wanted to say: "Honorable Judges, I really wasn't in the same league as these other fellows."*

Promptly at 10 A.M. the honorable judges filed in. They were an interesting lot.

* Omitted from this list of defendants was the worst Nazi killer of them all, Ernst Kaltenbrunner, second in command of the S.S.-Gestapo under Himmler, for whom he was substituted in this trial. Two days before the opening he had a cerebral hemorrhage and was unable to be present. Like Hitler, he was an Austrian. One of his assistants in the last years of the war was Adolf Eichmann, who organized the massacre of the Jews.

Dr. Robert Ley, the drunken head of the Labor Front, was also not present, though he was among the Nazi leaders originally indicted. Before the trial began, he hanged himself in his cell.

Lord Justice Geoffrey Lawrence, who will preside, is a fine old chunk of Britain with an ample Gladstonian forehead and the restrained self-assurance of all eminent British judges. . . . He will be firm, unemotional, and fair. His alternate is Sir Norman Birkett, . . . a thin, gangling fellow whom I had often seen at court in my younger days in London, where he was among the two or three greatest trial lawyers of our time.

Francis Biddle, our former attorney general, is a bit self-conscious, almost tripping on his robe as he mounts the bench. At his side is Judge John J. Parker, his alternate, a home-spun North Carolinian, whom an irate Senate had once kept out of the Supreme Court. Europe and especially the insane Nazi world are a bit strange to him. . . . The French judge, Donnedieu de Vabres, resembles Clemenceau one minute and Pétain the next. His alternate, Robert Falco, looks like any other French lawyer one used to see crowding the halls of the Palais de Justice in Paris. He seems to have a tendency to drool.

All these gentlemen wear black judicial robes, but the Russian judges, Major General Iona Timofeevich Nikitchenko, vice-president of the Supreme Court of the U.S.S.R., and his alternate, Lt.-Col. Alexander Fedorovich Volchkov, are in military uniform, resplendent with decorations.

The Nuremberg Trial went on for almost a year. More important to me than the trial itself was the making public by the prosecution of thousands of secret documents of the Nazi government, the Foreign Office, the S.S., the party and the three armed services which told a shocking tale of the rule in Germany and in conquered Europe of Hitler's barbarous regime. The documents, hundreds of tons of them, had been seized by the Allied armies before the Germans had time to destroy them. In these papers the Nazis in the dock convicted themselves of the most heinous crimes, though they were given every opportunity to defend themselves, which they did, with the help of their lawyers, at great length.

On October 1, 1946, the International Military Tribunal handed down its verdicts. Nineteen of the twenty-two defendants were found guilty on one or more counts of the indictment. Of these, twelve were sentenced to death by hanging, three to life imprisonment, and four to terms of ten to twenty years in prison. Three, Schacht, Papen and Fritzsche, to the surprise of many, were acquitted.* Hess, also to the surprise of many, since he was one of Hitler's

---

* Later all three were convicted by German denazification courts, Fritzsche receiving a sentence of nine years at hard labor, and Schacht and Papen eight years of the same. In the

key aides for so long, escaped with a life sentence as did Funk and Raeder. Speer and Schirach got twenty years in prison, Neurath fifteen, and Doenitz ten. The rest were sentenced to death on the gallows.

Sixteen days later, shortly after 1 A.M. on October 16, 1946, Ribbentrop mounted the gallows in the execution chamber of the Nuremberg prison. He was followed at brief intervals by Keitel, Kaltenbrunner, Rosenberg, Frank, Frick, Streicher, Seyss-Inquart, Sauckel and Jodl.

The turn of Hermann Göring never came. He avoided the hangman. Two hours before he was due to mount the gallows he swallowed a vial of poison that had been smuggled into his cell.

"Like his Fuehrer, Adolf Hitler, and his rival for the succession, Heinrich Himmler," I wrote in another place, "Goering had succeeded at the last hour in choosing the way in which he would depart this earth, on which he, like the other two, had made such a murderous impact."*

By that time I had returned home for the last time from Germany, making it, as I had five years before, just in time for Christmas with my family.

This time, at forty-one, after twenty years abroad, it was for good.

---

end, they served very little time.

Martin Bormann, a murky little character who acquired great power as Hitler's secretary during the latter part of the war, was tried in absentia, found guilty of two counts and sentenced to death. I'm convinced he was killed by Russian shells when he attempted to escape from Berlin the day after Hitler committed suicide. But for years rumors persisted that he had got away and was living well in South America. His rise to Nazi eminence came after I left Berlin in 1940.

* The last sentence of *The Rise and Fall of the Third Reich.*

Index

Deutsch ist die Saar